T0320989

THE
LSTA'S
COMPLETE
CREDIT
AGREEMENT
GUIDE

THE LSTA'S COMPLETE CREDIT AGREEMENT GUIDE

SECOND EDITION

Michael Bellucci and Jerome McCluskey

Milbank

New York   Chicago   San Francisco   Athens   London
Madrid   Mexico City   Milan   New Delhi
Singapore   Sydney   Toronto

8 9 10 LCR   22

ISBN   978-1-2596-4486-3
MHID   1-2596-4486-3

e-ISBN   978-1-2596-4487-0
e-MHID   1-2596-4487-1

This publication is designed to provide accurate and authoritative information in regard to the subject matter covered. It is sold with the understanding that neither the author nor the publisher is engaged in rendering legal, accounting, securities trading, or other professional services. If legal advice or other expert assistance is required, the services of a competent professional person should be sought.

> —*From a Declaration of Principles Jointly Adopted by a Committee of the American Bar Association and a Committee of Publishers and Associations*

McGraw-Hill Education books are available at special quantity discounts to use as premiums and sales promotions or for use in corporate training programs. To contact a representative, please e-mail us at bulksales@mheducation.com.

Library of Congress Cataloging-in-Publication Data

Names: Bellucci, Michael J.. author. | McCluskey, Jerome, author. | Wight, Richard, author. LSTA's complete credit agreement guide.
Title: The LSTA's complete credit agreement guide / by Michael J. Bellucci and Jerome McCluskey.
Description: 2E [edition]. | New York : McGraw-Hill, [2017] | Earlier edition authored by Richard Wight, with Warren Cooke and Richard Gray
Identifiers: LCCN 2016027124 (print) | LCCN 2016039668 (ebook) | ISBN 9781259644863 (alk. paper) | ISBN 1259644863 | ISBN 9781259644870 () | ISBN 1259644871
Subjects: LCSH: Credit.
Classification: LCC HG3701 .W54 2017 (print) | LCC HG3701 (ebook) | DDC 332.7—dc23
LC record available at https://lccn.loc.gov/2016027124

The authors wish to thank Richard Wight,
Warren Cooke, and Rick Gray. Richard, with the help of
Warren and Rick, authored the first edition, which was a herculean
effort that required a career's worth of knowledge and took years
to write. It quickly became a unique and valuable resource
for loan market participants. Our task in writing this book was
made immensely easier by being able to start with the first edition.
All commendations from this book are equally theirs;
any shortcomings are the responsibility of the authors
of the second edition.

CONTENTS

14 REGULATORY DEVELOPMENTS   647

PREFACE

As Richard Wight, Warren Cooke, and Rick Gray noted in the First Edition of the *Credit Agreement Guide*, standard practice for credit agreements evolves for many reasons. While documentary terms tighten and loosen to the rhythm of capital flows and the credit cycle, it is new case law, new tax rules and other regulatory pronouncements, new financing structures and new market entrants that concomitantly impact the loan market and its workhorse document, the credit agreement. Constant evolution is the normal course of things in the highly dynamic and increasingly global loan market. In ordinary times, this constant evolution would be reason enough to regularly revisit an overview guide to credit agreements. However, the past few years have been anything but ordinary times.

Since the initial printing of the *LSTA's Complete Credit Agreement Guide*, the debt markets have seen a lifetime's worth of turmoil. The global and U.S. financial systems suffered a financial shock the scale and depth of which had not been witnessed since the Great Depression. The steep falloff in lending and credit availability more generally was but one measure of the severity of the crisis. Looking at the potent amalgam of the aforementioned evolutionary market forces, the tempest that was the recent financial crisis and the regulatory aftershocks that followed, the authors saw many compelling reasons to survey the aftermath and produce this Second Edition. Richard, Warren, and Rick laid a formidable foundation with the First Edition and we hope that we have only added to the luster with this Second Edition. Our goal is to have provided the reader with a clear, accessible, and timely guide to the credit agreement and we hope that we have done so.

We wish to thank Bridget Marsh and Tess Virmani of the LSTA for their belief in this project, and their invaluable input and feedback. We could not have done it without their support.

Finally, we would like to thank our families for their patience and tireless support. We have already asked much of them in supporting our often unpredictable and demanding day jobs as New York banking lawyers. Their support of our authorial adventure went above and beyond. For that we are eternally grateful.

CHAPTER 1

The Credit Agreement

Neither a borrower nor a lender be;
For loan oft loses both itself and friend,
Hamlet Act I, Scene 3

Even Shakespeare understood the risk of making a loan. Not only can the loan be lost, but the cordial business relationship between the parties can be harmed along the way. There is no sure antidote to this hazard, but a clearly drafted agreement between borrower and lender that defines for each what to do and not to do certainly helps.

The credit agreement (also commonly referred to as a loan agreement) is but one of many genres of agreement under which a business can obtain borrowed funds. Other examples include agreements for the issuance of senior or subordinated debt securities in the public markets, private placement transactions, the issuance of commercial paper, and short-term repurchase agreements for Treasury securities. The list of structures is as numerous as deal transactors can invent. This volume focuses on the credit agreement and (if we succeed) provides a guide to some of its mysteries.

Traditionally, the credit agreement described the species of contract under which bank borrowings were effected. In the 1920s, a small shoe manufacturer in the mill towns of Massachusetts might sign a credit agreement with its local bank if it needed working capital to fund its business. Today, a large multinational telecommunications company may sign a credit agreement arranged by its principal investment bank leading a syndicate of dozens of lenders to provide funds for the acquisition of a business in Europe. Although the complexity of credit agreements may have grown over the decades, its basic form remains the same: borrow and repay funds with interest, make representations, agree to covenants, and accept events of default if the agreement is breached.

There may originally have been a distinction between a loan agreement and a credit agreement. The former historically may have referred to an agreement in which the lenders made one-time loans to the borrower (the "term loans" described in Chapter 2), while the latter may have referred to agreements that contained a revolving credit facility—hence the term *credit* agreement. Today many bankers and legal practitioners use the terms interchangeably.

Historically, a credit or loan agreement included only banks as lenders. That is no longer the case. With the expansion of nonbank institutional lenders (including investment banks, collateral loan obligation funds (or CLOs), credit hedge funds, mutual funds, and other funds and special-purpose vehicles) into the bank loan market, the typical syndicated credit agreement today will contemplate that both banks and nonbanks provide funds to the borrower. While banks still have the largest share of the market when it comes to negotiating, originating, and syndicating loan facilities, being a lender under these syndicated facilities is no longer the exclusive province of banks, as was the case until the early 1990s. In 2015 nonbank lenders represented about 86 percent of the participants in syndicated noninvestment grade credit facilities.[1] Many of the changes to credit agreement provisions described in this second edition are driven by the migration of the loan investor market from being comprised primarily of banks to being comprised primarily of nonbanks.

For the uninitiated, a credit agreement can appear to be a confused jumble of boilerplate and legalese. An agreement with one borrower blends mentally into that of another; one mass of paper appears essentially the same as the next and the novice might wonder what the fuss is all about. Why so many words? Why can't the lawyers just write a simple two-page agreement? Why must it be so complicated? Has no one heard of the KISS principle—keep it short and simple?

Of course, a loan transaction need not be complicated. A one-page promissory note containing the borrower's obligation to repay the loan and the lender's right to enforce that obligation will get the job done. The difference between a one-page promissory note and a 150-page credit agreement is an attempt to give the borrower certainty and flexibility. Although simple to document, a one-page promissory note (or other short-form credit agreement) is likely to be payable either on demand or within a very short time. It typically evidences an *uncommitted* line of credit and, having a short tenor, will not be treated as the

---

[1] See S&P Capital IQ LCD.

borrower's long-term debt for accounting purposes. It may also not have the locked-in stability that a borrower needs if its business is cyclical or subject to other unknown risks. A credit agreement, by contrast, gives the borrower *committed* funds as well as the business stability and long-term debt that comes with an agreed repayment schedule. For many borrowers, these benefits outweigh the complexity and cost of negotiating, drafting, and living with a 150-page credit agreement.

The purpose of the succeeding chapters is to explore the secrets (if that is the right term) contained in the market-standard credit agreement. Our goal is to explain many of the basic questions that a lender (or lender's counsel) will confront in drafting and reviewing a typical credit agreement. We also elaborate upon the historical rationale for many of the provisions in the credit agreement. Why is there a governing law clause? Why are there long pages of representations? In addition, we hope to unlock the mysteries of the many industry buzzwords that are thrown around whenever the initiated discuss a credit agreement. What is LIBOR? What is a yank-a-bank provision? A platform? A claw-back? A soft-call premium? An MFN provision?

For most issues, we provide sample language to show what customary provisions look like. In many cases we have excerpted clauses from the Loan Syndications and Trading Association (LSTA) Model Credit Agreement Provisions, which have been widely adopted by leveraged loan market participants. The sample language is not intended to prescribe the only *correct* way to write something, but rather is intended solely as a reference when reading the discussion of a particular clause, and should be used with these principles in mind.

When reading this volume, some key parameters should be remembered. First, we address only syndicated credit agreements for *nonbankrupt* borrowers; we do not generally address the unique issues that arise in the context of debtor-in-possession financings. Second, although we discuss some of the issues that arise with non-U.S. borrowers, the principal focus of this volume is credit facilities provided to domestic U.S. companies. Domestic U.S. companies represent a wide variety of borrower types with varying levels of risk from a loan underwriting perspective. A credit agreement for Microsoft will look very different than a loan to the local café. While acknowledging the difference in terms in a credit agreement for a "middle market" business versus a "large cap," this volume does not attempt to highlight and explain such differences on the theory that in the final analysis there are more similarities than differences. Third, we presume (unless indicated otherwise) that the credit agreement will be governed by New York law. We do not, for example, address issues that would arise with credit agreements under

English law or California law, although in a few instances we do distinguish U.S. market practice from U.K. market practice.

For ease of reading, we refer generally throughout this volume to provisions applicable to "the borrower." Nevertheless, other than in the context of the making of loans, the term should be understood to cover affiliated obligors; many provisions, including representations and warranties, covenants, and events of default, apply as well to other parties (subsidiaries, parent holding companies, guarantors, pledgors, and others) that support the credit. These chapters are not intended to read like a credit agreement (accompanying every reference to borrower with the litany "or subsidiary, guarantor, or other obligor or pledgor") and so should be read wearing a common-sense hat.

The discussion in this volume is intended to be solely an overview of the most common provisions found in a credit agreement. It cannot encompass the tremendous variety of provisions found in credit agreements, since borrowers and arrangers alike have an infinite capacity for creativity and negotiation. What is typical practice today will certainly evolve over time as new pricing options are created, new covenants are devised, new court decisions are rendered (perhaps requiring new waivers to be inserted), new tax structures evolve, and new regulations are implemented. Indeed a significant factor in publishing this second edition is to reflect in this volume the many changes in practice and credit agreement documentation that have occurred since the printing of the prior edition. We hope, nevertheless, that the reader will find the explanation here useful as a resource when reviewing or drafting the next credit agreement that comes across his or her desk.

CHAPTER 2

Commitments, Loans, and Letters of Credit

2.1 CREDIT VARIANTS

2.1.1 Loans

> **Box 2.1**
>
> (a) *Revolving Credit Loans.* Subject to the terms and conditions set forth herein, each Revolving Credit Lender agrees to make Revolving Credit Loans from time to time during the Revolving Credit Availability Period in an aggregate principal amount up to but not exceeding its Revolving Credit Commitment; *provided* that the aggregate outstanding principal amount of the Revolving Credit Loans *plus* the aggregate outstanding principal amount of Competitive Loans shall not at any time exceed the total Revolving Credit Commitments. Within the foregoing limits and subject to the terms and conditions set forth herein, the Borrower may borrow, prepay, and reborrow Revolving Credit Loans.
>
> (b) *Tranche A Term Loans.* Subject to the terms and conditions set forth herein, each Tranche A Term Lender agrees to make one or more Tranche A Term Loans to the Borrower during the Term Loan Availability Period in an aggregate principal amount not exceeding its Tranche A Term Loan Commitment. Amounts prepaid or repaid in respect of Tranche A Term Loans may not be reborrowed.
>
> (c) *Tranche B Term Loans.* Subject to the terms and conditions set forth herein, each Tranche B Term Lender agrees to make one or more Tranche B Term Loans to the Borrower on the Effective Date in an aggregate principal amount not exceeding its Tranche B Term Loan Commitment. Amounts prepaid or repaid in respect of Tranche B Term Loans may not be reborrowed.

> (d) *Competitive Bid Loans.* Subject to the terms and conditions set forth herein, from time to time during the Revolving Credit Availability Period the Borrower may request Competitive Bids and may (but shall not have any obligation to) accept Competitive Bids and borrow Competitive Loans; *provided* that the aggregate outstanding principal amount of the Revolving Credit Loans plus the aggregate outstanding principal amount of Competitive Loans shall not at any time exceed the total Revolving Credit Commitments.

In its simplest form, a credit agreement provides merely for loans. In more complex forms, it may encompass letters of credit, bankers' acceptances, deposit facilities, and other alternative ways to make credit available to a borrower. Even an agreement that provides only for loans may blossom into pages and pages of intricate mechanics if it contemplates multiple tranches of loans, or other loan variants that reflect practices the financial markets have developed over many decades. Here we discuss briefly the principal types of loans seen in credit agreements today.

2.1.1.1 Revolving Credit versus Term Loans

Revolving credit loans, as their name implies, "revolve" within "commitments" established by the lenders. To "revolve" in this sense means that the aggregate outstanding amount of the loans may increase and decrease during the commitment period. As provided explicitly in the language in Box 2.1, the borrower is allowed to borrow, repay, and reborrow the loans during the term of the commitments, so long as the outstanding amount does not exceed the aggregate revolving credit commitments and all applicable lending conditions are satisfied.

By contrast, term loans, once borrowed and repaid, may not be reborrowed (again, see the language in Box 2.1). This is not to say that term loans cannot be made available in multiple drawdowns (a so-called "standby" or "delayed draw" term loan facility), but simply that once the term loan has been repaid, the borrower has no right to reborrow the amount repaid. An easy analogy is to equate a revolving credit facility to your credit card or a home equity line during its availability period, while a term loan facility equates to your 30-year home mortgage.

Revolving credit loans are traditionally provided to borrowers that need working capital facilities. The classic example is a seasonal business such as a merchandise retailer where the amount of liquidity (cash) needed in its business fluctuates up and down as summer sales, back-to-school promotions, and holidays come and go. Term loans may also be used for working capital purposes, but since their principal amount does not fluctuate they are more often associated with a borrower's longer-term capital needs, such as to finance an acquisition, refinance other debt, or provide funds for capital improvements.

2.1.1.2 A and B Loan Tranches

Term loans have evolved over time into two principal types: so-called A loan tranches and B loan tranches. "A loans" are generally understood to be term loans that are made by bank lenders (as opposed to funds or other institutional investors) and have a tenor shorter than any B loan tranche (if there is one). Although A loans may have a "bullet" maturity—that is to say they are repayable in a single lump sum at final maturity with no prior amortization—they are more often entitled to the benefit of genuine amortization through the payment of installments over the term of the loan representing sizeable (and not just nominal) paydowns of the facility. An amortization schedule that provides for, say, equal quarterly installments each representing 1.25 percent to 5 percent or more of the original principal, is a typical repayment schedule for an A loan tranche.

By contrast, "B loans" are typically provided not by banks (except perhaps at initial syndication) but by funds or other institutional lenders, have a maturity longer than any related A loan (usually six months to a year longer), and have only nominal amortization until the final year. A typical B loan amortization provides for principal payments equal to 1 percent per year until the final year (or the final installment), whereupon the entire remaining principal balance becomes payable. It is the longer maturity and nominal amortization that define a B loan structure. Historically, this is because institutional investors were more willing than banks to accept longer maturities (akin to their bond investments) and, although they required some amortization, they were not fussy about much. Lower scheduled principal repayment and longer maturity together lead to more principal being outstanding for longer and thus additional repayment risks. As a result, generally speaking, lenders holding B loans are generally rewarded with higher pricing as compared to tranche A loans.

Revolving credit loans and A loans are often referred to as the *pro rata tranches* because the lenders who make available the revolving credit loans generally also make a ratable portion of the A loans; B loans are referred to as the *B tranche*. Herein, the latter term is used to refer collectively to all tranches that fit within a B loan repayment schedule like the one described earlier. Thus, even though a credit agreement may have multiple series of B loans (Series B, Series C, Series D, and so forth), any tranche that is in the mold of a B tranche is referred to as a B tranche, notwithstanding that the name assigned to that tranche uses another letter of the alphabet. This, of course, can lead to confusion if an agreement has a revolving credit commitment and two B tranches identified as Series A and Series B, but the point to remember is that a B tranche need not be labeled as such.

2.1.1.3 Competitive Bid Loans

As discussed in greater detail in Section 3.1, a credit agreement may also provide for so-called competitive bid or competitive access facilities. Facilities of this kind are most often offered to borrowers with high credit quality and are tied to revolving credit facilities. Lenders do not commit to make competitive bid loans; rather, these loans may be offered by the lenders at their individual options within the aggregate limits of the revolving credit commitments of all revolving credit lenders. A single lender can lend *more* than the amount of its own revolving credit commitment, so long as the aggregate of all revolving credit loans and all competitive bid loans does not exceed the aggregate of the revolving credit commitments of all the lenders. The purpose of competitive bid loans is to allow the lenders (if they choose) to provide loans to a borrower at rates lower than those otherwise available under the agreed pricing set out in the credit agreement.

The normal mechanism in a competitive bid facility is for the borrower to request its revolving credit lenders to submit offers to make loans for specified periods (usually corresponding to the permitted durations of interest periods) at specified interest rates or at specified margins over the London interbank offered rate (LIBOR). The lenders then compete to provide loans by making the best offers they can. The borrower has the option to accept (or reject) the offers made, although the credit agreement will stipulate that, if the borrower wishes to accept any offers, it will do so in ascending order by agreeing to offers for the lowest rates first. Whether a lender submits an offer is within its sole discretion.

2.1.1.4 Swingline Loans

Swingline loans are normally made available as an adjunct to the revolving credit facility by one of the revolving lenders designated as the "swingline lender." Swingline loans are designed to give the borrower more rapid access to funds than would otherwise be permitted by the notice periods prescribed in the credit agreement, which typically require at least three business days' notice for LIBOR loans and one business day's notice for base rate loans. (LIBOR and base rate are discussed in detail in Chapter 3.) Even where same-day availability is allowed for base rate loans, a swingline facility provides greater flexibility by permitting swingline loans to be made later in the day. Swingline loans can be made on such short notice because they are being advanced by only one lender, often (but not always) the lender serving as the administrative agent. Some agreements may contemplate more than one swingline lender, but rarely will the number exceed two or three. Revolving lenders may be named as swingline lenders in the agreement or may be designated as such at a later time by the borrower; however, it is typically within a lender's sole discretion whether or not to accept the designation as a swingline lender, and a swingline lender can typically resign from acting in such capacity.

A second purpose of a swingline facility is to give the borrower access to loans of lower minimum amounts than would otherwise be required for a syndicated borrowing from all the lenders participating in the revolving credit facility.

Swingline facilities have several key features. First, the swingline lender is customarily obligated to make swingline loans only within the limit of its revolving credit commitment and will never be required to make revolving credit loans and swingline loans in excess of that commitment. Second, a maximum amount of swingline loans is specified, usually a sublimit within the total revolving credit commitments. Third, swingline loans will normally be required to be repaid in a very short time, typically within five business days to two weeks and, sometimes, concurrently with the next regular borrowing under the credit agreement, whenever that occurs. They are intended only as a short-term stopgap until a revolving credit borrowing from the full syndicate can be made. Finally, in the event that for any reason the borrower does not repay the swingline loans within their prescribed maturity (including by reason of an intervening event of default or even bankruptcy), the other revolving credit lenders will be unconditionally obligated to purchase participations in the swingline loans so that the risk of the swingline loans is shared ratably among all revolving credit lenders and not borne disproportionately by the swingline lender.

2.1.2 Letters of Credit

Box 2.2

Subject to the terms and conditions set forth herein, in addition to the Loans provided for herein, the Borrower may request the Issuing Lender to issue, at any time and from time to time during the Revolving Credit

Availability Period, Letters of Credit in such form as is acceptable to the Administrative Agent and the Issuing Lender in their reasonable determination. The issuance of a Letter of Credit hereunder shall constitute utilization of the Revolving Credit Commitments. The aggregate Letter of Credit Exposures *plus* the aggregate outstanding principal amount of the Revolving Credit Loans and Competitive Loans shall not exceed the aggregate amount of the Revolving Credit Commitments.

"*Letter of Credit Exposure*" means, at any time, the sum of the aggregate face amount of all outstanding Letters of Credit plus the aggregate outstanding principal amount of all unreimbursed Letter of Credit drawings.

A credit agreement may provide that the revolving credit facility can be accessed not only through loans, but also through the issuance of letters of credit. In this case, the maximum amount of loans and letters of credit (and unreimbursed letter of credit drawings) is not permitted to exceed the total revolving credit commitments. Often, the aggregate face amount of letters of credit is also subject to a sublimit within the revolving credit commitments.

The content of the letter of credit provisions in a credit agreement is driven, in large part, by the nature of letters of credit and by bank supervisory regulations that constrain how letters of credit are to operate (see, for example, the requirements in Code of Federal Regulations (CFR) Title 12, Section 7.1016 (12 CFR § 7.1016) applicable to national banks). A little background may be helpful. Although a letter of credit is signed by only one party (the issuer), it arises out of an arrangement that has three principal parties: the issuer, an account party, and a beneficiary. The letter of credit itself is an undertaking by the issuer of the letter of credit (virtually always a bank, although legally it can be anyone) made directly to the beneficiary at the request of the account party or applicant (the borrower or, if the agreement allows it, an affiliate or other person designated by the borrower). Pursuant to the letter of credit, the issuer agrees to pay the beneficiary a specified sum upon delivery to the issuer of documents spelled out in the letter of credit. Typically, the account party requests the issuer to deliver a letter of credit to a beneficiary because the latter requires, as a condition to entering into the transaction, that a letter of credit cover the risk of the account party's not paying an obligation that it owes to the beneficiary.

In practical effect, therefore, a letter of credit is a guarantee by the issuer that a required payment by the account party will be made, subject only to the delivery of specified documents. The letter of credit obligates the issuer *unconditionally* to honor drawings under the letter of credit upon presentation of the prescribed documents. In the case of commercial letters of credit issued to support the purchase of goods (discussed in more detail below), the drawing under the letter of credit will itself constitute payment by the account party to the beneficiary. When payment is made upon a drawing under the letter of credit (assuming the documents appear on their face to be proper), the account party is obligated to reimburse the issuer for the amount paid. The net result of the entire structure is that the beneficiary has the credit strength of the issuer substituted for that of its customer, the account party, and it is the issuer that takes the credit risk of the account party.

The undertaking by the issuer under a letter of credit is independent of the contract between the account party and the beneficiary. The only requirement is that the documents presented conform to the conditions stipulated in the letter of credit; the issuer is not under any obligation to verify the truth of statements in the documents. It looks at documents and documents only. So long as the documents appear on their face to comply with the terms of the letter of credit, the issuer is obligated to pay.

Letters of credit can be "commercial" (or "trade") letters of credit (if they support the shipment of and payment for goods), standby letters of credit (if they support an obligation to make payments to the beneficiary), or performance letters of credit (if they support the performance of nonfinancial obligations). A commercial (or trade) letter of credit might be issued, for example, to support the import by a U.S. purchaser of electronic equipment from a Thai seller, where the seller wants assurance (before it loads boxes on a freighter) that the purchaser is money-good to pay for the shipment. The letter of credit obligates the issuer to pay the Thai seller the purchase price of equipment shipped upon delivery to the issuer, for example, of a draft, an invoice, a bill of lading showing that the equipment has been loaded on board a ship bound for the United States, evidence that the cargo is insured, and whatever other documents the buyer and seller have agreed (certificates of origin, proof of tax payments, customs documentation, and so on—the list can be endless). A standby letter of credit might be issued to support a borrower's obligation to an insurance company for workers' compensation payments, or payment of franchise obligations by a cable television company to a municipality, or an infinite variety of other obligations.

A performance letter of credit might support completion of reclamation obligations in a construction project, much like a reclamation bond. The documents required to be delivered upon a drawing under a standby or performance letter of credit are usually simpler than those for a commercial letter of credit—typically, just a certification from the beneficiary that the borrower is required to make payment to the beneficiary and has not done so.

Letters of credit are the product of centuries of trade practice out of which has grown a large body of law that defines the rights and duties of the issuer, the account party, and the beneficiary. The key principles, in the United States at least, are distilled into Article 5 of the Uniform Commercial Code. In addition, the International Chamber of Commerce (ICC) has issued rules for commercial and standby letters of credit that have gained wide acceptance and which are normally incorporated by reference into letters of credit. For commercial letters of credit, the Uniform Customs and Practice (UCP) for Documentary Credits (ICC Publication No. 600), effective July 1, 2007, is the latest revision of these rules. The corresponding rules for standby or performance letters of credit are the International Standby Practices (ISP; ICC Publication No. 590), 1998. The UCP and the ISP apply to a letter of credit only if the letter of credit states that it is subject to one or the other.

Some agreements may contemplate more than one letter of credit issuer but rarely will the number exceed two or three. If there are multiple letter of credit issuers, the credit agreement may specify the circumstances governing which letter of credit issuer will issue a particular letter of credit or it may permit the borrower to choose. Rarely will more than one letter of credit issuer issue a letter of credit to a beneficiary in response to an issuance request, as it would be impractical for a beneficiary to make a drawing upon more than one issuing bank. Letter of credit issuers may be named as such in the credit agreement or may be designated as such at a later time by the borrower; however, it is typically within a lender's sole discretion whether to accept the designation as a letter of credit issuer. A letter of credit issuer can typically resign from acting in such capacity. The effect of resignation is that the letter of credit issuer will no longer be obligated to issue letters of credit but will still be entitled to the benefits of the credit agreement with respect to outstanding letters of credit previously issued by it.

Given the purpose and legal structure of letters of credit described in the preceding paragraphs, the corresponding language set out in the typical credit agreement may seem self-evident. We discuss here the key provisions most often included in credit agreements that contemplate the issuance of letters of credit.

2.1.2.1 Application for Issuance

Box 2.3

If requested by the Issuing Lender, the Borrower shall submit a letter of credit application on the Issuing Lender's standard form in connection with any request for a Letter of Credit. In the event of any inconsistency between the terms and conditions of this Agreement and the terms and conditions of any such application (or any other agreement entered into by the Borrower with the Issuing Lender relating to any Letter of Credit), the terms and conditions of this Agreement shall control.

The party that requests issuance of a letter of credit is often referred to as an "applicant." The term arises out of the procedure under which letters of credit are most often issued by banks. Indeed, the vast majority of letters of credit are opened on a one-off basis for a bank's customer after completion by the customer of a standard-form application. The typical application requires the customer to spell out with particularity the terms of the letter of credit (identity of beneficiary, amount, expiration date, drawing conditions, and so forth) and then to agree to a jumble of fine print, including the obligation to reimburse the bank upon any drawing under the letter of credit, to post cash collateral if the bank ever "deems itself insecure," and to indemnify the bank for any liability associated with the issuance of the letter of credit. The substance of most of the provisions spelled out in the boilerplate for a standard letter of credit application will also appear in the letter of credit provisions of the typical syndicated credit agreement.

Letters of credit, even when issued under a syndicated credit agreement, are normally processed by the issuer's letter of credit department, just as the case with the customary one-off letter of credit described in the preceding paragraph. Department personnel will want the borrower to complete a letter of credit application in the same manner as would otherwise happen. The typical syndicated credit agreement allows this practice but, to avoid any inconsistency between the issuer's particular form of application and the credit agreement itself, it will state that the credit agreement controls in the event of conflicting provisions. This has the effect of superseding most of the fine-print boilerplate on the back of the letter of credit application, but leaving in place the letter of credit particulars (which is probably what the letter of credit department is most interested in anyway).

2.1.2.2   Form of Letter of Credit

> **Box 2.4**
>
> The issuance or modification by the Issuing Lender of any Letter of Credit shall, in addition to the conditions precedent set forth in Article____, be subject to the conditions that such Letter of Credit shall be in such form as is acceptable to the Administrative Agent and the Issuing Lender.

The application submitted by the borrower in connection with any request for issuance of a letter of credit sets forth the conditions to drawing that the borrower wishes to impose upon the beneficiary. In many cases the actual form of the letter of credit is not presented by the borrower to the issuer, and it is the issuer itself that prepares the letter of credit (on its standard form) and inserts the appropriate drawing terms. In some cases the borrower may try to impose upon the issuer a particular form of letter of credit that has been settled upon in negotiations with the beneficiary. To preclude the borrower from requesting a letter of credit that is not satisfactory to the issuer (perhaps the borrower insists upon a letter of credit written in Slovenian, or attempts to impose nondocumentary drawing conditions, or wants documents delivered to a branch of the issuer that is not equipped to handle the review responsibilities), the credit agreement typically gives the issuer veto rights over the actual form of any letter of credit.

2.1.2.3   Expiration Date

> **Box 2.5**
>
> Each Letter of Credit shall expire at or prior to the close of business on the earlier of (i) the date twelve months after the date of the issuance of such Letter of Credit (or, in the case of any renewal or extension thereof, twelve months after the then-current expiration date of such Letter of Credit) and (ii) the date that is five Business Days prior to the last day of the Revolving Credit Availability Period.

As with bank commitments generally, the regulatory regimes applicable to banks require that any letter of credit must be limited in duration or contain a specified expiration date. In the case of national banks, the Office of the Comptroller of the Currency (OCC) has broadened this somewhat by, among other things, allowing a letter of credit to have no expiration date if the bank has the ability to terminate the letter of credit on a periodic basis, or to obtain cash collateral from the account party upon demand (12 CFR § 7.1016(b) (1)(iii)). Although these regulatory requirements could be met by providing that any letter of credit must expire prior to the commitment termination date (which might be five or seven years after issuance), many credit agreements stipulate that any letter of credit issued under the agreement shall expire either within one year of issuance or, in the case of so-called "evergreen" letters of credit, within one year of its most recent renewal. The shorter, one-year maturity is inserted for the reasons discussed in Section 9.2.4, namely the risk that a bankruptcy court may reduce the issuer's claim in bankruptcy by its estimate of the probability of the letter of credit being drawn. Also, the regulatory capital treatment for a short-term letter of credit with a one-year term, although renewable, is more advantageous for a bank as compared with a longer-term letter of credit.

Evergreen letters of credit effectively allow for terms longer than one year without having the tenor at any given time exceed 12 months, since any renewal beyond one year is at the option of the issuer. In an evergreen letter of credit, the initial expiration date is automatically extended an additional year (or other period) unless the issuer gives the beneficiary advance notice (typically 30 days) that the letter of credit will not be renewed. The 30-day notice period itself is set out in the letter of credit and not in the credit agreement. Each year, as the new expiration date approaches, the same procedure kicks in so that, if the issuer never sends a notice to the beneficiary halting each automatic annual extension, the letter of credit term may run many years. Commercial letters of credit are typically for the shorter periods consistent with the amount of time it takes to assemble, pack, and ship the goods being purchased under the letter of credit; the evergreen option is, therefore, largely inapplicable to commercial credits.

A credit agreement, in any event, normally does not permit letters of credit to have an expiration date (taking into account evergreen renewals) beyond the termination date of the commitments. The language set out in Box 2.5 requires that any termination date actually occur five days before the commitment termination date so that whatever drawings are to be made under the letter of credit by reason of the termination can be paid prior to the borrower's loan and other obligations becoming due.

2.1.2.4   Limitations on Amount

> **Box 2.6**
>
> A Letter of Credit shall be issued, amended, renewed, or extended only if (and upon issuance, amendment, renewal, or extension of each Letter of Credit the Borrower shall be deemed to represent and warrant that), after giving effect to such issuance, amendment, renewal, or extension (i) the aggregate Letter of Credit Exposure shall not exceed $____ and (ii) the sum of the Revolving Credit Loans, Competitive Loans, and Letter of Credit Exposures shall not exceed the total Revolving Credit Commitments.

Bank regulations require that letters of credit include an amount limit. A letter of credit (at least if issued by a bank) may not, as an example, support a borrower's obligation to compensate a municipality for whatever damages (without limit) might occur to streets during the installation of underground fiber-optic cables. A letter of credit could support this type of liability only if it covered damages ". . . up to $____," so that there is a specified maximum limit beyond which the issuer is not obligated. Inserting a ceiling into a letter of credit allows the lenders to control their exposure to the borrower. As noted earlier in this chapter, where revolving credit commitments are available for loans and letters of credit, the maximum amount of both will not be permitted to exceed the total revolving credit commitments; often the letter of credit exposure is further subject to a sublimit within the revolving credit commitments.

2.1.2.5   Examination of Documents

> **Box 2.7**
>
> The Issuing Lender shall, within a reasonable time following its receipt thereof, examine all documents purporting to represent a demand for payment under a Letter of Credit. The Issuing Lender shall promptly after such examination notify the Administrative Agent and the Borrower by telephone (confirmed by telecopy) of such demand for payment and whether the Issuing Lender has made or will make a Letter of Credit Disbursement thereunder; *provided* that any failure to give or delay in giving such notice shall not relieve the Borrower of its obligation to reimburse the Issuing Lender and the lenders with respect to any such Letter of Credit Disbursement.

Obviously, if the issuer of a letter of credit makes payment only against documents, it must examine them. The language set out in Box 2.7 is a typical undertaking by the letter of credit issuer to the lenders and the borrower to examine drawing documents within a reasonable time. An issuer that does not examine documents within a reasonable time may be deemed, under both the Uniform Commercial Code (§ 5–108(b)) and the terms of the letter of credit itself (which, as noted in Section 2.1.2, normally incorporates the provisions of the UCP or ISP), to have approved the documents tendered and be bound to make payment. Uniform Commercial Code Section 5-108(b) defines a "reasonable time" to examine documents as no more than seven business days. The UCP stipulates a shorter period for commercial letters of credit (". . . a maximum of five banking days" (UCP 600, Article 14b)); the ISP prescribes a similar time for standby letters of credit (". . . beyond seven business days is deemed to be unreasonable" (ISP 590, Rule 5.01.a.i)).

2.1.2.6   Borrower's Reimbursement Obligation

Box 2.8

If the Issuing Lender shall make any Letter of Credit Disbursement in respect of a Letter of Credit, the Borrower shall reimburse the Issuing Lender in respect of such Letter of Credit Disbursement by paying to the Administrative Agent an amount equal to such Letter of Credit Disbursement not later than 12:00 noon, New York City time, on (i) the Business Day that the Borrower receives notice of such Letter of Credit Disbursement, if such notice is received prior to 10:00 a.m., New York City time, or (ii) the Business Day immediately following the day that the Borrower receives such notice, if such notice is not received prior to such time.

The Borrower's obligation to reimburse Letter of Credit Disbursements as provided herein shall be absolute, unconditional, and irrevocable, and shall be performed strictly in accordance with the terms of this Agreement under any and all circumstances whatsoever and irrespective of (i) any lack of validity or enforceability of any Letter of Credit, or any term or provision therein, (ii) any draft or other document presented under a Letter of Credit proving to be forged, fraudulent, or invalid in any respect or any statement therein being untrue or inaccurate in any respect, or (iii) any other event or circumstance whatsoever, whether or not similar to any of the foregoing, that might, but for the provisions of this Section, constitute a legal or equitable discharge of, or provide a right of setoff against, the Borrower's obligations hereunder; *provided* that the Borrower shall not be precluded from asserting any claim for direct (but not consequential) damages suffered by it to the extent, but only to the extent, caused by the willful misconduct or gross negligence of the Issuing Lender in determining whether a request presented under any Letter of Credit complied with the terms of such Letter of Credit.

For a bank to issue a letter of credit, the account party (the borrower) must be unconditionally obligated to reimburse the bank upon a drawing under the letter of credit. Some regulatory schemes may be more flexible on this point (the OCC, for example, has said that national banks need only be "fully collateralized or have a post-honor right of reimbursement from the account party or from another issuer [of a letter of credit] . . . ," 12 CFR § 7.1016(b) (1)(iv)), but credit agreements customarily follow the practice of including an absolute undertaking on the part of the borrower to pay when a drawing is made.

The typical credit agreement requires reimbursement to be made on the day on which a drawing under the letter of credit is honored (or, at most, one or a small number of business days later). Frequently, if reimbursement is to occur on the day of drawing, payment on the next day will be allowed in the event that notice of the drawing is not received in sufficient time for the borrower to take down a loan on that day. Sometimes the credit agreement states that the reimbursement claim automatically converts into revolving credit loans, with the lenders obligated to fund their portions of the loans so that the issuer obtains full reimbursement for the drawing. Either approach satisfies the regulatory requirement that the borrower be obligated to pay the issuer upon any drawing by the beneficiary.

Credit agreements describe the obligation of the borrower to reimburse the issuer as absolute and unconditional (or words to that effect). The borrower will be asked to waive certain particular excuses to payment that it might otherwise be permitted to raise (invalidity or unenforceability of the letter of credit and fraud or forgery in drawing documents) as well as "any other event or circumstance whatsoever" that might discharge the borrower. The latter catch-all waiver is, among other things, intended to prevent the borrower from asserting against the issuer defenses that the borrower may have against the beneficiary. As an example, the borrower may not refuse to reimburse the issuing lender on the ground that electronic components paid for through the drawing under a letter of credit are defective. Since a letter of credit is an obligation of the issuer *independent* of the agreement between the borrower and the beneficiary, if the bank must pay, the borrower must reimburse. The breadth of the waivers is driven by the need that the borrower's obligation be sufficiently absolute to satisfy regulatory requirements and by the purely commercial concern that any risk associated with the issuance of a letter of credit resides with the borrower.

There is one common exception to the general rule described in the preceding paragraph (that the borrower's reimbursement obligation be absolute). The exception permits the borrower to refuse reimbursement if the issuer, in determining whether a drawing request is rightful, is either grossly negligent or guilty of willful misconduct. (For a discussion of the term "gross negligence," see Section 10.1.4.) This, for example, protects the borrower against an issuing lender blithely honoring drawing requests without regard to whether the requests are proper. It protects the lenders as well, since their obligation to pay for their participation interests is contingent upon the borrower's defaulting on a reimbursement claim actually required to be made by it to the issuing lender (which would not be the case if the related drawing request was honored as a result of gross negligence or willful misconduct).

2.1.2.7 Participations by Lenders

> **Box 2.9**
>
> By the issuance of a Letter of Credit, and without any further action on the part of the Issuing Lender or the Revolving Lenders, the Issuing Lender hereby grants to each Revolving Lender, and each Revolving Lender hereby acquires from the Issuing Lender, a participation in such Letter of Credit equal to such Lender's Applicable Percentage of the aggregate amount available to be drawn under such Letter of Credit. Each Revolving Lender acknowledges and agrees that its obligation to acquire participations pursuant to this paragraph in respect of Letters of Credit is absolute and unconditional and shall not be affected by any circumstance whatsoever, including any amendment, renewal, or extension of any Letter of Credit, or the occurrence and continuance of a Default or reduction or termination of the Commitments. In consideration and in furtherance of the foregoing, each Revolving Lender hereby absolutely and unconditionally agrees to pay to the Administrative Agent, for account of the Issuing Lender, such Lender's Applicable Percentage of each Letter of Credit Disbursement made by the Issuing Lender promptly upon the request of the Issuing Lender at any time from the time of such Letter of Credit Disbursement until such Letter of Credit Disbursement is reimbursed by the Borrower. Such payment shall be made without any offset, abatement, withholding, or reduction whatsoever.

Although in the normal case only one bank issues any particular letter of credit, that bank will not want to assume for its own account the full credit exposure to the borrower in respect of the reimbursement obligation. In a syndicated facility, the exposure is, instead, shared by all of the revolving credit lenders ratably in accordance with their revolving credit commitments. The mechanism to effect this is through the acquisition by each lender, upon issuance of the letter of credit, of a participation in the letter of credit exposure (refer to Chapter 11 for a full discussion of the concept of participation). The language set out in Box 2.9 is a common approach. Payment for the participations is not required unless the borrower fails to reimburse the issuer.

The obligation to pay for the participation will, subject only to demand by the issuer, be absolute, regardless of whether any of the conditions for the making of loans under the credit agreement have been satisfied. Even bankruptcy of the borrower or reduction or termination of commitments will not excuse the lenders from their obligation to pay the issuing lender. The logic is that the conditions to the credit extension (the issuance of the letter of credit) were required to be satisfied at opening; once that has occurred, the conditions are no longer relevant, just as loan conditions are no longer pertinent once a loan is made.

In the past, there has been the worry that the obligation of a bank to purchase a participation in an issuing lender's letter of credit could be tantamount to an *ultra vires* guarantee of the borrower's obligations. This concern would exist particularly in cases where the borrower is first required to default on its reimbursement obligation in respect of a drawing before the participant is obligated to pay. At least in the context of national banks, this is probably no longer a concern. Interpretations issued by the Comptroller of the Currency have implicitly acknowledged that default by the account party (the borrower) can be a condition to the participant's obligation to pay the purchase price to the issuing lender in respect of its participation.[1]

2.1.2.8   Strict versus Substantial Compliance

Box 2.10

The Issuing Lender may accept documents that appear on their face to be in substantial compliance with the terms of a Letter of Credit

---

[1] See OCC Interpretive Letter No. 412, January 26, 1988, reprinted in [1988-1989 Transfer Binder]. Fed. Banking L. Rep. (CCH) 85,636.

without responsibility for further investigation, regardless of any notice or information to the contrary, and may make payment upon presentation of documents that appear on their face to be in substantial compliance with the terms of such Letter of Credit. The Issuing Lender shall have the right, in its sole discretion, to decline to accept such documents and to make such payment if such documents are not in strict compliance with the terms of such Letter of Credit. The foregoing shall establish the standard of care to be exercised by the Issuing Lender when determining whether drafts and other documents presented under a Letter of Credit comply with the terms thereof (and the parties hereto hereby waive, to the extent permitted by applicable law, any standard of care inconsistent with the foregoing).

A point that frequently arises in negotiating letter of credit provisions, whether in a single lender application or in a syndicated credit agreement, is what happens if the issuer wrongfully honors (or wrongfully dishonors) a drawing under a letter of credit. As noted earlier, a letter of credit requires that the beneficiary deliver documents to the issuer in order to effect a drawing. The documents may be as simple as a notice, but can be complex if the requirements of the underlying commercial transaction and the negotiation of the parties demand it. Whatever the required documents, the letter of credit issuer is instructed to pay only if the documents delivered meet the conditions spelled out in the letter of credit. So how much wiggle room is there if the documents are not exactly as prescribed?

Many facilities employ what can best be described as a double standard—perhaps a loaded term, but an approach blessed by the Uniform Commercial Code.[2] As against a beneficiary, the credit agreement allows the issuer to dishonor any drawing that does not "strictly" comply with the provisions of the letter of credit (the second sentence in Box 2.10). As against the borrower, however, the credit agreement allows the issuer to pay against documents that "substantially" comply with the terms of the credit (the first sentence in Box 2.10). Absent a contrary agreement of the parties, the Uniform Commercial Code requires that an issuer deny payment to a beneficiary if the documents presented do not *strictly* comply with the terms of the letter of credit.

Strict compliance is a term of art requiring that documents presented to an issuer under a letter of credit conform strictly to the terms

---

[2] See Comment 1 to UCC § 5-108.

specified in the letter of credit. If a letter of credit calls for presentation of a bill of lading referencing "java white granulated sugar" and the bill actually tendered refers to "java white sugar" the issuer is entitled to refuse payment as the documents do not strictly comply with the requirements of the letter of credit; see *Lamborn v. Lake Shore Banking & Trust Co.*, 188 N.Y.S. 162 (App. Div. 1st Dep't 1921), *aff'd* 231 N.Y. 616 (1921). Similarly, if a letter of credit calls for documents referencing "yellow pine flooring," but the bill of lading actually references "yellow pine lumber," the drawing is not in strict compliance; see *Brown v. Ambler*, 7 A. 903 (Md. 1887). In *Equitable Trust Co. v. Dawson Partners, Ltd.*, 27 Lloyd's List L. Rep. 49 (H.L. 1927), one English court famously pronounced that in letter of credit transactions, "there is no room for documents which are almost the same, or which will do just as well."

Although some cases have held that strict compliance does not mean "oppressive perfectionism" (see *New Braunfels Nat'l Bank v. Odiorne*, 780 S.W.2d 313 (Tex. Ct. App. 1989)), few issuers want to take the risk that if they honor a drawing the borrower will refuse reimbursement because the issuer paid against documents that did not strictly comply with the terms of the letter of credit. Accordingly, credit agreements normally give the letter of credit issuer an absolute right to be reimbursed so long as the drawing "substantially" complies with the letter of credit. Thus, a bill of lading for "grapes" could be satisfactory, insofar as reimbursement by the borrower is concerned, even though the letter of credit required delivery of a bill of lading for "Alicante Bouchez grapes"; see *Laudisi v. American Exch. Nat'l Bank*, 239 N.Y. 234 (1924). Technical misstatements (if not material to the drawing), although not complying *strictly* with the letter of credit, nevertheless comply *substantially* with its terms. The standard credit agreement protects the issuer against close judgment calls in reviewing documents.

2.1.2.9 Indemnification

Box 2.11

(a) *Indemnification by Borrower.* The Borrower shall indemnify the Issuing Lender against, and hold it harmless from, any and all losses, claims, damages, liabilities and related expenses (including fees and disbursements of counsel) incurred by or asserted against the Issuing Lender by the Borrower or any third party arising out of, in connection with, or as a result of any Letter of Credit or the use or proposed use of the proceeds therefrom (including any refusal by the Issuing Lender to honor a demand for payment under a Letter of Credit if the documents presented in connection therewith do not strictly comply with the terms of such Letter of Credit), *provided* that such indemnity shall not be available to the extent that such losses, claims, damages, liabilities, or related expenses (x) are determined by a court of competent jurisdiction by final and nonappealable judgment to have resulted from the gross negligence or willful misconduct of the Issuing Lender or (y) result from a claim brought by the Borrower against the Issuing Lender for breach in bad faith of the Issuing Lender's obligations hereunder or under any other Loan Document, if the Borrower has obtained a final and nonappealable judgment in its favor on such claim as determined by a court of competent jurisdiction.

(b) *Reimbursement by Lenders.* To the extent that the Borrower for any reason fails to indefeasibly pay any amount required under paragraph (a) above to be paid by it, each Revolving Lender severally agrees to pay to the Issuing Lender such Lender's Applicable Percentage of such unpaid amount, *provided* that the unreimbursed expense or indemnified loss, claim, damage, liability, or related expense was incurred by or asserted against the Issuing Lender in its capacity as such.

In addition to the general indemnification given by the borrower (and the corresponding backstop by the lenders) to the administrative agent and the lenders in the so-called boilerplate provisions of the credit agreement (see Sections 10.2 and 12.6), the borrower and issuing lenders will expect to be similarly indemnified in respect of letters of credit issued under the agreement. Typically, the credit agreement combines all indemnification provisions into one clause (consistent with the approach taken by the Model Credit Agreement Provisions of the Loan Syndications and Trading Association (LSTA)) and does not break them out separately. The language in Box 2.11 is an adaptation of the LSTA's Model Credit Agreement Provisions showing the letter of credit indemnification only and is not typical.

2.1.2.10 Cash Collateral

Box 2.12

Event of Default; Acceleration; Prepayment:

If either (i) any Event of Default shall occur and be continuing, on the Business Day that the Borrower receives notice from the Administrative Agent or the Required Lenders (or, if the maturity of the Loans has been accelerated, Lenders with Letter of Credit Exposure representing [more than 50%] of the total Letter of Credit Exposure) demanding the deposit of cash collateral pursuant to this paragraph, (ii) the Borrower shall be required to provide cover for Letter of Credit Exposure pursuant to Section [*Mandatory Prepayments*], the Borrower shall immediately deposit into an account established and maintained on the books and records of the Administrative Agent . . . an amount in cash equal to, in the case of an Event of Default, [105%] of the Letter of Credit Exposure as of such date *plus* any accrued and unpaid interest thereon and, in the case of cover pursuant to Section [*Mandatory Prepayment*], the amount required under said Section; *provided* that the obligation to deposit such cash collateral shall become effective immediately, and such deposit shall become immediately due and payable, without demand or other notice of any kind, upon the occurrence of any Event of Default with respect to the Borrower described in Section [*Bankruptcy Defaults*].

Such deposit shall be held by the Administrative Agent as collateral for the payment and performance of the obligations of the Borrower under this Agreement, and the Administrative Agent shall have exclusive dominion and control, including the exclusive right of withdrawal, over such deposit. Other than any interest earned on the investment of such deposit, which investments shall be made at the option and sole discretion of the Administrative Agent and at the Borrower's risk and expense, such deposit shall not bear interest.

* * * * * * * *

Defaulting Lender:

At any time that there shall exist a Defaulting Lender, within one Business Day following the written request of the Administrative Agent or any Issuing Bank (with a copy to the Administrative Agent) the Borrower shall Cash Collateralize the Issuing Banks' Fronting Exposure with respect to such Defaulting Lender (determined after giving effect to Section [*Defaulting Lender – Reallocation of Participations to Reduce Fronting Exposure*] and any Cash Collateral provided by such Defaulting Lender) in an amount not less than the Minimum Collateral Amount.

(a) *Grant of Security Interest.* The Borrower, and to the extent provided by any Defaulting Lender, such Defaulting Lender, hereby grants to the Administrative Agent, for the benefit of the Issuing Banks, and agrees to maintain, a first priority security interest in all such Cash Collateral as security for the Defaulting Lenders' obligation to fund participations in respect of L/C Obligations, to be applied pursuant to clause (b) below. If at any time the Administrative Agent determines that Cash Collateral is subject to any right or claim of any Person other than the Administrative Agent and the Issuing Banks as herein provided [(other than [specify applicable Permitted Liens])], or that the total amount of such Cash Collateral is less than the Minimum Collateral Amount, the Borrower will, promptly upon demand by the Administrative Agent, pay or provide to the Administrative Agent additional Cash Collateral in an amount sufficient to eliminate such deficiency (after giving effect to any Cash Collateral provided by the Defaulting Lender).

(b) *Application*. Notwithstanding anything to the contrary contained in this Agreement, Cash Collateral provided under this Section [*Cash Collateral*] or Section [*Defaulting Lender*] in respect of Letters of Credit shall be applied to the satisfaction of the Defaulting Lender's obligation to fund participations in respect of L/C Obligations (including, as to Cash Collateral provided by a Defaulting Lender, any interest accrued on such obligation) for which the Cash Collateral was so provided, prior to any other application of such property as may otherwise be provided for herein.

(c) *Termination of Requirement*. Cash Collateral (or the appropriate portion thereof) provided to reduce any Issuing Bank's Fronting Exposure shall no longer be required to be held as Cash Collateral pursuant to this Section [*Cash Collateral*] following (i) the elimination of the applicable Fronting Exposure (including by the termination of Defaulting Lender status of the applicable Lender), or (ii) the determination by the Administrative Agent and each Issuing Bank that there exists excess Cash Collateral; *provided* that, subject to Section [*Defaulting Lenders*] the Person providing Cash Collateral and each Issuing Bank may agree that Cash Collateral shall be held to support future anticipated Fronting Exposure or other obligations [and *provided further* that to the extent that such Cash Collateral was provided by the Borrower, such Cash Collateral shall remain subject to the security interest granted pursuant to the Loan Documents].

Letters of credit are different from loans in a fundamental way in that they cannot be unilaterally repaid or cancelled. A letter of credit is an irrevocable undertaking issued by an issuer at the request of an applicant and payable to a third party (the beneficiary). The borrower is unconditionally obligated to reimburse the issuer in the event of a drawing by the beneficiary under the letter of credit. Prior to a drawing, the reimbursement obligation is not even outstanding and therefore cannot be paid or prepaid; nothing is owed so nothing can be payable. Some letters of credit give the issuer the right to force a drawing by the beneficiary in order to crystallize a reimbursement claim but, absent such a provision, the issuer must either wait for a drawing or wait for the letter of credit to expire before the amount of the borrower's liability is settled.

To enable letters of credit nevertheless to be "repaid" (or "prepaid" in the case of a voluntary or mandatory prepayment), credit agreements often contemplate that the borrower provide cash collateral for its obligation to reimburse the issuer upon a drawing. In the context of voluntary prepayments, the agreement may also allow the borrower to cause a backstop letter of credit to be issued in favor of the issuing lender by a third-party bank. Whatever the form of support, the term "cover" (as in cover for the future, contingent letter of credit reimbursement claim) is often used to describe both cash collateral and backstop letters of credit. No distinction is intended between the two terms.

The sample language in Box 2.12 reflects typical provisions where the cover will consist of cash collateral. In this context, the obligation to provide cover is triggered by one of four events: an event of default, an acceleration, the occurrence of a mandatory prepayment event, or a revolving credit lender becoming a defaulting lender. The requirement to post cover based upon an event of default is dependent upon the administrative agent or the required lenders affirmatively demanding cover. The requirement to post cover based upon an acceleration may similarly be triggered by the administrative agent and the required lenders, but also by the lenders exposed on the letter of credit itself (including those lenders that have purchased participations in the letter of credit). The requirement to post cover upon the occurrence of certain bankruptcy events is triggered automatically without any requirement that the lenders request cover, just as is the case with the automatic acceleration of loans upon bankruptcy. Cash collateral upon an acceleration (including upon bankruptcy) is discussed in some detail in Section 9.2.4. The obligation to post collateral upon the occurrence of a mandatory prepayment event is automatic once the event occurs. However, as discussed in Section 4.8, letter of credit reimbursement obligations are normally not required to be covered until all outstanding revolving loans have first been reduced to zero. Cover in the context of voluntary prepayments, such as when a credit agreement is being terminated early, is discussed in Section 5.1.10. The obligation to post collateral upon a revolving credit lender becoming a defaulting lender is triggered by a request of the administrative agent or any issuing lender. The sample language in Box 2.12 under the caption "Defaulting Lender" is taken from the LSTA's Model Credit Agreement Provisions.

The amount of cash collateral (or, in the case of voluntary prepayments, the amount of a backstop letter of credit) typically required to be posted is not limited to the face amount of the letter of credit. It is customary, at least where the facility is to be prepaid in full (such as upon a full mandatory or voluntary prepayment, or an event of default), to require that an amount exceeding the face amount of the outstanding letters of credit be posted (in the form of cash or a backstop letter of credit) in order to cover letter of credit commissions, interest charges on any reimbursement obligation, and fees associated with any drawing under the letters of credit. A typical percentage to be posted ranges from 102 to 105 percent of the face amount of the letters of credit. When cash collateral is required as a result of a revolving credit lender becoming a defaulting lender, it is not the full face amount of the letter of credit that is required to be posted, but rather only the defaulting lender's proportionate share of it.

Deposits held in a cash collateral account will normally not bear interest or even be invested except in the discretion of the administrative agent. Cash collateral is intended to be a substitute for payment by the borrower and not an earning investment; cash, once posted with the agent, is not subject to control by the borrower. The purpose here is twofold. First, the lenders do not want to be subject to market-value fluctuations. If investments are ever allowed, they are normally limited to the safest and most short term of Treasury securities or similar high-quality cash assets. Second, all things being equal, the lenders much prefer to have a letter of credit replaced rather than remain outstanding (even if secured by cash) and so the negative arbitrage implicit in posting cash is a way to encourage the borrower to cancel or replace letters of credit as soon as possible.

2.1.3   Synthetic Letters of Credit

As discussed in Section 2.1.2, letters of credit are typically issued under revolving credit facilities. As a consequence, the liquidity provided by lenders (such as B lenders) that are unable or unwilling to participate in revolving credit facilities is not available to support the issuance of the typical letter of credit. To fill this gap, a financing structure (sometimes referred to as a "synthetic" letter of credit structure) has been devised to expand the universe of possible lenders that might participate in letter of credit facilities to include traditional term loan lenders.

The so-called *synthetic* letters of credit issued under this structure are not in fact a different type or species of letter of credit. From the perspective of borrowers and beneficiaries, they are as real as any letter of credit issued under a traditional revolving credit facility. From the perspective of the lenders, however, synthetic letters of credit are quite different. Whereas under a traditional letter of credit facility the lenders do not provide funds to the issuing lender unless and until a drawing is made and the borrower fails to reimburse the issuing lender, under a synthetic structure the lenders provide the full amount of their funds upfront on day one, just as they would if they were making a term loan (for this reason, this structure is also sometimes referred to as a "pre-funded" letter of credit structure). Each lender acquires a participation in each letter of credit issued by the issuing lender (as it does in a traditional structure) and the funds provided by such lender at closing are held by the issuer in a deposit (owned by the lender) as cash collateral for the lender's obligation to fund its participation if a drawing is not reimbursed by the borrower.

From the issuer's perspective, the synthetic letter of credit structure has another advantage besides expanding the potential lenders in the syndicate. Since the obligations of the participant are secured by cash, the issuer is spared the work of assessing the credit strength of the participant, as well as the burden of pursuing the participant in the event there is a drawing under the letter of credit and the participant fails to pay. The issuer, having possession of the cash collateral, is in the enviable position of simply having to grab the deposited cash when payment is due, rather than fret about sending notices and praying that an illiquid fund will make timely payment.

The issuing lender pays the lenders interest on the deposits, generally at a rate slightly less than LIBOR, and the borrower pays the lenders a facility fee. The sum of the interest on each deposit plus the facility fee payable to each lender is designed to be equal to the amount that the lender would receive for a term loan to the borrower. If the deposit is debited because a drawing is not reimbursed, whatever principal and interest the lender loses on the deposit is replaced with the borrower's obligation to the lender to reimburse it for having funded its participation in the drawing and to pay interest on the reimbursement claim until it is paid. What the borrower sees as a letter of credit facility the lenders see as a term loan facility.

The synthetic letter of credit structure described above results in a substantial risk that certain non-U.S. lenders (in particular, institutional lenders formed in the Cayman Islands, which include a large majority of the institutional lenders who participate in the U.S. domestic loan market) will be subject to U.S. withholding taxes on the interest and fees they receive in respect of synthetic letters of credit issued by a U.S. domestic borrower. As a result, such structures, as a practical matter, are viable only for non-U.S. borrowers or for lenders that are either in the United States or in jurisdictions that have withholding tax treaties with the United States providing for an exemption from U.S. withholding taxes. An alternative structure that is used for U.S. domestic borrowers is to have all or a portion of the proceeds from a tranche of term loans be deposited into a collateral account to secure the borrower's obligation to reimburse drawings under the synthetic letter of credit.

Multicurrency synthetic letter of credit facilities are rare because the lenders expect to see their credit exposure capped at the initial amount deposited by them in a particular currency (usually dollars) on day one. If letters of credit are issued in different currencies, fluctuations in foreign exchange (FX) rates could mean that the amounts on deposit may become insufficient to fund the issuing lender fully for drawings in those other currencies. Accordingly, in any multicurrency synthetic letter of credit facility, it is likely that the issuing lender will bear some of the credit risk for the borrower associated with fluctuations in FX rates.

2.1.4 Bankers' Acceptances

Box 2.13

Subject to the terms and conditions set forth herein, each Lender agrees to extend credit to the Borrower from time to time during the Availability Period, by creating and discounting Acceptances for the Borrower in the manner hereinafter provided up to but not exceeding its Commitment, *provided* that the sum of the total Acceptance Liabilities shall not at any time exceed the total Commitments.

Bankers' acceptances represent a means of financing associated with trade, particularly international trade. Essentially, an acceptance facility is a big-ticket check-writing arrangement used by importers and exporters. An importer that needs money to finance the importation of goods might draw a draft upon itself (much like writing a check to cash); take the draft to the importer's bank, which will "accept" the draft (equivalent to certifying a check); and then sell (discount) the accepted draft either to the bank that accepted the draft or in the secondary bankers' acceptance market. The proceeds are, in turn, used by the importer to pay the exporter for the goods. Conversely, an exporter might draw a draft upon itself and, following "acceptance" thereof by its bank, discount the same to its bank or into the market and apply the proceeds to manufacture or assemble goods that are to be exported. In either case, once the draft has been accepted, it becomes an obligation of both the bank and the drawer of the draft. As such, it is a highly marketable instrument.

The accepted draft is ordinarily a *time draft*. Unlike a check written to cash, which is payable immediately (the technical term is *at sight*), a time draft is payable on a future date specified on the instrument—usually one to six months after the date the draft is created. The term of the draft normally corresponds to the amount of time the importer anticipates will be necessary to begin converting the goods it has purchased into the cash needed to pay the draft when it comes due.

In a credit facility that provides for bankers' acceptances, the syndicate is made up of banks that agree with the borrower to accept drafts created by the borrower and to purchase the drafts so accepted at an agreed-upon discount and commission. An importing borrower might create a draft for $1,000,000 payable in three months. A syndicate bank would then accept the draft and purchase it from the borrower for, say, $985,000 and pay that amount to the borrower. The borrower presumably then uses those funds to pay the exporter for the trade transaction in respect of which the time draft was created. Three months hence, the borrower is obligated to pay the full $1,000,000 to the holder, yielding for the tenor of the acceptance an effective annual interest rate of 6.09 percent. The bank can either keep the accepted draft for that three-month period or rediscount it into the bankers' acceptance market either for its own or the borrower's account. In a syndicated bankers' acceptance facility, it is frequently difficult to have acceptances allocated ratably among the lenders (market custom requires that acceptances be in round numbers that are multiples of $100,000 or $1,000,000—not always achievable in a syndicate with multiple lenders). The credit agreement addresses this by requiring that the acceptances be allocated among the lenders to the maximum extent possible on a basis ratably with their commitments.

Bankers' acceptances are either "eligible" or "ineligible," a distinction made in the Federal Reserve Act when it was enacted in 1913. One of the Act's objectives was to encourage the development of a bankers' acceptance market in the United States to compete with the highly developed acceptance market that existed at the time in London. The Federal Reserve banks were authorized to purchase acceptances that were "eligible." Whether an acceptance was "eligible" was not dependent upon anything set out in the acceptance itself but rather a function of the transaction out of which the acceptance arose. The Act itself prescribed three very broad categories of eligibility: (1) drafts drawn in connection with the import or export of goods, (2) drafts drawn in connection with the domestic shipment of goods so long as shipping documents conveying or securing title are attached at the time of acceptance, and

(3) drafts secured by a warehouse receipt or other document conveying or securing title and covering readily marketable staples. With language as nebulous as this, it is not surprising that a great many arcane rules and interpretations were propounded to delineate the circumstances in which a draft could be eligible.

It is beyond the scope of this volume to dive into the details of the eligibility rules. This is not, however, a particular loss. Starting in the 1970s, the Federal Reserve determined that the acceptance market had matured sufficiently so that it no longer needed to be supported by Federal Reserve banks. Purchases of eligible bankers' acceptances were accordingly discontinued. The concept of eligibility today is therefore largely irrelevant. In fact, the only continuing practical consequence of eligibility is that an eligible acceptance is excluded from the definition of "deposit" under Regulation D and thus reserves need not be kept against the accepting bank's related liability (for a more detailed discussion of reserves, see Section 3.1.2.3). Bankers' acceptances continue to be created and traded in an active bankers' acceptance market (the Federal Reserve Board publishes current bankers' acceptance rates in its weekly H.15 bulletin), but, perhaps because of the reduced significance of eligibility, syndicated bankers' acceptance facilities that were historically quite common are rarely seen today.

2.2 COMMITMENTS

2.2.1 Several Liability

Box 2.14

The failure of any Lender to make any Loan to be made by it on the date specified therefor shall not relieve any other Lender of its obligation to make its Loan on such date, but neither any Lender nor the Administrative Agent shall be responsible for the failure of any other Lender to make a Loan to be made by such other Lender.

A commitment represents the obligation of a lender, at the request of the borrower, to make loans or issue letters of credit (or, in a bankers' acceptance facility, to accept and purchase bankers' acceptances). In a syndicated credit facility, each lender undertakes a separate commitment to the borrower; its commitment may be part of a tranche in which a number of other lenders participate, but each lender is individually obligated (that is, *severally* obligated) to make loans to the borrower. It is not, in other words, a condition to a lender's obligation to make a loan that other lenders are also making their loans. No lender is excused from making its loan if the conditions to lending are satisfied, even though one or more other lenders are refusing or defaulting on their obligation to lend. Moreover, no lender is obligated to step up for the failure of another lender to make its share of a loan available. The *several* liability of the lenders in a credit agreement contrasts with the typical securities underwriting agreement in which the underwriters agree to cover the purchase obligation of a defaulting underwriter in proportion to their commitments up to a specified amount (usually not to exceed 10 percent of the offering).

If a lender defaults, nothing prevents the borrower from requesting a new borrowing in the amount of a defaulting lender's portion. Thus, if a borrower were to request its lenders to make a $10,000,000 loan and one lender fails to participate so that the borrower only receives $9,000,000 in actual proceeds, it would be entitled to go back to the lenders again with a request for a second loan (this time in the amount of $1,000,000) in order to obtain the full amount of the proceeds ($10,000,000) that it had originally sought.

Note that in a loan facility where a minimum level of loan proceeds are necessary for the borrower to satisfy a condition precedent (for example, if the borrower needs $10,000,000 to consummate an acquisition), from a practical standpoint no lender will be obligated to make its loans unless all of the other lenders are concurrently making their loans, even though from a legal standpoint each lender's commitment remains several. Stated another way, if the only way for the borrower to obtain the $10,000,000 necessary to close the acquisition is for all the lenders to extend credit, then the obligations of the lenders are effectively linked and not several. But, of course, in this instance a lender would be declining to lend because the acquisition condition has not been satisfied and not because another lender has failed to provide its share of the funds.

2.2.2 Reducing Revolving Credit Commitments

Box 2.15

(a) The aggregate amount of the Revolving Credit Commitments shall be automatically reduced on each Revolving Credit Commitment Reduction Date set forth below by an amount equal to the reduction amount set forth below opposite such Revolving Credit Commitment Reduction Date:

[Schedule]

(b) The Borrower shall have the right at any time or from time to time to reduce the Revolving Credit Commitments, *provided* that no such partial reduction in the aggregate amount of the Revolving Credit Commitments on any date shall reduce the amount of any scheduled reduction in Revolving Credit Commitments pursuant to paragraph (a) above.

(c) If after giving effect to any reduction provided above the aggregate outstanding principal amount of the Revolving Credit Loans and Letter of Credit Exposure shall exceed the Revolving Credit Commitments, the Borrower shall forthwith prepay the Revolving Credit Loans (and provide cover for Letters of Credit) in an amount equal to the excess.

(d) The Revolving Credit Commitments once reduced may not be reinstated.

Credit agreements that contain a revolving credit facility almost uniformly allow the borrower to reduce (and, as described in Section 2.2.3, to terminate) the related commitments at any time, subject to giving prior notice. Paragraph (b) in Box 2.15 allows for this; paragraph (c) sets out the related obligation of the borrower to repay any portion of the loan principal that exceeds the reduced commitments. Sometimes the right to reduce revolving credit commitments is limited to the reduction of "unutilized commitments." There is little practical difference between such an approach and the one contemplated above, since a borrower can always create unutilized commitments by simply prepaying loans.

Just as term loan facilities can amortize by mandating that the loans be repaid in installments (see Section 4.2 for a discussion of term loan amortization), so also can revolving credit facilities "amortize" by providing that the commitments reduce in installments on scheduled "commitment reduction dates." The last such date is the date the commitments terminate.

A facility that provides for scheduled reductions of revolving credit commitments is a so-called reducing revolving credit facility. It is, in a sense, a hybrid of a revolver and a term loan facility because it forces the borrower progressively to repay its debt (as does a term loan), but allows seasonal fluctuations within the commitments (as does a revolver). The revolving credit "installments" are expressed as automatic reductions of the commitments coupled with a requirement that whenever the aggregate outstanding loans (together with outstanding letters of credit and unreimbursed drawings) exceed the amount of the commitments, the borrower must prepay the excess (paragraph (c) in Box 2.15).

In paragraph (b) in the example in Box 2.15, no partial voluntary reduction of the revolving credit commitments results in any adjustment to the amounts of scheduled reductions in the commitments. This has the effect of applying voluntary reductions to the schedule in the *inverse* order of maturity, with the result that the date upon which the commitments are ultimately reduced to zero will be earlier than if no voluntary reductions had occurred. Some agreements provide that voluntary reductions be made in the *direct* order of maturity. In this instance, any reduction has the effect of reducing the next subsequent installments in an equal dollar amount until total reductions in those installments equals the amount of the voluntary reduction. Other agreements have more complicated reduction formulae, such as requiring that the reductions be applied to the installments ratably. The variations of reduction principles here are limited only by the ingenuity and negotiation of the parties.

2.2.3 Terminating Commitments

Box 2.16

The Borrower shall have the right at any time or from time to time to terminate the Commitments of any Tranche, *provided* that, upon any such termination, the Borrower shall forthwith prepay the Loans of such Tranche in full.

A credit agreement virtually always gives the borrower the option to voluntarily terminate commitments for any tranche of loans at any time. Termination of the commitments, together with the ability to repay the loans, enables the borrower, in effect, to opt out of the requirements of the credit agreement and thereby be relieved of ongoing commitment fees, and any obligation that it comply with covenants. Under New York law, absent an express provision allowing the borrower to terminate commitments, a borrower's attempted election to do so would arguably be a breach of contract. Agreements customarily provide that upon any commitment termination the loans shall be paid in full. Some agreements, particularly those involving facilities (such as an asset-based lending facility) that require significant due diligence to implement and ongoing work to administer (such as asset reviews and appraisals), may require the payment of termination fees as a condition to the termination of commitments.

The remedies provisions of the credit agreement also provide that the commitments terminate (either automatically or at the election of the lenders) upon the occurrence of any event of default (see the discussion in Section 9.2).

2.2.4 Increasing Commitments: Accordion Features and Incremental Facilities

Many credit agreements accord the borrower the right to increase the amount of credit available under the agreement after the closing. Such an increase is typically offered in one of two forms: a so-called accordion feature or an incremental facility.

Under either the accordion or incremental option, no lender will at the outset commit to providing any increase (the credit agreement will be explicit on this point), but all of the lenders will, in effect, agree that, if the borrower is able to obtain the agreement of one or more lenders to step up for increased credit exposure, no further consent of the lenders is required to permit the *increasing* lenders to commit to the increase. The increase will be automatically entitled to the benefit of any guarantees or collateral security to which the closing date facilities are entitled, as if the accordion loans had been made at the initial closing. Because the documentation to implement an accordion or incremental option, as described below, is short and simple, borrowers often find that utilizing these options is preferable, from a cost- and timing-perspective, to negotiating standalone credit documentation for a new facility and any required intercreditor documentation to set forth the relative rights of the existing and new lenders.

2.2.4.1 Accordion Feature

Box 2.17

(a) *Requests for Increase.* The Borrower may, at any time, request that the Commitments be increased (each such requested increase being a *"Commitment Increase"*) by notice to the Administrative Agent, specifying each existing Lender (each an *"Increasing Lender"*) and each additional lender (each an *"Assuming Lender"*) approved by the Administrative Agent that is willing to provide an additional Commitment and the date on which such increase is to be effective (the *"Commitment Increase Date"*), which shall be a Business Day at least _____ Business Days after such notice and _____ days prior to the Commitment Termination Date. The minimum amount of the Commitment of any Assuming Lender, or increase of any Increasing Lender, shall be $_____ and, after giving effect to such Commitment Increase, the total Commitments shall not exceed $_____.

(b) *Effectiveness of Increase.* The Commitment Increase shall become effective upon (i) receipt by the Administrative Agent of an agreement from each Assuming Lender and Increasing Lender, in form and substance satisfactory to the Borrower and the Administrative Agent, pursuant to which such Lender shall, effective as of the Commitment Increase Date, undertake a Commitment or an increase of Commitment in the amount contemplated by the notice of Commitment Increase received from the Borrower, and (ii) satisfaction of the conditions to effectiveness specified therein.

(c) *Adjustments of Borrowings.* On the date of any Commitment Increase and notwithstanding the provisions of Section [*Pro Rata Treatment*] requiring that borrowings and prepayments be made ratably in accordance with the principal amounts of the Loans and Commitments held by the Lenders, the Borrower shall borrow from the Assuming Lenders and Increasing Lenders, and such Lenders shall make, Loans to the Borrower (in the case of LIBOR Loans, with Interest Period(s) ending on the date(s) of any then outstanding Interest Period(s), and the Borrower shall prepay Loans held by the other Lenders in such amounts as may be necessary, so that after giving effect to such Loans and prepayments, the Loans (and Interest Period(s) of LIBOR Loan(s)) shall be held by the Lenders pro rata in accordance with the respective amounts of their Commitments (as so increased).

An accordion commitment increase provision is normally used only for increases in a revolving credit facility. It works by allowing the amount of the commitments to go up (usually up to some specified maximum) if the borrower is able to convince new lenders to provide the increase, or existing lenders to increase their current commitments. Since the increase is to an already-outstanding facility, the interest, maturity, and other terms applicable to the increased loans will be identical to those of the existing revolving credit facility.

In some instances the increase is subject to conditions such as the absence of any default and the truth of representations. This is arguably not necessary given that the establishment of the increased commitments alone does not impose new obligations upon the borrower (beyond, perhaps, commitment or facility fees). The borrower does not incur additional obligations until loans are made that utilize the increase and those will, of course, be subject to the same conditions as any other loan—including the absence of defaults and truth of representations (see Section 5.2). However, in some facilities the conditions to an increase may go beyond the borrowing conditions by, for example, requiring that a leverage ratio fall below a certain level before an increase may become effective, or requiring evidence that another facility has been repaid or terminated. Whether or not conditions are specified in the accordion provision itself, nothing precludes any new or increasing lender from imposing any requirement it deems appropriate as a condition to its participation, including that new legal opinions be delivered, that up-front fees be paid, or even that the borrower post additional collateral (although the security would, of course, accrue to the benefit of all loans under the increased commitments).

The effectiveness of any increase is also subject to the execution by each new lender or increasing lender of an agreement approved by the borrower and the administrative agent. This is the instrument pursuant to which the new or increasing lender becomes bound to the increase. It does not normally require a new lender to execute a counterpart of the credit agreement, but would typically just be a one- or two-page document under which the new lender assumes its commitment as a lender under the facility. An increasing lender would, similarly, agree to the increase of its commitment.

As discussed in more detail in Section 10.4, it is a general principle of credit agreements that loans within a tranche are to be made (and held) ratably in accordance with the lenders' commitments in that tranche. Except in the rare case where a commitment increase is provided ratably by all existing lenders (with no new lenders assuming a commitment), a commitment increase results in outstanding loans and commitments being held by the lenders on a nonratable basis. Accordion clauses adjust the amounts of the loans so that ratability is achieved in one of several ways. Some agreements simply require that all outstanding loans be prepaid in full from the proceeds of new loans made by the entire syndicate under the increased commitments. Mechanically this works, but it may require the borrower to pay breakfunding fees on the entire facility (potentially a significant cost). Other accordion clauses (the example in Box 2.17 takes this approach) provide that, upon any increase, the loans will be adjusted through nonratable borrowings and prepayments in such amounts as are necessary so that the loans in the increased facility are held by the lenders ratably in accordance with their commitments. This results in breakfunding only with respect to the smaller portions being prepaid. In unusual cases the adjustment is handled through assignments of loan portions by existing lenders to the new or increasing lenders, who then make corresponding payments to buy into the existing loans. This latter approach is more complicated since it requires the agreement of existing lenders to cooperate with the reallocation, something they may not be inclined to do (they are, after all, not participating in the full increase, which may evidence dissatisfaction with the borrower and, even by assigning a loan, may suffer breakfunding costs).

2.2.4.2 Incremental Facilities

Box 2.18

In addition to the Loans made pursuant to Section _____, the Borrower and one or more Lenders (or other financial institutions agreed to by the Borrower and the Administrative Agent) may enter into commitments to make additional revolving credit or term loans (each an *"Incremental Loan"*) under this Section pursuant to an agreement setting forth the commitments of such Lenders (or financial institutions), the fees (if any) to be payable by the Borrower in connection therewith, and the interest rate, amortization schedule, and maturity date to be applicable thereto. The Incremental Loans made pursuant to any such agreement shall be deemed to be a separate "Series" of Incremental Loans. The minimum aggregate principal amount of any Series of Incremental Loan commitments shall be $_____ and the aggregate principal amount of all Incremental Loan commitments of all Series of Incremental Loans shall not exceed $_____. No Lender shall be required to provide any Incremental Loan except in its sole and absolute discretion.

An incremental facility, in comparison to an accordion clause, contemplates the creation of a new tranche of loans, or an increase in an existing tranche of term loans, rather than a mere increase in existing revolving commitments. The credit agreement may even allow for more than one incremental facility, although these are almost always capped at a dollar maximum. Depending upon the flexibility afforded to the borrower, the new tranches may be either revolving credit or term loan facilities. The pricing, payment, and other terms of an incremental facility, unlike an increase pursuant to an accordion, are not required to be the same as those of any other tranche in the credit agreement. The up-front fees, interest rate, maturity, amortization, and other terms of the incremental facility will be specified at the time the incremental facility is established. Accordingly, an incremental facility providing for term loans may result in either A or B loans. It is typical for the credit agreement to require that, relative to the existing tranches in the credit agreement, the incremental facility not have a later maturity or a shorter weighted average life-to-maturity and not share in mandatory prepayments on a greater-than-ratable basis. It is also typical for the credit agreement to require that the covenants and events of default applicable to the incremental facility not be more restrictive and that guarantees and collateral security supporting the incremental facility not be greater than those applicable to the existing tranches. The incremental commitments themselves will be set forth in a separate, usually short "incremental facility agreement" executed by the borrower, any guarantors, the administrative agent, and the lenders that are to provide the facility.

One concern that the initial syndicate members have with providing flexibility for incremental facilities to a borrower is the possibility that an incremental facility may have more favorable pricing than the existing tranches in the agreement. This can have the immediate effect of depressing the trading value of the original loan tranches. It may also strike the initial lenders as being fundamentally unfair. Many agreements that include an incremental option will therefore also provide for a so-called "most favored nation" (or "MFN") clause where the initial loan pricing will receive a concurrent bump-up in margin to the yield applicable to the incremental facility (or within, say, 25 basis points of the incremental facility yield). These provisions typically will take account of up-front fees payable to all lenders or issuance discount on the incremental facility, in addition to the interest rate margin, and equate those fees or discount to yield based upon an assumed life to maturity of the incremental facility. Most favored nation provisions reduce the sense of unfairness and the risk that the trading value of the existing tranches will be adversely affected. Some credit agreements that have MFN provisions utilize a so-called "MFN sunset," whereby the pricing protections embodied by an MFN clause cease to apply after a negotiated period of time.

As with an accordion clause, the lenders that provide the incremental facility are not necessarily limited to those already party to the credit agreement; any institution that is willing to provide the incremental facility is allowed to step up. The selection of any new institution is, of course, subject to the consent of the borrower, of the administrative agent, and of any issuer of letters of credit under the facility to the same extent that the consent of those parties would be required if the new institution were taking an assignment of loans.

In addition, as with an accordion feature, the requirements to be satisfied by the borrower as a condition to the incremental facility (such as delivery of opinions, issuance of governmental approvals, and adoption of board resolutions) are left to negotiation between the borrower and the incremental facility lenders. The credit agreement is normally silent except to provide, in the ongoing conditions clause, that each loan made under the credit agreement (including the incremental facility loans) is subject to the truth of representations and the absence of defaults.

Unlike an increase in commitments pursuant to an accordion clause, to become effective an incremental facility does not require an adjustment of outstandings so that the loans are held by the lenders ratably in accordance with their commitments. By definition, an incremental facility is an entirely *new* tranche and so no loans will be outstanding until the facility is activated.

2.2.4.3 Recent Developments

Since the financial crisis, incremental financing provisions in credit agreements have undergone much change. Purely as a matter of presentation, the incremental facility and accordion clauses are now rarely presented as separate provisions but rather appear in the same section of the credit agreement. It has become increasingly common for the credit agreement to permit the additional debt capacity afforded by incremental financing provisions to be in the form of pari passu secured notes (but, typically, not loans), subordinated secured loans or notes and/ or unsecured loans or notes pursuant to a separate credit agreement, indenture, or note purchase agreement. These so-called "sidecar facilities" or "incremental equivalent debt" utilize the credit agreement's incremental financing capacity (e.g., a dollar of debt incurred under a sidecar facility will reduce availability under the incremental financing facility by a dollar) and are subject to the same limitations.

Traditionally, credit agreements provided for the amount of permitted incremental financing capacity to be capped at a fixed dollar amount, with availability of such amount being subject to pro forma compliance with the credit agreement's financial covenants. Increasingly, credit agreements are providing for a dollar amount (based upon the borrower's EBITDA) plus an additional amount subject to pro forma compliance with a ratio of the borrower's debt to EBITDA. The ratio typically measures first lien secured debt when the loans to be incurred are secured by a pari passu lien on the collateral securing the credit agreement, secured debt and/or total debt when the debt to be incurred is secured by a lien that is subordinate to the lien on the collateral securing the credit agreement, and total debt when the debt to be incurred is unsecured.

Another feature in the ongoing evolution of incremental financing provisions is the incorporation of limited conditionality provisions in the acquisition finance context. When the proceeds of the incremental facility are to be used to consummate an acquisition that is itself not conditioned upon the borrower's receipt of debt financing (a so-called limited conditionality acquisition), some credit agreements will contain an exception to the ongoing conditions clause so that, as between the borrower and the existing lenders, the no default condition will not apply or will instead be limited to the absence of a payment or bankruptcy event of default. In addition, the truth of representations condition may not apply, or may be limited to so-called "Specified Representations" as described in Section 13.8. The incremental facility lenders, of course, will be free to impose any conditions they deem appropriate.

Because incremental financing provisions provide borrowers with potentially substantial additional borrowing capacity, these features have increasingly been the subject of scrutiny by bank regulators.

2.2.5 "Termout" of Revolving Credit Commitments

Box 2.19

The aggregate principal amount of Revolving Credit Loans outstanding on the close of business on the Revolving Credit Commitment Termination Date shall automatically convert into Term Loans and shall be repaid in installments as follows:

[Schedule]

Sometimes a credit agreement provides that, at the commitment termination date for revolving credit commitments, any outstanding revolving credit loans convert into term loans. This is usually referred to as a "termout" option. Such a conversion is normally automatic (as in the example in Box 2.19), and not subject to a bring-down of representations or the absence of a default. But in some agreements, conditions of this nature are required to be satisfied, as if the term loan were a new extension of credit under the agreement. Borrowers prefer the termout to be automatic since the imposition of conditions, in the eyes of rating agencies, may mean that the revolving credit loans during the twelve months prior to the commitment termination date should be treated as short-term rather than long-term debt.

2.2.6 Loan Commitment Letters

While a detailed discussion of loan commitment letters is beyond the scope of this volume, their impact on the terms of the related credit agreement warrants some mention. In connection with many loan financing transactions, the borrower will enter into a commitment letter for the applicable loan facilities. Under a commitment letter, one or more lenders will commit to provide the applicable loan facilities, subject to specified conditions precedent. Commitment letters are important to a borrower in situations where it needs certainty that the loan facilities will be available to the borrower when needed, but where the borrower does not want to incur the expense to fully negotiate the credit agreement and related documents. A common example is an acquisition financing. At the time the borrower signs the purchase and sale agreement and becomes legally obligated to purchase the target business, it wants to know that it has legal commitments in place for its debt and equity financing needs. This may enable the borrower to make a purchase offer that is not subject to a so-called "financing out"—a condition precedent in the purchase and sale agreement that excuses the borrower's performance if it is unable to obtain debt financing—and is, therefore, more attractive to the seller.

A commitment letter typically attaches a term sheet that sets forth some of the material terms of the loan financing to be provided. Terms not set forth in the term sheet are left to negotiation and must be mutually acceptable to the borrower and the lenders. So, for example, the amount and maturity of the loan would typically be specified in the term sheet, but other terms may be only briefly referred to. Historically, for example, references in the term sheet to the negative covenants would typically be brief and generic, such as "limitation on liens; indebtedness; investments; restricted payments; etc." with specific exceptions and basket levels left to be negotiated in the credit agreement. However, one of the conditions precedent set forth in a commitment letter is the negotiation, execution, and delivery of the credit agreement and related documents. As a result, the failure of the borrower and lenders to agree on the terms of the credit agreement would excuse the lenders from having to fund. To minimize this risk in the context of acquisition financings, term sheets for acquisition financings today are typically quite detailed (and lengthy) and set forth detailed covenant exceptions, basket levels, defined terms, and other provisions and, in many cases—particularly in the case of acquisitions by financial sponsors—reference a specific precedent credit agreement to serve as the fallback for terms that are not specifically set forth in the term sheet. Thus, in many loan financings, large portions of the credit agreement are pre-agreed well before the drafting process begins. See Section 5.3 for a detailed discussion of commitment letters and conditionality in acquisition financing transactions.

2.3 MULTICURRENCY FACILITIES

> **Box 2.20**
>
> *"Eligible Foreign Currency"* means Sterling, Euros, Canadian Dollars, and Japanese Yen and any other currency other than U.S. Dollars (a) that is readily available, freely transferable, and convertible into U.S. Dollars in the international interbank market and in which dealings in deposits are carried on in the London interbank market and (b) that has been approved by [each Lender] [the Required Lenders] [the Administrative Agent]. If, after the designation of any currency as an Eligible Foreign Currency, (x) currency control or other exchange regulations are imposed in the country in which such currency is issued with the result that different types of such currency are introduced or (y) such currency is, in the determination of the Administrative Agent, no longer readily available or freely traded, the Administrative Agent shall promptly notify the Lenders and the Borrower, and such currency shall no longer be an Eligible Foreign Currency until such time as all of the Lenders agree to reinstate such currency as an Eligible Foreign Currency.

U.S. credit agreements do not always contemplate loans only in U.S. dollars; in many cases the agreement will provide, at the borrower's option, that loans be made (or letters of credit be issued) in other currencies as well. Normally, the currencies to be made available do not constitute an open-ended list, but are instead spelled out in the agreement (major currencies such as British pounds sterling, Euros, Canadian dollars, and Japanese yen are most frequently seen). Although structuring and documenting multicurrency facilities can add considerable complexity (and legal and syndication costs) to a financing, such facilities can have the advantage of providing a natural hedge to borrowers that have revenues, assets, and liabilities in nondollar currencies, minimizing taxes (by creating local deductions and minimizing interest withholding taxes), and reducing the transaction costs of currency conversions that the borrower would otherwise incur to obtain funds that are legal tender in other jurisdictions.

Some agreements allow additional currencies to be designated after closing. In that case (other than, perhaps, in agreements contemplating local lines—see Section 2.3.3) the credit agreement will normally require that the currency be readily available, freely transferable, convertible into U.S. dollars, and dealt with in the London interbank deposit market (see clause (a) in the sample language quoted in Box 2.20). Beyond these conditions, there is wide disparity in credit agreements as to what level of lender approval is necessary for a new foreign currency to be approved. Most credit agreements require that even as to currencies that satisfy the listed conditions the approval of each lender in the relevant tranche is necessary. Some agreements may not require unanimous approval, but permit the required lenders or the administrative agent to consent to the new currency. In rare cases no approval of any type (whether by the lenders or the agent) is required; instead the syndicate relies solely on the listed conditions to ensure that the lenders are protected. If letters of credit are to be issued in a foreign currency, the approval of each issuing lender is required.

The concepts of availability, transferability, convertibility, and London interbank deposit-taking referenced in the language in Box 2.20 address the principal concerns that lenders face if a new currency is added after closing to their lending commitments. To begin with, lenders will want assurance that they have access to the currency in amounts sufficient to satisfy their commitments. Unless a lender maintains local branches at which it takes in local currency deposits, it will need access to the currency through the LIBOR market. The references to "ready availability" and the existence of a deposit market in London are intended to cover this concern. Second, lenders will want certainty that the interest earned on the loan will cover their costs of funding. Access in the London interbank market to deposits in the relevant currency comes into play here as well. If a lender can fund itself through taking Norwegian kroner deposits in London, its cost of funding is presumably covered by the stated interest on the loan since the latter is calculated on the basis of the LIBO rate for kroner deposits. Third, the lenders will want the currency to be convertible so that they have a basis upon which to measure the dollar exposure of the foreign currency commitments. Convertibility also affords the flexibility, should a default occur, of redenominating the entire foreign currency exposure into dollars. Lastly, the lender will want to know that payments in the particular currency are not subject to regulatory requirements of the country that issues the currency; in other words that the currency is free of any exchange controls. "Transferability" is the term that covers this point. Euros and sterling are freely transferable. Thailand bhat (as of the date of this volume) are not.

Multicurrency facilities can be structured in a variety of ways, depending upon the business needs of the borrower, the depth of the market for the currency, tax, and other considerations. The following are some common structures.

2.3.1 Ratable Committed Dollar/FX Loans

In a ratable committed dollar/FX loan structure, each lender in a tranche commits to make loans in dollars and in specified foreign currencies in each case ratably in accordance with their commitments of that tranche. Interest for the dollar loans is the same as that for a dollar-only facility based on the base rate or LIBOR. Interest for the foreign currency loans is most often based solely upon LIBOR for the relevant currency. However, if the LIBOR market for deposits in that currency is perceived as thin, such as is the case with Canadian dollars, it is customary to use local rates—the Canadian bankers' acceptance rate in the case of Canadian dollar loans.

In most cases, the lenders participating in a ratable committed dollar/FX loan tranche assess whether to participate in the tranche, and obtain credit approval, based upon the dollar exposure they will undertake. This necessitates some mechanism to measure the dollar equivalent of each foreign currency loan. The typical method to determine how much of the commitments is being used by any particular loan is to deem the amount of each foreign currency borrowing to be equal to its corresponding dollar amount. Thus, if the U.S. dollar/U.K. sterling exchange rate is 2 to 1 (two dollars for every pound) a request by the borrower for £10,000,000 will be treated for commitment utilization purposes as a request for a borrowing in the amount of $20,000,000. If the unutilized commitments are less than that dollar amount, then a borrowing of that size cannot be made. If after the borrowing the U.S. dollar/U.K. sterling exchange rate increases to 2.5 to 1 and the aggregate of the dollar loans and dollar equivalent of sterling loans exceeds the commitments then the borrower may be required to make a mandatory prepayment (see Section 4.7.8).

The ratable committed dollar/FX loan structure has the advantage of simplicity and is therefore relatively easy to administer (all lenders provide funds ratably and the administrative agent need not keep track of a confused bundle of nonratable loans). It suffers the disadvantage that each lender in the tranche must have access to each of the specified currencies. As a consequence, the universe of lenders to which the tranche can be syndicated may be constricted. In some cases this can be solved by imposing a sublimit on the aggregate amount of foreign currency loans that may be made. The size of any sublimit is subject to the depth of the market for the currency and the negotiated needs of the borrower for loans in that currency. The deeper the market, the more confident the lenders will be that they can have the access to funding in that currency. A sublimit, however, reduces flexibility for the borrower.

2.3.2 Nonratable Committed Loans

In this structure, a subgroup of lenders in a dollar tranche agrees to make loans in selected foreign currencies up to specified sublimits. There may be a different mix of lenders in each subgroup, so that lenders A through F make dollar and euro loans; lenders A, B, and E make loans in kroner; and lenders B, C, and F make loans in Swiss francs.

This structure enhances the number of foreign currencies that can be made available to the borrower, since not every lender is required to have access to all currencies. It has the disadvantage of being more difficult to administer, inasmuch as loans end up being made on a nonratable basis and the administrative agent is forced into a complicated monitoring function to ensure that no lender's dollar and dollar-equivalent exposure exceeds its commitment or foreign currency sublimit.

The structure also has the disadvantage of not spreading the credit exposure ratably among the lenders; which subgroup holds exposure at any given time is a function solely of which currencies have been borrowed. Thus, if lenders A, B, and E make kroner loans that use their full commitments and the borrower wants to take down Swiss franc loans, it will have to borrow from lenders C and F only, even though B has also agreed to make Swiss franc loans. If it later wants to borrow dollars, these may need to come from lender D if the Swiss franc loans utilize the full commitments of C and F. Depending upon the timing and currencies of borrowing, the mix of loans may be entirely different. If the borrower goes into bankruptcy after taking down solely the kroner loans, lenders A, B, and E are the only ones with exposure. This can, in theory, be solved through a true-up or collateral allocation mechanism (see Section 8.5), but that presents other difficulties. Either the other lenders (A, C, D, and F) must buy participations in kroner—a currency to which they may not have access—or the kroner loans first need to be converted to dollars—which may violate the automatic stay under the Bankruptcy Code without court approval. As a consequence, syndicating nonratable committed facilities to borrowers without an investment-grade credit standing (allowing the lenders to be less concerned with nonratable credit exposures) can be problematic.

2.3.3　Local Currency Tranches

In a local currency structure, a separate loan tranche is created for each foreign currency, with specified lenders (or, in some instances, a single lender) making loans directly to the borrower out of local offices in the relevant foreign country. As with a ratable committed dollar/FX loan tranche, this has the advantage of simplicity and being easy to administer. It eliminates the operational headaches described in Section 2.3.2 (the administrative agent is not forced to keep track of a shifting mix of lender-specific loan exposures), and has the advantage of increasing the number of currencies that may be made available. Because the lender will fund the local currency locally, it may even be willing to issue a commitment for a currency that does not satisfy the conditions described earlier of availability, transferability, convertibility, and London deposit-taking. Given that the loans are made out of local offices, a local currency tranche may also have the benefit of eliminating withholding taxes and, since funding will not be limited to the LIBOR market, may allow for shorter notice periods. Credit approval is presumably measured by reference to the foreign currency, and not to dollars.

A local currency tranche, however, has the disadvantage of breaking the total credit under the facility into multiple discrete, and sometimes small, segments; unused commitments in one currency cannot be accessed in other currencies. So, while the borrower may nominally have $100,000,000 of commitments in 15 currencies, the aggregate that it can borrow in sterling is limited by the sterling commitment even though no other borrowings are outstanding. Conversely, unused sterling commitments are not available for borrowings in dollars, except through borrowing sterling and converting them into dollars with the attendant currency conversion expenses.

The structure also does not solve (and may, indeed, exacerbate) the problem of the credit risk being spread unevenly among the lenders. Possible solutions are not terribly practical. A true-up mechanism has the same problems described in Section 2.3.2. Spreading the risk by supporting the local currency tranche with a letter of credit issued under the credit agreement is a possible approach. However, this results in the borrower paying letter of credit fees for the backstop letter of credit on top of the interest on the foreign currency loans themselves. Any backstop letter of credit in this circumstance would also, by definition, need to be in dollars rather than in the foreign currency and, to provide protection against exchange fluctuations, would need to be larger (say, 125 percent or 150 percent) than the beginning dollar equivalent of the foreign currency commitment. Of course, even a backstop letter of credit is impractical if the local currency is not convertible since the amount of a dollar equivalent would be guesswork not determined by a currency exchange market. All of this has the effect of raising the cost to the borrower of accessing the local currency. As with nonratable committed facilities, unless the lenders are indifferent to assuming more than their ratable share of the syndicate's exposure to the borrower (likely only when the borrower enjoys an investment-grade rating), syndicating a facility with local currency tranches can be challenging.

2.3.4 Uncommitted FX Loans

In this structure, the credit agreement contemplates that individual lenders may, on a basis to be separately negotiated with the borrower, make loans in an agreed foreign currency. Any such loans, if assented to, would be entitled to the benefits of the same guarantees and security enjoyed by the committed tranches, and the credit agreement would so specify. Limits on the aggregate uncommitted and committed loans would be spelled out in the credit agreement. In most cases, the mechanics of making such loans (including the business terms, such as interest, fees, and amortization) would be left to negotiation and separate documentation. The structure, therefore, has the advantage of simplicity, as the administrative agent will not be involved in funding and payment operations. It has the obvious disadvantage that the borrower does not have committed access to the foreign currency. Whenever it needs access to nondollar tender, it will be prey to one-on-one negotiation with individual lenders and to unearthing a lender that is willing to take on nonratable exposure.

2.3.5 Multicurrency Competitive Bid Loans

Multicurrency loans can also be made available through a competitive bid loan structure (see Section 2.1.1.3 for a discussion of how these work). In some sense, this structure is a more formalized uncommitted FX line. Multicurrency loans are made available by expanding a competitive bid facility to allow lenders to offer loans not only in dollars, but also in nondollar currencies. If the borrower needs loans to finance its operations in Hungary, it would simply request the lenders to submit offers in Hungarian forints. Each lender would be given the option to offer to make loans in the currencies requested by the borrower, but none would be obligated to make any offer. The borrower could either be overwhelmed with forints, or find that no lender was willing to make an offer for any amount in forints.

The multicurrency competitive bid loan structure solves many of the problems enumerated in the preceding paragraphs. Administratively it is no more complex than a dollar competitive bid facility and, as with dollar competitive bid loans, the lenders that make the offers understand, by necessity, that they will take on nonratable exposure. It has several disadvantages, however. To begin with, as with an uncommitted FX facility, the borrower is not guaranteed access to any particular foreign currency since no lender is issuing a commitment to make loans in any currency. This may not be problematic for major currencies like Euros, sterling, or yen, but is likely to raise difficulties for currencies with lower trading volumes, such as New Zealand dollars or Norwegian kroner (and likely forints as well). Second, competitive bid facilities work only as an adjunct to revolving credit facilities. If a borrower wants term loans in a particular currency, it needs commitments in that currency; a competitive bid structure will be unhelpful. Finally, as with dollar competitive bid facilities, the structure works best only for investment-grade borrowers where individual lenders will be amenable to taking on nonratable credit exposure.

2.4 SECOND LIEN AND UNITRANCHE FACILITIES

2.4.1 *General Observations*

Second lien facilities are not, in truth, any different than the facilities described earlier in this chapter—they typically provide for plain-vanilla term loans with the one quirk that, although secured, the priority of their liens with respect to the collateral is junior to identical liens in favor of a first lien lending syndicate. Normally, the first lien facility and the second lien facility are committed to, and documented and syndicated by, the same arranger and at the same time. Typically, a single counsel for the arranger also drafts the respective credit agreements and security documents for both facilities.

In a sense, a second lien facility is just one variety of a range of subordinations of one creditor to another. We discuss in Section 6.5.2, the concept of *contractual* subordination, and in Section 7.6.4.6, the concept of *structural* subordination. Second lien facilities are a third species: *lien* subordination.

The rationale behind second lien facilities is simple and perhaps best illustrated by examples. If a borrower is looking at a credit facility to consist of a revolver and term loan A and term loan B facilities, all of it secured, it may improve the pricing and other terms of the revolver and term loans if all or a portion of the term loan B facility is converted into a second lien facility. The second lien facility's interest margin will likely be higher, but that may be offset by the improvement in pricing on the revolver and remaining term loans. Similarly, if the borrower is looking at a senior secured credit facility and an unsecured bond financing, it may prefer to establish a second lien facility in lieu of the bond financing. The second lien facility, being secured, may attract more favorable pricing than the bond issuance with the reduced cost being sufficient to offset any disadvantages in the terms of the second lien loans over unsecured bonds, such as a shorter term and tighter covenants.

Many of the drafting complications associated with second lien facilities arise when articulating the intercreditor relationship between the first lien and second lien lending syndicates. In general, the first lien lenders want the second lien facility to be silent—put up and then shut up. "Silence" for these purposes has both prebankruptcy and postbankruptcy components. Prebankruptcy, the first lien lenders want to be in control. For example, if the first lien lenders determine to release collateral to enable the borrower to consummate a sale, they will want (and sometimes succeed in convincing) the second lien lenders to be forced to tag along, at least if the proceeds of the sale are to be applied to a permanent reduction of the first lien facility. If the first lien lenders determine to amend the first lien security documents, they will want the second lien lenders to amend the corresponding second lien security documents (though not if that involves a release of collateral outside the sale context or involves changing provisions that uniquely affect the second lien holders). Most important, the intercreditor arrangements will prohibit the second lien lenders from exercising any rights with respect to the collateral until the first lien lenders have been paid in full. This prohibition will apply even if it is provided that the foreclosure of the second priority liens leaves intact the first priority liens.

In assessing these intercreditor issues, it is important to remember that *lien* subordination is not the same as *contractual* subordination. In the typical second lien facility, the second lien lenders are not prohibited from accelerating their loans upon default or from suing the borrower to obtain recovery. With one big exception, there is also no payment block imposed upon the second lien holders nor any requirement that they turn over payments to the first lien holders. The exception, applicable both pre- and postbankruptcy, is where a payment represents proceeds of collateral that should have flowed through the intercreditor waterfall (the provision of the intercreditor agreement or security documents that describes how proceeds of collateral are to be paid to the respective parties in interest—normally first to the collateral agent, second to the first lien syndicate, third to the second lien syndicate, and last to the borrower). To that extent, whatever proceeds of collateral should, under the waterfall, have been remitted to the collateral agent or first lien lenders must, if received by the second lien lenders, be immediately paid over to those parties until they have been paid in full. Whether an amount is subject to the intercreditor waterfall or not means the difference between a junior creditor being repaid its loan or instead being forced to turn the amount over to the senior first lien creditors for repayment of that loan. Therefore the scope of intercreditor waterfalls can attract intense scrutiny, and even lawsuits, among senior and junior creditors alike.

Postbankruptcy, the first lien lenders also want to be in control, although the issues are different than those of prebankruptcy control and largely driven by the nuances of the Bankruptcy Code. A complete analysis of the bankruptcy-related issues between first and second lien lenders is beyond the scope of this volume; it is useful, however, to describe some of the key concerns that first lien syndicates want to see addressed in any first and second lien documentation (including any related intercreditor agreement).

2.4.2 Bankruptcy Issues

2.4.2.1 Post-Petition Interest

When a borrower files for bankruptcy, it is (at least initially) entitled to stop paying its creditors, including interest payments to its lenders. Even if the lenders ultimately receive their full interest entitlement at the end of the case, not receiving current interest can adversely affect them, perhaps most importantly by altering the tradability of their loans (and hence the ease with which they can turn over the bankruptcy headache to a willing assignee at a favorable price). Lenders do not lack remedies, however. Without setting out a broad treatise on the question of post-petition interest under the Bankruptcy Code, the general rule is that secured creditors are entitled to post-petition interest to the extent the value of their collateral exceeds the amount of their claim (if, in other words, they are *oversecured*). By way of example, if the first lien claims are $25,000,000 and the value of the collateral is $35,000,000, the first lien lenders should be able to convince the bankruptcy court to allow post-petition interest to be paid.

A different answer would follow if there were a second lien syndicate of $50,000,000 secured by the same collateral and the bankruptcy court were to treat the first and second lien claims as a single class. In that case, the total amount of the secured claims ($75,000,000) far outweighs the value of the collateral ($35,000,000) and so the first lien lenders might not be entitled to current post-petition interest payments. Having the first and second lien facilities treated as a single class should not, in this example, ultimately affect the ability of the first lien lenders to be paid their interest in full, but the inability to receive current interest can, as described in the preceding paragraph, adversely affect tradability. There is also the time-value cost of not receiving current interest.

First lien lenders try to solve these issues by structuring the first and second lien facilities in a way that increases the likelihood they will be treated as separate classes. Consequently, the first and second lien tranches are not typically documented in one credit agreement, but rather in two. Similarly, there will normally be separate security documents for the first and second liens, with separate grants of security to separate agents. These dynamics radically affect the way in which the facilities are papered, and can complicate the drafting and negotiating process.

Increasing the likelihood that the two facilities are treated as separate classes will also be helpful for the issue of plan confirmation discussed in Section 2.4.2.5.

2.4.2.2   Debtor-in-Possession Financing and Use of Cash Collateral

After the filing of a bankruptcy petition, whether voluntary or involuntary, if the debtor (the borrower) is seeking to reorganize under Chapter 11 of the Bankruptcy Code (most do) it will need cash to continue to run its business during the pendency of the bankruptcy case. Typically, therefore, one of the first orders granted by the bankruptcy court will be either to permit the use of cash collateral or to establish a debtor-in-possession (DIP) financing facility. Since DIP facilities prime any liens granted by the borrower pre-petition (including those of the first and second lien lenders), the first lien lenders are normally the ones eager to provide the DIP facility. They want any priming of liens to be done by themselves rather than by some potentially antagonistic third party.

In either case (whether allowing the borrower to use cash or providing a DIP facility), any secured creditor can object if it is not "adequately protected." If the first and second lien facilities are structured as separate classes (as described in Section 2.4.2.1), then the second lien lenders have a separate right to object that they are not adequately protected if the borrower is allowed to use cash or establish a DIP facility. To prevent the second lien lenders from taking a stance inconsistent with that of the first lien lenders, the first lien lenders will normally require that the second lien lenders preconsent to any use of cash or DIP financing that the first lien lenders agree to and will agree not to request adequate protection or other relief in connection with such use of cash or DIP financing. The first lien lenders will also typically want the intercreditor arrangements with the second lien lenders to preclude the latter from submitting their own, separate, DIP financing proposal.

2.4.2.3 Automatic Stay

The first lien lenders will want the second lien lenders to agree that, if the first lien lenders request (or consent to) the lifting of the automatic stay in bankruptcy, such as to permit a sale of collateral or to enable payments to be made to third parties, then the second lien lenders will remain silent and not object to the lifting.

2.4.2.4 Contest Rights

The first lien lenders will want the second lien lenders to agree not to contest the validity, priority, or enforceability of the liens of the first lien facility. Of course, this risk is, in theory, eliminated if the first and second liens are created pursuant to the same security documents (in that case, the second lien holders could not attack the first-priority liens without also attacking their own second-priority liens). However, as described in Section 2.4.2.1, this carries with it the disadvantage that the first and second lien lenders may be treated as a single class in the bankruptcy proceeding.

2.4.2.5 Plan Confirmation

As is the case with DIP financing and the use of cash collateral, if the first lien lenders support a reorganization plan, they will want the second lien lenders to support the plan as well. This is a perfect illustration of how the second lien lenders may be in a worse position than they would have been if they were simply unsecured, subordinated creditors of the borrower. Any class of creditors (and for these purposes unsecured subordinated creditors would be a distinct class from the secured lenders) would be entitled to vote to accept or reject the plan. Second lien lenders, by virtue of the silent second provisions in their intercreditor agreement with the first lien lenders, effectively lose their separate vote.

2.4.2.6 Aggregate Effect

The aggregate effect of the intercreditor provisions described above can be so draconian as to reduce the second lien lenders to a position *worse* than what they would have enjoyed had they simply agreed to a contractual subordination instead of a lien subordination. If the second lien lenders had been unsecured and were not subject to the standard second lien intercreditor shackles, they would generally be free to speak as they wanted before the bankruptcy judge to object to sales of collateral and the lifting of the automatic stay and to vote against a plan confirmation. It is not an answer for second lien lenders to rely upon unsecured creditors to do their bidding. The example earlier is a perfect illustration. If the aggregate of the first and second lien claims is $75,000,000 and if the value of the collateral (assuming it is effectively all of the assets of the borrower) is $35,000,000, no *unsecured* creditor will want to bother objecting to anything, or even to involve themselves in the case (except, perhaps, to contest the validity of the liens), since, regardless of the outcome given the level of secured debt, no money will ever trickle down to the unsecured creditors. For this reason, some second lien credit documentation gives second lien lenders the right to waive their rights to collateral security in exchange for relief from the intercreditor constraints. To address these issues, many intercreditor agreements contain a provision that permits second lien lenders to enforce rights and remedies against the debtors that are available to unsecured creditors, so long as they are not inconsistent with the express terms of the intercreditor agreement.

2.4.2.7 Recent Bankruptcy Decisions

The financial crisis brought about an increase in the number of bankruptcy filings and an increase in the number of skirmishes between first lien and second lien lenders.

In *In re Ion Media Networks, Inc.*, 419 B.R. 585 (Bankr. S.D.N.Y. 2009), the second lien lenders sought to challenge the validity of the first lien lenders' liens on FCC licenses and the proceeds of those licenses and to object to the debtor's proposed plan of reorganization. The applicable intercreditor agreement contained provisions pursuant to which the second lien lenders agreed not to contest the validity, priority, or enforceability of any of the first lien lenders' liens and agreed not to oppose, object to, or vote against any disclosure statement that has terms consistent with the first lien lenders' rights under the applicable security documents. The intercreditor agreement also contained a provision that permitted the second lien lenders to exercise rights and remedies against the debtors that are available to unsecured creditors, so long as they are not inconsistent with the express terms of the intercreditor agreement. The court rejected the ability of the second lien lender to assert unsecured creditor rights to challenge the validity of the first lien lenders' liens or to vote against the debtor's plan of reorganization, because those actions were expressly prohibited by the terms of the intercreditor agreement.

In *In re Boston Generating, LLC*, 440 B.R. 302 (Bankr. S.D.N.Y. 2010), the second lien lenders sought to object to the sale of substantially all of the debtor's assets pursuant to Section 363 of the Bankruptcy Code. The intercreditor agreement contained a provision pursuant to which the first lien lenders "shall have the exclusive right to enforce rights, exercise remedies . . . and make determinations regarding the release, sale, disposition or restrictions with respect to the Collateral without any consultation with the [second lien lenders]. . . ." Another provision of the intercreditor agreement stated that "the sole right of the [second lien lenders] with respect to the Collateral is to hold a Lien on the Collateral pursuant to the Second Lien Collateral Documents . . . and to receive a share of the proceeds thereof, if any, after the Discharge of the First Lien Obligations has occurred[,]" subject to certain exceptions, including the right to assert "any right and interest available to unsecured creditors in a manner not inconsistent with the Intercreditor Agreement."

The court noted that unlike the Model Intercreditor Agreement published by the American Bar Association, which contained an express waiver of the right of second lien lenders to object to a sale pursuant to Section 363 of the Bankruptcy Code, the applicable intercreditor agreement at issue in the case contained no such waiver. The court concluded that the second lien lenders retained the right to object as an unsecured creditor to the proposed Section 363 sale of collateral that was supported by the first lien lenders because there was "no provision [of the intercreditor agreement] which can be read to reflect a waiver of the [second lien lenders'] right to object to a section 363 sale motion, either in its capacity as a [s]ecured [p]arty or in its capacity as an unsecured creditor." The court noted that this result "goes against the spirit of the subordination scheme in the [i]ntercreditor [a]greement," but that the court was "constrained by the language of the [i]ntercreditor [a]greement."

In *In re MPM Silicones, LLC*, 518 B.R. 740 (Bankr. S.D.N.Y. 2014), the first lien lenders alleged that the second lien lenders violated their intercreditor agreement by, among other things, supporting the confirmation of the debtor's cramdown plan of reorganization over the objection of the first lien lenders.

The intercreditor agreement provided that "[the second lien lenders] will [not] take any action that would hinder any exercise of remedies undertaken by the . . . [first lien lenders] with respect to the Common Collateral under the Senior Lender Documents, including any sale, lease, exchange, transfer or other disposition of the Common Collateral, whether by foreclosure or otherwise; and each [second lien lender] hereby waives any and all rights it . . . may have as a junior lien creditor or otherwise to object to the manner in which . . . [first lien lenders] seek to enforce or collect the [first lien lenders' claims or the [l]iens granted in any of the [first lien lenders'] Collateral, regardless of whether any action or failure to act by or on behalf of . . . [first lien lenders] is adverse to the interests of the [second lien lenders]." However, the intercreditor agreement also provided, in Section 5.4, that "[n]otwithstanding anything to the contrary in this [a]greement, the [second lien lenders] may exercise rights and remedies as an unsecured creditor against the [borrower or any guarantor] in accordance with the terms of the applicable [second lien documents] and applicable law."

The court noted that, arguably, by supporting a cramdown plan the second lien lenders were opposing the first lien lenders' enforcement of their lien rights in the bankruptcy case, and further noted that because it was the debtors that advocated cramdown, any claim based on the second lien lenders support of the debtors' cramdown plan would have to be based upon the second lien lenders' encouragement of the debtors to proceed on that course. The court determined that any such encouragement by the second lien lenders was "the type of action, consistent with *Boston Generating* and in contrast with Judge Chapman's citation to *Ion Media*, that any unsecured creditor would rightly take." The court held that the second lien lenders' actions in support of the debtors' proper exercise of their duties to unsecured creditors with regard to the cramdown plan were permitted under Section 5.4 of the intercreditor agreement.

The court distinguished the intercreditor agreement in another bankruptcy case which contained "very tight language prohibiting the junior lien holders from taking almost every action against the general interests of the senior secured party—where the junior lien holders would, in the court's phrase, be 'silent seconds' and yield in all respects to the senior lien holder until the claim of the senior lien holder was fully satisfied" and observed: "[c]learly, more was required here to have rendered the [second lien lenders] silent on these types of issues."

The trend in the foregoing cases seems to be that courts will narrowly construe waivers by second lien lenders of their rights as unsecured creditors, but that express waivers of explicit rights are more likely to be upheld.

2.4.3 Unitranche Facilities

The past several years have seen a marked increase in the use of unitranche credit facilities for middle market borrowers. A unitranche credit facility combines into a single credit facility what would otherwise be separate first lien and second lien credit facilities. From a credit agreement perspective, the agreement is the same as with any other loan transaction. Namely, the borrower in a unitranche financing will have only a single set of covenants and reporting obligations to monitor and comply with, will pay a single blended interest rate on the unitranche loans (typically a cheaper rate than it would pay in aggregate for separate first and second lien loans), and will grant a single lien on collateral securing the unitranche loans. However, along with the typical credit agreement the lenders will also enter into a separate intercreditor agreement that is referred to as an agreement among lenders, or AAL. Pursuant to an AAL, which the borrower is not typically party to, the unitranche lenders will divide the unitranche loans into a first out tranche and a last out tranche. The AAL will contain a payment waterfall, under which the first out tranche will be entitled to be paid before the last out tranche and in exchange the last out tranche will be entitled to receive a larger share of the interest payments made by the borrower. The AAL will also typically set forth the relative rights of the first out tranche and the last out tranche with respect to voting, exercise of remedies, standstills, buyout rights, and bankruptcy matters.

Despite the cost and administrative benefits to borrowers of unitranche financings, there are also uncertainties regarding how AALs will be treated in bankruptcy. As a threshold matter, there is some uncertainty whether a bankruptcy court will determine that it has jurisdiction to enforce the AAL. Unlike most first/second lien intercreditor agreements, the borrower is typically not a party to an AAL, and therefore a bankruptcy court could determine that a dispute wholly among lenders is not sufficiently related to the borrower's bankruptcy case to confer jurisdiction. If that were the case, the lenders would have to try their dispute in a state court separately from the bankruptcy case, which could be time-consuming and inefficient. As of the date of this volume there has been only one bankruptcy case involving an AAL, *In re RadioShack Corp.*, 2016 Bankr. LEXIS 2006 (Bankr. D. Del. 2016). The bankruptcy court enforced the applicable AAL, to which the borrower was not a party. Although the court did not issue a precedential ruling based upon an interpretation of the Bankruptcy Code, practitioners have taken some comfort from the result.

Another uncertainty regarding AALs is whether a bankruptcy court will treat first out lenders and last out lenders as separate classes of creditors or as a single class of creditors. Treatment as a single class of creditors may have unfortunate results for the first out lenders. If the first out lenders are determined to be undersecured as a result of their claims being combined with the claims of the last out lenders, then the first out lenders could lose the right to receive post-petition interest or adequate protection (see the discussion in Section 2.4.2.1) and depending on the relative sizes of the two tranches, the last out tranche could potentially control the voting of the combined unitranche claim in the bankruptcy case.

2.5 MINIMUMS, MULTIPLES, AND FREQUENCY

A borrower sometimes pushes to have complete freedom to designate the dollar amount of any loan, regardless of whether that results in an extremely small loan or a loan with an odd value. It will want as much freedom to borrow $23.37 as to borrow $10,000,000. Similarly, a borrower might push to be able to have any number of separate LIBOR loans (separate LIBOR interest periods) outstanding at any time. All of this is in the name of flexibility.

Arguably, since the advent of computers, none of this should be an issue. However, both agents and lenders alike want to be spared the administrative nuisance of very small loans or of a multiplicity of LIBOR interest periods. In the context of LIBOR loans, a historical factor may also come into play; a small principal amount is inconsistent with the concept of "match funding," discussed in Section 3.1.2, since most deposits taken in the London interbank market are in minimums of $5,000,000. A lender is unlikely to find a deposit of $23.37 (let alone of its syndicate share of that amount, which would be even smaller). Although lenders in fact only rarely match funds, small LIBOR increments would nevertheless force the administrative agent and the lenders to track a potentially very large number of LIBOR loans with distinct interest periods and distinct interest rates. Accordingly, most credit agreements require that loans have relatively large minimums ($5,000,000 is typical for LIBOR loans, with somewhat smaller figures for base rate loans) and that the aggregate number of LIBOR loans be limited (ten is a typical maximum). Jumbo syndicates with commitments in the billions often have larger minimum amounts. All of these constraints operate to reduce the frequency of borrowings under the credit agreement, but of course also take away some flexibility from the borrower.

2.6   NOTICES AND MECHANICS OF FUNDING

Box 2.21

(a) *Notices.* To request a Borrowing, the Borrower shall notify the Administrative Agent of such request by telephone (i) in the case of a Eurodollar Borrowing, not later than 11:00 a.m., New York City time, three Business Days before the date of the proposed Borrowing, or (ii) in the case of an ABR Borrowing, not later than 11:00 a.m., New York City time, one Business Day before the date of the proposed Borrowing. Each such telephonic Borrowing Request shall be irrevocable and shall be confirmed promptly by hand delivery or telecopy to the Administrative Agent of a written Borrowing Request in a form approved by the Administrative Agent and signed by the Borrower. Each such telephonic and written Borrowing Request shall specify the following information: . . .

(b) *Funding.* Each Lender shall make each Loan to be made by it hereunder on the proposed date thereof by wire transfer of immediately available funds by 12:00 noon, New York City time, to the account of the Administrative Agent most recently designated by it for such purpose by notice to the Lenders. The Administrative Agent will make such Loans available to the Borrower by promptly crediting the amounts so received, in like funds, to an account of the Borrower maintained with the Administrative Agent in New York City and designated by the Borrower in the applicable Borrowing Request.

The credit agreement will require that the borrower give advance notice of any borrowing to the administrative agent, which will then notify the relevant lenders. Except in rare cases, notices are required to be delivered on "business days," and in the case of LIBOR loans are typically required to be delivered at least three business days prior to the date the loan is to be made, although there are occasionally credit agreements that permit LIBOR loans made on the closing date of the agreement to be made with one or two business days' notice. Base rate (or adjusted base rate or "ABR" for short) loans, depending on the number of lenders in the facility, may call for one business day's or same-day notice. The rationale for the longer notice periods for LIBOR loans in contrast to base rate loans is a function of the convention that the rate applicable to LIBOR loans is fixed two London banking days prior to the day the loan is made (see the discussion in Section 3.1.2.1).

The credit agreement almost always specifies a time of day by which notices are to be given and a time of day by which the lenders are to provide funds to the administrative agent. It does not ordinarily specify a time of day for the administrative agent to remit funds to the borrower, since the administrative agent does not have control over when it will receive funds. All notices are stated to be irrevocable, because it is presumed that the lenders will have allocated funds for the anticipated lending and, were the borrower to decline to take the loan, the lenders would not have an alternative for redeploying the funds that they lined up to lend to the borrower.

In almost all syndicated credit agreements, remittances between the borrower and the lenders pass through the administrative agent. Accordingly, when a loan is to be made, the lenders will be required to remit funds to the administrative agent, who will then disburse the funds to the borrower. This is usually the case even with competitive bid loans, though not necessarily for swingline loans (where the credit agreement may provide that the swingline lender remit proceeds directly to the borrower).

The administrative agent is the agent of the lenders, not of the borrower (except for the very limited role of maintaining the loan register as described in Section 11.2.6), and, consequently, the loan is not made when funds are received by the administrative agent from the lenders. Rather, the loan is made only when the administrative agent transfers funds to the borrower. The discussion of clawback clauses in Section 10.6, addresses what happens if a lender does not provide the administrative agent with its portion of a loan, but the administrative agent, not being aware that the lender has failed to remit funds, nevertheless forwards to the borrower an amount representing that lender's loan.

In some cases, when the borrower requires loan proceeds to make an acquisition and needs funds in the morning of the closing day, the parties may enter into a "prefunding" agreement, under which the lenders deposit funds with the administrative agent on the business day preceding the anticipated closing date and the borrower agrees to pay interest on such funds until the closing date, as if the loans had been made. If, for any reason, the closing does not occur on that day, the deposited funds are returned to the lenders by the administrative agent. This mechanism enables the administrative agent to know at the opening of business on the closing date that it has been put in funds by all lenders. In other cases, when the borrower requires loan proceeds to make an acquisition and there is a period of weeks or longer between when the credit agreement is executed and the acquisition is to occur, the lenders may prefer to fund the loan proceeds into an escrow account, so that they can earn full interest on the drawn loans rather than an undrawn commitment fee. In such circumstances, the escrowed loan proceeds will be released to the borrower upon the consummation of the acquisition and satisfaction of the other conditions precedent to the release or will instead be returned to the administrative agent to be applied to repay the loans.

Prefunding agreements are also sometimes used when a borrower wishes to take down LIBOR loans at closing and has not yet executed the credit agreement. (This is, of course, the normal case, since most credit agreements are not executed until the initial funding, even though the language of the credit agreement invariably contemplates that the funding is to occur some days after execution.) Since the credit agreement is not yet in effect, there is no agreement under which the borrower can give notice (and no agreement under which it is obligated to make "breakfunding" payments if for any reason the borrowing does not occur; see the discussion of breakfunding in Section 3.7.5). The prefunding agreement bridges this gap by having the borrower undertake that, if the closing does not happen when expected, it will make breakfunding payments as if the lenders had received a valid notice of borrowing.

2.7 AMEND AND EXTEND

Box 2.22

(a) The Borrower may, by written notice to the Administrative Agent from time to time, request an extension (each, an *"Extension"*) of the maturity date of any Class of Loans and Commitments to the extended maturity date specified in such notice. Such notice shall (i) set forth the amount of the applicable Class of Revolving Credit Commitments and/or Term Loans that will be subject to the Extension (which shall be in minimum increments of $[AMOUNT] and a minimum amount of $[AMOUNT]), (ii) set forth the date on which such Extension is requested to become effective (which shall be not less than [ten (10)] Business Days nor more than [sixty (60)] days after the date of such Extension notice (or such longer or shorter periods as the Administrative Agent shall agree in its sole discretion)) and (iii) identify the relevant Class of Revolving Credit Commitments and/or Term Loans to which such Extension relates. Each Lender of the applicable Class shall be offered (an *"Extension Offer"*) an opportunity to participate in such Extension on a pro rata basis and on the same terms and conditions as each other Lender of such Class pursuant to procedures established by, or reasonably acceptable to, the Administrative Agent and the Borrower. If the aggregate principal amount of Revolving Credit Commitments or Term Loans in respect of which Lenders shall have accepted the relevant Extension Offer shall exceed the maximum aggregate principal amount of Revolving Credit Commitments or Term

Loans, as applicable, subject to the Extension Offer as set forth in the Extension notice, then the Revolving Credit Commitments or Term Loans, as applicable, of Lenders of the applicable Class shall be extended ratably up to such maximum amount based on the respective principal amounts with respect to which such Lenders have accepted such Extension Offer.

(b) The following shall be conditions precedent to the effectiveness of any Extension: (i) no Default or Event of Default shall have occurred and be continuing immediately prior to and immediately after giving effect to such Extension, (ii) the representations and warranties set forth in Article *[Representations and Warranties]* and in each other Loan Document shall be deemed to be made and shall be true and correct in all material respects on and as of the effective date of such Extension, (iii) the Issuing Bank and the Swingline Lender shall have consented to any Extension of the Revolving Credit Commitments, to the extent that such Extension provides for the issuance or extension of Letters of Credit or making of Swingline Loans at any time during the extended period, and (iv) the terms of such Extended Revolving Credit Commitments and Extended Term Loans shall comply with paragraph (c) of this Section.

(c) The terms of each Extension shall be determined by the Borrower and the applicable extending Lenders and set forth in an Extension Amendment; *provided* that (i) the final maturity date of any Extended Revolving Credit Commitment or Extended Term Loan shall be no earlier than the Revolving Credit Maturity Date or the Term Loan Maturity Date, respectively, (ii)(A) there shall be no scheduled amortization of the loans or reductions of commitments under any Extended Revolving Credit Commitments and (B) the average life to maturity of the Extended Term Loans shall be no shorter than the remaining average life to maturity of the existing Term Loans, (iii) the Extended Revolving Loans and the Extended Term Loans will rank pari passu in right of payment and with respect to security with the existing Revolving Loans and the existing Term Loans and the borrower and guarantors of the Extended Revolving Credit Commitments or Extended Term Loans, as applicable, shall be the same as the Borrower and Guarantors with respect to the existing Revolving Loans or Term Loans, as applicable, (iv) the interest rate margin, rate floors, fees, original issue discount and premium applicable to [any Extended Revolving Credit Commitment (and the Extended Revolving Loans thereunder) and] Extended Term Loans shall be determined by the Borrower and the applicable extending Lenders, (v)(A) the Extended Term Loans may participate on a pro rata or less than pro rata (but not greater than pro rata) basis in voluntary or mandatory prepayments with the other Term Loans and (B) borrowing and prepayment of Extended Revolving Loans, or reductions of Extended Revolving Credit Commitments, and participation in Letters of Credit and Swingline

Loans, shall be on a pro rata basis with the other [Revolving Loans] or [Revolving Credit Commitments] (other than upon the maturity of the non-extended [Revolving Loans] and [Revolving Credit Commitments]) and (vi) the terms of the Extended Revolving Credit Commitments or Extended Term Loans, as applicable, shall be substantially identical to the terms set forth herein (except as set forth in clauses (i) through (v) above).

(d) In connection with any Extension, the Borrower, the Administrative Agent, and each applicable extending Lender shall execute and deliver to the Administrative Agent an Extension Amendment and such other documentation as the Administrative Agent shall reasonably specify to evidence the Extension. The Administrative Agent shall promptly notify each Lender as to the effectiveness of each Extension. Any Extension Amendment may, without the consent of any other Lender, effect such amendments to this Agreement and the other Loan Documents as may be necessary or appropriate, in the reasonable opinion of the Administrative Agent and the Borrower, to implement the terms of any such Extension, including any amendments necessary to establish Extended Revolving Credit Commitments or Extended Term Loans as a new Class or tranche of Revolving Credit Commitments or Term Loans, as applicable, and such other technical amendments as may be necessary or appropriate in the reasonable opinion of the Administrative Agent and the Borrower in connection with the establishment of such new Class or tranche (including to preserve the pro rata treatment of the extended and non-extended Classes or tranches and to provide for the reallocation of Revolving Credit Exposure upon the expiration or termination of the commitments under any Class or tranche), in each case on terms consistent with this Section.

Following the occurrence of the financial crisis, borrowers faced uncertain and illiquid loan market conditions. A large amount of pre-crisis loans were scheduled to mature at similar times, and borrowers were concerned that lenders would not be willing or able to make available sufficient amounts of loans at attractive interest rates to refinance all the maturing loans. This set of conditions has been referred to as a "refinancing cliff." As a refinancing alternative, borrowers sought to extend the maturities of their existing loans, typically in exchange for an increase in interest rates and/or the payment of fees. However, under most credit agreements these transactions needed to be effected by an amendment to the applicable credit agreement approved by the required lenders and, because extending the loan maturity is a "sacred" right requiring the consent of each affected lender, by each extending lender. If the amendment provisions of the applicable credit agreement required a unanimous rather than required lender vote, as a practical matter an amend and extend transaction would likely not be possible.

Over time, new credit agreements started to include mechanics that are referred to as amend and extend transactions that permitted the required amendments to be effected with the consent of only the extending lenders and not also the required lenders. The sample language in Box 2.22 is taken from the LSTA's Model Credit Agreement Provisions. The key features of the provisions in Box 2.22 are that (i) all lenders of the applicable class must be provided the opportunity to participate in the amend and extend transaction ratably and on equal terms and (ii) relative to the existing class of loans or commitments, the extended class (a) will not have a later maturity or a shorter weighted average life-to-maturity, (b) will rank pari passu in right of payment and security and have the same guarantors and collateral, (c) may share in mandatory prepayments on a ratable or less-than-ratable basis (but not a greater-than-ratable basis), (d) may have greater (or lower) interest rate margins, interest rate floors, fees, and premiums, as agreed by the borrower and the extending lenders, and (e) otherwise will have substantially identical terms. The amend and extend transaction is effected by an extension amendment, which may take the form of an amendment and restatement and may establish the extended loans or commitments as a separate tranche, executed by the borrower, the administrative agent, and each extending lender.

By way of contrast, European loan facilities address these refinancing concerns by using so-called forward start facilities. A forward start facility is a facility under which lenders under an existing credit facility commit, well in advance, to provide financing to repay the existing facility at its maturity. On the date that the existing facility matures, the borrower can draw down the forward start facility to repay it. Lenders who participate in a forward start facility provide commitments at least equal to their commitments under the existing facility. In exchange, they typically receive payments representing incremental increases over the interest margin and the fees payable under the existing facility. These top-up payments are designed to ensure that forward start facility lenders enjoy an immediate "marked to market" increase in the aggregate amount paid for their existing commitments (funded and unfunded) under the existing facility without increasing their overall exposure to the borrower.

The borrower, in turn, locks in the terms and pricing of a committed longer-term facility, in essence refinancing itself by extending its existing facilities. The forward start facility is a useful tool because it bypasses the unanimous lender consent that normally would be required to extend an existing facility. Forward start facilities are more difficult to utilize in the United States in part because many institutional B loan lenders cannot provide loan commitments (as would be required in a forward start facility), but instead purchase only funded term loans.

2.8 REFINANCING FACILITIES

Increasingly, credit agreements are including provisions permitting refinancing facilities that allow a borrower to refinance a class of loans or commitments in whole or in part, pursuant to a refinancing amendment that is required to be executed only by the lenders providing the refinancing loans or commitments and not by any other lenders. In the absence of such a provision, any such amendment would also require the consent of the required lenders or possibly all lenders of the classes not being refinanced. Refinancing facility provisions give borrowers an efficient way to take advantage of a favorable interest rate environment or otherwise manage their balance sheets without having to negotiate new standalone credit and security documentation and, potentially, intercreditor arrangements.

The typical requirements applicable to refinancing facilities are that relative to the class of loans or commitment being refinanced, the refinancing facility (a) will not have a greater principal amount (other than possibly by the amount of accrued unpaid interest and premium on the refinanced debt and any fees and expenses incurred in connection with the refinancing transaction), (b) will not have a later maturity or a shorter weighted average life-to-maturity, (c) if secured, will not have any greater collateral, (d) if guaranteed, will not have any additional guarantors, (e) may have greater (or lower) interest rate margins, interest rate floors, fees, and premiums, as agreed by the borrower and the extending lenders, and (f) otherwise may not have covenants and other terms that are more favorable to the lenders providing the refinancing facilities. The proceeds of the refinancing facility are contemporaneously applied to repay and satisfy the loans or commitment being refinanced. Other typical requirements include that the refinancing facility may be secured on a pari passu or junior basis with the remaining credit agreement facilities that are not being refinanced or may be unsecured, and if the refinancing facility is a term loan that is secured on a pari passu basis with any remaining term loan tranches that are not being refinanced, the refinancing term loans may share in voluntary and mandatory prepayments with the remaining term loan tranches on a ratable or less-than-ratable basis (but not a greater-than-ratable basis).

2.9 CASHLESS SETTLEMENT

Box 2.23

Notwithstanding anything to the contrary contained in this Agreement, any Lender may exchange, continue or rollover all or a portion of its Loans in connection with any refinancing, extension, loan modification or similar transaction permitted by the terms of this Agreement, pursuant to a cashless settlement mechanism approved by the Borrower, the Administrative Agent and such Lender.

In circumstances where a loan is being refinanced or amended and extended, the refinancing or amended credit agreement may permit a lender to continue its existing loans that are being refinanced or amended as new loans under the new agreement, or exchange its existing loans with refinancing or amended loans under the new agreement, in each case on a cashless basis. This is sometimes referred to as a "cashless roll." This is an attractive, administratively convenient option that obviates the need for the lender to fund new money and is particularly helpful for institutional lenders who may be subject to investment restrictions that limit their ability to make new cash investments.

The sample language in Box 2.23 is taken from the LSTA's Model Credit Agreement Provisions, and contemplates that the borrower, the administrative agent, and the applicable lender approve a mechanism for the cashless roll. Typically, the mechanism would be set forth in a cashless roll letter agreement. The LSTA has promulgated a form of such agreement.

CHAPTER 3
Interest and Fees

3.1 INTEREST

Unlike bond indentures or private placement documents, in which interest is nearly always calculated at a fixed rate for the life of the debt, credit agreements exhibit wide variability in pricing. They can (albeit rarely) provide for interest at a fixed rate. More commonly, though, the interest rate under a credit agreement will be floating and normally (in the case of U.S. dollar-denominated loans) is expressed as the sum of (1) a base component, usually either the prime or base rate or the London interbank offered rate (LIBOR, explained more fully in Section 3.1.2), that is reset from time to time, plus (2) a margin that is either fixed for the life of the transaction or subject to change based upon pre-agreed criteria.

Typically, floating rate pricing allows a borrower to elect to borrow either prime (or base rate) loans or LIBOR loans, or both simultaneously, with the borrower permitted to switch back and forth between the two types of loans at its option. Switching from one type to another is referred to as *conversion*. By way of illustration, a company might initially borrow $100,000,000, consisting of $10,000,000 of base rate loans and $90,000,000 of LIBOR loans; three months later, it could convert all of the base rate loans to LIBOR, so that the full $100,000,000 is outstanding as LIBOR loans; and six months further on it might convert some or all of the LIBOR loans back into base rate loans. In addition, as noted in Section 2.1, some credit agreements offer high-grade borrowers competitive bid or competitive access facilities, where the interest on loans is determined according to a bidding process among the lenders. The most common pricing options generally made available to borrowers are discussed here.

3.1.1   Base Rate Interest

Box 3.1

"*Alternate Base Rate*" means, for any day, a rate per annum equal to the greatest of (a) the Prime Rate in effect on such day, (b) the Federal Funds Effective Rate in effect on such day *plus* 1/2 of 1%, and (c) Adjusted LIBOR for a one-month Interest Period on such day (or if such day is not a Business Day, the immediately preceding Business Day) *plus* 1%, *provided* that, Adjusted LIBOR for any day shall be based on LIBOR at approximately 11:00 a.m. London time on such day, subject to any interest rate floors set forth therein. Any change in the Alternate Base Rate due to a change in the Prime Rate, the Federal Funds Effective Rate or Adjusted LIBOR shall be effective from and including the date of such change.

"*Prime Rate*" means the rate of interest per annum publicly announced from time-to-time by [Bank] as its prime rate in effect at its office at ____; each change in the Prime Rate shall be effective from and including the date such change is publicly announced as being effective.

The base rate (sometimes referred to as the alternate base rate, or ABR) is typically defined as the higher of (1) a specified bank's (normally the bank acting as administrative agent) publicly announced benchmark "base rate" or "prime rate" and (2) 50 basis points over the federal funds rate. Some banks prefer calling their publicly announced rate their "base rate" and others prefer "prime rate," but the two terms mean essentially the same thing. However captioned, the rate is the primary benchmark rate publicly announced by the bank for interest on its loans.

The definition "prime rate" has an interesting history. Originally, the prime rate was characterized by banks as the lowest rate offered in the United States to their "prime" or "best" customers for short-term loans. Sometimes it would be described as the "best" rate of interest generally charged to the bank's most creditworthy commercial borrowers for short-term commercial loans. With the broad expansion of the LIBOR market, these formulations left banks open to potential liability, since in many cases the prime rate ceased to be the best rate. LIBOR itself was being offered for short-term periods (as short as 30 days or even on an overnight basis) and could be *lower* than the prime rate. See *Michaels Bldg. Co. v. Ameritrust Co., N.A.*, 848 F.2d 674 (6th Cir. 1988), and *Haroco, Inc. v. American Nat'l Bank & Trust Co.*, 747 F.2d 384 (7th Cir. 1984), *aff'd*, 473 U.S. 606 (1985) for examples of attempted litigation under the Racketeer Influenced and Corrupt Organizations Act (RICO) based upon the disparity between the prime rate and other, lower, rates charged to corporate customers. The quick response of many banks was to rephrase the definition of prime rate so that it no longer claimed to be the lowest or best rate, but rather simply the rate *publicly announced* as the prime rate. In the consumer context the definition is sometimes even further clarified by stating expressly that the rate is not, and should not be considered to represent, the lowest or the best interest rate available to a borrower at any given time. These revised prime rate definitions have generally survived RICO attack. See *Lum v. Bank of Am.*, 361 F.3d 217 (3d Cir. 2004).

The base or prime rate has always been unilaterally determined by banks based on their cost of funds (whether from deposits, commercial paper, or other sources), competitive pressures, and other factors, including reserve requirements. In theory it could be changed at any time for any reason (or for no reason). Nevertheless, banks are reluctant to change their base or prime rates to reflect mere seasonal or other short-term increases in their cost of funds because of the rate's economic (and sometimes political) importance. Changes are relatively infrequent which, in turn, means that the rate may not accurately reflect on a daily basis their true cost of making loans.

As a consequence, when determining the ABR under a credit agreement, banks generally include a second component, the market-based federal funds rate. Incorporating the federal funds rate serves to protect lenders at times when the base or prime rate is not adjusting quickly or frequently enough to reflect the increased cost of funds. The federal funds rate is the interest rate at which banks that have a surplus in reserves at their Federal Reserve bank are willing to lend that surplus on an overnight basis to other banks. Most often, these overnight loans are used to satisfy reserve requirements, but they may also be a source of general funds for the borrowing bank. The federal funds rate is published daily by the Federal Reserve Bank of New York. For any day, the rate is the volume-weighted median rate on overnight federal funds transactions for the preceding business day. If that rate is not published, it is usually determined by the administrative agent based upon either actual quotes from federal funds brokers or the federal funds rate charged to the administrative agent bank. The additional 50 basis points are factored in to bring the federal funds rate and the base or prime rate closer to parity.

In addition, since the 2008 credit crunch, banks have typically included a third component to the definition of base rate, based upon one-month LIBOR. As is discussed further in Section 3.1.2.4, the interest rate applicable to base rate loans is typically higher than the interest rate applicable to LIBOR loans. For a time during the financial crisis, the base rate was lower than LIBOR. Because the applicable margin on base rate loans is typically lower than that on LIBOR loans (see Section 3.1.5.1), the overall interest rate (determined as base rate or LIBOR plus applicable margin) payable to lenders was reduced. This third component ensures that the base rate will never be lower than one-month LIBOR, as it changes each day.

Some agreements do not base the definition of "prime rate" upon the agent bank's announced prime rate, but rather make reference to the prime rate set out in the *Wall Street Journal* or other publicly available source. This avoids a potential verification problem if a lender is ever forced to prove that the calculation of interest is accurate. If the ABR is keyed to another bank's prime rate, the active cooperation of that bank would be required to determine what the prime rate was during, say, June 2005. This should not be an issue if the other bank is the administrative agent. It is more problematic if the relevant prime rate is that of a bank not associated with the credit agreement. Unfortunately, few banks make their historical prime rate information readily available through the Internet, in contrast to the financial press (where historical publications can almost universally be accessed on the Web).

3.1.2 LIBOR Interest

3.1.2.1 General Principles

Box 3.2

"LIBOR" means, with respect to any LIBOR Loan for any Interest Period, the rate appearing on Reuters Page LIBOR01[1] (or on any successor or substitute page or service providing quotations of interest rates applicable to dollar deposits in the London interbank market comparable to those currently provided on such page, as determined by the Administrative Agent from time to time) at approximately 11:00 a.m., London time, two Business Days prior to the commencement of such Interest Period, as the rate for dollar deposits with a maturity comparable to such Interest Period; *provided* that if such rate shall be less than [____], such rate shall be deemed to be [____] for the purposes of this Agreement; *provided further* that if such rate is not available at such time for any reason, then the "LIBO Rate" with respect to such LIBOR Loan for such Interest Period shall be the Interpolated Rate.

---

[1] Reuters Page LIBOR01 is the successor to page 3750 of the Moneyline Telerate Service in use for many years.

"Interpolated Rate" means, at any time, the rate per annum determined by the Administrative Agent (which determination shall be conclusive and binding absent manifest error) to be equal to the rate that results from interpolating on a linear basis between: (a) the rate as displayed on Reuters Page LIBOR01 (or on any successor or substitute page or service providing quotations of interest rates applicable to dollar deposits in the London interbank market comparable to those currently provided on such page, as determined by the Administrative Agent from time to time; in each case the *"Screen Rate"*) for the longest period (for which that Screen Rate is available) that is shorter than the Interest Period and (b) the Screen Rate for the shortest period (for which that Screen Rate is available) that exceeds the Interest Period, in each case, at approximately 11:00 a.m., London time, two Business Days prior to the commencement of such Interest Period; *provided* that if the Interpolated Rate shall be less than [____], such rate shall be deemed to be [____] for purposes of this Agreement.

For many decades, the London interbank market has been a major source of liquidity for banks seeking to fund loans whether denominated in U.S. dollars or in other currencies. The market has worked efficiently to enable banks in need of liquidity to obtain deposits from others with excess liquidity, whether on an overnight basis or for customary "interest period" tenors of one, two, three, or six months. The rates paid for these deposits have become the basis for LIBOR interest pricing in credit facilities.

Sometimes referred to as "LIBO rate," LIBOR is an acronym for London Interbank Offered Rate. It refers to the London-based unsecured wholesale market rates for jumbo deposits between major banks that are of varying durations and are denominated in certain designated currencies. As discussed in Section 3.1.2.5, there is a different LIBO rate for each of five currencies: U.S. dollars, Euros, British pounds, Swiss francs, and Japanese yen. This section will focus mainly on the U.S. dollar rate. Furthermore, each of the five LIBOR currencies also has seven different maturities or tenors ranging from overnight to 12 months. The LIBOR tenors are discussed in Section 3.1.2.2.

Since such deposits are often referred to as eurodollar deposits, the terms *eurodollar* and *LIBOR* are often used interchangeably; some credit agreements may even refer to "LIBOR (or LIBO rate) loans"; others simply refer to "eurodollar loans." The applicable LIBOR interest rate for a loan for any "interest period" is based upon the prevailing interest rate offered for eurodollar time deposits with matching beginning and ending dates.

Historically, "LIBOR" for any given bank was the rate that bank was *offered* funds by other banks in the London interbank deposit market (hence, the London Interbank *Offered* Rate). It was, in other words, the rate that depositors would *ask* to receive in order to induce them to place a deposit with a given bank. The latter might also *bid* for deposits, but the rate it quotes to take in funds would naturally be lower than the *ask* rate. The LIBOR that became the basis for calculating the interest rate for a particular loan, since it was the *offered* rate, was thus pegged to the higher ask rather than the lower bid quotes.

Historically, also, credit agreements provided that LIBOR for a given interest period was determined by averaging the individual LIBOR for such period quoted by several (usually two to five) "reference banks." Selection of reference banks would be the subject of negotiation between the parties, with the agent bank almost always included and other banks being selected (usually from participants in the syndicate) so that the reference bank pool contains both money center and middle-market institutions. The latter were included because the *ask* rate offered to money center banks was often lower than the *ask* rate offered to smaller middle-market banks, presumably to reflect the greater credit risk of the latter institutions (the risk that they might not be able to repay the deposit). Since a major portion of the lending syndicate would consist of non-money center banks, a blended LIBOR based upon quotes to multiple reference banks was thought to reflect more accurately the true cost of funds.

The LIBOR quotes assembled were stated to be those at approximately 11:00 a.m. London time. By market convention, banks in the London interbank market would record for future reference the rates as in effect at 11:00 a.m. The quotes collected would generally be for amounts "comparable" to the particular loan for the particular interest period. LIBOR quotes could vary depending upon the amount of the deposit (a jumbo deposit of $5,000,000 naturally attracts a higher interest rate than a deposit of $10,000). Similarly, a LIBOR quote for an interest period of one month could be different than a quote for an interest period of three or six months. The reference bank rates to be averaged, by referencing the interest period and amount, were intended to reflect the actual circumstances of the particular loan being made or continued.

For the most part, LIBOR is today no longer fixed by averaging reference bank rates but is instead determined by resort to a screen quote from Reuters or other market quotation service. Only if a screen quote is not available would the definition revert to reference banks.

The customary LIBOR quotation service, such as Reuters Page LIBOR01, employs rates compiled by ICE Benchmark Administration Limited. As described in the latter's website, which as of the date of this volume is www.theice.com/iba/libor, these are based upon quotes obtained from a broad spectrum of contributing banks (varying by currency), each of which is asked to submit the rate at which it could borrow funds were it to do so by "asking for and then accepting" interbank offers in a reasonable market size. This rate is thus equivalent to the *ask*, rather than the *bid*, side of the market for interbank deposits and should therefore (in theory) be economically equivalent to the historically determined LIBOR based on reference bank quotes.

Calculating LIBOR using a published rate (itself based upon the trimmed average of rates produced by a group of contributing banks and excluding the highest and lowest 25 percent of submitted quotes) may not diverge significantly from a reference bank system (based upon the average of rates produced by the reference institutions). Arguably, the essential difference between the two is simply the number of institutions that feed into the average. In a "reference bank" calculation, the number is from two to five; in a published rate calculation, the number is much larger (for 2016, ICE Benchmark Administration Limited cited 18 contributing banks for U.S. dollars).

Regardless of how LIBOR quotes are assembled (whether based on reference bank quotes or screen quotes), as is discussed further in Section 3.7.5, the assumption that underlies the pricing provisions for LIBOR loans is that each lender will fund its loan by accepting a eurodollar time deposit on which it will have to pay interest at a given rate, and that it will relend the funds to the borrower at the same rate (plus a margin that represents profit). This is so-called match funding. It is an assumption that drives many provisions of eurodollar credit agreements, both substantive and mechanical, and conforms LIBOR loans to the market practice for eurodollar deposits.

In the context of determining LIBOR itself, one of the provisions affected by this assumption is the rule that LIBOR quotes are fixed two London banking days prior to the first day of the interest period for the loan. Since the practice in the London interbank deposit market is to agree to the terms of a deposit two banking days prior to the deposit actually being received, and since it is assumed that each LIBOR loan is funded through a deposit made to the lender, a LIBOR-based interest rate must be similarly calculated for the same period as the deposit (the interest period). To ensure that the lender does not lose money by paying a higher interest rate on the deposit than it earns on the loan, the formula for calculating interest on the loan is tied exactly to the interest rate that the lender would pay on the corresponding deposit received on the day the loan is made. Consequently, the loan is priced two days in advance.

The convention of fixing interest on deposits in London two banking days prior to the first day of the deposit period itself likely has its origin in the practice of the foreign exchange market that a currency transaction (other than for a tourist or other buyer of paper money from a bank or currency dealer) is closed two banking days after the transaction is entered into. A purchase of Swiss francs with U.S. dollars on Monday will accordingly be closed on Wednesday (assuming Monday, Tuesday, and Wednesday are all banking days). Since LIBOR is based upon the trading of U.S. dollars in London, and dollars are a foreign currency in England, the interest rate for a deposit of dollars in London is similarly determined two banking days in advance of the actual deposit.

If a rate for a given interest period is unavailable on Reuters Page LIBOR01, a fallback method for determining the rate is needed. In the past, the parties would agree to a rate determined on the basis of quotes from designated "reference banks" as a first fallback measure and "market disruption event" (see Section 3.7.3) provisions as a second fallback measure. Today, use of an interpolated rate (as shown in Box 3.2) that interpolates between the rates for the next shorter and next longer interest periods for which screen rates are available is increasingly common as the first fallback. Another first fallback alternative sometimes used is the offered quotation rate to first class banks for deposits in the London interbank market by the administrative agent or a designated bank.

As shown in Box 3.2, it has also become common for LIBOR to have a floor rate below which LIBOR cannot go (even if the screen rate is in fact lower). These so-called LIBOR floors were first implemented in the wake of the 2008 credit crunch to address, in part, the disparity between the lower publicly quoted LIBOR and the reference rates actually paid by banks on eurodollar deposits (see discussion in Section 3.7.3.1) and provided for a minimum positive rate of interest, say, 1.0 percent. More recently, following the European Central Bank's reduction to below zero of a key interest rate in June 2014 (which was followed by central banks in Japan and several other European nations) and resultant concerns by lenders of possible negative interest rates on their loans, it has become common to have a LIBOR floor of zero if no higher floor is commercially agreed.

3.1.2.2 Interest Periods

> **Box 3.3**
>
> *"Interest Period"* means, for any LIBOR Loan, the period commencing
> on the date of such Loan (or its most recent Interest Reset), and ending
> on the numerically corresponding day in the calendar month that is one,
> two, three, or six months thereafter; *provided*, that (i) if any Interest Period
> would end on a day other than a Business Day, such Interest Period shall
> be extended to the next succeeding Business Day unless such next suc-
> ceeding Business Day would fall in the next calendar month, in which
> case such Interest Period shall end on the next preceding Business Day,
> and (ii) any Interest Period that commences on the last Business Day of
> a calendar month (or on a day for which there is no numerically corre-
> sponding day in the last calendar month of such Interest Period) shall end
> on the last Business Day of the last calendar month of such Interest Period.

Understanding how LIBOR works is largely a matter of remembering market convention and operational fictions. Perhaps the most
important feature to keep in mind is that the interest rate on LIBOR
loans is fixed for discrete periods, referred to as "interest periods,"
which correspond to the tenor of the hypothetical "matching" eurodollar time deposits. The durations of interest periods are, accordingly,
normally limited to the tenors for deposits commonly available in the
eurodollar market. The desired duration among these options is then
selected by the borrower. The most common tenors, and therefore the
most customary interest periods available to borrowers, are one, two,
three, and six months. Other interest periods are also often made available, but when they include tenors in which the eurodollar market is
less liquid, such as 12 months, or shorter than one month, unanimous
consent of the affected lenders is usually required because of the difficulty or expense of attracting the hypothetical matching deposits.
LIBOR for an interest period of an odd duration (such as one for
77 days) is determined by interpolating the rates for the next longer and
next shorter standard interest periods (in this example, interpolating
two- and three-month LIBOR).

The beginning and end dates of interest periods are subject to
rules that may seem somewhat arcane, and generally pertain to what
happens if the last day of an interest period would otherwise fall on a
nonbusiness day or when the relevant months do not have correspond-

ing days (for example, given that February 30 cannot be the one-month anniversary of January 30, does the anniversary become February 28 or perhaps March 2?). These rules are driven by the corresponding market conventions for eurodollar deposits. The month-end convention requires that interest periods end on the same day as they begin and if there is no corresponding day in the relevant subsequent month, the interest period expires on the last day of that month. A one-month interest period that begins on January 15 ends on February 15. A one-month interest period that begins on January 30 ends on February 28 (or, in a leap year, February 29). And if any of those end dates are not business days, the interest period ends on the *next following* business day, unless that day rolls into the next calendar month in which case the interest period ends on the *next preceding* business day.

At the borrower's election, it may have LIBOR loans with different interest periods outstanding simultaneously, with the maximum number of allowed interest periods limited as described in Section 2.5. Since, by market convention, the interest rate for a eurodollar deposit is set two business days before the deposit is accepted (its value is determined two business days forward), the interest rate for a LIBOR loan is set two business days before the interest period begins (for the meaning of "business day," see Section 3.5).

The interest rate for a LIBOR loan is fixed for the duration of its interest period, given that the interest rate for the hypothetical matching eurodollar deposit is also fixed for that period. If the borrower repays the LIBOR loan or converts it into a base rate loan in the middle of the interest period, the lenders are still obligated to maintain any matching eurodollar deposit. They could therefore incur a funding loss if interest rates have declined since the beginning of the interest period and they are unable to cover the interest they are paying on the matching eurodollar deposit by redeploying the proceeds of the repayment for the remainder of the interest period. Credit agreements require the borrower to indemnify the lenders for these losses (see Section 3.7.5). A few credit agreements prohibit voluntary repayments and conversions of LIBOR loans in the middle of interest periods. Virtually all credit agreements prohibit repayments of competitive bid loans prior to their maturity. Similarly, borrowers are sometimes prohibited from selecting interest periods that extend beyond the final maturity of the credit agreement or that straddle scheduled amortization dates if the amortization could force a repayment of LIBOR loans in the middle of an interest period.

At the end of each interest period for a LIBOR loan, the borrower is required to elect whether that loan will be converted into a base rate loan or be continued (or "rolled over") as a LIBOR loan (and, if the latter, to specify the new interest period). If the borrower fails to do so, the credit agreement normally provides for one of two fail-safes: either the LIBOR loan is automatically converted into a base rate loan or the LIBOR loan is automatically rolled over into another LIBOR loan with an interest period of one month. There are advantages to each fail-safe. The advantage to the borrower of an automatic conversion into a base rate loan is that its oversight may be corrected immediately without breakfunding, rather than waiting until the end of a one-month interest period. The advantage to the borrower of continuing the loan as a one-month LIBOR loan is that LIBOR, at least based upon historical experience, is likely to be lower than the base rate and will therefore result in lower interest charges. Breakfunding is never an issue for base rate loans, since base rate loans do not have interest periods; it is assumed that repayment of a base rate loan should not result in unanticipated costs to the lender since there are no matching deposits.

At least in U.S.-law credit agreements, when a base rate loan is converted into a LIBOR loan, or when a LIBOR loan is rolled over or converted into a base rate loan, it is normally *not* considered a new borrowing that requires the satisfaction of conditions precedent. It is treated merely as the resetting of interest on an outstanding loan, similar to the resetting of the interest rate from time to time on an adjustable-rate home mortgage loan.

Many credit agreements provide that whenever an event of default exists, LIBOR loans are no longer available or, if available, are available only for one-month periods. Sometimes this limitation becomes effective only if the administrative agent or required lenders so elect. The purpose is to minimize the lenders' breakfunding costs in the event the loans are accelerated and paid during the middle of an interest period.

3.1.2.3 Reserve Requirements

Box 3.4

"*Adjusted LIBO Rate*" means, with respect to any LIBOR Loan for any Interest Period, an interest rate per annum (rounded upwards, if necessary, to the next 1/16th of 1%) equal to (a) the LIBO Rate for such Interest Period *multiplied by* (b) the Statutory Reserve Rate.

"Statutory Reserve Rate" means, for the Interest Period for any LIBOR Loan, a fraction (expressed as a decimal), the numerator of which is the number one and the denominator of which is the number one *minus* the arithmetic mean, taken over each day in such Interest Period, of the aggregate of the maximum reserve percentages (including any marginal, special, emergency or supplemental reserves) expressed as a decimal established by the Board of Governors of the Federal Reserve System for eurocurrency funding (currently referred to as "Eurocurrency liabilities" in Regulation D of the Board).

The pricing of LIBOR loans is premised upon the assumption that lenders fund those loans with matching eurodollar deposits, so lenders consider this pricing to be "cost plus." They require compensation for any direct or indirect costs of funding LIBOR loans above the interest they pay on the eurodollar deposits. Most of these items are described in Section 3.7, but one, reserve requirements, merits special mention here.

When a bank is required to maintain reserves against a deposit, it will not have the full amount of the deposit available to it to lend to its customers. By way of example, if a bank is required to maintain a reserve equal to 3 percent of a deposit, it has only $9,700,000 available to lend from a $10,000,000 deposit. This means that to make a $10,000,000 LIBOR loan, it must fund itself with (and pay interest on) a larger eurodollar deposit (in this example, a deposit of $10,000,000 *divided by* 0.97, or $10,309,000). To cover the cost of obtaining a deposit of the appropriate size, the bank needs to receive interest (or at least LIBOR) on a notional loan of $10,309,000, even though it lends only $10,000,000.

Lenders are generally compensated for the additional cost of maintaining the larger eurodollar deposit by one of two methods. In each method, the interest calculation includes a gross-up for the reserve requirement. In the first method, the gross-up is based upon the *statutory* reserve requirement. The grossed-up LIBOR (sometimes referred to as "adjusted LIBOR" or the "adjusted eurodollar rate," if the gross-up is not contained in the definition of LIBOR itself) is written arithmetically as:

$$\text{Adjusted LIBOR} = \text{LIBOR}/(1 - R)$$

R here means the maximum gross percentage rate at which reserves are required to be maintained against eurocurrency liabilities, as defined in Regulation D, the applicable regulation of the Federal Reserve Board that establishes reserves against deposits. Since this method provides for recovery according to the maximum possible reserve rate, it is referred to as compensation for reserves on a "statutory maximum" basis. Lenders prefer this method because it is straightforward and easy to calculate, since it implicitly assumes that the full amount of the matching eurodollar deposit is a "Eurocurrency liability" within the meaning of Regulation D (see the definition of "statutory reserve rate" in Box 3.4). Of course, lenders, such as funds or insurance companies, that are not subject to any reserve requirements (or are subject to lower reserve requirements) may be overcompensated.

The second method to compensate lenders for reserve costs is based on the *actual* cost to the lender of maintaining reserves. The actual reserve cost suffered by a lender may not be at the full statutory rate, just as the income taxes an individual pays are not equal to the full tax rate *times* his or her taxable income. Eurocurrency liabilities, just like income taxes, are subject to a number of thresholds, offsets, and deductions which, in the case of eurocurrency liabilities under Federal Reserve Board Regulation D can change daily. For this reason, some borrowers insist upon indemnifying lenders for reserve costs only on an "as incurred" basis to reflect the true cost suffered by the lender. When calculated on an as incurred basis, the compensation is accordingly based upon the individual position of each lender. Consequently, nonbank institutional investors would not be entitled to any gross-up for reserve requirements.

Lenders have traditionally required, regardless of which method is used, that the resultant adjusted eurodollar rate be rounded; the example above contemplates rounding to the next highest 1/16 of 1 percent. Although rounding may have originally been inserted into rate calculations as an administrative convenience, there is now arguably no reason why it needs to jump by sixteenths. More recent market convention appears to contemplate rounding to the nearest 1/100 of 1 percent or to dispense with rounding altogether.

All of this notwithstanding, the reserve rate for so-called eurocurrency liabilities (those imposed by Regulation D on eurodollar funding) has been zero for many years. Nevertheless, adjustment language to compensate for these costs continues to be included in eurodollar credit agreements because it is always possible that the Federal Reserve could reset the reserve requirement to a level higher than zero.

3.1.2.4 Why LIBOR?

It should be apparent that the need for LIBOR loans to follow certain conventions of the eurodollar market reduces the flexibility of this pricing option for borrowers. The list of special conventions, however, goes beyond the interest period and reserve requirement fictions described above. For example, the fact that eurodollar deposits are priced two London business days prior to the delivery of funds means that the typical credit agreement requires notices of borrowings, prepayments, and conversions for LIBOR loans at least three business days in advance. The question arises, why do borrowers elect LIBOR loans over base rate loans?

The answer is easy: the interest on LIBOR loans has almost invariably been lower. Indeed, the more apt question is, why do borrowers ever elect base rate loans? Here, the answer goes back to the need for flexibility. In the context of an acquisition with a moving closing date or another urgent need for financing without much advance notice, the three business days' requirement for borrowing LIBOR loans may not be practicable. Similarly, a borrower's cash management may result in frequent borrowings and repayments, and the advance notice requirements and restrictions on repayments of LIBOR loans in the middle of interest periods (or the requirements for breakfunding if such repayments do occur) may lead a borrower to maintain at least a portion of its loans as base rate loans.

3.1.2.5 LIBOR Scandal and Recent Developments

In 2012, European and American regulatory authorities uncovered a widespread LIBOR-fixing scheme. Major financial institutions on both sides of the Atlantic were accused of artificially manipulating LIBOR to their benefit and ultimately paid fines in the billions of dollars to settle claims. As a result of the scandal, regulators sought to reform common LIBOR practices and Martin Wheatley, the former chief executive officer of the United Kingdom's Financial Conduct Authority, submitted a report detailing numerous suggested reforms to LIBOR. Several noteworthy reforms have been implemented, which are discussed below.

Beginning in 2014, the British Bankers' Association ceased to be the authority in charge of administering and maintaining LIBOR. Those responsibilities were transferred to ICE Benchmark Administration Limited, an independent subsidiary of the private exchange operator, Intercontinental Exchange.

Furthermore, as suggested in Wheatley's report, the number of currencies quoted by LIBOR was reduced. As of the date of this writing LIBOR reports rates for only five currencies, U.S. dollars, pounds sterling, Euros, Japanese yen, and Swiss francs. This is a reduction from the 10 LIBOR currencies reported prior to the implementation of the reforms.

As of the date of this writing there are seven lengths of maturity for which LIBO rates are reported: one day, one week, one month, two months, three months, six months, and twelve months. Of these, only four of them—one month, two months, three months, and six months—are typically offered to borrowers. Prior to the implementation of the reforms, LIBO rates were also reported for periods of two weeks, four months, five months, seven months, eight months, nine months, ten months, and eleven months. These rates were discontinued with the aim of improving the ability to verify submissions and focus on the more frequently used benchmark rates.

The LIBOR market reforms also increased the size of the banking panel reporting borrowing rates for the U.S. dollars from 16 banks to 18 banks. As of the date of this writing, these banks include Bank of America, BNP Paribas, Citibank, JP Morgan Chase, Royal Bank of Canada, the Norinchukin Bank, Bank of Tokyo-Mitsubishi UFJ, Credit Agricole, Deutsche Bank, Lloyds Banking Group, Société Générale, The Royal Bank of Scotland Group, Barclays Bank, Credit Suisse, HSBC, Rabobank, Sumitomo Mitsui Banking Corporation, and UBS.

3.1.3 Competitive Bid Loans

As noted in Section 2.1.1.3, some credit agreements offer high-grade borrowers competitive bid or competitive access facilities, for which the interest on loans is determined according to a bidding process among the lenders. When the borrower requests a competitive bid loan, the lenders compete to offer the lowest rate so as to capture a greater portion of the borrowings made under the credit agreement than would otherwise be the case if they merely lent their allocated percentage of the commitments. To initiate the bid process, the borrower makes a formal request of the administrative agent to solicit offers from the lenders to make competitive bid loans. The borrower specifies (1) the total amount of loans needed, (2) whether the offers should be expressed as a margin above LIBOR or should be expressed as a flat rate, (3) if the offers are for LIBOR-based loans, the tenors for which offers are solicited (which generally must conform to the same conventions described earlier for interest periods for LIBOR loans), and (4) if the offers are solicited for flat-rate loans, the tenors for which offers are solicited (which generally are between seven and 180 days).

Lenders at their option may provide offers in response to the borrower's request, and the borrower may at its option accept any offers made (although if it does accept offers, it must accept them in ascending order, taking up the offers for the lowest rates first). If an offer is accepted by the borrower, the lender is then obligated to make a competitive bid loan on the terms of the offer—amount, interest rate, and tenor.

The interest rate for competitive bid LIBOR loans is calculated by adding the accepted margin, if any, to the relevant LIBOR determined two business days before the loans are made, in accordance with the eurodollar convention discussed earlier. The interest rate for flat-rate loans is the flat rate accepted by the borrower.

The competitive bid lending provisions in a credit agreement prescribe a complex set of rules and procedures to ensure that the bid process is both timely and fair. All communication is through the agent—requests by the borrower for bids from the lenders, communication of bids by the lenders, acceptance of bids by the borrower, and notification by the agent of which lenders have had their offers accepted. Precise times for submitting offers are specified, including (to ensure fairness) that, if the agent bank is to submit a bid, it must do so before any other bids are required to be given to the agent. Similarly, if bids from more than one lender offer the same margin or flat rate, the bid rules specify that accepted loans are allocated among those lenders ratably in accordance with the principal amounts offered. The typical credit agreement provides that the borrower pays the agent a negotiated fee on the occasion of each bid request to compensate the agent for the administrative hassle of processing the bid request and resultant offers.

The interest rate on a competitive bid loan is fixed for the tenor of the loan, which may be called an interest period, even though competitive bid loans are not necessarily LIBOR based. The loans are generally not prepayable during the interest period, and the lender will be entitled to breakfunding if the loans are nevertheless paid during the interest period. One major difference between a competitive bid loan and the loans otherwise available under the credit agreement is that a competitive bid loan becomes due and payable on the last day of its interest period. It may not be converted or continued as a new competitive bid loan. If the borrower wishes to roll over a competitive bid loan, it must borrow new competitive bid loans (which, of course, will be subject to the satisfaction of conditions precedent and the bid procedure described earlier) and apply the proceeds to repay the maturing competitive bid loans. Alternatively, it must repay the loan either from funds available to it or from the proceeds of loans made under the revolving commitments under the credit agreement.

If, because of an intervening event, conditions cannot be satisfied and the borrower is unable to take down a replacement competitive bid loan or to borrow under the revolving credit commitments, the borrower will be in default under the credit agreement, and a serious one at that—namely, the failure to pay the full principal of the competitive loan at the end of its interest period. As a consequence, competitive bid loans, if drawn down, have the potential to convert a mere inability to borrow (something that would not normally even be a technical default) into a full-blown principal payment default.

3.1.4   Other Pricing Options

Over the years, the bank loan markets have seen a variety of other pricing options tied to various indices. These have included pricing determined by reference to certificate of deposit rates and term federal funds rates. LIBOR (London; U.S. dollars, pounds sterling, Swiss francs, and Japanese yen) has spawned EURIBOR (Europe; Euros), CDOR (Canada; Canadian dollars), HIBOR (Hong Kong; Hong Kong dollars and Chinese yuan), SIBOR (Singapore; Singapore dollars), and IBOR (indeterminate global markets). Since 2008, the loan market has seen the introduction of pricing based on the borrower's credit default swap (or CDS) spread. CDS-based pricing may be seen in credit agreements for higher rated companies with widely traded debt covered by a liquid CDS market. The pricing options explained here reflect the predominant preferences in today's markets. There are scores of others and will doubtless be still more that come into and go out of vogue over time.

3.1.5   Applicable Margins

Box 3.5

"Applicable Margin" means, for any day, with respect to any Base Rate Loan or LIBOR Loan, the Applicable Margin per annum set forth below based upon the [Index Debt ratings by the Rating Agencies] [Leverage Ratio]. . . .

3.1.5.1   General Principles

As noted earlier, the interest rate on each base rate loan and each LIBOR loan normally includes an additional, or "applicable," margin, sometimes also referred to as the *spread*. The applicable margin is, in some cases, a flat rate that is fixed for the life of the agreement, but in other instances it increases over time, or increases or decreases dependent on the credit ratings and/or a financial test (such as leverage) of the borrower. Whichever approach is taken, the applicable margin for LIBOR loans is always higher than the applicable margin for base rate loans in order to bring the two rates closer to parity. The difference has historically been 100 basis points, although the applicable margin for base rate loans would not be less than zero even if the applicable margin for LIBOR loans were less than 1 percent.

A flat margin or one that increases by the passage of time is rather straightforward and requires no further explanation. When the applicable margin is dependent on the credit rating and/or a financial test of the borrower, the various rates are set forth in the credit agreement in the form of a grid that varies by type of loan (by tranche and by pricing option) and the relevant financial measure (hence the term *grid pricing*). In addition, when the grid is based upon a leverage or other financial test, the credit agreement sometimes stipulates that the margin bumps up to the highest level during any event of default and whenever the borrower is late in delivering financial statements upon which the interest margin is to be calculated. The bump-up will be in addition to any default interest that may become payable by reason of an event of default.

3.1.5.2 Margins Based upon Credit Ratings

Box 3.6

"Applicable Margin" means, for any day, with respect to any ABR or LIBOR Loan, the applicable rate per annum set forth below under the caption "ABR Spread" or "LIBOR Spread," as the case may be, based upon the ratings by Moody's and S&P, respectively, applicable on such date to the Index Debt:

Index Debt Ratings	ABR Spread	LIBOR Spread
A–/A3 or more		
BBB +/ Baa1		
less than BBB +/Baa1		

For purposes of the foregoing [Grid], (i) if a Rating Agency shall not provide a Relevant Rating, the Applicable Margin shall be the highest rates provided above; (ii) if the Relevant Ratings shall fall within different Categories, the Applicable Margin shall be based on the [lower/higher] of the two ratings [unless one of the two ratings is two or more levels lower than the other, in which case the Applicable Margin shall be determined by reference to the level next above that of the lower of the two Ratings]; and (iii) if the Ratings by a Rating Agency shall be changed (other than as a result of a change in rating system), such change shall be effective as of the date on which it is first announced by such Rating Agency, irrespective of when notice of such change shall have been furnished. Each change in the Applicable Margin shall apply during the period commencing on the effective date of such change and ending on the date immediately preceding the effective date of the next such change.

When grid pricing is based upon credit ratings, the relevant parameters include reference debt (sometimes referred to as the "index debt"), the identity of the credit rating agencies to be relied upon (Moody's, Standard and Poor's, and Fitch are the most frequently used), and the treatment of split ratings (when different rating agencies assign different ratings to the same index debt). The index debt can be the loans under the credit agreement, a specific issue of debt securities of the borrower, or unspecified non-credit-enhanced, publicly issued debt of the borrower. Often, when there is a split rating, the higher of the two ratings is used, but when the ratings differ by more than one level (with each movement from "–" to flat or flat to "+" constituting a level), the most standard approach is to use the level immediately above the lower of the two ratings. Typically, any change in the applicable margin takes place either when the borrower notifies the administrative agent of the change in the rating or simultaneously when the change in rating occurs. If the index debt is rated by only one of the rating agencies or ceases to be rated at all, the applicable margin reverts to the highest rate in the grid.

3.1.5.3 Margins Based upon Financial Tests

Box 3.7

"*Applicable Margin*" means, for any day, with respect to any ABR or LIBOR Loan, the applicable rate per annum set forth below under the caption "ABR Spread" or "LIBOR Spread," as the case may be, based upon the Leverage Ratio as at the most recent determination date:

Leverage Ratio	ABR Spread	LIBOR Spread
≥5.00 to 1		
>5.00 to 1 and ≥4.00 to 1		
<4.00 to 1		

Each change in the "Applicable Margin" based upon any change in the Leverage Ratio shall become effective hereunder on the date three Business Days after the delivery to the Administrative Agent of the financial statements of the Borrower for the most recently ended fiscal quarter pursuant to Section [*Financial Statements*], and shall remain effective for such purpose until three Business Days after the next delivery of such financial statements to the Administrative Agent hereunder, *provided* that the Applicable Margin shall be the highest rates provided above if such financial statements shall not be delivered by the times provided herein (but only with respect to periods prior to the delivery of such statements).

In the event that any financial statement or compliance certificate delivered pursuant to Section [*Financial Statements*] is inaccurate (regardless of whether this Agreement or the Commitments are in effect when such inaccuracy is discovered), and such inaccuracy, if corrected, would have led to the application of a higher Applicable Margin for any period (an "*Applicable Period*") than the Applicable Margin applied for such Applicable Period, then (i) the Borrower shall immediately deliver to the Administrative Agent a corrected financial statement and a corrected compliance certificate for such Applicable Period, (ii) the Applicable Margin shall be determined based on the corrected compliance certificate for such Applicable Period, and (iii) the Borrower shall immediately pay to the Administrative Agent (for the account of the Lenders during the Applicable Period or their successors and assigns) the accrued additional interest owing as a result of such increased Applicable Margin for such Applicable Period. This paragraph shall not limit the rights of the Administrative Agent or the Lenders with respect to Section [*Default Interest*] and Article [*Events of Default*], and shall survive the termination of this Agreement.

When grid pricing is based upon leverage (or some other financial benchmark), the relevant date on which to test leverage is usually the end of the borrower's most recent fiscal quarter. Changes therefore occur no more frequently than quarterly, but they do not take place at the end of fiscal quarters. Rather they occur when the borrower delivers to the administrative agent financial information for the quarter setting out the current leverage ratio (or other financial test). The reason for this delay in adjustment is a practical one. If the interest margin were to change at the end of a quarter, the parties would not know whether an adjustment has occurred until financial statements for that quarter are delivered. The borrower could thus easily be required to make payments of interest *before* knowing what the appropriate interest figure is. Consequently, credit agreements frequently provide for the applicable margin to change upon delivery of the relevant leverage information or within two or three business days thereafter. Often the borrower is required to deliver a certificate for these purposes that sets out the leverage ratio. The applicable margin is then recalculated again when the borrower furnishes information for its subsequent fiscal quarter, in which case the applicable margin is reset (or continues) based upon the new information. Alternatively, if the borrower fails to furnish the financial information for any quarter on a timely basis, the applicable margin reverts to the highest rate in the grid effective on the latest date by which the information is to be delivered. This protects the lenders against the borrower not wanting to deliver bad news in order to keep the interest margin at a previous, lower, rate.

One problem that this approach raises is what happens if the underlying financial information or certificate for a particular quarter end is later discovered to be inaccurate. This is the issue addressed by the U.S. Bankruptcy Court for the Southern District of New York in *In re Adelphia Communs. Corp.*, 342 B.R. 142 (Bankr. S.D.N.Y. 2006). The case arose out of the Adelphia Communications bankruptcy proceedings filed in June 2002. In that case, seven different credit agreements for seven different borrowers each had grid pricing like that described above, with interest margins changing upon delivery of a compliance certificate that set out a leverage ratio at the end of each fiscal quarter. Early in the bankruptcy case, all of the lenders agreed to forego default interest in exchange for immediate payment of all pre-petition interest and the debtors' agreement to pay the lenders interest at the nondefault interest rate on a current basis going forward. Later, however, it was discovered that the financial information upon which pre-petition compliance certificates had been based (and the leverage ratios calculated) was inaccurate. The lenders sought bankruptcy court approval for a retroactive recalculation of pre-petition interest based upon the correct financial information. Their aggregate claim was alleged to be in excess of $187,000,000.

The lenders' plea was summarily rejected by the court. Reading the language in each definition of "applicable margin," the court noted that the spread was determined "based upon" (the words used in each underlying credit agreement) the quarterly compliance certificate. The court, in other words, held that the margins were determined in each case by reference to the leverage ratio set forth in the compliance certificate rather than by what the leverage ratio actually was. The court supported its reasoning by reference to other provisions of the credit agreements, including that delivery of an inaccurate compliance certificate had its own remedy, namely that it constituted an event of default entitling the lenders to interest at the much higher default rate. But, of course, the lenders in the *Adelphia* case had previously given up any claim for default interest in exchange for payment of pre-petition interest and current post-petition interest and so were barred from seeking the higher default rate. The court noted also that none of the credit agreements contained any language that provided for retroactive adjustment of interest margins if a leverage ratio calculation was later determined to be inaccurate.

As a result of the *Adelphia* case, credit agreements now typically insert express language to allow for retroactive adjustment of interest margins if the benchmark financial test or compliance certificate is later discovered to have been inaccurate. The last paragraph in Box 3.7 is an example. Typically this language is one-way. It will not provide for retroactive *reduction* of interest margins if the borrower subsequently learns that it overpaid interest, although logically the adjustment should run both ways. An easier way to accomplish retroactive adjustment (both up and down) without a long, sometimes contentiously negotiated, paragraph that mandates subsequent recalculation might be simply to remove the concept that the margin is based upon financial statements or a certificate and instead require the margin to be based upon the actual ratio. The applicable margin definition would thus state that it is calculated by looking at the leverage ratio and changes upon *delivery* of financial statements for the relevant quarter, not that it is based upon the financial statements themselves or upon a calculation of the leverage ratio prepared by the borrower.

Retroactive adjustment, if it were ever required, could present an enormous headache for an administrative agent to determine who is entitled to what interest and at what rate. This is particularly the case where the adjustment follows par (as opposed to distressed) trades. For example, in the par trade context, the assignee does not normally purchase interest claims. The assignment agreement instead contains an agreement of the administrative agent to remit to the assignors interest accrued for periods prior to the trade. If a retroactive adjustment of interest were ever required, the administrative agent could find itself having to track down former holders of loans going back (potentially) several years in order to allocate additional (or recover excess) interest payments. The headache becomes a migraine if the inaccuracy is discovered after the loans have been paid in full.

3.1.6   Interest Payment Dates

Box 3.8

Accrued interest on each Loan shall be payable in arrears on each Interest Payment Date for such Loan and, in the case of Revolving Credit Loans, upon termination of the Commitments; *provided* that (i) interest accrued pursuant to Section [*Default Interest*] shall be payable on demand, (ii) in the event of any repayment or prepayment of any Loan (other than a prepayment of an ABR Revolving Loan prior to the end of the Revolving Credit Availability Period), accrued interest on the principal amount repaid or prepaid shall be payable on the date of such repayment or prepayment, and (iii) in the event of any conversion of any LIBOR Loan prior to the end of the current Interest Period therefor, accrued interest on such Loan shall be payable on the effective date of such conversion.

"Interest Payment Date" means (a) with respect to any ABR Loan (other than a Swingline Loan), the __ day of each [March], [June], [September], and [December] and (b) with respect to any LIBOR Loan, the last day of the Interest Period for such Loan and, in the case of a LIBOR Loan with an Interest Period of more than three months' duration, each day prior to the last day of such Interest Period that occurs at intervals of three months' duration after the first day of such Interest Period.

The credit agreement specifies the dates on which interest is to be paid. In the case of base rate loans, most credit agreements provide for quarterly payment dates (often at the end of calendar quarters or on quarterly anniversaries of the closing date). In the case of LIBOR loans and competitive bid loans, interest is payable on the last day of each interest period and, if any interest period is longer than three months, on each quarterly anniversary of the first day of the interest period. The result is that if the borrower has multiple LIBOR loans outstanding, it may be paying interest frequently during the course of a quarter as interest periods come and go. Most credit agreements also provide that, for all loans, interest is payable on the date that the principal is paid or the loan is converted to a different type. In some cases, the latter rule does not apply to base rate loans, on which interest may be payable only at quarterly dates. Default interest is payable on demand as described in Section 3.1.8.

3.1.7   PIK Interest and "Toggle" Loans

Although interest is generally payable in cash, some credit agreements, particularly where the borrower has near-term liquidity concerns, allow interest to be paid by adding some or all of the accrued amount to the principal. This is so-called pay-in-kind (PIK) interest. Traditionally in such agreements, either it is specified up-front whether interest is to be payable in cash or PIK'd, or the borrower is given the option each time an interest payment is to be made of either paying the interest in cash or adding it to the principal. The election is often required to be made in advance of a borrowing or interest period, but there are examples of credit agreements that permit the borrower to make that election near the end of an interest period. These are referred to as "toggle" loans, and they can be complicated assets to trade and settle in the secondary loan market.

Typically, in par trading, performing loans are sold without accrued interest. The assignor retains the right to be paid interest for periods prior to the effective date of the assignment and the assignee is entitled to be paid interest for periods subsequent to the effective date subject, of course, to any delayed compensation that may be payable under the LSTA's trading documentation as a result of a late settling trade. An assignor will be content with this arrangement if all interest is payable in cash since, even in the context of a complete sell-down of its loans, the assignor knows it will receive its full retained interest component in cash on the next interest payment date. However, if any portion of the interest is payable on a PIK basis, trading that loan becomes far more complicated, especially where a borrower is permitted to make the election near the end of the interest period. Under the LSTA's trading documentation, all PIK interest that is capitalized or accreted on or after the relevant trade date is for the assignee's account for no additional consideration. Thus, parties may not know how to price a loan if, at the time of trade, the borrower has not yet elected to pay cash or PIK interest.

If the assignor and assignee know whether interest is to be payable in cash or PIK'd, they can enter into the trade (and appropriately price the payment for the interest component) with full knowledge of what portion is payable in cash and what portion is to be added to the principal. Because PIK interest typically accrues at a higher rate, normally 75 basis points over the cash interest spread, guessing wrong can have economic costs. Although the secondary market issues surrounding the trading of toggle loans were not resolved in 2007, fortunately for the secondary loan market, there have been only a few new toggle deals since the financial crisis.

3.1.8 Default Interest

Two principal approaches to default interest (an increase in interest rate that occurs by reason of default) are seen in credit agreements. One approach requires default interest to be paid only on amounts that are not paid when due. If the overdue amount is the principal of a loan, then the interest rate on that amount is increased to the default rate. For example, if loans in the amount of $100,000,000 are outstanding and the borrower fails to pay an installment of $10,000,000, then the increased interest rate applies only to the overdue amount of $10,000,000. (Of course, if all of the loans are accelerated because of the payment default, then all of the loans are overdue and therefore attract the higher interest rate.) When the overdue amount is something other than the principal, say interest or fees, then interest is paid on that overdue amount at the default rate.

A second approach provides for interest to be paid at the default rate on the entire amount of the loans whenever an event of default exists, regardless of whether the event of default involves nonpayment. Using the previous example, if loans in the amount of $100,000,000 are outstanding and the borrower fails to pay an installment of $10,000,000 (or, say, if a financial covenant is breached), and such failure (or breach) constitutes an event of default, then the increased interest rate applies to the full $100,000,000. Since it is not feasible to apply interest to accruing obligations like interest and fees until they are overdue, even when an event of default exists, the default interest rate applies to the amount of these obligations only once they become due and are not paid.

The default rate of interest for the principal amount of any loan under both approaches is usually 2 percent above the then-applicable rate for that loan. The default rate of interest for other amounts is usually 2 percent above the then-applicable rate for base rate loans, since there is no rate otherwise applicable to such amounts. Although a lender might be tempted to exact a higher bump-up in interest when a default occurs, there is a risk that an excessive increase would be deemed to be a penalty, and thus unenforceable. An increase limited to 2 percent has been held by at least one court not to constitute a "penalty," see *Ruskin v. Griffiths*, 269 F.2d 827 (2d Cir. 1959). Greater increases, however, have been rejected. See the cases discussed in *In re Vest Assocs.*, 217 B.R. 696 (Bankr. S.D.N.Y. 1998). The increase of 2 percent is in addition to whatever applicable margin is in effect. As noted earlier, it is customary that interest accruing at the default rate be payable on demand rather than on the regularly scheduled dates otherwise provided in the credit agreement.

Another aspect of default interest is worth noting. When an event of default exists, it is possible that lenders may become concerned about the likelihood of repayment. They may consider accelerating the maturity of loans. They may be willing (indeed, eager) to accept prepayments of LIBOR loans in the middle of interest periods. To minimize funding losses in this context, credit agreements are often structured so that, while a default is ongoing, LIBOR interest periods are either required to be short in duration (one month is typical) or LIBOR loans are simply made unavailable and forced to be converted into base rate loans as interest periods roll off. Sometimes the restrictions upon LIBOR occur automatically upon notice of a default, but more commonly they kick in once an explicit notification to that effect is delivered to the borrower by the administrative agent or the lenders.

3.2   FEES

Fees in credit agreements typically include some combination of the following: commitment fees, facility fees, utilization fees, letter of credit fees, swingline fees, upfront fees, and administrative agency fees.

3.2.1   Commitment Fees

Commitment fees are compensation for the lenders' contractual commitments to make loans. Typically, they are charged on revolving credit commitments, usually based on the daily average of the unused portion of each lender's outstanding revolving credit commitment. They can also be charged on term loan commitments, depending upon the transaction and the length of the period for which the commitments are outstanding. The rate at which commitment fees are payable is generally either flat for the duration of the credit agreement or subject to grid pricing. Accrued commitment fees are generally payable quarterly in arrears.

In calculating the unused amount of revolving credit commitments, all outstanding loans, undrawn letters of credit, and outstanding reimbursement obligations for payments under letters of credit are normally considered utilizations of the revolving credit commitments, though the practice is not uniform. In credit agreements with swingline loans, the amount of outstanding swingline loans is generally not deducted for purposes of calculating commitment fees (even though it is considered a utilization of the revolving credit commitments for other purposes). This is so because the lenders that have not advanced swingline loans nevertheless remain committed to extend credit to the borrower in the amount of those loans, whether by funding participations in the swingline loans or by making revolving credit loans for the purpose of repaying the swingline loans, and will want to be compensated for this commitment. The contrast between letter of credit participations, which are treated as a utilization for commitment fee purposes, and the possible future swingline loan participations, which are not treated as a utilization for commitment fee purposes, is explained very simply. Swingline lenders are not entitled to share in swingline interest until the participation is actually funded. Letter of credit participants, however, are paid their ratable share of letter of credit fees once the participation arises, regardless of whether the participation is ever funded.

Term loan commitments sometimes accrue a commitment fee known as a "ticking fee." Ticking fees are most commonly found in commitment letters (or related fee letters) for committed term loan financings for which the commitment period is relatively long. The ticking fee may start to accrue immediately or after some period of time following the effectiveness of the commitment letter and will typically accrue until and be payable on the closing date. The rate of the ticking fee may be fixed, or may increase with the passage of time. Ticking fees may be documented in the credit agreement, but do not need to be if they are in a commitment or fee letter.

3.2.2 Facility Fees

In contrast to commitment fees, which are computed on unused commitments, facility fees are computed on the total amount of revolving credit commitments, both used and unused. Facility fees generally do not apply to term loan facilities. Commitment fees and facility fees are mutually exclusive—the same revolving credit facility would not provide for both. Facility fees are most often seen either when the usage of a revolving credit facility is expected to be low or when the facility provides for competitive bid loans. Like commitment fees, facility fees are either calculated at a flat rate or subject to grid pricing, and are generally payable quarterly in arrears. Some credit agreements provide that facility fees are payable only until the revolving credit commitments terminate. Others, however, provide that facility fees are payable until the later of the termination of the revolving credit commitments or the repayment in full of the loans and termination of all other extensions of credit. This latter structure is designed to avoid a reduction in the aggregate pricing of the facility when the commitments expire, but loans and letters of credit continue outstanding. After termination of the revolving credit commitments, the fee is payable on the total amount that would have been considered utilization of the revolving credit commitments had those commitments remained in effect.

3.2.3   Utilization Fees

For transactions in which the revolving credit commitments are not expected to be heavily utilized, the commitment fee or facility fee may be lower than in other comparable transactions. However, to address the possibility that utilization may turn out to be high, the credit agreement may provide for an additional fee to be payable if utilization exceeds a certain percentage (say, 30 percent or 50 percent) of the commitments. On each day that this percentage is exceeded, the fee is payable on all utilizations of the revolving credit facility and not merely on the portion in excess of the 30 percent or 50 percent threshold.

In contrast to the approach used to calculate the commitment fee, utilization for this purpose is more likely to be defined broadly, including not only outstanding revolving credit loans, letters of credit, and reimbursement obligations, but also swingline loans and competitive bid loans. Like commitment fees and facility fees, utilization fees are either calculated at a flat rate or subject to grid pricing. Approaches vary as to whether accrued utilization fees are payable quarterly in arrears or concurrently with payments of interest on the related loans, although quarterly payments are more common. Utilization fees are characterized under some credit agreements as additional interest on loans because interest may receive more favorable treatment than fees under the Bankruptcy Code.

3.2.4   Letter of Credit Fees

As letters of credit are issued under a revolving credit facility, all of the revolving credit lenders share in the credit exposure, even if they are not the letter of credit issuer, since each acquires a participation in any letter of credit upon its issuance. Accordingly, borrowers are obligated to pay to each revolving credit lender a letter of credit fee that accrues at an agreed per annum rate on its participation in the undrawn amount of each outstanding letter of credit. In the case of the issuer of each letter of credit, its participation therein for purposes of this calculation is deemed to be its remaining credit exposure after subtracting the participations of the other revolving credit lenders. It is very common for the letter of credit fee rate to be the same as the applicable margin for LIBOR loans, taking into account the use of any applicable grid pricing.

Even though all revolving credit lenders share in the credit exposure to the borrower, the letter of credit issuer bears an additional risk—the risk that one or more of the revolving credit lenders might not fund their participations in a letter of credit if the borrower fails to reimburse the issuer. Letter of credit issuers are compensated by borrowers for this additional risk in the form of a fronting fee (so-called because the issuer "fronts" the letter of credit for the other revolving credit lenders). The fronting fee accrues at a modest agreed per annum rate on the undrawn amount of each outstanding letter of credit, and the rate is generally flat rather than based on grid pricing.

These letter of credit fees and fronting fees are customarily payable quarterly in arrears, although they are often paid two or three business days after the quarterly period ends in order to give the administrative agent sufficient time to make the necessary calculations. In addition to these fees, the letter of credit issuer may impose administrative charges for issuing, amending, and making payments under letters of credit.

3.2.5 Swingline Fronting Fees

Swingline lenders bear a fronting risk similar to that of a letter of credit issuer. If a revolving credit lender refuses or is unable to fund new revolving loans intended to repay a swingline loan (or to fund a participation in a swingline loan), the swingline lender will end up with greater exposure to the borrower than contemplated by the relative size of its commitment. Swingline lenders are often compensated for this risk with a swingline fronting fee that operates, and is payable, much like the letter of credit fronting fee.

3.2.6 Upfront Fees

Upfront fees are compensation to lenders for making a loan. Unlike the other fees referred to in this discussion, upfront fees do not accrue over time but instead are payable on the closing date as a percentage of the lender's term loan amount or revolving commitment amount. Upfront fees are often netted by term loan lenders from the proceeds of the loans they fund at closing. Upfront fees can be so netted by revolving lenders only to the extent they fund their revolving commitments at closing (often they do not) and otherwise must be paid as a cash fee. Credit documentation often refers to upfront fees and original issue discount (or "OID") interchangeably. OID is a tax-related term that represents the discount from the par amount of a debt instrument at the time that it is issued. Under relevant tax rules, if more than a *de minimis* amount, OID is accrued over the life of the debt instrument and is generally treated as a form of taxable interest, which is required to be recognized when it accrues, whether or not the borrower actually makes an interest payment. Upfront fees are sometimes referenced in the credit agreement, but like ticking fees discussed in Section 3.2.1 do not need to be if included in a commitment or fee letter.

3.2.7 Administrative Agency Fees

Administrative agency fees are payable by the borrower to the administrative agent, for its own account, to compensate the administrative agent for the services it performs in connection with the credit agreement. The fee is typically payable as a fixed dollar amount, either quarterly or annually in advance. The credit agreement itself may refer to the administrative agency fee, but the fee will typically be set forth in a separate fee letter between the borrower and the administrative agent, so that both parties can keep the amount of the fee confidential.

3.3 COMPUTATION OF INTEREST AND FEES

Box 3.9

All interest hereunder shall be computed on the basis of a year of 360 days, except that interest computed by reference to the Alternate Base Rate at times when the Alternate Base Rate is based on the Prime Rate shall be computed on the basis of a year of 365 days (or 366 days in a leap year), and in each case shall be payable for the actual number of days elapsed (including the first day, but excluding the last day).

Two methods are generally used under the typical credit agreement to calculate the accrual of interest and fees. The first method computes the accruing amount on the basis of a year of 360 days and actual days elapsed. The second method determines the accruing amount on the basis of a year of 365 days and actual days elapsed.

A few illustrations may clarify the distinction. Assume the interest rate for a LIBOR loan determined in accordance with the formulae set out earlier in this chapter (see Section 3.1.2.3) is 6 percent per annum.

Calculating interest on the basis of a 360-day year and actual days elapsed means that the actual interest charged on the loan is 6.08 percent, as shown by the following arithmetical computation:

$$6.00\% \times 365/360 = 6.08\%$$

Calculating interest on the basis of a 365-day year results in no adjustment to the formula LIBOR under the credit agreement, since the mathematical computation looks like this:

$$6.00\% \times 365/365 = 6.00\%$$

The reason the first computation produces a slightly higher effective interest rate is the fiction that a year has only 360 days. A year of 360 days requires that the full 6 percent be recovered within 360 days. But since a year is, in fact, longer (365 or 366 days), those extra five or six days attract interest on top of the 6 percent produced by the LIBOR formula. Hence computing interest on a 360-day basis always produces a higher interest rate.

An obvious question is why a borrower would ever allow interest to be calculated on a 360-day basis. The answer is a function of market convention and business negotiation. From the inception of the eurodollar market, computing interest on a 360-day basis has been the method used to determine interest on LIBOR deposits. Since, as discussed earlier in this chapter, LIBOR loans were historically funded with a direct match to eurodollar deposits, interest on LIBOR loans was also computed on the basis of a 360-day year. What was initially a necessity to ensure that deposit costs were fully covered by interest earnings on a loan became a market convention. A 360-day year is now universally used when calculating the interest on LIBOR loans. The same is true for competitive bid LIBOR loans and for competitive bid flat-rate loans. Whether a 360-day year is used in other contexts (such as to calculate base rate interest or commitment or facility fees) is largely a matter of negotiation. There is really no "fair" or "unfair" result here, so long as the lender, when preparing a term sheet that lays out projected interest rates, is clear how interest will be computed.

A third method of calculating interest is also seen in the fixed interest context of bond indentures and private placements. This method calculates interest on the basis of a year that consists of twelve 30-day months. Although it would appear that this is another way of accruing interest on the basis of a 360-day year (it is a fiction to assume that a year has twelve 30-day months), over a full year the formula is equivalent to calculating interest on a 365-day basis. By way of illustration, if the stated interest rate on a bond is 6 percent per annum, the rate for a full year (12 months) is 6% × 1/12 × 12 = 6% per annum. Of course, for individual months, the formula can produce distortions inasmuch as the rate for any given calendar month is 6% × 1/12 = 0.5%, regardless of how many days there actually are in that month (28, 29, 30, or 31). Thus, interest for the month of February is overstated (28 or 29 days is not 1/12 of a year), while interest for the month of March is understated (31 days is more than 1/12 of a year). The method is nevertheless used in the bond and private placement contexts because bonds and private placement notes generally tend to have a tenor that is a multiple of full years with interest payable on semiannual dates, and because the method allows for easy calculation of the interest payable every six months.

3.4 ACCRUAL CONVENTIONS

When calculating interest and fees, one final principle should be borne in mind. If a loan is made on Monday and repaid on Tuesday, for what day is interest payable? Stated another way, if the base rate is 6 percent on Monday and 6.25 percent on Tuesday, what is the interest rate on the loan? Market convention provides that interest (with the exception of that on intraday loans) is charged for the day on which the loan is made and each day thereafter that it is outstanding, but *not* for the day on which it is repaid. In this example, therefore, interest would be payable at 6 percent. Fees are calculated on a similar basis.

Some agreements expressly provide that ". . . in the computation of periods of time from a specified date to a later specified date, the word 'from' means 'from and including' and the words 'to' and 'until' each mean 'to but excluding.'. . ." The typical credit agreement then provides that interest is paid *from* a given date *to* a second date. Whether or not these definitional prescriptions are set out in the credit agreement, market custom (as well as the plain dictionary meaning of the terms) produces the same result: interest is paid for the first day of a period but not the last. New York Gen. Constr. Law, Article 2 § 20 also stipulates the same result.

3.5 BUSINESS DAY CONVENTIONS

Box 3.10

"Business Day" means any day that is not a Saturday, Sunday or other day on which commercial banks in New York City are authorized or required by law to remain closed; *provided* that, when used in connection with a Eurodollar Loan, the term "Business Day" shall also exclude any day on which banks are not open for dealings in dollar deposits in the London interbank market.

Bankers and borrowers (and their lawyers too) like to take weekends off. Who wants to be sending and receiving notices, funding loans, and allocating payments and prepayments when the sun is out and the day is warm? Who would be around anyway? To alleviate the inconvenience and trauma of working on weekends and holidays, a credit agreement typically provides that no activity is required (or permitted) on days that are not "business days." The definition is used to determine notice periods for borrowings and prepayments and other actions to be taken under the agreement, and also to determine when loans are available or payments to be made. Loans are made and repaid only on business days.

The definition of "business day" normally has two components. First, it sets out a general rule as to what constitutes a business day in the jurisdiction in which the administrative agent is located. This lets the agency personnel at least enjoy their weekend. But there is a rub. What is good for New York should be good for London as well. Simply because we do not celebrate England's late May "Spring Bank Holiday" (the successor to Queen Victoria's birthday) should not mean that we make our British compatriots work the holiday to make LIBOR determinations. The markets would not, in any event, be open. So a definition of a business day, at least if the credit agreement provides for LIBOR loans, lays out a second set of rules applicable to determine LIBOR business days. Insofar as a "business day" relates to LIBOR, the term refers to any New York business day (as determined in accordance with the general rule) that is *also* a day on which dealings in dollar deposits (or other relevant currency) are carried out in the London interbank market. Consequently, the typical notice period for a LIBOR loan (three days) needs to allow for three full New York and London business days. A request for a LIBOR borrowing made on a Thursday when the Friday is a holiday in New York and the Monday is a holiday in London results in the borrowings not being available until Thursday of the following week.

In a New York–law agreement, the general rule states that a business day is any day other than a day on which banks are required or authorized to close. This is *not* equivalent to days on which the stock exchanges are open (the approach customarily seen in bond indentures), nor does it include Saturdays. Even though many banks may be open on Saturdays, they are in fact authorized to close, so Saturdays, under the definition, do not constitute business days. Days upon which banks are authorized to close may also happen unexpectedly if, for example, there is a blackout or some other disaster and the governor or other appropriate official issues an order that banks are authorized to close.

Sometimes a borrower pushes to have the business day definition include the jurisdiction in which it is located, so that, for example, the base definition for a Boston-based borrower consists of New York and Massachusetts business days. This lets our Boston friends celebrate Patriots' Day (the third Monday in April), even though New York ignores what happened in Lexington and Concord two centuries ago. Administrative agents generally resist this approach because of the complications it creates when determining LIBOR business days (these are customarily just New York and London) and the concern that it opens a Pandora's box: if the borrower gets its holiday, why not each of the lenders? Given the hodge podge of state bank holidays (and religious and other holidays in other countries) an expansive definition of "business day" could theoretically result in administrative activity occurring only on one or two days each week.

3.6 LENDING OFFICES

Box 3.11

"Applicable Lending Office" means, with respect to any Lender, in the case of a Base Rate Loan, such Lender's "Domestic Lending Office" and, in the case of a LIBOR Loan, such Lender's "LIBOR Lending Office", in each case specified opposite its name on Schedule ___, or in either case such other office of such Lender as it may from time to time specify to the Borrower and the Administrative Agent.

When the LIBOR market first developed, since LIBOR funding was from offshore deposits and LIBOR borrowers were foreign, it was natural that the branches from which LIBOR loans were made were situated outside of the United States as well. Even when LIBOR lending was expanded to domestic borrowers, and the funding of LIBOR loans was no longer sourced exclusively from LIBOR deposits, banks continued the practice of making LIBOR loans only from nondomestic offices. This contrasted with prime or base rate loans, which were always made from domestic offices.

The offshore offices used were frequently shell branches in the Caribbean—the Bahamas and the Cayman Islands were popular—set up for the sole purpose of making LIBOR loans. Lending from offices outside the United States was done for a variety of reasons. Making a loan from a Cayman branch (and having the branch take in the necessary deposits to fund the loan) meant that the transaction taken as a whole was free from Federal Reserve Board reserve requirements, Federal Deposit Insurance Corporation (FDIC) deposit insurance assessment charges, taxes, and other regulatory burdens. Lending from a nondomestic office also allowed the lender to distinguish its eurodollar loans from its base rate loans. As noted in Section 3.1.1, the prime rate was historically characterized as the "lowest" rate offered to a bank's "best customers" in the United States. With the advent of LIBOR, which was most often *lower*, the traditional definition of prime rate became problematic. A way to distinguish the two rates was therefore to make all LIBOR loans from lending offices located outside the United States and all prime rate loans from offices within the United States. In this way, LIBOR could continue to be offered without making the description of prime rate untrue.

The definition of "prime rate" now refers simply to a publicly announced rate and consequently most credit agreements today give lenders complete flexibility to specify whatever lending offices they desire—domestic or foreign—for whatever class of loan. A typical lending office clause allows each lender at its option to book a loan at any domestic or foreign branch or affiliate of the lender as it shall choose. Although some agreements create formal definitions of an "applicable lending office," as illustrated in the language in Box 3.11, many agreements are simply silent on the point and allow the bank's own internal bookkeeping to establish the office from which any particular class of loan is made. This approach is certainly less cumbersome than defining "applicable lending office" inasmuch as the lender can freely shift offices during the term of the agreement without having to send a notice to the borrower and the administrative agent.

3.7 YIELD PROTECTION

Lenders do not like making loans that lose money. LIBOR lending incurs the theoretical risk that the cost of the loan (meaning the cost of the underlying deposit that nominally funds the loan) can rise after the loan is made without the rate of interest on the loan increasing to compensate. It also suffers the risk that the agreed LIBOR quotes will not accurately reflect the true cost of funding the loans. Enter the yield protection clause. The yield protection clause, as the name implies, is intended to protect the lender's yield on a loan to the borrower. While originally conceived to address yield issues as they relate to LIBOR loans and the obligation to make LIBOR loans, today yield protection clauses generally apply to all loans and obligations to make loans, notwithstanding that changes that affect the underlying cost of base rate loans are passed on to borrowers through changes in the prime rate.

The original focus of yield protection clauses on LIBOR borrowings is a product of how LIBOR loans are nominally funded. As described earlier in this chapter, the theory that underlies a LIBOR loan is that a bank takes in a succession of deposits in London for relatively short terms (say, three or six months) and lends the proceeds of the deposits to its customer for a longer term (say, five or seven years). The interest rate on the loan is simply the sum of the interest paid by the lender on the deposits *plus* an interest margin increased, if necessary, to compensate for reserve requirements. LIBOR is adjusted every three or six months as deposits are renewed or "rolled over" by the lender in London to maintain the loan outstanding to its customer, and any change in pricing (whether higher or lower) is passed on to the customer. LIBOR loans are, in essence, a cost-plus loan product.

When the LIBOR market first developed, the practice of taking in a particular deposit to provide funding for a particular loan was nearly universally employed by banks that made LIBOR loans. The practice was described as "match funding," a term that refers to the "matching" of a loan to a deposit. Today, with the LIBOR market having developed to the point where many billions of deposits are traded each day, few banks will match fund. Nonbank lenders will not, in any event, match fund because they do not take deposits. Nevertheless, the principle of match funding still lives in the yield protection clauses of credit agreements as a way to protect the lenders against unexpected events that adversely affect their ability to make, maintain, and earn money from LIBOR loans.

In decades past, yield protection clauses were the source of long, agonizing negotiations between borrowers and lenders. In recent years, the language has become more settled. The LSTA's Model Credit Agreement Provisions include market-standard yield protection clauses. Although yield protection clauses can vary widely, they almost always consist of the provisions described below and are included in credit agreements notwithstanding that (apart from breakfunding) the number of times that lenders have invoked the clauses since the creation of the LIBOR market (even including the credit crisis of 2008) can probably be counted on a single hand. Lenders remain convinced that the potential damage to them from omitting the clause far outweighs any detriment to borrowers having to cover lenders for unknown costs if a yield protection event were ever to occur.

Yield protection clauses come in a variety of flavors (increased costs, capital costs, LIBOR market disruption, illegality, breakfunding, and taxes), each of which addresses a distinct risk to which a lender could be prey when making a loan. These are discussed in turn below.

3.7.1 Increased Costs

Box 3.12

If any Change in Law shall:

(i) impose, modify or deem applicable any reserve, special deposit, compulsory loan, insurance charge or similar requirement against assets of, deposits with or for the account of, or credit extended or participated in by, any Lender (except any reserve requirement reflected in the Adjusted LIBO Rate) or any Issuing Bank;

(ii) subject any Recipient to any Taxes (other than (A) Indemnified Taxes, (B) Taxes described in clauses (b) through (d) of the definition of Excluded Taxes and (C) Connection Income Taxes) on its loans, loan principal, letters of credit, commitments, or other obligations, or its deposits, reserves, other liabilities or capital attributable thereto; or

(iii) impose on any Lender or any Issuing Bank or the London interbank market any other condition, cost or expense (other than Taxes) affecting this Agreement or Loans made by such Lender or any Letter of Credit or participation therein;

and the result of any of the foregoing shall be to increase the cost to such Lender or such other Recipient of making, converting to, continuing or maintaining any Loan or of maintaining its obligation to make any such Loan, or to increase the cost to such Lender, such Issuing Bank or such other Recipient of participating in, issuing or maintaining any Letter of Credit (or of maintaining its obligation to participate in or to issue any Letter of Credit), or to reduce the amount of any sum received or receivable by such Lender, Issuing Bank or other Recipient hereunder (whether of principal, interest or any other amount) then, upon request of such Lender, Issuing Bank or other Recipient, the Borrower will pay to such Lender, Issuing Bank or other Recipient, as the case may be, such additional amount or amounts as will compensate such Lender, Issuing Bank or other Recipient, as the case may be, for such additional costs incurred or reduction suffered.

"Change in Law" means the occurrence, after the date of this Agreement, of any of the following: (a) the adoption or taking effect of any law, rule, regulation or treaty, (b) any change in any law, rule, regulation or treaty or in the administration, interpretation, implementation or application thereof by any Governmental Authority or (c) the making or issuance of any request, rule, guideline or directive (whether or not having the force of law) by any Governmental Authority; *provided* that notwithstanding anything herein to the contrary, (x) the Dodd-Frank Wall Street Reform and Consumer Protection Act and all requests, rules, guidelines or directives thereunder or issued in connection therewith and (y) all requests, rules, guidelines or directives promulgated by the Bank for International Settlements, the Basel Committee on Banking Supervision (or any successor or similar authority) or the United States or foreign regulatory authorities, in each case pursuant to Basel III, shall in each case be deemed to be a "Change in Law", regardless of the date enacted, adopted or issued.

"Recipient" means (a) the Administrative Agent, (b) any Lender or (c) any Issuing Bank, as applicable.

As discussed briefly above, when the London interbank eurodollar market was developing an early concern of lenders was that the cost of a deposit taken into their London branches to provide funds for a loan might increase during the term of the deposit because of a change in law, such as the imposition of a tax, a new reserve, or some other new regulatory requirement. The increased costs clause of a credit agreement was therefore invented to protect the lender against this risk (consistent with the cost-plus assumptions of LIBOR loans) by allowing it to pass on those costs to the borrower in the event of a "regulatory change" or a "change in law." These terms were defined broadly to pick up not only changes in law, rules, and regulations, but also requests, guidelines, or directives from a government authority "whether or not" these have the force of law. The latter was intended to address the approach taken by central banks (particularly the Bank of England and the Bank of Japan) to implement action (such as the maintenance of additional reserves) through informal "requests" rather than setting out requirements in explicit published regulations. Although couched in terms of a request, there is no ambiguity as to a bank's having to comply. "Costs" for purposes of the clause are not limited to out-of-pocket cash costs, but also include reductions in the return for a lender (as would be the case if it were required to maintain reserves against a deposit that funds the loan).

The sample language in Box 3.12 is taken from the LSTA's Model Credit Agreement Provisions. It is not limited in scope to agreements with LIBOR-based loans. Even in a facility with only base rate pricing, the borrower is required to pay increased costs resulting from changes in law. The definition of Change in Law in Box 3.12 specifies that (x) the Dodd-Frank Wall Street Reform and Consumer Protection Act ("Dodd Frank") and all requests, rules, guidelines, or directives thereunder or issued in connection therewith and (y) all requests, rules, guidelines, or directives promulgated by the Bank for International Settlements, the Basel Committee on Banking Supervision (or any successor or similar authority) or the United States or foreign regulatory authorities, in each case pursuant to Basel III, will in each case be deemed to be a "Change in Law," regardless of the date enacted, adopted, or issued. Dodd Frank was passed in 2010 and the United States endorsed the adoption of Basel III in 2010, both of which will require an increase in capital requirements for certain financial institutions. While banking regulators have implemented most of the regulations required under Dodd Frank, as of the date of this writing additional regulations are expected to be promulgated under both Dodd Frank and Basel III. Accordingly, lenders want clarity in credit agreements that the adoption of further regulations under Dodd Frank or Basel III will constitute increased costs for which they are entitled to reimbursement.

An increased costs clause normally provides that the amount of the cost incurred by a lender (and which it may pass on to a borrower) be determined by the lender acting in good faith, and that the determination is conclusive "absent manifest error," or words of similar import. The clause may, in some cases, require the lender to deliver supporting calculations for its determination. The latter can be a point of contention. An institution with many hundreds of millions (or billions) of offshore deposits having different tenors, located in different legal jurisdictions and in different currencies, and funding many different loans, could face difficulty assembling cost data for any particular loan and, indeed, may be reluctant to share with borrowers what might be highly confidential funding strategies.

Yield protection provisions, therefore, do not generally require a detailed analysis of the cost determinations by a lender for reimbursement from a borrower. Reliance on the lender acting in good faith coupled with delivery of a certificate is assumed to be sufficient. The certificate is often stated to be conclusive "absent manifest error" or words of similar import. "Manifest error" has generally been construed by courts as an error that is ". . . plain and indisputable, and that amounts to a complete disregard of the . . . evidence." See *Guy v. Crown Equip. Corp.*, 394 F.3d 320 (5th Cir. 2004). In the context of a credit agreement this probably requires the certificate to contain an arithmetical mistake (such as a misplaced decimal point or obvious extra zeros, or a blunder in simple addition) to be "manifest." Given that the typical certificate sets out only the amount to be compensated without any backup calculation, the circumstances in which an error could be manifest are likely very limited (see Section 13.4).

Sometimes a borrower attempts to limit a lender's ability to request compensation to situations in which the lender is seeking similar compensation in similar amounts from other customers "similarly situated." Although superficially appealing, lenders tend to resist an approach that requires customers to receive "equal" or "similar," or "comparable" treatment. To begin with, there is the difficulty of determining what "similarly situated" means in any given circumstance. Does it require that a lender make increased cost requests of all borrowers, or can it distinguish based upon credit quality? Or on deal size? What if there are differences in wording in the increased cost clauses? Even if a lender is rigorously consistent when it possesses drafting control for increased cost clauses, it is still likely to agree to many variants when it participates as a syndicate member in deals led by other arrangers. Are all of these "similarly situated"? For these reasons, and to avoid putting the lender in the difficult position of reviewing potentially hundreds or thousands of agreements to catalog individual variances, few agreements give a borrower this right.

Another issue generally addressed in the clause is the ability of a lender to seek retroactive reimbursement for increased costs. One concern that lenders have is that, because of the difficulty of working through the implications of regulatory changes for institutions with loan portfolios in the billions, they may discover after the fact that an increased cost event has occurred. A common resolution is to allow the lender to seek recovery for costs for some retroactive period from, say, three, six, or nine months prior to the effectiveness of the regulatory change. Costs incurred prior to that period are solely for the account of the lender.

Increased cost provisions are frequently qualified by several provisions inserted for the protection of the borrower; these provisions are discussed in Sections 13.2, 13.3, and 13.4.

3.7.2 Capital Costs

Box 3.13

If any Lender or Issuing Bank determines that any Change in Law affecting such Lender or Issuing Bank or any lending office of such Lender or such Lender's or Issuing Bank's holding company, if any, regarding capital or liquidity requirements, has or would have the effect of reducing the rate of return on such Lender's or Issuing Bank's capital or on the capital of such Lender's or Issuing Bank's holding company, if any, as a consequence of this Agreement, the Commitments of such Lender or the Loans made by, or participations in Letters of Credit or Swingline Loans held by, such Lender, or the Letters of Credit issued by any Issuing Bank, to a level below that which such Lender or Issuing Bank or such Lender's or Issuing Bank's holding company could have achieved but for such Change in Law (taking into consideration such Lender's or Issuing Bank's policies and the policies of such Lender's or Issuing Bank's holding company with respect to capital adequacy), then from time to time the Borrower will pay to such Lender or Issuing Bank, as the case may be, such additional amount or amounts as will compensate such Lender or Issuing Bank or such Lender's or Issuing Bank's holding company for any such reduction suffered.

Bank regulators exist, among other reasons, to help avoid bank collapses. Public confidence in banks contributes to a prospering economy. Over the decades, a wide variety of measures have been adopted in an effort to ensure that the banking system is stable, including regular investigations by bank examiners, the institution of federal deposit insurance, and the requirement that banks satisfy certain minimum capital standards.

Capital requirements have been in place for many decades, although capital rules were historically not uniform among the major countries in which banks are organized. In a global economy this led to unfairness and inconsistent regulation. To address these issues, in July 1988, the Basel Committee on Banking Regulations and Supervisory Practices issued proposals (known as the Basel I Accord) for a risk-based capital framework to be applicable to bank supervisory authorities in the G10 countries (these include, among others, the United States,

Canada, the United Kingdom, France, Germany, Italy, and Japan). The Accord contemplated that each participating authority would phase in new capital requirements upon banks under its supervision so that, when fully implemented, the capital requirements of each country would conform to the uniform standards set out in the Accord. In the United States, the phase-in was to take place over the course of several years starting in 1989.

Before the new standards and implementation steps were announced (in the United States this was done in coordinated fashion by the Federal Reserve Board, the Comptroller of the Currency, the FDIC, and other federal regulators of depository institutions) bank lenders were afraid that the initial capital requirements contemplated by the Accord would adversely affect their profitability by increasing the amount of capital they were legally required to maintain as support for their assets. A lender that, prior to Basel I, maintained capital of 3 percent (or $300 million) against assets of $10 billion would, assuming the cost of capital is 6 percent, pay $18 million per year to induce investors to supply that capital. If, under the Accord, the bank were required to increase its capital to 5 percent (or $500 million), it would need to pay out $30 million each year, assuming the same 6 percent cost of capital. The additional $12 million payout would need to be covered somehow by earnings on its assets, including on loans made under credit facilities extended by it. Fearing the unknown and being unable to calculate exactly what the new capital requirements were to be, lenders wanted protection against whatever increased costs might result from the new rules issued by the Federal Reserve Board (or other relevant supervisory authority). Banks also wanted protection against subsequent changes to capital requirements, such as in fact occurred in September 1996 and, again, after the announcement of Basel II guidelines in 2004 and Basel III guidelines in 2010. The capital costs clause in a credit agreement addresses these risks and, following the announcement of Basel III guidelines, which included proposals regarding minimum liquidity, also now typically address changes in law regarding liquidity requirements.

Borrowers can make a logical argument that the uncertainties of capital costs should not be passed on to them. As shown with the preceding example, an increase in the cost of capital operates very differently than an increase in the cost of funds. The increased costs clause in a credit agreement is designed to preserve a lender's return on a cost-plus deal. LIBOR or the base rate is cost and the margin is the plus, or profit. Capital costs, on the contrary, are arguably no different than overhead costs and (or so the reasoning goes) should not be entitled to a special compensation regime like that for increased costs.

This is not an argument that borrowers have won. Due to the uncertainty of the effect upon lenders of changes in capital standards, credit agreements commonly include a clause designed to protect them against unanticipated capital costs. The sample language in Box 3.13 is taken from the LSTA's Model Credit Agreement Provisions. The clause is not limited in scope to agreements with LIBOR-based loans. Even in a facility with only base rate pricing, the borrower is required to indemnify the lenders against increased capital costs.

The clause entitles a lender to compensation not just for the increased costs suffered by the lender itself, but for the increased capital costs of its holding company. Why is this appropriate? After all, it is the bank rather than the holding company that makes the loans. The answer lies in the different bank ownership structures prevalent in different jurisdictions and the fact that capital requirements in the United States are imposed on both the bank and its holding company. In most countries, the Basel Accord capital requirements are implemented directly at the bank level since most countries do not structure their banking system through the mechanism of holding companies; the United States is one of the few countries that does so. The cost that a German or French bank incurs for increased capital is, in the United States, most likely to be incurred by the U.S. bank's holding company on a consolidated basis. To avoid the quirk of non-U.S. bank lenders being compensated for increased capital costs while U.S. banks go uncovered, the capital adequacy clause is written to encompass bank holding companies as well as banks.

The sample language cited in Box 3.13 covers a lender for capital costs imposed by a change in law after "taking into consideration such lender's policies" with respect to capital adequacy. The guidelines set out in the regulations implementing the Basel Accord are meant to be *minimum* capital requirements. Bank lenders may, for their own reasons, wish to have higher internal capital requirements and the typical capital adequacy provision could therefore be triggered by these higher, more restrictive, standards.

The cost calculation is made on a lender-by-lender basis. A less creditworthy bank lender (one that has a higher cost of capital) could, in the event of a change in capital requirements, submit a bigger claim than would a first-tier bank. Additionally, a nonbank institutional lender or other vehicle that participates in B tranche loans, is unable to submit any claim since such an entity is not subject to bank supervision and thus not vulnerable to the increased capital costs of the Basel Accords.

3.7.3   LIBOR Market Disruption

> **Box 3.14**
>
> If prior to the commencement of any Interest Period for a LIBOR Borrowing:
>
> (a) the Administrative Agent determines (which determination shall be conclusive absent manifest error) that adequate and reasonable means do not exist for ascertaining LIBOR for such Interest Period; or
>
> (b) the Administrative Agent is advised by the Required Lenders that LIBOR for such Interest Period will not adequately and fairly reflect the cost to the Lenders of making or maintaining the Loans for such Interest Period;
>
> then the Administrative Agent shall give notice thereof to the Borrower and the Lenders as promptly as practicable thereafter and, until the Administrative Agent notifies the Borrower and the Lenders that the circumstances giving rise to such notice no longer exist, (i) any request to convert any Borrowing to, or continue any Borrowing as, a LIBOR Borrowing shall be ineffective and (ii) any requested LIBOR Borrowing shall be made as an ABR Borrowing.

3.7.3.1   Background

From its inception, lenders have been concerned that the mechanism to determine LIBOR as set out in the typical credit agreement might not accurately reflect the true cost of making a LIBOR loan. Lenders feared the possibility that some "disaster" could occur in the LIBOR market that would result in lenders being unable to obtain LIBOR quotes at the beginning of an interest period, or that the quotes obtained would not adequately reflect the cost to the lenders of making a loan. In the early days of the LIBOR market, the former (absence of quotes) might occur for reasons as simple as a London-wide blackout or as problematic as The Bank of England imposing legal restrictions on deposit-taking activity. The latter (quotes not reflecting true cost) might occur if the LIBOR market started tiering banks based upon credit quality so that depositors insisted upon a premium to place funds with weaker institutions. During the credit crunch in the second half of 2008, there was a broader fear that the quotations assembled by the British Bankers' Association (BBA) and other pricing services simply did not reflect the true cost to the lenders of obtaining euromarket funds.

Several possible explanations have been proposed for this perceived disparity between the publicly quoted LIBOR and the actual rates on eurodollar deposits. The most often cited is that, for reputational reasons, banks on the BBA panels may have been unwilling to report their true, higher cost of funds because it might have reflected a desperate need for cash. Another possible explanation is that, during a credit crunch, the eurodollar market became relatively thin, particularly for deposits with longer tenors. While depositors may have been willing to place funds overnight or for other short periods, it may have been difficult for some banks to obtain deposits for, say, three or six months. Rates quoted by the panel banks for longer-term deposits therefore might have contained some element of artificiality and not have been completely reliable. The brunt of any illiquidity in the interbank dollar market is borne by non-U.S. banks since they do not have a broad U.S. dollar deposit base as do U.S. banks. In late 2008, for example, it was reported that rates paid by many European banks for overnight deposits were double the rates paid by U.S. banks.

As discussed earlier in this chapter, in syndicated loan transactions, the assumption underlying LIBOR loans is that banks are able to obtain eurodollar deposits for specific periods and re-lend the amounts of those deposits to borrowers. Since credit agreements usually determine LIBOR for this purpose by reference to the rate publicly announced by Reuters (or by using reference banks) rather than by reference to the actual rate paid on eurodollar deposits by each lender, the disparity referred to above between publicly quoted LIBOR and actual eurodollar deposit rates means that a bank may lose money on a loan if its funding cost exceeds the interest it receives. This risk is especially high for loans to investment-grade borrowers (where the slim profit margins are quickly eroded by the funding loss) than for leveraged loans (where the higher margins provide more cushion).

3.7.3.2 Components of the Market Disruption Clause

The solution invented by early drafters of LIBOR-based credit agreements to address the potential disparity in rates was the so-called "market disruption clause," often referred to as the "alternative interest rate provision" or, more ominously, the "eurodollar disaster clause." The original purpose of the clause was to protect lenders against exactly the circumstances described above, either (a) the quoted LIBO rates are somehow "tainted," in that they do not reflect actual market rates, or (b) a tiering has occurred within the bank ranks resulting in some banks incurring higher costs than others to obtain eurodollar deposits. An example of a typical market disruption clause is shown in Box 3.14.

The clause has two principal components. The first component is the trigger event that entitles lenders to suspend making loans bearing interest at rates calculated by reference to LIBOR. In the sample clause above, the trigger event is a determination by the required lenders that LIBOR for an interest period will not "adequately and fairly" reflect the cost to the lenders of making or maintaining the loans for the interest period. Mandating that the required lenders invoke the trigger means that lenders holding a substantial portion of the loans must suffer funding losses before the clause may be invoked. In contrast, British-style syndicated credit agreements often require a lower percentage, perhaps as low as 30 percent. At whatever level fixed, the purpose of a minimum percentage is to strike a balance between providing real protection to the lenders without subjecting the borrower to idiosyncratic conditions affecting only one or very few of the lenders. Some credit agreements, however, provide that the administrative agent make the determination whether the trigger has been met with respect to the required threshold of lenders.

The second component of the disruption clause is the *consequence* of lenders invoking their rights. In the sample language above, the clause requires that all loans otherwise bearing interest calculated by reference to LIBOR become base rate borrowings instead. The reason that base rate pricing is used as the fallback (at least in domestic agreements providing for both base rate and LIBOR pricing) is that the base rate has, with rare exceptions, always exceeded LIBOR. Even though using the base rate in this circumstance is potentially expensive for the borrower, it is short and easy to draft.

However, in loan transactions where the borrower is not U.S.-based and syndication takes place primarily outside of the United States, the base rate interest option may not be practical. In these cases, the clause will typically provide for one of two potential approaches. A simple approach allows each lender invoking the clause to charge interest on its loans equal to its cost of funds plus the applicable margin. The cost of funds is generally not defined, but each lender is usually required to certify its cost to the borrower. Another approach, more complex though arguably more fair, is to set out a procedure whereby the borrower and the lenders agree to negotiate a "substitute basis" upon which to price the loans. Typically, the negotiations for an alternative interest rate will be required to be completed within some relatively brief period of time, say 30 or 45 days. The interest rate would not need to be agreed to by each lender, but only by the required lenders of the relevant tranche. Absent agreement between the borrower and the required lenders, each lender would be entitled to charge interest based upon its cost of funds.

A borrower can always, of course, refinance the loans if it does not like the alternative rates specified by the lenders, though if the LIBOR market has collapsed completely, this option may not be particularly economic. Some borrowers press for the ability to repay selectively those lenders that specify the highest alternative interest rates. Lenders resist this approach since, if the borrower's credit quality has begun to deteriorate, it rewards lenders that prescribe higher rates by allowing them to exit the facility early.

3.7.3.3 Historical Issues with the Market Disruption Clause

The market disruption clause is often regarded as mere legal boilerplate, and like other yield protection clauses has rarely, if ever, been invoked. In the early 1990s, when the Japanese economy slipped from its previously dominant position, many Japanese banks paid premiums in order to attract eurodollar deposits, pushing their costs of funding above the rates paid by leading banks from other parts of the world. But since the number of affected banks in any given syndicate was generally below the threshold of "required lenders," invoking the market disruption clause was difficult if not impossible.

Arrangers, not wanting to forfeit the ability to syndicate to Japanese banks, looked for an alternative solution. At the time, the historical practice of calculating LIBOR based upon eurodollar deposit rates quoted by several syndicate-member "reference banks" prevailed. Consequently, to address the concerns of affected Japanese lenders, where the opportunity arose, credit agreements were amended or new credit agreements were entered into providing for the reference banks to include Japanese banks so that the Japanese premium would be taken into account when calculating LIBOR.

The clause came into focus again during the credit crisis of 2008. Lenders and leading industry groups devoted countless hours pondering how to protect lenders against the problem of the published rates arguably not reflecting the true cost of funding. Yet, despite the frustration expressed by many, there were only a small number of cases where the market disruption clause was invoked indicating, perhaps, the difficulty of even the most well-crafted LIBOR disaster clause to help in a real-world situation.

A variety of possible explanations for the failure of the clause to protect lenders effectively has been offered. To begin with, just as banks on the BBA panels may not have wished to report their true, higher cost of funds because it may have been seen as reflecting a critical need for cash, syndicate members might have been reluctant to invoke the clause and, thereby, reveal that their cost of funds was higher than other institutions. Further, even though credit agreements normally provide that rate quotes by lenders are "conclusive," the risk remains that a quote which purports to reflect the cost of funding to a lender might be challenged. This could force a lender to reveal closely guarded secrets (in public if the issue went before a court) as to how it funds its lending operations.

There is also the risk that the "cure" of invoking the clause may be worse than the "disease" of living with below-cost LIBOR quotes. Although, as already noted, LIBOR has generally been lower than the base rate, the relationship between these rates can in rare cases invert, as happened in late 2008. Thus, where a credit agreement contemplates base rate pricing as the fallback if LIBOR does not reflect the genuine cost of funds, resorting to the market disruption clause would have the ironic effect of *lowering* yields, although today most credit agreements mitigate this risk by including a prong in the base rate that is based upon one-month LIBOR plus 100 basis points (see Section 3.1.1).

Other problems exist as well. For example, because the market disruption clause has been so seldom invoked, lenders may be concerned about strong negative reactions from borrowers. Indeed, during the credit crunch of 2008, the British Association of Corporate Treasurers published a press release on September 28, 2008, discouraging lenders from invoking the clause, except as a last resort. And even when eurodollar market conditions affect a large number of lenders, it may be difficult either to coordinate action or to achieve the threshold number of lenders required to invoke the clause. For all of these reasons, the utility of the LIBOR market disruption clause, despite the seeming clarity of its language, may be limited.

With the passage of LIBOR determination from the unregulated British Bankers' Association to the regulated ICE Benchmark Administration, and the resulting reforms and safeguards described in Section 3.1.2.5, it is expected that it will be less likely that LIBOR fails to reflect the lenders' funding costs.

3.7.4 Illegality

> **Box 3.15**
>
> If any Lender determines that any Law has made it unlawful, or that any Governmental Authority has asserted that it is unlawful, for any Lender or its applicable lending office to make, maintain, or fund Loans whose interest is determined by reference to LIBOR, or to determine or charge interest rates based upon LIBOR, or any Governmental Authority has imposed material restrictions on the authority of such Lender to

purchase or sell, or to take deposits of, Dollars in the London interbank market, then, upon notice thereof by such Lender to the Borrower (through the Administrative Agent), (i) any obligation of such Lender to make or continue LIBOR Loans or to convert Base Rate Loans to LIBOR Loans shall be suspended, and (ii) if such notice asserts the illegality of such Lender making or maintaining Base Rate Loans the interest rate on which is determined by reference to the LIBOR component of the Base Rate, the interest rate on which Base Rate Loans of such Lender shall, if necessary to avoid such illegality, be determined by the Administrative Agent without reference to the LIBOR component of the Base Rate, in each case until such Lender notifies the Administrative Agent and the Borrower that the circumstances giving rise to such determination no longer exist. Upon receipt of such notice, (x) the Borrower shall, upon demand from such Lender (with a copy to the Administrative Agent), prepay or, if applicable, convert all LIBOR Loans of such Lender to Base Rate Loans (the interest rate on which Base Rate Loans of such Lender shall, if necessary to avoid such illegality, be determined by the Administrative Agent without reference to the LIBOR component of the Base Rate), either on the last day of the Interest Period therefor, if such Lender may lawfully continue to maintain such LIBOR Loans to such day, or immediately, if such Lender may not lawfully continue to maintain such LIBOR Loans and (y) if such notice asserts the illegality of such Lender determining or charging interest rates based upon LIBOR, the Administrative Agent shall during the period of such suspension compute the Base Rate applicable to such Lender without reference to the LIBOR component thereof until the Administrative Agent is advised in writing by such Lender that it is no longer illegal for such Lender to determine or charge interest rates based upon LIBOR. Upon any such prepayment or conversion, the Borrower shall also pay accrued interest on the amount so prepaid or converted, together with any additional amounts required pursuant to Section [*Breakfunding*].

With some historical justification, lenders have been concerned that a credit agreement once signed (or a loan once made) might become illegal. When the LIBOR loan market first developed, for example, lenders were afraid that making or continuing a loan based upon LIBOR might be made illegal. The worry was that a regulatory change could give rise to more than just increased costs; it might involve a flat prohibition against pricing loans based upon offshore deposit-taking. This scenario became more real in the late 1960s when, with the issuance by President Nixon of interest equalization regulations, it was feared that the newly developing LIBOR market might be seen as circumventing the regulations. This could, in turn, have led the U.S. government to prohibit U.S. banks from making LIBOR loans.

Another worry has been the possibility that a government might ban *all* loans (not just LIBOR loans) to a particular type of borrower. In the United States, such restrictions now exist under U.S. Foreign Assets Control Regulations (which bar loans to entities in or owned by North Korea, for example) and anti-terrorist legislation (which prohibits loans to any of thousands of designated "terrorist" organizations or individuals). See Section 6.1.10. Similar restrictions arose in 1982 during the Falklands War when the United Kingdom decreed that transactions (including loan facilities) with Argentine entities were illegal.

Despite the interest equalization regulations, the United States never took action to constrain lenders based upon LIBOR funding; illegality clauses nevertheless became common. Under the clause, if a regulator outlaws funding based on LIBOR, or if a legislature or executive prohibits banks in its jurisdiction from making loans to borrowers in a particular country, one of two consequences follow: either the borrower is obligated to repay the loan either at the end of its current interest period (if it is legally permissible to keep the loan outstanding) or immediately (if not) as illustrated in the language in Box 3.15 or, if the restrictions relate to the nature of a lender funding its loans, interest is shifted to a different interest rate basis (the base rate or a substitute basis as described Section 3.7.3). Neither of these options is likely to be palatable to the borrower. Requiring the loan to be repaid may force the borrower to find an alternative source of funds; it also allows the affected lender to be repaid on a nonratable basis to the potential detriment of other lenders. And if the borrower is unable to repay the loan, both the lender and borrower could still be in violation of law. If the nature of funding is the problem, shifting to a different interest rate is little better since it can result in substantially increased costs for the borrower. In both cases, however, inclusion of the clause allows the lender to argue that it has done everything possible to comply with applicable law and that any violation by it was solely attributable to a pesky borrower in breach of its undertaking to repay.

In recent years illegality clauses, when they exist, are limited to LIBOR loans, rather than all loans. However, there is an emerging consensus that illegality clauses may no longer be necessary. The reasoning is that, given the tremendous growth in international financial markets since the LIBOR loan market was first created, it is almost inconceivable that a government or regulator would today declare LIBOR-based loans unlawful in the manner contemplated by the clause. The risk of a subsequently arising general illegality is ignored on the theory that even governments understand that if a loan has already been made there is little that a lender can do to remedy the illegality, short of waiting until maturity. As a consequence, some credit agreements today no longer include an illegality clause.

3.7.5 Breakfunding

Box 3.16

In the event of (a) the payment of any principal of any LIBOR Loan other than on the last day of an Interest Period applicable thereto (including as a result of an Event of Default); (b) the conversion of any LIBOR Loan other than on the last day of the Interest Period applicable thereto; (c) the failure to borrow, convert, continue, or prepay any LIBOR Loan on the date specified in any notice delivered pursuant hereto; or (d) the assignment of any LIBOR Loan other than on the last day of the Interest Period applicable thereto as a result of a request by the Borrower pursuant to Section [*Replacement of Lenders*], then, in any such event, the Borrower shall compensate each affected Lender for the loss, cost, and expense attributable to such event.

Such loss, cost, or expense to any Lender shall be deemed to include an amount determined by such Lender to be the excess, if any, of (i) the amount of interest that would have accrued on the principal amount of such Loan had such event not occurred, at the Adjusted LIBO Rate that would have been applicable to such Loan, for the period from the date of such event to the last day of the then current Interest Period therefor (or, in the case of a failure to borrow, convert, or continue, for the period that would have been the Interest Period for such Loan), over (ii) the amount of interest that would accrue on such principal amount for such period at the interest rate which such Lender would bid were it to bid, at the commencement of such period, for dollar deposits of a comparable amount and period from other banks in the eurodollar market.

A certificate of any Lender setting forth any amount or amounts that such Lender is entitled to receive pursuant to this Section shall be delivered to the Borrower and shall be conclusive absent manifest error. The Borrower shall pay such Lender the amount shown as due on any such certificate within 10 days after receipt thereof.

Despite common perception, lenders really do *not* want their loans repaid (unless, of course, the borrower is a deadbeat). Not the least of the lender's worries (for LIBOR loans) would be what to do with all the deposits it has accepted, and commercial paper and other securities it has issued, to provide a source of funding for those loans. In the typical bond indenture or private placement, this problem is normally solved by simply prohibiting prepayment or requiring payment of a premium upon early redemption. In a bank credit agreement, it is the breakfunding clause that jumps into the breach.

3.7.5.1 General Principles

Under the theory of match funding, if a borrower repays a LIBOR loan in the middle of an interest period (which notionally corresponds to the term of a deposit taken in by the lender), the lender is deprived of an interest stream (namely, the one on the loan) intended by the lender to service the payments that the lender must make to its depositor at the end of the deposit term. A lender is faced with a similar problem if a borrower requests a LIBOR loan and then, for whatever reason, declines to take down the loan; the lender will (notionally) have obtained a deposit in London two business days prior to the anticipated borrowing date and yet find itself in the position of having the deposit proceeds not being put to work. In either case, the lender is forced to find an alternative use to span the balance of the deposit term (interest period) for the money repaid, or not used, by the borrower. An alternative deployment by the lender may yield a lower interest coupon than the rate that was to be paid by the borrower. Other examples of "breakfunding" situations are recited in the first paragraph of Box 3.16, including conversion of a LIBOR loan into a base rate loan in the middle of an interest period and the forced assignment of a LIBOR loan other than on the last day of an interest period.

The breakfunding clause is intended to address the possibility that the source of funds for interest on the deposit (namely, the anticipated interest payments to be made by the borrower on its loan) is "broken" in the middle of the deposit term. The breakfunding clause, in essence, allows the lender to be compensated for any shortfall between the amount of interest that would have accrued on the loan (usually not including the margin) for the balance of the interest period and the amount of interest that the lender is able to earn by reinvesting the prepaid proceeds into alternative assets for that period.

Breakfunding clauses take two basic forms. One form allows the lender in its good faith to specify the cost suffered by it through having to redeploy the repaid loan proceeds. This approach is consistent with the approach of the increased costs clause in that no detailed mathematical calculation of the loss to the lender is made. The clause customarily permits the lender, in determining its loss, to assume that it funded each LIBOR loan by taking in a deposit in the London interbank market in an amount, and for a term, equal to the interest period for the LIBOR loan. In other words, the lender is deemed to have match funded all of its LIBOR loans and can base the calculation of its loss upon that presumption.

Another form of the clause, such as that shown in the second paragraph of Box 3.16, sets out an arithmetical formula to calculate the minimum amount that should be payable to the lender as a result of the breakfunding event. The formula assumes match funding, but because the math is explicit, a statement confirming the assumption is not express. The formula also assumes that the lender reinvests the funds in the LIBOR market (as opposed to, say, reinvesting in U.S. Treasuries at what would likely be a much lower rate) for the balance of the term of the broken interest period. Sometimes the shortfall payable to the lender includes the interest margin, but in most cases the borrower is required to make up the difference in LIBOR only for the two periods (LIBOR for the originally selected interest period and LIBOR for a hypothetical interest period for the remaining portion of the original interest period that follows the breakfunding event).

An illustration of the calculation may be useful. Assume that a $1,000,000 LIBOR loan has a six-month interest period and a rate of 6 percent, consisting of LIBOR of 5 percent for that interest period and an interest margin of 1 percent. Assume next that the borrower prepays the $1,000,000 in full at the fourth month. Assume, finally, that at the time of the prepayment, LIBOR for a two-month interest period is 4.5 percent. The lender is unable to reinvest the funds at a sufficient rate to cover the hypothetical six-month deposit that it took in to fund the loan. The borrower is, therefore, required to pay breakfunding of $833, which represents 5 percent *minus* 4.5 percent, or the difference in LIBO rates, *times* $1,000,000 (the amount prepaid) *times* 2/12 (the number of months of the original interest period remaining *divided by* the number of months in a year). If the lender is compensated for the loss of interest margin as well, the amount payable by the borrower increases to $2,500, which represents (6 percent *minus* 4.5 percent) *times* $1,000,000 *times* 2/12.

3.7.5.2 Breakfunding upon Initial Drawdowns

Breakfunding concerns arise not just in the context of prepayments, but also in the context of borrowings, particularly the initial drawdown. Even though credit agreements generally contemplate that the initial borrowing or closing occurs at a date later than execution, this is largely a fiction. Most domestic credit agreements are signed by the parties concurrently with the initial drawing (if there is to be one). The obvious issue becomes how a borrower gives notice of a LIBOR borrowing in advance of the closing when the credit agreement has not yet become effective and there is no breakfunding protection for the lenders in place if the closing does not occur when scheduled.

The solution in many cases is to require that initial loans be base rate loans, though borrowers understandably resist this given the greater effective cost of base rate loans. Another solution, more palatable to borrowers, is a so-called prefunding agreement. Under a prefunding agreement (generally a simple one- or two-page letter agreement executed between the borrower and the administrative agent), the borrower agrees to make to the lenders the same breakfunding payments it would be required to pay under the credit agreement if the closing does not occur when scheduled. If the credit agreement never becomes effective, the lenders have resort to the prefunding letter to obtain appropriate compensation (see Section 2.6).

3.7.5.3 Sell-Down Costs

One cost that a breakfunding clause does not cover is that incurred by lead banks that undertake a sell-down to syndicate members immediately following a closing. This occurs not infrequently when the credit agreement provides for a B loan tranche. Often B lenders, for tax reasons, are prepared to purchase loans in the secondary market only after the loans have been made. In this circumstance, the lead bank makes all or a substantial portion of the B loans to the borrower at closing and then, in the first weeks thereafter, settles the primary loan trades with the B loan syndicate members. If the initial loans are made as LIBOR loans, the selling bank may (depending upon how LIBOR has moved) suffer breakfunding costs for the broken initial interest period. The purchasing lenders could, alternatively, find themselves holding a loan for the balance of that interest period with a LIBOR below the LIBOR that would have otherwise applied had the loan been made on the date of the secondary purchase. Generally, the arranger and syndicate members absorb these costs. In some cases, however, the credit agreement provides that the initial interest period for all LIBOR loans must be a short period (not exceeding a month), with the intention that all sell-downs occur on the last day of the first interest period, thus avoiding any breakfunding costs. In rare cases the base rate solution referred to in the preceding paragraph is employed; the credit agreement provides that, for an interim period, or at least until the postclosing sell-down is completed, all loans must be base rate loans.

3.7.5.4   Compared to Prepayment Premiums

Breakfunding clauses are sometimes compared to prepayment premiums and make-whole payments seen in bond indentures and private placements. Prepayment premiums are normally computed at a flat percentage of the principal paid (without reference to the interest rate). Make-whole payments are typically calculated by first discounting to present value (at a rate based upon U.S. Treasury securities) the stream of payments (principal and interest) that, but for the prepayment, would have been received by the note holder and then subtracting from the resulting figure the amount of principal to be prepaid.

Prepayment premiums and make-whole calculations have been the subject of a number of judicial decisions, some of which have imposed constraints on their enforceability. The general rule is that such clauses are enforceable so long as the parties are able to show that the premium or make-whole was not intended as a penalty, but was a reasonable attempt to estimate the loss resulting from the prepayment. Courts have struggled with the idea that the U.S. Treasury rate can be a proxy for the rate of interest to be earned on a corporate credit. Some courts have held that for a make-whole to be enforced, the discount rate employed must exceed the U.S. Treasury rate, reflecting the fact that a loan to the typical borrower is more risky than the purchase of U.S. Treasuries. Other courts have held that a premium or make-whole cannot be enforced if a loan is accelerated or becomes subject to a mandatory prepayment, although more recent decisions have upheld payment if the relevant agreement is explicit that a premium or make-whole is payable upon an acceleration.

The general consensus is that these court decisions do not impact the enforceability of breakfunding clauses. Although superficially similar, breakfunding provisions in credit agreements are quite different from prepayment premiums and make-whole payments. Prepayment premiums, since not related to the rate of interest on the note or bond, can represent a substantial dollar cost for an issuer that wants to redeem bonds or notes prior to scheduled maturity. A 5 percent premium on a note that bears interest at 5 percent represents an entire year's extra interest on the amount prepaid. Make-whole payments are also quite different. The latter are intended to compensate the note holders for the loss of interest that would have been earned over the entire term of the notes, not just to the end of the next interest period, again potentially resulting in a much higher dollar cost to the borrower. Also, in the case of make-whole payments, the discount rate (being based upon U.S.

Treasury securities) is normally much lower than the LIBOR used to calculate breakfunding and further removed from corporate interest rates. The effect of these two factors is that a prepayment premium or make-whole provision can produce a much higher prepayment cost to the issuer than a LIBOR breakfunding clause. This may explain the paucity of court decisions that address the enforceability of breakage provisions.

3.7.6 Taxes

Box 3.17

"Excluded Taxes" means any of the following Taxes imposed on or with respect to a Recipient or required to be withheld or deducted from a payment to a Recipient, (a) Taxes imposed on or measured by net income (however denominated), franchise Taxes, and branch profits Taxes, in each case, (i) imposed as a result of such Recipient being organized under the laws of, or having its principal office or, in the case of any Lender, its applicable lending office located in, the jurisdiction imposing such Tax (or any political subdivision thereof) or (ii) that are Other Connection Taxes, (b) in the case of a Lender, U.S. federal withholding Taxes imposed on amounts payable to or for the account of such Lender with respect to an applicable interest in a Loan or Commitment pursuant to a law in effect on the date on which (i) such Lender acquires such interest in the Loan or Commitment (other than pursuant to an assignment request by the Borrower under Section [*Replacement of Lenders*]) or (ii) such Lender changes its lending office, except in each case to the extent that, pursuant to Section [*Taxes*], amounts with respect to such Taxes were payable either to such Lender's assignor immediately before such Lender became a party hereto or to such Lender immediately before it changed its lending office, (c) Taxes attributable to such Recipient's failure to comply with Section [*Taxes – Status of Lenders*] and (d) any U.S. federal withholding Taxes imposed under FATCA.

"FATCA" means Sections 1471 through 1474 of the Code, as of the date of this Agreement (or any amended or successor version that is substantively comparable and not materially more onerous to comply with), any current or future regulations or official interpretations thereof and any agreement entered into pursuant to Section 1471(b)(1) of the Code.

"Indemnified Taxes" means (a) Taxes, other than Excluded Taxes, imposed on or with respect to any payment made by or on account of any obligation of [the Borrower] [any Loan Party] under any Loan Document and (b) to the extent not otherwise described in (a), Other Taxes.

"Other Connection Taxes" means, with respect to any Recipient, Taxes imposed as a result of a present or former connection between such Recipient and the jurisdiction imposing such Tax (other than connections arising from such Recipient having executed, delivered, become a party to, performed its obligations under, received payments under, received or perfected a security interest under, engaged in any other transaction pursuant to or enforced any Loan Document, or sold or assigned an interest in any Loan or Loan Document).

"Other Taxes" means all present or future stamp, court or documentary, intangible, recording, filing, or similar Taxes that arise from any payment made under, from the execution, delivery, performance, enforcement or registration of, from the receipt or perfection of a security interest under, or otherwise with respect to, any Loan Document, except any such Taxes that are Other Connection Taxes imposed with respect to an assignment (other than an assignment made pursuant to Section [*Mitigation Obligations; Replacement of Lenders – Replacement of Lenders*]).

"Recipient" means (a) the Administrative Agent, (b) any Lender, or (c) any Issuing Bank, as applicable.

"Taxes" means all present or future taxes, levies, imposts, duties, deductions, withholdings (including backup withholding), assessments, fees, or other charges imposed by any Governmental Authority, including any interest, additions to tax, or penalties applicable thereto.

* * * * * * * * *

(a) *Defined Terms.* For purposes of this Section [*Taxes*], the term "Lender" includes any Issuing Bank and the term "applicable law" includes FATCA.

(b) *Payments Free of Taxes.* Any and all payments by or on account of any obligation of [the Borrower] [any Loan Party] under any Loan Document shall be made without deduction or withholding for any Taxes, except as required by applicable law. If any applicable law (as determined in the good faith discretion of an applicable Withholding Agent) requires the deduction or withholding of any Tax from any such payment by a Withholding Agent, then the applicable Withholding Agent shall be entitled to make such deduction or withholding and shall timely pay the full amount deducted or withheld to the relevant Governmental Authority in accordance with applicable law and, if such Tax is an Indemnified Tax, then the sum payable by [the Borrower] [the applicable Loan Party] shall be increased as necessary so that after such deduction or withholding has been made (including such deductions and withholdings applicable to additional sums payable under this Section) the applicable Recipient receives an amount equal to the sum it would have received had no such deduction or withholding been made.

(c) *Payment of Other Taxes by the Borrower.* [The Borrower] [The Loan Parties] shall timely pay to the relevant Governmental Authority in accordance with applicable law, or at the option of the Administrative Agent timely reimburse it for the payment of, any Other Taxes.

(d) *Indemnification by the Borrower.* [The Borrower] [The Loan Parties] shall [jointly and severally] indemnify each Recipient, within 10 days after demand therefor, for the full amount of any Indemnified Taxes (including Indemnified Taxes imposed or asserted on or attributable to amounts payable under this Section) payable or paid by such Recipient or required to be withheld or deducted from a payment to such Recipient and any reasonable expenses arising therefrom or with respect thereto, whether or not such Indemnified Taxes were correctly or legally imposed or asserted by the relevant Governmental Authority. A certificate as to the amount of such payment or liability delivered to the Borrower by a Lender (with a copy to the Administrative Agent), or by the Administrative Agent on its own behalf or on behalf of a Lender, shall be conclusive absent manifest error.

(e) *Indemnification by the Lenders.* Each Lender shall severally indemnify the Administrative Agent, within 10 days after demand therefor, for (i) any Indemnified Taxes attributable to such Lender (but only to the extent that [the Borrower] [any Loan Party] has not already indemnified the Administrative Agent for such Indemnified Taxes and without limiting the obligation of [the Borrower] [the Loan Parties] to do so), (ii) any Taxes attributable to such Lender's failure to comply with the provisions of Section [*Successors and Assigns – Participations*] relating to the maintenance of a Participant Register, and (iii) any Excluded Taxes attributable to such Lender, in each case, that are payable or paid by the Administrative Agent in connection with any Loan Document, and any reasonable expenses arising therefrom or with respect thereto, whether or not such Taxes were correctly or legally imposed or asserted by the relevant Governmental Authority. A certificate as to the amount of such payment or liability delivered to any Lender by the Administrative Agent shall be conclusive absent manifest error. Each Lender hereby authorizes the Administrative Agent to set off and apply any and all amounts at any time owing to such Lender under any Loan Document or otherwise payable by the Administrative Agent to the Lender from any other source against any amount due to the Administrative Agent under this paragraph (e).

It is said that life has only two certainties: death and taxes. Not much can be done about the former. Lenders look to the taxes clause to beat the latter, and with some success. Under the clause, whatever taxes the lender has to pay that are directly attributable to a loan will—with some exceptions, including a big one for net income taxes—be passed on to the borrower.

Why is any of this necessary? After all, are taxes not just another cost of doing business? Why does the lender not just charge a high-enough interest rate to cover its cost of doing business? Why should the borrower have to indemnify a lender against taxes that a lender is itself responsible for?

The answer is simple. Although a lender understands it may have to pay income taxes to its own local jurisdiction (and does not demand that its borrowers cover that cost of doing business), when it comes to interest on a loan (and fees in respect of a loan facility), it expects to receive what the agreement prescribes. In this regard, the lender is not asking for anything more than any other business. When a toy retailer, for example, sells a doll for $19.95, it expects to receive $19.95. So if sales tax of 7 percent (or $1.40) must be paid, the retailer commonly passes that cost on to the customer rather than resetting the price at $18.64 so that, with the tax, the total charge remains unchanged. The product a lender sells are loans, rather than dolls, and it looks for the same monetary gross-up. If the stated interest under the credit agreement is 8 percent, the lender must receive 8 percent. A particular creation of taxing authorities called the withholding tax can, however, get in the way of the lender's interest stream and is a major motivation for the taxes clause. A withholding tax is typically imposed by a country on interest payments made by a borrower in that country to lenders in another country. Normally, the foreign lender (not the borrower) is the one legally liable for the tax but, to ensure payment, the borrower is required by tax regulations to withhold from each interest payment made to the lender an amount equal to the tax. The lender may become liable for the tax (and even penalties) if the borrower fails to withhold.

The rate of withholding by a country (the United States is no different on this score) may vary on a country-by-country basis depending on the locations of the bank lenders. This is because the withholding rate may be reduced under a tax treaty between the payor country and the recipient country. Treaty rates diverge. The interest paid by a U.K. borrower to a U.S. lender is generally not subject to withholding, while, absent an applicable domestic exemption, interest payments by a U.K. borrower to a Thai bank may be subject to a high rate of withholding.

Taking a concrete example, interest payments by a Mexican borrower to a lender (at least as of the date of this publication and with various exceptions) are subject to withholding at a rate of 35 percent. A loan made by a U.S. lender to a Mexican borrower accordingly requires that $35 of every $100 of interest be withheld from each interest payment and forked over to Mexico City. Now the lender is not going to want to end up with only $65 when it was expecting $100. To the rescue comes the tax gross-up clause. Under the clause the borrower is required to "gross up" the interest payment so that the lender realizes an amount in cash that, after deduction for the withheld taxes (including further withholding taxes on the gross-up payment), is equal to the stated interest on the loan. The clause will also try to capture other taxes that might be imposed on the loan, such as any stamp taxes, documentary taxes, intangible taxes, recording taxes, and so forth. The definition of "Other Taxes" set out in Box 3.17 is an illustration of the all-encompassing approach customarily taken.

An illustration of how the typical gross-up works may be helpful. Assume that interest on a loan to the Mexican company made by a bank located in the United States is equal to 6 percent. With Mexico imposing a withholding tax of 35 percent, absent a gross-up the lender will receive only 3.9 percent per annum on its loan: $6\% \times (100\% - 35\%) = 3.9\%$. The gross-up clause eliminates this shortfall by grossing up (increasing the amount of) the interest payment to a rate equal to 9.23 percent ($6\% \div 0.65 = 9.23\%$). When the 35 percent withholding is then applied to the 9.23 percent, the lender will receive cash interest equal to the full, contracted, 6 percent ($9.23\% \times 0.65 = 6\%$).

So why does the syndicate not just charge interest at 9.23 percent in the first instance? If the interest rate were fixed for the entire term of the loan, this might be a solution. But interest rates under credit agreements typically float, and the stated rate of 6 percent is, in actuality, a composite of a floating base (LIBOR or the base rate) plus a margin. The rate of 9.23 percent may be the appropriate gross-up rate when the contractual formula produces a rate of 6 percent. It is not the appropriate rate if LIBOR or the base rate (or the margin) goes up or down and a higher or lower rate begins to accrue.

There is another, perhaps more compelling, reason why coverage for withholding taxes is accomplished through a gross-up formula rather than by specifying a prescribed rate. Different lenders are subject to different withholding rates. We can look again to Mexico as a perfect example. As noted earlier, the withholding rate generally applicable to interest payments to a lender by a Mexican borrower is 35 percent. However, certain banks that are registered for Mexican tax purposes as "foreign financial institutions" with the Mexican Ministry of Finance and Public Credit, and that fund their loans through branches either in Mexico or in a jurisdiction with which Mexico has entered into an appropriate tax treaty, are entitled to a lower withholding tax rate. Since a syndicate may consist of lenders subject to different withholding tax rates, it is more advantageous to a borrower to gross up interest on a lender-by-lender basis rather than through an across-the-board increase in the stated rate of interest under the credit agreement.

In forming a syndicate, the borrower and the administrative agent will seek to minimize the amount of withholding that the borrower must pay to the tax authorities and, therefore, be required to gross up. Lenders that are in jurisdictions where payments from the borrower's country incur high withholding rates are likely not to be included in the syndicate. For those lenders that do join the syndicate, either because they are not subject to withholding or because they are subject to a very low rate of withholding, the gross-up clause, in effect, becomes a change-in-law provision. A lender is entitled to a gross-up only to the extent that at the inception of the loan (the closing or the date on which the lender acquires a loan by assignment) the lender is exempt from withholding or subject to withholding at the agreed lowest rate. The clause thus protects against new taxes or adverse changes in tax rates or tax treaties.

The sample language in Box 3.17 sets forth the general tax indemnification provisions (including the gross-up language) contained in the LSTA's Model Credit Agreement Provisions.

Paragraph (e) in Box 3.17 specifies that if the borrower fails to gross-up the administrative agent for withholding taxes attributable to a particular lender, that lender must indemnify the agent for the shortfall. This indemnification obligation is similar to the general backup indemnification obligation that lenders have (described in Section 10.2) for the borrower's failure to make indemnification payments to the agent. That paragraph also requires a lender to indemnify the administrative agent for that lender's failure to maintain a participant register as described in Section 11.3 and for any Excluded Taxes paid or payable by the administrative agent (whether or not correctly asserted by the applicable government authority).

Clause (d) in the definition of "Excluded Taxes" in Box 3.17 addresses a 2010 change in law. The Foreign Account Tax Compliance Act provisions, generally referred to as "FATCA," were included in the Hiring Incentives to Restore Employment (HIRE) Act. FATCA was adopted to detect tax evasion by U.S. persons who hide their U.S. income through the use of offshore accounts and foreign entities. Generally, foreign financial institutions (FFIs) and non-financial foreign entities (NFFEs) are required under FATCA to collect and report to the U.S. Treasury Department certain information about their U.S. investors. To encourage institutions that may otherwise be outside U.S. jurisdiction to comply and provide this information, FATCA imposes a 30 percent withholding tax on certain payments, including interest payments made by U.S. borrowers to FFIs and NFFEs that do not comply with information reporting requirements of FATCA. In addition, starting on January 1, 2019, FATCA will also impose a 30 percent withholding tax on principal payments made by U.S. borrowers to noncompliant FFIs and NFFEs. FATCA went into effect on July 1, 2014, but grandfathered its application to any loan that closed prior to that date, unless the terms of the loan are "significantly modified" on or after that date. As can be seen by the inclusion of clause (d) in the definition of "Excluded Taxes" in Box 3.17, market practice has generally allocated to lenders the risk of FATCA withholding taxes, as borrowers do not gross-up for Excluded Taxes.

3.7.6.1   Evidence of Payments

> **Box 3.18**
>
> (f) *Evidence of Payments.* As soon as practicable after any payment of Taxes by [the Borrower] [any Loan Party] to a Governmental Authority pursuant to this Section [*Taxes*], [the Borrower] [such Loan Party] shall deliver to the Administrative Agent the original or a certified copy of a receipt issued by such Governmental Authority evidencing such payment, a copy of the return reporting such payment or other evidence of such payment reasonably satisfactory to the Administrative Agent.

As described above, although it is normally the borrower that physically remits a withholding tax to the appropriate tax authority, in many countries the lender is legally responsible for paying the tax. No lender wants to trust a borrower completely, so the typical tax provision requires that the borrower promptly provide to the lender a tax receipt or other evidence of each payment of a withholding tax. This not only enables the lender to confirm that payment has been made, but also provides it with the relevant documentation for any foreign tax credit or refund it may be able to claim (these are discussed in further detail below). Also, the general indemnification provision puts the borrower on the hook for any penalties associated with payments made (or not made) under the credit agreement, so if the borrower fails to withhold taxes from an interest payment it is obligated to reimburse the lender for any extra taxes, fees, interest, or penalties assessed by the relevant tax authority.

3.7.6.2   Actions by Lenders to Minimize Taxes

> **Box 3.19**
>
> *"Foreign Lender"* means (a) if the Borrower is a U.S. Person, a Lender that is not a U.S. Person, and (b) if the Borrower is not a U.S. Person, a Lender that is resident or organized under the laws of a jurisdiction other than that in which the Borrower is resident for tax purposes.
>
> *"U.S. Person"* means any Person that is a "United States Person" as defined in Section 7701(a)(30) of the Code.

Tax rules are never simple. Exceptions and limitations, exclusions, and exemptions are the nature of the beast. Borrowers understandably want lenders to minimize withholding taxes in order to minimize the gross-up. If a credit agreement written on purple paper is exempt from withholding tax in Sloboda, you can expect all Slobodan borrowers to insist that purple paper be used. More realistically, if a lender is registered for Mexican tax purposes as a "foreign financial institution" with the Mexican Ministry of Finance and Public Credit, the borrower will want the lender to supply evidence to that effect so that the lower Mexican withholding tax rate described earlier is applicable.

The tax indemnification clause as shown in the LSTA's Model Credit Agreement Provisions addresses this concern in the language cited in Box 3.19. This approach is typical of tax indemnification clauses. In effect, it requires a lender to cooperate with the borrower by delivering to it whatever evidence will permit interest payments to be made without withholding or at a reduced rate of withholding. A covenant in this form is easy for a lender to accept, and there is generally little resistance to its inclusion.

3.7.6.3   Refunds and Credits

> **Box 3.20**
>
> (h) *Treatment of Certain Refunds.* If any party determines, in its sole discretion exercised in good faith, that it has received a refund of any Taxes as to which it has been indemnified pursuant to this Section [*Taxes*] (including by the payment of additional amounts pursuant to this Section [*Taxes*]), it shall pay to the indemnifying party an amount equal to such refund (but only to the extent of indemnity payments made under this Section with respect to the Taxes giving rise to such refund), net of all

out-of-pocket expenses (including Taxes) of such indemnified party and without interest (other than any interest paid by the relevant Governmental Authority with respect to such refund). Such indemnifying party, upon the request of such indemnified party, shall repay to such indemnified party the amount paid over pursuant to this paragraph (h) (plus any penalties, interest or other charges imposed by the relevant Governmental Authority) in the event that such indemnified party is required to repay such refund to such Governmental Authority. Notwithstanding anything to the contrary in this paragraph (h), in no event will the indemnified party be required to pay any amount to an indemnifying party pursuant to this paragraph (h) the payment of which would place the indemnified party in a less favorable net after-Tax position than the indemnified party would have been in if the Tax subject to indemnification and giving rise to such refund had not been deducted, withheld or otherwise imposed and the indemnification payments or additional amounts with respect to such Tax had never been paid. This paragraph shall not be construed to require any indemnified party to make available its Tax returns (or any other information relating to its Taxes that it deems confidential) to the indemnifying party or any other Person.

As discussed earlier, when a withholding tax is paid to the tax authorities, it is paid on behalf of the lender. It is the lender's tax and the lender's payment, even though the actual remittance is effected by the borrower. What happens if a U.S. lender is able to take a credit against its United States income tax for the amount withheld? What if later it receives a refund of the amount paid from the borrower's country? In either case, the lender has accomplished the impossible: it has got its cake and eaten it too. Borrowers may cry foul.

Notwithstanding the seeming unfairness of a lender's glomming on to a double recovery, lenders typically resist agreeing to reimburse the borrower for the benefit derived from foreign tax credits. They do this because of the practical and administrative difficulties of tracing particular credits to particular loans. Money is fungible, so if an aggregate of $1,000,000 of withholding taxes has been paid by a lender to Mexico in respect of multiple loans and that lender receives a credit of $700,000 on its home tax return, which loans do the credit relate to? Would it be fair to apportion, and, if so, how? From a lender's perspective there is a certain rough justice to ignoring credits because borrowers normally refuse to cover the lender's additional net income taxes that result from the payment of the larger grossed-up amount (a so-called spiral gross-up or super-gross-up), even when the lender cannot obtain benefit from the additional foreign tax credits (for example, because the lender already has more credits than it can use, given the complex limitations that apply). Also, no lender wants to have its books examined to determine whether a credit is attributable to loan X or loan Y. The upshot? Tax indemnification clauses rarely, if ever, allow a borrower to receive reimbursement for credits in the nature of an indirect income tax benefit such as foreign tax credits.

A different approach is taken when it comes to refunds. Lenders are generally willing to show more flexibility in rebating refunds to a borrower because it is more likely to be possible to match a refund to a loan. The language set out in Box 3.20, which is the approach taken in the LSTA's Model Credit Agreement Provisions, still allows the lender in its discretion to match loan to refund. Having the verification of a match be in the lender's discretion avoids the concern of a lender opening up its books to the borrower. Once the match is made, the clause requires the lender to return to the borrower whatever excess it paid.

3.7.6.4 Exclusions

Notwithstanding the general requirement of a gross-up described above, the typical taxes clause incorporates several big exclusions. To begin with, ordinary taxes on overall net income or franchise taxes (or comparable taxes, however denominated) imposed on the lender by the jurisdiction where it is organized or has its principal office or lending office are normally excluded. Other exclusions for activities unrelated to any specific loan are also fairly typical.

For example, in putting together a credit facility a lender may have conducted significant activity in a particular country (marketing the customer, performing due diligence, negotiating with the borrower, and closing the facility) that may or may not be the borrower's jurisdiction. The tax authorities in that jurisdiction may, in turn, feel it is appropriate to treat income on the loan as attributable to any branch office that the lender may have in that country. The lender would, of course, typically respond that its "booking" the loan at a different branch deemed to be the "applicable lending office" should override these considerations, but that may not deter the taxing authorities.

When negotiating the gross-up clause, a borrower's counsel typically seeks to exclude net income taxes imposed by any country where the lender is engaged in business (or otherwise has activities unrelated to the specific loan that result in tax being imposed) and not merely exclude the country where the lender's "applicable lending office" is situated. Similarly, borrowers may seek to limit coverage under the gross-up to taxes imposed by the country where the borrower is resident (and perhaps also those where it is engaged in business) on the theory that each party should bear the risks it brings to the table by reason of the manner in which it conducts its business, but not imponderable risks like the assertion of taxing rights by some (perhaps overly aggressive) third country. Borrowers typically make this last point in vain. From the perspective of a lender, it will take the obvious position that any and all "imponderable" risks must be for the borrower's account and not the lender's.

Borrowers may also attempt to backstop the exclusions agreed to in the gross-up clause by removing from coverage any tax that arises from a failure on the part of the lender to comply with its own obligations under the clause—typically the requirement to provide forms that minimize taxes. Because, with some exceptions, lenders are required to provide such forms, this might seem like harmless duplication, but lenders generally resist on the theory that they have a right to be paid first and face action later by the borrower for any breach of their obligations, rather than have the borrower refuse to pay based upon an alleged breach. This avoids the lender having to itself demonstrate that it complied with the tax provisions and shifts the burden to the borrower to show that it was the lender that defaulted.

3.8 INTEREST SAVINGS CLAUSES

> ### Box 3.21
>
> Notwithstanding anything herein to the contrary, if at any time the interest rate applicable to any Loan, together with all fees, charges, and other amounts which are treated as interest on such Loan under applicable law (collectively the "*Charges*"), shall exceed the maximum lawful rate (the "*Maximum Rate*") which may be contracted for, charged, taken, received or reserved by the Lender holding such Loan, the rate of interest payable in respect of such Loan hereunder, together with all related Charges, shall be limited to the Maximum Rate. To the extent lawful, the interest and Charges that would have been payable in respect of a Loan, but were not payable as a result of the operation of this Section, shall be cumulated and the interest and Charges payable to such Lender in respect of other Loans or periods shall be increased (but not above the Maximum Rate therefor) until such cumulated amount, together with interest thereon at the Federal Funds Effective Rate to the date of repayment, shall have been received by such Lender.

For millennia, laws have imposed limits upon the amount of interest that may be charged on loans. Exceeding the maximum permitted amount is called "usury." Every state in the United States has its own version of these limits today. So what happens if the fees and interest rate set out in a credit agreement exceed the maximum allowed under law? No banker wants to find out. Many credit agreements therefore contain a so-called interest savings clause designed to rescue the lender should it cross the usury line.

This can occur in a variety of ways. The simplest case arises when the stated interest rate under a credit agreement is higher than the permitted limit in the borrower's home jurisdiction. Few lenders are so stupid as to do this. Exceeding the usury limits occurs most often because interest rate laws contain many traps for the unwary. For example, the general usury limit in New York, before taking into account the numerous exceptions built into the statute, is 16 percent per annum. Although this rate has historically been well in excess of LIBOR, once up-front fees are taken into account (some of which may qualify as "interest" for purpose of the statute), the 16 percent limit could be exceeded. To illustrate, if on initial syndication the borrower paid a 1 percent up-front fee to each lender and the initial loan interest rate is 10 percent, the actual stated rate of interest should the loan be accelerated and repaid in 30 days would be 22 percent. Although voluntary prepayment has been uniformly held not to result in loan interest exceeding the usury rate (see *Saul v. Midlantic Nat. Bank/South*, 572 A.2d 650 (N.J. Super. Ct. App. Div. 1990)), acceleration of a loan might not be accorded the same favorable treatment.

Some usury laws, if violated, can have draconian effects on lenders. Lenders might be required, for example, to return *all* interest (not just the excess interest) or even a multiple of the interest paid. Under New York law (General Obligations Law Section 5-511) the basic rule is that a usurious transaction shall be "void," which means that the offending lender would not just lose interest, but *principal* as well. See *Szerdahelyi v. Harris*, 67 N.Y.2d 42 (1986). As a practical matter, because of numerous exceptions to the application of the usury laws, few of the extreme penalties are ever imposed upon lenders. Most states, for example, exempt corporations from the application of usury laws. In New York, General Obligations Law Section 5-501.6.b provides that any loan of $2,500,000 or more, or any loan made under a facility that provides for aggregate loans of $2,500,000 or more, is not subject to usury limitations (not even the 25 percent criminal usury limits set out in Sections 190.40 and 190.42 of the New York Penal Law). Under this rule, a credit agreement under which a term loan of $2,500,000 or more has been made may provide for any rate of interest. Even if the actual loan made is less than $2,500,000, if the agreement contemplates multiple loans, or a commitment for revolving credit loans, of $2,500,000 or more, no usury limit is applicable (at least so long as the amount of the facility was not manipulated solely for purposes of evading the usury statute).

Large New York law credit agreements, therefore, are free of usury limitations. This does not mean, however, that an interest-savings clause becomes superfluous. The selection of New York law to govern the agreement does not necessarily override the more restrictive usury law of the state where the borrower is located. For example, a borrower headquartered in Texas that intends to use all of the proceeds in Texas, that never comes to New York to negotiate the agreement, and that executes and closes the agreement in Texas might have a basis to convince a Texas court to ignore the choice of New York law and instead apply Texas usury principles to the loan. That a local court could override a valid choice of New York law is a particular risk in states, such as Texas, where the statute provides that merely *contracting for* interest in excess of the limit can result in usury.

The interest-savings clause inserted in many credit agreements generally serves two purposes. First, it allows a lender to claim that the contract itself was never usurious since the parties expressly agreed pursuant to the clause that interest is never to exceed the maximum permitted rate. Second, the clause may include so-called "spreader" language to address what is to be done with excess interest if it is ever paid. Here the savings clause takes one of two forms. One version, such as that shown in the sample above, provides that any interest paid on a loan in excess of that permitted under applicable law will be cumulated and added to interest on other loans with the intent that the aggregate interest charged on the facility (regardless of the interest rates otherwise provided for in the agreement) will be the maximum rate that may be charged under applicable usury laws (but not one penny more). Another approach (not illustrated above) simply deems the excess interest paid to have been applied to the prepayment of principal on the loan. Under either approach, if interest were ever discovered to have exceeded the maximum rate, complicated after-the-fact calculations would need to be made by the agent.

Do these clauses work? Probably yes. The few court decisions that construe interest-savings clauses have generally upheld them. For an example, see *Bernie's Custom Coach, Inc. v. Small Business Admin.*, 987 F.2d. 1195 (5th Cir. 1993), which upheld a savings clause on the ground that it expressed the intent of the parties not to charge a usurious interest rate.

It is also worth noting that under the National Bank Act (NBA), national banks may be sued for usury only if they charge an interest rate higher than that allowed by their home state.[2] All other usury claims against national banks are preempted by the NBA. There are similar provisions in Section 27 of the Federal Deposit Insurance Action (FDIA) that preempt the application of usury laws to state-chartered banks.[3]

In May 2015, the United States Court of Appeals for the Second Circuit held in *Madden v. Midland Funding, LLC*, 786 F.3d 246 (2d Cir. 2015), that a non-national bank assignee of debt originated by a national bank could not rely on the NBA for preemption of state usury laws. Citing the relevant preemption standard set forth by the Supreme Court, the Second Circuit wrote that "[t]o apply NBA preemption to an action taken by a non-national bank entity, application of state law to that action must significantly interfere with a national bank's ability to exercise its power under the NBA." The court then held that no such "significant interference" would occur if assignees of debt originated by national banks were prevented from relying on NBA preemption of state usury laws. In reaching its decision, the Second Circuit did not address at all an independent basis for finding that the interest charged by defendants was valid: the longstanding and widely relied-upon common law principle that "[t]he non-usurious character of a note should not change when the note changes hands"—the so-called Valid-When-Made Doctrine.[4]

Madden has caused substantial uncertainty in the lending industry as a whole and especially in secondary loan markets. Secondary loan markets have historically been liquid in part because the Valid-When-Made Doctrine provided financial institutions comfort that loans originated by federal or state-chartered depositary institutions would remain non-usurious after assignment. Unless it is overturned or qualified, *Madden* has important implications for the lending market.

---

[2] See 12 U.S.C. § 85; 12 C.F.R. § 7.4001.
[3] See 12 U.S.C. § 1831d.
[4] *FDIC v. Lattimore Land Corp.*, 656 F.2d 139, 148-49 (5th Cir. 1981) (citing cases).

CHAPTER 4

Amortization and Maturity

4.1 PAYMENTS GENERALLY

4.1.1 Immediately Available Funds

Box 4.1

(a) *Advances by Lenders*. Each Lender shall make each Loan to be made by it hereunder on the proposed date thereof by wire transfer of immediately available funds by 12:00 noon, New York City time, to the account of the Administrative Agent most recently designated by it for such purpose by notice to the Lenders.

(b) *Payments by Borrower*. The Borrower shall make each payment required to be made by it hereunder (whether of principal, interest, or fees, or of amounts payable under Section [*Yield Protection*], or otherwise) prior to 12:00 noon, New York City time, on the date when due, in immediately available funds, without deduction, setoff or counterclaim.

Credit agreements are about money and getting it now. A borrower wants loan proceeds that it can use the instant received (and interest begins to accrue). Delivery by the lenders to a New York borrower of a check drawn on a bank in Alaska that takes 10 days to clear is not good enough. Similarly, lenders want payment from a borrower that they can redeploy straight away; again, payment to a group of New York lenders by means of a check drawn on a bank in Hawaii will not suffice. Stated another way, when loans are made and payments received, the borrower and lender want money that is just like *cash*. Of course, they do not actually want suitcases of cash. Rather, they want its equivalent deposited to an account for instantaneous use.

What both parties really want is something called "immediately available funds." Credit agreements accordingly, with rare exception, stipulate that loans must be advanced to the borrower (and payments be made to the lenders) in funds that are immediately available. The phrase "immediately available funds" is a term of art that refers to funds that can be used at the place of payment instantly upon receipt. Payment by check is generally not in immediately available funds, since, before the recipient can have access to the funds represented by the check, it must first be collected (which may take several business days, depending upon where the bank on which the check has been drawn is located).

Real-time funding and payment is typically accomplished in one of two ways. For advances of funds to the borrower, the lenders normally send money through the Fedwire Funds Service, Federal Reserve's wire transfer system (or in Europe with respect to Euro-denominated fundings, the Trans-European Automated Real-time Gross Settlement Express Transfer or "TARGET2" payment system) to the administrative agent. Funds sent in this way are immediately available when received by the agent and can be immediately deposited to an account of the borrower or remitted as the borrower directs. Payments by a borrower to the lenders are effected in the same way if funds come to the administrative agent from another bank. More frequently, the borrower maintains a deposit account at the administrative agent and instructs the agent to debit the account in the required amount whenever payment is to be made. Since the agent itself knows the balance of the funds in the account, payments made in this manner to the agent are immediately available and can be remitted by the agent to the lenders as such.

4.1.2   Time of Payment

Credit agreements almost uniformly require that payments be made by a particular time on a specified date. The language set out in Box 4.1 is an example of this approach. One might ask why lenders bother to specify a *time* of payment as opposed to merely the *day* of payment. Is this yet another example of unnecessary wordiness?

There are two answers to this question. First, absent specification of a time of payment, a borrower would be permitted to tender payment at any time up to the close of business on the date that the payment is due. Under New York law, merely spelling out a date of payment has been held to preclude the exercise of certain remedies by the lenders if payment is not made until the business day following the date upon which the payment becomes due. Accordingly, exercise of a right of setoff, institution of suit, foreclosure on collateral, and perhaps even acceleration of the loan would not be permissible until the next business day; see *Marine Midland Bank-New York v. Graybar Electric Co.*, 41 N.Y.2d 703 (1977). As a consequence of the *Graybar* case, credit agreements since 1977 have almost uniformly prescribed a time of day by which payment is to be made, thus allowing the lenders to claim that a default occurs at the specified time (if payment is not received) rather than having to wait until the next business day.

Of course, any time prior to close of business works for purposes of the *Graybar* decision. The time actually specified is a function of the second consideration motivating lenders to indicate a particular hour by which payments must be made. For a lender, the later in the day funds are received, the more difficult it becomes to redeploy those funds into alternative assets, such as an investment in commercial paper, certificates of deposit, Treasury bills, or, in the best case, new loans to other borrowers. Lenders that receive funds later than 2:00 p.m. or 3:00 p.m. at the place of payment might be forced to keep those funds unused until the next business day (this could be three days over a holiday weekend) and so suffer a lost opportunity cost that could be substantial when spread generally to credit agreements over time. Most credit agreements, therefore, specify that all payments must be made between 11:00 a.m. and 1:00 p.m. to ensure that both the *Graybar* issue and the reinvestment concerns are addressed.

4.1.3 Extensions for Nonbusiness Days

Box 4.2

If any payment hereunder shall fall due on a day that is not a Business Day, the date for payment shall be extended to the next succeeding Business Day, and, in the case of any payment accruing interest, interest thereon shall be payable for the period of such extension.

Under New York law (General Construction Law, Article 2, § 25), if a payment is due on a day that is not a business day (such as a Saturday, Sunday, or public holiday), then (unless otherwise agreed) the due date is automatically extended to the next succeeding business day, but no interest is payable for the period of the extension. Lenders, of course, abhor words such as "no interest." As a consequence, although the General Construction Law provides an alternative date if a date of payment is not a business day, credit agreements as a rule try not to rely upon the statute and instead require that all payments be made on business days (avoiding in this way any extension where interest would not accrue). An example of this can be found in the structure of LIBOR interest periods discussed in Section 3.1.2.2; such interest periods are always designed to both begin and end on business days.

Nevertheless, nonbusiness days can occur unexpectedly (see Section 3.5). Credit agreements accordingly include the language allowed by the General Construction Law to the effect that interest is payable for the period of any extension.

4.1.4   Obligation to Repay Absolute

Imagine the scenario in which a borrower requests a loan and signs a credit agreement with a group of its favorite lenders. Time passes and the loans are made and become due. On an unrelated matter, however, the borrower has sued one of the lenders because (or so it alleges) the lender wrongfully debited the borrower's demand deposit account. Can the borrower deduct from the payment it must make to the agent an amount equal to its claim against the lender? Can it create litigation or settlement leverage in this way?

The answer under virtually all credit agreements is "no." Credit agreements almost universally stipulate that the obligations of the borrower to the lenders are not subject to setoff or counterclaim (and, hence, absolute; see the sample language in Box 4.1). This approach is taken for at least two reasons. First, there is the purely operational issue. In the example above, since the administrative agent is, as a result of standard *pro rata* payment provisions (see Section 10.4), required to divide the payment shortfall among all of the lenders, the borrower would be penalizing all of the lenders and not just the lender with whom it has a dispute. Second, lenders have a strong aversion to giving borrowers a defense based on unrelated (or even related) disputes whenever payment is due under a credit agreement. Were the rule otherwise (or so lenders fear), a borrower might refuse to make a payment based upon any dispute with a lender—such as by alleging that a lender caused the borrower harm by wrongfully declining to do business with the borrower in a separate transaction. The remedy for the borrower, the lender would say, is to sue the lender directly for whatever harm it suffered, not to reduce the amount of the payment (see Section 9.7 for the hurdles that a borrower faces in asserting damages against a lender). Waivers of setoff and counterclaim are generally enforceable, absent special circumstances (such as fraud). See *Frankel v. ICD Holdings S.A.*, 930 F. Supp. 54 (S.D.N.Y. 1996) and *Barclays Bank of New York, N.A. v. Heady Electric Co.*, 571 N.Y.S.2d 650 (App. Div. 3d Dep't 1991).

4.2 SCHEDULED REPAYMENT

> **Box 4.3**
>
> The Borrower will repay the principal amount of each Revolving Credit Loan on the Revolving Credit Commitment Termination Date. The Borrower will repay each Swingline Loan on the earlier of the Revolving Credit Commitment Termination Date and the date _____ Business Days after the date such Loan is made. The Borrower will, commencing on [Date] and thereafter on each Tranche A Principal Payment Date, pay the principal amount of the Tranche A Term Loans in 20 consecutive equal quarterly installments. The Borrower will, commencing on [Date] and thereafter on each Tranche B Principal Payment Date, pay the principal amount of the Tranche B Term Loans in 24 consecutive quarterly installments, the first 23 of which will each be in an amount equal to 0.25% of the original principal amount thereof, and the final installment of which will be in an amount equal to 94.25% of the original principal amount thereof.

As hard as lenders work to find companies that want to borrow money, they ultimately want their loans back. A credit agreement, accordingly, always includes a maturity date—indeed, as a regulatory matter, it would be imprudent or even illegal for a bank to make a loan without a maturity date. The exact date is, of course, determined by negotiation, and there is no general custom as to what the maturity should be, except that revolving credit and A loan tranches (discussed in Section 2.1.1) rarely extend beyond six years and B loan tranches rarely extend beyond seven years. Additionally, B loan tranches nearly always mature well after any revolving credit or A loan tranche set out in the same credit agreement. All of this contrasts with bond indentures and private placements, in which maturities from 8 to 10 years or more are common. Any borrower that truly seeks long-term money and does not care about the advantages of a credit facility (lower interest, more flexible covenants, and easy prepayment ability) may therefore want to issue bonds or enter into a private placement financing.

Term loans either have a so-called "bullet" maturity or are repayable in installments. A loan with a bullet maturity is payable in one installment in the full principal amount on the maturity date. Lenders often prefer a loan to be repayable in installments because of the discipline a repayment schedule imposes on the borrower, since it is thereby required to ensure that its business throws off enough cash to make principal payments as they come due. As noted earlier (see Section 2.1.1.2), the installments for a B loan tranche are generally nominal until the final year; the installments for an A loan tranche are larger throughout its term, so that the loan is substantially repaid by the time it matures. For a B loan, an illustrative amortization might be one that provides for payments of 1 percent per year for seven years with a final installment of 93 percent in the eighth year. For an A loan, an illustrative amortization might be one that provides for 28 equal quarterly installments through year seven.

As discussed in Section 2.2.2, a revolving credit facility can be reduced in installments as well; this is effected by providing for the commitment to decrease in accordance with a specified commitment reduction schedule. As the maturity date (the commitment termination date) approaches, the commitment grows smaller and smaller. The borrower is required to repay any outstanding loans so that at no time does the sum of the loans and any letters of credit exceed the commitment as reduced. Commitment reduction schedules for a revolving facility are not, however, the rule. In most cases a revolving credit commitment has a bullet maturity: the entire commitment is available until maturity, and then the whole amount terminates.

As illustrated in the example above (and discussed also in Section 2.1.1.4), swingline loans generally have short maturities, typically within five business days to two weeks.

4.3 ADVANCING THE MATURITY DATE

Box 4.4

Notwithstanding the foregoing, if on any date (the "*Test Date*"), the maturity date for any then-outstanding Public Notes of the Borrower shall fall within six months of the Test Date then, if the aggregate principal amount of all such Public Notes that mature is at such time greater than $_____ and the Required Lenders do not elect otherwise, the Tranche A Term Loans shall be paid in full on the Test Date.

Section 2.2 describes the so-called accordion feature that allows commitments to be increased at the option of the borrower (assuming that it finds willing lenders). To confuse things, bankers also use the term "accordion" to describe a quite different feature whereby the maturity date for a loan is advanced because of an intervening bond maturity or other event. An example might arise when a loan is made with a seven-year maturity, while at the same time a large subordinated bond indenture, scheduled to mature in five years, is outstanding. As a credit matter, lenders may find this situation unacceptable, but may nevertheless make the loan with the expectation that the borrower will refinance the bonds in advance of their maturity. In another example, the lenders might want the borrower to issue an agreed amount of additional equity by a date prior to maturity of the loans. To ensure that the borrower completes the refinancing (or issues additional equity) in a timely fashion, the credit agreement may provide that, if the bonds are still outstanding on (or if equity has not been issued by) the agreed date (in the example above, six months prior to maturity of the bonds), the maturity date for the loans is automatically advanced to that date. Like an "accordion," the maturity folds in upon itself to an earlier date.

The credit agreement could, of course, accomplish the same result by including a default that is triggered on the relevant date if the bonds are not repaid or additional equity issued. Similarly, the same result could be achieved through a covenant—the additional equity could, for example, be mandated by stipulating that the equity capital or net worth of the borrower must increase by the agreed amount by a particular date. Borrowers are reluctant, nevertheless, for cosmetic purposes to achieve this through a default or covenant. The accordion feature looks more borrower-friendly even though it leads to the same result.

4.4 364-DAY FACILITIES

> **Box 4.5**
>
> (a) *Requests for Extension.* The Borrower may, by notice to the Administrative Agent (who shall promptly notify the Lenders) not earlier than 45 days and not later than 35 days prior to the Commitment Termination Date then in effect hereunder (the *"Existing Commitment Termination Date"*), request that each Lender extend such Lender's Commitment Termination Date for an additional 364 days from the Existing Commitment Termination Date.
>
> (b) *Lender Elections to Extend.* Each Lender, acting in its sole and individual discretion, shall, by notice to the Administrative Agent given not earlier than 30 days prior to the Existing Commitment Termination Date and not later than the date (the *"Notice Date"*) that is 20 days prior to the Existing Commitment Termination Date, advise the Administrative Agent whether or not such Lender agrees to such extension. Each Lender that determines not to so extend its Commitment Termination Date (a *"Non-Extending Lender"*) shall notify the Administrative Agent of such fact promptly after such determination (but in any event no later than the

Notice Date) and any Lender that does not so advise the Administrative Agent on or before the Notice Date shall be deemed to be a Non-Extending Lender. The election of any Lender to agree to such extension shall not obligate any other Lender to so agree.

(c) *Notification by Administrative Agent.* The Administrative Agent shall notify the Borrower of each Lender's determination under this Section no later than the date 15 days prior to the Existing Commitment Termination Date (or, if such date is not a Business Day, on the next preceding Business Day).

(d) *Additional Commitment Lenders.* The Borrower shall have the right on or before the Existing Commitment Termination Date to replace each Non-Extending Lender with, and add as "Lenders" under this Agreement in place thereof, one or more Eligible Assignees (each, an *"Additional Commitment Lender"*) with the approval of the Administrative Agent and the Issuing Lender (which approvals shall not be unreasonably withheld), each of which Additional Commitment Lenders shall have entered into an agreement in form and substance satisfactory to the Borrower and the Administrative Agent pursuant to which such Additional Commitment Lender shall, effective as of the Existing Commitment Termination Date, undertake a Commitment (and, if any such Additional Commitment Lender is already a Lender, its Commitment shall be in addition to such Lender's Commitment hereunder on such date).

(e) *Minimum Extension Requirement.* If (and only if) the total of the Commitments of the Lenders that have agreed so to extend their Commitment Termination Date and the additional Commitments of the Additional Commitment Lenders shall be more than [____%] of the aggregate amount of the Commitments in effect immediately prior to the Existing Commitment Termination Date, then, effective as of the Existing Commitment Termination Date, the Commitment Termination Date of each Extending Lender and of each Additional Commitment Lender shall be extended to the date falling 364 days after the Existing Commitment Termination Date (except that, if such date is not a Business Day, such Commitment Date as so extended shall be the next preceding Business Day) and each Additional Commitment Lender shall thereupon become a "Lender" for all purposes of this Agreement.

(f) *Conditions to Effectiveness of Extensions.* Notwithstanding the foregoing, the extension of the Commitment Termination Date pursuant to this Section shall not be effective with respect to any Lender unless:

(x) no Default or Event of Default shall have occurred and be continuing on the date of such extension and after giving effect thereto;

(y) the representations and warranties contained in this Agreement are true and correct on and as of the date of such extension and after giving effect thereto, as though made on and as of such date (or, if any such representation or warranty is expressly stated to have been made as of a specific date, as of such specific date); and

(z) on or before the Commitment Termination Date of each Non-Extending Lender, (1) the Borrower shall have paid in full the principal of and interest on all of the Loans made by such Non-Extending Lender to the Borrower hereunder and (2) the Borrower shall have paid in full all other amounts owing to such Lender hereunder.

On the date of any extension and notwithstanding the provisions of Section [*Pro Rata Treatment*] requiring that borrowings and prepayments be made ratably in accordance with the principal amounts of the Loans and Commitments held by the Lenders, the Borrower shall borrow from the Lenders (other than the Non-Extending Lenders), and such Lenders shall make, Loans to the Borrower (in the case of LIBOR Loans, with Interest Period(s) ending on the date(s) of any then-outstanding Interest Period(s)), and the Borrower shall have prepaid Loans held by the other Lenders in such amounts as may be necessary, so that after giving effect to such Loans and prepayments, the Loans (and Interest Period(s) of LIBOR Loan(s)) shall be held by the Lenders pro rata in accordance with the respective amounts of their Commitments (as so extended).

Lenders are always looking for new ways to compete. Any structure that allows a lender to lower the all-in cost to the borrower of a facility without reducing the lender's return is like squaring the circle. The so-called 364-day credit facility may come close to doing this. The 364-day facility has its origin in the capital requirements issued by the Federal Reserve Board (for a discussion of capital requirements generally, see Section 3.7.2). Among the many factors lenders take into account when they determine the appropriate commitment fee for a loan are the capital costs of the commitment. The commitment fee is fixed at levels that are designed to cover these costs based upon capital regulations in effect at the time the commitment is issued. At the same time, the lenders protect themselves against future increases of these costs by inserting a capital costs provision into the yield protection clause.

One type of loan commitment, however, is entitled to reduced capital requirements, namely any commitment that has a term of one year or less. Factoring this rule into a deal structure, lenders early on created the concept of a 364-day facility under which a borrower is offered a reduced commitment fee that, in effect, credits to the borrower the capital cost savings of the facility. Although Federal Reserve rules stipulate that the reduced capital requirement applies to any facility of "one year or less," the market practice calls for these facilities to expire one day earlier than a full year, namely on the 364th day. The Federal Reserve also allows reduced-capital treatment for 364-day facilities that have a term-out option at the end of the commitment so long as the commitment otherwise satisfies the durational requirements for reduced-capital treatment.

There is, of course, a big difference between a facility available for only 364 days and a facility that has a duration of three to five years. There is, therefore, a cost to a borrower who pays the reduced commitment fee of a 364-day facility. In an attempt to overcome the short-term character of a 364-day facility, it is common in the credit agreement to build in an extension mechanism (discussed below) which provides that when the expiration of the 364-day facility nears, the facility can be extended for another 364 days. To benefit from the extension mechanism, however, a borrower needs to be comfortable that the lenders will, in fact, be willing to extend when the commitment expiration approaches. As a practical matter, therefore, 364-day facilities are most often found in credit agreements for investment-grade borrowers, who are likely to have the requisite level of comfort that an extension will be forthcoming.

Nevertheless, any extension must be at the sole and absolute discretion of each lender. If it were not (if the lender were in any way legally committed to extend the facility prior to the actual expiration date), the lender would in effect have a commitment of longer than one year and the facility could lose the reduced-capital treatment. This risk notwithstanding, the borrower wants to know whether or not the lenders are going to exercise their discretion to extend the facility sometime prior to the expiration date. Otherwise, it may not have sufficient time to find alternative lenders and execute a replacement facility. Borrowers therefore want the lenders to commit to the extension *before* the current expiration date. This is where a 364-day facility begins to get complicated.

Helpfully, the Federal Reserve has recognized that from the standpoint of business practicality, lenders need (at least for some brief period prior to each expiration date) to be committed for a period longer than a year. However, it has given only very general guidance as to how such extensions must be effected in order that the facility not lose the reduced-capital treatment. Two key time frames have been described in interpretations. With certain exceptions for "complex" facilities, a borrower may not request an extension earlier than 45 days prior to the current commitment expiration date and lenders may not commit to an extension earlier than 30 days prior to the expiration date. As a result, assuming a lender agrees to an extension on the 30th day, it could have a commitment under a 364-day facility with a duration of 394 days. A "complex" facility is any facility that has at least 15 lenders or is in an amount of $1,000,000,000 or more. In a complex facility, the extension request may be made as early as 60 days prior to the current commitment expiration date.

A properly drafted extension clause needs to address more issues than merely the 45- and 30-day periods noted above. The borrower and lenders normally want to include a mechanism for additional lenders to join the syndicate and replace any lenders that choose not to extend. Similarly, the lenders expect the extension itself to be subject to certain conditions, such as the truth of representations, the absence of defaults, and the execution of an appropriate extension agreement. As a consequence, a market practice has developed for the credit agreement to lay out very explicit extension procedures that incorporate the Federal Reserve's timelines and other mechanics. The LSTA's Model Credit Agreement Provision set out in Box 4.5 incorporates these concepts and is language that has been formally blessed by the Federal Reserve.

Despite the inclusion of extension language in a 364-day credit agreement, the actual extension of the commitments under a 364-day facility is often effected through informal procedures rather than by using the formal extension mechanism set out in the agreement. In such cases, the administrative agent and the borrower accomplish an extension by communicating verbally with the syndicate, receiving their nonbinding oral commitments to extend, and then providing for a short extension agreement to be executed on the commitment termination date.

4.5 STRIPPED LOAN FACILITIES

"Stripped" loan facilities are largely an historical anachronism, although a few credit agreements may, from time to time, still adopt this format. The concept behind a stripped loan facility is that, instead of a single revolving credit or term loan being outstanding for a tenor of, say, five years, the lenders agree to make a series of back-to-back loans, each with a short-term maturity, over a period of five years. If the borrower elects continually to roll over each short-term loan into a new short-term loan, it will have the principal outstanding for the full five-year period equivalent to what it would have had with a single, five-year term loan.

In a stripped loan facility, each loan made under the agreement (whether a base rate loan or LIBOR loan) is assigned a single "interest period." Base rate loans are typically given an "interest period" of 30 or 90 days; LIBOR loans have interest periods of the durations customary for non-stripped credit facilities. Each loan then matures and must be paid in full at the expiration of its base rate or LIBOR interest period. If the borrower wants to continue a loan, it must reborrow the principal at the end of the interest period and apply the proceeds to the payment of the maturing loan.

This structure works fairly easily in the context of a revolving credit facility, since there is already a commitment in place under which the borrower can make a drawing to repay maturing loans at the end of their interest periods. For the stripped loan structure to work in the context of a term loan facility, a different approach must be taken. In a normal (non-stripped) term loan facility, the commitments expire immediately upon the loans being made. A stripped term loan facility is structured so that the commitments continue until the final maturity date. This establishes a commitment for new loans that provides funds to repay outstanding loans at the end of each interest period. So as not to convert the term loan facility into a revolving credit facility, any drawing after the initial drawing is permitted to be applied only to the repayment of the outstanding term loans of the same tranche that are then maturing. Any unused term loan commitments automatically terminate—thus, the total of the commitments never exceeds the outstanding principal of the related term loans.

Lenders originally employed the stripped loan structure because they wanted to benefit from certain favorable accounting and regulatory rules. Normally, a loan carried as an asset on a lender's balance sheet cannot be deemed sold if there is any obligation on the part of the lender to repurchase the loan prior to maturity. So a lender that wanted to take advantage of the market for short-term loans by selling a five-year loan only for a 90-day period (with an undertaking to repurchase the loan at the end of that period) would not be able to treat the loan as having been sold. Accounting rules, however, allowed a 90-day loan to be treated as sold even if there were a commitment on the part of the lender to make a new loan at maturity that would repay the old loan, at least if there were customary conditions to the commitment. Regulatory accounting rules, initially, also accorded similar treatment to sales of short-term loans within a longer-term commitment.

These rules spawned the development of stripped loan facilities. Their shelf-life, however, proved to be short. Banks and their regulatory supervisors quickly became uncomfortable with sale treatment for short-term loans assigned in this manner. Resistance from borrowers also increased as they began to realize that, upon each rollover, they needed to satisfy the truth of representations and absence of default conditions. Failure to satisfy these conditions (and to effect the rollover) had the ability to create a massive payment default in the middle of what had been intended as a stable, five-year facility for events that would otherwise never cause a lending syndicate to want to accelerate. These pressures proved to be the downfall for stripped loan facilities, and they have now largely disappeared.

4.6 VOLUNTARY PREPAYMENTS

Box 4.6

The Borrower shall have the right at any time and from time to time to prepay any Loan in whole or in part, without premium or penalty (other than as provided in Section [*Breakfunding*]), subject to prior notice in accordance with Section [*Notices*]. Prepayments of Term Loans under this paragraph shall be applied (i) as between each Class of Term Loan, *pro rata* in accordance with the respective aggregate principal amounts of the Loans of such Class outstanding on the date of prepayment and (ii) as within each such Class of Loans, to the respective installments thereof ratably in accordance with the respective principal amounts of such installments. Each notice of prepayment shall be irrevocable; *provided* that a notice of full prepayment may state that such notice is conditioned upon the effectiveness of other credit facilities, in which case such notice may be revoked by the Borrower (by notice to the Administrative Agent on or prior to the specified effective date) if such condition is not satisfied.

Credit agreements with limited exceptions (including, most notably, the exception for so-called "soft call" protection applicable to B loans described in Section 4.11) do not restrict prepayments or impose prepayment premiums. The ability to prepay a loan facility is, in fact, one of the big advantages of credit agreements over bond indentures and private placements. The latter severely restrict the right of a borrower to make early prepayments by typically barring any payment during the first three to five years and mandating payment of a premium or make-whole amount each time an early payment occurs thereafter (see Section 3.7.5.4).

By way of legal background, the general rule under New York law is that a loan may not be prepaid without the consent of the lender. See *Troncone v. Canelli*, 538 N.Y.S.2d 39 (App. Div. 2d Dep't 1989). The theory is that the lender has contracted for a loan of a particular term and that it would constitute a breach of that contract were the borrower to pay early. Credit agreements, however, commonly expressly override this general rule and allow the borrower to prepay loans at any time at its option. There are exceptions, such as with respect to competitive bid loans (most credit agreements do not permit these to be prepaid), and any payment of a LIBOR loan prior to the expiration of its interest period needs to be accompanied by a breakfunding payment (described in Section 3.7.5).

In the case of the prepayment of a loan that is otherwise payable in installments, the prepayment provision addresses how the prepayment is to be applied to the installments. Absent specification, under New York law the borrower is free to apply the prepayment to whichever installments it chooses.[1] Lenders may prefer to have prepayments applied to installments in inverse order (which is to say, starting with the last installment and then working forward), so that the credit exposure is shortened and the borrower remains subject to the discipline of having to make the regular agreed-upon installments of principal initially contemplated by the parties. Borrowers prefer the opposite, namely, that prepayments be applied to installments in the direct order of maturity or in whatever other order they may choose. Some agreements (as demonstrated in the sample language in Box 4.6) compromise on the two extremes by stipulating that prepayments are applied to installments ratably. Other twists are also seen, such as applying prepayments first to, say, the next four installments and then ratably or in inverse order. There are few limits as to what the parties can negotiate.

Credit agreements may also address allocation between loans within a particular tranche. This might occur, for example, if the loans outstanding under a tranche consisted of base rate loans, LIBOR loans with an interest period expiring in a week, and other LIBOR loans with an interest period expiring in four months. To minimize breakfunding costs, the borrower will want to prepay the base rate loans first and then the LIBOR loans with the interest period expiring in one week. Credit agreements often allow the borrower to pick and choose among these loans to minimize its costs, since the lenders are essentially indifferent as to which loan is repaid if breakfunding is payable. Sometimes, however, the credit agreement locks in this type of allocation by an express statement that base rate loans are to be paid first and then LIBOR loans are to be paid in the order in which their interest periods expire.

Voluntary prepayments may usually be made only upon notice given by the borrower to the administrative agent (who then advises

---

[1] See Restatement of Contracts 2d, § 258.

the appropriate lenders). For a LIBOR loan, the notice period is typically two or three business days; for a base rate loan, the notice period is normally one day in advance or same day (notice on the day of the prepayment). A notice, once given, is irrevocable because it is presumed that the lenders, in reliance on the notice, will have committed to redeploy the funds to be repaid to an alternative asset (though a borrower is often allowed to issue a revocable notice of prepayment in connection with an anticipated refinancing).

As with the making of loans, prepayments are required to be in stated minimum amounts (and sometimes multiples in excess of those minimums) to ease the administrative burden of dealing with small funds transfers.

4.7 MANDATORY PREPAYMENTS

Voluntary prepayments are at the *option* of the borrower. Mandatory prepayments are prepayments that are *required* to be made upon the occurrence of specified events. Except in a credit agreement with an investment-grade borrower, it is common for the agreement to contain at least one mandatory prepayment provision of the types described below.

Mandatory prepayments should be contrasted with the corresponding requirements in bond indentures, in which a required prepayment (which is usually confined to asset sales and changes of control) is normally structured as an "offer to prepay" made to all bondholders rather than as an obligation that bonds be prepaid or redeemed. There are at least two substantive differences between the credit agreement approach and the bond indenture approach. First, in a credit agreement, the prepayment is usually required to be made immediately (or virtually so). In a bond indenture, the process can take up to 90 or more days after the triggering event, with the issuer given 30 or more days in which to make an offer, the bondholders given another 30 or more days to accept or reject the offer, and the issuer granted yet more time in which to make payment. The second major difference is that in a credit agreement, the lenders (with the exception of B loan tranches, as described later in Section 4.10) are not given the opportunity to opt out of a prepayment. In the bond indenture context, whether or not a particular bondholder is prepaid is purely a function of whether it elects to be prepaid by accepting the offer to prepay. What follows is an overview of the mandatory prepayment provisions most commonly included in credit agreements.

4.7.1   Revolving Clean Downs

Box 4.7

The Borrower will from time to time prior to the Revolving Credit Commitment Termination Date prepay the Revolving Credit Loans, and provide cover for Letters of Credit, in such amounts as shall be necessary so that for a period of at least _____ consecutive days at any time during the _____ fiscal quarter of each fiscal year, the total Revolving Credit Loans and Letter of Credit Exposure shall [not exceed $_____] [be zero].

In a revolving credit facility, a clean-down requirement forces the borrower, typically for a period of 30 days during each calendar year, to have no outstandings under the revolving credit commitments. This type of mandatory prepayment requirement is customarily applied to a borrower with a seasonal business; the company, if it is successful, should be able to reduce its loan balance to zero (or some reduced base amount) at least once each year. An example might be a borrower engaged in a retail merchandising business who, after an intense holiday sale season and during the months of January or February, should be flush with cash and able to reduce its outstanding loans. The prepayment is, in effect, a control against adverse developments in the borrower's business.

4.7.2   Borrowing Base

Box 4.8

The Borrower will from time to time prior to the Revolving Credit Commitment Termination Date prepay the Revolving Credit Loans, and provide cover for Letters of Credit, in such amounts as shall be necessary so that at all times the total Revolving Credit Loans and Letter of Credit Exposure shall not exceed the Borrowing Base.

* * * * * * * *

"*Borrowing Base*" means, as at any date, the sum of (a) [_____] % [(or such other percentage as the Required Revolving Credit Lenders shall, in their discretion, specify to the Borrower as being appropriate for these purposes)] of the aggregate amount of Eligible Receivables at such date *plus* (b) [_____] % [(or such other percentage as the Required Revolving Credit Lenders shall, in their discretion, specify to the Borrower as being appropriate for these purposes)] of the aggregate value of Eligible Inventory at such date. The *"value"* of Eligible Inventory shall be determined at the lower of cost or market in accordance with GAAP, except that cost shall be determined on a first-in-first-out basis.

* * * * * * * *

The Borrower will deliver a Borrowing Base Certificate as at the end of each [weekly] [monthly] accounting period setting forth a determination of the Borrowing Base as at the last day of such accounting period.

For highly leveraged borrowers, the syndicate may want to implement a so-called borrowing base structure in which the availability of loans (typically revolving credit loans) is tied to an agreed valuation (the "borrowing base") of the collateral security. If, giving effect to a borrowing, the amount of the loans and letters of credit exceeds the borrowing base, the lenders are not obligated to honor the borrowing request. Similarly, if the amount of the borrowing base falls below the aggregate outstanding loans and letters of credit, the borrower is required immediately to repay a sufficient amount of the loans to eliminate the shortfall.

Borrowing bases are used primarily in so-called "asset-based" transactions. Normally, the credit facility is secured by the assets included in the borrowing base. As the example above illustrates, a borrowing base is typically structured around the value of easily liquidated collateral, such as accounts receivable and inventory, though sometimes other assets may be included, such as real property or equipment. The borrowing base is usually calculated as the sum of an agreed percentage (the "advance rate") of each class of assets included in the collateral security.

The percentage advance rate for each type of collateral is determined by the lenders after extensive analysis of the assets to be included in the borrowing base. In many cases the analysis starts with formal appraisals of those assets. The appropriate advance rates for any class of assets will be fixed at the percentage that the syndicate believes it can realistically realize in the event it is forced to foreclose upon and sell the assets. If the borrower has receivables from large, creditworthy customers, the lender might settle upon an advance rate of 80 percent or 85 percent. If the borrower has receivables from less creditworthy customers who have a history of defaulting on their receivables, a lower advance rate would be set. Similarly, for inventory, the lender may be willing to give a higher advance rate to raw materials (which can be resold to a wider range of potential purchasers) than for a finished product (which may have a narrower market). In a syndicated credit facility, the determination of advance rates is normally undertaken by the administrative agent.

Other refinements may also be factored into each class of assets before running the arithmetic calculation. To improve further the chances that the borrowing base assets, when liquidated, will be sufficient to repay the secured loans, the typical borrowing base definition applies the advance rates only to "eligible" accounts receivable and "eligible" inventory. It is beyond the scope of this chapter to discuss in detail typical eligibility criteria. However, by way of illustration, an account receivable denominated in a foreign currency, or from a bankrupt customer, or that is more than 90 days old, or (in a domestic U.S. facility) from a non-U.S. customer, would normally be treated as ineligible. Inventory that consists of work-in-process held at third-party warehouses or located outside of the United States might also be treated as ineligible.

The borrowing base is typically computed by the borrower on a weekly or monthly basis and set forth in a borrowing base certificate delivered to the lenders. Failure to deliver the certificate when required usually results in an immediate event of default because of the potential that the failure to deliver the certificate may be masking a required prepayment.

The borrowing base prepayment has an effect very similar to that of the clean-down prepayment described previously. In a seasonal business, when the borrower is flush with cash (and therefore when its receivables and inventory are relatively low), shrinkage in the borrowing base forces it to reduce its outstanding loan balance. For this reason, the two prepayments are often used in tandem.

4.7.3 Asset Sales

Box 4.9

On any date on which the Borrower or any of its Subsidiaries shall receive Net Cash Proceeds from any Asset Sale, the Borrower shall apply an amount equal to 100% of such Net Cash Proceeds to the prepayment of the Loans (and cover for Letters of Credit) and the reduction of the Commitments as set forth below; *provided* that, if prior to such date the Borrower shall notify the Administrative Agent that it wishes to reinvest such Net Cash Proceeds into Qualifying Reinvestment Assets, then the

Borrower shall be permitted to defer such prepayment, cover and reduction of Commitments for a period of up to 360 days after the date of such Asset Sale (and, if the Borrower shall have committed to reinvest within such 360-day period, such deferral shall be extended for an additional 180 days) and on such 360th day (or, if so committed to be reinvested, the 180th day following such 360th day) shall be required to make such prepayment, provide such cover and reduce Commitments to the extent that such reinvestment shall not have been made. Such Net Cash Proceeds shall be applied first to the prepayment of outstanding Term Loans and, after repayment in full of all Term Loans, to the prepayment of Revolving Credit Loans and cover for Letters of Credit, and to the reduction of Revolving Credit Commitments.

* * * * * * * *

"*Asset Sale*" means a sale, assignment, conveyance, transfer, or other disposition to, or any exchange of property with, any Person (other than the Borrower or any of its Subsidiaries), in one transaction or a series of transactions, of all or any part of the businesses, assets, or properties of the Borrower or any of its Subsidiaries of any kind, whether real, personal, or mixed and whether tangible or intangible, whether now owned or hereafter acquired, other than (i) inventory (or other assets) sold, leased or licensed in the ordinary course of business, and (ii) dispositions of assets for aggregate consideration of less than \$_____ during any fiscal year.

"*Net Cash Proceeds*" means, with respect to any Asset Sale, an amount equal to: (a) Cash payments received by the Borrower or any of its Subsidiaries from such Asset Sale (including any Cash received by way of deferred payment pursuant to, or by monetization of, a note receivable or otherwise, but only as and when so received), *minus* (b) any bona fide direct costs incurred in connection with such Asset Sale, including (i) income or gains taxes payable by the seller as a result of any gain recognized in connection with such Asset Sale and (ii) payment of the outstanding principal amount of, premium or penalty, if any, and interest on any Debt (other than the Loans) that is secured by a Lien on the stock or assets in question and that is required to be repaid under the terms thereof as a result of such Asset Sale.

Depending upon the strength of the borrower's credit, lenders can be sensitive to a borrower's sale of assets, particularly if the sale is material. In most credit agreements there is some form of asset sale covenant that addresses this directly (see Section 7.6.6). Many credit agreements (particularly for noninvestment grade companies), however, go beyond a mere covenant and impose an asset sale prepayment requirement along the lines sampled above that forces the borrower to prepay loans upon any sale of assets out of the ordinary course of business beyond an agreed-upon threshold. In many cases the asset sale prepayment ends up being redundant with the asset sale covenant in that a sale that requires a prepayment may also be a sale that must first be consented to by the lenders. In theory, therefore, no asset sale prepayment should be necessary, since lenders are always free to impose conditions on their consent to the sale (such as requiring prepayment), whether or not the credit agreement incorporates a mandatory prepayment.

This fact notwithstanding, many agreements include both the covenant and the prepayment. Traditionally there may have been some logic to this because of the different voting percentages required to waive these provisions. An asset sale covenant can typically be waived by the required lenders, while changes in the prepayment provision historically required the approval of a higher percentage (or all) of the lenders. To avoid, therefore, the required lenders consenting to a sale without imposing a prepayment condition, the asset sale prepayment was inserted. Voting provisions tend no longer to be crafted in this manner, and credit agreements now routinely provide that prepayment requirements, unless they adversely affect one lender or tranche when compared to others, can be modified with the consent of the required lenders. The double treatment of asset sales (as both a prepayment and a covenant) nevertheless continues, perhaps as an acknowledgment by the borrower that a portion of the proceeds of any asset sale is expected to be applied to reduce the loan balance.

Typically, the asset sale prepayment allows the borrower a period within which to reinvest the proceeds before being required to make the prepayment. The reinvestment is normally required to be made into replacement or equivalent assets which provides the lenders some comfort that the sold assets are being replaced with like assets and the collateral base is not being fundamentally altered to their detriment. The covenant sometimes, however, permits the reinvestment to be applied to "capital expenditures" generally (see the discussion regarding capital expenditures in Section 7.4.4.5) or, more expansively, to the purchase of assets useful in the borrower's business. Lenders frequently grant the borrower up to a year to make a reinvestment. It has become increasingly common to allow an extended reinvestment period if the borrower commits within the initial period to make the reinvestment. This additional period may be helpful if the borrower is reinvesting in assets that will be acquired or constructed over time and where payment in full is not required to be made upfront. Only if a reinvestment does not occur within the specified time frame is the borrower required to make a prepayment. In highly leveraged, fully secured deals, it is not uncommon for the borrower to be required to pledge the proceeds to the administrative agent (or collateral agent) pending reinvestment, or to apply the proceeds to revolving credit loans until they are borrowed to make a reinvestment.

In drafting an asset sale prepayment provision, lenders must assure that it is not inconsistent with the asset sale provisions of any outstanding bond indentures. For example, if a bond indenture specifies a reinvestment period of 180 days, the credit agreement should not specify a longer period; otherwise the bonds might be paid before the loans. Similarly, if the bond indenture specifies dollar thresholds over which prepayments are to be made, the dollar thresholds in the credit agreement should not be higher.

A borrower also wants to be alert to the problem that a dollar of asset sale proceeds does not result in two dollars of required prepayments. This could arise if a borrower has an asset sale prepayment in both a credit agreement and one or more bond indentures. The typical solution may already be incorporated into the bond indenture. The latter normally treat any prepayment of credit agreement debt as a deduction from the asset sale proceeds, and thus avoids any double count. However if the borrower has outstanding other debt that is secured on a pari passu basis with the credit agreement, care should be taken to require that only the respective pro rata portions of the asset sale proceeds (rather than 100 percent) be required to make prepayments under the credit agreement and such other debt.

A prepayment is required upon the occurrence of an asset sale only to the extent there are cash proceeds. Many asset sale covenants permit sales (at least in part) for noncash consideration (see Section 7.6.6.2) and the value of that noncash consideration is not taken into account for purposes of the prepayment requirement. The amount of the prepayment required upon the occurrence of an asset sale is customarily equal to a percentage of the "net cash proceeds" of the sale. Net cash proceeds are typically defined as all cash proceeds received by the borrower net of transaction costs (including transfer taxes) and typically also net of income taxes that the borrower anticipates having to pay by reason of the sale. The borrower is sometimes allowed to estimate these taxes in "good faith," even though there may be potential for abuse in that regard. Net cash proceeds may also include promissory notes or deferred installments received in connection with a sale, as and when the cash realized on the notes or installments is actually remitted to the borrower.

4.7.4   Casualty Events

> **Box 4.10**
>
> Not later than _____ days following the receipt by the Borrower of the proceeds of insurance, condemnation award, or other compensation in respect of any Casualty Event affecting any property of the Borrower or any of its Subsidiaries, the Borrower shall apply an amount equal to 100% of such Net Cash Proceeds to the prepayment of the Loans (and cover for Letters of Credit) and the reduction of the Commitments as set forth below; *provided* that, if prior to such date the Borrower shall notify the Administrative Agent that it wishes to reinvest such Net Cash Proceeds into Qualifying Reinvestment Assets, then the Borrower shall be permitted to defer such prepayment, cover and reduction of Commitments for a period of up to 360 days after its receipt of such proceeds (and, if the Borrower shall have committed to reinvest within such 360-day period, such deferral shall be extended for an additional 180 days) and on such 360th day (or, if so committed to be reinvested, on the 180th day following such 360th day) shall be required to make such prepayment, provide such cover and reduce Commitments to the extent that such reinvestment shall not have been made. Such Net Cash Proceeds shall be applied first to the prepayment of outstanding Term Loans and, after repayment in full of all Term Loans, to the prepayment of Revolving Credit Loans and cover for Letters of Credit, and to the reduction of Revolving Credit Commitments.
>
> * * * * * * * *
>
> "*Casualty Event*" means, with respect to any property of any Person, any loss of or damage to, or any condemnation or other taking of, such property for which such Person or any of its Subsidiaries receives insurance proceeds, or proceeds of a condemnation award or other compensation.
>
> "*Net Cash Proceeds*" means, with respect to any Casualty Event, an amount equal to: (a) Cash payments received by Borrower or any of its Subsidiaries from such Casualty Event, *minus* (b) any bona fide direct costs incurred in connection with such Casualty Event, including payment of the outstanding principal amount of, premium, or penalty, if any, and interest on any Debt (other than the Loans) that is secured by a Lien on the stock or assets in question and that is required to be repaid under the terms thereof as a result of such Casualty Event.

A sale of an asset is a voluntary act of the borrower. A casualty event is akin to an involuntary sale of an asset; property of the borrower disappears in exchange (hopefully) for compensation in the form of insurance or condemnation payments. From the perspective of a lender, the two are equivalent and many credit agreements for noninvestment grade borrowers therefore include a mandatory prepayment tied to the involuntary loss of property by the borrower or any of its subsidiaries and that prepayment provision is typically similar to that for an asset sale.

The involuntary disappearance of property can occur in two basic ways. One is through loss or destruction by *force majeure*, or an "Act of God"; for example, a factory burns to the ground or a tornado blows off its roof. The second can occur through a condemnation (referred to often as an exercise by the government of its powers of eminent domain); for example, the local municipality decides to widen a road and so forces a warehouse to be torn down, or wants to build a public park and needs to flatten an office building.

In either of these events, the borrower should be compensated. In the case of a loss or destruction of property, it should receive proceeds of casualty insurance. In fact, the lenders, pursuant to an insurance covenant (see Section 7.5.3), are likely to have required the borrower to maintain sufficient insurance to protect itself (and the lender) against unforeseen destruction of property. In the case of property subject to a lien, the administrative agent is normally also a named loss payee on the insurance policy itself so that the cash proceeds of the loss or destruction are paid directly to the lender. In the case of a condemnation, the government is required to provide "just compensation" for the taking of the property, though what compensation is just for these purposes is often the subject of negotiation and litigation. Nevertheless, whatever is paid to the borrower by the relevant government agency will be available for prepayment of the loans.

As with an asset sale, it is customary in a casualty event prepayment to allow the borrower a period of time in which to replace the lost asset (see the sample language in Box 4.10). Some credit agreements go further and permit the borrower to simply invest the proceeds into similar assets rather than replace the particular assets lost or destroyed.

4.7.5 Debt and Equity Issuances

Box 4.11

Upon any Equity Issuance or Debt Incurrence [if after giving effect thereto the [*Leverage Ratio*] shall be _____ to 1 or greater], the Borrower shall prepay the Loans (and provide cover for Letters of Credit), and reduce the Commitments as set forth below, in an aggregate amount equal to _____ % of the Net Cash Proceeds of such Equity Issuance and 100% of the Net Cash Proceeds of such Debt Incurrence, *provided* that, notwithstanding the foregoing, the Borrower shall not be required to make a prepayment under this clause to the extent that (A) the Borrower advises the Administrative Agent at the time of the relevant event that it intends to use such Net Cash Proceeds to finance one or more acquisitions pursuant to Section [*Acquisitions*], (B) such Net Cash Proceeds are held by the Borrower in a segregated investment or other account (or, alternatively, applied to the prepayment of Revolving Credit Loans) until so used to finance one or more acquisitions as contemplated above), and (C) such Net Available Proceeds are in fact so applied to such acquisition(s) within _____ days of such event or applied to the prepayment of Loans and cover for Letters of Credit, and to the reduction of Commitments as provided above. Such Net Cash Proceeds shall be applied first to the prepayment of outstanding Term Loans and, after repayment in full of all Term Loans, to the prepayment of Revolving Credit Loans and cover for Letters of Credit and to the reduction of Revolving Credit Commitments.

* * * * * * * *

"*Debt Incurrence*" means the incurrence by the Borrower or any of its Subsidiaries after the Effective Date of any Debt, other than. . . .

"*Equity Issuance*" means any issuance or sale by the Borrower after the Effective Date of (i) any of its capital stock, (ii) any warrants or options exercisable in respect of its capital stock (other than any warrants or options issued to directors, officers, or employees of the Borrower or any of its Subsidiaries pursuant to employee benefit plans established in the ordinary course of business and any capital stock of the Borrower issued upon the exercise of such warrants or options) or (iii) any other security or instrument representing an equity interest (or the right to obtain any equity interest) in the Borrower.

"*Net Cash Proceeds*" means, in the case of any Equity Issuance or Debt Incurrence, the aggregate amount of all cash received by the Borrower and its Subsidiaries in respect of such Equity Issuance or Debt Incurrence, as applicable, net of reasonable expenses incurred by the Borrower and its Subsidiaries in connection therewith.

Issuance of equity is rarely restricted by the covenants in a credit agreement. In contrast, issuance of additional debt is routinely constrained by debt covenants or leverage ratios. Yet, despite the different attitudes that lenders may have toward equity and debt, in highly leveraged deals for noninvestment grade borrowers mandatory prepayments tied to the issuance of equity and debt are not uncommon.

Much of the logic behind these two prepayment triggers is visceral. The lender reasons that if it is going to stick its neck out for a borrower leveraged to the hilt, any unexpected cash coming in after the closing ought to prepay the loans. Stated another way, apart from running its business, the lenders feel (and expect the agreement to reflect) that the sole objective of the borrower in a highly leveraged transaction is to reduce its debt as quickly as possible. Since the lenders always view the credit agreement as sitting at the top of the capital structure food chain, they expect the loans to have first claim on that unexpected cash.

As set out in the language in Box 4.11, the prepayment applies only to *cash* proceeds. Accordingly, if newly issued equity of the borrower is used as currency for an acquisition, no prepayment results, since no cash proceeds are yielded to the borrower. The same applies for debt issued to the seller of property (though the debt and leverage covenants are likely to limit the incurrence of additional debt used for that purpose).

Apart from a lender simply wanting to be prepaid as fast as possible after closing, there are other reasons why these prepayments are often seen in credit agreements for highly leveraged borrowers. In the case of an equity issuance, for example, the lenders may perceive that there is limited capacity for the borrower to issue stock before it becomes so diluted that additional issuances are no longer available.

In the case of the incurrence of debt, the lenders want to ensure that any extraordinary issuance of debt (even if permitted by the covenant) does not result in an aggregate increase of leverage. As new debt comes in the front door, the lenders want the proceeds simultaneously to exit the back door in the form of a permanent reduction of the loan balance. The lenders want this notwithstanding that the incurrence of additional debt is likely already controlled by the negative covenants or financial ratios, and the lenders could always (as with asset sales) require prepayment as a condition to their consent of an incurrence not otherwise allowed. The prepayment provision is included as a form of up-front acknowledgment by the borrower that it is the expectation of all parties that the lenders will be prepaid. The acknowledgment avoids the argument that the request for prepayment is a new (arguably unreasonable) condition the lenders are imposing as the price of their approval.

Some credit agreements are so-called "bridge" facilities, which is to say that the borrowing of the loans is an interim measure bridging to a more permanent issuance of debt or equity. In this circumstance, therefore, the mandatory prepayment is simply designed to ensure that the credit facility functions as a short-term agreement. Another way to accomplish the same goal, of course, would be simply to shorten the maturity of one or more tranches of the facility to six months or a year, forcing the borrower to refinance those tranches as quickly as possible from equity or replacement debt.

Several carveouts are often seen in the equity/debt issuance prepayment. First, at least in respect of the issuance of equity, it is not uncommon for only a portion (less than 100 percent) of the proceeds of the issuance to be applied to the prepayment of the loans. The sample language in Box 4.11 takes this approach. Some of the logic here is that a potential purchaser of equity may not want to invest in the borrower if 100 percent of the proceeds are going to retire debt rather than be made available for capital expenditures or other investments in the business of the borrower. Many credit agreements do not include an equity issuance prepayment at all, particularly where the borrower is a public company or where it is owned by a private equity sponsor that wants the ability to make ongoing equity investments to finance the borrower's ongoing business operations or growth. Second, in the case of both equity and debt, the borrower may want to have the ability to apply the proceeds to consummate an acquisition or make other strategic investments. Finally, it is not uncommon for the entire prepayment requirement to fall away once a leverage or other ratio is reduced below an agreed level.

4.7.6 Excess Cash Flow/Cash Sweep

Box 4.12

Not later than _____ Business Days after the delivery by the Borrower of its annual audited financial statements pursuant to Section [*Financial Statements*] for each fiscal year of the Borrower ending on or after _____, 20 _____, the Borrower will prepay the Loans (and provide cover for Letters of Credit) and reduce the Commitments as set forth below in an aggregate amount equal to the excess of (i) the ECF Percentage of the Excess Cash Flow for such fiscal year over (ii) the sum of (x) all optional prepayments of the Term Loans made during such fiscal year and (y) the aggregate amount of all prepayments of Revolving Credit Loans made during such fiscal year occurring after the Term Loans have been paid in full to the extent accompanied by permanent optional reductions of the Commitments. Such percentage of Excess Cash Flow shall be applied first to the prepayment of outstanding Term Loans and, after repayment in full of all Term Loans, to the prepayment of Revolving

Credit Loans and cover for Letters of Credit, and to the reduction of Revolving Credit Commitments.

* * * * * * * *

"ECF Percentage" means, for any fiscal year of the Borrower, (a) [75]%, if on the last day of such fiscal year the Leverage Ratio shall be greater than ____ to 1, (b) [50]%, if on the last day of such fiscal year the Leverage Ratio shall be greater than ____ to 1 but less than or equal to ____ to 1, (c) [25]% , if on the last day of such fiscal year the Leverage Ratio shall be greater than ____ to 1 but less than or equal to ____ to 1, and (d) [0]%, if on the last day of such fiscal year the Leverage Ratio shall be less than or equal to ____ to 1.

"Excess Cash Flow" means, for any period, the excess of (a) EBITDA for such period over (b) the sum of (i) Capital Expenditures made during such period plus (ii) the aggregate amount of Debt Service for such period *plus* (iii) the Tax Payment Amount for such period plus (iv) any decreases (or minus any increases) in Working Capital from the first day to the last day of such period.

For highly leveraged borrowers, a lender reasons that if it stretches its normal credit criteria to the limit, the borrower ought to return the favor when it begins to flourish by applying a portion of its "excess" cash flow to repay the loans. It is not unusual to see the excess cash flow prepayment requirement step down and ultimately fall away if a leverage or other ratio is reduced below an agreed level (as is shown in the language in Box 4.12).

The prepayment provision typically requires that a specified percentage (the number is strictly up for negotiation, although a fixed percentage or, in the case of a provision that steps down, a starting percentage of 50 percent or 75 percent is common) of the borrower's excess cash flow for an agreed accounting period is applied to prepay outstanding term loans. Contrast this with the asset sale, casualty event, and debt and equity prepayments which are discussed above and which each generally requires 100 percent prepayment though the exact percentage may be a topic of negotiation. (As shown in the language in Box 4.12, the covenant does not usually require application of prepayments to revolving loans, or reduction of revolving commitments, until after all term loans are paid in full.) Normally, to avoid the effects of seasonality, the relevant accounting period is the borrower's fiscal year with the actual prepayment being required to be made only after the financial statements for that year have been prepared and excess cash flow can be definitively calculated.

The key to the prepayment is to define what cash flow should be treated as "excess." The object is to determine the amount of cash the borrower generates that it truly needs to operate its business and to treat any additional cash as excess and, therefore, subject to the prepayment requirement. Many hours of lender diligence and borrower-lender negotiation can be spent on this topic. The typical starting point is the borrower's earnings or what the accountants refer to as "EBITDA." EBITDA is shorthand for "earnings before interest, taxes, depreciation, and amortization," and, in most cases, it represents a good proxy for the cash thrown off by the borrower's business *operations* (excluding, therefore, non-operation-related revenues and costs, such as financing costs and taxes). Adjustments are then made to EBITDA to arrive at a suitable "excess cash flow" for the borrower's particular business, in other words by allowing the borrower to *deduct* from EBITDA those cash needs that should trump prepayment of the loans. Typical deductions include capital expenditures, interest, and taxes, and scheduled principal payments.

Sometimes scheduled dividend payments are subtracted as well, particularly if the dividend payments relate to preferred stock that, if not paid, will either result in a bump-up of dividend rates or other monetary costs, or grant the holders of the preferred stock representation on the borrower's board of directors. Noncash accounting expenses (such as any charge for stock option plans that reduce EBITDA) might be *added* to arrive at the true excess cash thrown off by the borrower's business. The sample definition set out above also picks up changes in working capital (see the discussion in Section 7.4.3 on the meaning of working capital). If working capital increases from the beginning to the end of the year, excess cash flow is reduced and, conversely, if working capital decreases, excess cash flow increases. The result of all of these additions and subtractions then becomes the "excess cash flow" to be divided between the borrower and the lenders. It is not unusual in credit agreements for borrowers owned by private equity sponsors for the definitions of the terms "excess cash flow" and "EBITDA" each to run for multiple pages. A recent trend in credit agreements for such borrowers is for the excess cash flow formula to start with consolidated net income rather than EBITDA. The negotiating dynamic with such borrowers allows them, in a way, to have their cake and eat it too—by starting with consolidated net income for both defined terms and adding numerous items to arrive at a larger amount for EBITDA (which borrowers want to be a higher figure because it improves the calculation of financial ratios), while subtracting numerous items to arrive at a smaller amount for excess cash flow (which borrowers want to be a lower figure to result in a smaller prepayment obligation).

One of the issues that any excess cash flow prepayment provision should address (not all credit agreements do) is how to treat voluntary prepayments of term loans made during the fiscal period for which excess cash flow is calculated. Should voluntary prepayments be treated as a credit against the required prepayment? The answer for both borrowers and lenders should be yes. Particularly if no revolving credit loans are outstanding that can be temporarily prepaid and later reborrowed, the borrower will likely want any voluntary prepayment to reduce the mandatory prepayment. Otherwise, a prepayment of term loans that it makes in July has to be made again in March when the excess cash flow calculation is run. Absent a credit, there would be a strong disincentive for the borrower to tender the prepayment in July even though, for a variety of reasons, including saving itself interest costs and improving leverage ratios, it might otherwise wish to do so. Similarly, the lenders should want to remove any disincentive to a prepayment—better to get the cash today than await an uncertain tomorrow. The solution (illustrated in the sample language in Box 4.12) is to grant the borrower a full dollar-for-dollar credit for any voluntary prepayment made during the excess cash flow calculation period. Thus, a $1,000,000 voluntary prepayment of term loans in July reduces by $1,000,000 the mandatory term loan prepayment in March, when the excess cash flow prepayment comes due.

Some borrowers also seek to reduce the amount of the required excess cash flow prepayment by the amount of voluntary prepayments made during the fiscal period for which excess cash flow is calculated for other debt that is secured on a pari passu basis with the credit agreement. The logic here is not compelling. In the absence of a voluntary prepayment of the other debt, the borrower would have had to make a mandatory prepayment under the credit agreement with a like amount of excess cash flow. Unlike the example described in the preceding paragraph in which the difference was one of timing, the reduction here permits the borrower to change the amount of the prepayment obligation owing to one creditor group as a result of a prepayment made to another creditor group. While lenders resist this, on occasion borrowers owned by private equity sponsors successfully negotiate to include it.

4.7.7 Change of Control

Box 4.13

Upon the occurrence of any Change in Control, the Borrower shall prepay the Loans (and provide cover for Letters of Credit) in full and reduce the Commitments to zero.

* * * * * * * *

"Change in Control" means (a) the acquisition of ownership, directly or indirectly, beneficially or of record, by any Person or group (within the meaning of the Securities Exchange Act of 1934 and the rules of the Securities and Exchange Commission there-under as in effect on the date hereof) [other than the Grandfathered Shareholders], of Equity Interests representing more than [_____]% of the aggregate ordinary voting power represented by the issued and outstanding Equity Interests of the Borrower; (b) a majority of the seats (other than vacant seats) on the board of directors of the Borrower shall be occupied by Persons who were neither (i) nominated by the board of directors of the Borrower nor (ii) appointed by directors so nominated; or (c) the acquisition of direct or indirect Control of the Borrower by any Person or group [other than the Grandfathered Shareholders].

One of the fundamental principles of sound banking is the "know your customer" rule. Knowing the customer includes knowing who ultimately controls the customer. This principle is the genesis of the change of control provision in the typical credit agreement. If control of the customer devolves upon a new entity, the lenders may want the right to exit the facility.

Credit agreements vary as to whether a change of control is an event of default or a mandatory prepayment event. Traditionally, change of control protection was reflected as an event of default. However, since the borrower may regard the event as being outside its control, it may prefer that a change of control be a prepayment event rather than a default. There is little substantive difference, though it may look better if it is a prepayment event. By contrast, the near-uniform practice in bond indentures is to require the issuer to make an offer to prepay upon the occurrence of a change of control rather than have it trigger a default.

A change of control can be defined in several ways. One approach is to mandate that existing shareholders continue to hold a minimum percentage of the borrower's total equity. Another approach is to trigger the change of control when one or a group of shareholders, other than the controlling shareholders at the inception of the deal, acquires a specified percentage of the outstanding shares, or a percentage greater than that held by the existing shareholders. It can also be triggered if a majority of the board of directors is replaced by new directors not approved by the existing board. Depending upon whether the borrower is a privately held company or a public company, there is some customary variation as to which of these approaches is used.

In the case of a privately owned company, the lenders are most concerned with the continued influence and ownership stake of the existing equity holders, the presumption being that they can trust their integrity, competence, strategy, policies, and management style; the lenders will not want them replaced without their concurrence. In many cases, therefore, the "change of control" definition may simply focus on voting power (and not factor in any nonvoting equity) by ensuring that the current shareholders maintain a minimum percentage or that their voting percentage not be exceeded by another shareholder or group. In other cases, the lenders may factor in a nonvoting equity stake by requiring that the existing owners continue to have sufficient "skin in the game." Depending upon the amount of proceeds paid to the existing owners, the prepayment or default could be triggered even upon a sale of nonvoting stock. The theory here is that if the sponsor or investor has already realized its target return on the investment, it may have less incentive to support (or focus management attention on) the borrower.

In the case of a public company, the definition is normally triggered if any person or group obtains control by acquiring a percentage of the outstanding shares greater than a negotiated threshold (typically, 20 percent to 30 percent). The assumption is that so long as the borrower's shares are widely held, its character will not change. A change of control in a public company may also be triggered by changes to the board of directors, such as if a majority of the board cease to be "continuing directors" (usually defined as new directors that have been approved by incumbent directors). This might occur if a competing shareholder or group were to attempt to take over the borrower through a proxy fight, and as a result the continuing directors prong of a change of control is commonly referred to as a "proxy put."

Although the concept of a change of control provision sounds entirely lender favorable (and borrower hostile), certain classes of borrowers may actually want a change of control provision to be included in a credit agreement, viewing it as a form of "poison pill"—another hurdle that a potential acquirer of the borrower would need to overcome if it wanted to make a hostile bid for the borrower.

A number of recent cases in Delaware have addressed proxy puts. In *San Antonio Fire & Police Pension Fund v. Amylin Pharmaceuticals, Inc.*, 983 A.2d 304 (Del. Ch. 2009), the Delaware Court of Chancery construed a proxy put in an indenture. The court found that the board of directors may approve the nomination of a slate of directors proposed by dissident shareholders in order to avoid triggering a change of control under the indenture, while at the same time opposing the election of those same nominees and instead endorsing its own slate of nominees, as long as the directors take such action in conformity with the indenture's implied covenant of good faith and fair dealing and in accordance with their normal fiduciary duties.

In *Kallick v. SandRidge Energy, Inc.*, 68 A.3d 242 (Del. Ch. 2013), the Delaware Court of Chancery construed a proxy put in both a credit agreement and an indenture. The court took *Amylin* a step further and ruled that "where an incumbent board cannot identify that there is a specific and substantial risk to the corporation or its creditors posed by the rival [dissident] slate, and approval of that slate would therefore not be a breach of the contractual duty of good faith owed to noteholders with the rights to the proxy put, the incumbent board *must* approve the new directors as a matter of its obligations to the company and its stockholders, even if it believes itself to be better qualified and have better plans for the corporation than the rival slate." (Emphasis added.) Failure to do so is likely a breach by the incumbent directors of their fiduciary duties.

In *Pontiac Gen. Employees Ret. Sys. v. Healthways, Inc.*, C.A. No. 9789-VCL (Del. Ch. 2014) (transcript ruling), the Delaware Court of Chancery construed a so-called "dead-hand" proxy put in a credit agreement for Healthways, Inc. In a dead-hand proxy put, the dissident slate of directors cannot be "continuing directors" even if approved by the incumbent directors if that slate was initially nominated as the result of an actual or threatened proxy solicitation. Thus, the incumbent board is unable to take action such as that taken in *Amylin* and *SandRidge* to avoid the occurrence of a change of control under the credit agreement. The case involved a suit against the incumbent directors for breach of fiduciary duty for agreeing to the inclusion of the dead-hand proxy put in the credit agreement and against the administrative agent under the credit agreement for aiding and abetting the fiduciary duty breach. The court noted (alluding to *Amylin* and *SandRidge*) that "[t]here was ample precedent from this Court putting lenders on notice that these provisions were highly suspect and could potentially lead to a breach of duty on the part of the fiduciaries who were the counter-parties to a negotiation over the credit agreement."

In the wake of *Healthways*, there have been several similar cases brought against the directors of and lenders to public companies that have credit agreements or indentures that contain dead-hand proxy puts. As a result, many banks have eliminated the use of these proxy puts, in some cases altogether, but more commonly just the dead-hand variety, to minimize the risk of being involved in litigation.

4.7.8 Currency Adjustments in Multicurrency Deals

Box 4.14

The Administrative Agent will determine the Dollar Amount of (i) each Loan as of the date three Business Days prior to the Borrowing Date or, if applicable, the date of conversion or continuation thereof, and (ii) all outstanding Loans as of the last Business Day of each quarter and other Business Day elected by the Administrative Agent in its discretion or upon instruction by the Required Lenders. Each day as of which the Administrative Agent determines Dollar Amounts as described in the preceding sentence is herein described as a *"Computation Date."* If at any time the Dollar Amount of all outstanding Loans (calculated, for Loans denominated in an Agreed Foreign Currency, as of the most recent Computation Date with respect to such Loans) exceeds 105% of the aggregate amount of the Revolving Credit Commitments, the Borrower shall immediately repay Loans and provide cover for Letters of Credit in an aggregate principal amount sufficient to cause the remaining outstanding Loans and Letter of Credit Exposure not to exceed the aggregate amount of the Revolving Credit Commitments.

****

"Dollar Amount" of any Agreed Foreign Currency at any date means the equivalent in Dollars of the amount of such currency, on the basis of the rate at which such currency may be exchanged into Dollars on such date at the [Relevant Time] on the Reuters Currency pages for such currency.

Lenders do not like comparing apples and oranges any more than you or I do. If a commitment is expressed in dollars, but contemplates that loans can be made in Euros, the lenders nevertheless want to think in dollars. They want the amount of each Euro loan to be measured in dollars. Compare apples to apples; convert Euros to dollars and then compare the "dollarfied" Euros to dollars.

This is the purpose of the currency adjustment prepayment. As with a credit agreement for dollars only, a domestic U.S. credit agreement with a tranche available in both dollars and one or more other currencies normally delineates the amount of the tranche by reference to a dollar commitment level. Consequently, although loans may be available in Euros, the credit agreement typically stipulates that if the commitments total $100,000,000 the borrower can borrow Euros only so long as the total of the dollar equivalent of the Euros plus the dollar amount of the dollar loans does not exceed $100,000,000. This ensures that the total exposure is consistent with the credit approvals obtained internally by each lender at the inception of the loan.

What happens if the dollar equivalent of Euros increases after a loan is made so that the total exposure increases above $100,000,000? Euros could start out at an exchange ratio of one dollar to one Euro and increase later to a ratio of 1.40 dollars to Euro. What was initially an exposure of $100,000,000 (€100,000,000 = $100,000,000 at a 1 to 1 exchange ratio) becomes $140,000,000 (€100,000,000 = $140,000,000 at a 1.4 to 1 exchange ratio). The aggregate dollar exposure of the lenders has effectively been increased.

To address this risk, when a tranche allows loans to be made in more than one currency, a credit agreement customarily requires a periodic recalculation (typically quarterly, but sometimes more frequently, or at every borrowing) of the aggregate amount of loans and letters of credit. The recalculation takes into account any fluctuations in currency values. The normal approach (such as illustrated in the sample language in Box 4.14) is to require a prepayment be made down to an exposure level equal to 100 percent of the commitment amount, but only to the extent that the aggregate exposure upon recalculation exceeds 105 percent of the commitment amount. Taking the example above, once the dollar/Euro exchange rate exceeds 1.05 to 1 and the dollar exposure therefore increases to above $105,000,000, the borrower is required to prepay some portion of the loans (or, if there were letters of credit, to terminate or provide cover for the letters of credit) so that the total exposure does not exceed the aggregate commitment level of $100,000,000.

The currency adjustment prepayment does *not* apply if the particular tranche contemplates loans be made only in a single foreign currency. In this case, it is presumed that the initial credit approval of the lenders was couched in terms of that particular foreign currency and, therefore, no exposure adjustment is necessary.

4.8 ALLOCATION OF PREPAYMENTS

> **Box 4.15**
>
> Prepayments and/or reductions of Commitments pursuant to this Section [*Mandatory Prepayments*] shall be applied as follows: *first*, ratably among the Tranches of Term Loans in accordance with their respective outstanding principal amounts and *second*, after the payment in full of the Term Loans, to reduce the aggregate amount of the Revolving Credit Commitments (and to the extent that, after giving effect to such reduction, the aggregate principal amount of the Revolving Credit Exposure shall exceed the Revolving Credit Commitments, the Borrower shall first prepay Revolving Credit Loans, and second provide cover for Letters of Credit, in an aggregate amount equal to such excess). Each such prepayment of Term Loans shall be applied to the installments thereof in inverse order of maturity.

Credit agreements thrive on specificity. Spelling out the mandatory prepayments to be made as time passes without identifying the particular loans to which the prepayment is applied is not sufficient in a credit agreement with both revolving and term loan tranches, or with multiple term loan tranches.

The obvious and immediate question is how the prepayment is to be allocated among the different classes of loans. The order of prepayment between tranches is frequently the subject of negotiation, but several considerations are customarily taken into account by the parties in determining an appropriate allocation. For example, in a transaction that includes both a term loan facility and a revolving credit facility, the borrower normally does not want to lose the liquidity afforded by the revolving credit commitments until the last possible moment. As a consequence, the credit agreement customarily provides that all term loans must be paid in full before any reduction of the revolving credit commitments occurs.

In an agreement with multiple term loan tranches, the formula may be more complex, since the borrower must determine whether it prefers to pay first the more expensive, but longer-term, B loan tranches, or the less expensive, but shorter-term, A loan tranches. In an ideal borrower world, the borrower wants the flexibility to pick and choose among the tranches at the time the prepayment is to be made. Frequently, however, in structuring the agreement, the administrative agent or arranger anticipates that the potential syndicate will want certainty as to how any prepayment of term loans is to be allocated among the various tranches.

One common approach is to allocate the payment ratably among the tranches, although in agreements in which a term loan tranche is, in actuality, a bridge to an equity or debt offering, the prepayment is allocated solely to the tranche that functions as a bridge.

If the revolving credit commitments provide for letters of credit, the prepayment provisions also typically specify that revolving credit loans must be paid in full first before any prepayment proceeds are applied to provide cover for letters of credit. Providing cover is, of course, more expensive for the borrower because of the negative arbitrage it entails (see the discussion that follows in Section 4.9).

4.9 COVER FOR LETTERS OF CREDIT

Since letters of credit cannot be unilaterally repaid, a mandatory prepayment with respect to letters of credit must be effected through the borrower's posting cash collateral (or "cover") for its future, contingent reimbursement obligation in respect of the letter of credit (see the discussion in Section 2.1.2.10 for the mechanics of the borrower's providing cover in the context of prepayments).

4.10 PREPAYMENT OPT OUTS

> ### Box 4.16
>
> If, upon receipt by the Administrative Agent from the Borrower of any notice of any prepayment pursuant to this Section [*Mandatory Prepayments*], there shall be outstanding any Tranche A Term Loans, the Administrative Agent shall deliver a notice of such prepayment to each of the Tranche B Lenders advising each of such Lenders that it shall have the right to decline all or any portion of such prepayment that would otherwise be applied to the Tranche B Term Loans and that any amount so refused will be applied to prepay the Tranche A Term Loans to the extent of the Tranche A Term Loans. The Administrative Agent shall prescribe such procedures as it shall deem appropriate to implement such right to decline any such prepayment.

As noted previously, one of the basic differences between the prepayment provisions of a credit agreement and those of a bond indenture is that in the credit agreement, prepayments work automatically, while in a bond indenture they are often structured as an offer to prepay. In the latter, the holders of the bonds are therefore given the option either to accept the prepayment offer or to decline the offer and continue to hold the bonds. As a consequence, mandatory prepayments in the case of bonds are *optional* on the part of the holders; mandatory prepayments in the case of credit agreements are truly *mandatory*, both for the borrower and the lenders.

One exception to this general rule is sometimes seen in the market: B loan lenders are from time to time given the right to decline or opt out of a mandatory prepayment (but not an optional prepayment). Sometimes (the language in Box 4.16 is an example), the opt-out is granted only if there are A loans outstanding, so that the monies that would otherwise be applied to the B loans are applied instead to the A loans. More commonly, the opt-out is granted whether or not there are A loans outstanding and the borrower is permitted to retain those monies. Whether B loans are afforded this option is strictly a question of negotiation. Borrowers may want to resist the option since it removes some of their flexibility to pay higher interest debt. Nevertheless, if that is the price of syndicating a favorable B loan tranche, they may have little choice.

4.11 PREPAYMENT PREMIUMS

Box 4.17

Hard Call:

Upon any prepayment of Tranche B Term Loans the Borrower shall pay to the holders of such Loans a prepayment premium in respect of the principal amount of such Loans so prepaid in an amount equal to (i) _____% of such principal amount for any prepayment made on or before the first anniversary of the Closing Date and (ii) _____% of such principal amount for any prepayment made after such first anniversary and on or before the second anniversary of the Closing Date. No prepayment premium shall be required pursuant to this paragraph in respect of any prepayment of such Loans made after such second anniversary.

* * * * * * * *

Soft Call:

In the event that all or any portion of the Tranche B Term Loans is (i) repaid, prepaid, refinanced or replaced (including as a result of an assignment pursuant to Section [*Yank-a-Bank*]) or (ii) repriced or effectively refinanced through any waiver, consent or amendment, in each case pursuant to a Repricing Transaction occurring on or prior to the first anniversary of the Closing Date, such repayment, prepayment, refinancing, replacement or repricing will be made at 101.0% of the principal amount so repaid, prepaid, refinanced, replaced or repriced.

* * * * * * * *

"*Repricing Transaction*" means (a) any waiver, consent or amendment to the Tranche B Term Loans directed at, or the result of which would be, the lowering of the effective interest cost or the weighted average yield of the Tranche B Term Loans or (b) the incurrence of any debt financing having an effective interest cost or weighted average yield that is less than the effective interest cost or weighted average yield of the Tranche B Term Loans.

As discussed in Section 3.7.5, bond indentures and private placements traditionally compensate the holders for early prepayment through imposing a prepayment premium. Credit agreements normally take an opposite tack: they do not impose a fee as the price of a prepayment, but instead only look to cover losses with respect to their cost of funds for any current LIBOR interest periods.

As with any discussion that relates to credit agreements, there are exceptions to the general rule, and prepayment premiums for B loan tranches constitute one instance, particularly in second lien credit agreements. In some facilities the borrower is required to pay a premium in respect of B loan tranches upon any early payment of the loans (the language in Box 4.17 under "Hard Call" is an example). B loan prepayment premiums tend to be lower than those in the bond indenture or private placement context, for which premiums may start as high as 5 percent or 6 percent of the amount of the prepayment and descend to zero over a period of years. In a credit agreement, the prepayment premiums for B loans are ordinarily much lower (typically 2 percent descending to 1 percent), and are likely to apply only to prepayments made during the first or second year after the closing. This type of prepayment premium is a so-called "hard call."

It has become common for credit agreements to provide for a prepayment premium for B loans when the source of the prepayment is a refinancing by the borrower with cheaper debt—this approach is a so-called "soft call." The theory behind the soft call is that if the borrower is prepaying B loans from the proceeds of an asset sale, earnings, or cash on hand, it should be free to do so without paying the premium, but that if the borrower is fleeing to cheaper financing it should be required to pay the premium. Typically, the soft call provision is written broadly to pick up not only a true refinancing but also a repricing amendment, and would also be triggered by a forced assignment pursuant to the credit agreement's yank-a-bank provision (discussed in Section 13.3) resulting from a lender's not consenting to the repricing amendment. The language in Box 4.17 under "Soft Call" is an example of a soft-call premium.

4.12 MULTIPLE BORROWERS

Box 4.18

It is the intent of the parties hereto that the Borrowers shall be jointly and severally obligated hereunder and under the Notes, as co-borrowers under this Agreement and as co-makers on the Notes, in respect of the principal of and interest on, and all other amounts owing in respect of, the Loans and the Notes. In that connection, each Borrower hereby (i) jointly and severally and irrevocably and unconditionally accepts, not merely as a surety but also as a co-debtor, joint and several liability with the other Borrowers with respect to the payment and performance of all of the obligations hereunder, it being the intention of the parties hereto that all such obligations shall be the joint and several obligations of each Borrower without preferences or distinction among them and that the obligations of each borrower hereunder shall be unconditional irrespective of any circumstance whatsoever that might otherwise constitute a legal or equitable discharge or defense of a guarantor or surety, and (ii) further agrees that if any of such obligations are not paid in full when due (whether at stated maturity, as a mandatory prepayment or cash collateralization, by acceleration or otherwise), the Borrowers will, jointly and severally, promptly pay the same, without any demand or notice whatsoever. All Borrowers acknowledge and agree that the delivery of funds to any Borrower under this Agreement shall constitute valuable consideration and reasonably equivalent value to all Borrowers for the purpose of binding them and their assets on a joint and several basis for the obligations hereunder.

From a lender's standpoint having a claim against one entity is essential; having a claim against more than one entity is better yet. Normally, the support of additional entities is effected through guarantees (see Chapter 8). Sometimes, however, credit agreements structure the facility not as a loan to a *single* borrower under the guarantee of one or more subsidiaries or parent entities, but instead provide that the loans are deemed made to *multiple* borrowers, with each borrower being jointly and severally obligated to repay all loans. This is sometimes referred to as a "co-borrower arrangement."

There is little practical legal difference between having a single borrower supported by guarantees and having a co-borrower structure, but some believe that the latter may provide a slight advantage under fraudulent conveyance rules (see Section 6.2.7), in that it may be easier to argue that each co-borrower received the full amount of the loan proceeds. Receipt of loan proceeds is one of the bases upon which to defeat a fraudulent conveyance claim. It is unclear that a bankruptcy court would give much credence to this argument if it can be shown that the proceeds, in fact, went to a particular borrower or subsidiary and not to *all* borrowers, but when lenders are looking for even a remote legal advantage, co-borrower structures are not uncommon.

There are also instances, such as on occasion when a non-U.S. borrower is seeking to raise loan financing, that institutional lenders may require or prefer that there be a U.S. co-borrower. For example, an institutional lender may not be permitted under its organizational documents to own a loan of a Peruvian borrower but can own that same loan if jointly borrowed with a U.S. co-borrower. The use of a U.S. co-borrower in these circumstances makes a loan eligible for investment by the institutional lenders. While the U.S. co-borrower could be another entity in the borrower's corporate group, often the co-borrower is specially formed for that purpose, has no material assets, and does not provide any meaningful credit support for the loan.

CHAPTER 5

Conditions Precedent

5.1 EFFECTIVENESS CONDITIONS

The conditions precedent in a credit agreement are, in essence, a simplified closing list, although given the tendency to detail in more recent credit agreements, they are often neither short nor simple. The conditions specify what documents the borrower must deliver to the lenders (or the administrative agent), what actions it must take, and what other circumstances must exist in order for credit to be available. Customarily, the conditions are broken out into two types: those to be satisfied at closing and those to be satisfied both at closing and at each borrowing or other extension of credit or other extension of credit thereafter (the latter are the so-called "ongoing conditions").

Normally, a majority vote is required to waive any of the conditions precedent, although some credit agreements require unanimity for changes to the closing date conditions. However, unless the lenders have waived a condition, any lender that believes a condition has not been satisfied is legally entitled to decline to lend (and, thereby, pick a fight with the borrower) even if the other lenders believe the condition to have been satisfied. As discussed in Section 2.2.1, a refusal by one lender to make a loan does not by itself affect the obligation of any other lender to make a loan since each lender is *severally* obligated to extend credit under the agreement.

The particular conditions set out in a credit agreement are typically crafted (and negotiated) for the specific credit facility, though certain conditions are so basic that they are contained in nearly every credit agreement. These are conditions that relate to execution of documents, corporate matters, opinions, and the material adverse change (or MAC) condition and are discussed first below. Inclusion of the other conditions discussed below are dependent upon factors such as whether the facility is secured, whether the borrower is organized outside the

United States, whether the proceeds will finance an acquisition, and whether the proceeds of new debt or equity are to be received before the loans are made.

5.1.1 Signing versus Closing

> **Box 5.1**
>
> The obligations of the Lenders to make Loans hereunder shall not become effective until the date on which each of the following conditions is satisfied (or waived in accordance with Section [*Waivers*]): . . .

One final point must be made for a full understanding of conditions precedent. The typical lead-in to the conditions precedent provision (see the sample in Box 5.1) reflects a fiction that underlies most credit agreements, namely that there is a gap in time between the date of the credit agreement (which is typically the date it is executed, but may precede that date) and the date upon which the obligation to lend becomes effective—the "closing date" or "effective date." By way of example, the credit agreement may be dated January 2, but the conditions precedent will be drafted as if they could be satisfied on January 2 or at any time thereafter up to an explicit drop-dead date spelled out in the agreement.

For many credit agreements the idea of a gap between signing and effectiveness is just that: a fiction. The vast majority of credit agreements, even agreements with large syndicates, see signature pages floating into the agent concurrently with the borrower's and arranger's lawyers furiously assembling closing documents. For other credit agreements, the dating convention is real. A credit agreement for a non-U.S. borrower may need to be executed before the closing if delivery of a fully executed agreement is necessary before final foreign exchange approvals or enforceability opinions can be issued. Similarly, a credit agreement that is intended to finance an acquisition may need to be executed in advance of closing if the buyer (the borrower) wants to see the financing locked in before funds are needed for the purchase, which is not uncommon in the United Kingdom (see the discussion of certain funds requirements and interim loan agreements in Section 5.3), but rarely occurs in the United States. In these cases, necessity requires that an agreement be signed in advance of effectiveness or of the initial extension of credit.

5.1.2   Execution; Lender Addenda; Fronting Letters

> **Box 5.2**
>
> The Administrative Agent (or its counsel) shall have received from each party hereto either (i) a counterpart of this Agreement signed on behalf of such party or (ii) written evidence satisfactory to the Administrative Agent (which may include telecopy transmission of a signed signature page of this Agreement) that such party has signed a counterpart of this Agreement. In addition, the Administrative Agent (or its counsel) shall have received from the Borrower and each of its Subsidiaries the following additional documents, in each case signed on behalf of each such Person in a manner satisfactory to the Administrative Agent: _____.

The old maxim "Get it in writing" applies to credit facilities as much as to any other business arrangement. No lender has an appetite to seek enforcement before a judge of an *unsigned* credit agreement. And certainly no lender has patience for a lawyer that does not obtain all necessary signatures. Perhaps the most basic of conditions precedent is therefore the requirement that the credit agreement (and all other related contracts) be executed by all parties before any money is lent.

The language in Box 5.2 is a typical example of this condition. It takes into account the varying methods through which execution of a document can be evidenced to the administrative agent. Physical signature by all parties gathered together in a conference room is, of course, the most obvious. Such a closing, or any closing where originals of documents are exchanged through mail or courier, is generally referred to as a "paper closing." However, although once common practice, in-person closings (or other paper closings), for large syndicated credit facilities at least, are now relatively rare. Today, most closings are accomplished by delivery of e-mail signatures. For a discussion of the validity of documents executed in this way, see Section 12.10.

Large syndicated credit facilities can present some peculiar logistical problems when it comes to executing a credit agreement. Particularly when one of the facilities is a B loan tranche, the lenders themselves may not be identifiable and commitments may not be allocated until just prior to (or, in some cases, the day of) the closing. Even from those so identified, it often cannot be determined until the closing date whether a lender is to execute the agreement or to become a lender by purchasing a piece of the tranche through post-closing assignment from the lead bank or arranger.

Preparing a credit agreement in these circumstances with a full set of signature pages and a completed commitment schedule becomes impossible. A practice that developed to address this issue is the so-called "lender addenda." Lender addenda permit the credit agreement itself (the 150-page document, including the signature pages) to be silent as to who actually provides the B loan tranche. Instead, at least as it relates to that tranche, the credit agreement is executed between the borrower and the administrative agent, and each lender (other than those joining through post-closing assignments) becomes a party to the agreement by signing a separate one-page lender addendum. Under the addendum, the add-on party agrees to be a "lender" under the credit agreement with a "commitment" of the relevant tranche in an amount specified in the addendum. It becomes the addendum there-fore, rather than the credit agreement, that spells out the identity and commitment of each lender.

Delivery of lender addenda is no different in legal effect than returning executed signature pages, except that lender addenda are drafted to refer expressly to the credit agreement (not the case with a mere signature page) and also to specify the amount of the lenders' com-mitments. Lender addenda, in short, are a way to have lenders become original signatories to the credit agreement even up to the last hour or minutes before the closing without having to distribute a changed com-mitment schedule to all lenders on the day of the closing.

The more common practice at the time of this writing is for the arranger or its lending affiliate to fund the entire amount of the B loan tranche and then to sell the B loans by post-closing assignments to the B loan lenders (these lenders are still considered original lenders). If there are multiple arrangers, the lead arranger (or more precisely, the lead left arranger, so-called because its name appears first or farthest to the left on any marketing material listing of the arranger banks) or its lending affiliate will fund the entire amount of the B loan tranche. If the sale of the B loan tranche has not been fully settled to B loan lenders by a specified date after the closing date (30 to 45 days is typical), the other arrangers (or their lending affiliates) will typically be required, pursuant to the terms of a fronting letter agreement entered into by all the arrangers, to purchase from the lead arranger or its lending affiliate their pro rata shares of the B loans (determined based on their com-mitment amounts) subject to any primary trades that have not settled. In this way, the lead arranger is fronting for the other arrangers, but if the syndication of the B loan tranche is not successful, the arrangers as a group will bear that risk. In practice, however, the date by which the primary trades must settle is often extended, instead of requiring the other arrangers to acquire their pro rata shares of the unsettled primary trades. The LSTA has promulgated a form of fronting letter that evidences the agreements of the arrangers to front loans and share the risk of primary allocation with trades that have not settled.

5.1.3 Matters Relating to Organization and Authorization

> **Box 5.3**
>
> The Administrative Agent (or its counsel) shall have received such documents and certificates as the Administrative Agent (or its counsel) may reasonably request relating to the organization, existence and good standing of the Borrower, the authorization of the Transactions and any other legal matters relating to the Borrower, this Agreement, or the Transactions, all in form and substance satisfactory to the Administrative Agent and its counsel.

As discussed in detail in Section 6.1.1, when making a loan, a lender wants its borrower to *exist*—to be alive if an individual and to be an entity with legal life if created by law or statute. The purpose of a credit agreement is not to give money away to the ether, but to *lend* money to a legal entity that can own assets and incur liabilities and that can be sued in court, if it comes to that. For an individual this is easy. The lender simply needs to be satisfied that its borrower is breathing and competent (not a juvenile or mentally impaired) when it establishes the credit.

For a legal entity (a corporation, limited liability company, partnership, or other construct), checking for the regular intake of oxygen and outflow of carbon dioxide will not work. Something different is needed, and this is the rationale behind the condition for matters that relate to organization and authorization. For entities created by law, the lending syndicate wants to know essentially two things: first, that the borrower exists as a legal entity and, second, that it has the legal capacity to sign, and then perform, the credit agreement and has appropriately authorized and executed the credit agreement. These correspond, roughly, to breathing and competence in an individual.

The full list of what must be delivered to establish existence, capacity, and authorization is set out in the detailed closing list prepared by counsel for the borrower and arranger. As illustrated in the language in Box 5.3, the condition precedent that appears in the credit agreement itself describes what needs to be delivered (and what will therefore appear in the closing list) in broad terms. Proof of existence is established through delivery of organizational documents, which, in the case of a U.S. corporation, starts with a certificate of good-standing from the relevant Secretary of State and includes the certificate of incorporation and bylaws and, in the case of a partnership or limited liability company, includes the relevant partnership or limited liability company (or operating) agreement. Proof of capacity and authorization is established through delivery of relevant board or shareholder resolutions coupled with evidence of the incumbency of officers (confirming that the relevant individual has been duly elected as an officer, such as "Vice President for Credit Agreement Finance") and a sample (or specimen) signature of the officer who will execute the credit agreement.

Normally, the documentary elements of the "proofs" described above are set out in a certificate of an officer of the borrower or other obligor, attaching the organizational documents and the relevant board or shareholder resolutions, and setting forth also the statement of incumbency and specimen signatures. Delivery of a false certificate is an event of default. In addition, delivery of a deliberately false certificate to a bank risks a violation of the Federal Bank Fraud statute (18 U.S.C. § 1344), which makes it a felony knowingly to either "defraud a financial institution" or obtain monies or funds "by means of false or fraudulent pretenses, representations, or promises." Violation of the statute could lead to a heavy fine for the borrower and a heavy fine or imprisonment for the falsely certifying officer.

Why should a lender care about seeing evidence of the existence, capacity, and authorization of its corporate, partnership, or limited liability company borrower? If an officer of a corporation, or a general partner of a partnership, signs the agreement is that not sufficient? The answer is *probably* yes. The president of a corporation (or the managing member of a limited liability company or the general partner of a partnership) may well have sufficient authority under general legal principles to bind the borrower, even for a very large financing. However, many credit agreements are not, in fact, signed by the president, managing member, or general partner, but rather by an executive of lower rank, such as a treasurer or chief financial officer. Further, in the case of a corporation, execution of an agreement that is "material" to the borrower normally requires board of directors approval. Board approval is normally also necessary to authorize the *borrowing* of the loans (as distinct from signing the credit agreement and taking on the covenants). For these reasons it is inadvisable for a lending syndicate to rely merely upon the "apparent authority" of a president, managing member, or general partner, and the inclusion of a condition precedent relating to organizational and authority matters is consequently standard in credit agreements.

In the context of an acquisition financing, the target company will typically sign loan documents on the closing date. The target company's board of directors generally will be asked to resign upon the closing of the acquisition and so does not want to authorize (and thereby take fiduciary responsibility for) the loan financing transaction. It is common practice for the individuals who will become the new board of directors to authorize the loan financing transaction prior to actually becoming directors and to deliver that authorization "in escrow"—meaning to be released and to become effective upon the closing of the acquisition, when the current board would resign and the new board would be appointed.

In *U.S. Bank National Association v. Verizon Communications Inc.*, 2012 U.S. Dist. LEXIS 103900 (N.D. Tex. 2012), the court determined that board resolutions could not be signed in advance by incoming board members prior to their actually becoming directors. The court observed that "individuals who have not yet been elected to a corporation's board of directors cannot act as directors. . . . Therefore, actions taken by individuals that are not members of a corporation's board of directors are a nullity. This is true even if these individuals are subsequently appointed as members of the board of directors."

For a time, the *Verizon* decision resulted in a more cumbersome closing process for acquisition financing transactions. In response to the *Verizon* decision, the Delaware General Assembly amended the Delaware General Corporation Law effective August 1, 2014, to permit board consents to be signed by persons who are not at the time directors, be placed in escrow, and then be released from escrow and become effective when those persons subsequently become directors.

5.1.4 *Opinions*

Box 5.4

The Administrative Agent shall have received (a) a favorable written opinion (addressed to the Administrative Agent and the Lenders and dated the Effective Date) of _____, counsel for the Borrower, substantially in the form of Exhibit _____, and covering such other matters relating to the Borrower, this Agreement and the transactions contemplated hereby as the Administrative Agent or its counsel shall reasonably request (and the Borrower hereby instructs such counsel to deliver such opinion to the Lenders and the Administrative Agent) and (b) a written opinion (also addressed to the Administrative Agent and the Lenders and dated the Effective Date), of counsel for the Administrative Agent, substantially in the form of Exhibit _____.

Everybody loves to hate the attorneys. Shakespeare even penned, "The first thing we do, let's kill all the lawyers" (*King Henry VI*, Act 4, Scene 2). Of course, Shakespeare probably never saw a large, syndicated credit facility or he might have said let's kill all the lawyers *after they first render their legal opinions*. Legal opinions are, in one sense, the capstone for the credit agreement. Once the lawyers have spent hours and hours negotiating and then drafting the agreement, formal written opinions are a way to have them confirm that the result of all that effort was worthwhile—that the agreement is legal and enforceable, that the borrower exists and has authorized all documents, that all necessary government approvals have been obtained, and so on. A large body of literature spells out what opinions should say and what they mean. It is not the purpose of this volume to substitute for that learning, but rather to explain briefly the opinion requirements that appear in virtually every credit agreement as a condition to closing.

This condition precedent typically mandates delivery of a legal opinion from counsel to the borrower and (although less frequently in U.S.-based financings) from counsel to the administrative agent or lead bank. The sample language in Box 5.4 is consistent with the two-opinion approach. The opinion rendered by the borrower's counsel will cover matters such as the due organization of the borrower, its power to enter into the financing, its authorization of the transaction, and the like ("corporate" matters), as well as the legality, validity, binding effect, and enforceability of the agreement (collectively, *enforceability*). Normally, if the borrower has retained outside counsel to assist in connection with the credit agreement, the outside counsel renders the opinion. Sometimes, however, all or a portion of the borrower's opinion is given by the borrower's internal counsel. When in-house counsel provides the opinion, it is most often with respect to issues over which he or she may have peculiar competence, such as matters that relate to the due organization of the borrower or due authorization of the transaction, or the absence of conflicts with other contracts. Receipt of an opinion from in-house counsel is generally acceptable to the lenders, given that inside counsel is, in most cases, likely to have greater day-to-day familiarity with such issues. Nonetheless, the independence of outside counsel is an important countervailing factor that tends to argue for an outside opinion. In addition, if the borrower has a large legal department, the lenders may be uncomfortable accepting an opinion from a relatively junior staff attorney.

The second opinion, if the conditions provide for one, is given by the firm identified as legal counsel to the administrative agent or the lead bank and is typically limited to the question of enforceability as described above. This opinion can be particularly important in cases where the agreement is governed by a law normally applicable to the lead lender's agreement (such as New York or California), but when borrower's counsel is not admitted in that jurisdiction and, therefore, may not speak to that law. An opinion from the borrower's Kansas counsel that a New York law credit agreement is enforceable is useful, particularly if enforcement is sought in Kansas, but it is generally not considered sufficient for the lending syndicate which wants to know that the New York law agreement is enforceable under New York law. The opinion from counsel to the administrative agent or lead lender fills this void. Although the sample condition precedent set out in Box 5.4 includes an express requirement for an agent or lead bank legal opinion, many credit agreements are silent. This can mean one of two things. It can mean that, although the opinion will be issued, it is not a condition to the lenders' obligations to extend credit. It can also mean, as is becoming the more frequent practice, that no opinion from counsel for the lenders (or the agent) will be issued at all.

Legal opinions always speak as of their date, and the opining firm has no obligation to update the opinion unless it otherwise agrees to do so. This sometimes leads to the question of what that date should be: the date of *execution* of the agreement or the date of the *closing* (when the first loans are made)? Traditionally, the date of all opinions was the date of closing, the theory being that the important event for the lenders was the date they forked over the money, not the date the borrower signed the closing documents. Nevertheless, traditional practice has evolved over the years so that the execution date (or effective date) is now often used, regardless of whether any credit is extended on that date.

Typically, the proposed forms of legal opinion are attached to the credit agreement as exhibits. This helps assure that the lenders are aware of their content prior to signing, and provides certainty to the borrower that an opinion in the prescribed form satisfies the conditions. It also results in buy-in from the borrower and its counsel that they are actually able to render the opinion. Sometimes, however, as in the sample language in Box 5.4, the condition may contemplate that additional issues will be covered if *reasonably* requested by the administrative agent or its counsel. The logic here is simple, although not always acceded to by borrowers. By way of illustration, if upon review of the closing documents the agent's counsel discovers ambiguous language in the borrower's charter or bylaws, or perhaps confusing language in the resolutions, it may want the borrower's opinion to address expressly the ambiguity. Ideally, of course, the agent's counsel will have reviewed all of these documents in advance of the opinion exhibit form being finalized, but this is not always the case. The requirement that any request be *reasonable* is intended to protect the borrower against the agent or lenders (or their counsel) effectively ignoring the exhibit form.

What issues the opinions cover are not set in stone. The required scope can expand with the circumstances of particular financings. If there are ancillary agreements, such as guarantees and security agreements, the closing opinions are expected to cover them. If collateral security is being granted, the opinions are expected to address the matters discussed in the second paragraph below. If material borrower parties (including guarantors) are in multiple jurisdictions, the lenders are likely to want opinions to cover each relevant jurisdiction. If the borrower is a regulated entity, such as an electric utility, the opinion will confirm that all appropriate agency approvals have been obtained. An opinion may be required to cover the status of the borrower under the Investment Company Act of 1940, matters that relate to the Federal Communications Act, or issues that arise under other regulatory statutes. And if the borrower is located in a foreign country, a raft of other opinions enters the fray, such as the ability of the lenders to sue the borrower in New York and to export a judgment from New York to the foreign country without having the courts in the foreign country reexamine issues from scratch.

The language of the typical closing opinion is the product of many years of developing custom elaborated upon in the literature referred to earlier. In addition, opinion givers endeavor to ensure that the scope and language of their opinions are consistent with customary practice as well as with their internal policies (most law firms have opinion committees that establish what may be said in a closing opinion and what due diligence is required to say it). Among the principal sources of opinion practice today are published reports by New York's "TriBar" Opinion Committee, which began its existence as a group formed by three New York bar associations, but which today includes representatives from a number of states and Canada. Despite the emphasis on customary practice, however, there is still considerable divergence in approach from one law firm to another, and discussion of opinion forms for a particular transaction is often needed.

In a secured credit facility, a number of specialized opinions have become customary. Thus, an opinion may be required to confirm the *creation* of the relevant security interests (a "creation" opinion is regarded as distinct from an opinion that the security agreement is enforceable), sometimes to confirm the *perfection* of the security interests (although such opinions require a host of exceptions and qualifications), and in rare cases to address the *priority* of the security interests. The manner in which a security interest is perfected, and which law governs its perfection, varies with the kind of collateral involved and various other factors. In addition, the question of perfection of a security interest is not necessarily governed by the same law that determines the enforceability of the credit agreement or even of the security agreement itself. As a consequence, many law firms are reluctant to render legal opinions on either the perfection or the priority of a security interest. There are, however, some limited exceptions: for example, an opinion may be given that the pledgee of certificated securities is, subject to certain assumptions, a "protected purchaser" as that term is defined in Article 8 of the Uniform Commercial Code (an opinion that is equivalent to a first-priority perfected lien opinion).

Legal opinions express legal conclusions and do not generally cover factual matters, such as the accuracy or completeness of financial statements. One exception is the so-called no-litigation opinion, in which the opinion giver confirms that there is no pending or threatened litigation or proceedings against the client. However, past litigation (see *Dean Foods Co. v. Pappathanasi*, 18 Mass. L. Rep. 598 (Super. Ct. Suffolk County 2004)) against law firms with respect to no-litigation opinions has made such opinions, at least by outside counsel, a rare phenomenon, and many firms will not give them under any circumstances. (So-called negative assurance in 10b-5 opinions in connection with securities transactions and law firm responses to audit letters, each of which may address the question of material litigation, involve considerations that are not present in the typical loan financing, and are beyond the scope of this chapter.)

Opinions are typically addressed to the administrative agent, the collateral agent (if the financing is secured), and the lenders. The historical practice (at least in the United States) has been for all lenders (whether lenders at closing or that subsequently become lenders) to be addressees. However, there are some firms that limit (or attempt to limit) the opinion addressees to those lenders that are party to the credit agreement at closing or who become lenders within a short post-closing period such as 90 days (to allow for lenders, such as B loan lenders, who acquire their loans following the closing to have the benefit of the opinion). This practice is common in Europe, but is less commonly accepted in the United States. Some firms, rather than addressing their opinion to all lenders, will limit the opinion addressees to closing date lenders but then permit subsequent lenders to rely on the opinion. Such a distinction is simply a matter of form over substance. Still other firms will permit reliance by subsequent lenders only if reliance is "actual and reasonable" at the time and based upon then existing circumstances and the knowledge of the assignee. The latter formulation is intended to limit the ability of an assignee in a distressed scenario to become a lender with the intention of buying a cause of action against the opining firm.

The rationale for obtaining legal opinions at a credit agreement closing is not solely to give the lenders a law firm to sue in the event that the conclusions set out in the opinion are incorrect. Many other considerations come into play. Delivering an opinion forces the opinion giver to go through a due diligence process that ideally has the beneficial result of making the conclusions accurate by, for example, forcing any corporate deficiencies to be fixed, clarifying board resolutions, obtaining necessary third-party consents, and the like. It is not enough, in other words, that the opinion giver believes that a legal conclusion is correct; it is more important that the conclusions in fact be correct, and the due diligence required for an opinion helps assure this.

There are at least two other reasons for an opinion to be required at closing. First, bank regulators often expect to see an opinion in the loan file. Second, an opinion from the borrower's counsel can be valuable in the event that, at enforcement of the loan, the borrower attempts to raise defenses that are addressed by the opinion. A borrower that tries to defend against a suit under the credit agreement by contending that the transaction had not been properly authorized or that it violated some law or contract would face a heavy burden indeed once the legal opinion is shown to the judge. In this context, the opinion could have significant estoppel value.

The case of *Fortress Credit Corp. v. Dechert LLP*, 934 N.Y.S.2d 119 (App. Div. 2011) explored issues relating to the liability of an opinion-giving firm (Dechert) to a recipient (Fortress) that is not the firm's client. Dechert was retained by Marc Dreier to provide an opinion to Fortress, the lender in a loan transaction. The borrowers were clients of Dreier's (who was then an attorney), collectively referred to as Solow Realty. Dreier himself was a guarantor of the financing. It turns out that Solow Realty knew nothing of the financing. Dreier fraudulently falsified documents, forged the Solow Realty signatures, and misappropriated the loan proceeds. It was alleged that in providing its opinion, Dechert did not undertake sufficient diligence. Fortress sued Dechert to recover damages alleging fraud, legal malpractice, negligence, and negligent misrepresentation. Fortress asserted that it relied upon Dechert's opinion that the loan documents were duly executed and delivered and were a valid and binding obligation of Solow Realty.

The Appellate Division of New York's Supreme Court dismissed the legal malpractice claim because there was no attorney-client relationship between Dechert and Fortress. It also dismissed the fraud claim, finding a lack of scienter (knowledge of the fraud), which is an essential element to a fraud claim.

The court did, however, determine that despite the lack of a contractual relationship between Dechert and Fortress ("privity" is the legal term) there was a relationship of "near-privity" that would support a cause of action of negligence or negligent representation. The court went on to dismiss those causes of action as well, noting that the "complaint fails to allege (a) that [Fortress] informed [Dechert] that its obligations were not limited solely to a review of relevant and specified documents or (b) that [Fortress] informed [Dechert] that it was to investigate, verify and report on the legitimacy of the transaction. Absent such factual allegations, [Fortress] cannot establish that [Dechert] breached a duty of care." The court noted further that Dechert had no reason to suspect fraud by Dreier and stated, "[t]he opinion was clearly and unequivocally circumscribed by the qualifications that [Dechert] assumed the genuineness of all signatures and the authenticity of the documents, made no independent inquiry into the accuracy of factual representations or certificates, and undertook no independent investigation in ascertaining those facts. Thus, [Dechert's] statements as contained in the opinion, were not misrepresentations."

It should be noted that Fortress's claims survived a motion to dismiss in the Supreme Court, meaning that unlike the Appellate Division, the Supreme Court did not believe that even if all the facts alleged in the complaint were true there was no sustainable cause of action. The Supreme Court's ruling in 2010 alarmed opinion practitioners who take comfort from the Appellate Court's contrary decision, which most opinion practitioners believe was correctly decided.

5.1.5   Government Approvals

> **Box 5.5**
>
> The Administrative Agent shall have received evidence that the execution, delivery and performance of this Agreement, the borrowing of loans hereunder, and the granting of liens to the Administrative Agent for the benefit of the Lenders pursuant to the Security Documents have been approved by an order of _____, and such order shall be final and non-appealable and not subject to further review.

Legislators rarely see an activity they can refrain from regulating in some way, large or small. Fortunately (at least from the standpoint of preparing for the closing), only in rare cases does such regulation extend to something a borrower or lenders want to do under a credit agreement. There are exceptions, however. Certain regulated public utilities require approval from state public utility commissions of the terms of any debt before the debt can be incurred. Sometimes the commission must also approve the terms of any collateral security. Borrowings by companies in non-U.S. jurisdictions that are subject to foreign exchange regulations often require approval from the central bank to incur debt denominated in a foreign currency, such as U.S. dollars (see Section 5.1.9).

No lender (or borrower, for that matter) wants to run afoul of any of these strictures. Not to obtain approval of a public utility commission may render the loan or collateral security void. To extend credit to a non-U.S. borrower without first obtaining exchange control approval may also render the loan void, or could at least make the borrower unable to obtain dollars from its central bank to make the payments of principal and interest required under the credit agreement. In cases where the credit agreement, or the borrowings or collateral security thereunder, requires government approval, it is customary for the conditions to state expressly that evidence of approval has been delivered to the lenders. The issuance of the approval is typically also supported by a legal opinion. Evidence normally consists of a copy of the approval certified by an officer of the borrower.

The reference in the sample language in Box 5.5 to the final and nonappealable nature of the approval reflects the reality that, in many cases, the order of a regulatory agency can be appealed by third parties. Simply because the Iowa Utilities Board approves a $100,000,000 credit agreement does not prevent a competitor, or interested citizens, from going to court to contest the approval order. The condition should not be deemed satisfied until the time period for an appeal or review has expired—in other words, until the order is "final and nonappealable."

5.1.6 The MAC Condition

> **Box 5.6**
>
> Since _____, 20 _____, there has been no material adverse change in the business, condition (financial or otherwise), assets, operations or prospects of the Borrower and its Subsidiaries, taken as a whole.

Lenders do not look at borrowers with Pollyannaish eyes. They do, however, expect a borrower only to grow stronger (or, at least, not deteriorate) after the lender has completed its due diligence, obtained internal credit approvals, and delivered an executed commitment letter. The lenders therefore normally insist that the credit agreement conditions protect against the borrower suffering what is called a "material adverse change," or MAC. Although there are many possible formulations of the MAC, a typical approach is set out in the sample language in Box 5.6. In most cases (certain exceptions are discussed below), the MAC condition needs to be satisfied each time there is a borrowing or other extension of credit under the facility, even if that takes place years after the closing.

A MAC condition can be reflected into a credit agreement in two ways. One is to expressly provide in the conditions that no MAC has occurred—the technique shown in Box 5.6. This is the approach normally taken when the MAC condition need only be satisfied at effectiveness or closing. A second, more common approach, is for the borrower to state in the representations that no MAC has occurred since a given date. As discussed in Section 5.2, the continued accuracy of representations is generally a condition precedent to new loans or extensions of credit under a credit agreement (including those made at closing). Thus, if a material adverse change has occurred, the MAC representation cannot be truthfully made, and the obligations of the lenders to make loans or extend other credit would, as a consequence, be suspended for so long as the material adverse change continues (unless the condition is waived).

The typical MAC clause tests whether a material adverse change has occurred since a particular date. The date selected is generally the date of the most recent *audited* financial statements of the borrower delivered to the lenders prior to their committing to sign the credit agreement. The audited financials are normally referenced because they set forth the most reliable financial information for the borrower available when the lenders made their credit decision to enter into the credit agreement. However, audited financial statements are not always available (for example, if the borrower at closing is acquiring a new business unit) and in such cases unaudited or pro forma financial statements must be used. See the discussion in Section 6.2.1 for an explanation of the differences between audited, unaudited, and pro forma financial statements.

Measuring change from a specified date protects the lenders against deterioration in the borrower's condition that gradually becomes material over time, as well as against a single dramatic event that is material by itself. A Category 5 hurricane that destroys the borrower's only manufacturing facility is a single extraordinary event that would likely result in a MAC (at least if the borrower is uninsured or, even if insured, if reconstruction would take many months). Even if no hurricane strikes, if the borrower suffers a 35 percent decline in sales each year from closing through year five as a result of a condition that portends continuing worsening in future years, a MAC would likely have occurred. Comparing its condition in year five to its condition at closing might show as extreme a change as a single devastating hurricane.

Since a MAC clause removes some of the certainty that the borrower can access funds under the credit agreement, borrowers sometimes seek to reduce the uncertainty by providing that the clause incorporate a built-in change to the benchmark date against which a material adverse change is measured. For example, instead of specifying a single fiscal date that occurs prior to the closing date, a MAC condition might look to whether a material adverse change has occurred "since the date of the latest financial statements delivered to the lenders under" the agreement. The clause would, in other words, have a floating benchmark date. Since financial statements are usually delivered quarterly, this would mean that the MAC clause would test whether there has been a material adverse change over a period of generally no more than 90 days before the borrowing. Using a floating benchmark date in this manner may deprive the lenders of protection against a steady, incremental deterioration in the borrower's condition. It may also allow the borrower to wipe out a catastrophic adverse change simply by delivering a new set of financials. Go back to our hurricane. After its plant is destroyed, the borrower could arguably eliminate any MAC that results from the hurricane through the simple expedient of serving up financials that reflect a reduction in the book value of its fixed assets to zero. Unless a *second* hurricane (or other similarly adverse event) occurs subsequent to the date of the new financials, the borrower has evaded a MAC.

Just as a borrower may seek to reduce its risk by changing the benchmark date for testing a material adverse change, it may alternatively request a cutoff date for the period over which a material adverse change is measured. It might, for example, request that the clause measure whether a material adverse change has occurred only during the time from a fiscal end date (prior to the closing date) to the closing date. Alternatively, the list of representations that must be brought down as a condition precedent to each borrowing could explicitly exclude the MAC clause. Regardless of the approach used, to change the standard MAC condition in this way can be even more disadvantageous to lenders than to employ a floating benchmark date, since it excludes from the MAC any material adverse change that occurs *after* the cutoff date (in this example, the closing date). This type of MAC clause is, nevertheless, used in certain credit agreements. One example is a revolving credit facility to be used as a backup line for commercial paper or the like. Rating agencies may consider that the more traditional MAC condition renders the facility too conditional to support a desired credit rating. Another example is a credit facility for strong investment-grade companies, where borrowers use their negotiating muscle to suspend the MAC after the closing date.

The litany of items to be tested for a material adverse change—in the language above, "business, condition (financial or otherwise), assets, operations or prospects"—is intentionally broad and overlapping. Although this is a common formulation, the MAC clause is often negotiated. This is particularly the case as to the reference to "prospects." Borrowers frequently object that they should not be disqualified from borrowing until a bad event or condition actually materializes and not simply because one is expected to materialize. Otherwise, or so a borrower would argue, it might be prevented from accessing the credit facility once the National Weather Service projects a hurricane's path will run directly through the borrower's manufacturing facility, even though landfall is days away. Nevertheless, from the perspective of the lenders, although they are likely to agree that "prospects" is not intended to protect against wind-blowing hurricanes, they would argue they should be protected against financial or operational "hurricanes." The latter could affect a borrower's future performance (and therefore its ability to repay the loans) just as disastrously, or so the lenders would say, even though not yet resulting in measurable consequences. Examples might include the permanent loss of a material license or the borrower's being required, for product safety reasons, to pull a major product line from the market, even though the consequences of either is only the loss of future (as opposed to current) revenues.

Borrowers occasionally request other exceptions to the MAC clause. A frequent plea is that the MAC provision exclude changes that arise from general macroeconomic circumstances, or changes that affect the borrower's industry generally. Courts are split as to whether a broad MAC clause, such as that illustrated above, is triggered by general economic or business factors not unique to the borrower. Contrast *Pittsburgh Coke & Chemical Co. v. Bollo*, 421 F. Supp. 908 (E.D.N.Y. 1976), which holds that it would be "patently unreasonable" to permit "technological and economic changes" that affect the business of all in an industry to constitute a MAC, with *In re IBP S'Holders Litig. v. Tyson Foods*, 789 A.2d 14 (Del. Ch. 2001), which holds the opposite: "had IBP wished such an exclusion [for industry-wide or general factors] . . . IBP should have bargained for it." Most MAC clauses assume that the rule in the *IBP* case is applicable and that, unless expressly excluded, the term "material adverse change" factors in general economic and industry circumstances. Lenders frequently resist inserting an express exclusion, notwithstanding that such events or circumstances are general in nature and not peculiar to the borrower, since they can, nevertheless, have a material adverse impact on the borrower's ability to repay the loans. Ultimately, whether these (or any other) exceptions are included in any given transaction depends on how the parties agree these risks are most appropriately allocated.

The entities to be covered by a MAC clause are those companies whose creditworthiness is the basis of the lending decision. These companies are usually the borrower and its subsidiaries, and any guarantor and its subsidiaries, but in an acquisition financing, the target company and its subsidiaries may also be included. In the context of an acquisition, it is not uncommon for the language of the MAC clause to follow the corresponding language in the acquisition agreement, at least insofar as the target is concerned, since a borrower does not want to be contractually bound to complete a purchase if lenders suspend funding on the basis of a different MAC provision for the target. The borrower may even insist that its determination of whether a MAC at the target has occurred under the acquisition agreement should govern whether the corresponding MAC has occurred under the credit agreement. See Section 5.3 for a discussion of the MAC in the context of an acquisition financing.

Whether a material adverse change has occurred is best described as a complicated question of fact. If the issue comes before a court in litigation, it could be up to a jury, consisting of persons who may be quite ignorant of business practices and terminology, to decide whether a bank has correctly determined that a MAC has transpired. It may be in part for this reason that lenders are generally reluctant to invoke the MAC clause as a basis to refuse to lend if all other conditions are satisfied. In many instances there will be no legal certainty as to whether the circumstances constitute a material adverse change.

The few court decisions that have explored the meaning of "material adverse change" tend to be in the acquisition or merger context. The *IBP* decision referred to above is an example. The court there said that a material adverse change clause is a provision that protects against the occurrence of *"unknown* events that substantially threaten the overall earnings potential of the target in a *durationally significant* manner." Requiring that an event be "unknown" at the time of the closing may lead a borrower to argue that the event does not qualify if already covered by a covenant or representation.

Hexion Specialty Chemicals v. Huntsman Corp., 965 A.2d 715 (Del. Ch. 2009) is another example. *Hexion* involved the proposed acquisition of Huntsman by Hexion. In *Hexion*, Delaware Court of Chancery ruled on Hexion's request for relief from its contractual obligations to consummate its merger with Huntsman. The court there noted that "Delaware courts have never found a material adverse effect to have occurred in the context of a merger agreement. This is no coincidence."

The court then went on to address several important contractual interpretation issues. First, the court held that "absent clear language to the contrary, the burden of proof with respect to a material adverse effect rests on the party seeking to excuse its performance under the contract." Thus, the court placed the "heavy burden" on Hexion to establish that Huntsman had in fact suffered a MAC within the meaning of their merger agreement.

Second, the court adopted the "durationally significant" rationale of *IBP*, noting that "the important consideration therefore is whether there has been an adverse change in the target's business that is consequential to the company's long-term earnings power over a commercially reasonable period, which one would expect to be measured in years rather than months."

Third, the court determined that in a cash acquisition the appropriate "benchmark to use in examining changes in results of business operations post-signing of the merger agreement" to determine whether a MAC has occurred is the results of operation of the business, commonly referred to as "EBITDA." The court rejected the use of earnings per share for that purpose, observing that it is very much a function of the capital structure of a company, reflecting the effects of leverage, and largely irrelevant in the case of a cash acquisition in which the capital structure of the target company is being replaced.

Fourth, in determining over which periods of time changes in EBITDA should be examined, the court noted that the terms "financial condition, business, or results of operations" used in the definition of MAC are "terms of art" to be understood with reference to the meanings given to them in rules adopted by the Securities and Exchange Commission in connection with periodic reporting by registered companies. The court determined that "[t]he proper benchmark then for analyzing these changes [in EBITDA] with respect to [a MAC] . . . is to examine each year and quarter and compare it to the prior year's equivalent period." The court also noted that because the merger agreement's MAC definition referred not just to events that have had a MAC, but also to events that could be "reasonably expected to have" a MAC, "the expected future performance of the target company is also relevant to a material adverse effect analysis."

Fifth, the MAC definition in the merger agreement contained an exception for "any . . . change . . . that affects the chemical industry generally . . . except in the event, and only to the extent, that such . . . change has had a disproportionate effect on the Company and its Subsidiaries, taken as a whole, as compared to other Persons engaged in the chemical industry. . . ." Hexion focused its MAC argument on the performance of Huntsman relative to the rest of the chemical industry and offered evidence that Huntsman had been disproportionately adversely affected, relative to its chemical industry peers, by market and industry conditions. However, the court made it clear that the first step in the analysis must be a determination as to whether a MAC has occurred at all, noting that "Huntsman's performance being disproportionately worse than the chemical industry in general does not, in itself, constitute [a MAC]. Thus, unless the court concludes that the company has suffered [a MAC] as defined in the language coming before the proviso, the court need not consider the application of the chemical industry carve-outs."

Sixth, the court rejected Hexion's argument that "Huntsman's failure to hit its forecasts" supported a determination whether a MAC occurred, noting that the merger agreement explicitly disclaimed any representation or warranty with respect to projections.

Using the rationale of *IBP* and *Hexion*, a borrower might contend (rightly or wrongly) that a credit agreement containing a cash flow covenant (such as a leverage test to measure debt or interest expense to cash flow) should prevent a lender from invoking a MAC based upon a mere decline in earnings. Similarly, a borrower might argue that the requirement of *IBP* and *Hexion* that an event be "durationally-significant" should preclude basing a MAC solely upon the adverse impact of predictable business or commodity price cycles. The *IBP* court wrote that to a short-term speculator, the failure of a company to meet its projected earnings for a quarter could be highly material; for a longer-term investor (lenders under a multiyear credit agreement are likely to fall in this category) such a failure would be less significant. In the context of a credit agreement, "durationally-significant" may therefore depend upon whether a court concludes that the lenders are taking a short-term or long-term view of their borrower.

5.1.7 Conditions That Relate to Perfection of Collateral

Box 5.7

The Borrower shall have delivered to the Administrative Agent the results of recent lien searches in relevant jurisdictions satisfactory in scope to the Administrative Agent and such searches shall reveal no liens on any of the assets of the Borrower or its Subsidiaries except for liens permitted under Section [*Lien Covenant*] or liens to be discharged on or prior to the Effective Date. The Borrower shall have taken such action (including recordings and filings, delivery of appropriate instruments and certificates, and execution of third-party control agreements) as the Administrative Agent shall have requested to perfect the security interests created pursuant to the Security Agreement and the Mortgages in the manner, and with the priority, contemplated therein. In addition, in the case of the Mortgages, the Borrower shall have (i) procured mortgagee policies of title insurance on forms of and issued by one or more title companies satisfactory to the Administrative Agent, insuring the validity and priority of the liens created under the Mortgages in amounts, and subject to such exceptions and exclusions as are satisfactory to the Administrative Agent and (ii) delivered to the Administrative Agent evidence that the Borrower has paid all expenses and premiums in connection with the issuance of such policies and all recording and stamp taxes payable in connection with the recording of the Mortgages.

All other things being equal, lenders prefer a secured credit facility over an unsecured credit facility. From a lender's perspective, having a first claim on the borrower's assets if the arrangement turns south is a powerful weapon to gain maximum recovery when a borrower's financial condition goes sour. That said, whether a credit agreement is secured (and, if secured, the scope of the security—is it just stock of subsidiaries or does it encompass other assets as well, such as real property, inventory and receivables, trademarks, and other property) is strictly a matter of negotiation and largely driven by the financial strength of the borrower. Investment-grade borrowers are rarely forced to grant security to their lenders; noninvestment-grade leveraged borrowers routinely grant security.

Assuming a facility is to be secured, the conditions precedent normally require evidence of two things: first, that each lien granted to the lenders has been *perfected* and, second, that it has the agreed-upon *priority* over other liens on the property. Although volumes have been written on the meanings of "perfection" and "priority," it is worth a brief discussion here to explain the difference.

"Perfection" means, in general terms, that steps have been taken to give public notice of the security interest and to make it enforceable against other creditors of the borrower. If a lien is not perfected, it may be set aside if the grantor files for bankruptcy. An unperfected lien is usually regarded as valueless. "Perfection" is a term of art that originates in the Uniform Commercial Code, but it is often used in the United States to refer generally to the creation of an enforceable lien. The term is not commonly used outside the United States, though the objective of taking security (that is, creating a lien good against third parties in an insolvency of the borrower) is fundamentally the same. Brazil is no different than Kansas in this regard.

Perfection may involve a number of different steps, depending upon the kind of asset subject to the lien. Liens on most kinds of personal property (as distinct from real property) may be perfected by filing a simple "financing statement" under the Uniform Commercial Code, normally at a designated central location in the state of organization of the grantor of the collateral. For a Delaware corporation, the place to file is the Secretary of State of Delaware. For other types of collateral, such as collateral that consists of "instruments" under the Uniform Commercial Code (promissory notes or bankers' acceptances are examples) or "certificated securities" (such as stock certificates for subsidiaries), perfection may also be accomplished by taking possession of the collateral. For certain categories of collateral (such as deposit accounts and letter of credit rights), neither of these steps perfects the lien, and the secured party must take "control" as defined in the Uniform Commercial Code. A mortgage (or, as the terminology has it in certain states, a "deed of trust") that covers real estate must be duly recorded in the real estate records.

Perfection of a lien is necessary, but not sufficient, for a lender that expects to have a special claim against the assets of the borrower encompassed within the collateral. The lending syndicate still wants to know that the lien is prior or senior to other liens (or, if not senior, at least is subject only to those other liens that are allowed under the business deal). Taking a lien upon inventory worth $100,000,000 when there is a prior lien on the same inventory that secures debt of $200,000,000 is likely to be of little value.

The conditions precedent in the credit agreement address priority in two ways. First, the lenders will insist that appropriate lien searches or other due diligence be conducted with respect to the property that is to serve as collateral for the credit facility to ascertain whether anyone already has a lien against the same property. For most personal property, lien searches are relatively easily conducted under the Uniform Commercial Code. For certain kinds of personal property, however (such as property as to which a lien may be perfected by taking possession), the lenders as part of their due diligence will want to confirm that no other debt holder (or trustee or agent for a debt holder) has possession or control over the collateral. For real property, the lien searches are not as simple. To determine whether a parcel of real property is subject to other liens, the lenders need to conduct a search in the local land office where the property is located. This is usually conducted by a title company and typically requires a metes and bounds description of the parcel in order to locate the property in the relevant land records.

Other classes of collateral require searches in other offices, such as certain vessels or aircraft. The range of methods to perfect collateral (and, therefore, the means to conduct lien searches) is beyond the scope of this volume. It would take tomes to address the myriad ways in which liens may be perfected in jurisdictions outside the United States. Consultation with local counsel is essential in these cases.

Once lien searches have been completed, it is necessary to review the search results and determine whether they show that the lenders will receive the priority they are entitled to under the business deal. Lenders generally expect that the credit agreement will enjoy a *first priority* lien; in other words, a lien not subject to the lien of any other creditor. The search results should confirm this (or, at worst, show only liens that are either permitted under the exceptions to the lien covenant or that are to be repaid upon closing). If there is a second lien credit facility (see the discussion in Section 2.4), the liens securing it will typically be created and perfected in tandem with a first lien credit agreement, so that two simultaneous credit facilities cover identical collateral, with the second lien facility being subject only to the first lien facility (and to no other debt).

Although not an element of perfection, in the case of real estate collateral, title insurance is often obtained to insure that the mortgage lien created has been perfected and is entitled to the priority that the parties intended. Title insurance policies can be complex and are usually prepared and reviewed only by specialists. They can, however, give the lender protection (in the form of monetary compensation) for any loss attributable to a bad or imperfect lien that covers real property. Title insurance can be quite expensive and the scope of the coverage is generally the subject of negotiation, since the lenders expect the cost of the insurance to be for the account of the borrower.

In addition, in the case of improved real estate collateral located in a "special flood hazard area" designated in any Flood Insurance Rate Map published by the Federal Emergency Management Agency, regulated lending institutions (this includes national banks, state member banks, and state insured banks) must make certain that borrowers carry flood insurance before the lenders extend credit secured by improved real estate. See Section 7.5.3 for a more detailed discussion of flood insurance requirements.

5.1.8 Promissory Notes

> **Box 5.8**
>
> The Administrative Agent shall have received, for the account of each Lender requesting the same, a duly completed promissory note in the form of Exhibit _____ evidencing the Loans to be made by such Lender to the Borrower hereunder.

For centuries, it was unthinkable for a bank to make a loan without obtaining a promissory note from the borrower. "No note, no loan" was the universal refrain. The historical rationale behind promissory notes was simply to evidence a loan with the best documentation possible. A note was felt to be the most powerful acknowledgment by a borrower of its obligation to repay, and infinitely preferable to a loan or credit agreement standing alone. The practice, with some modifications, continues to this day.

There is little magic to the form of note commonly used under credit agreements. A recitation of the amount of the loans made, a reference to the credit agreement, the fact that it requires the payment of principal and interest, and a signature by the borrower are the essential elements typically required. Most notes under a credit agreement are not negotiable (a term of art under the Uniform Commercial Code). Accordingly, transferees of a note are not typically entitled to "holder in due course" status and thus will not be free of any defenses the maker of the note might seek to raise.

In a revolving credit facility, a so-called grid note is customarily used. In a grid note, the face of the note specifies a dollar amount that corresponds to the *commitment* of the lender, but the text of the note provides that the true amount payable is the aggregate of all the loans actually advanced and outstanding. Details of the loans actually made can be set forth in a schedule (or grid) attached to the note. To deal with the possibility that a borrower may object to the amount entered on the grid, the credit agreement (and the note) usually provide that the entries on the grid are "prima facie" accurate or accurate "absent manifest error." This, in effect, shifts to the borrower the burden of establishing that the notations were wrong.

Apart from the benefits of an acknowledgment by the borrower of its obligations, there are other motivations to evidence loans with a note. For example, in New York under Section 3213 of the New York Civil Practice Law and Rules (CPLR) a note that is "an instrument for the payment of money only" is entitled to summary enforcement— basically an expedited proceeding to obtain judgment from a court. Not all notes qualify as instruments for the payment of money "only," though courts have held that the fact that the note references another agreement (such as the credit agreement), or that the interest rate must be determined externally (such as if it accrues at LIBOR or the base rate), does not prevent the note from being an instrument for the payment of money only. See *Cmty. Nat'l Bank & Trust Co. of N.Y. v. I.M.F. Trading, Inc.*, 561 N.Y.S.2d 578 (App. Div. 1st Dep't 1990). It is less certain that a grid note would qualify as such an instrument (no reported cases address this situation as of the date of this volume), though logically if presenting external evidence to prove the amount of interest does not disqualify a note from Section 3213 treatment, external evidence should be permissible to prove the amount of the principal.

Although CPLR Section 3213 is a provision of New York law, other jurisdictions accord similar benefits to promissory notes as well. In most civil law Latin American jurisdictions, for example, it is common practice to require the borrower to execute an instrument that qualifies as a *pagaré* under local law because of significant procedural and other advantages it affords (though, to qualify, an instrument may not be able to attach a grid). In addition to the availability of expedited proceedings akin to a summary judgment motion (the local equivalent of CPLR Section 3213), a *pagaré* is typically entitled to a presumption of authenticity and subject to strictly limited defenses. There is also the theoretical ability in certain countries (Mexico is an example) to obtain prejudgment attachment (levying on the borrower's assets at the inception of litigation rather than only after a favorable judgment has been obtained). This right can be a tremendous hammer in the hands of a lender; at a minimum it puts the borrower into a talking mood and makes it more willing to resume payments (even if on a restructured basis). Last (but certainly not least) possessing a *pagaré* can simplify litigation since the *pagaré* will not be perceived by the local courts as complicated or novel, such as might be the case when a lender attempts to sue upon a 100-page U.S.-style credit agreement. The *pagaré* is also normally executed in Spanish or Portuguese and consequently avoids the burdens of obtaining an official translation, as well as myriad other local-law procedural hurdles (powers of attorney to prosecuting lawyers, affidavits, increased court fees, and the like).

Historically, for banks in the United States, there was an additional reason to obtain notes, namely the ability to pledge them to a Federal Reserve bank at its discount window pursuant to Regulation A of the Federal Reserve Board. The discount window is an easy way for a bank to obtain back-up or short-term, seasonal, or emergency funds, and traditionally was available only if the bank could pledge a physical note to the relevant Federal Reserve bank. However, under revisions to its discount window policies, which became effective in the late 1990s, noteless loans now also qualify for pledging to the Federal Reserve, so physical notes are no longer necessary. There may, nevertheless, be a continuing advantage for banks to use physical notes under Regulation A. A pledge by a bank to the Federal Reserve of a physical note can be perfected by simple delivery of the note; a pledge of a noteless loan requires the filing of a Uniform Commercial Code financing statement against the pledgor. Some bank lenders have been reluctant to let this occur, and for this reason still insist upon physical notes.

The willingness of the Federal Reserve to discount noteless loans has provided encouragement to a practice in the bank syndication market of dispensing with notes altogether—or at least to require any lender that wanted a promissory note to request one expressly. This is the so-called "note-option" structure whereby the lenders (at least those that are comfortable without a note) rely instead upon the credit agreement itself to evidence the borrower's obligation to repay the loans. The language set out in Box 5.8 is an example of a note-option condition precedent.

Despite the advantages under CPLR Section 3213, with few exceptions lenders today no longer generally request promissory notes of the borrower, though some bank lenders still have internal policies that require all loans to be evidenced by notes. In addition, certain fund investors may be required under their organizational documents to obtain a note in order to have an instrument that may be pledged as security for financing being provided to the fund.

Promissory notes can, in some places, be subject to stamp taxes, which are taxes imposed upon the instrument itself, or the execution thereof. Many non-U.S. jurisdictions impose these taxes, and even some U.S. jurisdictions do so (Florida's Documentary Stamp Tax is an example). A number of devices are used to avoid or minimize these taxes, such as to execute the notes outside the taxing jurisdiction (this is frequently done in the case of the Florida Documentary Stamp Tax) or, in the case of non-U.S. borrowers, to restructure the transaction so that a subsidiary in a nontaxing jurisdiction becomes the borrower under the guaranty of the company that would otherwise have been the borrower. In cross-border transactions, it is customary to have local counsel opine that no stamp taxes are payable in connection with the credit agreement.

5.1.9 Special Conditions Applicable to Non-U.S. Borrowers

Box 5.9

The Administrative Agent shall have received (a) an acceptance from the Process Agent of its appointment by the Borrower pursuant to Section [*Process Agent Appointment*] and (b) confirmation that the transactions contemplated hereby have been approved by the Central Bank of _____ for purposes of [U.S. dollar availability].

Cross-border lending by U.S. lenders to non-U.S. borrowers can raise a number of special issues. Some of these are addressed in Chapters 6, 7, and 12. Several special conditions precedent can also be relevant to non-U.S. borrowers. The sample language in Box 5.9 sets out two common examples: the acceptance from a process agent of its appointment by the borrower, and confirmation that any necessary foreign exchange approvals have been obtained.

The rationale for a process agent is discussed in more detail in Section 12.8.1. The objective is to designate a person to whom notice of litigation can be delivered. In circumstances when a process agent is appointed—generally limited to situations where the borrower is located outside the United States—the conditions precedent sometimes include a requirement that evidence of the acceptance of the appointment be returned by the process agent itself. A process agent must, as a rule, be located in the jurisdiction where the lenders want to be able to commence litigation. This means that if the lenders want to sue the borrower in New York (this would almost certainly be the case if the credit agreement is stated to be governed by New York law), the process agent needs to have an office in New York to which notice of the suit can be delivered. The process agent, subject to certain exceptions (embassies and consulates, for example), can be anyone located in the desired jurisdiction. It can be an individual, though that is likely a bad idea since when the individual expires, or flees the jurisdiction, so does the process agent. The borrower sometimes wants to appoint its U.S. law firm as the process agent, though many firms are unwilling to take on the responsibility of functioning as an agent for the full duration of the credit facility (at a minimum there is a duty to notify the borrower if the process agent ever receives notice of a suit); in addition, law firms, just like individuals, have been known to disappear.

Most lending syndicates therefore insist that one of the commercial companies in the business of serving as process agents be appointed. These companies are quite willing to be an agent for anyone so long as the requisite annual fee is paid. For a credit agreement with a five-year term, the lending syndicate wants to know at closing that the full fee has been paid for each of the five years plus an additional period of normally up to one year. This allows suit to be commenced even after maturity if the loan is not paid when it comes due.

The acceptance by a process agent of its appointment generally includes three key elements: a formal acceptance by the process agent, an agreement to maintain an office in New York during the term of the appointment, and a confirmation that the fee for the full term of the appointment has been paid. With this in hand, the lenders then know that if they want to commence suit against their Zambian borrower, they can do so in New York rather than traveling to Lusaka. Winning the suit and collecting a judgment are, of course, separate issues and are also discussed in Section 12.8.

Obtaining foreign exchange control approval is a second condition precedent that comes into play for non-U.S. borrowers. Most countries in the developed world have freely exchangeable currencies and so lending into those countries does not raise exchange control issues. Lending to countries in the developing world can be subject to a different set of rules, which raises two concerns, practical and legal. From the practical standpoint, if a required exchange control approval is not obtained, the borrower may be unable to obtain the dollars (or other freely exchangeable currency in which the loans are denominated) that are essential to permit timely repayment of the loans. It is not enough that the borrower be super-profitable and awash with cash in Argentine pesos. It must have the legal right to convert those pesos into dollars at the Argentine Central Bank; otherwise the lenders will simply not be paid in dollars.

The legal concern arises out of Article VIII of the Bretton Woods Agreement pursuant to which the International Monetary Fund (IMF) was established. Section 2(b) thereof provides that:

> . . . exchange contracts which involve the currency of any member and which are contrary to the exchange control regulations of that member maintained or imposed consistently with this Agreement shall be unenforceable in the territories of any member.

At least one commentator has argued that a cross-border credit agreement is a type of "exchange contract" under the IMF Agreement. The one court decision in the United States that directly addressed this issue, however, concluded that a loan agreement is not such a contract. See *Libra Bank, Ltd. v. Banco Nacional de Costa Rica, S.A.*, 570 F. Supp. 870 (S.D.N.Y. 1983). Courts in other IMF member states have adopted a broader interpretation of the same language and treat a loan agreement as an "exchange contract."[1] If, notwithstanding the *Libra Bank* holding, a U.S. court were to conclude that a credit agreement was an exchange contract, then making loans to a borrower in a country that has imposed exchange controls without obtaining necessary exchange control approvals could result in the credit agreement being *unenforceable* in the territory of any IMF member country, including the United States, because of the application of Article VIII, Section 2(b). Since virtually all countries are members of the IMF, and those few that are not members are (with the exception of Taiwan) unlikely places for borrowers to be doing business—North Korea and Andorra, to name a few—the risk of unenforceability is real.

Given both the practical and legal risks associated with not obtaining required foreign exchange approvals, lenders generally take three steps to ensure that any necessary approvals have been obtained. Of course, when lending into countries where it is obvious that controls are not in place—Canada, most European countries, Japan, Australia, New Zealand, for example—these steps are usually ignored. First, the arranger consults with its own local counsel regarding the applicability of exchange controls. Second, the borrower's local counsel is required to state in its opinion that no approval is necessary or, if required, that

---

[1] See *Colloquium: 2(b) or not 2(b): Fifty Years of Questions—The Practical Implications of Article VIII Section 2(b)*, 62 Fordham L. Rev 1931 (May, 1994).

approval has been obtained. Third, in those cases for which approval is obligatory, the conditions precedent require that evidence of the approval be obtained prior to the first extension of credit under the agreement. The sample language in Box 5.9 shows this approach.

5.1.10   Repayment of Other Debt

> **Box 5.10**
>
> The Administrative Agent shall have received evidence that the principal of and interest on, and all other amounts owing in respect of, the Debt (including any contingent or other amounts payable in respect of letters of credit) indicated on Schedule _____ that is to be repaid on the Effective Date have been, or shall be simultaneously, paid in full (or arrangements for such payment satisfactory to the Administrative Agent shall have been made), that any commitments to extend credit under the agreements or instruments relating to such Debt have been canceled or terminated, and that all Guarantees in respect of, and all Liens securing, any such Debt have been released (or arrangements for such release satisfactory to the Administrative Agent shall have been made).

A thorough credit approval process always includes an analysis of the borrower's debt levels after closing. Out of this process (and negotiation with the borrower) a debt or leverage covenant may be incorporated into the credit agreement that limits the debt of the borrower (by class, on an aggregate basis, or both). The lenders want any debt that does not fit within the covenants to be repaid as a condition to the initial loans under the credit agreement. The language in Box 5.10 is a typical repayment condition. It does not require that the proceeds of the loans be directly applied to the repayment of the scheduled debt. This reflects the reality that a borrower often repays other debt from a combination of proceeds of the loans, cash on hand, and, perhaps, other concurrent borrowings.

To repay debt is, in most instances, straightforward. The borrower simply remits the requisite funds to the lender or other debt holder and instructs that they be applied to outstanding principal and interest (and any breakfunding or premium or other payments). Sometimes, however, the other debt may not be prepayable, such as is often the case with bonds which, during their early years, generally do not permit redemption. In this case, the borrower may need to resort to alternative strategies. One is to purchase the outstanding bonds in the open market. This is almost never completely successful (there will always be some holders that, whether willfully or inadvertently, will not sell).

Another strategy is to *defease* the bonds, although this solution is not practical unless interest on the bonds is at a fixed rate. Often included in bond indentures, defeasance provisions require satisfaction by the debt issuer (the borrower) of a number of conditions. The most important of these stipulates that the borrower post cash and U.S. Treasury securities with the indenture trustee in an amount sufficient to cover all future principal and interest payments to be made on the bonds until maturity (or, in some cases, until the earliest prepayment or redemption date). The cash and treasuries are specifically dedicated to the repayment of (and, in effect, secure) the bonds and become the source of the scheduled payments of principal of and interest on the bonds. Other conditions to defeasance include delivery to the trustee of various opinions of counsel and officers' certificates. Although defeasance tends to be a very expensive "repayment" option for borrowers, in most cases it removes the defeased debt for accounting purposes from the borrower's balance sheet. It is thus a quasi-repayment option available when a bond indenture does not otherwise permit early redemption.

Another quasi-repayment option that is sometimes seen may be employed when a bond maturity follows relatively quickly after the credit agreement closing, or when the closing must occur prior to the completion of the 30- or 60-day redemption notice period required under the typical bond indenture. In these circumstances, formal defeasance is not undertaken (this avoids the borrower having to deliver the numerous certificates and opinions, and to satisfy the other conditions, that are prerequisite to a defeasance), but an amount equal to the required principal, interest, and premium is deposited in escrow with the bond trustee or the credit agreement administrative agent or third party. When the maturity date arrives, the escrow funds are then applied to repay the bonds. The escrow structure carries with it some risks if the borrower declares bankruptcy prior to the dissolution of the escrow. The cash held in escrow could theoretically be taken by the now-bankrupt borrower, replaced with alternative (much less liquid) collateral, and then used by the borrower in its business—perhaps never to be seen again. This risk notwithstanding, the escrow approach is employed from time to time as an alternative repayment option.

When the target debt to be repaid includes letters of credit, a different set of issues arises. Letters of credit cannot be unilaterally repaid, as loans or bonds can, by merely paying (or defeasing) outstanding principal and interest. Since a letter of credit is an unconditional obligation of the issuer to the beneficiary, it cannot be cancelled by the issuer without the beneficiary's consent. Nor can the reimbursement obligation be paid until a drawing occurs and a reimbursement claim becomes payable by the borrower. The only way a letter of credit may be "refinanced" is by causing a replacement letter of credit to be issued to the beneficiary and having the beneficiary consent to the termination of the original letter of credit under the target debt agreement. To coordinate this at a closing can be difficult, especially if many letters of credit are outstanding.

An alternative custom that has developed is for the letters of credit under the target agreement to remain outstanding even after the closing, on the condition that the borrower either post cash collateral for its contingent reimbursement obligation or post a backstop letter of credit from another institution to support the reimbursement obligation. Thus, the agent under the new facility would ensure that a portion of the proceeds of the initial loans is deposited with the letter of credit issuer under the existing facility, or alternatively would arrange for the letter of credit issuer under the new facility to issue to the agent under the old facility a letter of credit to backstop the existing letters of credit. In either event, the amount of cash posted or the face amount of the backstop letter of credit is normally 102–105 percent of the potential reimbursement claim, in order to cover letter of credit fees and any default interest that might accrue on the reimbursement obligation. At the same time, the borrower undertakes with both the old and new agents to replace all backstopped letters of credit within some relatively short period—30 to 60 days. (See Section 2.1.2.10 for other aspects of letter of credit cover.)

The alternative repayment mechanics of the defeasance or escrow arrangements described above, and the specialized "repayment" mechanics for letters of credit discussed in the preceding paragraph, are contemplated in the sample language in Box 5.10 through the reference to arrangements for payment "satisfactory to the administrative agent." These arrangements should provide the agent with sufficient flexibility to consent to the numerous substitute repayment options that can sometimes be required at closing.

5.1.11   Other Conditions

A variety of other conditions are, from time to time, inserted into credit agreements. Some of these are discussed in this section.

5.1.11.1 Appraisals

Box 5.11

The Administrative Agent shall have received an appraisal from a nationally recognized appraisal firm selected by the Borrower and satisfactory to the Administrative Agent setting forth a recent appraisal of the fair market value of the borrower's [inventory] [real property satisfying the requirements of the Financial Institutions Reform, Recovery and Enforcement Act of 1989] [other specified assets].

Appraisals are sometimes required as a condition to the extension of credit under an agreement. Where they are not required it is when loans are made against the cash-generating potential of the borrower and not against raw asset values. It is also a function of the due diligence process. Whatever concerns the lenders have regarding asset values are usually addressed at the due diligence stage *before* a commitment letter and term sheet are delivered to the borrower and not as a condition to the initial loans under the agreement. There are two exceptions to this general rule, however.

The first arises in the context of asset-based lending transactions. As discussed briefly in Section 4.7.2, in an asset-based lending transaction the amount of available credit is measured by a borrowing base that is determined by reference to the value of inventory, receivables, or other liquid assets. In most cases, the determination of values is based upon the values of the inventory and receivables carried on the balance sheet of the borrower. Often, however, the lending syndicate wants independent validation that the balance sheet amounts reflect the true market value of the assets. An appraisal addresses these concerns. It is frequently undertaken by an affiliate of the lead bank.

The second context in which appraisals arise is when loans are made against the security of real property, unless the real property security is either taken out of "an abundance of caution" or "for purposes other than the real estate's value." The Financial Institutions Reform, Recovery, and Enforcement Act of 1989 (FIRREA), as implemented by regulations (those for national banks are at 12 C.F.R. § 34.43), requires that an appraisal be performed for all real estate–related financial transactions (these include loans secured by real estate) by any federally regulated bank. The appraisal must be obtained *before* the transaction is consummated. There are, however, several listed exceptions to the FIRREA requirement, including the two noted above: abundance of caution and purposes other than the real estate's value. A credit agreement that is secured by a single real estate asset—such as a hotel or a housing development—probably requires an appraisal. Lending to a manufacturing company, where security is taken in all of the borrower's assets, including its factories, probably does not require an appraisal since the purpose of the security is to obtain a blanket lien and not to lend solely against the value of the factories.

5.1.11.2 Solvency

Box 5.12

The Administrative Agent shall have received a certificate from a the chief financial officer of the Borrower to the effect that, as of the Effective Date and after giving effect to the initial extension of credit hereunder and to the other transactions contemplated hereby, (a) the present fair salable value of the assets of the Borrower and its Subsidiaries on a consolidated basis (i.e., the amount that may be realized within a reasonable time, considered to be six months to one year, either through collection or sale at the regular market value, conceiving the latter as the amount that could be obtained for the property in question within such period by a capable and diligent businessperson from an interested buyer who is willing to purchase under ordinary selling conditions) is not less than the amount that will be required to pay the probable liability of the Borrower and its Subsidiaries on their debts (including contingent, unmatured, and unliquidated liabilities) as they become absolute and matured, (b) the Borrower and its Subsidiaries will not, on a consolidated basis, have an unreasonably small capital in relation to their business or with respect to any transaction then contemplated and (c) the Borrower and its Subsidiaries, on a consolidated basis, will have sufficient cash flow to enable them to pay their debts as they mature.

Lenders do not like lending to insolvent borrowers (with the exception, perhaps, of debtor-in-possession financings made under the supervision of a bankruptcy court), and, in most cases, the credit review process that the lenders undertake prior to establishing a facility will demonstrate to their satisfaction that the borrower is solvent and able to repay the loan. A condition precedent, such as that set out in Box 5.12, is therefore not normally included in the credit agreement.

Such a condition might, however, be inserted if the terms of the credit facility give rise to fraudulent conveyance or fraudulent transfer issues. These are discussed in detail in Section 6.2.7. Examples might include facilities where the proceeds of the loans are to pay a large dividend to shareholders, or where upstream guarantees from subsidiaries are taken. Such a condition has also become common in acquisition finance credit agreements. In such cases, a condition like that set out in Box 5.12 would be intended to give the lenders confirmation that they could later show a court (if the borrower were to go bankrupt) to demonstrate the borrower's financial condition at the time of the loan closing and show that it was solvent. Whether any of this works is open to question. Understandably, in assessing whether a fraudulent conveyance has occurred, bankruptcy judges acquire a great deal of 20/20 hindsight about the borrower's condition at closing, if for no other reason because the borrower has landed in bankruptcy court. Nevertheless, having a certification from the borrower's chief financial officer (or other senior financial officer) that confirms the borrower's (or guarantying subsidiaries') solvency should, at a minimum, make it more difficult to prove that the loan transaction gave rise to a fraudulent conveyance.

When they first appeared in credit agreements, solvency conditions typically required that an independent specialist or appraisal firm provide a detailed solvency report and analysis, rather than a conclusory certification from a financial officer of the borrower. Lenders took comfort from the independence of the third-party provider. Today, independent reports are the exception, not the least because of their questionable value in front of a court, but also because of their significant expense.

5.1.11.3 Environmental Due Diligence

Box 5.13

The Administrative Agent shall have received a [Phase I] [Phase II] environmental survey and assessment prepared by a firm of licensed engineers (familiar with the identification of toxic and hazardous substances) selected by the Borrower and satisfactory to the Administrative Agent, such environmental survey and assessment to be based upon physical on-site inspections by such firm of each of the existing sites and facilities owned, operated or leased by the Borrower and its Subsidiaries, as well as a historical review of the uses of such sites and facilities and of the business and operations of the Borrower and its Subsidiaries (including any former Subsidiaries or divisions of the Borrower or any of its Subsidiaries that have been disposed of prior to the date of such survey and assessment and with respect to which the Borrower or any of its Subsidiaries may have retained liability for Environmental Claims). In addition, if requested by the Required Lenders (through the Administrative Agent), the Borrower shall have completed (and delivered to each Lender) an environmental risk questionnaire in a form provided to the Borrower by the Administrative Agent (and containing such inquiries with respect to environmental matters as shall have been requested by any Lender, through the Administrative Agent, to be included in such question-naire). The results of such survey and assessment and the responses to such questionnaire (and the underlying facts and circumstances shown thereby) shall be in form and substance satisfactory to the Required Lenders.

As discussed more fully in Section 6.3.8, borrowers that have environmental problems may face significant capital costs or potential liabilities that could compete for funds needed to operate the business and ultimately repay the loans. Several provisions are often included in a credit agreement to address these risks, including the representa-tions discussed in Chapter 6 and the default discussed in Section 9.1.8. In some cases, especially if the initial due diligence at the credit review stage indicates that there may be environmental issues or if there is sig-nificant real property collateral, the credit agreement may also include a condition precedent providing for an environmental due diligence report to be prepared with respect to properties owned, leased, or operated by the borrower (or that were previously owned, leased, or operated by the borrower if the borrower retains potential liability) and demonstrating either that such problems do not exist or that they are not material.

Such a report, which is generally undertaken by an engineer, can be either a so-called Phase I Report (for which the engineer looks at public records and performs a physical inspection of the property) or a Phase II Report (for which the engineer may conduct groundwater test-ing, take sample soil borings, and perform other more detailed inves-tigations). Most credit agreements, if they contain an environmental condition precedent at all, require delivery of a Phase I Report only. A Phase II Report is generally reserved for those circumstances in which the Phase I Report indicates there is a risk of material environmental liabilities or costs. The Phase II Report is then obtained so that those costs or potential liabilities can be quantified.

In many cases the lenders are willing to have the borrower merely complete a questionnaire (usually prepared by counsel for the arranger) as a way to identify any potential environmental problems. A question-naire is, of course, only as good as the questions and the frankness of the answers, and is therefore not as reliable as an independent report.

However, since questionnaires do not involve a physical inspection of properties by a third party, they are cheaper and far less time-consuming than Phase I or Phase II Reports, and are an alternative sometimes pushed for by borrowers.

5.1.11.4 Insurance

> #### Box 5.14
>
> The Administrative Agent shall have received certificates of insurance evidencing the existence of all insurance required to be maintained by the Borrower pursuant to Section [*Insurance*] and the designation of the Administrative Agent as the loss payee or additional named insured thereunder [(or, in the case of key-person life insurance, assignments of insurance)] to the extent required by said Section, such certificates to be in such form and contain such information as is specified in said Section.

In most credit agreements (with the exception, perhaps, of agreements for investment-grade borrowers), the lenders insist upon a covenant that sets out certain minimum requirements for insurance to be maintained by the borrower. This covenant can be simple or complex, as is discussed in more detail in Section 7.5.3. Particularly in credit facilities that are secured, the insurance covenant is more detailed and is also accompanied by a condition precedent pursuant to which the borrower is required to deliver independent confirmation of the existence of the insurance under the covenant. Typically, this confirmation is effected through the delivery by the borrower's insurance broker of a "certificate of insurance" that lays out a summary of the policies, and their limits and deductibles, carried by the borrower.

In a secured credit facility, the covenant normally requires that the agent, on behalf of the lenders, be designated pursuant to endorsements as the loss payee (under property insurance policies) and as an additional named insured (under liability policies). In these cases, evidence of the endorsements is set forth on the certificate of insurance.

Since the certificate of insurance is issued by the borrower's insurance broker, it does not actually bind the insurance carrier. The certificate is also only a *summary*; it does not spell out the details of coverage (and exclusions) set forth in the insurance policies themselves. By way of example, the certificate of insurance may indicate "all-risks" coverage for damage to property, but will not explain that "all-risks" does not cover floods from water-main breaks caused by terrorist attack, or environmental damage caused by the bursting of an underground fuel-storage tank. As a consequence, in agreements for which the value of an asset is critical, such as for an asset-based, project finance, or aircraft or ship financing, the certificate of insurance is not sufficient, and the lenders will want to obtain copies of and review the actual policies (and all endorsements). Having the policies in hand eliminates the two risks of relying upon a certificate of insurance: the policies come from, and bind, the insurance carrier and the policies (and endorsements) contain all of the details of coverage that the lenders need to ensure that the borrower (and they) are protected against losses.

5.1.11.5 Patriot Act

Box 5.15

The Lenders shall have received, sufficiently in advance of the Effective Date, all documentation and other information required by bank regulatory authorities under applicable "know your customer" and anti-money laundering rules and regulations, including without limitation, the United States PATRIOT Act (Title III of Pub. L. 107-56 (signed into law October 26, 2001)) including the information described in Section [*PATRIOT Act*].

As discussed more fully in Section 12.12, following September 11, 2001, the United States enacted the so-called USA PATRIOT Act, which, in addition to banning business with known or suspected terrorists or terrorist organizations, mandates that *financial institutions* compile information on borrowers and ensure that they are not doing business with people designated as "terrorists" or their associates. The PATRIOT Act additionally requires, under the so-called "know your customer" rules, that financial institutions notify borrowers that this information is being collected. The boilerplate provisions of the credit agreement will, as a consequence, typically include a notice to this effect (see the sample language in Box 12.20).

Some credit agreements go further and throw in a condition precedent along the lines set out in Box 5.15 so that, as drafts of the credit agreement are prepared, the borrower knows that it is expected to cooperate with the prospective syndicate to assemble the necessary documents and information. In any event, whether the condition is included or not, no lender subject to the Act wants to sign a credit agreement until it has first completed its PATRIOT Act diligence on the borrower and has determined that the latter is not on the list of "Specially Designated Nationals." The condition is therefore less a condition to effectiveness or lending and more a condition to execution and, as such, is technically unnecessary. Nevertheless, it has become common to include such a provision in syndicated credit agreements with any U.S.-based lender.

5.1.11.6   The Catchall

> ### Box 5.16
>
> The Administrative Agent shall have received such other documents as the Administrative Agent [or any Lender] or special New York counsel to [the Arranger] may reasonably request.

The "modern" credit agreement, as compared with those of 30 years ago, is nothing if not explicit. The development of a strong syndicated loan market has led to longer and denser credit agreements. While 60 pages may have been a lengthy credit agreement in 1980, it is today considered almost too short for comfort—an approach to be employed only for the strongest, most creditworthy companies.

The conditions precedent set out in credit agreements have joined in the drift to detail; in many cases they border on being a full closing list of what the borrower must deliver. Arrangers may still, however, want to have a catchall clause in addition to all of the other conditions, at least in those cases (admittedly relatively rare) where there will be a lapse of time between signing and effectiveness. The reasoning is that too much can happen, or be discovered, in the theoretical time period between execution of the final agreement and closing. If the borrower is organized in a developing country, perhaps it becomes suddenly subject to foreign exchange controls so that the lenders want to see an appropriate approval. Perhaps it is named in a billion dollar lawsuit and the lenders seek a fuller understanding of the litigation and the impact it will have upon the borrower's ability to repay. The final review of the borrower's charter documents might indicate that a special vote of preferred shareholders must be obtained before any borrowing is taken down. The agent may want the right to insist this be done before the agreement is deemed effective.

A "catchall" condition along the lines set out above is the common solution to these concerns. It allows the administrative agent (some agreements even give the right to individual lenders) to request additional documents that it "reasonably requests." The condition is rarely invoked, primarily because any truly serious issue should have been ferreted out during due diligence, and intervening events or discoveries (including all of the examples above) are probably already covered by representations. Borrowers may also resist the inclusion of this condition on the ground that whatever the lenders need should already be spelled out in the agreement. These factors notwithstanding, arrangers may be reluctant to remove the condition in agreements where there is to be any significant lapse of time between execution and closing.

5.1.12   Effectiveness

Box 5.17

The Administrative Agent shall notify the Borrower and the Lenders of the Effective Date, and such notice shall be conclusive and binding. Notwithstanding the foregoing, the obligations of the Lenders to make Loans shall not become effective unless each of the foregoing conditions is satisfied (or waived pursuant to Section [*Amendments and Waivers*]) on or prior to 3:00 p.m., New York City time, on _____, 20_____ (and, in the event such conditions are not so satisfied or waived, the Commitments shall terminate at such time).

Without limiting the generality of the provisions of Section [*Agent Exculpations*], for purposes of determining compliance with the conditions specified above, each Lender that has signed this Agreement shall be deemed to have consented to or accepted each document or other matter required thereunder to be consented by or acceptable to such Lender unless the Administrative Agent shall have received notice from such Lender prior to the Effective Date specifying its objection thereto.

Unless otherwise stated, a credit agreement becomes effective as a contract when all parties have executed and delivered counterparts thereof. However, the obligation of the lenders to extend credit under the agreement is treated separately. That obligation does not become effective until the borrower satisfies all of the "effectiveness date" conditions. The typical credit agreement does not, however, give the borrower an open-ended period within which to satisfy such conditions, and instead sets out a cutoff date beyond which the borrower may no longer make the agreement effective. The language in Box 5.17 is a typical example of a provision that imposes a cutoff date.

Although not so stated in the typical effectiveness language, the administrative agent has an important role in confirming the satisfaction of the conditions. It is normally the arranger's and agent's counsel that assembles and reviews the closing documents. The arranger or agent is also heavily involved in making sure that signature pages are received. It is logical, therefore, that the administrative agent be the one to advise the lenders of the agreement's effectiveness by posting a notice to that effect on the credit facility's website (see the discussion in Section 12.1.2). Providing for a notice of effectiveness from the agent also avoids any ambiguity as to whether the agreement is effective, since there is a single, clear act necessary before anyone (borrower or lender) can contend the agreement has gone live.

The effectiveness notice normally states merely that *documentary* conditions have been satisfied—in other words, only that the conditions to effectiveness, and not the conditions to each drawing, have been satisfied. The latter are not typically documentary in nature. The administrative agent is accordingly not responsible to ascertain compliance with such standard conditions as to the absence of any actual or incipient event of default, the truth of representations, or that the lenders themselves are satisfied as to matters within their discretion. It is, however, responsible to ensure that the borrower delivers any necessary certificates that swear to the absence of defaults and truth of representations. As to the documentary conditions, it is not uncommon for the credit agreement to include a provision (see the second paragraph in the sample language in Box 5.17) to the effect that the administrative agent may presume that each lender is satisfied with the conditions unless it receives notice to the contrary. Although this may appear repetitive of the agency exculpations (see Section 10.1.4), many agent institutions insist upon inclusion of additional language to this effect.

5.2 ONGOING CONDITIONS

Box 5.18

The obligation of each Lender to make any Loan is subject to the satisfaction of the following conditions:

(a) the representations and warranties of the Borrower set forth in this Agreement shall be true and complete on and as of the date of such Loan as if made on and as of such date (except to the extent that such representations and warranties expressly relate to an earlier date, in which case they shall be true and complete as of such earlier date); and

(b) at the time of and immediately after giving effect to such Loan, no Default shall have occurred and be continuing.

> Each Borrowing shall be deemed to constitute a certification by the Borrower on the date thereof as to the matters specified in the preceding sentence.

The previous sections of this chapter describe the conditions to be satisfied at closing in order for the lending commitments to become effective. Those conditions, once satisfied, no longer need to be looked at each time the borrower wants an extension of credit under the facility, except to the extent that their continued satisfaction is required through compliance with the representations in the credit agreement.

There are, however, additional conditions that must be satisfied *both* at the time of effectiveness and at the time of each drawing under the facility. Most credit agreements, for example, require at each borrowing or other extension of credit that all representations be true and that no actual or incipient event of default be outstanding. An agreement for a revolving credit facility in which availability is subject to a borrowing base may also include a condition that total exposure (loans and letters of credit) not exceed the borrowing base. Note that conversions of loans from one pricing option to another are not normally subject to a bring-down of ongoing conditions (but see the discussion in Section 4.5).

At initial drawdown (or effectiveness) the conditions that the representations be true and that no default exists are normally confirmed by the delivery by a senior officer (usually the chief financial officer) of the borrower of a certificate to this effect on the closing date. The agreement does not customarily require delivery of a similar certificate at later borrowings. However, the conditions precedent will likely include language similar to that set forth in Box 5.18, namely that each borrowing is *deemed* to constitute a certification by the borrower that the representations continue to be true and that no default exists. The purpose of the deemed certification is to trigger an event of default in the event that the representations are not, in fact, true at drawing, or an event of default is outstanding (see the discussion in Section 9.1.2).

Although satisfaction of the representations and no-default condition is confirmed by a certificate, credit agreements do not normally allow the mere delivery of the certificate to satisfy the condition itself; rather, the condition goes to the underlying facts. If the lenders have reason to believe that the certificate is inaccurate, they are not barred from asserting that the condition has not been satisfied.

Some key principles should be borne in mind when reading the ongoing conditions provision of a credit agreement.

5.2.1 Representations

The condition generally requires that all representations be true and complete on the date of a borrowing "as if made on and as of that date." In other words, if a borrowing is requested in July following a closing date in March, the representations must be true in July as if they were being made in July (having been true in March is not sufficient). There is one exception to this general rule, shown in paragraph (a) in Box 5.18. It is customary for representations that refer to a specific date (such as a list of the subsidiaries of the borrower "on the [signing date]") to be required to be true only as of that specific date. This allows borrowings to be made without updating those representations (for example, a representation that lists all subsidiaries of the borrower as of the signing of the agreement does not fail to be satisfied at a later date because of the establishment of new subsidiaries).

Some credit agreements require that representations need be true and complete only "in all material respects." This can lead to potential interpretation issues and may be redundant to the extent the representations themselves are already qualified by materiality. It has, however, become fairly standard in the market. One way that this is often addressed is to require representations that are qualified by materiality be true in all respects and those that are not be true in all material respects.

In credit agreements for investment-grade borrowers, and where the facility is to backstop commercial paper, this condition may expressly exempt the MAC clause and the litigation representation (and, sometimes, the Employee Retirement Income Security Act (ERISA) representation) for any borrowing or other extension of credit made after the closing date. Consequently the borrower would be permitted to borrow or obtain other credit even though a material adverse change or material adverse litigation has occurred (or an adverse ERISA event has developed).

5.2.2 Defaults

The ongoing conditions also include a requirement that no default or event of default exists at the time of or when effect is given to a borrowing or other extension of credit. The distinction between a default and an event of default is discussed in the opening paragraphs of Chapter 9. The basic rule is that, although the loans may be accelerated only if an event of default occurs, the lenders are entitled to refuse to increase their exposure (by making additional loans) if a mere default exists.

5.3 SUNGARD CONDITIONALITY IN ACQUISITION FINANCINGS

Box 5.19

Notwithstanding anything in this Commitment Letter, the Fee Letter, the Loan Documents or any other letter agreement or other undertaking concerning the financing of the transactions contemplated hereby to the contrary, (a) the only representations the accuracy of which shall be a condition to availability of the Loans on the Closing Date shall be (i) such of the representations made by or on behalf of Acquired Business in the Acquisition Agreement as are material to the interests of the Lenders, but only to the extent that you have the right to terminate your obligations under the Acquisition Agreement (or decline to consummate the Acquisition) as a result of a breach of such representations in the Acquisition Agreement (the *"Specified Acquisition Agreement Representations"*) and (ii) the Specified Representations (as defined below), and (b) the terms of the Loan Documents shall be in a form such that they do not impair the availability of the Loans on the Closing Date if the conditions set forth herein are satisfied (it being understood that, to the extent any Collateral (including the perfection of any security interest therein) is not or cannot be provided on the Closing Date (other than the perfection of Collateral with respect to which a security interest may be perfected by means of (x) filing a Uniform Commercial Code financing statement, (y) delivery of certificated equity securities, or (z) filing a notice with the United States Patent and Trademark Office or the United States Copyright Office), after your use of commercially reasonable efforts to do so, the perfection of such security interests in such Collateral shall not constitute a condition precedent to the availability of the Loans on the Closing Date but shall be required to be provided within 60 days (or such longer period as the Agent may agree) after the Closing Date pursuant to arrangements to be mutually agreed). For purposes hereof, *"Specified Representations"* means the representations and warranties of the Borrower and the Guarantors set forth in the Loan Documents relating to corporate existence; power and authority to enter into the Loan Documents; due authorization, execution, delivery and enforceability of the Loan Documents; Federal Reserve margin regulations; no conflicts of the Loan Documents with organizational documents, applicable law or material agreements; solvency; the Investment Company Act of 1940; the USA PATRIOT Act; creation, validity and perfection of security interests (subject to the limitations set forth in clause (b) above); and status as senior debt.

When negotiating acquisition agreements, buyers sometimes include a condition precedent that would permit them not to close under the acquisition agreement if they were unable to obtain the financing required to complete the acquisition (a so-called "financing out"). However, during the seller-favorable acquisition market in the mid-2000s the financing out was largely replaced with a reverse break-up fee, which the buyer was required to pay to the seller if the buyer could not close the acquisition due to its inability to obtain the required financing.

In 2005 a consortium of seven private equity sponsors bidding for SunGard Data Systems, Inc. negotiated a limitation on conditionality in the commitment letter for their bank financing that has come to be known as SunGard conditionality. This limitation was intended to minimize the divergence between the acquisition agreement conditions and the commitment letter conditions, thus minimizing the borrower's risk of being required to close an acquisition without its committed financing being available. SunGard conditionality has since become widely adopted in commitment letters for acquisition financings. The language in Box 5.19 is an example.

As shown in Box 5.19, and contrary to the customary practice described in Section 5.2.1, it is not a requirement that all of the credit agreement representations and warranties be true on the date of the borrowing that finances the acquisition. Rather, only the Specified Acquisition Agreement Representations and the Specified Representations must be true. The Specified Acquisition Agreement Representations are those that relate to the target company and its business. The key consideration from the borrower's perspective is that the truth of these representations does not condition the availability of the financing unless the borrower has the right to terminate the Acquisition Agreement (or decline to close the acquisition) as a result. The Specified Representations are a limited subset of the credit agreement representations that relate more to integrity of the financing structure than to the target company and its business.

The language in clause (a) in Box 5.19 specifies that it is the *accuracy* of the designated representations that is a condition to the availability of the financing. This formulation requires that the borrower make all of the credit agreement representations, but only the Specified Representations must be true as a condition to funding. If the non-Specified Representations are untrue, the lenders must still lend but there will be an immediate event of default entitling the lenders to exercise the remedies described in Section 9.2. Borrowers often argue for the *making* of the designated representations to be the condition. In this formulation, the borrower does not even make the non-Specified Representations on the closing date, so no event of default is triggered if those representations are untrue.

In a typical secured financing outside of the acquisition context, collateral security must be in place and properly perfected before lenders are willing to fund. The language in clause (b) in Box 5.19 specifies, in effect, that as a condition to funding, the borrower must only perfect liens that can be perfected by simple Uniform Commercial Code or intellectual property filings or by delivery of physical equity securities (typically the stock certificates acquired in the acquisition) and must use only commercially reasonable efforts to perfect the liens on other collateral. If the liens on that other collateral cannot be perfected at closing, the borrower will have a post-closing period (60 days is typical) to perfect those liens. Perfecting liens on other types of collateral may require more involvement of the target company (examples include negotiating a control agreement with the target company and the bank that maintains its accounts; or obtaining a title insurance policy in connection with a mortgage over real property), which is harder to obtain before the buyer owns and controls it. Borrowers sometimes negotiate for an exception from even having to create a lien over collateral that they would not have to perfect. This makes little sense in most cases, since typically liens can be created merely by signing a security agreement and target companies routinely sign agreements as a condition to closing the financing.

In addition to the language in Box 5.19, SunGard conditionality involves a few other concepts. First, the list of conditions precedent is typically limited and clearly defined. There is no catchall like that described in Section 5.1.11.6 or otherwise an ability for the lenders to request additional items. Second, the condition requiring the absence of a material adverse change with respect to the target company (the "Target MAC") will either be defined in the commitment letter exactly as it is defined in the acquisition agreement (and accordingly will include all the carveouts negotiated by the buyer and seller) or will simply cross-reference the definition in the acquisition agreement. Third, the absence of defaults condition referred to in Section 5.2.2 will not be applicable. Fourth, the commitment letter will typically reference agreed "precedent" documentation that will be the fallback if the parties cannot agree on terms not detailed in the term sheet included as part of the commitment letter. Fifth, with the exception of the solvency representation included in the Specified Representations and the Target MAC, lenders must rely on the acquisition agreement for protections relating to the target company and it is typically a condition to the availability of the loan facility that the acquisition must be completed in accordance with the terms of the acquisition agreement and that the acquisition agreement cannot be modified or waived in a manner materially adverse to the lenders without the consent of the lead arranger(s). Finally, even if the acquisition loan facility is syndicated to lenders prior to funding, the lender(s) that signed the commitment letter will be responsible to fund the loans on the closing date if the syndicate lenders fail to do so and retain sole voting control to grant waivers on the closing date.

Note that SunGard's special conditionality applies only on the closing date, when the loans that will finance the acquisition are funded. For a subsequent borrowing of revolving loans, all the representations and warranties in the credit agreement must be true, there must be no default and the absence of a material adverse change will be determined by reference to the credit agreement definition of that term and not to the Target MAC.

Note that the typical SunGard conditionality for U.S. acquisition financings bears some similarities and some differences with the "certain funds" practice in the United Kingdom. The certain funds practice derives from statutory requirements applicable to certain U.K. public companies. The City Code on Takeovers and Mergers requires "[a]n offeror must announce a bid only after ensuring that he/she can fulfil in full any cash consideration, if such is offered, and after taking all reasonable measures to secure the implementation of any other type of consideration." A financial advisor is also required to provide a "cash confirmation," confirming that the bidder has the necessary financial resources available to satisfy full acceptance of an offer. By market convention, a similar approach of not having financing conditions in acquisition agreements has been adopted for private acquisitions.

Unlike in U.S. acquisition financings, in which the acquisition agreement is signed with committed financing evidenced only by a commitment letter and term sheet, in U.K. "certain funds" financings the parties will also typically sign an interim loan agreement at the same time the acquisition agreement is signed. The interim loan agreement will have a short maturity (60 to 90 days is typical), limited representations and covenants that apply only to the borrower and not to the target company. In addition, the interim loan agreement will have limited conditions precedent that relate to the borrower (and are within its control) and the acquisition agreement (and, indirectly, the target company), and will require that the conditions contained in the acquisition agreement are satisfied. As is the case with U.S. commitments, the certain funds financing conditions will prohibit the acquisition agreement conditions from being waived without the consent of the lenders. The interim loan agreement will also typically contain a limitation on the ability of the lenders to assign their commitments, similar to the requirement in U.S. commitment letters that obligates the commitment letter lenders to fund the loans on the closing date if the syndicate lenders fail to do so.

It is typically not expected that interim loan agreements will be drawn. Rather, the borrower and lenders will expect to have negotiated and signed the permanent loan agreement containing the terms set forth in the commitment letter and term sheet by the time the acquisition is to close. Use of the interim loan agreement provides somewhat greater certainty of financing than the U.S. approach that uses a commitment letter, term sheet, and agreed precedent financing documents as a fallback for terms that have not been agreed.

CHAPTER 6

Representations

Representations are best viewed as *affirmations* by the borrower of facts or conclusions the lenders want to know are true. They are inserted into a credit agreement as a way to confirm the fundamental assumptions upon which the lenders agree to extend credit to the borrower. Although typically referred to as "representations," a credit agreement normally provides that the borrower makes both representations and "warranties" to the lenders. When used together, the terms may be viewed as interchangeable, although there is an historical distinction between the two, at least in the insurance context. A *warranty* was always deemed part of the insurance policy and had to be strictly complied with whether material to the loss or not. In contrast, a *representation* was deemed separate from the policy and affected the validity of the policy only if material. See *De Hahn v. Hartley*, 1 T. R. 344 (Kings Bench, 1786).

The purported distinction between representations and warranties has, in any event, long been roundly criticized (see *The History of the Development of the Warranty in Insurance Law,* by W. Vance, 20 Yale L.J. 523, 531–32 [1911]). In the insurance context, the distinction has also been statutorily overridden in a number of states, including New York (New York Insurance Law § 3106). Nevertheless, in the case of agreements of all kinds (including credit agreements, purchase agreements, employment agreements, and many others) the full phrase "represent and warrant" is still used with near universality. This practice probably continues more out of fear that using only one of the terms will somehow disadvantage a party rather than for any cogent legal distinction between the two.

Although the representations discussed in this chapter are written as if they are to be made only by the borrower, in a credit agreement that has multiple obligors (such as one with guarantors) each credit party typically provides representations as to itself and the ancillary documents that it signs. Representations address legal and financial issues, matters that relate to the business and capital structure of the borrower and its subsidiaries, and various other matters of concern to the lenders (such as whether the disclosures made by the borrower as a whole are complete). Of course, a borrower may be unable to make a representation in the form originally proposed by an arranger's counsel in the first draft of a credit agreement. The borrower can hardly affirm to the lenders that no material litigation exists if it is a defendant in a trillion dollar lawsuit. The solution is to allow the borrower to qualify a representation by reference to information set out in a disclosure schedule that is either attached to the credit agreement or separately delivered to the lenders prior to their execution of the agreement. The lenders are entitled not to sign the agreement if they do not like what is disclosed. The disclosure schedules themselves, when complete, become a very useful tool for the lenders to understand the borrower's business.

Some representations, particularly those that relate to legal condition, are also covered by the opinion of the borrower's counsel. To that extent, the representations and the legal opinion provide double confirmation of the same underlying issues. There is a difference, however, between the two. If a legal opinion is inaccurate, the lender's remedy, if any, is against the counsel that delivered the opinion. If a representation is inaccurate, the lender's remedy is more powerful: it can cut off additional credit and even demand repayment of the loans (at least if the representation is material and a breach thereof results in an event of default; see Section 9.1.2).

Borrowers sometimes push for representations to be qualified by knowledge. A borrower might want to say that "to its knowledge" it is duly organized, or "to its knowledge" its financial statements are accurate. In some instances, knowledge qualifications are appropriate, as is explained below. For example, the borrower is normally required to disclose threatened lawsuits that exist to its knowledge. However, to broaden this approach beyond the few narrow instances where it is customary may defeat the entire purpose of representations, which is to place the risk of a breach (even if in good faith) squarely with the borrower. It is the borrower, and not the lender, that is in the best position to verify the truth of the representations and, for this reason, knowledge qualifications are sparingly used.

Certain representations are qualified by reference to materiality, eliciting whether a circumstance "could" or "would" or "could reasonably be expected to" or "would reasonably be expected to" have a material adverse effect. Credit agreement drafters sometimes negotiate passionately over which of these approaches to take and it is important to understand the subtle difference between the two. That difference is grounded in the distinction between *can* and *will*. "Could" asks whether there is any circumstance (regardless of how likely) in which a material adverse effect could occur. A patently frivolous lawsuit for $1 trillion has the potential, if lost (since it *can* under some far-fetched scenario be lost), to produce a material adverse effect. The borrower would therefore be unable to represent that there is no litigation that *could* have a material adverse effect. "Would" asks whether the suit is likely to be lost. In other words, taking into account the strength of the case against the borrower, does it appear likely (*will*) it be lost, and, if lost, will it have a material adverse effect?

"Could reasonably be expected to" or "would reasonably be expected to" probably just soften (or confuse) the distinction by requiring that any determination be "reasonable." However, these formulations may cut both ways; they may help or hurt both borrower and lender. They may prevent the borrower from being too carefree in making a determination whether a suit should be disclosed, but they may also allow the borrower to argue that determining materiality must take into account the likelihood of liability. The formulations may thus also give the borrower grounds to argue that the frivolous $1 trillion lawsuit should be ignored (even if the word *could* is used) because it is, well, frivolous.

Lenders, in any event, much prefer the "could" formulation because it allows them (even if qualified by reasonableness) to make a credit judgment based upon the worst-case scenario that the outcome of all litigation will be adverse to the borrower. Borrowers naturally prefer the "would" formulation because it relieves them from having to disclose litigation that they conclude will be decided favorably. Any related disclosure schedule accordingly becomes much shorter, with the consequence that the usefulness of the representation as a disclosure device to enable the lenders to learn as much as possible about the borrower and its business is limited.

The purpose of representations is threefold. First, representations give the lenders a basis upon which to refuse to lend if they discover that a representation is not true. Second, in the worst case, since a breach of a representation is a default, the representations provide a basis to accelerate the loans if the underlying statements made by the borrower are not true. And, finally, representations may affirm the good faith of the lenders, a fact that could be important if, for example, the margin regulations representation is not true or if a necessary foreign exchange approval is not obtained—either of these could potentially result in a violation of law by the lenders. The representation gives the lenders something to point to if a government entity or regulator questions whether the lenders took the care they should to comply with relevant law.

It should be noted that under New York law, when a representation and warranty is made in a contract, the party to whom the warranty has been made may recover damages for a breach of that warranty, regardless of whether it relied upon the truth of the warranty or believed that it was true. In *CBS, Inc. v. Ziff-Davis Publishing Co.*, 75 N.Y.2d 496 (1990), the New York Court of Appeals held that "[t]he critical question is not whether the buyer believed in the truth of the warranted information . . . 'but whether [it] believed [it] was purchasing the [seller's] promise [as to its truth]. . . .' This view of 'reliance' i.e., as requiring no more than reliance on the express warranty as being a part of the bargain between the parties reflects the prevailing perception of an action for breach of express warranty as one that is no longer grounded in tort, but essentially in contract. . . . Once the express warranty is shown to have been relied on as part of the contract, the right to be indemnified in damages for its breach does not depend on proof that the buyer thereafter believed that the assurances of fact made in the warranty would be fulfilled." See Section 12.11, and Box 12.19, which contains customary credit agreement language regarding survival of representations and warranties regardless of any investigation made by any party and notwithstanding whether the administrative agent or any lender had notice or knowledge that any representation or warranty was incorrect. This stands in contrast to the type of reliance that must be established in a tort action based on fraud or misrepresentation for a claim of breach of express warranty—namely, a belief in the truth of the representations made in the express warranty and a change of position in reliance upon that belief.

6.1 LEGAL MATTERS REPRESENTATIONS

Legal matters representations address the legal status of the borrower and its subsidiaries. These representations are rarely, if ever, removed—even for investment-grade borrowers—since they help establish the good faith of the lenders in the event that, for any reason, any of the representations proves to be untrue. Given the overlap between legal matters representations and the legal opinions delivered at closing, some have argued that it is unnecessary to include such representations in the credit agreement. Although superficially logical, to keep the lenders in the same substantive position it would be necessary to rewrite the default provisions to permit acceleration upon the conclusions in a legal opinion being inaccurate. Such an approach would be highly unusual.

6.1.1 Organization, Existence, Power, and Qualification to Do Business

---

Box 6.1

The Borrower represents and warrants to the Lenders and the Administrative Agent that the Borrower and each of its Subsidiaries is duly organized, validly existing and in good standing under the laws of the jurisdiction of its organization, has all requisite power and authority to execute, deliver, and perform this Agreement and the other Loan Documents to which it is a party and to carry on its business as now conducted and, except where the failure to do so, individually or in the aggregate, could not reasonably be expected to have a Material Adverse Effect, is qualified to do business in, and is in good standing in, every jurisdiction where such qualification is required.

The organization and existence representation tells the lenders four things about the borrower: that it is organized, that it exists, that it has certain powers, and that it is qualified to do business where required. For a borrower that is an individual, none of this is necessary, so long as the lender can verify that the borrower is alive and legally competent (meaning that he or she is of age and *compos mentis* and, in some states, has not been deprived of the right to enter into contracts, such as by a conviction for a felony). A representation to that effect in an agreement with a two-legged borrower would, however, look exceedingly silly since confirming that a walking, talking person is alive and competent is easily covered by external diligence.

For a borrower created by law, such as a corporation, limited liability company, partnership, or other kind of legal entity, existence, organization, power, and qualification to do business are not as obvious. Obtaining a representation becomes one element of several to confirm that these characteristics are satisfied; each is important. Take existence as an example. Contracting with an entity that a lender believes is a corporation, but which, in fact, does not exist as a corporation, could thrust the lender into a morass of truly unwanted legal questions, such as whether the credit agreement was properly authorized and executed, whether the borrower can permissibly hold all necessary licenses and conduct business in states where it owns property and has operations, how the borrower is taxed, whether the lenders are entitled to the "corporate" usury exception for interest on the loans, and a host of other issues (if, for example, a subsidiary does not subsist as a corporation its shareholder— the borrower—may not have the benefit of limited liability).

Each of these four attributes—organization, existence, power, and qualification to do business—has a distinct meaning and purpose. They have been the subject of numerous court decisions and treatises and come with an accumulation of market lore as to how they should be used.

"Organization" means that an entity is properly incorporated or formed ("due incorporation," in the case of corporations, or "due formation," in the case of partnerships or limited liability companies) and that other steps required under state law to complete the organizational process have been accomplished. By way of illustration, a corporation is generally duly incorporated once all of the statutory elements to the creation of a corporation are completed, including the preparation and execution of a charter document with the minimum legally required provisions—in New York these include name, purpose, county of location, aggregate authorized shares, as well as other items—together with the submission of the charter to the relevant state filing office and the issuance by that office of a certificate of incorporation. Similar requirements apply for partnerships and limited liability companies, with a certificate of formation or organization generally used in place of a charter.

To make the due organization representation, however, the borrower must also be satisfied that any additional organizational steps required by law have been taken. In the case of a corporation, these include the adoption of bylaws, the appointment of officers, the issuance of stock, and satisfaction with minimum capital requirements. For a partnership or limited liability company, execution of a partnership or operating agreement and the receipt of initial capital contributions from members are among the necessary actions.

When delivering opinions lawyers resist strenuously issuing the due organization opinion because to determine whether many of the required additional steps have been completed necessitates an inquiry into facts. The common practice is, therefore, to write the representation to address "due organization," but to draft the opinion to cover solely "due incorporation" or "due formation." Even here, however, if the attorney or firm that renders the opinion did not participate in the organization process, or if the entity was not recently organized, an accepted practice is for the opinion not to address organization, incorporation, or formation at all, but rather simply to state that the entity "validly exists." An exact congruence, therefore, between the scope of the due organization representation and the corresponding legal opinion rarely occurs.

The second element of the due organization and existence opinion, namely "existence," refers to whether the entity still exists as the corporation, partnership, or limited liability company that was created. A corporation can be duly organized and yet cease to exist for a number of reasons. It may have been dissolved voluntarily by action of the shareholders, or judicially by action of the state for any number of reasons, including that the corporation exceeded its powers, conducted a fraudulent business, or failed to pay taxes. Unless provided otherwise in a partnership agreement, a partnership can cease to exist upon the death or dissolution of one of the general partners. Any of these entities (corporation, partnership, or limited liability company) may also, upon creation, have had a limited life. Although rare today, limited-life corporations were in the past more frequent and it is not unheard of to learn at a closing that a subsidiary created in 1920 had a 75-year life and no longer exists.

The reference to "good standing" in the phrase "validly existing and in good standing" simply means that the borrower has filed all necessary annual reports and tax returns with the relevant tax and other authorities of the organizing state. The representation, in effect, provides comfort that the borrower is not subject to imminent judicial dissolution for failure to comply with these legal requirements. The concept of "good standing," common for companies in the United States, generally does not exist for non-U.S. entities.

"Power," of course, refers to whether an entity has the power to undertake the obligations under the credit agreement (or other loan documents) and to conduct the business that it is engaged in. A corporation that accepts deposit accounts from customers must be organized as a bank, and not merely under the business corporation statute, to have the requisite power. A life insurance company may not have the power to guarantee the obligations of a subsidiary (or even to pledge the stock of a subsidiary) to support credit agreement obligations. Similarly, certain banks under the legal scheme pursuant to which they are organized are restricted, with limited exceptions, from guaranteeing obligations on behalf of a customer, except through the device of a letter of credit. A purported guarantee in any other form might be *ultra vires* (beyond the power) of the bank and perhaps unenforceable. See *OCC Interpretive Letter No. 1010*, September 7, 2004, and related amendments under 73 Fed. Reg. 22215 for this rule as it applies to national banks.

The powers of an entity are set out in two places—in its organizational documents and in applicable statutes. Every certificate of incorporation for a corporation, and every partnership or limited liability company agreement, contains a declaration of what the powers of the entity are, even if only a brief statement that it has all of the powers "prescribed or allowed by law." State statutes also set forth the powers permitted to entities created under its law. Here is where, for example, the business of banking and issuing insurance are reserved to banks and insurance companies and not permitted for ordinary business corporations.

The litany in the sample language set out in Box 6.1, to the effect that the borrower has the power to "execute, deliver, and perform" the agreement, is used in a number of other representations as well (see Sections 6.1.2, 6.1.5, and 6.1.6). Each of these words has a distinct meaning. "Execution" refers to the signature by the borrower of the agreement. "Delivery" refers to the act, following signature, of handing over (delivering) the agreement to the lenders with the intent that it be treated as an effective and binding agreement between the borrower and each of the other parties. "Performance" refers to the ability of the borrower to pay interest, to repay principal, to comply with affirmative and negative covenants, and to undertake all of the other obligations (such as indemnities and submission to jurisdiction) set out in the typical credit agreement.

"Qualification to do business" refers to the legal right of an entity to do business where it owns property and conducts operations. It applies when an entity is organized in one state, but does business in another. A Delaware corporation may not, for example, conduct business in New York or New Jersey or North Dakota, for that matter, unless it has first been authorized by those states to do business there. The authorization process typically requires completion of an application containing, among other things, the appointment of the secretary of state as a process agent for suit in that state and an agreement to pay taxes. The secretary of state, in turn, confirms that the name of the entity is not already used by, or confusingly similar to, the name of a local (or previously qualified) corporation or other entity. An entity that passes these tests, and continues to file annual reports and pay taxes, is "qualified" to do business in that state.

A corporation, partnership, or limited liability company that is not "qualified" to do business in a state, but which nevertheless conducts business in that state may be liable for penalties, fines, and other charges. In addition, many states have so-called "door-closing statutes" that prevent a nonqualified entity from resort to the courts of that state to enforce contracts. So, conducting business in New Jersey (and contracting with New Jersey people) without being qualified in New Jersey could make for a very short litigation indeed should the nonqualified entity try to sue in New Jersey for a breach of contract.

Most door-closing statutes permit after-the-fact cure of failure to qualify, though this normally necessitates payment of all back taxes (and penalties and fines) and is not necessarily something done quickly.

The qualification to do business representation is typically conditioned by reference to materiality. This is based upon several factors. First, the criteria for determining when an entity crosses the threshold of business activity that necessitates that it qualify in a particular state are often obtuse. It is not difficult for a business to conduct marginal activity in a jurisdiction that passes the magic threshold and yet be unaware that it has done so. Second, perhaps as a corollary of the first, it is generally conceived as unfair to penalize a borrower—by withholding credit or accelerating— for failure to qualify in a state where the consequences are not material to the business of the borrower and its subsidiaries as a whole.

The representation shown in the language in Box 6.1 covers each of the four critical elements of organization, existence, power, and qualification. The typical credit agreement does not, however, stop there, but in addition looks for these four attributes to be confirmed by due diligence and delivery of documents at closing (see Section 5.1.3) as well as by appropriate closing opinions.

6.1.2 Due Authorization

Box 6.2

The Borrower represents and warrants to the Lenders and the Administrative Agent that the execution, delivery, and performance of this Agreement and the other Loan Documents have been duly authorized by all necessary corporate and, if required, shareholder, partner, or member action on the part of the Borrower and its Subsidiaries.

Once the organization, existence, and power of the borrower are established (see the discussion above), the next inquiry focuses on whether the credit agreement and related instruments have been duly *authorized*. For an individual (except if the signer is acting for another under a power of attorney), the concept of authorization is irrelevant, so long as he or she is alive and competent—the act of execution is the only "authorization" needed. For a corporation, partnership, or limited liability company, however, additional action is normally necessary.

What action is required for all of the different species of borrower (corporation, partnership, limited liability company, trust, association, government or government agency, and so on) to authorize an agreement is well beyond the scope of this volume. It is useful, how-ever, to state a few general principles. In general, for a corporation, the execution of a contract by an appropriate officer (for example, the chief executive officer or, for a financial contract, the chief financial officer) is often sufficient authorization as a matter of corporate law, at least in the absence of a provision in the applicable corporate law statute or the corporation's organizational documents requiring board approval. That said, it is the near universal practice in lending transactions, as well as good corporate governance, to require that material contracts be approved by the board of the corporation, which can be either by way of a special resolution that expressly authorizes the credit agreement or through a general resolution that gives officers the authority to enter into agreements for borrowings. Materiality for these purposes is dependent upon the assets and credit strength of the borrower. A $1,000,000 loan facility for a corporation with assets of $2,000,000 is probably material and should be authorized by resolution. A $100,000,000 loan facility for one of the top ten Fortune 500 companies is akin to petty cash and is probably not material and probably does not need authorization by resolution. Shareholder approval is normally not required unless the charter or the corporate law under which the borrower is organized so provides. A sale of all or substantially all of the assets of a corporation, for example, often requires shareholder approval; if the credit agree-ment is to finance the purchase of all or substantially all of the assets of a selling corporation, the lenders will want to be satisfied that the requisite seller shareholder approval has been obtained.

For a partnership or limited liability company, authorization by a general partner or managing member is normally sufficient for the entity. If, however, the partner or member is itself a corporation, the lenders will want to know that the partner or member is itself autho-rized to execute the agreement on behalf of the borrower. In the lan-guage in Box 6.2, this point is covered by the reference to partner or member action "if required."

Other entities (associations, trusts, foreign governments, or agen-cies), all have their own specialized rules with respect to authorization.

A representation that an agreement has been duly authorized does not in and of itself supply authorization if one is missing. However, if an agreement has not been duly authorized, including the representa-tion in the credit agreement may bolster a lender's argument that it relied upon the "apparent authority" of the officer, partner, or member that executed the agreement. If the relevant person *appeared* to have authority to bind the borrower—as should be the case given the rep-resentation, unless the lender knows otherwise—the lender should be protected at least to the extent of money advanced. That said, when seeking repayment of loans, no lender wants to go before a court and argue the endlessly fascinating issue of apparent versus actual authority. A due authorization opinion is therefore helpful but, by itself, not sufficient and so, as discussed in Section 5.1.3, lenders' counsel always insists upon seeing the paper—charter, bylaws, resolutions, and so forth—that evidence actual authorization of the facility.

6.1.3 Due Execution

> **Box 6.3**
>
> The Borrower represents and warrants to the Lenders and the Administrative Agent that this Agreement and the other Loan Documents have been duly executed and delivered by the Borrower and its Subsidiaries party thereto.

The reference in Box 6.3 to the agreement being "duly executed" tells the lenders two things: first, that the agreement has, in fact, been executed and, second, that the individual who signed the agreement on behalf of the corporation, partnership, or limited liability company that is the borrower is, in fact, the one authorized to bind the borrower. So, if the president and any vice president of a corporation have been authorized by board resolution to execute a credit agreement, signature by a director will likely not amount to "due execution." Due execution also carries with it other helpful baggage, such as a confirmation that multiple signers have executed the agreement if that is what the charter, bylaws, or resolutions require. In the case of an individual, the concept of "due execution" confirms that the agreement has been signed either by the individual or by another under a power of attorney that has not been revoked (whether by death of the individual or other circumstance) and that grants the signer the authority to bind the individual to the agreement.

In the United States (unlike many civil law jurisdictions), agreements do not need to be notarized in order to be duly executed. This is generally even the case for mortgages and deeds of trust, which can be duly executed without notarization, although notarization is required for them to be in recordable form. Notarization is, however, a useful evidentiary action that makes it more difficult (particularly if the signer is an individual) to argue that the signature is forged or fraudulent, since the notary is, in effect, a state-licensed witness that swears to the execution of a document.

The due execution representation also normally includes an affirmation that the agreement has been duly delivered. "Delivery" in this context refers to the tendering by the signer for the borrower of the executed agreement to the lenders with the intent that it constitute a binding agreement. Execution of an agreement alone is not sufficient, since execution is purely mechanical: it might be effected by an officer who expects to be enroute to Europe during the closing and who signs the agreement with instructions to junior officers that his or her signature be delivered only if they are satisfied with the final version of the document. "Execution and delivery" conveys the two essential ingredients to a binding agreement—signature and supplying a copy (whether electronic or paper) to the lenders and the administrative agent.

6.1.4   Enforceability

Box 6.4

The Borrower represents and warrants to the Lenders and the Administrative Agent that this Agreement and the other Loan Documents each constitutes a legal, valid, and binding obligation of the Borrower and its Subsidiaries party thereto, enforceable in accordance with its terms, subject to applicable bankruptcy, insolvency, reorganization, fraudulent conveyance or transfer, moratorium, or other similar laws affecting creditors' rights generally, and subject to general principles of equity, regardless of whether considered in a proceeding in equity or at law.

The litany "legal, valid, binding, and enforceable" has near-religious status as a way to express the ultimate worth of an agreement. Certainly this is the case for legal opinions for which numerous bar reports, discussions, and treatises have been devoted to the precise meaning (or lack thereof) of these terms, often referred to (in the opinion context) as the "remedies opinion." Historically, the phrase was not included in agreements on the theory that if the other legal-oriented representations (organization, authorization, execution, and compliance with law) were given, a statement as to legality, validity, binding effect, and enforceability was unnecessary. Modern practice, however, is to include the representation as a matter of course.

It might be thought that each of these four words has a distinct and agreed meaning, but they are, in fact, often viewed as interchangeable or redundant. The *1998 Report of the TriBar Opinion Committee*, 53 Bus. Law. 591 (1998), stated that "the remedies opinion may take a number of forms without any difference in meaning. Some . . . include the word 'legal'. . . . Others omit one or both of the words 'valid' or 'binding.' Still others omit the word 'enforceable.' Neither the inclusion of 'legal' nor any of these omissions expands or limits the generally understood meaning of the remedies opinion." The general consensus for opinion practice, therefore, is that these words simply express that an agreement is enforceable as against the borrower.

This does not mean that it is enforceable in each and every respect. Opinions customarily set out in detail the ways in which the agreement is not enforceable, for example with respect to participant offset rights (see Section 10.5) or the submission to jurisdiction clause insofar as it applies to federal courts (see Section 12.8.1). Opinions also normally include a qualification for the effects of bankruptcy and similar events (in a case under federal bankruptcy law, all enforcement becomes subject to bankruptcy court approval), as well as for "equitable remedies" (this refers to remedies, such as ordering "specific performance," that are in a court's discretion). Confusingly, to list all the ways in which the enforceability representation is *not* true is not the practice in agreements—few borrowers even make the request. The only standard qualification taken for the enforceability opinion is that shown in the sample language in Box 6.4, namely the bankruptcy and equitable remedies exceptions. The underlying theory must simply be that a lender would be laughed out of court (and may even subject itself to potential liability) were it to accelerate loans based upon its sudden "discovery" that, horrors, the participant offset right is unenforceable. This is especially the case given that all lenders will have been put on notice of the infirmity by dint of the qualifications to the borrower's legal opinion.

6.1.5   No Conflict

Box 6.5

The Borrower represents and warrants to the Lenders and the Administrative Agent that the execution, delivery, and performance of this Agreement and the other Loan Documents (a) will not violate any applicable law or regulation, (b) will not violate the charter, bylaws, or other organizational documents of the Borrower or any of its Subsidiaries or any order of any Governmental Authority, and (c) will not violate or result in a default under any indenture, agreement, or other instrument binding upon the Borrower or any of its Subsidiaries or its assets, or give rise to a right thereunder to require any payment to be made by the Borrower or any of its Subsidiaries, and will not result in the creation or imposition of any Lien on any asset of the Borrower or any of its Subsidiaries [except to the extent provided in the Security Documents].

The no-conflicts representation covers three classes of potential conflicts: conflict with law, conflict with organizational documents, and conflict with other agreements to which the borrower may be party. It is customary also for the no-conflicts representation to state that the agreement will not give rise to a lien on the borrower's property (other than, of course, in favor of the lenders). The purpose of these representations is simple. An agreement that violates law or a borrower's organizational documents may very well be unenforceable. An agreement that violates other agreements to which the borrower is a party may subject the lender to liability for intentionally inducing breach of the other agreement and, if the other agreement is a debt instrument, may result in acceleration of outstanding amounts. The latter event, in particular, might adversely affect the borrower's credit profile. Breaching a debt covenant in a bond indenture or violating a government regulation could dramatically affect the borrower's ability to service the loans if the bonds are accelerated or a compliance proceeding is instituted by a regulatory agency against the borrower.

The representation that there is no conflict with applicable law or regulations may arguably make redundant the separate representation (discussed below) that all necessary government filings or approvals have been made or obtained. A borrower could not, presumably, warrant that the agreement does not violate applicable law if it neglects to obtain a legally required government consent, such as a foreign exchange approval. There are, however, a number of other ways in which the execution, delivery, or performance of a credit agreement could violate law. The agreement may provide for interest in excess of the applicable usury limit. It may violate the margin regulations, although that is typically the subject of a separate representation (see Section 6.1.12). If the borrower is a company regulated by state public utility boards, it may violate short-term or long-term debt limits to which the borrower is subject.

Compliance with law can be particularly important in cross-border transactions and lenders and their counsel should take all appropriate steps to try to assure that the obligations of the non-U.S. borrower are lawful. For one thing, even assuming that New York law is the governing law of the contract, under some circumstances New York law will recognize a defense of illegality under other law. For example, a payor whose obligations are payable in a foreign jurisdiction, and were undertaken in violation of the laws of that jurisdiction, may be able to assert the defense of illegality in a U.S. court, at least if the payee knew or should have known of the illegality. See *Lehman Bros. Commer. Corp v. Minmetals Int'l Non-Ferrous Metals Trading Co.*, 179 F. Supp.2d 118 (S.D.N.Y. 2000).

The opinion of the borrower's counsel customarily includes a statement that the agreement does not violate applicable law, though it is normally subject to a number of conditions. It is, for example, typically limited to the law of the particular state or foreign country in which the counsel is admitted (this may or may not be the state or country in which the borrower conducts its principal operations and where the lenders may want to enforce their loans) and limited also to the kinds of laws that the counsel could reasonably expect to be applicable to a loan transaction. The opinion accordingly does not, in the United States, address municipal laws or regulations, zoning regulations, or laws that may be peculiarly applicable to the borrower by reason of its business. The corresponding representation, in contrast, is unqualified. It is a flat statement that the agreement does not violate any *applicable* law. Qualifications of the type conceded in the opinion context by reason of the opinion giver's limited knowledge are not appropriate when the borrower makes a representation, since the borrower is presumed to be familiar with all laws that could be applicable to the loan transaction.

The representation with respect to organizational or governance documents addresses many of the same issues that are covered in the due authorization representation discussed in Section 6.1.2. After all, failure to obtain a required shareholder, partner, or member approval before entering into a credit facility may not only result in an unauthorized borrowing, but may conflict with the corporate charter, partnership agreement, or operating agreement of the borrower as well. However, this is not always the case. If the limited liability company operating agreement of a proposed parent guarantor expressly states that the limited liability company may not guarantee the debt of others, an amendment, rather than a mere authorization, is in order. To ignore a prohibition on guarantees may result in an unenforceable guarantee (and perhaps even risk of liability to members). If the preferred stock provisions of a corporate charter prohibit secured debt in excess of a given percentage of the equity capital of the borrower, violation of such a restriction could lead to a shift of board control to the holders of preferred stock—a development that the lending syndicate may or may not have anticipated.

The no-conflicts representation addresses two issues in addition to compliance with law and organizational instruments: the relationship of the credit agreement to other agreements that bind the borrower and whether the credit agreement will give rise to liens upon the borrower's property.

The representation with respect to other agreements is fairly straightforward. If another contract to which the borrower is a party (typically this will be another debt instrument) prohibits the loans contemplated by the credit agreement at least two potentially bad things can happen. First, as noted earlier, breach of the other debt agreement may adversely impact the credit standing of the borrower. Once it borrows the loans and thereby contravenes covenants in the other agreement, the other debt may be accelerated and the interest payments be bumped up to a default rate. The borrower may simply be unable to pay or refinance such a large amount of debt. And for the lending syndicate the situation may be equally disastrous, even if the lenders benefit from a cross-default and can accelerate their own loans (see Section 9.1.4). They will not want to be competing with a group of other lenders (whether in or out of bankruptcy) for the borrower's precious dollars.

There is a second concern as well. If another agreement prohibits additional debt (such as the loans under the credit agreement), the lenders may expose themselves to liability to the other debt holders under the tort doctrine of intentional interference with contractual relations (also called tortious interference). Although it did not involve a debt agreement, this is the mess that Texaco fell into in 1984 when it signed an agreement with the Getty Oil Company to acquire all Getty stock. Getty had several days previously signed a letter of intent with Pennzoil to sell a 43 percent stake. Pennzoil sued Texaco (in Texas) and won an $11 billion judgment for its alleged interference with the Pennzoil–Getty "agreement" (there was, naturally, considerable question as to whether the letter of intent constituted an agreement, but a jury found that it did). After a four-year legal battle, which included Texaco's ultimately being forced to file for bankruptcy, the dispute was settled with a $3 billion payment by Texaco to Pennzoil.

Whether a clean no-conflicts representation protects a group of lenders against a claim of tortious interference depends upon the facts of any particular transaction. Case law delineates five elements to tortious interference (the existence of a valid contract between the plaintiff and a third party, defendant's knowledge of that contract, defendant's intentional procurement of the third-party's breach of the contract without justification, actual breach of the contract, and damages resulting therefrom) and a clean representation from the borrower helps counter two of them: knowledge of the contract and intentional procurement of a breach. See *Lama Holding Co. v. Smith Barney Inc.*, 88 N.Y.2d 413 (1996).

The no-conflicts representation also has the borrower confirm that the execution of the agreement does not result in any lien upon property of the borrower. Although such a lien is unlikely to arise if the credit facility is unsecured, it could occur if the facility is secured and the borrower has another debt agreement with a so-called "equal and ratable sharing clause." This kind of provision is discussed in more detail in Section 7.6.2. Equal and ratable sharing clauses are commonly seen in bond indentures in which the issuer agrees that it will not grant liens to secure debt (subject, of course, to a long list of negotiated, but standard, exceptions) without making provision to "equally and ratably" secure the bonds. Thus, granting liens to a lending syndicate may require granting liens to the bondholders and a failure to do so may not only result in acceleration of the bonds, but could also cast a cloud over the validity of the lenders' own liens. In some cases, the equal and ratable sharing clause may even purport to work automatically, so that the lenders that expected to be the only secured creditors suddenly find themselves sharing with a mass of other debt. The representation provides confirmation to the lenders that their liens are not subject to any equal and ratable sharing clause.

Borrowers often request that the no-conflicts representation be qualified by reference to materiality. An example might be a statement to the effect that the credit facility will not give rise to any breach of a law, organization document, or agreement that would have a "material adverse effect." More commonly, the request is to limit the representation to "material" agreements and to offer a clean representation as to matters of law and organizational documents.

A qualification that requires a conflict to have a material adverse effect can be problematic. If the "material adverse effect" is defined by reference only to the financial condition of the borrower (and not to include reference to the enforceability of the agreement), the representation will miss the mark. To take an exaggerated example, if by reason of a violation of law the agreement is unenforceable, the borrower might conclude that the conflict is in fact entirely *favorable*; it gets the proceeds without a corresponding obligation to repay! Some lenders (and their counsel) therefore strenuously resist qualifying the no-conflict-with-law representation by reference to materiality.

Qualifying the no-conflicts representation by reference to *material* agreements is less troublesome, though which agreements are "material" can be subject to dispute, and even a nonmaterial debt agreement can inflict a substantial burden on a borrower if it must be refinanced on short notice. Large corporate borrowers with far-flung operations may, nevertheless, respond that they have no way of knowing whether a subsidiary in, say, Mauritius has executed an agreement that will be breached by virtue of the credit agreement (although they are prepared to say that any such breach will not be material). The normal response from the lenders is one of risk allocation. If the borrower is concerned about what its Mauritius subsidiary may have done, how is it that the lenders are not to be concerned? This issue is typically resolved through negotiation, due diligence, and finger-crossing (by either the lenders or the borrower); no completely uniform practice has developed.

6.1.6 Government Approvals

Box 6.6

The Borrower represents and warrants to the Lenders and the Administrative Agent that the execution, delivery, and performance of this Agreement and the other Loan Documents do not require any consent or approval of, registration, or filing with, or other action by, any Governmental Authority, except such as have been obtained or made and are in full force and effect [or that consist of filings and recordings in connection with the liens created under the Security Documents].

"*Governmental Authority*" means the government of the United States of America or any other nation, or of any political subdivision thereof, whether state or local, and any agency, authority, instrumentality, regulatory body, court, central bank, or other entity exercising executive, legislative, judicial, taxing, regulatory, or administrative powers or functions of or pertaining to government (including any supra-national bodies such as the European Union or the European Central Bank).

The government approvals representation has the borrower confirm that all necessary government filings and approvals with or from any "Governmental Authority" have been obtained in connection with the agreement. The term "Governmental Authority," as shown in the sample language in Box 6.6, is normally defined broadly to pick up not just federal and state government agencies, but also courts, foreign governments, central banks, and even municipalities.

Since the representation sweeps in any filing or approval necessary for the execution, delivery, or *performance* of the credit agreement, borrowers typically want to be very careful not to make a flat statement that no actions from or with governmental authorities are necessary. A borrower might, for example, fear that the representation requires it to affirm that all business licenses and permits (including, say, environmental permits) have been obtained given that it can hardly perform the agreement if its sole chemical plant must be shut down because of a missing approval. This may be one rationale for the exception shown in the language in Box 6.6 that no filings or approvals are necessary other than those already obtained. From the perspective of the lender, this approach nevertheless begs the question as to what actions relating specifically to the agreement are, in fact, necessary. Therefore, in cases where the parties know of a particular government filing or approval (some examples are identified in the next paragraph), the general practice is to list these specifically or to set them out in a disclosure schedule.

As discussed in more detail in Section 5.1.5, approvals required for the execution, delivery, or performance of a credit agreement can take a variety of forms, including foreign exchange approvals (for loans to non-U.S. borrowers in countries that have exchange controls), state public utility commission authorizations (for loans to certain state-regulated utilities), and bankruptcy court orders (for debtor-in-possession financings). In an acquisition context notice under the Hart–Scott–Rodino Act and approval by the Justice Department of the acquisition itself may be necessary. Additionally, if the acquisition involves a foreign investment in a U.S. entity, a voluntary notification to the Committee on Foreign Investment in the United States (known as CFIUS), an interagency committee that reviews the national security implications of foreign investment in the U.S. economy, may also be advisable in order to obtain CFIUS clearance that would protect the transaction from future scrutiny. If the acquisition involves the transfer of licenses or permits, the approval of local government authorities may also be required. Although neither of these latter examples is strictly needed for the credit agreement to be enforceable, if any portion of the funding for the acquisition is to be provided by the credit facility, the borrower may insist that the exception language of the representation be broad enough to cover these ancillary approvals—hence the approach shown above to reference other (unnamed) approvals that have "been obtained."

The government approvals representation also covers registrations and filings with government entities. Filings and recordings necessary to perfect liens are the classic example; these are normally handled through a general statement like that shown in brackets in Box 6.6 rather than through an explicit list of required security filings. Sometimes, also, after-the-fact filings can be important for the enforceability of the credit facility, such as lodging a final execution copy with a central bank to seal the effectiveness of a foreign exchange approval and, in these instances, a specific exception needs to be written into the representation; by definition, this is not an action that can have already been effected when the agreement is first executed. The representation is generally understood not to pick up filings that the borrower may itself be required to make for it to comply with law. An example of the latter is the filing of the credit agreement with the Securities and Exchange Commission (SEC) if the agreement crosses the materiality threshold set out in the securities laws.

6.1.7   Compliance with Law; Licenses

Box 6.7

The Borrower represents and warrants to the Lenders and the Administrative Agent that each of the Borrower and its Subsidiaries is in compliance with all laws, regulations, and orders of any Governmental Authority applicable to it or its property and all indentures, agreements, and other instruments binding upon it or its property, except where the failure to do so, individually or in the aggregate, could not reasonably be expected to have a Material Adverse Effect.

While the no-conflict and government approvals representations discussed in Sections 6.1.5 and 6.1.6 confirm that the credit agreement does not itself violate law or require a filing or approval, the compliance with law representation addresses the operation of the borrower's business generally. It answers the question whether the borrower's business operations comply generally with law and whether it has obtained all necessary licenses. The representation is normally qualified by reference to materiality (consistent with the approach described in Section 6.1.1 for qualifications to do business) on the theory that, given the intensity of government regulation, it is unfair to penalize a borrower for breaches that are immaterial to its business. The failure to obtain a fire-code exemption is thus not treated the same as a radio station that operates without a broadcast license or an electric utility without a certificate of public convenience and necessity.

The purpose of the compliance with law representation is less to allow the lending syndicate to argue that they acted in good faith (as is the objective generally of the legal representations explained earlier in this chapter) and more to give the syndicate leverage *vis-à-vis* the borrower in the event it is suspected the latter may be in material breach of legal standards. Examples abound. The lenders may discover that a proposed waste project does not comply with municipal zoning regulations, a cable television company is submitting bills to its customers without proper fee disclosures, or a chemical processing company is spewing noxious fumes into the atmosphere in violation of environmental emissions standards. These may or may not be material, but with the representation the lenders are at least able to request a "serious talk" (code for threatening to refrain from making additional loans or even to accelerate the loans) to determine the question of materiality and hear how the borrower proposes to remedy any breach.

6.1.8 Investment Company Act

Box 6.8

The Borrower represents and warrants to the Lenders and the Administrative Agent that neither the Borrower nor any of its Subsidiaries is, or is affiliated with, an "investment company" as defined in, or subject to regulation under, the Investment Company Act of 1940.

The Investment Company Act representation has the borrower affirm that it is not an "investment company," or otherwise "affiliated with" an investment company, as those terms are defined in the Investment Company Act of 1940, or otherwise subject to regulation under the Act. An investment company under the Act that does not register under the Act is prohibited from engaging in a wide variety of business activities (subject to a number of exceptions that are beyond the scope of this volume). As a consequence, lending to an unregistered investment company can lead to two potentially very serious adverse consequences for a lending syndicate. First, the credit agreement itself may be unenforceable. Second, as the borrower conducts business, it may expose itself to potential criminal sanctions and the inability to enforce its contracts in court, neither of which is helpful to the credit standing of the borrower.

6.1.9 Anti-Corruption Regulations

Box 6.9

None of the Borrower or any of its Subsidiaries nor, to the knowledge of the Borrower, any director, officer, agent, employee, or other person acting on behalf of the Borrower or any of its Subsidiaries has taken any action, directly or indirectly, that would result in a violation by such persons of the Foreign Corrupt Practices Act of 1977, as amended, and the rules and regulations thereunder (the *"FCPA"*) or any other applicable anticorruption law; and the Loan Parties have instituted and maintain policies and procedures designed to [promote and achieve] [ensure] continued compliance therewith.

The Foreign Corrupt Practices Act of 1977 (FCPA) prohibits issuers of U.S. securities, U.S. domestic concerns, and non-U.S. persons that take certain actions within the United States, from "corruptly" offering or giving "anything of value" to a non-U.S. government official, directly or indirectly, in order to influence official action or otherwise obtain an improper business advantage.

In the past decade, there has been a substantial increase in FCPA-related investigations and enforcement actions, a number of very large FCPA-related settlements involving the Department of Justice and SEC and financial institutions. Worldwide there has been greater crossborder cooperation among enforcement authorities who have simlarly relied on analogous laws such as the UK Bribery Act 2010 in England to regulate and enforce illegal activity.

Lenders are not required to guarantee that borrowers with whom they enter into financing relationships will not, in the future, violate the antibribery provisions of the FCPA, and there is no basis for lender liability for planned or future FCPA violations by a borrower based merely on the financing relationship. The only arguable basis for FCPA liability for a lender would be in the extreme case where the lender was aware at the time the financing agreement was entered into that the proceeds of the loan were likely to be used for the purpose of paying a bribe or bribes in violation of the FCPA and lent the money for the purpose of furthering the illegal bribes. As a practical matter, a lender will want to take reasonable steps to mitigate its FCPA risk, such as conducting due diligence and including anticorruption provisions in a credit agreement in appropriate circumstances (see Section 7.5.4.4).

Beyond the regulatory risks that lenders face, they also face the potential for reputational damage if a borrower commits an FCPA or other similar violation. There is also financial exposure to lenders if the borrower is subjected to such a large regulatory fine that the borrower cannot repay the loan or suffers collateral consequences, such as exclusion or debarment from government contracting or other loss of revenue, that may impair the actual or perceived ability of the borrower to repay or the value of the borrower's collateral.

The sample representation in Box 6.9, as well as the foregoing discussion generally, is from the regulatory guidance published by the LSTA entitled "Anti-Corruption Issues in Lending Transactions" (December 1, 2014).

6.1.10   Office of Foreign Assets Control Regulations

Box 6.10

None of the Borrower, any of its Subsidiaries or[, to the knowledge of the Borrower,] any director, officer, [employee, agent, or affiliate] of the Borrower or any of its Subsidiaries is an individual or entity ("*Person*") that is, or that is owned or controlled by Persons that are: (i) the [subject/target] of any sanctions administered or enforced by the U.S. Department of the Treasury's Office of Foreign Assets Control ("*OFAC*"), the U.S. Department of State, [the United Nations Security Council, the European Union, Her Majesty's Treasury of the United Kingdom, or other relevant sanctions authority] (collectively, "*Sanctions*"); or (ii) located, organized or resident in a country or territory that is, or whose government is, the subject of Sanctions [including, without limitation][currently,] Cuba, Iran, North Korea, Sudan, Syria, and the Crimea region of the Ukraine.

The Office of Foreign Assets Control (OFAC) of the U.S. Department of the Treasury is the primary federal agency tasked with administering and enforcing U.S. economic sanctions programs against countries, governments, entities, and individuals (U.S. Sanctions). U.S. Sanctions are designed, implemented, and enforced to promote and achieve U.S. national security and foreign policy objectives. U.S. Sanctions may be imposed against geographical areas and all persons from or within those areas, or against designated "persons" (which term includes governments, organizations, individuals, and entities) wherever located.

Under regulations administered by OFAC, U.S. persons are generally prohibited from engaging in transactions, directly or indirectly, with persons and countries targeted by U.S. Sanctions, unless the transactions are exempt or licensed by OFAC. U.S. persons are also generally prohibited from "facilitating" actions of non-U.S. persons, which—although they may be entirely legal for a non-U.S. person to perform—may not be directly performed by U.S. persons due to prohibitions under U.S. Sanctions.

At the time of this writing, the following countries and territories are targets of countrywide or territorywide U.S. Sanctions (often referred to as "comprehensive" sanctions): Cuba, Iran, Sudan, Syria, North Korea, and the Crimea region of the Ukraine. The governments of Cuba, Iran, Sudan, Syria, and North Korea are sanctioned, including their political subdivisions, agencies and instrumentalities, and entities they own or control directly or indirectly. In most cases, persons located, organized, or resident in a country or territory that is the target of comprehensive U.S. Sanctions are themselves also targeted under such sanctions, such that the provision or export to any such person by a U.S. person of goods or services (including financial services), directly or indirectly, is prohibited.

Since its December 2014 announcement of a shift in longstanding foreign policy toward Cuba, the U.S. government has taken steps to incrementally reduce the extent of U.S. Sanctions against Cuba by authorizing certain limited, narrowly defined transactions by U.S. persons with Cuba and Cuban nationals. Upon implementation of the July 2015 nuclear deal between the P5 + 1—the United States, the United Kingdom, France, China, Russia, and Germany—and Iran, the U.S. government suspended its nuclear-related secondary sanctions against Iran (secondary sanctions apply only to non-U.S. persons); virtually all elements of the primary sanctions against Iran, which apply to U.S. persons, remain unchanged. Despite these recent changes in the U.S. Sanctions targeting Cuba and Iran, both countries remain targeted under comprehensive U.S. Sanctions such that U.S. persons are broadly prohibited from engaging, directly or indirectly, in dealings in, with, or involving such countries, subject to limited exceptions.

OFAC also administers "list-based" sanctions that are imposed on persons designated under various programs based on their commission of or support for certain activities. These persons are generally identified on OFAC's List of Specially Designated Nationals and Blocked Persons. Designated persons include: (1) persons involved in narcotics trafficking, terrorism and terrorist financing, transnational crime, proliferation of weapons of mass destruction, piracy and malicious cyber-enabled activities; and (2) persons in, or related to, former regimes in the Balkans, Côte d'Ivoire, Iraq, and Libya and persons in current regimes of, or involved in certain activities in, Belarus, Burma, Burundi, Central African Republic, the Democratic Republic of the Congo, Lebanon, Russia, Somalia, South Sudan, Ukraine, Venezuela, Yemen, and Zimbabwe. U.S. persons are generally prohibited from conducting, directly or indirectly, financial or commercial transactions with or involving these designated persons or their property, including entities 50 percent or more owned by one or more of such designated persons, and any assets that these designated persons may have within the United States or within the possession or control of any U.S. person are required to be "frozen" or "blocked."

The main prohibitions of concern for U.S. lenders are: (1) the prohibition on the exportation of services or the provision of funds to any person or country targeted by U.S. Sanctions; and (2) the prohibition on the "facilitation" by U.S. persons of any non-U.S. person's activities that a U.S. person could not perform directly due to U.S. Sanctions. Lenders that are U.S. persons must ensure that they do not provide any benefit, directly or indirectly, to any person or country targeted by U.S. Sanctions by, for example, making loans to such targeted persons or countries, or to borrowers that use proceeds from such loans to finance business with such targeted persons or countries.

Given the aggressive enforcement posture of OFAC, as evidenced by a number of very large settlements between OFAC and financial institutions in recent years, U.S. and non-U.S. financial institutions have become increasingly conservative in managing their sanctions-related risks. In addition to liability risks, lenders are generally committed to protecting themselves against franchise and reputational risks resulting from sanctions violations and, in some cases, lawful transactions that have some nexus to persons and countries targeted by U.S. Sanctions.

The sample representation in Box 6.10 and the foregoing discussion generally are based on the regulatory guidance published by the LSTA entitled "US Sanctions Issues in Lending Transactions" (September 1, 2016), and have been updated to take account of recent developments and changes in law and practice.

6.1.11 USA PATRIOT Act

Box 6.11

The Borrower represents and warrants to the Lenders and the Administrative Agent that neither the Borrower nor any of its Subsidiaries (i) is a Person described or designated in the Specially Designated Nationals and Blocked Persons List of the Office of Foreign Assets Control or in Section 1 of the Anti-Terrorism Order or (ii) engages in any dealings or transactions with any such Person. The Company and its Subsidiaries are in compliance, in all material respects, with the USA PATRIOT Act.

The provisions of the USA PATRIOT Act are explained in detail in Sections 5.1.11.5 and 12.12. As discussed in those sections, the provisions of the Act impose upon *financial institutions* the responsibility to verify that their customers are not on a list of known or suspected terrorists or terrorist organizations (the Specially Designated Nationals and Blocked Persons List of the Office of Foreign Assets Control). Of course, no financial institution could comply with the Act simply by obtaining a representation to the effect set out above if its borrower is, in fact, wholly owned by a terrorist organization. Because the list of "Specially Designated Nationals" put out by the U.S. Department of Treasury is an ever-growing compendium of names (running, as of the date of this volume, to more than 950 three-columned, finely printed pdf pages), there is some justification, therefore, to have the borrower make the representation since it gives the lenders grounds upon which to decline further loans or to accelerate should any of these prohibited activities be engaged in.

This logic notwithstanding, credit agreements rarely include a representation that addresses PATRIOT Act issues other than (sometimes) to reference it expressly in the compliance with law representation. The more typical approach in this regard is for credit agreement simply to include the notice discussed in Section 12.12.

6.1.12 Margin Regulations

Box 6.12

The Borrower represents and warrants to the Lenders and the Administrative Agent that neither the Borrower nor any of its Subsidiaries is engaged principally, or as one of its important activities, in the business of extending credit for the purpose, whether immediate, incidental, or ultimate, of buying or carrying Margin Stock and no part of the proceeds of any Loan hereunder will be used to buy or carry, or to extend credit to others to buy or carry, any Margin Stock [in violation of Regulations T, X, or U].

The so-called "margin regulations" (Regulations T, X, and U) have been promulgated by the Board of Governors of the Federal Reserve System under authority of Section 7 of the Securities Exchange Act of 1934. After the market crash of 1929, Congress authorized the Board to prescribe the amount of credit that may be extended against any security. Congress was motivated in part by the perception that over-extension of credit on inflated stock contributed to the market frenzy of the 1920s, ultimately leading to the crash. The remedy was to have the Board control the amount of credit that could be extended against equity and certain other securities. To implement this control, the Board issued three Regulations: Regulation T, Regulation X, and Regulation U.

Regulation T applies to brokers and dealers. Regulation X applies to borrowers, and Regulation U applies to banks and certain other lenders.

The basic rule of Regulation U as currently in effect is that no lender may make a loan to enable a borrower to buy or carry margin stock if the loan is "directly or indirectly" secured by margin stock, unless the amount of the security is twice the amount of the loan. Note that the loan must *both* be made to buy or carry margin stock and be directly or indirectly secured by margin stock before it is required to satisfy the two to one collateral coverage ratio (although the margin stock that is purchased and the margin stock that serves as direct or indirect security need *not* be the same margin stock). To illustrate, neither borrowing against the shares of a public company to buy a new factory nor borrowing against a factory to buy the shares of a public company requires compliance with the ratio. A loan that is completely unsecured (neither *direct* nor *indirect* security) raises no Regulation U issues. And a loan that is secured by margin stock and by adequate nonmargin assets could, under complex interpretive rulings issued under Regulation U, also comply. If a loan violates the margin regulations, it may be void.

"Margin stock" is defined, with limited exceptions, as any equity security publicly traded on the domestic markets, including American Depositary Shares (ADSs), warrants, and debt that is convertible into publicly traded equity securities. A loan is deemed secured by margin stock not only in the situation where the borrower grants a lien on margin stock to the lenders to secure the loans ("directly secured"), but also where there is any restriction upon the borrower's ability to create liens on margin stock in favor of third parties or to sell margin stock to third parties ("indirectly secured"). However, if not more than 25 percent of the assets of the borrower and its subsidiaries subject to the restriction consist of margin stock, the loan is not deemed to be indirectly secured by margin stock by reason of such restrictions.

In the event that a loan is directly or indirectly secured by margin stock (whether or not the loan is used to buy or carry margin stock), the lender is required, under Regulation U, to obtain from the borrower an appropriately completed Form U-1. The form requires the borrower to certify the purpose of the loan and in this way enable the lender to determine whether or not the loan complies with Regulation U.

Credit agreements include a representation as to compliance with the margin regulations to mitigate the potential consequences of violating the regulations. To begin with, there is criminal liability. Although actual prosecutions are extremely rare, violations are made criminal offenses under Section 32 of the Act punishable by fine and imprisonment for up to 20 years. There is also the risk of rescission. The Act has been held to grant borrowers a right to rescind a loan made in violation of Regulation U without being required to restore the proceeds to the bank (at least where the borrower itself did not commit fraud). See *Daley v. Capitol Bank & Trust Co.*, 377 F. Supp. 1065 (D.C. Mass. 1974). At a minimum, violations of the margin regulations can be grounds for criticism by bank examiners.

Lastly, a loan to finance a tender offer that is not structured to comply with Regulation U can have potentially disastrous implications for both the borrower and the lending syndicate, particularly if the tender offer is hostile. The lenders face the consequences of violating the rule. The borrower faces the consequences of the target asking a court to enjoin the offer since Regulation U is about to be breached. A target has this ability even though courts have held that there is ". . . no implied private remedy to sue under Federal Reserve Board Margin Regulations." See *Polaroid Corp. v. Disney*, 862 F.2d 987 (3d Cir. 1988). The target can, however, get to the same point indirectly by forcing the acquirer to prove that its tender-offer disclosures are accurate. If there is a violation of Regulation U and the disclosure materials state that the margin regulations will be complied with (as they must if the tender is being financed), then the offer could be enjoined.

The purpose of the margin representation is to minimize these consequences. As with other representations, it gives the lender an argument that it acted in good faith if the borrower were to seek rescission based upon a violation of the regulations or an examiner were to criticize the arrangement. The mere fact of including a specific statement with respect to Regulation U also improves the likelihood that the parties will think carefully about the margin regulations before executing the agreement.

The representation quoted in Box 6.12 is a typical formulation. It states that the loan proceeds will not be applied to "buy or carry" margin stock and that the loans will not be secured "directly or indirectly" by margin stock. To "carry" margin stock basically means to refinance other debt originally incurred to purchase margin stock. Sometimes the representation contains the bracketed language in Box 6.12 to the effect that the loan proceeds will not be used to buy or carry margin stock "in violation of Regulation U." This approach, by having the borrower simply give a conclusory statement that the margin regulations are not violated, arguably defeats the objective of making the parties focus on exactly how the regulations will be complied with.

6.2 FINANCIAL CONDITION REPRESENTATIONS

The financial condition representations address the financial and other business attributes of the borrower and its subsidiaries. Representations covering financial statements, taxes, and Employee Retirement Income Security Act (ERISA) matters, like the legal matters representations, are considered "boilerplate" and are generally included in agreements for virtually any kind of borrower, including investment-grade borrowers. Others (projections and solvency, for example) are inserted only for highly leveraged borrowers.

6.2.1 Financial Statements

Box 6.13

The Borrower represents and warrants to the Lenders and the Administrative Agent that it has heretofore furnished to the Lenders its consolidated balance sheet and statements of income, stockholders equity, and cash flows (i) as of and for the fiscal year ended [_____], 20[_____], reported on by [_____], independent public accountants, and (ii) as of and for the fiscal quarter and the portion of the fiscal year ended [_____], 20[_____] certified by its chief financial officer. Such financial statements present fairly, in all material respects, the financial position and results of operations and cash flows of the Borrower and its consolidated Subsidiaries as of such dates and for such periods in accordance with GAAP, subject to year-end audit adjustments and the absence of footnotes in the case of the statements referred to in clause (ii) above. Except as set forth therein, as of the respective dates of such financial statements, there were no material contingent liabilities, material liabilities for taxes, material unusual forward or long-term commitments or material unrealized or anticipated material losses from any unfavorable commitments of the Borrower or any of its Subsidiaries.

To prepare the credit agreement and obtain the necessary internal credit approvals, the lenders examine the borrower's recent financial statements, typically the most recent annual audited statements and, if available, the most recent interim unaudited statements. There are, of course, exceptions, such as if the borrower is newly formed and does not have any historical financial statements (in which case the borrower typically represents that it has been capitalized as required by the lenders and has no liabilities apart from the credit facility).

Another example might arise if the facility is to finance an acquisition of assets, in which case the best that the borrower can deliver may be so-called "pro forma" financial statements that show what the borrower will look like (or would have looked like at a recent quarter end) assuming the acquisition had been consummated. All of these financial statements (including any pro formas) will almost certainly be included as part of any confidential information memorandum given to the lenders in the syndication process. In many cases the syndicate will also have been supplied "consolidating" financial statements and, in that instance, the representation references these as well. Consolidating statements are not typically audited, so they are certified only by an officer of the borrower and not by the independent accountants. Consolidating statements are discussed in more detail in Section 7.5.1.1.

The financial statements representation has the borrower affirm that all listed statements have been prepared in accordance with GAAP, and that they are "complete and correct" (or, alternatively, that they "fairly present" the borrower's financial condition) in "all material respects." "Complete and correct" is perhaps more precise; "fairly present" is the phrase generally used by accountants when writing their audit report and is the approach taken in the sample language in Box 6.13. (For a fuller discussion of GAAP, see Section 7.3.1.)

The financial statements representation sometimes also includes language to the effect that the statements and footnotes reflect all material liabilities or unusual forward or long-term commitments of the borrower (see the final sentence in Box 6.13). There does not appear to be a uniform practice in this regard and some agreements simply rely upon the "Completeness of Disclosure" representation discussed in Section 6.5.1 to protect the lenders. Including an express statement that there are no undisclosed material or unusual liabilities or commitments has one key purpose. Liabilities and commitments of this sort are not necessarily required by GAAP to be disclosed in the financial statements or footnotes. For example, that a borrower has agreed to supply oil to third parties at $20 a barrel when the cost of producing the oil has jumped to $40 a barrel and the market price is $120 a barrel probably does not appear anywhere in the financial statements or the footnotes. Sometimes borrowers request that the reference to liabilities and commitments be qualified by GAAP—in other words to recast the representation to assert that the financial statements reflect all material liabilities and unusual commitments *required to be disclosed under GAAP*. This approach effectively defeats the purpose of having the language in the first place, since the borrower is already telling the lenders in the heart of the representation that the financial statements have been prepared "in accordance with GAAP."

6.2.2 Material Adverse Change

Box 6.14

The Borrower represents and warrants to the Lenders and the Administrative Agent that, since [_____], 20[_____], there has been no material adverse change in the business, condition (financial or otherwise), assets, operations, or prospects of the Borrower and its Subsidiaries, taken as a whole.

With limited exceptions, most credit agreements include a representation to the effect that the borrower has not suffered a material adverse change or MAC (see Box 6.14, "no material adverse change in the business, condition (financial or otherwise), assets, operations or prospects"). For a detailed discussion of the MAC condition (and representation) see Section 5.1.6.

6.2.3 Litigation

Box 6.15

The Borrower represents and warrants to the Lenders and the Administrative Agent that there are no actions, suits, proceedings, or investigations by or before any arbitrator or Governmental Authority pending against or, to the knowledge of the Borrower, threatened against or affecting the Borrower or any of its Subsidiaries (i) as to which there is a reasonable possibility of an adverse determination and that, if adversely determined, could reasonably be expected, individually or in the aggregate, to have a Material Adverse Effect (except as disclosed on Schedule_____) or (ii) that involve this Agreement or the transactions contemplated hereby.

Lenders care about litigation for the same reasons that they care about the borrower's tax and pension liabilities discussed below. Adverse litigation has the potential, if lost, to alter radically the financial strength of the borrower by introducing a new creditor to compete with the lenders for the borrower's precious funds. The purpose of the litigation representation is, therefore, to force the borrower to identify on a disclosure schedule any "material" litigation or threatened litigation (including arbitrations, regulatory proceedings, and investigations) to which the borrower or any of its subsidiaries may be subject. The statement in the sample language in Box 6.15 also includes investigations. The results of an investigation by a government authority can be potentially just as devastating to a borrower as the loss of a lawsuit, at least if the investigation concludes that the borrower's business practices resulted in a violation of law. Such a conclusion could easily be the precursor to a raft of damage claims made by injured customers, vendors, or other parties while the lenders' commitments (and loans) remain outstanding.

One of the problems that a borrower confronts in completing any disclosure schedule is to determine whether an item of litigation or investigation (threatened or existing) actually rises to the level of materiality. As discussed in Section 5.1.6, deciding whether an event or condition is material is a complicated question of fact. The SEC (Regulation S-K) allows a safe harbor for litigation in which the damages sought are less than 10 percent of the borrower's consolidated *current* assets. Litigation claims below that amount need not be disclosed. The safe harbor does not, however, mean that all litigation that seeks more than 10 percent of current assets is necessarily "material." Faced with the lack of clear guidelines, some borrowers throw up their hands and just list all litigation to which they are party. This may not be particularly helpful to the borrower, since it might suggest that a $500 lawsuit is material and consequently impact the meaning of "material" as used in other contexts in the agreement—"material adverse effect," for example. Borrowers may try to override this implication by stating expressly in the disclosure statement that the mere listing of an item of litigation does not concede that it is, in fact, material.

This latter approach can, however, produce a problem for the lenders. Lenders normally want to investigate thoroughly the nature of any listed litigation and evaluate whether it might eventually impair the borrower's ability to satisfy its obligations under the credit agreement. Overinclusive listing by borrowers makes this task much more burdensome.

For a lender to assess whether it cares about a particular lawsuit or other proceeding, it typically must answer two questions: the likelihood of loss and the amount of liability (or other consequences) if a loss occurs. It is often difficult for borrowers to be helpful in this process. To begin with, if the borrower is a public filer, it will already have disclosed material litigation in its submissions to the SEC, usually accompanied by statements to the effect that it has "meritorious" defenses and intends to contest the action "vigorously." The borrower will not want to say anything other than this to a lending syndicate.

Even if the borrower is not a public filer, its natural inclination is to say as little as possible about the suit. That leaves the lenders with the option of trying to assess on their own the merit (or lack thereof) of the suit and the borrower's defenses. It is, in many cases, impracticable for lenders to dig out the relevant facts. The borrower itself may not yet have collected evidence and, even if it has, it will be difficult for the lenders' counsel to make an intelligent appraisal without spending the same amount of time (months or years) that the borrower's counsel has expended. Simplistically, the approach to take is to ask the borrower's own counsel for their opinion of the facts and their view of the strengths and weaknesses of the defense and the strategy they propose to take. But to disclose any of that to the lenders can easily waive the borrower's attorney-client privilege. As a consequence, the due diligence undertaken by lenders frequently consists of looking at briefs (if the case has progressed that far), listening to an explication by the borrower's counsel of the procedural posture of the case (is it in early discovery, has a trial date been set, have there been any settlement discussions, what is the status of any appeals?), and then engaging in a great deal of guesswork as to the likely outcome of the litigation.

Although in most cases determining whether litigation is material is a function of the amount of damages demanded by the plaintiff, this is not necessarily the case. Litigation could be material even if it does not seek monetary damages. For example, a suit might request a ruling that a license held by the borrower is no longer exclusive or that a borrower engages in a product-pricing practice that violates applicable antitrust laws. In either instance, the resultant change to the borrower's business (or its competition) could materially adversely affect it and therefore requires disclosure to the lenders.

6.2.4 Projections

Box 6.16

The Borrower represents and warrants to the Lenders and the Administrative Agent that it has heretofore furnished to the Lenders projections of anticipated cash flows for, and of inventory and receivables levels as at the end of, each fiscal year through [_____], 20[_____]. All such projections reflect the Borrower's good-faith estimates as of the date of preparation hereof, based upon methods and data the Borrower believes to be reasonable and accurate, but actual results during the periods covered by such projections may differ materially from such projections.

No one can predict the future. Beyond its own belief in the future ability of its business to make payments of principal and interest on the loans when they become due and to comply with financial covenants, no borrower wants to be on the hook for what its financial figures will actually look like after closing. Not surprisingly, therefore, borrowers are reluctant to make the same kinds of representations with respect to projections as they make with respect to historical financial statements.

That said, projections are frequently included in confidential information memoranda given to prospective syndicate members and, as discussed in Section 6.5.1, the borrower may be forced to represent that the financial and other information delivered by it are not in the aggregate misleading. That aggregate information, of course, includes whatever projections are delivered to the lenders. The second sentence in Box 6.16 is an example of qualification language inserted to make the (obvious) point that a borrower cannot say more about projections than that they have been prepared in good faith based upon assumptions that the borrower deems reasonable and that actual results may vary from projected performance.

6.2.5 Taxes

Box 6.17

The Borrower represents and warrants to the Lenders and the Administrative Agent that the Borrower and its Subsidiaries have timely filed or caused to be filed all tax returns and reports required to have been filed and have paid or caused to be paid all taxes required to have been paid by it, except (i) taxes that are being contested in good faith by appropriate proceedings and for which the Borrower or such Subsidiary, as applicable, has set aside on its books adequate reserves or (ii) to the extent that the failure to do so could not reasonably be expected to have a Material Adverse Effect.

Taxes come in all shapes and sizes and governments are not charitable if they are not paid. When collecting past-due taxes, the tax collector does so with the full force of the law. He or she is much more than just another aggrieved contract party. When not paid, property taxes, for example, give rise to a lien on the property being taxed (in most cases senior to all other liens, including preexisting mortgages in favor of a lending syndicate). A syndicate that thinks it has a first mortgage on the borrower's factory, could suddenly be junior to hundreds of thousands of dollars (or more) in property taxes. For a corporation, failure to pay franchise taxes can give the state the right to seek judicial dissolution. For any entity, failure to pay taxes where operations are conducted can result in the entity no longer being qualified to do business (with the consequences described in Section 6.1.1). Not paying income taxes can be worse still because it may give rise to a lien in favor of the Internal Revenue Service (IRS), or the equivalent state taxing authority, on *all* of the borrower's property. Although the lien is not automatically senior to all other liens (so the lenders' lien, if perfected first, may remain in first rank), it may nevertheless capture property not covered by the lien in favor of the lenders. In any event, in an unsecured deal the priority status of tax authorities gives the IRS (or state agency) the status of a secured creditor, while the lenders remain unsecured down at the level of all other general unsecured creditors, each fighting for the borrower's precious dollars.

The taxes representation does not solve or cure the borrower's tax problems, but it does have the borrower confirm that it is current on all taxes and gives the lenders leverage if the representation is false. It is customarily subject to the two exceptions shown in the sample language in Box 6.17. These are discussed below.

The first standard exception is for taxes in dispute. Given the complexity of tax determinations this is perhaps not surprising. For property taxes there can be endless debate about whether an assessed valuation is correct; for income taxes, there is a natural impetus for the company to exploit deductions, credits, exclusions, carrybacks, and other items to the maximum extent possible; and even for franchise taxes there can be disputes as to the appropriate measure of taxable capital. As a consequence, the relevant tax authority does not always agree with the (perhaps overly aggressive) determinations made by the borrower. There is, of course, nothing inherently wrong with a company pushing to minimize its tax bill. Nevertheless, to guard against a borrower's being too cavalier in contesting tax items, the exception requires that the dispute be "in good faith" and that adequate reserves be maintained against the borrower's ultimate tax liability. Sometimes the representation states that reserves are being kept "in accordance with GAAP," but the reference to GAAP is probably unnecessary given that all accounting terms in the agreement are deemed to be determined in accordance with GAAP anyway (see Section 7.3.1).

The reference to "reserves" merits some discussion as it is used in several contexts in the typical credit agreement; tax is only one of them. It may come up also in the litigation representation or the payment of obligations covenant (see Section 7.5.4). It is an accounting term that is intended to describe a charge against income taken in anticipation of possible future costs or losses. To illustrate, if a borrower believes it may ultimately have to pay $6,000,000 in disputed taxes, it can choose to deduct that amount from the current year's income and make an equivalent accounting entry on the liability side of its balance sheet (probably titled "Tax Reserve") until the contest is resolved. If three years later it loses its dispute with the tax authority, it will have a reserve against which to charge the full loss and need not, at that time, take a hit against its income. The exact amount of reserve to be posted in any situation is largely within the discretion of the borrower and its accountants (although, in theory, it should reflect the probability of loss based on the event reserved against). The term does not mean that the borrower maintains a lockbox filled with cash in an amount equal to the reserve. Consequently when the loss ultimately occurs, the borrower may not necessarily have cash ready at hand to cover the loss.

So why does the lending syndicate care if a reserve has been taken if it does not represent cash set aside to cover the adverse contingency? The reason flows from the reduction to the borrower's income taken when the reserve is established. From a lender's perspective, it means that the borrower is not overstating its true income or net worth and means that the financial covenants *may* be more reflective of the borrower's true financial performance. This should, at least, be the case where a net worth or income-based covenant is employed; it may not be the case where cash flow-based-covenants are used, since the establishment of the reserve does not reduce the cash flow for any period.

The second standard exception is for taxes that are too immaterial to be of significance to the borrower. Hence the qualification shown in Box 6.17 for taxes that, if not paid, "could not reasonably be expected to have a Material Adverse Effect." Failure to pay a $60 tax lien on a mega corporation's corporate headquarters, or neglecting to pay state income taxes that represents less than 1 percent of the company's total tax liability, should not result in the representation being false. (See Section 5.1.6 for a discussion of the meaning of "material adverse effect.")

6.2.6   Pension and Welfare Plans

Box 6.18

The Borrower represents and warrants to the Lenders and the Administrative Agent that no ERISA Event with respect to the Borrower or any of its ERISA Affiliates has occurred or is reasonably expected to occur that, when taken together with all other such ERISA Events for which liability is reasonably expected to occur, could reasonably be expected to have a Material Adverse Effect. The present value of all accumulated benefit obligations under all underfunded Employee Benefit Plans (based on the assumptions used for purposes of Statement of Financial Accounting Standards No. 158) did not, as of the date of the most recent financial statements reflecting such amounts, exceed [an amount that would reasonably be expected to have a Material Adverse Effect] [by more than $[____] the fair market value of the assets of such underfunded Plans].

Pension plan liabilities can be much like tax liabilities—if not paid, the borrower may have to face down a government agency (in this case the Pension Benefit Guaranty Corporation, or PBGC) and explain its behavior. The PBGC was established under the Employee Retirement Income Security Act of 1974 (ERISA). ERISA and the volumes of regulations issued thereunder amount to a complex gaggle of federal rules intended to protect the pension rights of employees. The pension funding provisions of ERISA were enacted in response to notorious insolvencies in the late 1960s, when employees who had worked for many years with the expectation that they would be entitled to a retirement payment suddenly discovered that no funds were available to pay the benefit. Anticipating a comfortable retirement, they faced instead a future living on social security.

At the risk of oversimplification, ERISA categorizes pension plans into two groups: defined *contribution* plans and defined *benefit* plans. A defined contribution plan describes a pension plan in which the employer makes a specified contribution each year to an employee's pension account. Under ERISA, these contributions must be held in a trust that is not subject to claims of the employer's creditors. When the employee retires he or she receives retirement payments from whatever has accumulated in the account as contributions and as earnings on investments made with those contributions. The employer does not guarantee any particular yield on the investments or any particular level of retirement payments, but commits only to the level of contributions to be made each year while the employee continues to work. By contrast, a defined benefit plan refers to a plan in which the employer undertakes to make specified (or defined) payments to the employee once he or she retires. The benefit is typically an amount based upon an arithmetical formula that takes into account years of service and average salary. As with defined contribution plans, the employer makes periodic payments into a trust. In the case of defined benefit plans the amount required to be deposited into trust each year is determined under complex actuarial calculations intended to ensure that sufficient funds are held in trust to make the defined pension payments as employees retire. ERISA does not require that an employer actually provide a pension to its employees, but simply regulates the way in which pension plans, if established, are funded and administered, and includes vesting, disclosure, plan termination, and other requirements intended to protect employees.

The ERISA representation (and the other ERISA provisions set out in a credit agreement) are, as a general rule, concerned only with defined benefit plans, since it is a breach of ERISA requirements in respect of such plans that has the most potential to cause financial problems for the borrower. Compliance is relevant to a lending syndicate for two reasons. First, failure to satisfy ERISA requirements may subject the borrower (and, as discussed below, its 80 percent or more owned affiliates) to liens and potential penalties. Second, to guard against employees being left in the lurch when a company with a defined benefit plan becomes insolvent, the PBGC provides insurance to continue benefit payments if an underfunded defined benefit plan is terminated, such as could happen when the employer (and its 80 percent or more affiliates) file for bankruptcy. To fund this insurance, employers that maintain defined benefit plans must pay the PBGC an annual assessment.

If an employer with an underfunded defined benefit plan fails to make the required annual contributions, the plan is entitled to a lien (to be enforced by the PBGC) on the assets of the employer equivalent to the tax lien granted in favor of the IRS described in Section 6.2.5. Since under ERISA, any company and any 80 percent or more owned entity in the same consolidated group (the "ERISA Affiliate" referred to in the language in Box 6.18) are each jointly and severally liable for the pension liabilities of the entire group, the tax lien can be imposed upon any 80 percent or more owned entity in that group. So if the borrower is the only creditworthy corporation in an otherwise insolvent corporate group, it is liable (and may have a lien imposed on its assets) for the underfunded pension obligations of a sister corporation three times removed. Lenders accordingly have a keen interest in knowing that the borrower and all of its ERISA affiliates are complying with the requirements of ERISA and that the syndicate will not be forced to compete with the PBGC for payment should the borrower become insolvent.

The sample representation above has two basic parts. First, the borrower confirms that no "ERISA Event" has occurred and second the borrower addresses the issue of potential funding deficiencies. A full discussion of "ERISA Event" as set out in the typical credit agreement is beyond the scope of this volume. In general, however, the term is designed to capture any event that affects the borrower (or any of its subsidiaries or affiliates under at least 80 percent common control with the borrower) that will give rise to a current or future risk of liability under ERISA and the Internal Revenue Code provisions that relate to defined benefit pension plans. Thus, for example, receipt of a notice from the PBGC of potential liability or of the appointment of a trustee for a defined benefit plan is included in the definition. The incurrence by a borrower of liability in respect of the termination of a defined benefit plan is also normally swept in, as well as potential liabilities because of a complete or partial withdrawal from a "multiemployer" pension plan (such as a regional Teamsters' plan); multiemployer plans are generally maintained under collective bargaining agreements.

With respect to funding deficiencies, the representation asks the borrower to tell the lenders what shortfall, if any, it faces under its defined benefit pension plans. As noted earlier, an employer that maintains a defined benefit plan is required to make annual contributions to a trust to fund the plan's future pension obligations. ERISA does not, however, require that at any point in time these future payments be fully covered by assets currently held in trust, since the average employee covered by the plan probably does not retire for another 15 or 20 years and amounts held in trust will continue to grow (through both contributions and earnings) during that period. ERISA simply requires that the level of contributions (determined under the complex actuarial rules referred to above) be maintained so that sufficient funds will be held in trust to make the defined pension payments as employees retire. The typical representation, as illustrated in the language in Box 6.18, addresses this issue by having the borrower either confirm the aggregate amount of accumulated unfunded liabilities under all underfunded plans or confirm that the aggregate deficiency will not have a material adverse effect. (See Section 5.1.6 for a discussion of the meaning of material adverse effect.)

As noted, ERISA does not require an employer to establish a pension plan. In cases where the borrower does not maintain a plan and is not obligated in respect of a plan terminated in earlier years (or a plan maintained, or recently terminated, by an affiliate under 80 percent or more common control), the representation may simply be a statement to this effect.

Sometimes in highly leveraged transactions, the representation also requires that the borrower confirm that it is in compliance with the provisions of ERISA and other state and federal law that relates to *all* employee benefit plans, including 401(k) and other defined contribution plans, and health and welfare benefit plans. Much of this is redundant with the compliance with law representation discussed earlier in this chapter and, where included, is frequently incorporated into the labor representation (see Section 6.3.6).

6.2.7 Solvency

> **Box 6.19**
>
> The Borrower represents and warrants to the Lenders and the Administrative Agent that it is Solvent. For purposes hereof, *"Solvent"* means, on any date, that the Borrower and its Subsidiaries on a consolidated basis are "solvent" within the meaning given that term and similar terms under applicable laws relating to fraudulent transfers and conveyances, including that (a) the present fair salable value of the assets of the Borrower and its Subsidiaries on a consolidated basis (i.e., the amount that may be realized within a reasonable time, considered to be six months to one year, either through collection or sale at the regular market value, conceiving the latter as the amount that could be obtained for the property in question within such period by a capable and diligent businessperson from an interested buyer who is willing to purchase under ordinary selling conditions) is not less than the amount that will be required to pay the probable liability of the Borrower and its Subsidiaries on their debts (including contingent, unmatured, and unliquidated liabilities) as they become absolute and matured; (b) the Borrower and its Subsidiaries will not, on a consolidated basis, have an unreasonably small capital in relation to their business or with respect to any transaction then contemplated; and (c) the Borrower and its Subsidiaries, on a consolidated basis, will have sufficient cash flow to enable them to pay their debts as they mature.

When first inserted into credit agreements, the solvency representation was intended for those situations in which a transaction gave rise to concerns under the so-called fraudulent conveyance or fraudulent transfer laws. Examples included credit facilities in which the proceeds of the loans were to be applied to pay an extraordinary dividend or distribution to shareholders or in which the loans were to be guaranteed by subsidiaries. However, many agreements now include solvency representations as a matter of course, regardless of whether there are structural issues that raise fraudulent conveyance concerns. Indeed, in some cases, a credit agreement goes further and requires the borrower to deliver a professional evaluation from an independent appraisal firm, known as a "solvency opinion," that confirms that the borrower (or a guarantor) will not be rendered insolvent by the financing (see Section 5.1.11.2).

Fraudulent transfer laws are designed to protect against the transfer of assets by any debtor (including an individual or any corporation, partnership, or limited liability company) in a way that prefers one set of creditors over another when the person or entity is insolvent. Originated by statute many centuries ago, they have been continued through modern legislation in every state and have also been incorporated into the Federal Bankruptcy Code. The laws invalidate any transaction that is undertaken with intent to "hinder, delay, or defraud" any creditor (actual fraud). They also address any transaction in which (1) a debtor undertakes an obligation or transfers property without receiving "reasonably equivalent" value and (2) the debtor is insolvent at the time of, or would be rendered insolvent as a result of, the transaction (constructive fraud).

A simple illustration of how the fraudulent transfer laws work may be helpful. Suppose a penniless musician, mad as hell at the bank where he has overdrawn his checking account, decides to fix the bank once and for all by selling his priceless Stradivarius to his brother for $1.00. The musician then proposes to declare bankruptcy and wipe out what he owes to all creditors (including his bank). This transaction almost certainly violates the fraudulent transfer laws. To begin with, a court would probably conclude that the sale was undertaken with the intent to hinder, delay, or defraud the bank. However, even absent bad intent on the part of the musician, a fraudulent transfer has likely occurred, since $1.00 is not a "reasonably equivalent" value for the sale of a valuable Stradivarius, and the musician is insolvent at the time of the sale to his brother.

In the corporate lending context, fraudulent conveyance issues arise in a variety of ways. The most common is perhaps in the context of guarantees by subsidiaries of the borrower. Except to the extent the loan proceeds are being advanced to the subsidiary, the latter is unlikely to receive reasonably equivalent value. It will be guaranteeing the full amount of the loans but receiving only a portion (or none) of the proceeds. The guarantor takes on an obligation (the guarantee) and receives nothing in exchange. Another example might arise in the context where the loans are to finance the payment of a dividend or distribution. Although the borrower receives loan proceeds in an amount equal to the repayment obligation it assumes, courts will look to the ultimate purpose of the loan. See *United States v. Gleneagles Inv. Co.*, 565 F. Supp. 556 (M.D. Pa. 1983). The borrower probably does not in this circumstance receive reasonably equivalent value once the payment of the dividend is taken into account. Indeed, it will likely receive no value at all. It transfers cash (to its shareholders) in exchange for nothing other than the shareholders' undying appreciation for the money received, which does not qualify as "value" for these purposes. Restructuring a deal in these circumstances to eliminate the upstream guarantees or the dividend is normally not an option.

To overcome completely the fraudulent conveyance concerns of the types described above is generally not possible. However, in many cases fraudulent conveyance risk is not, in fact, material since lenders do not ordinarily make credit available to borrowers that are insolvent (at least once the borrower's consolidated group is factored in) or to borrowers that are attempting to defraud other creditors. The solution therefore most often adopted in credit agreements is to have the borrower represent that it is "solvent." In the credit agreement, the term *solvent* is defined as the obverse of the term *insolvent* as used in fraudulent transfer laws. Although statutes vary in the precise language used, several common definitions of insolvency are used, including (1) when an entity's liabilities (including contingent liabilities) exceed its assets, (2) when its property or capital is unreasonably small in relation to its business or the obligations being undertaken under the credit agreement, and (3) when it cannot pay its debts as they come due.

Note that the sample representation above only asks for confirmation from the borrower on a consolidated basis that it is solvent; guarantors are not asked to make a similar confirmation. Some credit agreements, however, apply the representation to guarantors as well, by requiring that each entity obligated on the loan, whether borrower or guarantor, confirm that it is solvent on an *individual* basis. This is probably unfair for guarantors, at least in those cases in which guarantees come from entities that are subsidiaries or sisters of the borrower. A subsidiary or sister company may have a much smaller balance sheet than the borrower and, if considered individually, may very well not be solvent once the guarantee obligations are assumed. Only if the guarantee limitations and cross-contribution claims (discussed in detail in Section 8.2.9) are taken into account can a subsidiary or sister make the representation. But once those are factored in, the representation by the subsidiary or sister *individually* is essentially the same as a representation that the obligor group on a *consolidated* basis is solvent—in other words, the approach taken in the language in Box 6.19.

As described earlier, the solvency representation is occasionally further supported by a solvency opinion from an independent third party.

While this was conventional in leveraged acquisition financings in the early 1990s, the more common practice today is for the lenders to conduct their own independent analysis of the borrower's solvency and not to rely upon the conclusions of an (expensive) appraisal firm.

6.2.8   Material Agreements

Box 6.20

The Borrower represents and warrants to the Lenders and the Administrative Agent that neither the Borrower nor any of its Subsidiaries is in default in the performance or observance of any of the obligations, covenants, or conditions contained in any agreement or instrument to which it is a party, which default could reasonably be expected to have a Material Adverse Effect.

Some agreements, in addition to the no-conflicts representations discussed earlier in this chapter (which have the borrower confirm that the credit agreement itself does not conflict with other agreements), contain a material agreements representation along the lines sampled in Box 6.20. It asks the borrower to tell the lending syndicate that there are no other agreements to which it is a party that are in default. The other agreements referenced are not just debt documents, but could include operating agreements, such as supply and sales contracts, licensing arrangements, franchise agreements, and management contracts that, if breached, could have a material adverse effect. This representation is rarely, if ever, seen in agreements for investment-grade borrowers.

6.3   REPRESENTATIONS AND DISCLOSURES REGARDING THE BUSINESS

While the financial condition representations address the financial or other business *condition* of the borrower, the representations set forth in this section disclose particular *facts* about its property or business—the substance of these representations is often set out on disclosure schedules attached to the agreement. None of these representations is considered "boilerplate." Whether included or not in any particular credit agreement is strictly a matter of negotiation, though in a highly leveraged transaction it is not unusual to see them all.

6.3.1 Capitalization

Box 6.21

The Borrower represents and warrants to the Lenders and the Administrative Agent that the authorized capital stock of the Borrower consists, on the date hereof, of an aggregate of [____] shares of common stock, with [no] par value [of $____ per share], of which, as of the date hereof, [____] shares are duly and validly issued and outstanding, each of which shares is fully paid and nonassessable and all of which are held beneficially and of record by [____]. As of the date hereof, (x) there are no outstanding Equity Rights with respect to the Borrower and (y) there are no outstanding obligations of the Borrower or any of its Subsidiaries to repurchase, redeem, or otherwise acquire any shares of capital stock of the Borrower nor are there any outstanding obligations of the Borrower or any of its Subsidiaries to make payments to any Person, such as "phantom stock" payments, where the amount thereof is calculated with reference to the fair market value or equity value of the Borrower or any of its Subsidiaries.

The capitalization representation has four principal purposes. First, in the case of a corporation, such as in the sample in Box 6.21, it tells the lending syndicate the aggregate number of shares that the borrower is authorized to issue. Of course, the authorized capital can normally be determined by reviewing the charter of the corporation, but having the representation confirm the amount authorized serves as a useful benchmark for the balance of the representation. If the borrower is a partnership or limited liability company with an equivalent concept of authorized capital (this is not normally the case), the representation will contain a corresponding statement to this effect.

Second, the representation tells the syndicate who owns the outstanding shares of stock or partnership or membership interests in the borrower. Obviously, if the borrower is a public company the representation is appropriately reworded, although if there is a substantial block owned by an individual person or group, then that would be set out in a disclosure schedule. Knowing who owns the equity of the borrower serves as a yardstick against which the lenders can measure whether or not a change of control has occurred. (See Section 9.1.9 for a discussion of the change of control concept.) The representation also has the borrower confirm to the lenders the due diligence they will have undertaken as to who owns the borrower. One might argue that the ownership of the borrower is unrelated to the creditworthiness of the borrower. Nevertheless, it is a maxim of bank lending to "know your borrower."

That includes knowing, and being comfortable with the sagacity and judgment of, the people who control your borrower.

The representation with respect to outstanding equity also includes a statement as to whether the equity has been paid for. The typical litany, at least in the context of a corporation, asks for confirmation that the stock has been duly and validly issued and is fully paid and nonassessable. Having the borrower confirm that it has received cash (or the equivalent in property) as consideration for the issuance of equity tells the lender that the outstanding capital of the borrower is real and that it need not rely upon the creditworthiness of third parties (those obligated to purchase the additional equity) for the borrower to be fully capitalized.

Third, the representation identifies whether there are any rights of others to acquire equity interests in the borrower, through the exercise of warrants or options, the conversion of nonequity securities into equity, or the right to subscribe for equity. These are the "Equity Rights" in the sample language in Box 6.21. Having the borrower tell you that its founder and guiding genius owns 60 percent of its equity is severely tainted if you learn that Godzilla, the infamous corporate raider, as part of an earlier investment holds warrants that, if exercised, will reduce that 60 percent to 20 percent.

Finally, the representation identifies whether there are any obligations of the borrower to repurchase outstanding equity. It is important to know whether the borrower has any liability in this regard for at least two reasons. First, such an obligation is probably not reflected on the balance sheet and may not be picked up by other representations in the credit agreement (although, in theory, it should be picked up by the declaration in the financial statements representation to the effect that there are no unusual or material contingent liabilities). Second, if an obligation of this sort does exist, and presuming that the lenders are comfortable with the scope of the obligation, it needs to be grandfathered as a permitted purchase under the dividends and equity repurchases covenant (see Section 7.6.12).

6.3.2   Subsidiaries and Investments

Box 6.22

The Borrower represents and warrants to the Lenders and the Administrative Agent that:

(a) *Subsidiaries.* Set forth in Schedule _____ is a complete and correct list of all of the Subsidiaries of the Borrower as of the date hereof, together with, for each such Subsidiary, (i) the jurisdiction of its organiza-tion, (ii) each Person holding ownership interests in such Subsidiary, and (iii) the nature and percentage of the ownership interests held by such Person. Except as disclosed in said Schedule, (x) each of the Borrower and its Subsidiaries owns, free and clear of Liens [(other than Liens created pursuant to the Security Documents)], and has the unencumbered right to vote, all outstanding ownership interests in each Person shown to be held by it in said Schedule, (y) all of the issued and outstanding equity capital of each such Person is validly issued, fully paid, and nonassessable and (z) there are no outstanding Equity Rights with respect to such Person.

(b) *Investments*. Set forth in Schedule _____ is a complete and correct list of all Investments (other than Subsidiaries and other than Investments permitted under Section [*Investments*] (excluding clause [*Grandfathered Investments*]) held by the Borrower or any of its Subsidiaries in any Person on the date hereof and, for each such Investment, (x) the identity of the Person or Persons holding such Investment and (y) the nature of such Investment. Except as disclosed in said Schedule, each of the Borrower and its Subsidiaries owns all such Investments, free and clear of all Liens [(other than Liens created pursuant to the Security Documents)].

(c) *Restrictions on Subsidiaries*. None of the Subsidiaries of the Borrower is, on the date hereof, subject to any indenture, agreement, instrument, or other arrangement of the type described in Section [*Dividend Blockers*].

The subsidiaries and investments representation covers, as its title indicates, the ownership of subsidiaries, the ownership of investments, and whether there exist any restrictions upon subsidiaries paying divi-dends to their parent entities. One could question whether any of this is logically necessary in the typical credit agreement. After all, the agree-ment does not normally ask the borrower to identify which members in the consolidated group own which factory or licenses or inventory or receivables. And having the borrower state that its subsidiaries and investments are owned free and clear of liens is arguably duplicative of the existing debt and liens and title to property representations dis-cussed in Sections 6.3.4 and 6.3.5.

The representation nevertheless has a purpose. Insofar as subsidiaries are concerned, it sets out the necessary detail for the lenders to understand the ownership structure of the borrower and its subsidiaries, and to deter-mine whether, in negotiating the agreement, they have taken the right guarantees from subsidiaries and the correct pledges of subsidiary equity. The disclosure detail itself is normally set out in a schedule attached to the credit agreement and in some cases, perhaps more helpfully for the lending syndicate, the agreement requires that the borrower attach an organizational chart displaying the ownership structure for all subsidiaries. With respect to investments, the representation enables the lenders to understand the true scope of the grandfathered investments clause in the investments covenant—absent that disclosure they have no basis upon which to determine what investments they are actually consenting to.

The confirmation with respect to liens provides much more detail than is found in the existing debt and liens and title to property representations (see Sections 6.3.4 and 6.3.5). The representation, for example, addresses the nature of the ownership interests in subsidiaries and whether subsidiary equity is fully paid and nonassessable with the borrower and its subsidiaries having the right to vote the equity held by them. Shares might be subject to a voting trust agreement that could adversely affect the borrower's control over a subsidiary (its right to vote the equity). The borrower might also be obligated to make further mandatory contributions to subsidiary capital because its shares were not "fully paid and nonassessable." The representation forces potential problems of these types to be set out on a disclosure schedule.

Paragraph (c) in Box 6.22 tells the lending syndicate whether or not subsidiaries are subject to so-called dividend blockers. Dividend blockers are discussed in more detail in Section 7.6.14, but, in general, they describe a covenant restriction contained in a debt or other agreement to which a subsidiary is subject that would prevent the subsidiary from paying dividends to the borrower. Particularly where a borrower is a holding company and totally dependent upon funds being dividended from subsidiaries in order to meet its payment obligations (payroll, accountants, lawyers, overhead, and, not the least, principal and interest on its credit agreements), knowing that such payments can be freely made is essential.

6.3.3   Real Property

Box 6.23

The Borrower represents and warrants to the Lenders and the Administrative Agent that Schedule____ sets forth a complete and correct list, as of the date hereof, of all of the real property interests held by the Borrower and its Subsidiaries, indicating in each case whether the respective property is owned or leased, the identity of the owner or lessee, and the location of the respective property [and the borrower's good-faith estimate of the fair market value of the interest of the Borrower or Subsidiary in the respective property].

The real property disclosure representation is normally inserted into a credit agreement only when mortgages and deeds of trust on real property are to be executed in favor of the lenders. It functions as the basis for the parties to discuss which properties will secure the lending syndicate and which will remain unencumbered. This can be a frequent source of contention between borrower and arranger. Although in most cases the term sheet spells out that real property is to be taken as collateral, once the parties actually look at the list of the borrower's real property interests, resistance to the lenders' taking a lien on *all* such interests often surfaces. The borrower may (with considerable justification) say that it is not worth the effort to prepare and record mortgages (and obtain title insurance and surveys) over fee-owned properties that are nominal in value. Similarly, it may point out that leasehold mortgages normally require the cooperation and consent of the landlord and, unless the lease covers a material property of the borrower, it may not be worth the effort (and cost) of obtaining that consent. The borrower also typically observes that, if the lease consists of office space, such consent is rarely, if ever, granted. The representation in Box 6.23 attempts to address some of these issues by having the borrower state its good-faith determination of the fair market value of its interest in each property listed.

In a few instances, however, even low-value property interests are taken. A cable television company may, for example, have many head-end sites; a wireless tower company may have many disparate tower locations; a gasoline retailer may have many service stations spread over a wide geographic area. Any individual property may have relatively little value, but the separate properties taken as a whole can have substantial value—indeed, may be the only significant assets that the borrower has. In these instances, although taking the real property liens can be an arduous task, the effort is nevertheless made and the detailed list of real property interests disclosed in the representation becomes critical.

6.3.4 Existing Debt and Liens

Box 6.24

The Borrower represents and warrants to the Lenders and the Administrative Agent that:

(a) *Debt.* Set forth in Schedule _____ is a complete and correct list of each credit agreement, loan agreement, indenture, purchase agreement, guarantee, letter of credit, or other arrangement providing for or otherwise relating to any Debt or any extension of credit (or commitment for any extension of credit) to, or guarantee by, the Borrower or any of its Subsidiaries outstanding on the date hereof the aggregate principal or face amount of which equals or exceeds (or may equal or exceed) $____, and the aggregate principal or face amount outstanding or that may become outstanding under each such arrangement is correctly described in said Schedule.

(b) *Liens.* Schedule ____ is a complete and correct list of each Lien securing Debt of any Person outstanding on the date hereof the aggregate principal or face amount of which equals or exceeds (or may equal or exceed) $____ and covering any property of the Borrower or any of its Subsidiaries, and the aggregate Debt secured (or that may be secured) by each such Lien and the property covered by each such Lien is correctly described in said Schedule.

The primary purpose of a debt and liens representation is to create a schedule that can be referenced in the negative covenants to grandfather debt and liens that would otherwise be prohibited. A secondary purpose is to compel the borrower to provide greater detail (as to both debt and liens) than what GAAP requires to be set out in the financial statements. The representation forces the borrower, for example, to confirm the aggregate *unutilized* commitments and not just the outstanding debt balance, and also to verify the exact property subject to liens. Of course, much of the lien information as to property covered by Uniform Commercial Code (UCC) filings can be derived by the lenders' conducting a UCC search, but that does not work for real property, or for stock pledges or cash collateral arrangements, for which UCC filings are not required.

The benefits described above notwithstanding, many credit agreements, even for highly leveraged borrowers, dispense with the representation and reference instead the schedule in the negative covenants themselves. In these cases, the title to property representation described in Section 6.3.5 becomes of greater importance.

6.3.5   Title to Property

Box 6.25

The Borrower represents and warrants to the Lenders and the Administrative Agent that each of the Borrower and its Subsidiaries has good and marketable title to, or valid leasehold interests in, all of its real and personal property material to its business, except for minor defects in title that do not interfere with its ability to conduct its business as currently conducted or to utilize such properties for their intended purposes and except for liens permitted under Section [*Lien Covenant*].

The title representation covers some of the same territory as the liens representation, although it does not ask for a detailed listing of liens. The representation, however, goes well beyond liens. It asks that title not only be "good," but that it also be "marketable." The seminal New York case on the subject, *Moore v. Williams*, 115 N.Y. 586 (1889), somewhat confusingly said that "good title" means not merely a valid title, in fact, but a marketable title ". . . which can again be sold to a reasonable purchaser or mortgaged to a person of reasonable prudence as a security for the loan of money."

To begin with, for a title to be good, it must not only be free from liens, but it must also be free of other defects that would scare away a reasonable purchaser or prudent lender. Although perhaps a nebulous standard, at a minimum it undoubtedly requires (at least in the case of real estate) that the borrower be the *record* owner and not have leased the property to another (unless, of course, the borrower is in the leasing business). Being the record owner may not in itself be sufficient. In recent years a frequent worry has arisen in the northeast United States where Native American tribes have, based upon treaties signed many years ago, asserted ultimate ownership to vast tracts of land even though they are not listed as the record owners. As other examples of defects that might defeat the goodness (or validity) of title, a neighbor's parking lot or building might encroach on the borrower's property, the borrower might have originally acquired the property from a minor who did not have the capacity to sell the property, or title to the property could revert to a prior owner if its use is changed (perhaps an earlier deed required it to be devoted solely for religious purposes and the borrower wants to construct a new corporate headquarters on it).

The concept of "marketable" title is a term of art employed in the real estate context. To be "marketable," title to real estate must be free of the kinds of defects that would deter a prospective purchaser from acquiring the property. Examples of such defects might include easements for underground utility lines, installation of which requires destruction of the borrower's new office building, and metes and bounds descriptions in which the ending point does not loop back to the beginning point.

The illustrations here are largely in the real property context and that is where most court cases have construed the term "good title" or "marketable title." The representation intends that the borrower also address title to its personal property. The defects described above may be harder to envision in the personal property context, but the borrower might nevertheless breach the representation if, for example, it had transferred its property to a grantor trust, or the property were held by an affiliate rather than the borrower. Perhaps a Federal Communications Commission (FCC) license purportedly issued to the borrower, and necessary for it to operate its business, is held instead by a subsidiary or affiliate. Another classic example comes up in the context of artworks (albeit not normally relevant for corporate borrowers since they are not likely to interfere with the ability to conduct business). If the borrower's claim to that valuable Picasso hanging in its boardroom sits at the end of a long chain of ownership beginning with a confiscation in Nazi Germany, the borrower's title could be void.

The representation also requires that leasehold interests be "valid," and, although there are few court cases that construe the term, it presumably has a meaning similar to that for fee-owned property, including that the leasehold interest is free of liens and that the borrower is the named lessee and has not sublet the property to another.

6.3.6   Labor Matters

Box 6.26

The Borrower represents and warrants to the Lenders and the Administrative Agent that, except as set forth in Schedule _____, (a) as of the Effective Date, there are no collective bargaining agreements covering the employees of the Borrower or any of its Subsidiaries and (b) there is not pending, nor (to the knowledge of the Borrower) is there threatened, any strike, walkout, slowdown, or work stoppage, or any unfair labor practice complaint or grievance or arbitration proceeding arising out of or under any collective bargaining agreement covering the employees of the Borrower or any of its Subsidiaries that, individually or in the aggregate, could reasonably be expected to have a Material Adverse Effect. The hours worked and payments made to employees of the Borrower and its Subsidiaries have not been in violation in any material respect of the Fair Labor Standards Act or any other applicable law dealing with such matters. [Consummation of the Acquisition will not give rise to a

> right of termination or right of renegotiation under any collective bargaining agreement covering the employees of the Borrower or any of its Subsidiaries that, individually or in the aggregate, could reasonably be expected to have a Material Adverse Effect.]

Knowing that the borrower is at peace with its workforce eliminates one more risk of uncertainty that lenders fear. The labor matters representation attempts to address this issue. Unlike most of the representations discussed in this chapter, however, there is surprisingly little uniformity as to what lenders ask the borrower to say, an indication that the language is often closely negotiated to fit each borrower's circumstances.

The sample language in Box 6.26 sets out some of the more common matters covered. The representation typically begins with disclosure to the lenders of any collective bargaining agreements to which the borrower's employees may be subject. Often, the borrower also confirms that it has supplied copies of the collective bargaining agreements to the lenders, although in many cases the borrower will resist this out of concern that the exact provisions of the agreements must remain confidential. The representation then continues with an affirmation from the borrower that there are no disputes with its employees (strikes, grievance proceedings, or the like) that could have a material adverse effect. Some agreements also include a representation to the effect that the borrower is in compliance with the Fair Labor Standards Act, although this is largely redundant with the compliance with laws representation.

Finally, in agreements that finance an acquisition, the representation may ask the borrower to confirm that the transaction itself will not result in termination or renegotiation of any collective bargaining agreement. In many cases this issue is likely to be covered by the relevant acquisition agreement, and borrowers may for this reason resist inserting into the credit agreement a representation that no termination or renegotiation will occur. This fact notwithstanding, whether included or not, the possibility of termination or renegotiation is normally a subject of the lenders' due diligence and, if the risk is substantial (and the consequences potentially material), the lenders may simply not commit to provide the facility in the first instance.

6.3.7 Intellectual Property

Box 6.27

The Borrower represents and warrants to the Lenders and the Administrative Agent that each of the Borrower and its Subsidiaries owns, or is licensed to use, all trademarks, trade names, copyrights, patents, and other intellectual property material to its business, and the use thereof by the Borrower and its Subsidiaries does not infringe upon the rights of any other Person, except for any such infringements that, individually or in the aggregate, could not reasonably be expected to have a Material Adverse Effect.

Ultimately, every borrower has some important intellectual property (if nothing else, its name). For a borrower such as a chemical company that is heavily dependent on patents or a wine and spirits company that cannot sell product except by using trademarks, intellectual property can be vital. Of course, all businesses rely upon intellectual property (such as the operating system for internal computers, and accounting and word-processing software used in daily operations), although in these instances making the representation is relatively straightforward. The purpose of the representation is to have the borrower affirm that it has all intellectual property (patents, trademarks, and copyrights) necessary for it to operate its business. It is customary for the representation to be qualified by materiality.

6.3.8 Environmental Matters

Box 6.28

The Borrower represents and warrants to the Lenders and the Administrative Agent that, except as set forth in Schedule _____, and except with respect to any other matters that, individually or in the aggregate, could not reasonably be expected to have a Material Adverse Effect, neither the Borrower nor any of its Subsidiaries (i) has failed to comply with any Environmental Law or to obtain, maintain, or comply with any permit, license, or other approval required under any Environmental Law, (ii) has become subject to any Environmental Liability, including related to the Release of any Hazardous Materials, (iii) has received notice of any claim with respect to any Environmental Liability, or (iv) knows of any basis for any Environmental Liability.

One of the many concerns lenders take into account when extending credit is whether the borrower has environmental problems (current or former) that could require expenditure of capital or have an adverse effect on borrower's operations during the term of the loan. Foreign, federal, and state environmental laws and regulations are comprehensive and relate to a wide range of environmental issues, including pollution, air emissions, wastewater discharges, waste disposal, and exposure to hazardous materials. The underlying strict requirements can affect the way in which companies conduct business by, for example, requiring various permits and imposing various emission limits. Environmental law also frequently changes, which can lead to significant costs to comply with any new obligations. In addition, many companies can face significant clean-up responsibilities for hazardous materials on properties currently or formerly owned or leased by them, or on property owned by others on which hazardous substances have been released by the borrower.

Under the federal Superfund law, any past or present contributor of hazardous materials to a Superfund site (such as a landfill) may be jointly and severally liable with all other contributors for the entire clean-up cost, regardless of fault. Former property owners or operators could also be jointly and severally liable for contamination that was caused during the period of ownership or operation. Such liability can arise even if all actions that led to the contamination were in compliance with the law. A company that 25 years earlier thought it was a good corporate citizen by having an environmental service firm clean out all polychlorinated biphenyls (PCBs) from its on-site electric transformers could find itself jointly and severally liable for a billion dollar clean-up if those PCBs were disposed of by the service firm in a Superfund waste site. However, in such a case, liability would typically be spread out and allocated to different companies based, among other things, on the volume and type of waste that was generated. As a practical matter, so-called *de minimis* contributors may be able to settle for relatively small amounts, but other examples abound. While industries such as mining, power, chemical, and heavy manufacturing can be expected to be subject to substantial environmental regulation, material environmental liabilities can also arise in unexpected areas. A suburban office complex built on land that, unbeknownst to all, was a petroleum storage facility during World War II could involve the tenants in costly remediation if cumulative oil spills over the years have descended into the groundwater. A television station with a 40-year-old underground tank that holds fuel oil for its winter furnace may discover that the tank has been leaking and must be dug up along with a substantial portion of the surrounding earth, and replaced with unpolluted soil at a significant cost.

In order to help identify any potential environmental exposures or provide more information with respect to known environmental matters, lenders often request that a Phase I environmental site assessment or a Phase II environmental report be prepared with respect to the properties owned or operated by the borrower. (See Section 5.1.11.3 as to the distinction between these two categories of reports.) To supplement (or substitute for) such due diligence, lenders generally expect the credit agreement to include an environmental representation (and list any exceptions in a disclosure schedule).

Some borrowers object to inclusion of any environmental representation at all. Many investment grade public companies, for example, insist that the representation is inappropriate because they are already required to disclose any material contingent environmental liabilities in SEC filings, and that the completeness of disclosures representation discussed in Section 6.5.1 should fully protect the lenders. Although, as a general proposition, this logic may be reasonable, lenders not infrequently want detailed disclosure schedules that go beyond SEC filing requirements. Particularly, if the borrower is engaged in a manufacturing, refining, chemical processing, extraction, or other similar business, lenders may want a more focused confirmation from the borrower that, except as listed, it does not face any significant environmental liabilities or expenditures. As a consequence, most credit agreements for non-investment-grade borrowers (public or private) include the representation.

In its simplest form (such as the language in Box 6.28), the representation generally has the borrower confirm that it is not subject to any environmental liability, that it is in compliance with applicable environmental laws, and that it has not received notice of (and does not know of) any potential environmental liability. In its more comprehensive form, the representation may ask the borrower to list in disclosure schedules not only exceptions to the representation, but information about any asbestos or PCBs on its premises, any underground storage tanks, and any releases of hazardous materials that it has been required to report to regulatory agencies.

As with the litigation representation discussed in Section 6.2.3, the representation is typically qualified by a materiality threshold so that only serious liabilities need be listed. This spares the borrower from having to list every spill of cleaning liquid by its night janitors (any such spill could technically be a "release" of "hazardous materials" for purposes of environmental regulations). Representations sometimes use dollar thresholds (rather than the more nebulous "materiality" test) as a cut-off for inclusion in the disclosure schedules. Either approach covers the relevant issues and which tack is used is left to negotiation.

6.3.9   No Burdensome Restrictions

Box 6.29

[The Borrower represents and warrants to the Lenders and the Administrative Agent that neither the Borrower nor any of its Subsidiaries is a party to any agreement, or subject to any provision of law, compliance with which could, individually or in the aggregate, reasonably be expected to have a Material Adverse Effect.]

[The Borrower represents and warrants to the Lenders and the Administrative Agent that none of the Borrower or any of its Subsidiaries is, on the date hereof, subject to any indenture, agreement, instrument, or other arrangement (i) of the type described in Section [*Dividend Blockers*] or (ii) that would restrict the ability of the Borrower or any Subsidiary to grant a lien on its property to secure, or from guaranteeing, the obligations of the Borrower and its Subsidiaries under this Agreement and the other Loan Documents, or require that other obligations be secured or guaranteed concurrently with any such grant of security or guarantee in favor of the Lenders.]

Term sheets often throw in a requirement that the borrower tell the lenders that it is not subject to any "burdensome restrictions." This somewhat cryptic language is incorporated into credit agreements in two quite different ways. Some agreements (illustrated in the first bracketed paragraph in Box 6.29) want the borrower to represent that it is not subject to agreements that could materially constrain its business. Examples might include an agreement that limits the borrower's ability to use a patent to compete against a new product, a contract that requires the borrower to purchase a product from a supplier at above-market prices, or a trademark license that prevents the borrower from effectively marketing a product under the borrower's logo.

Other credit agreements express the "burdensome restrictions" allusion in a completely different sense, to require that the borrower tell the lending syndicate whether its subsidiaries are subject to any "dividend blockers" (see the detailed discussion of these in Section 7.6.14) and whether the borrower or its subsidiaries are prevented in any way from granting liens on their properties to secure the credit agreement or to guarantee the credit facility. For cases in which the credit facility, at inception, is neither guaranteed nor secured, the representation becomes a way to assure the lenders that, should financial difficulties develop, the borrower is free to provide additional credit protection for the exclusive benefit of the lenders.

Which of these two variants is inserted into any credit agreement is strictly a matter of negotiation and the understanding of the parties at the time that the term sheet is drafted.

6.4 REPRESENTATIONS BY FOREIGN BORROWERS

For a borrower that is not organized in the United States, the credit agreement may contain certain additional representations that cover matters unique to nondomestic borrowers, including the language in Box 6.30.

6.4.1 Commercial Activity

Box 6.30

The Borrower represents and warrants to the Lenders and the Administrative Agent that it is subject to civil and commercial law with respect to its obligations under the Loan Documents, and the making and performance of the Loan Documents by the Borrower constitute private and commercial acts rather than public or governmental acts. The Borrower is not entitled to any immunity on the ground of sovereignty or the like from the jurisdiction of any court or from any action, suit, setoff, or proceeding, or the service of process in connection therewith, arising under the Loan Documents.

If the borrower is a "foreign state" under the U.S. Foreign Sovereign Immunities Act of 1976 (the FSIA), it is entitled to immunity from court jurisdiction and its property is entitled to immunity from attachment or execution. That makes it hard to enforce a credit agreement against a sovereign entity—not only are the lenders prevented from suing the borrower in any U.S. federal or state court, but even if they should obtain a judgment in the borrower's home country or other jurisdiction, they would be prevented from enforcing the judgment by attaching or executing against assets in the United States. Since no lender wants to lend money to a borrower if it is unable to enforce the credit agreement, credit facilities to "foreign states" routinely include a waiver of sovereign immunity. The waiver, as well as a more general discussion of the FSIA, is discussed in Section 12.8.3.

A waiver of immunity is not always effective. Part of the difficulty comes from the breadth of the term "foreign state." It includes not only a foreign government, but any agency or instrumentality of a foreign government, such as a government-owned bank or airline. Under this standard, a borrower that at closing was privately owned could, during the term of the facility, become a "foreign state" if a majority of its shares are acquired by a foreign government. Consequently, loans to any borrower organized outside the United States routinely include a waiver to guard against the possibility that the borrower becomes entitled to immunity at a later date. It is not, however, clear that a waiver of immunity by a private entity will be effective once it becomes an agency or instrumentality of a foreign government (Section 1610(a)(1) of the FSIA requires that waivers be by a "foreign state;" a waiver granted upon execution of the credit agreement by a private borrower is arguably not a waiver by a "foreign state"). As a consequence, legal opinions in transactions with nongovernmental borrowers routinely include a qualification as to the enforceability of future waivers of immunity.

The purpose of the commercial activity representation is to cover the risk that the waiver of immunity by a private borrower will not be upheld once it becomes a "foreign state" under the FSIA. The representation springs out of the so-called commercial activity exception in Section 1605(a)(2) of the FSIA, which provides, in general, that no immunity attaches to commercial activity carried on by a foreign state. By having the (private) borrower acknowledge at inception that the loan is "commercial," the lenders have another basis upon which to argue that the FSIA does not prevent enforcement, attachment, or execution in the United States against the borrower.

6.4.2 Pari Passu *Ranking*

Box 6.31

The Borrower represents and warrants to the Lenders and the Administrative Agent that the payment obligations of the Borrower hereunder and under the Notes are and will at all times be unsubordinated general obligations of the Borrower, and rank and will at all times rank at least *pari passu* with all other present and future unsubordinated unsecured Debt of the Borrower.

Where the status as senior debt representation discussed in Section 6.5.2 tells the lenders that their debt is senior to subordinated debt of the borrower, the *pari passu* ranking representation tells the lenders that they are not themselves subordinated to other debt. *Pari passu* is Latin for "side by side" and, in the context of debt instruments, is understood to mean that two claims are to be treated equally and without preference of one over the other.

As discussed in Section 6.5.2, a claim against a borrower can be preferred over another claim either in right of security or in right of payment. Credit agreements provide assurance that the lending syndicate is not primed in right of security through the liens and title representation and through the lien covenant discussed in Section 7.6.1. Credit agreements provide assurance that the syndicate is not primed in right of payment through the *pari passu* representation. In the United States, except for certain narrow priorities granted by statute, and except for the doctrine of equitable subordination (see Section 6.5.2), one creditor cannot be subordinated to another without the express consent of the former. For this reason, the *pari passu* representation does not appear in domestic credit agreements, the assumption being (even if not always true!) that the lenders will know whether the document they have signed provides for their claims against the borrower to be subordinated.

If the borrower is located outside of the United States, however, different legal rules (that may not be waivable) may apply that could subordinate a creditor to other claims against a borrower without the consent of the creditor. Examples include the adoption by Argentina in the early 1970s of laws to subordinate external debt claims in the insolvency of an Argentine borrower to debt claims held by Argentine creditors. Some corporate law regimes in non-U.S. jurisdictions may rank debt issuances in order of issuance; bonds issued in 1990 would therefore have precedence over loans made in 2016. Certain civil law countries (Spain and the Philippines are historic examples) have legal doctrines to the effect that registration of a debt agreement before a notary public can give the agreement priority over nonregistered claims. Such registration can often be done without the knowledge or assent of third-party creditors. Thus, while a lending syndicate sleeps, a crafty bond trustee can register the indenture before a notary and thereby raise to preferred status the borrower's bond obligations above its credit agreement obligations.

The *pari passu* representation and its companion, the *pari passu* covenant (see Section 7.5.7), together attempt to address these concerns. The representation, of course, has the borrower affirm to the lenders that no other debt holder (lender, bondholder, or other claimant) has priority over the syndicate. Presumably, to make the representation, a careful borrower (along with the lending syndicate as part of its own due diligence process) will consult local counsel to ensure that the representation is, in fact, true. If any kind of priority exists, it should in theory be discovered (and in this way disclosed to the lenders). In contrast, the covenant will require the borrower to take whatever actions are necessary to ensure *pari passu* treatment (and refrain from taking actions, such as joining in the registration of a third party's debt claim, that could result in the lending syndicate being primed by another creditor).

To appreciate fully the implications of the representation and covenant, it may be useful to understand further what *"pari passu"* does and does not mean. To begin with, although contrary arguments have been raised by debt holders in a handful of cases,[1] the clauses have historically been understood not to force a borrower to make concurrent ratable payments outside a bankruptcy or insolvency context. As discussed below, the recent case involving Argentinian bonds represents an exception though an exception noted by the courts to be a narrow exception borne of a unique fact pattern. Nevertheless, if a borrower wishes to prepay syndicate B without also prepaying syndicate A when both are *pari passu*, it is generally understood that the borrower is free to do so. Even if it is in default to syndicate A, subject to preference rules or the like in a bankruptcy or insolvency proceeding, the borrower would be permitted to pay or prepay syndicate B without also prepaying other similarly situated creditors.

Stated another way, the *pari passu* representation and covenant have traditionally been intended only to address whether one creditor has a *legal right* to be paid before another creditor; neither clause is intended to prevent a borrower from being friendlier to one claimant over another, or from managing its balance sheet intelligently by paying higher-cost debt or earlier-maturing debt before lower-cost, later-maturing claims, or even from curing defaults by refinancing a creditor at the brink of acceleration while leaving other debt outstanding. Any lending syndicate that believes it needs protection against the borrower's prepaying other debt normally addresses that risk explicitly by inserting a mandatory prepayment provision into the credit agreement requiring ratable reduction of the facility upon any payment or prepayment of other target debt, or by insisting that an intercreditor agreement that requires sharing of nonratable payments be executed with the target debt holders. Additionally, the lenders in any facility that is in default can protect themselves by accelerating and forcing the borrower into an insolvency proceeding in which all similarly situated creditors are required (at least by most countries' laws) to be treated equally.

In the context of sovereign (rather than corporate) debt, however, where insolvency proceedings are unavailable, the operation of the *pari*

---

[1] See the useful discussion of these attempts set out in *The Pari Passu Clause in Sovereign Debt Instruments*, 53 Emory L.J. 869 (2004).

passu clause has historically been less clear, although a recent court case, *NML Capital, Ltd. v. Republic of Argentina*, 699 F.3d 246 (2d Cir. 2012) *cert. denied*, 134 S.Ct. 201 (2013) has provided some guidance. Argentina defaulted on certain bonds in 2001, following which its president declared a moratorium on payment of more than $80 billion of its public debt. The Argentine legislature then passed legislation in each subsequent year renewing the moratorium. In 2005 and 2010 Argentina made exchange offers to holders of the defaulted bonds to exchange their bonds for new exchange bonds, which Argentina has made current payments on, while not making any payment on the defaulted bonds. The Argentine legislature also passed a law that prohibited the reopening of the exchange offer, prohibited Argentina from conducting any in-court, out-of-court, or private settlement with respect to the defaulted bonds, and required the delisting of the defaulted bonds from all foreign and domestic securities markets and exchanges. Holders of the defaulted bonds that did not exchange their defaulted bonds for the exchange bonds sued Argentina for, among other things, breaching the *pari passu* clause applicable to the defaulted bonds. The court in *NML Capital* held that "[i]n short, the combination of Argentina's executive declarations and legislative enactments have ensured that plaintiffs' beneficial interests do *not* remain direct, unconditional, unsecured and unsubordinated obligations of the Republic and that any claims that may arise from the Republic's [exchange bonds] *do* have priority in Argentinian courts over claims arising out of the Republic's [defaulted bonds]. Thus we have little difficulty concluding that Argentina breached the *Pari Passu* Clause [applicable to the defaulted bonds]." The Second Circuit Court of Appeals in *NML Capital* affirmed the injunction imposed by the District Court intended to remedy the breach of the *pari passu* clause by directing that whenever Argentina paid on the exchange bonds it must also make a ratable payment to the plaintiffs that held defaulted bonds. Argentina ultimately reached a settlement with defaulted bondholders. A key takeaway from this case is that when there is disparate treatment between creditors that can be viewed as tantamount to de facto subordination (as the trial and appellate courts seemed to find in connection with Argentina's actions toward the defaulted bonds), then there is a risk of breaching the pari passu provision. It remains to be seen whether such an interpretation of *pari passu* would apply beyond the unique facts in the above case and whether the interpretation holds true beyond the sovereign debt realm.

Second, the *pari passu* representation and covenant are intended only to address disparate treatment of creditors *in right of payment* and not *in right of security*. So a representation that credit agreement debt is *pari passu* to other debt of the borrower does not say that the borrower has no outstanding secured debt. The sample language in Box 6.31 is unequivocal on this point because it refers to the ranking of the credit agreement only as against other *unsecured* debt. Many *pari passu* clauses do not expressly compare the credit agreement to other unsecured debt. Nevertheless, the clause, even when silent, is generally understood to refer only to other unsecured claims. Any preference that other creditors may have in right of security is addressed by the liens and title representations and covenants.

Third, *pari passu* clauses are intended to guarantee only the ranking of the credit agreement against other "Debt" as it is defined in the credit agreement. They are not intended to be a representation that the credit agreement is equal in rank to all other claims, since that would include creditors that even in the United States have a preference by statute, such as the priority accorded federal and state tax authorities. In many countries, the list of priority creditors is expanded considerably and could include pension and deposit liabilities, wages, and even certain preferred vendors.

Fourth, although the sample *pari passu* representation set out above refers to any other "unsubordinated unsecured Debt," and does not draw a distinction between claims payable to internal creditors and claims owed to external creditors, many *pari passu* clauses require only that the credit agreement rank on an equal footing with other *external* debt. Which formulation is used is largely a function of the foreign jurisdiction's legal rules (and perhaps also negotiation). If the borrower is situated in a jurisdiction that contains a rule such as that discussed above for Argentina, then the reference to external debt is obviously necessary for the representation to be true.

6.4.3 Legal Form

Box 6.32

The Borrower represents and warrants to the Lenders and the Administrative Agent that this Agreement is, and each Note when duly executed and delivered by the Borrower will be, in proper legal form under the laws of [Borrower's Country] for the enforcement thereof against the Borrower under such law, and if this Agreement were stated to be governed by such law, it would constitute a legal, valid, and binding obligation of the Borrower under such law, enforceable in accordance with its terms, subject to applicable bankruptcy, insolvency, reorganization, fraudulent conveyance or transfer, moratorium, or other similar laws relating to or

---

affecting the rights of creditors generally, and subject to general principles of equity, regardless of whether considered in a proceeding in equity or at law. All formalities required in [Borrower's Country] for the validity and enforceability of each of the Loan Documents have been accomplished, and no Taxes are required to be paid and no notarization is required, for the validity and enforceability thereof [except for . . .].

With rare exception, every credit agreement includes the enforceability representation discussed earlier in this chapter (see Section 6.1.4). However, since the agreement is typically governed by New York or California (or some other state's) law, a non-U.S. borrower may be willing to make the enforceability representation based simply upon the wide freedom of contract afforded in U.S. law jurisdictions. This may not be sufficient if the borrower is located outside the United States, where less flexible rules govern the scope of what two parties can contract to.

For non-U.S. borrowers, therefore, it is customary to ask for more. The sample language above has the borrower cover two issues beyond mere New York (or California) law enforceability. To begin with, it asks the borrower to answer a hypothetical question whether, under the assumption that the credit agreement were governed by the borrower's local law, it would be enforceable. Problems are sometimes identified. One issue that often surfaces is with respect to the boilerplate provision requiring that the borrower submit to the jurisdiction of a court in the United States. Under New York law, this can generally be done with a simple clause set out in the credit agreement (see Section 12.8.1). Under the laws of a non-U.S. jurisdiction, however, a submission to the jurisdiction of a foreign court (a U.S. court is *foreign* from the perspective of the borrower's local jurisdiction) might need to be effected pursuant to a notarized power of attorney. Accordingly, a representation that asks whether the agreement would be enforceable if governed by the law of Mexico could not be made without appropriate qualification and disclosure to the lending syndicate of the submission to jurisdiction clause. The purpose of asking for the representation will have been served.

Second, the legal form representation asks the borrower to confirm that the agreement is in proper form to be enforceable. This may appear wholly duplicative of the enforceability representation discussed earlier in this chapter but it addresses other risks. An agreement could, for example, be binding and enforceable, yet not be in proper form to be submitted to a court in an enforcement action. Perhaps it needs to be notarized and to have an *apostille* affixed under the Hague Apostille

Convention (a sometimes cumbersome process that requires that the notary's signature itself be authenticated by the state authority pursuant to which the notary is regulated). Perhaps it needs to be translated into the local language and then certified before a public official. Conceivably, it needs to be printed on special paper and sealed with wax. The possibilities are myriad. In some cases, even if all of these actions are taken, a stamp tax might need to be paid for the agreement to be introduced into evidence in court.

The legal form representation addresses these issues by making the borrower (and its local counsel) focus more precisely upon the types of actions that might be necessary for the credit agreement to be fully enforceable under local law. Some of the redundancy with the enforceability representation may come from the experience of U.S. lawyers with counsel in other jurisdictions in which language barriers can impede a complete understanding of what the lending syndicate's counsel is asking. A U.S. counsel might, for example, ask local counsel if any *taxes* are payable when the agreement is signed and receive an answer of no. But if the U.S. counsel asks whether a *fee* is payable, perhaps the answer changes to yes. Even if local counsel responds that no "tax" or "fee" is payable, a different answer might be obtained if the question is formulated as a "court charge." The legal form representation (together with due diligence and careful questioning of local counsel) attempts to identify these risks.

6.4.4   Foreign Taxes

Box 6.33

The Borrower represents and warrants to the Lenders and the Administrative Agent that there is no Tax of any kind imposed by [Borrower's Country] (or any municipality or other political subdivision or taxing authority thereof or therein that exercises *de facto* or *de jure* power to impose such Tax) either (a) on or by virtue of the execution or delivery of the Loan Documents or (b) on any payment to be made by the Borrower pursuant to the Loan Documents, other than any such tax, levy, assessment, impost, deduction, charge, or withholding imposed on any Person as a result of such Person's being organized under the laws of [Borrower's Country] or by virtue of its having a permanent establishment in [Borrower's Country] to which income under this Agreement and the Notes is attributable or its Applicable Lending Office being located in [Borrower's Country].

In Section 3.7.6, we discussed briefly the tax gross-up provisions of a credit agreement that are designed to indemnify the lenders against taxes (principally withholding taxes) directly attributable to a loan (subject to the exceptions described in Chapter 3). The taxes representation goes hand-in-hand with the yield-protection provision by requiring a borrower to make a representation as to what taxes, if any, are imposed by its local country and to identify at the time of preparation of the credit agreement whether any taxes, in fact, need to be covered by payments from the borrower under the yield-protection provisions. As with the yield protection clause, the term "tax" is defined broadly to pick up any tax, levy, assessment, impost, deduction, charge, withholding, or any other similar monetary burden that might be imposed by a government or its tax arm.

The representation set out in Box 6.33 is sometimes, for convenience, physically situated in the yield-protection clause itself, rather than in the representations and warranties section.

6.4.5   Sovereign Borrowers

Box 6.34

The Borrower represents and warrants to the Lenders and the Administrative Agent that (i) the Republic is a member in good standing and eligible to use the general resources of the International Monetary Fund and (ii) the obligations of the Borrower hereunder are entitled to the full faith and credit of the Republic.

In the case of a loan to a sovereign borrower (a government, central bank, or majority-owned government agency), the lenders will want to confirm that the borrowing country is a member in good standing of the International Monetary Fund (IMF) and is eligible to use the resources thereof under Article V, Section 3, of the Articles of Agreement of the IMF.[2] They do this for two reasons. First, failure to be in good standing with the IMF can be evidence of larger financial difficulties. As with the ERISA or tax representation, if the borrower cannot make the representation cleanly, there may be more serious problems with which the lenders should be concerned. Second, access to funds may be essential to servicing the credit facility. Eligibility to use the resources of the IMF

---

[2] See Articles of Agreement of the International Monetary Fund at https://www.imf.org/external/pubs/ft/aa/pdf/aa.pdf.

entitles a member state to obtain currencies of other member states through the auspices of the IMF. If a sovereign borrower does not itself have a convertible currency, its ability to obtain U.S. dollars (or Euros or whatever other convertible currency the loans are denominated in) may be critical to paying the principal and interest on the credit facility.

When the borrower is a government agency, it is also customary to request the borrower to represent that its obligations under the credit agreement are entitled to the "full faith and credit" of the country. Typically, a request for this representation leads to a conversation with the borrower's counsel as to what full faith and credit means. Its essential meaning is that the government (the sovereign) is obligated to use its taxing power to provide funds to the agency to make payments on the credit facility. This assures the lenders that the loans are not payable solely from a narrow source of funds (such as what happens to be available to the agency), but rather are payable from the general revenue of the country. Often, the conversations regarding the meaning of the term result in the representation being adjusted to refer to the specific *statute* or *decree* that provides for the sovereign to make its tax revenues available to service the credit facility. The representation is not normally included in facilities made directly available to a sovereign, since it is presumed that the sovereign *ipso facto* has access to its own tax revenues to pay the loans.

6.5 OTHER REPRESENTATIONS

6.5.1 Completeness of Disclosures

Box 6.35

The Borrower represents and warrants to the Lenders and the Administrative Agent that it has disclosed to the Lenders all agreements, instruments, and corporate or other restrictions to which it or any of its Subsidiaries is subject, and all other matters known to it, that, individually or in the aggregate, could reasonably be expected to have a Material Adverse Effect. Neither the Information Memorandum nor any of the other reports, financial statements, certificates, or other information furnished by or on behalf of the Borrower to any Lender in connection with the negotiation of this Agreement or delivered hereunder (as modified or supplemented by other information so furnished) contains any material misstatement of fact or omits to state any material fact necessary to make the statements therein, in the light of the circumstances under which they were made, not misleading; *provided* that, with respect to projected financial information, the Borrower represents only that such information reflects the Borrower's good-faith estimates as of the date of preparation thereof, based upon methods and data the Borrower believes to be reasonable and accurate, but actual results during the periods covered by such projections may differ materially from such projections.

The completeness of disclosure representation is modeled after similar representations commonly seen in securities underwriting agreements that are intended to protect the underwriters against liability under Rule 10b-5 when they resell securities purchased from an issuer. In general, Rule 10b-5, which has been promulgated under the Securities Act of 1933, makes unlawful the purchase or sale of securities using manipulative or deceptive devices. Violators can be subject to liability for damages as well as enforcement action by the SEC.

Since commercial credit agreements are generally structured so that the loans are not securities (see Section 11.6), Rule 10b-5, as such, does not normally apply to loans made under a credit facility. The representation is, nevertheless, inserted to afford to the lenders much of the same protection that Rule 10b-5 gives to the sale of securities, but without the hurdles that apply to 10b-5 claims, such as the requirements that the party to whom the securities are sold *reasonably* relies upon the statements made by the seller and that the seller acts with *scienter* (or intent). The representation also forces the borrower to step up affirmatively to the accuracy and completeness of any confidential information memorandum that is distributed in connection with the syndication of the facility, which lawyers for the borrower may not review with the same care as they would an offering circular or prospectus for the sale of securities (and which counsel for the arranger may not review at all).

The representation has the borrower confirm that the information supplied in connection with the credit agreement (including all financial statements, any confidential information memorandum, and other disclosures), when taken as a whole, is accurate and complete and does not omit any information necessary to be not misleading. The representation thus provides comfort to the lenders that the borrower is not selectively supplying information that, individually, is perfectly accurate, but that, in the aggregate, is deceptive. Insofar as it covers projections, the representation contains the same qualifications described under Section 6.2.4.

Absent the completeness of disclosure representation, in any agreement with an integration clause (see Section 12.9.3), the lenders might be barred from claiming that misstatements or omissions in the process of drafting and syndicating the credit facility gave them grounds upon which to declare a default.

6.5.2   Status as Senior Debt

> **Box 6.36**
>
> The Borrower represents and warrants to the Lenders and the Administrative Agent that the obligations of the Borrower under this Agreement constitute "senior indebtedness" under and as defined in the [Identify Subordinated Notes Indenture] entitled to the benefits of the subordination provisions therein.

One of the things that lenders look to when they assess the credit strength of a borrower is whether it has a solid capital structure consisting of senior debt supported by equity and junior or subordinated debt. Equity, reflected in the capital stock portion of the balance sheet, represents the sum of what has been paid into the borrower in exchange for the issuance of ownership interests (stock or partnership or membership interests) plus accumulated earnings. Mathematically, it can be viewed as the excess of the book value of a company's assets over its aggregate liabilities. In a bankruptcy or insolvency of the borrower, the equity receives money last; all liabilities must be paid in full first before any funds are delivered to the equity holders. Liabilities in a bankruptcy are all paid with equal priority unless any claimant is entitled to seniority (by security or otherwise). The question for the lenders in making their credit decisions is therefore whether they want a senior or preferred status or whether they are willing to be at the same level as other liabilities, including trade claims (vendors), wages, taxes, short-term and long-term debt and other nonequity items. This is the point at which lenders decide whether to ask for security or for a portion of the borrower's outstanding liabilities to be subordinated.

For a lending syndicate, there are in substance two flavors of preferred status or seniority—seniority in right of security and seniority in right of payment. Seniority in right of security occurs when the syndicate is granted liens while other creditors remain unsecured, or where one syndicate is granted first-priority liens while another syndicate is granted second-priority liens. It is discussed in more detail in Chapter 8. Secured creditors have first claim upon the proceeds of any collateral. If the syndicate is secured by a borrower's inventory and receivables, then upon a liquidation the borrower must pay the full amount of the proceeds of the inventory and receivables exclusively to the secured creditors (first, to first-lien creditors, and then, to second-lien creditors, if any) until they have been paid in full before distributing any portion thereof to its other creditors.

To simplify somewhat a dreadfully complex area of the law, seniority in right of payment can arise in one of three ways: by statute, by contract, and by a bankruptcy court's equitably subordinating the claims of one creditor to others. A detailed discussion of statutory seniority is beyond the scope of this chapter. It would not, in any event, ever benefit a lending syndicate. Examples of statutory seniority include the preference granted to claims of the U.S. government in nonbankruptcy proceedings under 37 U.S.C. § 3713 and the preference granted to taxes and other administrative claims in bankruptcy cases by Section 503 of the Bankruptcy Code (11 U.S.C. § 503). A detailed discussion of equitable subordination is also beyond the scope of this chapter. It is a remedy imposed by a bankruptcy court under Section 510(c) of the Bankruptcy Code (11 U.S.C. § 510(c)) and is available when a creditor engages in inequitable conduct to favor its position as a creditor against other claimants. Examples of behavior that could lead to equitable subordination might include a creditor using its power as a controlling shareholder to improve the priority of its claims over others or using information available to it through a board membership to buy in debt from creditors that do not have access to the same information. Equitable subordination can benefit a lending syndicate. Indeed, it is often a threat used by syndicates as leverage against perceived bad actors in a borrower's bankruptcy. In rare cases equitable subordination can even be used *against* a lending syndicate.

Contractual subordination is the seniority that the senior indebtedness representation addresses. It arises, as its name indicates, pursuant to contract. If the borrower has issued senior subordinated bonds, the governing indenture will contain subordination provisions that subordinate the claims of the bondholders to "senior indebtedness," as defined in the indenture. The bondholders by accepting the bonds will, under the language of the indenture, be deemed to have agreed to all of the terms and conditions of the indenture, including that the bonds are subordinated to the defined senior indebtedness, which should include the debt under the credit agreement. Bonds are not the only examples. Subordinated debt can also arise in other circumstances, such as through advances from a corporate parent or affiliate, or pursuant to an agreement to subordinate management fees payable to a managing investor.

There are two principal effects of claims being subordinated: payment blockage and the double dividend. The payment blockage provisions of a subordination agreement (these include the subordination provisions of an indenture) define the circumstances in which payment of principal or interest on the subordinated debt is prohibited. The degree of blockage determines whether the subordination is *shallow* or *deep*. The very deepest of subordination provides that the subordinated debt is not payable at all if any senior debt is outstanding. This kind of subordinated debt is typically only seen when advances have been made by a principal shareholder or affiliate. The shallowest of subordination incorporates a blockage provision preventing payment of the subordinated debt only if the borrower is in bankruptcy. Intermediate positions might block only junior payments if there is a default in respect of the senior debt (or, alternatively, if there is a senior payment default). Historically, in the context of subordinated bond indentures, long and agonizing negotiations took place between the potential senior lending syndicate and the underwriters for the new issue of subordinated debt to determine the payment blockage provisions. In more recent years, a market standard has developed that provides for an automatic block if a senior payment default occurs (including by reason of acceleration) and a block for 179 days if any nonpayment default occurs of which the senior creditors notify the borrower and subordinated debt holders (or their trustee).

The other feature of contractual subordination is the so-called double dividend. Double-dividend provisions (alternatively referred to as turnover provisions) stipulate that any payment received by a subordinated debt holder in violation of the relevant provisions of the indenture or other subordination agreement must be held by the debt holder in trust for the benefit of the holders of senior debt and immediately paid over directly to the senior debt holders. In a bankruptcy, this means that if all creditors are to be paid 15¢ for each dollar of debt, the senior creditors will ultimately receive their 15¢ plus the 15¢ being paid to the subordinated debt holders. The latter end up with zero until the senior debt has been paid in full. The moniker "double dividend" refers to the right of the senior claimants to, in effect, collect *two* claims.

The status as senior debt representation is intended to be nothing more than an affirmation from the borrower that its obligations under the credit agreement constitute "senior indebtedness" for purposes of any outstanding subordinated debt. The same conclusion may also be confirmed in an opinion of counsel though such an opinion is rarely requested and even more rarely provided. Of course, the inclusion in a credit agreement of a representation does not by itself convert a general claim against the borrower into a senior claim, and lenders therefore independently satisfy themselves, as part of their due diligence, that the credit facility is senior. Notwithstanding that the representation may state the obvious, it nevertheless gives the lenders an argument (if any subordinated debt holder should assert otherwise) that they acted in good faith in believing their loans were senior.

6.5.3 Perfection and Priority of Security

Box 6.37

The Borrower represents and warrants to the Lenders and the Administrative Agent that the Security Agreement and Mortgages, upon execution and delivery thereof by the parties thereto, are effective to create in favor of the Administrative Agent, for the ratable benefit of the Lenders, a legal, valid, and enforceable security interest or mortgage lien in the collateral intended to be covered thereby, which security interest or mortgage lien, upon the filing in the appropriate filings offices of Uniform Commercial Code financing statements with respect to the security interests created under the Security Agreement, and copies of the respective Mortgages in the appropriate real property recording offices with respect to the Mortgages, will constitute a perfected security interest or mortgage lien in or on , all right, title, and interest of the Borrower in and to the collateral intended to be covered thereby (other than collateral in which a security interest may be perfected only by the taking of control), in each case prior to the rights of all third persons and subject to no Liens except Liens expressly permitted by Section [*Lien Covenant*].

Notwithstanding that credit agreements place the legal responsibility for creating and maintaining liens on the borrower, to a great extent, whether liens are valid, enforceable, perfected, and prior to other claims on the borrower's property is a practical responsibility of the lenders. It is almost universal practice for the lenders (typically through the administrative agent) to undertake the job of recording mortgages, filing UCC financing statements, and taking other lien perfection actions; rarely is this task entrusted to the borrower. For this reason, the representation with respect to perfection and priority of security is different from all other representations. While the latter are within the ken of the borrower, the lien representation is more within the ken of the lenders. The purpose of the representation is actually, therefore, a means to make lien perfection the responsibility of the borrower as well as of the lenders. A similar point underlies the insertion of the lien default (see Section 9.1.10).

With narrow exceptions, liens in the United States are created by the execution of an appropriate security agreement (in the case of personal property) and mortgage or deed of trust (in the case of real property and certain other assets, such as vessels, railroad equipment, or aircraft), together with the lenders giving "value" and the borrower having ownership or (in the case of property subject to the UCC) "rights in the collateral." At least in the context of personal property as to which the rules of the UCC apply, a commitment to lend is "value" for these purposes. Although the sample language in Box 6.37 is designed to cover both personal and real property (the terms used do not satisfactorily fit vessel, rail, or aircraft liens), for clarity's sake most credit agreements break out each category of liens into separate representations: personal property liens, mortgage liens, and other liens (if relevant).

Liens on property outside the United States are also typically dealt with in a separate paragraph since the sample language in Box 6.37 is not easily adapted to non-U.S. collateral. Foreign counsel, whether representing the borrower or the lenders, may object that the concepts of "creation," "value," and "perfection" have no meaning under non-U.S. law. This can often lead to a long and pedantic discussion to describe their equivalents under foreign law and adapt the representation accordingly. Two things should be borne in mind. First, the essential element of any lien is to grant the lenders a senior and exclusive claim, priming third-party claimants, over the property of the borrower intended to be covered by the lien. Simply having the borrower represent that this is the effect of a lien in Lower Transmania may be sufficient. Second, as noted previously, the lending syndicate (through the administrative agent) almost universally takes responsibility for perfection. Whether, therefore, the borrower speaks to Transmanian law may not be particularly significant.

6.6 THE SPECIAL CIRCUMSTANCES OF ACQUISITION FINANCINGS

It has become quite common in the acquisition context to have the arduously negotiated representations described in this chapter limited substantially as they relate to a target, its subsidiaries, or its business. As discussed in more detail in Section 5.3, often the only representations made by the borrower (or at least the only representations that condition the availability of the acquisition loans) are the so-called specified acquisition agreement representations (i.e., those representations that are set forth within the acquisition agreement itself and, if untrue, permit the acquirer/borrower to terminate, or decline to close, the acquisition) and the so-called specified representations (i.e., a limited subset of the credit agreement representations that relate more to integrity of the financing structure than to the target, its subsidiaries, or its business).

CHAPTER 7

Covenants

7.1 SOME GENERAL PRINCIPLES

Covenants can be divided into three categories: financial covenants, affirmative covenants, and negative covenants. Many credit agreements create a separate section or article for each of the three categories, but frequently financial covenants are treated as negative covenants and included within the same section. As the labels might suggest, affirmative covenants stipulate what borrowers must do, negative covenants describe what borrowers are prohibited from doing (though subject to highly negotiated permissive exceptions), and financial covenants require the borrower to hit certain financial performance targets.

Beyond these pithy descriptions, there also is a deeper substantive difference between the types of covenants that has roots in historic lender liability concerns. Affirmative covenants generally cover ministerial matters such as the delivery of periodic reporting information, providing notices, compliance with applicable laws, payment of taxes and other expenses, and similar items. Negative covenants, on the other hand, go to the heart of management's execution on its business plan by regulating how much additional debt may be incurred and on what terms and conditions, what investments may be made and on what terms and conditions, under what scenarios dividends to shareholders are permitted to be made, and other mission-critical items. If lenders are viewed as relying on contractual covenants to call the shots on such key business decisions, it has been argued that such lenders are thereby exercising such a significant amount of control over the borrower, that they are de facto managers of the business and should be held accountable to shareholders and affected third parties for any fallout from such business decisions. In order to undercut the reality and appearance of lender control, lenders avoid being seen as affirmatively directing (i.e., thou shalt incur $x million in secured debt and thou shalt invest in $x million in permitted acquisitions, etc.) any borrower on major business decisions. Phrasing covenants in the negative has historically been held to lessen this risk.

Another principle to note with covenants is that each covenant is independent of each other covenant. Accordingly, if a transaction that the borrower wishes to undertake is within the reach of more than one covenant, it must be allowed under each covenant. An illustration of this might arise in the context of a borrower's proposal to guarantee the debt of a valued customer. Guarantees of this type are likely to be controlled by the debt covenant (since this is a guarantee of debt) and by the investments covenant (since a guarantee of the debt of a third party is often also treated as an investment in the third party). To issue the guarantee, the borrower would therefore need to find a basket or other exception in each of the debt and investments covenants.

7.2 SCOPE OF COVENANT COVERAGE

7.2.1 Subsidiaries Generally

The covenants (and certain other provisions) in most credit agreements apply not only to the borrower, but to the borrower and its subsidiaries. The financial strength of the borrower is only as good as the strength of the entire group of companies of which the borrower is the parent. Especially if the parent borrower is a holding company and the business operations and assets are at the subsidiary level, it is a logical extension to go right to the source and also regulate subsidiaries through covenants.

Box 7.1

"Subsidiary" means, with respect to any Person (the *"parent"*) at any date, any corporation, limited liability company, partnership, association, or other entity the accounts of which would be consolidated with those of the parent in the parent's consolidated financial statements if such financial statements were prepared in accordance with GAAP as of such date, as well as any other corporation, limited liability company, partnership, association, or other entity (a) of which securities or other ownership interests representing more than 50% of the equity or more than 50% of the ordinary voting power or, in the case of a partnership, more than 50% of the general partnership interests are, as of such date, owned, controlled, or held, or (b) that is, as of such date, otherwise controlled by the parent, or one or more subsidiaries of the parent, or by the parent and one or more subsidiaries of the parent.

As the sample language in Box 7.1 illustrates, "subsidiary" is normally defined as any entity that either is consolidated with the borrower in the preparation of financial statements or a majority of whose voting equity is owned or controlled by the borrower or another subsidiary. The term includes a limited partnership, the sole general partner of which is wholly owned by the borrower, even though the limited partnership interest is held by an unrelated third party and constitutes 99 percent of the equity. A sole general partner, by definition, controls the partnership and under the standard definition that makes the partnership a "subsidiary" irrespective of whether under accounting principles (see FASB Accounting Standards Codification Topic 810, for example) the limited partnership is consolidated with the general partner.

The term also includes an entity in which the borrower has *no* ownership interest if under GAAP or International Financial Reporting Standards, referred to as "IFRS," (see the discussion of these terms in Section 7.3.1) the entity should be consolidated with the borrower. This might occur if the borrower has such extensive debt and other contractual arrangements with the subsidiary that an accurate representation of the borrower's financial condition and operations can be accomplished only by consolidating the entity with the borrower.

Borrowers sometimes object to the breadth of the definition of "subsidiary." They argue that, even if an entity must be consolidated with the borrower under GAAP, unless the borrower has de facto control over the entity it should not be treated as a subsidiary for purposes of the covenants. If the borrower has no control, so the argument goes, how can it force the entity to maintain insurance or licenses and how can it prevent the entity from incurring debt or granting liens not permitted by the negative covenants? Although there may appear to be some justification in this example to exclude the entity from the negative and affirmative covenants, but include it for purposes of the financial covenants, few credit agreements provide for a split subsidiary definition in this fashion. The approach taken in any particular credit agreement is strictly a matter of negotiation.

Borrowers sometimes also argue that even if they control an entity (such as a partnership in which the borrower or a subsidiary is the general partner), if their ownership interest is, in fact, insignificant (say, the 1 percent general partnership interest described above), the entity should not be treated as a subsidiary for financial covenant purposes given that such a small portion of the economic pain or gain of the entity passes back to the borrower. Similarly, the borrower may argue that the entity should not be treated as a subsidiary for purposes of the affirmative and negative covenants, since it would be "unfair" to the major equity holders for the entity of which they are the principal owners to be subject to the covenants in the credit agreement of a minor equity holder. Lenders, in response, point out with some justification that, even though the borrower may have a mere 1 percent general partnership interest, being a general partner makes it legally obligated for all of the debt and other liabilities of the partnership and, therefore, the lenders have an interest in controlling the level of exposure of the borrower in respect of those liabilities. There is no right or wrong answer to these questions. It is not unusual, however, to see entities over which the borrower has control but in which its ownership interest is minor, excluded from the subsidiary definition.

7.2.2 Restricted and Unrestricted Subsidiaries

Box 7.2

"Restricted Subsidiary" means any Subsidiary of the Borrower other than an Unrestricted Subsidiary.

"Unrestricted Subsidiary" means any Subsidiary of the Borrower that (a) shall have been designated as an "Unrestricted Subsidiary" in accordance with the next sentence and (b) any Subsidiary of an Unrestricted Subsidiary. The Borrower may at any time designate any Subsidiary as an "Unrestricted Subsidiary" by notice to the Administrative Agent accompanied by an Officer's Certificate stating that the conditions set forth below have been satisfied, *provided* that no such designation shall be effective unless (x) at the time of such designation and after giving effect thereto, no Default or Event of Default shall have occurred and be continuing and (y) at the time of such designation and at all times thereafter:

(a) except as permitted under Section [*Debt*], no portion of the Debt or any other obligation (contingent or otherwise) of such Unrestricted Subsidiary (i) is guaranteed by the Borrower or any Restricted Subsidiary or (ii) is recourse to or obligates the Borrower or any Restricted Subsidiary, directly or indirectly, contingently or otherwise, to satisfaction thereof, and

(b) such Unrestricted Subsidiary has no Debt or any other obligation that, a default on which in any respect (including a payment default), would permit (upon notice, lapse of time, or both) any holder of any other Debt of the Borrower or any Restricted Subsidiary to declare a default on such other Debt or cause payment thereof to be accelerated or payable prior to its stated maturity.

Any designation of a Subsidiary as an Unrestricted Subsidiary shall be deemed an Investment in an amount equal to the fair market value of such Subsidiary (as determined in good faith by the Board of Directors of the Borrower) and shall be permitted only if it complies with the provisions of Section [*Investments*]. Any designation of an Unrestricted Subsidiary as a Restricted Subsidiary shall be deemed an acquisition of such Unrestricted Subsidiary and shall be permitted only to the extent permitted as an acquisition under Section [*Acquisitions*].

Bond indentures and, in recent years increasingly, credit agreements frequently include a concept of "restricted" and "unrestricted" subsidiaries. Credit agreements for smaller middle market borrowers make this distinction less frequently. In agreements that incorporate the concept, the motivation is to create a class of subsidiary (the unrestricted subsidiaries) that is free from the representations, covenants, and events of default to which subsidiaries would otherwise be subject. For example, the borrower could allow an unrestricted subsidiary to incur debt (and, if desired, grant liens on its own property to secure the debt), make acquisitions, and undertake riskier business activities without having to worry about the impact upon financial tests and without using up the negotiated, dollar-limited baskets in negative covenants.

In a credit agreement with both restricted and unrestricted subsidiaries, the restricted subsidiaries are subject to all of the representations, covenants, and defaults, while unrestricted subsidiaries are typically subject to none of these. An exception may, however, be made for those representations, covenants, or defaults covering an event or condition at an unrestricted subsidiary that could affect the consolidated group, such as a failure of an unrestricted subsidiary to pay taxes or Employee Retirement Income Security Act (ERISA) liabilities (which, as to subsidiaries organized in the United States that are 80 percent or more owned by a common parent, become under federal law the joint and several liability of every entity in the consolidated group). In these instances, unrestricted subsidiaries are not treated differently from restricted subsidiaries.

Although unrestricted subsidiaries afford greater flexibility to the borrower, they come with a disadvantage: they are treated essentially in the same way as unrelated third parties. For example, the earnings of an unrestricted subsidiary are excluded from the borrower's consolidated EBITDA. Also investments in unrestricted subsidiaries by the borrower and its restricted subsidiaries are controlled just as are investments in third parties, and the financial attributes of unrestricted subsidiaries (earnings, interest expense, debt service, working capital, and the like), whether positive or negative, are excluded when the corresponding financial attributes of the borrower and its restricted subsidiaries are determined. Unrestricted subsidiaries are treated as affiliates for the purposes of the affiliate transactions covenant, which forces transactions with unrestricted subsidiaries to be on an arm's-length basis.

There is nothing inherent or automatic about becoming an unrestricted subsidiary. Rarely are there unrestricted subsidiaries in existence at the time a credit agreement is entered into; generally unrestricted subsidiaries must be designated post-closing and only then upon satisfaction of certain conditions precedent. Designation of subsidiaries as restricted or unrestricted is usually at the discretion of the borrower or its board of directors, and frequently an effective designation is conditioned upon the absence of any default after giving effect to the designation and upon the satisfaction of certain other requirements. The mechanism for designation in credit agreements is typically less formal than that in bond indentures (a bond indenture customarily requires a board resolution), but many of the conditions for designation seen in bond indentures are the same. As a drafting matter, the conditions to designation may be spelled out in the definition section (as shown in Box 7.2) or, more often, the conditions are set forth as a standalone affirmative covenant provision. There is no substantive difference, only a stylistic difference, between the two drafting approaches.

The two conditions set out in paragraphs (a) and (b) of the sample language in Box 7.2 are quite common. To be unrestricted, neither a subsidiary nor any of its subsidiaries may have debt or other liabilities guaranteed in any way by the borrower or its restricted subsidiaries nor may such unrestricted subsidiary otherwise derive credit support from the credit group by being a stockholder in the borrower or any restricted subsidiary or owning property or liens in property of the credit group. Along the same lines, the unrestricted subsidiary may not have any outstanding debt or other liabilities that will be accelerated upon a default under the credit agreement.

The theory here is that an unrestricted subsidiary should, in all cases, behave as if it were a completely unrelated entity. Adverse events at an unrelated third party do not normally trigger potential defaults at the borrower and the same should be the case for an unrestricted subsidiary. If a borrower has guaranteed an unrestricted subsidiary's debt, or if borrower debt goes into default when the unrestricted subsidiary's debt suffers a default, the impact is not the same as if the subsidiary were unrelated. The cross-default condition—paragraph (b) in the definition in Box 7.2—is particularly subtle. Even though the borrower satisfies the condition that it not guarantee any obligations of the unrestricted subsidiary, if there is a cross-default to borrower debt, the borrower will likely want to rescue the unrestricted subsidiary just as if it were restricted, with the attendant occupation of management time and borrower funds.

Other conditions to designation often include the requirement that the investment in a restricted subsidiary designated as unrestricted be within whatever limits are imposed in the agreement upon investments in third parties. Conditions upon the obverse, a designation of an unrestricted subsidiary as restricted, normally include a requirement that the designation be treated as an acquisition of the unrestricted subsidiary (as well as incurrence of debt and liens to the extent such items remain in place postdesignation), just as if the borrower purchased the unrestricted subsidiary from a third party. The redesignation of a restricted subsidiary to an unrestricted subsidiary and back to a restricted subsidiary may be permitted, and each separate designation will of course be subject to the conditions of designation described above.

Subsidiaries of unrestricted subsidiaries are always treated as unrestricted. To provide for the contrary would lead to perverse results. The positive results of earnings at the restricted subsidiary would, for example, be included in the financial tests of the borrower yet, because the parent of the restricted subsidiary is unrestricted, the borrower would have no control over how those earnings are applied once the dividends go to the unrestricted parent.

7.2.3 Significant Subsidiaries and Immaterial Subsidiaries

Box 7.3

"*Significant Subsidiary*" means, at any time, each Subsidiary of the Borrower that meets the definition of a "significant subsidiary" under Regulation S-X of the Securities and Exchange Commission, or any successor thereto.

"*Immaterial Subsidiary*" means, as of any date, any Subsidiary of the Borrower (a) having Consolidated Total Assets in an amount of less than [% of Consolidated Total Assets of the Borrower and its Subsidiaries and (b) contributing less than [ ]% to consolidated revenues of the Borrower and its Subsidiaries, in each case, for the most recently ended Test Period for which financial statements have been delivered pursuant to Section [*Financial Reporting*]; *provided* that the Consolidated Total Assets (as so determined) and revenue (as so determined) of all Immaterial Subsidiaries shall not exceed [ ]% of Consolidated Total Assets of the Borrower and its Subsidiaries or [ ]% of the consolidated revenues of the Borrower and its Subsidiaries for the relevant Test Period, as the case may be.

If the borrower is a large corporation or other entity with many subsidiaries, it often pushes for a concept of "significant subsidiaries" and attempts to limit the application of the representations, covenants, and defaults solely to these entities. A typical definition, such as the sample in Box 7.3, defines a significant subsidiary as any subsidiary that meets the definition of a "significant subsidiary" under Regulation S-X of the Securities and Exchange Commission (SEC). Regulation S-X sets out accounting principles that both overlap and supplement GAAP. Legally, Regulation S-X is applicable only to entities that file financial reports with the SEC, but its convenience as a reference has made its use in credit agreements for nonreporting companies common.

Regulation S-X defines as "significant" any subsidiary that has 10 percent or more of the assets or 10 percent or more of the income of the borrower's consolidated group. In its narrowest application, the concept of significant subsidiary appears only in the bankruptcy default. In this case, the insolvency of a subsidiary gives rise to an event of default only if the subsidiary is "significant," but the balance of the defaults, and all representations and covenants, encompass all subsidiaries. Depending upon the negotiation between the parties, other credit agreements expand the concept further. Subject to the caveats described in the next paragraph, there is no logical limit to how the term should be used and, in its broadest application, it could apply to all representations, covenants, and defaults. The borrower's argument for broad application is that the lenders should not be concerned with bad events or conditions at subsidiaries that do not themselves rise to the level of being significant. Why, so a borrower might reason, should the lending syndicate be bothered by events at an Alaskan subsidiary that is responsible for less than 1 percent of the borrower's net income? Why should they care if the subsidiary fails to qualify to do business or loses a material (to the subsidiary) license?

There are situations in which a broad use of the significant subsidiary concept is inappropriate. As with the term "unrestricted subsidiaries," certain representations should logically encompass all subsidiaries (the tax and ERISA representations are examples) because liabilities at any subsidiary, even a truly insignificant one, can be the responsibility of all members in the consolidated group (including, therefore, the borrower). The Alaskan subsidiary may contribute less than 1 percent of the borrower's annual income, but if it has material pension liabilities, or if it has substantial debt outstanding that is guaranteed by the borrower, it can hardly be treated as insignificant. Similarly, if a borrower, though large, has many subsidiaries none of which rise to the 10 percent thresholds under Regulation S-X, using the definition everywhere may have the effect of dispensing with covenants on subsidiaries generally. For this reason, most credit agreements (with, perhaps the exception of agreements for high-quality investment-grade borrowers) limit the application of the "significant subsidiary" term to selected defaults (bankruptcy, cross-defaults, and judgments) and to particular representations (due organization and qualification; compliance with laws, title, and liens; and certain other disclosure matters are prime examples).

An alternative to the "significant subsidiary" concept is the converse concept of an "immaterial subsidiary." While the former seeks to *include* only its number under the scope of representations, covenants, and defaults, the latter seeks to *exclude* its number from covenants, defaults, and certain other provisions. In particular, a borrower seeking to carve out smaller subsidiaries from the requirement to become a guarantor or from triggering bankruptcy defaults will often seek to include an "immaterial subsidiary" concept. An immaterial subsidiary is commonly defined as any subsidiary that holds less than a minimal percentage of the group's consolidated total assets or consolidated revenues (often in the 3 percent to 5 percent range or approximately half of the significant subsidiary threshold discussed above). Along with this individual subsidiary-level cap, the concept will include an aggregate cap prohibiting the total amount of assets and revenue that can potentially be carved out through the "immaterial subsidiary" concept.

7.3 COVENANT DEFINITIONS

7.3.1 Definitions Generally; GAAP and IFRS

Box 7.4

"GAAP" means generally accepted accounting principles in the United States of America.

"IFRS" means the International Financial Reporting Standards as issued by the International Accounting Standards Board.

In any agreement, definitions are the building blocks upon which all other provisions are based. This is particularly true when it comes to covenants. The operative principle to keep in mind (at least when reading definitions that are relevant for negative covenants) is that definitions are often worded to have sweeping effect. Verbosity is deliberate here, motivated, to a great extent, by unfortunately worded court decisions refusing to give a term its natural meaning. To illustrate, a court may rule that a reference to a "car" cannot mean a sports utility vehicle or a van or even a taxi or a limousine or a rental. The definition of "lien" not only covers liens as they are normally understood, but also includes all charges, security interests, pledges, mortgages, encumbrances, assignments, and other similar arrangements and so forth ad nauseam. Similarly, the definition of "dividend" refers not just to dividends and distributions, but to redemptions of stock, payments to sinking funds for that purpose, and even "phantom stock" arrangements.

Perhaps the most basic building block is the definition of GAAP. Credit agreement covenants are normally based upon the borrower's historical and projected financial statements. These are required by the credit agreement to be prepared upon the basis of generally accepted accounting principles "consistently applied." That is to say, if the borrower delivered financial statements for its two most recent fiscal years, the statements must not have employed one set of principles in one year and a different set of principles in the second year. To take an example, the statements must not calculate inventory on a first-in, first-out (FIFO) basis in the first year and on a last-in, first-out (LIFO) basis in the second.

Accordingly, the *historical* financial statements delivered to the lenders and used as the basis for determining financial covenant levels must be "consistent." This raises the question of whether the borrower in preparing its financial statements after the closing is free to change accounting principles—for example, to switch from LIFO to FIFO? Or what if the borrower wants to make a more sweeping change from GAAP to IFRS? Borrowers may want precisely this flexibility. They may even need this flexibility to obtain financial statements that are reported upon by independent auditors, since under accounting rules those statements must be based upon generally accepted accounting principles that reflect changes continually being implemented by the accounting profession. From their standpoint, the lenders will want the principles used in calculating covenants (as distinct from those applied in preparing the statements themselves) to remain stable and not to reflect changes if those changes would affect the outcome of covenant compliance. Borrowers may care less whether changes in principles affect covenant compliance because they likely have more control over how (and the time frame within which) changes are implemented.

The definition of GAAP in a credit agreement normally takes one of two approaches. Some agreements ignore the impact upon covenants and allow them to be calculated in accordance with generally accepted accounting principles as they change and as they are applied from time to time by the borrower. This approach leaves the borrower complete flexibility to modify the basis upon which it prepares its financials. Other agreements lock in the financial presentation as it relates to determining compliance with covenants. Naturally, the variant preferred by borrowers is to have GAAP defined as generally accepted accounting principles "as in effect from time to time." The variant preferred by lenders is to have GAAP (at least for covenant calculation) frozen in time to those principles that were in effect at closing and that were used to prepare the statements upon which the covenants were originally determined. Although the borrower may object that this requires it to prepare two sets of financial statements, a middle-ground solution is often adopted along the lines discussed in Section 7.6.18.

Foreign borrowers, U.S. subsidiary borrowers of foreign parents, or U.S. borrowers with substantial overseas operations may desire the flexibility to move from reporting under GAAP to reporting under widely adopted IFRS. In those credit agreements that provide the right to switch, there are a few elements in common. First, all that is typically required to commence the conversion process from GAAP to IFRS is a simple borrower election and notice to the administrative agent. Following such election and notice, the borrower may start reporting in IFRS. Second, following election and notice, a borrower cannot switch back to reporting under GAAP and the decision becomes irrevocable. Third, financial reporting is required to subsequently conform to IFRS standards. As noted in the introduction, in this volume we are generally concerned with New York-law governed credit agreements and lenders in such facilities by and large expect GAAP financial reporting from their borrowers. While it may be rare for a credit group to request to switch whole cloth from GAAP to IFRS, it is a reality that some part of a multinational credit group's operations may be reported under IFRS and credit agreements increasingly take that into account.

7.3.2   Key Financial Definitions

Financial definitions are, in large part, accounting based and heavily negotiated. The variants are not infinite, however, and in looking at definitions to decipher covenants, some fundamental concepts should be kept in mind.

7.3.2.1 Debt

> **Box 7.5**
>
> "*Debt*" of any Person means, without duplication, (a) all obligations of such Person for borrowed money or with respect to deposits or advances of any kind; (b) all obligations of such Person evidenced by bonds, debentures, notes, or similar instruments; (c) all obligations of such Person upon which interest charges are customarily paid; (d) all obligations of such Person under conditional sale or other title-retention agreements relating to property acquired by such Person; (e) all obligations of such Person in respect of the deferred purchase price of property or services (excluding current accounts payable incurred in the ordinary course of business); (f) all Debt of others secured by (or for which the holder of such Debt has an existing right, contingent or otherwise, to be secured by) any Lien on property owned or acquired by such Person, whether or not the Debt secured thereby has been assumed; (g) all Guarantees by such Person of Debt of others; (h) all Capital Lease Obligations of such Person; (i) all obligations, contingent or otherwise, of such Person as an account party in respect of letters of credit and letters of guarantee; (j) net obligations of such Person under Hedging Agreements (the amount of such obligations to be equal at any time to the net payments under such agreement or arrangement giving rise to such obligation that would be payable by such Person at the termination of such agreement or arrangement); and (k) all obligations, contingent or otherwise, of such Person in respect of bankers' acceptances. The Debt of any Person shall include the Debt of any other entity (including any partnership in which such Person is a general partner) to the extent such Person is liable therefor as a result of such Person's ownership interest in or other relationship with such entity, except to the extent the terms of such Debt provide that such Person is not liable therefor.

"Debt" is not a GAAP concept, but a term created in finance documents for purposes of financial tests, restrictive covenants, and defaults. The intent is to capture all nonordinary course claims against the borrower. Consistent, therefore, with the general principle of completeness (see Section 7.3.1), the definition of debt normally starts with all balance-sheet liabilities and sweeps in other specified liabilities not required under GAAP to be shown on the balance sheet. Certain ordinary course items (examples include tax liabilities, current accounts payable, and accrued expenses) are then carved out.

There are exceptions to the carveouts, however. While a purchase of inventory that must be paid within 60 days is not ordinarily thought of as debt, a purchase of inventory that may be paid in installments over a period of three years is indistinguishable from other categories of debt (such as borrowed money), even though it may still be classified as an "account payable" under GAAP. The exclusion for accounts payable and accrued expenses is thus, as the language in Box 7.5 illustrates, confined to "current" accounts payable and accrued expenses. Some agreements explicitly define "current" to mean only obligations payable within a specified number of days (60 or 90 days are typical periods).

The balance-sheet claims incorporated into the definition typically include debt for borrowed money, debt under bonds, debentures, notes, and other instruments, capitalized lease obligations, conditional sales agreements, the deferred purchase price of property and services, and bankers' acceptances. Non-balance-sheet claims sweep in guarantees of other debt (guarantees are normally only footnoted in financial statements and are not carried as liabilities on a balance sheet), synthetic leases, obligations related to off-balance financing such as hedging arrangements (on a net basis), factoring, receivables financing and securitization arrangements.

The definition includes all letters of credit, although borrowers frequently negotiate for the exclusion of trade letters of credit using the argument that these are ordinary course. In general, lenders are amenable to such a request, though if the letters of credit are issued under the credit agreement itself they are normally included on the theory that any usage of the facility should be included as part of the financial covenant tests.

The definition also picks up obligations that, under GAAP, are sometimes (though less obviously) shown on the balance sheet, such as obligations of third parties secured by a lien on assets of the borrower whether or not assumed by the borrower and obligations for which a person may be liable by virtue of its ownership interest in another (such as by reason of its being a general partner in a partnership). In the case of obligations of third parties secured by liens, the amount thereof treated as debt is often limited to the value of the property subject to the claim. That may not, however, be the correct result given Section 1111 of the Bankruptcy Code, which in some circumstances allows a creditor to submit a full claim against the borrower in a bankruptcy proceeding, even if the borrower has not assumed the debt.

Many credit agreements state that debt includes obligations under derivative contracts, even though a proper determination of the amount thereof leads to time-consuming calculations. For example, to establish the amount of a derivative, a borrower cannot look simply at an internal statement of account. Instead, it needs to ascertain from market quotes (potentially on a daily basis) the liability that would arise upon the termination of the derivative contract. Determining the amount becomes even more complicated where master netting arrangements are in place between the borrower and hedge counterparties and the aggregate net obligations across a hedge portfolio need to be calculated. While some credit agreements treat derivatives as investments or have a separate derivatives covenant (see Section 7.6.10), the more common approach is to treat the net obligation as debt under the credit agreement.

Recent credit agreements often include provisions that are designed to restrict the impact of any borrower's use of fair value accounting for reporting debt liabilities. Following the recent financial crisis, the global accounting rulemaking bodies, the Financial Accounting Standards Board (FASB) and International Accounting Standards Board (IASB), developed new accounting standards for reporting financial statement items on a fair value basis. By many measures, the use of fair value reporting has expanded in the wake of these pronouncements. The fair value rules allow an issuer to elect fair valuation reporting for financial liabilities as opposed to reporting liabilities solely at principal face value. In reaction to the risk of debt liabilities being reported at a fraction of what is actually owed, an increasing number of credit agreements include language overriding any fair value election for purposes of covenant calculation. Specifically, the language (1) expressly deems all debt to be carried at 100 percent of the outstanding principal amount for purposes of covenant calculations and (2) expressly disregards the applicable fair value pronouncements for such purpose.

7.3.2.2   EBITDA

Box 7.6

"EBITDA" means, for any period, the sum, for the Borrower and its Subsidiaries (determined on a consolidated basis without duplication in accordance with GAAP), of the following: (a) net operating income for such period, calculated before federal, state, and local income taxes; Interest Expense; extraordinary and unusual items; and income or loss attributable to equity in Affiliates, *plus* (b) noncash items for such period in each case to the extent deducted in determining net operating income, including depreciation and amortization, impairment charges with respect to goodwill and other intangibles, unrealized gains or losses on financial instruments (such as contemplated by FAS 133), noncash financing losses on the extinguishment of debt, and the noncash portion of postretirement benefits.

EBITDA is an acronym for "earnings before interest, taxes, depreciation and amortization." The term is an important building block for financial covenants, for interest margins (to the extent that margins are determined with reference to a debt ratio that incorporates EBITDA as one of its elements), and for excess cash-flow prepayment provisions. Some agreements use the term *cash flow* or *operating cash flow* in lieu of EBITDA.

The purpose of the term is to capture the amount of cash thrown off by the borrower's business before taking into account nonoperating expenses, such as interest and taxes. Depreciation and amortization are added back because, although they reduce the level of operating earnings, they do not diminish the amount of cash generated during any calculation period. EBITDA is intended to be a predictor of the ability of a borrower to pay interest, principal, and the other types of "fixed charges" discussed below. The debt ratio, interest coverage ratio, debt service coverage ratio, and fixed charges coverage ratio (discussed in greater detail later in this chapter), each of which has EBITDA as a component, test the amount of cash available to the borrower against these corresponding needs.

Set forth in Box 7.6 is a simplified version of an EBITDA definition. Most credit agreements contain much more detailed language that prescribes numerous additional adjustments to net operating income that must be made to reach an EBITDA number. These adjustments, otherwise known as "add-backs," are heavily negotiated and generate significant attention from borrowers and lenders alike as add-backs can meaningfully swing EBITDA to the benefit of the borrower and in turn weaken the effectiveness of covenants.

It is beyond the scope of this volume to spell out all of the add-backs variables that can go into a full-blown definition. We note that in recent years even bank regulators looking at the leveraged loan market have increasingly scrutinized the extent to which EBITDA add-backs are realistic and corroborated. For example, the Shared National Credits Program 2014 Leveraged Loan Supplement issued by the three main U.S. federal banking regulatory bodies criticized "difficult-to-support adjustments, such as unrealized cost savings from mergers and acquisitions."[1] At the time of this writing, bank regulators have continued to scrutinize EBITDA add-backs and are continuing to insist that

---

[1] See *Shared National Credits Program 2014 Leveraged Loan Supplement*, Board of Governors of the Federal Reserve System, Federal Deposit Insurance Corporation and Office of the Comptroller of the Currency November 2014 (referred to herein as the "2014 SNC Supplement").

credit agreements define add-backs in ways that allow enhancements to EBITDA only to the extent they are reasonably supportable.

7.4 FINANCIAL COVENANTS

Financial covenants, as the name indicates, test the financial performance of the borrower. Are its earnings and EBITDA meeting certain levels preagreed at the time the facility is negotiated? Does EBITDA adequately cover interest and debt service? Has the borrower overcommitted to make capital expenditures? These issues are discussed in this part.

7.4.1 Date-Specific versus Performance versus Hybrid Covenants; Annualized and Rolling Periods

Financial covenants can be divided into three categories: those that test the borrower's financial position at a particular date (such as a net worth or current ratio covenant), those that test its performance over one or more fiscal periods (such as a fixed charges or interest coverage covenant), and those that are a hybrid of the first two and contain both date-specific and performance elements, such as a debt ratio covenant that tests the ratio of debt at a particular date to earnings for a specified fiscal period ending on that date.

Date-specific covenants are typically measured at fiscal end dates or on dates upon which the borrower prepares accounting reports (even if those reports are purely internal and are not publicly disclosed). The dates chosen to test compliance with the covenant are primarily a function of practicability. Since net worth is a balance-sheet concept that is calculated only when a balance sheet is prepared, it is not practical to ask a borrower to comply with a net worth covenant recalculated on a daily basis. Rather it is normally done at the end of an annual or quarterly fiscal period or, if the borrower prepares monthly financial reports, at the end of monthly accounting periods. Other date-specific covenants, such as the current ratio or working capital covenants, which are based upon outstanding inventory and receivables, may be more easily calculated each day, though it is still rare to see a credit agreement that forces these covenants to be tested other than on accounting period end dates.

A performance-based covenant tests the borrower's financial performance for an agreed fiscal period. The period may be short, long, or rolling, depending in large part upon the nature of the borrower's business and the negotiating ability of the borrower to make the covenant fit the business. Although it is risky to generalize when it comes to financial covenants, as a general rule shorter performance test periods are used much less frequently than longer or rolling periods. Only in rare cases (companies in workout are a prime exception) is performance tested on a quarter-by-quarter basis. This is a reflection of the reality that any business can have a bad quarter (and should not be penalized if it quickly recovers in subsequent quarters), and also that most businesses are cyclical to some degree (and should be allowed to sweep in good quarters with the bad). As a consequence, it is much more common for the relevant performance period to consist of two or four fiscal quarters. An interest coverage covenant that tests the ratio of EBITDA to interest expense annually for each full fiscal year is an example.

Most often, however, covenants are tested for a so-called rolling period that consists of the borrower's two or four most recent fiscal quarters. This allows compliance with the financial covenants to be assessed on a frequent (quarterly) basis, but for performance periods that are longer in duration. Consequently, if the rolling period is four quarters, when testing the covenant at the end of December, the relevant test period is the four quarters that end December 31. When testing again at the end of March, the relevant period is the four quarters that commenced on April 1 of the preceding year and end on March 31 of the current year. The benefit of this approach (from the standpoint of both the borrower and the lenders) is that it avoids the borrower's falling into default either because of a bad quarter or because of seasonality issues, which might otherwise occur if only the most recent single fiscal quarter were tested.

Hybrid covenants test two indicia of the borrower's business, one date-specific and one period-specific. An example is a leverage ratio that compares debt at a fiscal end date to EBITDA for the four quarters that end on that date. Sometimes, in this case, the performance may be "annualized." To illustrate, the leverage ratio could be defined as the ratio of debt at the fiscal end date to earnings for the most recent fiscal quarter *times* four (or the two most recent fiscal quarters *times* two). Annualizing, in most cases, exacerbates the risks of a single bad quarter or cyclicality. However, the approach can be useful for a start-up borrower, whose earnings are expected to begin low but grow quickly from quarter to quarter. Annualizing may also be employed in the acquisition context as discussed in Section 7.4.2. Technically annualizing is not necessary—the lender could simply adjust the maximum permitted debt ratio until the borrower's operations have ramped up—but cosmetically (and cosmetics often matter when crafting a credit agreement) it looks better to have a debt ratio maximum of 5 to 1 rather than 20 to 1.

7.4.2 Phase-In and Pro Forma Treatment

An issue that comes up in the context of credit agreements that finance acquisitions is how to deal with the impact of an acquisition upon performance-based covenants. For example, if an acquisition doubles the size of the borrower's business, it may make little sense to measure EBITDA on a strictly historical rolling four-quarter basis, since (at least at inception) most of the rolling four quarters reflect a lower preacquisition EBITDA. Similarly, to test interest expense only for the historical period understates the borrower's future interest costs as a result of the increased acquisition borrowing. The solution most often adopted in credit agreements is to calculate performance numbers (such as EBITDA, interest expense, capital expenditures, debt service, taxes, and the like) on a hypothetical (or pro forma) basis as if the acquisition had occurred at the beginning of the rolling four-quarter period.

Particularly in calculating EBITDA, this can lead to a tangled discussion between the parties. The lenders simply want to add the borrower's and the target's *actual* EBITDA figures for the relevant periods to obtain the pro forma numbers. Borrowers, on the other hand, often want to take into account cost savings that they anticipate realizing once the acquisition occurs. The combined business will not have two finance departments, or so the borrower will argue, so EBITDA should be appropriately adjusted upward to reflect the elimination of redundant personnel. Lenders will counter that there may be one-time costs associated with integrating the two businesses. The borrower will then say those costs should be capitalized and should not reduce current earnings. And so the negotiation goes. Unfortunately, resort to a theoretically unbiased third party (such as the borrower's independent accountants) is not generally helpful because no GAAP rules spell out in an *objective* manner how such cost savings or other pro forma adjustments should be calculated. The parties are, therefore, usually left to themselves to find a middle ground. SEC pro forma rules that apply to public reporting companies provide one possible basis for scoping out a middle ground for the determination of pro forma adjustments. Namely, Article 11 of Regulation S-X contains principle-based requirements for the presentation of pro forma financials. Pro forma adjustments, such as cost savings, must be (1) directly attributable to the subject transaction, (2) expected to have a continuing impact on the borrower, and (3) factually supportable. Even though Article 11 does not apply to loans or other nonsecurities transactions, many credit agreements nonetheless refer to Article 11, directly or indirectly, by incorporating its criteria as the standard for making pro forma determinations. These rules of pro forma calculation, which are most frequently employed in connection with determining compliance with credit agreement incurrence covenants, are typically set forth in a defined term or interpretational provision. It is not only acquisitions but other material transactions, including dispositions, debt incurrences, and the making of investments and dividends and other restricted payments, that can trigger the use of pro forma calculations under a credit agreement.

One approach sometimes used to ameliorate the difficulty of running pro forma calculations is to annualize the relevant earnings and other numbers until a full four quarters (or other relevant roll-up period) have elapsed after the acquisition. Using this approach, at the end of the first fiscal quarter after the acquisition, EBITDA for that quarter would be multiplied by four. At the end of the second fiscal quarter, EBITDA would be calculated for two quarters and multiplied by two. At the end of the third fiscal quarter, EBITDA would be calculated for three quarters and multiplied by 4/3. Only after four full fiscal quarters have elapsed subsequent to the acquisition is the performance period rolled forward at the end of each fiscal quarter. Annualizing in this way may simplify (or eliminate) pro forma calculations—a borrower may still of course complain that finance department savings will not be fully realized during the first quarter following the acquisition—but it does not avoid the risks of a bad quarter or the cyclical nature of the combined business. For this reason, the pro forma calculation approach is used more often than annualization.

Because accountants do not normally calculate earnings for odd periods, a more refined way to annualize interest expense is sometimes seen that is not available to determine EBITDA. The approach employed for interest expense is to calculate first the expense for the period from the closing to the test date and then to multiply the result by an appropriate fraction to bring it up to a full 365-day year. For example, if an acquisition occurs on February 17, interest expense for March 31 would be annualized by multiplying the actual interest for the 42-day period between February 17 and March 31 by a fraction, the numerator of which is 365 and the denominator of which is 42. A similar calculation would be run at the end of June 30 (the fraction being 365/133) and at the end of each quarter thereafter until four full quarters have elapsed subsequent to the acquisition.

7.4.3 Date-Specific Financial Covenants

As discussed in Section 7.4.1, date-specific covenants test an element of the financial condition of the borrower on particular dates. These dates may be at the end of fiscal quarters or other accounting periods, or may be on every day. The net worth, current ratio, and working capital covenants discussed below are examples only (and not a complete list) of the types of date-specific covenants included in credit agreements.

7.4.3.1 Net Worth

Box 7.7

"Tangible Net Worth" means, as at any date, the sum for the Borrower and its Subsidiaries (determined on a consolidated basis without duplication in accordance with GAAP), of the following:

(a) the amount of capital stock; *plus*

(b) the amount of surplus and retained earnings (or, in the case of a surplus or retained earnings deficit, *minus* the amount of such deficit); *minus*

(c) the cost of treasury shares; *minus*

(d) the sum of the following: the book value of all assets that should be classified as intangibles (without duplication of deductions in respect of items already deducted in arriving at surplus and retained earnings), but in any event including goodwill, minority interests, research and development costs, trademarks, trade names, copyrights, patents and franchises, unamortized debt discount and expense, all reserves, and any write-up in the book value of assets resulting from a revaluation thereof subsequent to [Date of Base Financials].

* * * * * * * * * * * *

The Borrower will not permit its Tangible Net Worth at any time to be less than the sum of (x) $_____ *plus* (y) ___% of the aggregate net income of the Borrower and its Subsidiaries (determined on a consolidated basis without duplication in accordance with GAAP and for which purpose any net loss shall be deemed to be a net income of zero) for the period commencing on [Date of Base Financials] and ending at the time of determination.

The tangible net worth (or, less frequently, net worth) covenant tests the balance-sheet shareholders' equity of the borrower at a specific date (normally a fiscal quarter or fiscal year end). "Net worth" refers generally to the excess of the borrower's assets over its liabilities, and sometimes the definition of the term is couched in precisely those terms (assets *minus* liabilities). More often, though, the definition is built up from paid-in capital and retained earnings less treasury stock as shown in paragraphs (a) through (c) of the sample for a corporate borrower in Box 7.7. Mathematically the two approaches are the same. The difference between net worth and *tangible* net worth is that the latter tries to capture the value of the hard or verifiable assets of the borrower and to exclude speculative or intangible assets. Tangible assets can be characterized as those that a business person can prove exist by, say, pointing to a factory or inventory or equipment sitting on dirt, or by pointing to a bank or securities account or stock certificate that shows a credit balance of cash or investment property. It also includes accounts receivable (verifiable by invoices). Intangible assets, by way of contrast, typically consist of the items described in paragraph (d) in Box 7.7, such as goodwill, the value of intellectual property (trademarks, trade names, copyrights, or patents), research and development costs, reserves, and asset write-ups.

Although the existence of intangible "assets" is certainly evidenced by numbers shown on a balance sheet of the borrower, the intangible assets themselves are not otherwise independently verifiable. Their value is also more speculative than that of tangible assets. Goodwill, for example, represents the amount paid when a company acquires a business or division over the book value of the assets acquired. If the target business has balance-sheet property, plant, equipment, inventory, receivables, and cash totaling $10,000,000 and the acquirer pays $50,000,000, the difference ($40,000,000) will be carried on the latter's balance sheet as goodwill. Whether that $40,000,000 constitutes actual value for the buyer is a guess; it may represent either the genuine worth to the buyer of a future income stream, or simply its overpayment for the target. Write-ups in assets are similarly speculative. Although not generally allowed under GAAP or, for public companies, by the SEC, in those rare cases in which they are permitted (foreign accounting practices may, for example, allow write-ups) the tangible net worth definition forces them to be excluded.

The covenant itself, because it requires that tangible net worth (or net worth) remain at a preset, negotiated level during the term of the credit agreement, in effect compels the borrower not to suffer an earnings loss that would reduce tangible net worth (or net worth) below that level. As with any covenant, the required minimum is, at the time the agreement is drafted, set so as to give the borrower some cushion in the event it should suffer a loss for a fiscal year or other period. Any major loss, however, will trigger the covenant. The covenant also prevents the borrower from paying a large dividend to its shareholders that has the effect of reducing its capital below the agreed number.

The covenant is typically drafted so that the initial agreed cushion does not grow excessively as the borrower earns money. If the borrower's initial net worth is $100,000,000 and the covenant is set at $80,000,000 (with, therefore, a cushion of $20,000,000), each year that the borrower earns money, 80 percent of the earnings amount might be added to the minimum. If after three years the borrower has realized an additional $50,000,000 in profits that have been added to its tangible net worth, the new minimum will be $120,000,000 ($80,000,000 + 80 percent of $50,000,000). The cushion has grown (as is probably fair given the borrower's improved performance), but not so much as to make the covenant irrelevant (a cushion of $30,000,000 has some bite whereas a cushion of $70,000,000 may have none).

7.4.3.2   Net Worth Ratio

Box 7.8

The Borrower will not permit the Net Worth Ratio to exceed ___ to 1 as at the last day of any fiscal [quarter] [year].

* * * * * * * * * * * *

"Net Worth Ratio" means, at any time, the ratio of Total Liabilities to Tangible Net Worth at such time.

A net worth ratio measures the aggregate liabilities of a borrower against its tangible net worth (or net worth). The objective is to test whether the borrower has sufficient equity capital to support the liabilities carried on its balance sheet. *"Total liabilities"* is defined as just that: all liabilities carried on the balance sheet plus any non-balance-sheet liabilities that, under the typical debt definition, would be treated as debt. Although at one time the net worth ratio covenant was popular, it is used less frequently today since most lenders believe a leverage ratio covenant (see Section 7.4.5.1) that measures debt to EBITDA is a more accurate predictor of future performance.

7.4.3.3   Current Ratio/Working Capital

Box 7.9

Current Ratio. The Borrower will not permit the ratio of current assets to current liabilities to be less than ___ to 1 at any time.

Working Capital. The Borrower will not permit the excess of current assets over current liabilities to be less than $_____ at any time.

* * * * * * * * * * * *

For purposes of this Agreement, the terms *"current assets"* and *"current liabilities"* shall have the respective meanings assigned to them by GAAP, [*provided* that in any event there shall be included in current assets the undrawn availability under the Revolving Credit Commitments, and there shall be excluded from current liabilities the current portion of all Debt hereunder].

The purpose of the current ratio and working capital covenants is to ensure that the borrower has sufficient liquid, quickly realizable assets to cover liabilities that will come due in the next 12 months. The covenants attempt to test, in other words, whether the borrower faces an impending cash bind or liquidity crisis (scary words for a lender). The current ratio covenant measures the ratio of current assets to current liabilities at a given date. The working capital covenant calculates the excess of current assets over current liabilities at a given date. An agreement rarely has both covenants and, in fact, the frequency of these covenants (other than, perhaps, in asset-based financings) has declined considerably in recent years as lenders focus increasingly upon a borrower's cash flow rather than its assets.

The two financial elements used in these covenants (current assets and current liabilities) are accounting terms that look to what assets will be converted into cash within one year and what liabilities will become payable within one year (short-term liabilities). Current assets normally consist of cash, marketable securities, and accounts receivable. Current liabilities include accounts payable and accrued expenses (including wages), as well as the current portion of long-term debt (the portion of the principal of outstanding debt that must be paid within the next year). Current assets and current liabilities are required under GAAP to be identified as such on a balance sheet.

Whether to include the bracketed language shown in Box 7.9 is strictly a matter of negotiation. Adding availability under the credit facility to "current assets" avoids penalizing the borrower if it applies excess cash to prepay revolving loans. The rationale for excluding the current portion of the outstanding loans under the credit agreement may be less compelling. If the borrower's business is highly seasonal, simply because a borrower does not have cash today to cover principal payments under the agreement does not mean it cannot realize sufficient cash to pay the principal during its high-sales season. Excluding the current portion of credit agreement loans may be appropriate in that case. But if the borrower's business is not seasonal, there may be logic to forcing its current assets to cover the current portion of the loans, just as it must cover the current portion of any other debt.

7.4.4   Performance-Based Financial Covenants

Performance-specific covenants, as noted earlier, test the financial performance of the borrower over an agreed fiscal period, which may be as short as one month or as long as a full year. As with date-specific covenants, the examples set out in Sections 7.4.4.1 to 7.4.4.5 are not intended to be a comprehensive list of all performance-based covenants that could appear in a credit agreement.

7.4.4.1   Interest Coverage Ratio

Box 7.10

The Borrower will not permit the Interest Coverage Ratio to be less than ___ to 1 at any

* * * * * * * * * * * *

"Interest Coverage Ratio" means, as at any date, the ratio of (a) EBITDA for the period of four fiscal quarters ending on or most recently ended prior to such date to (b) Interest Expense for such period.

"Interest Expense" means, for any period, the sum, for the Borrower and its Subsidiaries (determined on a consolidated basis without duplication in accordance with GAAP), of the following: (a) all interest in respect of Debt (including the interest component of any payments in respect of Capital Lease Obligations) accrued or capitalized during such period (whether or not actually paid during such period) *plus* (b) the net amount payable (or *minus* the net amount receivable) under Hedging Agreements relating to interest during such period (whether or not actually paid or received during such period).

The interest coverage covenant is designed to ensure that the borrower has sufficient available cash to pay interest on its outstanding debt (including that outstanding under the credit agreement). It measures the ratio of EBITDA for a fiscal period (typically the most recently ended rolling four quarters) to interest expense for that same period. Note that, although the sample covenant above requires that the interest coverage ratio not be less than the prescribed ratio "at any time," the definition of "Interest Coverage Ratio" refers back to the most-recently ended fiscal quarter date. A daily recalculation of the ratio is thus not required.

"Interest expense" is normally defined to include only cash interest; pay-in-kind (PIK) interest and capitalized interest charges are often excluded (though interest that accrues on such amounts will be included to the extent payable in cash). The interest expense definition

in Box 7.10, however, is an example of the broader formulation that counts both cash and noncash interest. *"Cash interest"* will not be literally confined to interest paid in cash *during* a particular period, but rather will measure interest payable in cash *for* the particular period. To provide otherwise potentially allows a borrower to manipulate interest expense (and, thereby, covenant compliance) by paying interest a day before the beginning (or a day after the end) of a fiscal period. Also, interest expense normally reflects payments made (or cash received) under interest hedging agreements. The reasoning here is to give the borrower the benefit of hedging agreements which, after all, are intended to protect the borrower against adverse fluctuations of interest, and should therefore be factored in when measuring compliance with interest coverage.

The level set for the interest coverage ratio is strictly a subject of negotiation based upon the projections prepared by the borrower to be used as a basis to fix covenant minimums and normally takes into account the desired need for some cushion. That said, an interest coverage minimum of less than 1.00 to 1 is highly unlikely; otherwise the lenders would essentially be admitting that the borrower cannot generate sufficient funds (EBITDA) during the year to service its interest payments! Similar considerations come into play when a number is fixed for the debt service coverage and fixed charges coverage ratios (see Sections 7.4.4.2 and 7.4.4.3).

7.4.4.2 Debt Service Coverage Ratio

Box 7.11

The Borrower will not permit the Debt Service Coverage Ratio to be less than ___ to 1 at any time.

* * * * * * * * * * * *

"Debt Service Coverage Ratio" means, as at any date, the ratio of (a) EBITDA for the period of four fiscal quarters ending on or most recently ended prior to such date to (b) Debt Service for such period.

"Debt Service" means, for any period, the sum, for the Borrower and its Subsidiaries (determined on a consolidated basis without duplication in accordance with GAAP), of the following: (a) all regularly scheduled payments or prepayments of principal of Debt (including the principal component of any payments in respect of Capital Lease Obligations and any payment required as a result of a scheduled reduction of lending commitments, including the Revolving Credit Commitments hereunder) made during such period *plus* (b) all Interest Expense for such period.

The debt service coverage covenant is virtually identical to the interest coverage covenant except that it factors in payments of principal in addition to payments of interest. As its name indicates, it measures the ratio of EBITDA for a fiscal period (similar to the interest coverage ratio, this is typically the most-recently ended rolling four quarters) to debt service for that period. "Debt service" consists of interest expense and *scheduled* principal payments. By limiting payments to those that are scheduled, mandatory prepayments (such as excess cash flow, disposition, or debt and equity issuance prepayments) are not included. Voluntary prepayments are also excluded. It does, however, include scheduled reductions of revolving commitments if that requires a payment of debt.

As with the interest coverage ratio, determining the appropriate level of the debt service coverage ratio is a matter of negotiation between the parties. A minimum level of less than 1.00 to 1, however, normally raises a red flag.

7.4.4.3 Fixed Charges Coverage Ratio

Box 7.12

The Borrower will not permit the Fixed Charges Coverage Ratio to be less than ___ to 1 at any time.

* * * * * * * * * * * *

"Fixed Charges Coverage Ratio" means, as at any date, the ratio of (a) EBITDA for the period of four consecutive fiscal quarters ending on or most recently ended prior to such date to (b) the sum, for the Borrower and its Subsidiaries (determined on a consolidated basis without duplication in accordance with GAAP), of the following: (a) Debt Service for such period *plus* (b) Capital Expenditures for such period *plus* (c) federal, state, and local income taxes for such period [*plus* (d) dividend payments required to be made in respect of the Borrower's ___ preferred stock during such period].

The fixed charges coverage covenant builds upon the debt service coverage covenant and factors in other so-called "fixed charges," such as capital expenditures, taxes, and preferred stock dividend payments. It tests the ratio of EBITDA to fixed charges during a fiscal period (again, as with interest coverage and debt service coverage, this is typically the most recently ended rolling four quarters). The purpose of the covenant is to test the ability of the borrower to generate sufficient cash during a period to service all of its nonoperating cash needs during that period (operating cash needs are implicitly covered by the borrower's having a positive EBITDA). Whether to treat dividend payments as a fixed charge (as contemplated in the bracketed language in Box 7.12) is a matter of negotiation, though the lending syndicate may often want to include such payments, particularly if a failure to pay preferred dividends gives the preferred stockholders onerous covenant rights or results in a change of control of the borrower's board of directors or managers.

As with the interest coverage and debt service coverage ratios, the minimum level fixed is determined by negotiation. A compliance point of less than 1.00 to 1 would, as with the other ratios, be problematic, though in rare cases (particularly in the context of workouts) a ratio of less than 1.00 to 1 may be specified. The parties, in this case, in effect acknowledge that a portion of the fixed charges need to be paid with additional borrowings under the credit agreement or otherwise.

7.4.4.4 Lease Payments

Box 7.13

The Borrower will not permit the aggregate amount of payments to be made in respect of Operating Leases to exceed [$_____ during] [___% of EBITDA for] any fiscal year.

* * * * * * * * * * * *

"*Attributable Debt*" means, with respect to any lease (other than a Capital Lease) at any date, the total net amount of rent required to be paid under such lease during the remaining term thereof, discounted from the respective due dates thereof to such date at the rate per annum borne by the [specify debt instrument] compounded annually. In determining the net amount of rent required to be paid under any lease, amounts required to be paid on account of maintenance and repairs, insurance, taxes, assessments, water rates, and similar charges shall be excluded.

Credit agreements sometimes limit the aggregate lease payments made by the borrower during an agreed fiscal period on the theory that, to the extent the borrower does not own its assets (whether land or equipment), its obligation to make lease payments is essential to preserve the viability of its business. If it stops paying rent on its factory property, it will be difficult to continue making widgets. The lease obligations, viewed this way, are akin to secured debt; when the borrower fails to pay rent, the landlord or owner is, under most state laws and lease contracts, entitled to recover the leased property from the borrower. In many cases this can be done without the need to overcome the borrower-protective hurdles imposed upon foreclosure by a secured lender.

Payment obligations in respect of capitalized leases under GAAP are included in the definition of debt and therefore limited by the debt covenant (see Section 7.3.2.1). At the time of this writing, FASB and IASB have issued new accounting standards that will lead to the elimination of the operating lease category. Nonetheless, rather than bring what are currently deemed as operating lease obligations to the borrower's balance sheet for financial covenant purposes, some credit agreements expressly exclude these current operating leases from debt treatment. To the extent that operating leases are not counted as debt for covenant purposes, credit agreements may still regulate payment obligations under operating leases. These agreements take one of the two approaches (illustrated in the sample language in Box 7.13) to control operating lease obligations. The most direct method is simply to limit by a dollar cap, or to a percentage of EBITDA, the aggregate lease payments that the borrower makes in any single year. The second approach, used much more often, is to create a definition of "attributable debt." The latter attempts to delineate the (hypothetical) corresponding debt amount attributable to the lease payments by discounting to present value at an agreed rate (usually a rate of interest applicable to other debt of the borrower) the future rental stream required to be paid by the borrower. "Attributable debt" is then included in the definition of debt and controlled by the debt covenant itself. Note that other credit agreements may define "attributable debt" to include the capitalized amount of any capitalized lease obligations appearing on the borrower's balance sheet. In this latter formulation, operating lease obligations will also be picked up as debt (and regulated by the debt covenant) but only to the extent that operating leases are deemed to be capital leases under the new lease accounting standards.

Many borrowers argue that all of this is unnecessary, since operating lease payments are an operating expense and, therefore, reduce EBITDA. To the extent the credit agreement has covenants based on EBITDA (the debt ratio, interest or debt service coverage ratio, and fixed charges coverage ratio), they contend that the lenders are already adequately protected. Whether this reasoning wins out is largely a function of negotiation and the degree to which the borrower's key assets are leased. If its leased property is relatively small in relation to its total assets, the lenders often simply ignore the issue. If, however, the borrower's leased property is extensive in relation to total assets, they are more likely to insist upon some kind of lease covenant.

7.4.4.5 Capital Expenditures

Box 7.14

The Borrower will not permit the aggregate amount of Capital Expenditures to exceed $_____ during any fiscal year. Notwithstanding the foregoing, if the aggregate amount of Capital Expenditures during any fiscal year shall be less than such amount, then such shortfall shall be added to the amount of Capital Expenditures permitted during the immediately succeeding (but not any other) fiscal year.

* * * * * * * * * * * *

"Capital Expenditures" means, for any period, expenditures (including the aggregate amount of Capital Lease Obligations incurred during such period) made by the Borrower or any Subsidiary to acquire or construct fixed assets, plant, and equipment (including renewals, improvements, and replacements, but excluding repairs) during such period computed in accordance with GAAP.

When a credit agreement includes a capital expenditures covenant, it is commonly included in the financial covenants section of a credit agreement. However, the capital expenditures covenant is perhaps more accurately characterized as a negative covenant rather than a performance-based covenant. The provision limits the aggregate capital expenditures that the borrower may make during a fiscal quarter or fiscal year. "Capital expenditures" are typically defined to include any expenditures that give rise to a capital asset of the borrower; they are expenditures that are not factored in as a deduction when the borrower's income is calculated, but are rather added directly to the asset side of the borrower's balance sheet (normally to property, plant, and equipment). Under this principle, repairing a building damaged in a windstorm is more likely be an operating expense than a capital expenditure; erecting a new building as part of an expansion of the borrower's business will likely constitute a capital expenditure.

The covenant is calculated for discrete fiscal periods (one quarter or one year), rather than on a rolling basis. Once the maximum levels are set, the debate between the borrower and the lender often revolves around carryovers; how much of one period's unused capital expenditure capacity may be carried forward into a future period. The borrower pushes for unlimited carry forwards, while the lenders (as shown in the sample in Box 7.14) will want to limit carryovers to one or two years (or permit none at all).

One could question why a lending syndicate should limit the amount of capital expenditures in the first place. After all, is not any expenditure by the borrower in its business *ipso facto* good for the business and, therefore, good for the lenders? Part of the answer to this question stems from the fact that many companies have a basic level of capital expenditures that they *must* make every year to continue to survive as a business. A wireless telecommunications company or a cable television company, for example, must continually invest in the next generation of capital equipment to remain competitive. A supermarket chain must constantly renovate stores to present a modern and clean appearance that appeals to customers (and, therefore more attractive than the store down the street). These amounts are colloquially referred to as "maintenance capital expenditures."

In each of these cases, however, the lenders may have a concern that the borrower not go wildly above what is necessary from a maintenance capital expenditures perspective by committing to make expenditures in any year beyond its capacity to fund those expenditures. Borrowers that want an extra allocation for capital expenditures, as a consequence, often negotiate for the permitted amount during any period to be increased by some portion of the borrower's so-called "excess" cash flow for that period, or by the amount of the proceeds of new equity capital received by the borrower during (or prior) to that period. Permitted capital expenditures out of "excess" funds such as these can bridge the desire of the borrower for greater flexibility and the desire of the lending syndicate that the borrower not overcommit.

7.4.5 Hybrid Financial Covenants

7.4.5.1 Leverage Ratio

Hybrid financial covenants compare a date-specific element to an element based upon performance over a period. The classic example is the leverage ratio; others may appear in specialized agreements.

Box 7.15

The Borrower will not permit the Leverage Ratio to exceed ___ to 1 at any time.

* * * * * * * * * * * *

"*Leverage Ratio*" means, as at any date of determination thereof, the ratio of (a) [Debt] [Debt that is secured by a Lien on any asset or property] of the Borrower and its Subsidiaries (determined on a consolidated basis, without duplication, in accordance with GAAP) as at such date to (b) EBITDA for the period of four fiscal quarters ending on or most recently ended prior to such date.

Typically, the leverage ratio (sometimes also referred to as the *debt ratio* or *cash flow ratio*) is defined as the ratio of debt (or in the case of a secured leverage ratio, secured debt) at a given date to EBITDA for the rolling four quarters most recently ended prior to that date. Sometimes credit agreements provide for the determination of the leverage ratios after netting out the borrower's cash and cash equivalents. This is the so-called net leverage ratio. Under the net leverage formulation, the numerator of the leverage formula is reduced dollar-for-dollar by the amount of the borrower's unrestricted cash and cash equivalents (which cash netting may be capped by a fixed dollar amount or otherwise, depending on what the parties negotiate). The debate in negotiating the credit agreement is whether the leverage ratio should be tested only at the end of a fiscal quarter (the end of the relevant rolling period) or whether it should be tested each day during the year. To test only on the last day of fiscal quarters allows the ratio during a fiscal quarter (between quarter ends) to exceed the maximum otherwise required at the end of the quarter. To test each day during the year avoids this, but borrowers frequently object that they cannot possibly calculate the ratio each day during a period because the covenant is performance-based.

This objection is misplaced. It ignores that the covenant is a hybrid with both performance and date-specific elements. The performance element (EBITDA) continues to be calculated only for discrete rolling four-quarter periods. The date element (debt) is calculated each day, which should be a simple arithmetic calculation for any borrower with adequate internal financial controls. To permit the leverage ratio to exceed the covenant levels between quarter ends risks the borrower being out of compliance once the test date comes. A borrower may say that this is a problem for it to manage itself, but lenders, being conservative and cautious, may view that to give the borrower flexibility in this regard simply affords it the freedom to fail.

7.5 AFFIRMATIVE COVENANTS

Affirmative covenants tell the borrower what it must do (as opposed to what it may not do). Whether the distinction between affirmative and negative is due to historical lender liability concerns or just for clarity's sake, it is helpful to distinguish the discussion of what is *required* (affirmative covenants) from what is *prohibited* (negative covenants).

7.5.1 Disclosure Covenants

Once lenders have made (or purchased) loans under the credit agreement, they focus on monitoring the performance of the borrower. As a consequence, credit agreements invariably require borrowers to supply reams of financial information and other data for the borrower and its subsidiaries, the more the better. Monitoring is done for two reasons. First, lenders want to discover earlier, rather than later, if a borrower encounters financial difficulties that may impede its ability to service the loan. Second, equally important, under principles of safe and sound banking, banks must collect regular and periodic financial information on their borrowers. Credit agreements therefore require at a minimum that the borrower deliver annual audited and quarterly unaudited financial statements. The typical agreement, however, goes far beyond and requires that the lenders be furnished everything from compliance certificates to projections, accountants' letters, notices of default, and other adverse events and volumes of dull, impenetrable, ERISA material. The key elements of these disclosure covenants are discussed here.

7.5.1.1 Financial Statements

Box 7.16

(a) *Annual Statements.* The Borrower will furnish to the Administrative Agent and each Lender, within [90] days after the end of each fiscal year, its audited consolidated balance sheet and related statements of operations, stockholders' equity, and cash flows as of the end of and for such year, setting forth in each case in comparative form the figures for the previous fiscal year, all reported on by [_____] or other independent public accountants of recognized national standing (without a "going concern" or like qualification or exception and without any qualification or exception as to the scope of such audit) to the effect that such consolidated financial statements present fairly in all material respects the

financial condition and results of operations of the Borrower and its consolidated Subsidiaries on a consolidated basis in accordance with GAAP
consistently applied.

    (b) *Quarterly Statements.* The Borrower will furnish to the
Administrative Agent and each Lender within [45] days after the end
of each of [its] [the first three] fiscal quarters of each fiscal year, its consolidated [(and consolidating)] balance sheet and related statements of
operations, stockholders' equity, and cash flows as of the end of and for
such fiscal quarter and the then elapsed portion of the fiscal year, setting
forth in each case in comparative form the figures for the corresponding
period or periods of (or, in the case of the balance sheet, as of the end
of) the previous fiscal year, all certified by one of its Financial Officers
as presenting fairly in all material respects the financial condition and
results of operations of the Borrower and its consolidated Subsidiaries on
a consolidated [(or, in the case of consolidating statements, individual)]
basis in accordance with GAAP consistently applied, subject to normal
year-end audit adjustments and the absence of footnotes.

Delivery of quarterly and annual financial statements, as noted
above, is the minimum ongoing financial disclosure required by the
typical credit agreement. In the case of foreign borrowers, however, for
which quarterly financial statements may not be regularly prepared,
the covenant may limit the required financial statements to semiannual
or perhaps only annual statements. In specialized situations (such as
highly leveraged or asset-based facilities), financial statements may be
required to be delivered monthly.

    Annual financial statements are normally required to be audited
by the borrower's independent public accountants; interim financial
statements are usually required to be certified only by the chief financial
officer or other appropriate financial officer of the borrower. The financial statements to be delivered are typically the big four prepared by
the accountants: the balance sheet, income statement, statement of cash
flows, and changes to stockholders' equity. The precise descriptions
of these statements in the covenant, as a rule, match the terminology
employed by the borrower. If it prepares statements of operation rather
than income statements, the former term appears in the credit agreement. A borrower that is a partnership or limited liability company has
partners' or members' equity rather than stockholders' equity.

    The financial statements to be delivered are normally "consoli-
dated" (will consolidate the borrower with its subsidiaries) and, in some
cases, are also "consolidating" (will show how the balance sheet and

the results of operations for each entity in the consolidated group were added together to produce the consolidated statements). Consolidating statements are useful because they show more clearly which entities in the consolidated group are responsible for the assets and earnings. It is accordingly another method by which the lenders can determine that they have guarantees and security from the proper entities in the consolidated group. Borrowers sometimes resist delivery of consolidating financial statements and contend that to put them in a form for presentation to the lending syndicate is needless additional work for the benefit gained. As a practical matter, however, the preparation of *consolidated* statements begins with *consolidating* statements so the extra effort on the part of the borrower should be minimal. Accountants do not report on consolidating statements, so the credit agreement requires that they be certified only by an appropriate financial officer of the borrower.

One issue that often arises is whether delivery of financial statements with a "going concern" qualification can satisfy the covenant. Borrowers frequently resist the requirement that financial statements be free of such a qualification, and reason that, if a particular condition is not a default under the financial covenants or other provisions of the agreement, it should not become a default through the inability to deliver unqualified financial statements. In other words, they argue, whether the borrower is in default should be determined by reference to the negotiated tests incorporated in the credit agreement and not by whether the accountants have determined that a going-concern qualification should be taken. Despite the borrower's seeming logic on this point, most credit agreements do not allow financial statements with a going-concern qualification to satisfy the covenant requirement.

7.5.1.2 Compliance Certificates

Box 7.17

(c) *Compliance Certificates.* The Borrower will furnish to the Administrative Agent and each Lender, concurrently with any delivery of the annual and quarterly financial statements above, a certificate of a Financial Officer of the Borrower (i) certifying as to whether a Default has occurred and, if a Default has occurred, specifying the details thereof and any action taken or proposed to be taken with respect thereto, (ii) setting forth reasonably detailed calculations demonstrating compliance with Sections [____] and (iii) stating whether any change in GAAP or in the application thereof has occurred since the date of the audited financial statements referred to in Section [*Financial Statement Representations*] and, if any such change has occurred, specifying the effect of such change on the financial statements accompanying such certificate.

(d) *Accountants' Statements.* The Borrower will furnish to the Administrative Agent and each Lender concurrently with any delivery of annual financial statements above, a certificate of the accounting firm that reported on such financial statements stating whether such firm obtained knowledge during the course of their examination of such financial statements of any Default (which certificate may be limited to the extent required by accounting rules or guidelines).

Concurrently with the delivery of quarterly or annual financial statements, the borrower is typically also required to prepare a compliance calculation for financial and other number-based covenants. The compliance calculation, as with the unaudited financial statements, is required to be certified by a senior financial officer of the borrower. As discussed in Section 7.3.1, most credit agreements provide that financial levels are to be calculated in accordance with GAAP as in effect, and as applied, for purposes of the base financial statements referred to in the representations. In such cases, the lenders want the borrower to disclose any changes in GAAP, or in the application thereof, that has occurred after the execution of the credit agreement so that the lenders can know what adjustments to the current financial statements were necessary for the borrower to certify compliance with the covenants.

Lenders frequently ask for the borrower's independent accountants to confirm compliance with the covenants. This is often met with resistance. Borrowers largely object on economic grounds; if accountants are requested to say anything beyond their customary audit confirmation, they will increase their audit fees. However, even assuming the borrower is willing to pay increased audit fees, the accountants themselves will resist saying anything beyond a negative assurance that in the course of their examination they did not become aware of any default under the applicable covenants "insofar as relating to accounting matters." This limitation is grounded in pronouncements of the American Institute of Certified Public Accounts (AICPA; see CLARIFIED STATEMENTS on Auditing Standards, AU-C Section 806, (Am. Inst. of Certified Pub. Accountants 2015)). The sample language in Box 7.17 seeks somewhat broader assurance and allows the accountants to qualify their certificate "to the extent required by accounting rules or guidelines."

Whether this debate is actually important is unclear. It may, indeed, be a case in which credit agreement language diverges from business practice. Often, neither the lenders nor the borrower focuses on whether a certification comes from the accountants, either because they ignore the covenant language entirely or because they presume that the qualification exempts the borrower from requiring its accountants to deliver anything. As a practical matter, therefore, inclusion of the right to a backstop calculation from the borrower's accountants may be fantasy.

The borrower's own certificate is, in credit agreements, normally executed by only one officer. This is in contrast to the practice in bond indentures in which certifications have long been required to be made by *two* senior officers, customarily defined as "responsible officers." For a while, after the enactment of the Sarbanes–Oxley Act, credit agreements began to require that two officers sign compliance certifications, but this practice has largely disappeared.

7.5.1.3 Notices of Material Events

Box 7.18

(e) *Notices of Material Events.* The Borrower will furnish to the Administrative Agent and each Lender notice of the following [promptly after any Senior Officer obtains knowledge thereof]:

(i) the occurrence of any Default;

(ii) the filing or commencement of any action, suit, or proceeding by or before any arbitrator or Governmental Authority against or affecting the Borrower or any Subsidiary that, if adversely determined, could reasonably be expected to result [in a Material Adverse Effect] [liability in an aggregate amount exceeding $[____]];

(iii) the occurrence of any ERISA Event that, alone or together with any other ERISA Events that have occurred, could reasonably be expected to result in liability in an aggregate amount exceeding $[____];

(iv) the assertion of any Environmental Claim by any Person against, or with respect to the activities of, the Borrower or any Subsidiary and any alleged violation of or noncompliance with any Environmental Laws or any permits, licenses, or authorizations, other than any Environmental Claim or alleged violation that, if adversely determined, could not reasonably be expected to result [in a Material Adverse Effect] [liability in an aggregate amount exceeding $[____]]; and

(v) any other development that results in, or could reasonably be expected to result in, a Material Adverse Effect.

Each notice delivered under this Section shall be accompanied by a statement of a Financial Officer or other executive officer of the Borrower setting forth the details of the event or development requiring such notice and any action taken or proposed to be taken with respect thereto.

As part of the lenders' ongoing monitoring of the borrower, the credit agreement typically includes a requirement that the borrower notify the lenders of any default or other material event that affects the borrower or any of its subsidiaries. Accordingly, the borrower is required to notify the lenders of the occurrence of any default, the institution of any material litigation, or the occurrence of any ERISA event or environmental claim that exceeds a specified dollar threshold, or could result in a material adverse change (MAC), and of any other event that results or could be expected to result in a MAC.

Borrowers often press for the notice covenant not to be triggered unless a senior officer or group of senior officers (defined to include the financial officers responsible for monitoring the borrower's compliance with the covenants) obtain "knowledge" of the existence of the event that requires disclosure. Many agreements go further and require that the officers have "actual knowledge" rather than mere "knowledge." Regardless of the precise words used, the rationale from the borrower's perspective is to avoid its breaching an agreement in circumstances (constructive knowledge) in which an officer did not know, but arguably should have been able to ascertain that a default had occurred. This reflects the sharp distinction historically drawn between the two, with actual knowledge held to consist of "express information" of a fact and constructive knowledge being in the nature of a "legal inference." See *Colby v. Riggs Nat'l Bank*, 92 F.2d 183 (D.C. Cir. 1937). Section 1-201(25) of the Uniform Commercial Code (UCC) lays out a more modern approach by legislating that the two have essentially the same meaning. However, inertia and the fact that the UCC as a technical matter does not apply to credit agreement transactions lead borrowers to continue to push for "actual knowledge" rather than "knowledge."

The borrower's concerns here may, however, be misplaced. Even if a borrower breaches the credit agreement because it fails to advise the lenders of a default of which its officers had constructive knowledge, once the lenders learn of the breach, the fact that they were not told earlier simply means the borrower has defaulted twice rather than once. This may be somewhat like a robber failing to tell the police that he just held up a bank. Once the police learn of the theft the fact that the robber failed to tell them earlier becomes largely irrelevant; so it is with a credit agreement. Once the lenders learn of the default, they may be miffed that they were not notified of its occurrence, but with one exception their remedies are not thereby increased. The exception is found in those agreements that make the failure to notify the lenders of a breach an *immediate* event of default in circumstances in which the breach would otherwise enjoy a grace period. In that instance, failure to tell the lenders about the breach converts the future event of default into a present event of default—no grace period need run (see the discussion on this point in Section 9.1.3).

7.5.1.4 Catchall Provisions

Box 7.19

(f) *SEC Reports*. The Borrower will furnish to the Administrative Agent and each Lender, promptly after the same become publicly available, copies of all periodic and other reports, proxy statements, and other materials filed by the Borrower or any Subsidiary with the Securities and Exchange Commission, or any successor; and

(g) *Information Upon Request*. The Borrower will furnish to the Administrative Agent and each Lender promptly following any request therefor, such other information regarding the operations, business affairs, and financial condition of the Borrower or any Subsidiary, or compliance with the terms of this Agreement, as the Administrative Agent or any Lender may reasonably request.

The disclosure covenant almost always includes what can be described as catchall provisions that require the borrower to supply the lenders copies of reports filed with the SEC (and sometimes with securities exchanges) and additional financial or other information requested by the lenders from the borrower. The required information with respect to SEC reports is limited to information supplied *by the borrower*. Information filed by shareholders with respect to changes in their equity ownership is not included.

The right to request additional information from the borrower can be particularly important if the lenders have reason to believe that the borrower's financial condition may have deteriorated. The quarterly unaudited and annual audited financial statements, for example, may not provide divisional or product-line information, may not include consolidating statements (unless expressly specified in the covenant), and may not normally contain details with respect to a host of other contingencies that could be of concern to the lenders (litigation, tax, and ERISA issues; pending license and trademark disputes; subsidiary-specific information; and so forth).

The frequent debate with respect to information that may be requested by the lenders, however, revolves less around the scope of what can be asked for and more around whether any lender may *individually* make the request or whether the request must be made by the administrative agent (or, perhaps, by the lender through the administrative agent). Except in rare cases, most credit agreements allow information to be requested by individual lenders; to provide otherwise, at least for banks, may create regulatory concerns. The inability to request information may, under some circumstances, mean that the banks have not made a "loan" at all, but rather have purchased an investment security, which may be beyond their statutory power. It might also be criticized on review by bank examiners as an unsafe and unsound banking practice.

7.5.1.5 Delivery

Box 7.20

Documents required to be delivered pursuant to this Section may be delivered electronically and, if so delivered, shall be deemed to have been delivered on the date (i) on which the Borrower posts such documents, or provides a link thereto, on the Borrower's website or (ii) on which such documents are posted on the Borrower's behalf on Intralinks™ or another relevant website (whether a commercial, third-party website or whether sponsored by the Administrative Agent), if any, to which each Lender and the Administrative Agent have access without charge. Notwithstanding anything contained herein, in every instance the Borrower (x) shall be required to provide paper copies of the certificates required under this Section to the Administrative Agent and (y) shall notify any Lender when documents required to be delivered pursuant to this Section have been delivered electronically to the extent that such Lender has requested so to be notified.

Delivery of financial statements and other borrower information has traditionally been made by the borrower sending the disclosure material directly to lenders. However, as the size of lending syndicates has expanded and Web-based posting services (such as Intralinks™ or Debtdomain) have become widely adopted, financial statements are now routinely made available to lenders through posting on either the borrower's own website (to the extent that the information to be supplied by the company is public) or Internet platforms maintained by the administrative agent (used regardless of whether the information is public).

Certain lenders, referred to as "public-side lenders," want to receive only publicly available information or, if dealing with purely private borrowers, information that is of a type that would be made publicly available if the borrower had public securities and do not want to receive any material nonpublic information, or MNPI. Due to securities laws restrictions, the receipt of MNPI will taint or restrict a person's ability to trade in securities. Even for a purely private borrower, receipt of MNPI may complicate the ability to trade in loans especially if such then-private borrower issues public securities in the near future. Therefore public-side lenders want some mechanism through which they can control the type of information they are furnished. In the case of online platforms this is accomplished through Web-page warnings (colloquially referred to alternatively as splash pages, click-thru screens, or just "click-thrus") that identify those areas of the site that may contain MNPI. For cases in which information is being delivered physically to the lenders, informal procedures with the borrower and administrative agent are normally established to ensure that public-side lenders are not furnished MNPI. Except in rare cases, agents insist that the borrower identify MNPI at the time it is delivered to the agent for posting or further delivery to the lenders and do not want to assess themselves whether the information is MNPI. The logic here is simple: the borrower is in a better position than anyone else to assess whether an event or condition rises to the level of MNPI. If the borrower fails to identify such material as containing MNPI, the administrative agent will usually have the express right to assume that the material contains MNPI and, to avoid the risk of "tainting" public-side lenders, will only make such materials available on the portion of the online platform accessible to private-side lenders who have not expressed any desire to avoid MNPI. [2]

---

[2] For a further discussion of MNPI considerations, please refer to the LSTA "Statement of Principles for the Communication and Use of Confidential Information by Loan Market Participants" (December 11, 2006).

7.5.2   Inspection Rights

> **Box 7.21**
>
> The Borrower will, and will cause each Subsidiary to, permit any representatives designated by the Administrative Agent or any Lender, upon reasonable prior notice [and at the expense of the borrower], to visit and inspect its properties, to examine and make extracts from its books and records, and to discuss its affairs, finances, and condition with its officers and independent accountants, all at such reasonable times and as often as reasonably requested.

Potentially one of the most important rights granted by borrowers to lenders is the so-called visitation or inspection right. Failure to include the right, like failure to grant lenders the right to request additional information, may constitute an unsafe and unsound banking practice. Bank regulators, in any event, consider the visitation or inspection right important and may criticize agreements that do not accord this right to the lenders.

The sample language in Box 7.21 is deceptively simple. Borrowers may push to qualify the right in a variety of ways. Perhaps the most common request is that the lenders be entitled to the inspection right only once a default has occurred. Conditioning the right in this way largely undercuts the purpose of the inspection privilege in the first place, namely to determine whether or not a borrower really is in default, or is approaching default. When financial difficulties first arise, it is precisely because the lenders do *not* know whether the borrower is in default that they may wish to visit its business and look at records. Accordingly, credit agreements generally do not limit the inspection right in this manner.

Second, borrowers often request that the inspection right be constrained so that the lenders may talk with officers of the borrower only and not with its independent accountants. Much of the impetus for this comes from the accountants themselves who fear direct liability to lenders if they discuss the borrower's financial condition and statements with lenders. Borrowers are also reluctant to give lenders unrestrained access to accountants who may not be able (or willing) to explain or tell the borrower's "story" as it relates to adverse information with the same earnestness and conviction as the borrower itself. Therefore borrowers may negotiate for a right to participate in any discussions that the agent and lenders may engage in with its accountants. Relatedly, borrowers also may raise concerns about waiving attorney-client privilege that may arise from having to disclose privileged materials. Whether materials are in fact privileged may lead to vigorous debates if this exception is ever relied upon but nonetheless, lenders are increasingly being asked to include this exclusion. Lastly, borrowers often request that the lenders treat the information supplied confidentially. Although facially unobjectionable, confidentiality language in the inspection rights provision is redundant (and, if inserted, may end up inconsistent) with the general confidentiality provision that is customarily set forth in the credit agreement (see Section 13.9). Most credit agreements, as a consequence, do not include such language in the inspection covenant.

Borrowers also resist agreeing to pick up the expenses of the lenders in connection with their visitation rights (the bracketed language in Box 7.21), at least if no default has occurred. In most cases this is consistent with the approach taken in the expenses provision (see Section 12.5), which typically requires the borrower prior to a default to pay only the costs and expenses of the administrative agent and not of individual lenders. Borrowers argue, with some justification, that if they were obligated to pick up the expenses of each lender's inspections they could be overwhelmed with visits, particularly if their corporate headquarters is located in a desirable climate (Hawaii or Arizona anyone?).

7.5.3 Insurance

Box 7.22

(a) *Insurance Generally.* The Borrower will, and will cause each Subsidiary to, maintain, with financially sound and reputable insurance companies, insurance in such amounts and against such risks, and with such deductibles, as in each case are customarily maintained by companies engaged in the same or similar businesses, owning similar properties and operating in the same or similar locations.

[Without limiting the foregoing, such insurance shall include (i) physical hazard insurance on an "all risk" basis, (ii) commercial general liability insurance against claims for bodily injury, death, or property damage covering any and all insurable claims, (iii) business interruption insurance, (iv) worker's compensation insurance and such other insurance as may be required by law, and (v) such other insurance as the Administrative Agent may from time to time require (such policies to be in such form and amounts and having such coverage as may be reasonably satisfactory to the Administrative Agent).

All such insurance shall (i) provide that no cancellation, material reduction in amount, or material change in coverage thereof shall be effective until at least 30 days after receipt by the Administrative Agent of written notice thereof, (ii) name the Administrative Agent on behalf of the Lenders as loss payee (in the case of property insurance) or additional insured (in the case of liability insurance), as applicable, (iii) if reasonably requested by the Administrative Agent, include a breach of warranty clause, and (iv) be reasonably satisfactory in all other respects to the Administrative Agent.]

[Notwithstanding the foregoing, the Borrower and its Subsidiaries may maintain, in lieu of any such insurance required under this paragraph (a), a system of self-insurance consistent with sound practices of companies engaged in the same or similar businesses, owning similar properties and operating in the same or similar locations, and shall maintain adequate insurance reserves in accordance with GAAP and sound actuarial and insurance principles].

(b) *Flood Insurance.* If at any time the real property covered by any Mortgage is located in a "special flood hazard area" designated in any Flood Insurance Rate Map published by the Federal Emergency Management Agency (or any successor agency), the Borrower will obtain flood insurance in such reasonable total amount as the Administrative Agent may from time to time reasonably require, and otherwise comply with the National Flood Insurance Program as set forth in the Flood Disaster Protection Act of 1973, as amended.

(c) *Key Person Life Insurance.* The Borrower will maintain insurance on the life of [key person] in an amount not less than $_____ and shall assign the policies for such insurance to the Administrative Agent, on behalf of the Lenders, pursuant to an assignment in form acceptable to the Administrative Agent.

Lenders like predictability. As part of the credit approval process for any prospective borrower, they look at a long list of factors in an effort to forecast whether the borrower can service and repay the proposed credit facility, including historic and projected cash flows, depth and quality of management, asset values, competing product lines and companies, and general economic conditions. The credit approval process tries to reduce the number of unknowables to zero, but of course this is not possible when it comes to earthquakes, floods, or fires that destroy factories; employees that steal millions from corporate coffers; or unidentified product liability claims that arise out of defects in a borrower product line. To protect against unpredictable damages or liabilities such as these, lenders expect the borrower to carry insurance. Expectation leads to covenant. Most lenders are reluctant to lend to a company—except the strongest investment-grade borrowers—if they know the borrower does not carry insurance.

For these reasons, almost every credit agreement for leveraged borrowers (and even some for investment-grade borrowers) includes an insurance covenant. In its simplest form, the covenant requires the borrower to maintain insurance in amounts and against risks *customarily* maintained by other businesses in the same industry and geographic location. This approach is laid out in the sample in Box 7.22 in the first, unbracketed, portion of paragraph (a). The exact types of insurance, appropriate deductibles, limits on self-insurance, and covered risks are left to the borrower (subject, of course, to the lenders' ability to point out to the borrower that, for example, to carry *no* fire insurance is not customary for companies in the retail clothing business). In its simple form, the covenant does not attempt to name covered risks, amounts, deductibles, and other elements of the borrower's insurance policies.

In its more complex form, such as in highly leveraged secured transactions or project financings, the covenant is more detailed as to the risks to be covered and the deductibles or self-insurance to be permitted. The additional language set out in the first two bracketed paragraphs in paragraph (a) in Box 7.22 is an example of a more detailed approach. The key element of this language is the requirement that the borrower maintain "such other insurance" as the administrative agent may require and that all insurance be reasonably satisfactory to the agent. This gives the administrative agent a much more powerful tool than to simply plead with the borrower that its coverage is not up to "industry standards."

In a secured transaction, the lenders also want to designate the agent on behalf of the lenders as the "loss payee" or "additional insured." Being designated as loss payee in respect of casualty insurance means that if a factory blows up, the insurance proceeds are paid directly to the agent and not to the borrower. Being designated as additional insured for liability insurance means, in essence, that if anyone asserts liability against the lenders (for example, for making loans to the borrower that enable the manufacture of defective toys), the lenders would, if the policies are properly worded, be entitled to coverage under the company's liability policies. The requirement that any insurance provide for notice to the agent before cancellation or material change in the policy theoretically allows the lenders on their own initiative to continue the insurance policies—perhaps the reason for the cancellation is the failure of the borrower to pay premiums. The lenders may want to pay the premiums themselves rather than allow their collateral to be subject to the risk of casualty events. The so-called "breach of warranty" clause protects the lenders against an insurance carrier's holding against the lenders an alleged breach by the borrower of warranties it made to the insurance carrier. So if the borrower's factory did not have a sprinkler system contrary to the information given to the insurance company, the lenders are still entitled to payment when the factory burns down.

Some insurance covenants go even further than the example in Box 7.22 and mandate that the borrower deliver an annual insurance compliance certificate to the administrative agent. The certificate will demonstrate that all insurance required to be maintained under the covenant continues in effect, that all applicable premiums have been paid, and that the agent is still the loss payee and additional insured on the policies. This more extreme oversight might be expected in an asset-based facility or project financing when the value of the assets itself is normally a significant component of the borrower's capacity to repay the loan. It might also be seen in a secured bond transaction for which the bondholders want the trustee to have a tool to monitor the insurance covenant—if the certificate is not delivered, it would set in motion a process that could ultimately lead to acceleration. Of course, an insurance compliance certificate is only as good as any other certificate; it depends upon the veracity of the borrower in order to provide any real protection to the lenders.

Some credit agreements also address two other kinds of insurance: flood hazard insurance and key-person life insurance. When Congress established the National Flood Insurance Program (pursuant to the National Flood Insurance Act of 1968 and the Flood Disaster Protection Act of 1973), it mandated that regulated lending institutions (this includes national banks, state member banks, and state insured banks) must make certain that borrowers carry flood insurance before the lenders extend credit secured by improved real estate. These requirements were implemented pursuant to regulations issued by the relevant regulatory agencies (an example of these for national banks may be found at 12 C.F.R. Part 22). These provide that a regulated lending institution may not "make, increase, extend or renew" any loan secured by improved property that is located in a flood zone until it has verified that the borrower maintains appropriate flood insurance. The lenders' responsibility starts with consulting registries maintained by the Federal Emergency Management Agency to determine whether the real property is in a flood zone. If it is, and if the loan is secured by a building located on the property, then the lenders must notify the borrower that the property is in a flood zone and that should it be unable to obtain insurance privately it may do so under the National Flood Insurance Program. All of this finds its way into credit agreements through a covenant that requires that the borrower maintain flood insurance in accordance with the provisions of the National Flood Insurance Act. Some also attempt to insert the notice to the borrower into the credit agreement (on the theory that this permits only one notice to be given to the borrower rather than one from each regulated institution), but, although logical and practical, this may not technically comply with the regulations, which contain very specific requirements as to what any such notice must say. For suggested market best practice, see the LSTA "Market Standards for Flood Insurance Processes in Syndicated Lending" (revised December 19, 2014).

Key-person life insurance is insurance maintained on the life of a key officer or key employee. It is usually required by lenders in those circumstances in which one person is critical to the success of a company. Perhaps the founder and CEO of the company possesses unique industry knowledge and, were he or she to die, the borrower's competitive position would be severely damaged. Alternatively, a company might be dependent upon a research chemist's genius at exploiting patents and would see its competitive edge impaired if he or she were to be hit by the proverbial bus. In each of these cases, key-person life insurance at least softens the financial blow of tragedy. The purpose of the insurance, however, is not normally to repay the loan (except in unusual cases, the amount of insurance is far less than the outstanding loans), but rather to create a pot of money from which the borrower could pay an incentive bonus or the like to induce a replacement from another company to step in and take over for the officer or employee who has died.

7.5.4 Miscellaneous "Who-Can-Object" Covenants

A number of affirmative covenants in effect require the borrower to do nothing more than any right-minded borrower would do in the first place. They are like strawberries and fresh air (who could possibly object to their presence in a credit agreement?) and are inserted to guard against those situations in which a borrower is so abjectly sloppy or incompetent that it fails to run its business in the manner customarily expected of any good management team. The following are some examples.

7.5.4.1   Books and Records

> **Box 7.23**
>
> The Borrower will, and will cause each Subsidiary to, keep proper books of record and account in which full, true and correct entries are made of all dealings and transactions in relation to its business and activities.

Few borrowers fail to keep proper books and records, and, if they do, the lender probably has bigger problems than just the borrower's bad accounting. Nevertheless, the covenant is included so that, if in exercising its inspection rights, a lender determined that inadequate books and records were being maintained, the lender could point to the covenant as a basis for taking remedial action.

7.5.4.2   Properties

> **Box 7.24**
>
> The Borrower will, and will cause each Subsidiary to, keep and maintain all property material to the conduct of its business in good working order and condition, ordinary wear and tear excepted.

This covenant requires maintenance of all properties, although there is normally a materiality qualifier. So if a borrower fails to repair its factory roof after a tornado and the roof is necessary to keep its chocolate candy line clean and dry, then the lenders could claim a default if a construction crew is not quickly on site to repair the damage. Similarly, an airline that elects to reduce operating costs by deferring scheduled maintenance on its fleet might also be in breach of its maintenance covenant. As these examples illustrate, it is hard to see how any borrower would ever take (or fail to take action) that would trigger a breach of this covenant, but in an egregious case it could be useful to have the covenant in a credit agreement.

7.5.4.3   Existence and Franchises

> **Box 7.25**
>
> The Borrower will, and will cause each Subsidiary to, do or cause to be done, all things necessary to preserve, renew, and keep in full force

and effect its legal existence and the rights, licenses, permits, privileges, and franchises material to the conduct of its business; *provided* that the foregoing shall not prohibit any merger, consolidation, liquidation, or dissolution permitted under Section [*Fundamental Changes*].

This covenant requires that the borrower maintain franchises and licenses necessary for the conduct of its business. As with the maintenance of properties covenant, there is usually a materiality qualifier. If the borrower's business is heavily dependent upon particular licenses (such as Federal Communications Commission (FCC) licenses if the borrower is a television station or wireless company, or a certificate of public convenience and necessity if the borrower is a public utility), the credit agreement probably deals more explicitly, usually in the defaults, with what happens if any material licenses or franchises are revoked or not renewed. Although not generally stated, the reference to licenses is understood to mean *governmental* licenses and not intellectual property licenses or the like.

7.5.4.4 Compliance with Law; Sanctions and Anticorruption Laws

Box 7.26

(a) The Borrower will, and will cause each Subsidiary to, comply with all laws, rules, regulations, and orders of any Governmental Authority applicable to it or its property, except where the failure to do so, individually or in the aggregate, could not reasonably be expected to result in a Material Adverse Effect.

(b) The Borrower will not, directly or indirectly, use the proceeds of the Loans, or lend, contribute, or otherwise make available such proceeds to any subsidiary, joint venture partner, or other Person, [(i)] to fund any activities or business of or with any Person, or in any country or territory, that, at the time of such funding, is, or whose government is, the subject of Sanctions, [or (ii) in any other manner that would result in a violation of Sanctions by any Person (including any Person participating in the Loans, whether as underwriter, advisor, investor, or otherwise)][3].

(c) No part of the proceeds of the Loans will be used, directly or indirectly, in furtherance of an offer, payment, promise to pay, or

---

[3] Clause (b) is quoted from LSTA's publication "US Sanctions Issues in Lending Transactions" (September 1, 2016).

authorization of the payment or giving of money, or anything else of value, to any Person in violation of the United States Foreign Corrupt Practices Act of 1977, as amended ("*FCPA*") or any other applicable anti-corruption law. The Borrower will maintain in effect policies and procedures designed to promote compliance by the Borrower, its Subsidiaries, and their respective directors, officers, employees, and agents with the FCPA and any other applicable anticorruption laws.[4]

The compliance with law covenant is designed to do several things. First, it gives the lenders a remedy in the event they discover their borrower is a modern-day Jesse James or Al Capone or, more realistically, just a business that has a careless disregard for legal rules. Perhaps it runs a manufacturing facility that suffers an epidemic of Occupational Safety and Health Administration (OSHA) violations, or is a public filer that always skates at the edge of securities law requirements. By requiring the borrower to comply with law (at least if failure to do so would materially impact its business), the lenders reduce the risk of events that affect the borrower's financial condition adversely. Including the covenant in the credit agreement may also give the lenders an argument that they acted in good faith in extending credit to the borrower and are thus free of responsibility if a government authority should later seek to charge them with aiding and abetting the borrower's violation of law. Sometimes the covenant explicitly states that the laws with which the borrower is to comply include environmental laws (in case there were any doubt), but otherwise it simply obligates the borrower to do something that it should be doing already.

In recent years government regulators have placed an increasingly intense focus in the lending area on compliance with sanctions and antiterrorism regulations as well as regulations combating corruption of public officials. (See the discussion in Section 6.1.10.) To comprehend the seriousness of the issue, one only has to peruse the headlines about financial institutions finding themselves subject to governmental investigations that have resulted in billion-dollar fines and other serious enforcement actions. In addition to financial penalties, the reputational damage to a financial institution can be severe. Recognizing the heightened regulatory focus on compliance with these regulations, the LSTA published two pieces of regulatory guidance, "US Sanctions Issues

---

[4] Clause (c) is quoted from LSTA's publication "Anti-Corruption Issues in Lending Transactions" (December 1, 2014).

in Lending Transactions" (September 1, 2016) and "Anti-Corruption Issues in Lending Transactions" (December 1, 2014).

In reaction to this increasingly aggressive enforcement environment, lenders frequently require covenants that clearly spell out exactly how the borrower will remain compliant when it comes to applicable sanctions regimes, antiterrorism regulations, and anticorruption regulations in particular. The covenants may be incorporated within the general compliance with laws or use of proceeds covenants or take the form of a standalone negative covenant. Whatever form the specific language takes, if diligence yields evidence of the borrower doing any sort of business in sanctioned jurisdictions or with sanction targets, specific tailored covenants will be necessary though not completely sufficient protection. At a minimum, lenders will need to confirm that none of the loan proceeds will be used to finance business with sanctions targets or to fund any payment in violation of applicable anticorruption laws and memorialize such understanding within the appropriate covenants. Some covenants go further and require the borrower's continued maintenance of policies and procedures aimed at ensuring compliance with laws in both areas.

7.5.4.5   Payment of Taxes and Other Obligations

Box 7.27

The Borrower will, and will cause each Subsidiary to, pay its obligations, including Tax liabilities, that, if not paid, could have a Material Adverse Effect before the same shall become delinquent or in default, except where (a) the validity or amount thereof is being contested in good faith by appropriate proceedings, (b) the Borrower or such Subsidiary has set aside on its books adequate reserves with respect thereto in accordance with GAAP, and (c) the failure to make payment pending such contest could not reasonably be expected to result in a Material Adverse Effect.

This covenant is much like the compliance with law covenant; it obligates the borrower to do something (pay its taxes and other obligations) that it should be doing already. It may even appear superfluous to require by contract something that the borrower is likely already doing, assuming that the borrower is a competently run organization. However, where the value of this covenant really comes into focus is during times of distress when the borrower may be trying to preserve liquidity by postponing, or even skipping entirely, the payment of such basic obligations.

This covenant is normally qualified in several respects so as to avoid duplication with the cross-default (discussed in more detail in Section 9.1.4). To begin with, it requires payment of only *material* obligations (obligations that, if not paid, would result in a MAC) and permits nonpayment if the tax and other obligations are being contested "in good faith," the borrower keeps "adequate reserves," and, pending the contest, nonpayment will not give rise to a separate MAC. Contesting a property tax under circumstances in which the local authority is still free to assert a tax lien and commence foreclosure on the borrower's factory would not be allowed under the covenant. Some of this is redundant with other provisions of the credit agreement. In the context of taxes, for example, any lien upon property is likely already captured by the negative pledge.

As with the compliance with law covenant, the payment obligations covenant may help insulate the lenders against an (admittedly far-fetched) claim by a contract counterparty or taxing authority that the lenders aided and abetted the borrower's breach of a contract or failure to pay taxes by acquiescing in its default on payment obligations. The lenders should, in theory, be able to point to the covenant and say that they acted in good faith vis-à-vis the borrower.

7.5.4.6   Government Approvals

Box 7.28

The Borrower will, and will cause each Subsidiary to, from time to time obtain and maintain in full force and effect all licenses, consents, authorizations, and approvals of, and make all filings and registrations with, any Governmental Authority necessary under the laws of [Borrower's Country] for the making and performance by it of this Agreement and the other Loan Documents.

The government approvals covenant is not inserted into the typical domestic credit agreement, except for cases in which the borrower operates a specialized business that requires approval for the loan. This can be the case if, for example, the borrower is subject to state public utility board regulation or is regulated by other governmental authorities. The covenant, however, is routinely inserted into credit agreements when the borrower is a non-U.S. entity, particularly if it is located in a jurisdiction where foreign exchange control approval is necessary. Normally, of course, any such approval should be obtained prior to the closing (see Section 6.1.6), but for cases in which an exchange approval must be reconfirmed the covenant obligates the borrower to do this so that the approval is continually maintained.

7.5.4.7 Substantive Consolidation

> **Box 7.29**
>
> The Borrower will, and will cause each Subsidiary to, maintain a separate and distinct existence from [Parent] and its other Subsidiaries (collectively, the "*Parent Group*") for the purpose of avoiding substantive consolidation of the assets and liabilities of the Parent Group with the Borrower and its Subsidiaries under Title 11 of the United States Bankruptcy Code. Without limiting the generality of the foregoing, the Borrower will, and will cause each Subsidiary to, conduct its business and operations separately from that of the Parent Group, including (i) not commingling funds or other assets of the Borrower and its Subsidiaries with the funds or other assets of the Parent Group; (ii) maintaining separate corporate and financial records and observing all corporate formalities (including, without limitation, the holding of regular board of directors' and shareholders' meetings, or the taking of actions pursuant to written consents in lieu of such meetings); and (iii) dealing with third parties in its own name and as a separate and independent entity.

When loans under a credit agreement are being made to a borrower that is part of a larger consolidated group of companies, the lenders may be concerned with substantive consolidation in bankruptcy. "Substantive consolidation" arises out of a line of bankruptcy cases that treats a group of affiliated entities as if they were a single company, so that the assets of each of the affiliated companies are deemed to be owned by one entity and the creditors of each of the affiliated companies are deemed to be creditors of one entity. A good explanation of the history and key elements of substantive consolidation is set forth in the decision of *In re Owens Corning*, 419 F.3d 195 (3d Cir. 2005). If, in making their original credit analysis, a group of lenders relied upon the borrower's having particular assets and liabilities, substantive consolidation in a bankruptcy of the borrower with other members of the affiliated group can run roughshod over the lenders' careful analysis. Similar unfairness could arise if the lenders take guarantees from subsidiaries in order to have a priority claim against the assets of the subsidiaries over other creditors of the borrowers.

Due to the risk of substantive consolidation, credit agreements sometimes include a covenant that requires the borrower to take appropriate actions to minimize the risk of consolidation. Although the list of factors that courts have looked to when they impose substantive consolidation is long, key elements often inserted into a covenant include such things as (1) to observe corporate formalities (in other words, to keep the borrower's assets identified and separate from affiliates' assets), (2) not to commingle borrower cash with affiliates' cash (although some agreements allow this if done pursuant to a cash-management agreement that precisely lays out the rights and liabilities of each entity that is a party to the agreement), (3) to deal with customers under the borrower's name (and not to use a common name for the group of companies as if they were all one entity), and (4) to maintain separate books and records.

Other factors that have influenced a court's determination of whether to substantively consolidate multiple entities are outlined in the *Owens Corning* decision referred to above. In that case, the court considered it critical that the lenders had performed a separate credit analysis of the borrower and each entity obligated on the loans (specifically, subsidiary guarantors) and took the position that to substantively consolidate the borrower with its subsidiaries would override the intention of the parties, when structuring the credit agreement, that the lenders be given a preference over other creditors of the borrower. The case suggests that to assess the strength of each support party and include in the credit agreement appropriate restrictions that emphasize its "stand-alone" value (such as those described in the preceding paragraph), and to allow lender visitation rights at the level of each support party, will make it less likely that a bankruptcy court will order substantive consolidation.

7.5.5 Use of Proceeds

Box 7.30

The proceeds of the Loans will be used only for [_____]. No part of the proceeds of any Loan will be used, whether directly or indirectly, for any purpose that entails a violation of any of the Regulations of the Board, including Regulations T, U, and X. Letters of Credit will be issued only to support [_____].

The use of proceeds covenant ensures that the borrower uses the loan proceeds for the purposes it specified at the time the credit agreement was entered into. If the credit agreement is to provide funds for a major financing, the conditions precedent themselves control the actual disbursement of proceeds, so there is little likelihood that the borrower could stray. Most agreements provide that the proceeds of term loans be used only for one-time expenditures, such as acquisitions or capital expenditures, or to repay other debt, and that revolving credit facilities are available for the working capital needs or general corporate purposes of the borrower. "General corporate purposes" is customarily construed so broadly as to have little practical impact in constraining the borrower's use of the loans. Thus, it might allow the use of revolving loan proceeds to finance acquisitions, repay debt, or pay dividends, though the term may not permit transformational acquisitions or extraordinary dividends of a substantial portion of a borrower's capital.

The use of proceeds covenant may (as does the sample in Box 7.30) also require that loan proceeds be used in accordance with applicable law (including the margin rules set forth in Regulations T, U, and X, discussed in more detail in Section 6.1.12). This is another instance in which a covenant is redundant with the compliance with law provision and which obligates the borrower to do something that it should already do anyway—not break the law. Including an express provision in the credit agreement with respect to the margin regulations may help give the lenders an argument that they did not, in making the loans, assist the borrower to use the proceeds for an unlawful scheme.

The use of proceeds covenant as it applies to letters of credit refers to the transactions *supported* by the letter of credit. Since the proceeds of a letter of credit are remitted to the beneficiary rather than to the borrower, this is the more logical approach; the borrower is not in a position (nor should the lenders care) to restrict the use of proceeds by the beneficiary.

7.5.6   Interest Rate Protection

> **Box 7.31**
>
> The Borrower will, within [90] [180] days after the Closing Date, enter into, and thereafter maintain in full force and effect, one or more Interest Rate Protection Agreements with one or more banks or other financial institutions [having capital, surplus, and undivided profits of at least $_____$], that effectively enable the Borrower (in a manner reasonably satisfactory to the Administrative Agent) to protect itself, for a term of not less than ___ years, against adverse fluctuations in three-month London interbank offered rates as to a notional principal amount which, together

with that portion of the aggregate outstanding principal amount of Debt of the Borrower and its Subsidiaries bearing a fixed rate of interest and any existing Interest Rate Protection Agreements or other arrangements, shall in the aggregate be at least equal to ___% of the aggregate outstanding principal amount of the Debt of the Borrower and its Subsidiaries.

As noted in Section 7.6, the credit agreement frequently restricts the borrower from entering into hedging or derivative transactions for "speculative" purposes. At the same time, the credit agreement may compel the borrower to undertake a certain minimum amount of interest hedging to guard against swings in interest rates that could jeopardize the borrower's ability to service interest on the loans. While an interest rate coverage covenant might arguably provide some assurance that the borrower's interest costs are not excessive in relation to its EBITDA (as discussed in Section 7.4, the calculation of interest costs for any period is adjusted downward by the payments received by the borrower under interest hedging agreements), that assurance is retrospective only. An interest hedging covenant attempts to provide some protection to the lenders on a prospective basis, usually for the first two or three years of the credit facility.

The approach often taken by the covenant requires that a percentage of the borrower's overall debt (including loans under the credit agreement) be hedged so that the aggregate portion of its floating-rate debt (taking into account the hedge) does not exceed a percentage (usually somewhere around 50 percent or 60 percent) of its total debt. The covenant is typically written, as the sample in Box 7.31 illustrates, to give the borrower credit for fixed-rate bond or private placement debt, since that is treated as "hedged" for these purposes.

Hedging covenants are customarily phrased fairly loosely: they obligate the borrower only to enter into the appropriate hedges within some period (commonly three or six months) after the closing and set out only general parameters as to the manner of the hedge (subject, typically, to administrative agent approval rights over final terms). Some hedge covenants explicitly require that any hedge counterparty have some minimum capital and surplus or credit rating on the theory that the borrower should not receive credit for complying with the covenant unless the counterparty has sufficient substance to perform under the hedge agreement. Most agreements, however, simply rely upon the broad right of the administrative agent to approve the "manner" in which the hedging is effected. Presumably the agent could "reasonably" object to the "manner" of the borrower's hedging arrangements if the borrower's hedge counterparty is Joe's Diner around the corner.

7.5.7 Pari Passu *Ranking*

> **Box 7.32**
>
> The Borrower will promptly take all actions as may be necessary to ensure that the payment obligations of the Borrower hereunder and under the Notes will at all times constitute unsubordinated general obligations of the Borrower ranking at least *pari passu* with all other present and future unsecured and unsubordinated Debt of the Borrower.

The *pari passu* covenant addresses the concerns outlined in Section 6.4.2. As described there, the provision is almost exclusively seen in agreements for a non-U.S. borrower and has the latter undertake to keep the claims of the lenders under the credit agreement at an equal rank with the claims of other unsecured and unsubordinated debt.

7.5.8 *Further Assurances*

> **Box 7.33**
>
> (a) *Further Assurances.* The Borrower will, and will cause each Subsidiary to, promptly upon request by the Administrative Agent (a) correct any material defect or error that may be discovered in any Loan Document or in the execution, acknowledgment, filing, or recordation thereof and (b) do, execute, acknowledge, deliver, record, re-record, file, re-file, register, and re-register any and all such further acts, deeds, certificates, assurances, and other instruments as the Administrative Agent may reasonably require from time to time in order to (i) carry out more effectively the purposes of the Loan Documents; (ii) to the fullest extent permitted by applicable law, subject any Loan Party's properties, assets, rights, or interests to the Liens now or hereafter intended to be covered by any of the Security Documents; (iii) perfect and maintain the validity, effectiveness, and priority of any of the Security Documents and any of the Liens intended to be created thereunder; and (iv) assure, convey, grant, assign, transfer, preserve, protect, and confirm more effectively unto the Administrative Agent and the Lenders the rights granted or now or hereafter intended to be granted to the Administrative Agent and the Lenders under any Loan Document or under any other instrument

executed in connection with any Loan Document to which any Loan Party is or is to be a party.

(b) *Annual Certificates.* The Borrower will furnish to the Administrative Agent on [May 15] in each year beginning with [May 15], 20___, a certificate of a senior officer [together with an opinion of counsel, each] dated as of such date stating that (x) all action has been taken with respect to the recording, registering, filing, re-recording, re-registering, and re-filing of all financing statements, continuation statements, or other instruments of further assurance as is necessary to maintain and perfect the Lien of the Security Documents and reciting with respect to the security interests in the Collateral the details of such action, and (y) based on relevant laws as in effect on the date of such certificate [and opinion], all financing statements and continuation statements have been executed and filed that are necessary as of such date and during the succeeding 12 months fully to preserve, perfect, and protect, to the extent such protection and preservation are possible by filing, the rights of the Administrative Agent and the Lenders hereunder and under the Security Documents with respect to the security interests in the Collateral.

The further assurances covenant is most often seen in security documents themselves as an undertaking on the part of the grantor of a lien to execute additional agreements and take other actions in order that the lenders have a good lien on the collateral intended to be covered. In that context, the covenant applies only to property that is specified as "collateral" in the relevant security document. The security document typically also contains a power of attorney in favor of the administrative agent (or collateral agent) that authorizes it to take any action that the grantor fails to take to perfect the lien on the intended collateral.

In addition to whatever further assurances provisions are set out in the security documents, secured credit agreements normally also include a further assurances covenant. It is normally more expansive than the corresponding security agreement provision because it sets out overarching rules (subject to negotiated exceptions and thresholds) that govern what entities are to guarantee the loans and what types of property are to constitute collateral. The covenant prescribes which subsidiaries (including new subsidiaries) are to become guarantors, and what additional or future actions the borrower must take to continue the perfected status and priority of liens that secure the credit facility. Depending upon the scope of the collateral security that is to secure the facility, if a new subsidiary is formed, the borrower is required to deliver the stock certificates representing the borrower's equity interest in the subsidiary. If a new parcel of real estate is acquired, the borrower is required to slap a mortgage on it. If a UCC financing statement is about to expire, the borrower is required to file a continuation statement. (Of course, in most cases, the administrative agent has a tickler system to catch expiring financing statements; nevertheless, the further assurances clause squarely imposes responsibility for continuation upon the borrower.) In some agreements the covenant is self-operative; in others the borrower is obligated to take action only if *requested* by the administrative agent.

In many cases the further assurances clause does not just state a broad general principle with respect to maintaining the perfection and proper priority of collateral (such as in the example in Box 7.33), but in addition lays out in detail actions that the borrower must take with respect to a host of matters—new subsidiaries, additional real estate, new deposit accounts—and requires delivery of corporate resolutions (if necessary), opinions of counsel, title policies, and the like. The level of detail depends in large part upon the creditworthiness of the borrower and the negotiation between the parties.

In some cases, credit agreements adopt an approach used in secured bond indentures by requiring that the borrower deliver an annual certificate (sometimes accompanied by an opinion of counsel) to the administrative agent to confirm that all actions necessary to continue the perfection of liens have been taken. Although seemingly logical, the covenant is still relatively rare in the credit agreement context because of the difference in role between an administrative agent and an indenture trustee. A trustee is much more passive than an administrative agent (which is normally the same institution as the lead lender under the facility). A trustee does not necessarily even meet borrower personnel (and almost certainly does not visit the borrower or, absent a default, follow business developments that relate to the borrower). A trustee, therefore, wants the bond issuer to tell it, in writing, what needs to be done to continue the perfection of liens. Annual certificates and reports are the result. An administrative agent, in contrast, seeks to stay abreast of what is happening at the borrower (if for no other reason than to be alert to new business opportunities). It will feel less need to receive formal periodic lien updates. And even though the credit agreement is explicit that an administrative agent is not required to monitor the borrower, including to supervise the perfection of the liens securing the facility (see Section 10.1), as a practical matter the agent, in consultation with its counsel, almost always watches the status of liens. For these reasons (and the fact that borrowers resist strenuously being obligated in this regard), it is generally not market practice for credit agreements to require annual certificates and opinions.

To state perhaps the obvious, a further assurances clause does not guarantee that the lenders have a perfected lien, but only that the borrower must take whatever action can be "reasonably required" to perfect the lien. If the local jurisdiction in which property is located does not permit perfection (in some foreign countries, for example, a lien on certain types of property is simply not provided for), the borrower would not be in default if it fails to deliver a valid lien. This principle is cogently illustrated by *Flag Telecom Holdings Ltd. v. Flag Telecom Group, Ltd.*, 337 B.R. 15 (S.D.N.Y. 2005). There, the borrower was held not to be in default of a further assurances clause in favor of a French lender even though it did not perfect the security agreement under Taiwanese law, because Taiwanese law (as admitted by all parties) simply did not allow perfection of a lien in favor of secured parties that were not "locally based."

7.6 NEGATIVE COVENANTS

Negative covenants tell the borrower what it may not do. Lenders, by definition conservative, press to curb risky activity by their borrowers—at least for highly leveraged borrowers—so the range of negative covenants is limited only by the imagination of dealmakers. Set out below are a variety of negative covenants most often inserted into credit agreements.

It is useful, perhaps, at the outset to illuminate a distinction between so-called *incurrence* tests and *maintenance* tests as used in negative covenants. The basic distinction is that an incurrence test is a one-time restriction, while a maintenance test is a continual or periodic restriction. A debt covenant that is an incurrence test might state that a company is prohibited from borrowing or issuing debt securities if, after giving effect thereto, the ratio of debt to EBITDA exceeds 5.00 to 1. Within that constraint, the company can take on debt without limit. But if it borrows up to the maximum permitted amount and in subsequent fiscal periods EBITDA declines sharply, so that the new ratio is 20.00 to 1, it would not be in default; the covenant is tested only when new debt is taken on (incurred) and not continually.

Stated another way, in an incurrence covenant, satisfaction of the financial test (usually the ratio of debt to EBITDA) is a condition precedent to borrowings not already permitted by specific exception, but it is not an ongoing covenant. The borrower is in default of an incurrence test only if it causes a breach of that test through a prohibited borrowing, and not solely by reason of a fall in EBITDA (if the debt amount remains constant). Satisfaction of the incurrence test is usually also a condition precedent to other actions—for example, one of the conditions precedent to paying a dividend may be the borrower's ability to borrow an additional $1 under the incurrence test. It is easy to see why a borrower prefers an incurrence test to a maintenance test, since it cannot run afoul of an incurrence test except by voluntary action.

By contrast, a maintenance covenant would mandate that the ratio of debt to EBITDA be *maintained* so that it never exceeds an agreed level. If EBITDA plummets the borrower would be in default regardless of whether this is the result of a voluntary action on its part. For example, if EBITDA was a component of a maintenance test, a fall in EBITDA for any reason (whether or not within the control of the borrower) could cause the financial covenant to be breached. As this illustration makes clear, financial covenants are by definition maintenance tests since they require the borrower to remain continually in compliance with the stipulated performance levels. Most negative covenants are also maintenance tests since they operate to limit continually the borrower's activities, such as liens, debt, investments, transactions with affiliates, and so forth. An exception to this might be the dividend covenant which, if it allows dividends at all, often limits it to some percentage of EBITDA, net worth, or another credit metric: once the dividends have been paid the covenant will not be breached if the EBITDA, net worth, or other metric subsequently declines.

Historically, a key differentiator between loans and bonds was the frequency with which incurrence covenants appeared in the latter (and were not used in the former). This historic difference has been obliterated in recent years, especially in the case of leveraged loans, where bond-style incurrence tests have widely replaced maintenance covenants. See the discussion of covenant lite loans at the end of this section.

One final introductory point on negative covenants is on the topic of covenant "baskets." As a drafting matter, negative covenants are intentionally formulated to embody sweeping prohibitions on certain categories of borrower behavior. While creditors know the broad types of borrower behavior that can hurt the creditworthiness and, ultimately, the value of their investment, no lender can predict borrower behavior and the various creative ways that equity holder and competing creditor interests may be benefited to the detriment of lenders. The expansive drafting approach provides the most efficient prophylactic to this lender conundrum. However, if there are no exceptions to such a broad negative covenant, no borrower could run its business. Too much of its daily activity would likely be swept up in the negative covenant net. This is where express exceptions to a broad negative covenant, or "baskets," enter the picture.

Baskets may be the most heavily negotiated aspects of a credit agreement. Baskets come in various shapes and sizes. A taxonomy of baskets would include those designed to allow for ordinary course activities (e.g., debt in the form of customary trade payables), de minimis activities that may or not qualify as ordinary course (e.g., minor liens or encumbrances) as well as more material transactions that are conducive to the borrower hitting its business plan (e.g., making permitted acquisitions within its industry, selling material assets and other divestitures, etc.). This last category of baskets is generally subject to some cap or other type of governor. A cap of a fixed dollar amount is a "hard cap" or "dollar" basket while a cap based on a percentage of some variable (e.g., a percentage of total assets, consolidated net income, or other variable) is a "grower" basket or "soft cap" while a basket that is sized by a percentage of cumulative consolidated net income or the borrower's cumulative excess cash flow that is retained by the borrower is referred to as a "builder basket" as it literally builds in size as the borrower's cumulative consolidated net income or retained excess cash increases over time. Below are a description of several common baskets that appear in negative covenants.

7.6.1 Lien Covenant

Box 7.34

The Borrower will not, and will not permit any Subsidiary to, create, incur, assume, or permit to exist any Lien on any property or asset now owned or hereafter acquired by it, or assign or sell any income or revenues (including accounts receivable) or rights in respect of any thereof, except:

(a) Liens securing obligations of the Borrower and its Subsidiaries in respect of the Loans;

(b) any Lien on any property or asset of the Borrower or any Subsidiary existing on the date hereof and set forth in Schedule ___; *provided* that (i) such Lien shall not apply to any other property or asset of the Borrower or any Subsidiary, (ii) such Lien shall secure only those obligations which it secures on the date hereof [and extensions, renewals, and replacements thereof that do not increase the outstanding principal amount thereof], and (iii) any Lien securing Debt that is to be repaid on the Closing Date shall be concurrently released;

(c) Permitted Encumbrances;

(d) Liens on fixed or capital assets acquired, constructed, or improved by the Borrower or any Subsidiary; *provided* that (i) such Liens secure Debt permitted by Section [*purchase money debt basket*]; (ii) such Liens and the Debt secured thereby are incurred prior to or within [90] days after such acquisition or the completion of such construction or improvement; (iii) the Debt secured thereby does not exceed [__]% of the cost of acquiring, constructing, or improving such fixed or capital assets; and (iv) such Liens shall not apply to any other property or assets of the Borrower or any Subsidiary;

(e) any Lien existing on any property prior to the acquisition thereof by the Borrower or any Subsidiary or existing on any property of any Person that becomes a Subsidiary after the date hereof prior to the time such Person becomes a Subsidiary; *provided* that (i) such Lien is not created in contemplation of or in connection with such acquisition or such Person becoming a Subsidiary, (ii) such Lien shall not apply to any other property of the Borrower or any Subsidiary, and (iii) such Lien shall secure only those obligations that it secures on the date of such acquisition or the date such Person becomes a Subsidiary, as the case may be [and extensions, renewals, and replacements thereof that do not increase the outstanding principal amount thereof]; and

(f) other Liens securing Debt in an aggregate amount not exceeding $_____.

* * * * * * * * * * * *

"*Lien*" means any mortgage, pledge, hypothecation, assignment, deposit arrangement, encumbrance, lien (statutory or other), charge, or preference, priority or other security interest, or any other type of preferential arrangement in the nature of a security interest of any kind or nature whatsoever (including any conditional sale or other title retention agreement, any easement, right of way or other encumbrance on title to real property, and any financing lease having substantially the same economic effect as any of the foregoing) and, in the case of securities, any purchase option, call, or similar right of a third party with respect to such securities.

The lien covenant (sometimes referred to as a "negative pledge") restricts the borrower's granting of security interests and other encumbrances. Its main purpose is to limit both the number of creditors and amount of competing claims that will enjoy a preferential status in a bankruptcy or insolvency of the borrower. Secured creditors are entitled to be paid the entire proceeds or value of the property in which they have a lien before any junior or unsecured creditors or equity holders can share in the proceeds or value. In addition, secured creditors normally vote as a separate class in a bankruptcy and so can have significant bargaining leverage over unsecured creditors.

The term "lien" is typically defined expansively to include all manner of liens, charges, encumbrances, pledges, security interests, and the like, whether consensual or nonconsensual, statutory, or contractual. The term also typically includes the interest of a lessee under a lease, a licensee under a license, and a vendor in a conditional sale. The definition also customarily encompasses "any other type of preferential arrangement," language that is intended to capture the circumstance in which, without granting a lien, the borrower attempts to prefer one creditor over another. An example of the latter is the practice (not infrequent in international trade or project financings) whereby a borrower might agree to set aside or designate certain revenues for the benefit of particular lenders without actually granting a security interest in them. See the complaint in *Citibank, N.A. v. Export-Import Bank*, No. 76 Civ. 3514 (CBM) (S.D.N.Y. filed August 9, 1976) in which the absence of this language led to litigation over whether a contractual dedication of revenues (through a requirement that all export proceeds be deposited into a special account maintained with a group of new lenders) would breach either a negative pledge or *pari passu* clause; the suit was settled before any decision on the point was rendered. Lastly, the term may include, in the case of securities or other assets, put and call options and other similar arrangements in favor of third parties.

With liens defined so broadly, it naturally follows that for the lien covenant to be workable it must contain numerous exceptions. These include, among others, those described in Sections 7.6.1.1 to 7.6.1.8 (see the sample language in Box 7.34).

7.6.1.1 Lender Liens

These are liens in favor of the lenders. In most cases, this exception automatically includes liens that secure increases under the credit agreement, even though not stated, as well as refinancings of credit agreement debt.

7.6.1.2 Grandfathered Liens

So-called "grandfathered" liens are liens in existence on the closing date (normally listed in a disclosure schedule if they exceed a dollar threshold). The agreement may permit these liens to be "extended, renewed, or refinanced," though it typically bars spreading the affected lien to cover new property. Liens that secure debt to be repaid on the closing date are required to be released on the closing date. See the discussion regarding the related closing condition in Section 5.1.10.

7.6.1.3 Permitted Encumbrances

"*Permitted encumbrances*" are usually defined to sweep up a wide variety of liens that any business enterprise cannot avoid incurring in the ordinary course of business, such as easements and rights of way; certain nonconsensual statutory liens like warehouse liens, workers' compensation liens, and mechanics' liens; utility pledges; rights of offset; and the like. Given the breadth of the lien definition, permitted encumbrances also include zoning rules and other restrictions upon the use of property. Inchoate tax liens may also be permitted if the tax is not yet due or is being contested in good faith by the borrower, consistent with the affirmative covenant to that effect (see the discussion in Section 7.5.4.5).

7.6.1.4 Purchase Money Liens

Purchase money liens cover property that secures financing for the purchase, construction, or improvement of the property. The lien could be in favor of the seller of the property or in favor of a bank that supplies funds to enable the property to be purchased. Typically, the lien is not allowed to exceed the cost of the property (or sometimes a percentage of the cost) and must be incurred within some short period (say, 90 days) of the property's acquisition. In addition, to qualify as a purchase money lien, the underlying obligation may not be secured by any other property of the borrower. Purchase money liens do not include liens in existence on the property at the time it was acquired; those liens need to fit into the acquisition lien basket, discussed next.

7.6.1.5 Acquisition Liens

Acquisition liens are in existence on property (or on property of a subsidiary) at the time the property (or subsidiary) is acquired. Liens created in anticipation of the acquisition do not qualify. As with purchase money liens, acquisition liens are not allowed to spread to any other property of the borrower.

7.6.1.6 Secured Debt Liens

While the liens permitted under the foregoing exceptions may secure obligations that constitute either debt or nondebt obligations, this basket is focused on debt obligations by providing certain specified categories of debt permitted under the debt covenant to be secured.

Since secured debt is generally the cheapest form of debt, borrowers will expect to rely on these baskets for cost-efficient debt raises while lenders will of course want to balance against substantial dilutions to their secured position. The amount of debt that can be so secured will typically be subject to a cap set forth in the applicable debt covenant. With competing secured creditors sharing in the collateral, lenders may require the entry of such new secured creditors into satisfactory inter-creditor agreements as a condition to the incurrence of secured debt under this basket.

7.6.1.7 Non-guarantor Liens

Non-guarantor liens generally refer to liens on assets of non-guarantor subsidiaries (i.e., subsidiaries that do not guarantee the debt under the credit agreement) securing the debt of such subsidiaries. The debt of such non-guarantors is already structurally senior to debt under the credit agreement and related guaranty obligations. The ability to "lien up" non-guarantor assets only permits the incurrence of cheaper secured debt while pushing the credit agreement debt further down in priority with respect to proceeds from such encumbered non-guarantor assets.

7.6.1.8 General Lien Basket

This lien basket refers to additional liens permitted without restriction up to a negotiated dollar threshold or some other negotiated limitation. This exception is included in many, though not all, credit agreements. To the extent a borrower may need to provide cash to cover hedging obligations that are "out of the money," it looks to the lien basket (unless, of course, it has a hedging exception). There is, therefore, pressure in many credit agreement negotiations to allow the borrower some flexibility on this score.

7.6.2 Equal and Ratable Sharing Clause

Box 7.35

The Borrower will not itself, and will not permit any Domestic Subsidiary to, incur, issue, assume, or guarantee any Debt secured by any Lien on any Principal Property, or any shares of stock of or Debt of any Domestic Subsidiary, without effectively providing that all amounts payable by the Borrower to the Lenders hereunder (together with, if the Borrower shall so determine, any other Debt of the Borrower or such

Domestic Subsidiary then existing or thereafter created which is not subordinate to the payment of principal of, and interest on the Loans), and all other amounts payable by the Borrower to the Lenders hereunder shall be secured equally and ratably with (or prior to) such secured Debt, so long as such secured Debt shall be so secured, unless after giving effect thereto, the aggregate amount of all such secured Debt plus all Attributable Debt of the Borrower and its Domestic Subsidiaries in respect of Sale and Leaseback Transactions would not exceed ___% of the Consolidated Net Tangible Assets; *provided* that this Section shall not apply to, and there shall be excluded from secured Debt in any computation under this Section, Debt secured by the following: _____.

The lien covenant described in Section 7.6.1 is normally seen in credit agreements. In the context of certain bond indentures and private placements (and, as a consequence, in credit agreements for those same companies for which the business understanding is that the credit agreement covenants replicate the corresponding provisions in the indenture or private placement), the lien covenant may take a different approach. Rather than prohibiting liens directly, as does the lien covenant seen in credit agreements, it simply provides that if liens (subject to listed exceptions) are granted by the borrower to a third party the lenders must be "equally and ratably" secured. This is the so-called equal and ratable sharing clause (although many commentators loosely refer to the clause also as a "negative pledge"). An example is in Box 7.35.

Although often viewed as a substitute for a negative pledge, the typical sharing clause in a bond indenture in fact has a much narrower scope. A negative pledge normally applies to *all* assets of the borrower and its subsidiaries. In contrast, a bond indenture's equal and ratable sharing clause customarily applies only to the borrower and its *domestic* subsidiaries, and to "principal properties" or stock and debt of domestic subsidiaries. Principal properties, depending upon the borrower's industry, as a rule only encompass fixed assets (such as major manufacturing facilities, mines or land, and, perhaps, related equipment) located in the United States that are either designated by the board as material or that have a value in excess of some percentage (1 percent or 2 percent are often seen) of the borrower's consolidated net tangible assets. Importantly, most equal and ratable sharing clauses in bond indentures do not apply to inventory, receivables, or intellectual property, or to properties located outside the United States, or to stock of non-U.S. subsidiaries. That lenders (or third parties) are free to take liens on those assets without having to enter into sharing arrangements aptly illustrates the weakness of equal and ratable sharing clauses when compared to a negative pledge.

The exceptions incorporated into the typical equal and ratable sharing clause are much like those described in the lien covenant above: grandfathered liens, permitted encumbrances, purchase money liens, acquisition liens, and basket liens. The one major difference from the lien covenant is that the equal and ratable sharing clause normally couches the basket in terms of a percentage (5 percent to 15 percent are customary) of the consolidated net tangible assets of the borrower. The basket consequently grows as the borrower grows. Many lending syndicates when granted security structure the facility to take full advantage of the indenture's lien basket. The credit facility might be secured by two separate liens taken under two separate sets of security documents, the first of which secures *only* the lenders in an amount up to the basket and the second of which (junior to the first) secures the lenders and the target debt equally and ratably. The lenders thus have first crack at the value of the pledged property and, only after they are paid in full, or the dollar proceeds reach the basket limit, does the indenture debt begin to share.

In the private placement world the equal and ratable sharing clause was historically used in conjunction with a lien covenant. The combined covenant would prohibit liens (usually covering all property, and not just principal properties or stock and debt of subsidiaries), but go on to say that if the borrower or issuer granted a prohibited lien to a third party, the forbidden lien must nevertheless equally and ratably secure the private placement. Sometimes the equal and ratable language would purport to be self-operative; in other words even if the borrower did not grant the equal and ratable lien it would be deemed to have been granted. The obvious question is what would such a compound covenant mean if incorporated into a credit agreement? Probably not much beyond giving the lenders two defaults instead of one. The only possible advantage to including the equal and ratable sharing provision at the end of the lien covenant may be to give the lenders an equitable argument in the borrower's bankruptcy that they are entitled to share in the offending lien even though the lien documents do not provide for the lenders to be secured. This benefit is ephemeral at best and likely explains why the standard lien covenant in credit agreements (and in most private placements today) does not include an equal and ratable sharing tag-on.

Few cases address how an equal and ratable sharing clause should be implemented once a borrower determines to grant security that triggers the clause. The rare court decisions that have addressed the issue focus on more basic concerns. *Kaplan v. Chase Nat'l Bank*, 281 N.Y.S. 825 (Sup. Ct. N.Y. County 1934) ruled that an indenture trustee could be held liable if, on the nontrust side of the institution, secured loans were made in a manner that violated a sharing clause set out in the indenture. *In re Associated Gas & Electric Co.*, 61 F. Supp. 11 (S.D.N.Y. 1944) and *Conn. Co. v. New York, N.H. & H.R. Co.*, 107 A. 646 (Conn. 1919) held that a corporation cannot avoid the clause by first transferring assets to a subsidiary and then having the subsidiary grant the lien. And in *Conn. Light & Power Co. v. Deering*, 7 A.2d 924 (Conn. 1939), the court held that the clause does not impose an equitable lien prior to the grant of an actual lien. In the absent of clear case-law, drafters are forced to rely upon unwritten lore for guidance.

Precisely how a group of lenders should take liens that will equally and ratably secure a group of bonds or notes is not an idle question for lending syndicates. Since securing a credit agreement is most frequently the event that triggers an equal and ratable sharing clause, implementing the clause is typically the responsibility (or headache) of the lenders. A number of issues arise and are normally handled as described in Sections 7.6.2.1 to 7.6.2.4.

7.6.2.1 Documentation Issues

The threshold question, when the borrower and the syndicate determine to secure the credit agreement, is whether the target debt (bondholders or note holders that are the beneficiaries of the clause) should participate in deciding how to put into effect the sharing clause. The short answer is no, unless the clause itself expressly grants the target debt holders the right to participate. There is both a practical and legal rationale for this and, as a consequence, in the normal case the beneficiaries of the clause are not even notified that security has been taken until after the fact.

The practical reason for not involving the bondholders (or, more accurately, the trustee for the bondholders) and note holders is that, unless they have been educated as to the reason to take collateral (and are *compensated* for the time involved in coming up to speed on the proposed security arrangements), they often have little interest in cooperating with the documentation process. Disinterest can, in turn, frequently upset the time frame for the borrower and the syndicate in granting security. Even beyond this, to ask a trustee to approve the implementation inevitably leads to fewer lender rights than remaining silent and so, out of self-interest, it is better for the lending syndicate to draft alone.

The legal reason not to involve the beneficiaries of the clause derives from the way the typical clause is drafted. Customarily, it only requires equal and ratable sharing *if* a lien is granted. Most practitioners construe this language to require nothing more than to deliver the trustee or note holders a copy of the security documents *after* they have been executed and not to ask them (or the trustee) to consent to the form of the lien documentation. Not being required to involve the target debt, the lenders choose to ignore them.

Only in the private placement world is it customary for the clause to accord the note holders the right to participate in the drafting (the usual language states that the note holders must be equally and ratably secured "in a manner satisfactory" to them). And, given this language, private placement note holders almost always insist that an intercreditor agreement be executed with the lenders (or the administrative agent) that grants them voting rights with respect to any of the actions discussed below. As a consequence, the issues described in the succeeding sections are effectively relevant only in the bond context; in the private placement context the note holders generally have control rights equivalent to that of the lenders with respect to the actions described.

7.6.2.2 Sharing Rights

As its moniker indicates, under the sharing clause collateral is to be shared *equally and ratably*. In this context, "equal" is generally understood to mean that the lien granted to the target debt must be equal in rank to that granted to the triggering debt (the credit agreement). "Ratable" means that the benefits of the collateral (the proceeds) are applied proportionately to the secured parties. At a minimum, this means that proceeds must be shared among the parties secured in accordance with the amounts then due, although it is customary to allow expenses of foreclosure and the like by the collateral agent to be paid off the top. More difficult questions arise if one of the secured groups (say, the bondholders) has not accelerated its debt while the other (say, the lenders) has declared all of the loans due. Some agreements specify that in this situation the money that would otherwise have been paid to the bondholders must be set aside or delivered to the indenture trustee to be held as security for the bonds. Others simply stipulate that available funds are allocated in accordance with what is at the time actually payable. The latter approach appeals to both borrower and lenders since neither likes to provide for money to be segregated and not immediately applied to payment. For a borrower, segregation results in negative arbitrage (earnings on the cash collateral will almost certainly be lower than interest on the bonds). For the lenders, they have a general aversion to seeing cash not reduce debt, even if it is not their own.

Another difficult issue arises with respect to sales by the borrower of collateral other than in a foreclosure or default context. Frequently, when the lending syndicate is secured it will have provided for mandatory prepayments to be made from the proceeds of asset sales. If the transaction is highly leveraged, the borrower may even have covenanted to sell assets within some relatively short period of time (12 to 18 months) and to apply the proceeds to repay the credit agreement. Will application of the proceeds of such sales (assuming they constitute collateral) run afoul of the equal and ratable concept? The interpretation most often applied is that nothing in the words "equal and ratable" requires sharing of asset sale proceeds in a nonforeclosure context. Consistent with the theory (described in the next sections) that the beneficiaries of the clause do not have a right to consent to releases of collateral (unless the borrower is in bankruptcy), it follows that asset sale proceeds outside of a bankruptcy can be allocated solely to the lenders. Stated another way, given that the lenders have exclusive release rights (see Section 7.6.2.3), they are free to release from the shared lien any property immediately prior to its sale. Once released, they should be free to stipulate that when it is sold the proceeds pay down their loans.

7.6.2.3 Voting Rights

A third key issue is the degree to which the beneficiaries of the clause are accorded voting rights on matters that affect the collateral. Secondarily, to the extent voting rights are given to the beneficiaries, how should they be structured (implementation agreements are not consistent on this)? Do the beneficiaries and the lenders each vote as separate groups, or do they vote together as one happy (or distraught) pool of creditors? And how expansive are the voting rights? Do the beneficiaries have the right to approve releases of collateral or the termination in whole of the liens? Do the beneficiaries have the right to consent to sales of collateral? What about decisions as to whether to foreclose on collateral? Or, once foreclosure starts, do they participate in the instructions given to the collateral agent (should the collateral agent foreclose first on subsidiary stock, or the borrower's bottleneck factory in Owaskaloosa)?

The customary answer to these questions, at least in the bond indenture context, is that the lending syndicate gives the bondholders as few consent rights as possible consistent with the obligation to share collateral (and proceeds). The words "equal and ratable," after all, only speak to liens and do not speak to the bondholders having approval rights over matters that relate to the collateral. (In this connection, the fact that most private placement documents explicitly grant the note holders participation rights over the documents that implement the clause only bolsters the argument that, if bondholders were to have rights beyond just sharing the lien, indentures would so provide.) Consequently, bondholder voting rights are normally conditioned upon the occurrence of some drastic triggering event, such as bankruptcy, acceleration by one or both of the secured groups, or specified events of default. Prior to a triggering event, most agreements will accord full control to the lending syndicate.

In re Solutia Inc., 379 B.R. 473 (Bankr. S.D.N.Y. 2007) is one of the rare instances in which a court has addressed how an equal and ratable sharing clause should be implemented. In that decision, the court approved a mechanism that allowed lenders (without the concurrence of bondholders) to terminate entirely the equal and ratable liens, so long as no triggering event (in *Solutia*, bankruptcy or the occurrence of any default under the indenture) existed. The court's ruling is particularly supportive of lending syndicate control over collateral in the absence of a triggering event. In *Solutia*, the lenders had initially provided for the equal and ratable sharing of liens with bondholders because the aggregate of the loans exceeded the relevant basket (15 percent of consolidated net tangible assets). Once the aggregate of the loans fell below 15 percent, the loans were refinanced and the equal and ratable liens were released with new, lender-only liens taken on much of the same collateral. Suit was commenced when, shortly after the release, Solutia filed for bankruptcy and the bondholders discovered they were unsecured.

7.6.2.4 Collateral Agent

Although not strictly an implementation issue, any administrative agent for a lending syndicate that wants to take liens shared with another group of debt holders faces the question of who should hold the collateral. The easy, tempting answer is that the liens should be granted to the administrative agent for the benefit of everyone. That, after all, puts the lending syndicate into the driving seat when defaults start to occur and, even once voting control shifts to both groups (upon a bankruptcy or foreclosure), the administrative agent makes discretionary decisions as to how to foreclose.

The simple answer, however, is not the structure normally employed. Most administrative agents are reluctant to assume the additional role of collateral agent because they then owe a duty to two sets of creditors with (potentially) inconsistent interests. Although inherently there is nothing wrong with this, an administrative agent for a lending syndicate that is also a collateral agent for the syndicate and a group of bondholders or note holders could be accused of having a conflict of interest. The tag-along debt may second-guess (and even commence litigation over) every decision made by the collateral agent. Was the decision to foreclose first on the bottleneck factory really in the interests of all secured parties, or just of the lenders? The note holders may take the longer view and want to wait out financial difficulties rather than commence an early exercise of remedies and, inevitably, force the borrower into bankruptcy. As a consequence, equal and ratable liens for two potentially conflicting creditor groups are normally granted to an independent collateral agent or trustee.

7.6.3 Negative Negative Pledge or Burdensome Agreements

> **Box 7.36**
>
> The Borrower will not, and will not permit any Subsidiary to, directly or indirectly, enter into, incur or permit to exist any agreement or other arrangement that prohibits, restricts, or imposes any condition upon the ability of the Borrower or any Subsidiary to create, incur or permit to exist any Lien upon any of its property or assets, except to the extent:
>
> (a) existing on the date hereof identified in Schedule ___ [and extensions, renewals and replacements thereof that do not expand the scope thereof];
>
> (b) consisting of customary provisions in leases and other contracts restricting the assignment thereof;
>
> (c) imposed by any agreement relating to secured Debt permitted by this Agreement if such restrictions or conditions apply only to the property or assets securing such Indebtedness; and
>
> (d) consisting of customary restrictions and conditions contained in agreements relating to the sale of a Subsidiary or property pending such sale, provided such restrictions and conditions apply only to the Subsidiary or property that is to be sold, and such sale is permitted hereunder.

A negative pledge, as described previously, limits the ability of the borrower to grant liens on its assets. A "negative negative pledge" or what is frequently referred to as a "burdensome agreements" or "limitation on burdensome agreements" provision, takes this one step further and limits the ability of a borrower to enter into negative pledges with third parties. If an agreement has a negative negative pledge, the borrower is prohibited from agreeing with a third party that its ability to grant liens will be constrained. A negative negative pledge, depending upon how it is written, also normally sweeps in an equal and ratable sharing clause. In the illustration in Box 7.36, the latter is barred by the requirement that the borrower not impose any "condition" upon its granting liens.

The principal reason why the lending syndicate wants a negative negative pledge is to ensure that the borrower is free to grant security to the syndicate in the future without having to obtain consent from any third party. This is the case even if the lenders at the outset are fully secured by all of the assets of the borrower. They do not want the borrower constrained in any way to grant additional liens on newly acquired assets, or to comply with its further assurance obligations in respect of liens already granted.

Since a borrower can be expected to be subject to many lien restrictions in the ordinary course of its business, a negative negative pledge covenant normally contemplates a long list of exclusions. Many of the same exceptions seen in the negative pledge or debt covenants are customary in the negative negative pledge, and include, among others those described in Sections 7.6.3.1 to 7.6.3.4.

7.6.3.1 Grandfathered Restrictions

These are preexisting limitations that are normally set forth in a schedule. Since the borrower may already be subject to restrictions on granting liens by reason of other outstanding debt instruments, there is nothing (short of requiring the borrower to repay the related debt) that can be done to eliminate the need for a schedule. The restrictions will, accordingly, be grandfathered and listed in a schedule attached to the credit agreement.

7.6.3.2 Boilerplate Restrictions

These refer to restrictions included as part of the so-called boilerplate in many contracts. Often agreements contain restrictions upon assignment (which could restrict the granting of liens on rights that the borrower has under the contract) and many leases prohibit the tenant from granting liens on its rights under the lease and on any property subject to the lease. These restrictions cannot as a practical matter be waived (or easily listed on a schedule as grandfathered restrictions—they are simply too numerous) and so are usually entitled to a separate exclusion.

7.6.3.3 Secured Debt Restrictions

These are restrictions associated with liens and debt permitted under the credit agreement. Any security agreement, mortgage, or similar lien document that places a lien upon property of the borrower as well as any debt instrument of such borrower virtually always also limits liens (even if junior) on the same property. For the borrower to have the flexibility, therefore, to use the exceptions it has negotiated in the lien and debt covenants, it must be free to agree not to grant liens upon the collateral security that use those exceptions.

7.6.3.4 Sale Restrictions

Sale restrictions are often imposed in connection with a sale of a subsidiary or property. If the borrower enters into a contract to sell a subsidiary or division (or even a particular piece of property), the sale agreement likely provides that, pending closing of the sale, the borrower may not grant a lien upon the subsidiary (including its stock or assets) or the division or property to be sold. For the borrower, therefore, to have the ability to enter into agreements to sell assets as permitted under the loan document it needs to have an exception to the negative negative pledge. Usually the exception requires that the sale of the subsidiary or property itself be permitted under the credit agreement.

7.6.4   Debt

Box 7.37

The Borrower will not, and will not permit any Subsidiary to, create, incur, assume, or permit to exist any Debt, except:

(a) Debt created hereunder;

(b) Debt existing on the date hereof and set forth in Schedule ___ [and extensions, renewals, and replacements thereof that do not increase the outstanding principal amount thereof];

(c) Debt of the Borrower to any Subsidiary and of any Subsidiary to the Borrower or any other Subsidiary;

(d) Debt of the Borrower or any Subsidiary incurred to finance the acquisition, construction, or improvement of any fixed or capital assets, including Capital Lease Obligations, and any Debt assumed in connection with the acquisition of any such assets or secured by a Lien on any such assets prior to the acquisition thereof; *provided* that (i) such Debt is incurred prior to or within [90] days after such acquisition or the completion of such construction or improvement and (ii) the aggregate principal amount of Debt permitted by this clause (d) shall not exceed $[_____] at any time outstanding;

(e) Debt of any Person that becomes a Subsidiary after the date hereof and [extensions, renewals, and replacements of any such Debt that do not increase the outstanding principal amount thereof];

provided that (i) such Debt exists at the time such Person becomes a Subsidiary and is not created in contemplation of or in connection with such Person becoming a Subsidiary and (ii) the aggregate principal amount of Debt permitted by this clause (e) shall not exceed $[_____] at any time outstanding; *provided, further,* that any such Debt of a Restricted Subsidiary that is not a Guarantor shall not exceed $[_____];

(f) Debt of Subsidiaries of the Borrower in an aggregate principal amount not exceeding $[_____] at any time outstanding;

(g) any other Debt; *provided* that the *[Financial Covenant]* shall not exceed [ ]:1.00, as of the last day of the most recently ended Test Period after giving pro forma effect to the incurrence of such Debt and the use of the proceeds thereof; *provided, further,* that any such Debt incurred by a Restricted Subsidiary that is not a Guarantor shall not exceed $[_____]; and

(h) other Debt in an aggregate principal amount not exceeding $[_____] at any time outstanding; *provided* that the aggregate principal amount of Debt of the Borrower's Subsidiaries permitted by this clause (h) shall not exceed $[_____] at any time outstanding.

The debt covenant restricts the incurrence by the borrower and its subsidiaries of "debt." As discussed in Section 7.3.2.1, *debt* may be defined expansively to capture not just balance-sheet debt, but a host of other obligations that under GAAP might be referenced only in footnotes. The objective of the covenant is to ensure that the borrower does not take on more liabilities than it can service given the cash being thrown off by its business. Customary exceptions in the covenant (corresponding to the somewhat simplified exclusions in Box 7.37) include those in Sections 7.6.4.1 to 7.6.4.7.

7.6.4.1 Lender Debt

This exclusion covers loans and letters of credit under the credit agreement. As with the parallel exception for liens that secure the credit agreement, this exception (although not written explicitly) includes any increases under the credit agreement as well as refinancings of like amounts of lender debt with new debt incurred under the credit agreement.

7.6.4.2 Grandfathered Debt

Debt in existence on the closing date that is to be permitted after the closing date will often be grandfathered by being listed in a disclosure schedule. Some agreements may alternatively permit all debt reflected on the base financial statements, though this may not be helpful to the borrower, since any debt incurred subsequent to the base financials and prior to the closing date would utilize the debt basket. Other agreements may permit any debt in existence on the date of the agreement, though this is not advisable from the lenders' standpoint since they will have grounded their credit judgment upon base financials that may not include all the debt being permitted by the exception.

As with the lien exclusion, the grandfathered debt exclusion normally permits extensions, renewals, and refinancings, though it also states that the principal amount of the debt that is extended, renewed, or refinanced may not be increased (other than for accrued interest and premiums). Any increase, therefore, forces usage of another basket. Absent an express reference, it is unclear that extensions, renewals, and refinancings would be allowed.

7.6.4.3 Intercompany Debt

This covers debt between and among the borrower and its subsidiaries. In some instances, the credit agreement provides that debt of the borrower to subsidiaries (as distinct from debt of subsidiaries to the borrower and intersubsidiary debt) must be subordinated to the claims of the lenders under the credit agreement. This is to prevent the subsidiaries (or, more importantly, creditors of any subsidiary that becomes insolvent) from competing with the lenders in obtaining payment of claims against the borrower.

7.6.4.4 Purchase Money Debt

Purchase money debt finances the purchase, construction, or improvement of property, whether in favor of the seller of property or in favor of a bank that supplies funds to enable the property to be purchased, constructed, or improved. Since this debt is normally secured by the underlying property, the exception may cross-reference the purchase money basket in the lien covenant. The debt must typically be incurred within some short period after the related purchase, construction, or improvement, so that it is notionally linked to the property.

7.6.4.5 Acquisition Debt

Acquisition debt exists at the time an entity becomes a subsidiary. As with acquisition liens, debt created in anticipation of the purchase does not qualify. As with grandfathered debt, extensions, renewals, and refinancings are normally allowed so long as the principal amount is not thereby increased. To limit the number and scope of non-guarantors that are acquired, agreements may impose caps on the amount of acquisition debt that may be incurred or assumed by non-guarantor subsidiaries as shown in clause (e) of Box 7.37.

7.6.4.6 Subsidiary Debt

In many cases the credit agreement limits the aggregate amount of third-party debt of subsidiaries to avoid so-called "structural subordination." The latter term arises out of the legal principle that, in a bankruptcy of a subsidiary, all claims against the subsidiary must be paid in full before any money may flow up to a shareholder (the borrower). If the credit facility is made available to the borrower without the benefit of subsidiary guarantees, those creditors will not include the syndicate and therefore, until all creditors of the subsidiary have been paid in full, no money can flow up from the subsidiaries to service the credit agreement. This is not significant if the borrower is itself a major operating company with only minor assets held by subsidiaries. But if the borrower is a holding company with all material assets, liabilities, and operations at the subsidiary level, then the lending syndicate, as against creditors of the subsidiaries, holds in essence the deepest of deeply subordinated debt (see the discussion on subordination generally in Section 6.5.2). Although in this circumstance there is no *contractual* subordination in the form of an agreement by the lenders that their debt is junior to that of the subsidiaries, there is nevertheless subordination by reason of the structure of the facility—*structural* subordination, in other words.

To ameliorate the impact of structural subordination, the credit agreement may either restrict debt at the subsidiary level entirely or, if any debt is permitted, severely constrain the amount that may be incurred. None of this helps with the subsidiary's trade liabilities (which it is normally not practicable to limit and as to which the lenders will remain structurally subordinate); the only way to avoid subordination to the latter is to require the subsidiaries to guarantee the credit facility so that the lenders are direct creditors of the subsidiaries.

7.6.4.7 Debt Basket and Ratio Debt Basket

As with the lien basket, this is a basket for debt that does not fit into any of the other listed exceptions. Sometimes the portion of the basket debt that may be utilized by subsidiaries is limited because of the structural subordination issues referred to in Section 7.6.4.6.

Clause (g) of Box 7.37 is a basic example of a "ratio debt" basket. Historically a bond indenture basket, keeping with the theme of convergence of bond-style and credit agreement covenants, ratio debt baskets have increasingly shown up in recent years in credit agreements.

The typical covenant is styled as an incurrence test requiring the pro forma satisfaction of a certain credit ratio as a condition to incurring debt under the basket. Structural subordination concerns may also lead to express limits on the ability of non-guarantor subsidiaries to incur ratio debt.

Occasionally the debt basket may split out additional public or quasi-public debt, such as a senior or subordinated high-yield bond. Normally debt of this type is subject to constraints as to aggregate amount, tenor (typically not earlier than 90 days after the maturity of the loans under the credit agreement), weighted average life to maturity (not earlier than that for the loans under the credit agreement), and redemption requirements and covenants. Sometimes the covenants must be approved by the required lenders, but more frequently the credit agreement simply mandates that they satisfy the market standard in effect at the time the debt is issued.

If the credit agreement does not itself provide for revolving credit loans that can meet the operating needs of the borrower, the debt basket is either pegged at a sufficient size to permit working capital debt to be incurred within the basket, or splits out a separate basket for working capital financing. Since working capital debt can often be short term or even payable on demand (and, therefore, in a stronger position to compete for the borrower's attentions than the lazy old five-year credit facility), the credit agreement may impose limitations on the amount of such short-term debt and the institutions from which it may be incurred.

7.6.5 Disqualified Stock

Box 7.38

"Disqualified Stock" means any capital stock or other ownership interest that, by its terms (or by the terms of any security into which it is convertible, or for which it is exchangeable, in each case at the option of the holder thereof), or upon the happening of any event, (a) matures or is mandatorily redeemable, pursuant to a sinking fund obligation or otherwise, or redeemable at the option of the holder thereof, in whole or in part, within [90] days of the maturity of the Loans; (b) is secured by any assets of the Borrower or any Subsidiary; (c) is exchangeable or convertible at the option of the holder into Debt of the Borrower or any Subsidiary; or (d) provides for the mandatory payment of dividends regardless of whether or not the board of directors has declared any dividends.

Notwithstanding the preceding sentence, any capital stock or other ownership interest that would constitute Disqualified Stock solely because the holders thereof have the right to require the Borrower to repurchase such capital stock or other ownership interest upon the occurrence of a change of control or an asset sale shall not constitute Disqualified Stock [if the terms of such capital stock or other ownership interest provide that the Borrower may not repurchase or redeem any such capital stock or other ownership interest pursuant to such provisions unless such repurchase or redemption complies with the provisions of Section [Dividends].

Although normally included as part of the debt definition (and, therefore, controlled through the debt covenant or leverage tests rather than a separate "disqualified stock" covenant), some credit agreements control the issuance of stock that contains debt-like provisions, or that is convertible into debt-like instruments at the option of the holder.

The obvious example of disqualified stock is a series of preferred stock that is entitled to mandatory redemption at a future specified date. Generally, if that date is within a defined period (typically 90 days or a year) *after* the maturity date for loans under the credit agreement, the lenders want to treat the preferred stock as equivalent to debt. The theory here is that if the stock needs to be paid so soon after the maturity of the loans themselves, it will effectively compete for the borrower's available funds at that time. The borrower might be forced into a more difficult refinancing upon the loan maturity (since the preferred stock would also need to be refinanced) making it less certain that the lenders will be paid in full in a timely fashion.

Disqualified stock also includes any equity security that requires the payment of mandatory dividends since any such instrument effectively acts as if it were interest-bearing debt. Failure to pay the dividends can either subject the borrower to suit (if the stock is truly debt-like) or to a change of control on its board of directors by giving the holders of the preferred stock the right to nominate additional members to represent the preferred. An equity security, even if it does not have these debt-like features, also constitutes "disqualified stock" if the holder, at its option, can convert the security into another instrument that is either debt itself or that has debt-like terms, or if the preferred stock has mandatory redemption features. The one exception to the rule against mandatory redemption is for changes of control or asset sales (see the second paragraph in the definition in Box 7.38) if the terms of the preferred stock explicitly provide that it may not be redeemed except in compliance with the credit agreement's dividend covenant.

7.6.6 Fundamental Changes, Asset Sales, and Acquisitions

The objective of each of the fundamental changes covenant, asset sale covenant, and permitted acquisition covenant is to prevent transactions that would change in a fundamental way the business or assets of the borrower upon which the lenders' initial credit decisions were made. Corporate mergers, consolidations, liquidations, and dissolutions (which all fall under the purview of a fundamental changes covenant) as well as asset sales and acquisitions can dramatically alter (and from a lender's perspective, sometimes adversely alter) the borrower's business and asset mix. A merger of Exxon and Microsoft would likely alter radically the lenders' credit judgment with respect to loans to Microsoft, even if the combined company were financially stronger. To take one example, financial covenants crafted for a software company probably do not test adequately the performance of a combined software and oil company. Similarly, the need for constant innovation, research, and development that drives the success of a software company has little relevance to the commodity price swings that influence the profits of a petroleum business. While the example of a merger of operating companies in completely different industries illustrates how radically credit underwriting assumptions can be overturned, one doesn't even need to imagine such a far-fetched example to understand lenders' concerns. The corporate landscape is littered with the detritus of disastrous mergers of businesses in the same or related industries.

The approach taken to each of these three elements (fundamental changes, dispositions, and acquisitions) have their own nuances. Some agreements will address each of the three transaction categories, or some combination of the three, in a single fundamental changes covenant. The more common practice for modern credit agreements is to cover mergers, consolidations, and liquidations under the fundamental changes covenant while regulating asset sales under its own separate covenant and acquisitions either under its own covenant or under the investments covenant.

7.6.6.1 Fundamental Changes

Box 7.39

The Borrower will not, and will not permit any Subsidiary to, merge into or consolidate with any other Person, or permit any other Person to merge into or consolidate with it, or liquidate or dissolve, except that, if at the time thereof and immediately after giving effect thereto no Default shall have occurred and be continuing (i) any [Subsidiary/Person] may merge into the Borrower in a transaction in which the Borrower is the surviving corporation, (ii) any [Subsidiary/Person] may merge into any Subsidiary in a transaction in which the surviving entity is a Subsidiary, and (iii) any Subsidiary may liquidate or dissolve if the Borrower determines in good faith that such liquidation or dissolution is in the best interests of the Borrower and is not materially disadvantageous to the Lenders.

The limitation on mergers restricts the ability of the borrower to merge or consolidate with other entities. There can be exceptions that can be broadly distinguished between interfamilial mergers within the corporate family and mergers with unaffiliated third parties. In terms of intrafamilial mergers, almost universally a credit agreement permits mergers of subsidiaries with the borrower if the borrower is the surviving or continuing corporation. Similarly, intersubsidiary mergers are also allowed provided that there are generally limits on guarantor subsidiaries merging into non-guarantor subsidiaries and vice versa. In the category of mergers with unaffiliated third parties, a credit agreement may permit nonsubsidiaries to merge with the borrower (or subsidiaries) if the borrower (or subsidiary) is the surviving entity. Mergers involving borrowers or subsidiaries organized in the United States will often be conditioned on the surviving entity continuing to be organized domestically. The freedom to merge is not a license to reorganize into a jurisdiction that lenders may not have anticipated and, in the event of a distressed borrower, which could result in an unfamiliar offshore insolvency or bankruptcy proceeding. A merger of a third party into the borrower or subsidiary is, of course, nothing other than an acquisition. To the extent that acquisitions are separately controlled by the covenants, the requirement in the sample language in Box 7.39 that no default exist after the merger assures that the acquisition and investments limitations are also satisfied.

The requirement in credit agreement merger covenants that the borrower (or subsidiary) survive contrasts with the approach typically found in bond indentures, in which mergers are normally permitted even when the issuer is not the survivor. A bond indenture instead constrains the issuer by requiring that the surviving entity assume the issuer's obligations under the indenture and that the survivor satisfy certain other tests, such as that it is organized in the United States, does not have a reduced net worth, and is able to incur at least $1.00 of additional debt. It is not uncommon for indenture-style merger covenants to be incorporated into credit agreements for investment-grade borrowers.

7.6.6.2 Asset Sales

Box 7.40

The Borrower will not, and will not permit any Subsidiary to, make any Dispositions except:

(a) dispositions of obsolete, worn-out, or surplus property, whether now owned or hereafter acquired, in the ordinary course of business and Dispositions of property no longer used or useful in the conduct of the business of the Borrower and its Restricted Subsidiaries;

(b) dispositions of inventory and other assets in the ordinary course of business;

(c) dispositions in the ordinary course of business of Cash Equivalents;

(d) leases, subleases, licenses, or sublicenses, in each case in the ordinary course of business and which do not materially interfere with the business of the Borrower and its Restricted Subsidiaries, taken as a whole; and

(e) any Dispositions for fair value, *provided* that (i) no Default or Event of Default exists or would arise as a result of the transaction and (ii) with respect to any Disposition pursuant to this clause (e), the Person making such Disposition shall receive not less than 75% of such consideration in the form of cash or Cash Equivalents.

"Disposition" means the sale, transfer, license, lease, or other disposition of any property by any Person (including any sale and leaseback transaction), including any sale, assignment, transfer, or other disposal, with or without recourse, of any notes or accounts receivable or any rights and claims associated therewith.

Sales of revenue-generating assets often raise concerns from lenders as to whether the borrower is selling the asset for what it is worth as well as how the sale proceeds are being reinvested in the business. When asset sales rise to the level of being material to the borrower's operations, lenders are faced with additional concerns of a fundamental change in the direction of the borrower's business strategy and risk profile that may accompany a new mix of assets.

The covenant that limits asset sales is usually in one of two forms: either it limits sales by the borrower of "all or substantially all" assets or it limits sales of "any assets." Some agreements attempt to set out a middle ground by restricting sales of a "substantial part" of the assets or using dollar amounts or attributable EBITDA to reach the same point.

Although few court decisions illuminate what "substantially all" means in this context, by analogy to the way the term is used in other contexts (such as state corporation law), some guidance can be found. In *Gimbel v. Signal Cos.*, 316 A.2d 599 (Del. Ch. 1974), the court ruled that if the sale of assets is "quantitatively vital to the operation of the corporation and is out of the ordinary and substantially affects the existence and purpose of the corporation," then it constitutes a sale of "all or substantially all" of the assets of the corporation and requires shareholder approval. The court in *Gimbel* held that the sale did not require shareholder approval because it represented only 26 percent of the total assets and, although it constituted 41 percent of total net worth, it generated only about 15 percent of total revenue and earnings. Another court, faced with different numbers (51 percent of total assets and 45 percent of net sales), concluded that the transaction constituted a sale of "all or substantially all" assets. See *Katz v. Bregman*, 431 A.2d 1274 (Del. Ch. 1981). The *Katz* court also contrasted the sale to *Gimbel* by noting that the *Gimbel* sale would not fundamentally change the company's business (its business was already diversified), whereas the sale in *Katz* represented a "radical departure" from its historically successful line of selling steel drums.

In one of the few cases to have construed an indenture asset sale clause, the Delaware Court of Chancery stated that "the critical factor in determining the character of a sale of assets is generally considered not the amount of property sold but whether the sale is in fact an unusual transaction or one made in the regular course of business of the seller." See *Philadelphia Nat'l Bank v. B.S.F. Co.*, 199 A.2d 557 (Del. Ch. 1964), *rev'd on other grounds*, 204 A.2d 746 (Del. 1964).

What is clear from all of these decisions is that there is no black-and-white test as to what constitutes "all or substantially all" and that "substantially all" is not intended (as its words might otherwise indicate) to be a reference to a percentage (say, 98 percent) just shy of 100 percent, but can bite at much lower asset proportions. That said, the "all or substantially all" restriction affords considerably greater flexibility from the viewpoint of the borrower than an "any assets" covenant. The latter needs (and customarily incorporates) a variety of exclusions including most commonly carveouts for sales of inventory in the ordinary course of business; sales of worn-out, obsolete, or redundant property or equipment; and asset transfers among subsidiaries. Asset dispositions that are not otherwise allowed under the ordinary course exceptions may be permitted under a general basket permitting any asset sale so long as the transaction is at fair market value and results in at least 75 percent of proceeds being in the form of cash.

Credit agreements will regularly require prepayments from the proceeds of nonordinary course asset sales. Therefore, asset sales are regulated in two places: the fundamental changes or standalone asset sales covenant as well as mandatory prepayment provisions. Traditionally, the same result was arrived at by requiring proceeds from asset sales that were not permitted under the credit agreement to be subject to mandatory prepayment. Now credit agreements, especially those with the "any assets" construct described above, routinely and expressly permit a wide variety of asset sales while nonetheless requiring that the proceeds of such permitted dispositions be applied to prepay the loans (or *pari passu* secured debt). Borrowers will frequently push for the flexibility to keep the sale proceeds in the business by negotiating for reinvestment rights in lieu of forced debt repayment.

7.6.6.3   Acquisitions

The fundamental changes covenant may also limit acquisitions by the borrower. Acquisitions are typically defined to capture not only acquisitions of the equity of another company but also acquisitions of a business or division of another company. The underlying theory, as with mergers and dispositions, is that an acquisition has the potential to alter fundamentally the nature of the business of the borrower and affect not only the relevance of the financial covenants (as a merger of Exxon and Microsoft might), but also strain the ability of management to run a radically different business. Similar to the limitation on mergers and dispositions, an exclusion is normally made for "acquisitions" that are transfers of assets between and among the borrower and its subsidiaries (although to avoid structural subordination—see the discussion in Section 7.6.4.6—transfers of assets by the borrower to subsidiaries may sometimes be limited).

7.6.7   Sale-Leasebacks

Box 7.41

The Borrower will not, and will not permit any Subsidiary to, directly or indirectly, enter into any arrangement providing for the sale or transfer any property, real or personal, used or useful in the business of the Borrower or any Subsidiary, whether now owned or hereafter acquired, and thereafter rent or lease such property or other property that any of them intend to use for substantially the same purpose or purposes as the property sold or transferred [unless (i) the sale of such property is permitted by Section [*Fundamental Changes*] and (ii) any Lien arising in connection with the use of such property is permitted by Section [*Liens*]].

Sale-leaseback covenants have been a standard feature for bond indentures for decades and similarly make frequent appearances in credit agreements. The basic purpose is to control a transaction in which the borrower sells an asset and then immediately leases it (or an equivalent asset) back under a capital or operating lease arrangement. A sale of the borrower's high-tech robotic stamping machine, if immediately followed by the borrower's leasing the machine back, is a sale-leaseback transaction. Even a leaseback of a replacement machine constitutes a sale-leaseback.

The rationale behind limiting sale-leasebacks (perhaps more accurately described as sales and *immediate* leasebacks) is that they are a form of secured financing. By selling an asset, the borrower transfers title to a third party and by leasing it back, the borrower demonstrates, in effect, that the asset is too important to its business to simply be exchanged for cash. Also by entering into a lease arrangement, the borrower incurs a debt-like obligation in the form of rent over the medium or long term. As with capitalized lease obligations more generally, the extent to which the aggregate rent obligation under the sale-leaseback is included in debt covenant calculations may be the subject of negotiation. The upshot is that the borrower continues to use the asset (indeed, from an accounting perspective, it may still be carried on its balance sheet), but with title now in the hands of the purchaser/lessor. In a bankruptcy of the borrower, the asset will not be part of its estate nor will it be included in the lending syndicate's sweeping security interest in "all" assets of the borrower.

Described in this way, it is apparent, in the context of a credit agreement (although perhaps not in the context of a bond indenture), that each of the elements of a sale-leaseback transaction should already be controlled by other covenants (among them the lien, debt, and fundamental changes or asset sales covenants) and mandatory prepayment requirements. From a technical standpoint, therefore, the restriction may be unnecessary. Nevertheless, it is sometimes inserted into credit agreements either to replicate an indenture covenant (consistent with the business deal) or to set minimum standards for how sale-leaseback transactions otherwise permitted within an applicable debt, lien, or dispositions basket are to be structured.

7.6.8 Investments

Box 7.42

The Borrower will not, nor will it permit any Subsidiary to, make or permit to remain outstanding any Investments except:

(a) Investments (including investments in the capital stock of Subsidiaries) outstanding on the date hereof and identified in Schedule ___;

(b) Cash and Cash Equivalents;

(c) [Investments by the Borrower in any Subsidiary and by any Subsidiary in the Borrower or any other Subsidiary] [loans or advances by the Borrower to any Subsidiary and by any Subsidiary to any other Subsidiary];

(d) Guarantees constituting Debt permitted by Section [*Debt*];

(e) Investments constituting Acquisitions permitted under Section [*Fundamental Changes*]; and

(f) other investments up to but not exceeding $_____ in the aggregate at any one time outstanding, *provided* that no Investment may be made pursuant to this clause (f) at any time that a Default exists or if a Default would result therefrom.

* * * * * * * * * * * *

"*Investment*" means, for any Person: (a) the acquisition (including pursuant to any merger with any Person that was not a Subsidiary prior to such merger) of capital stock, bonds, notes, debentures, partnership, or other ownership interests or other securities of any other Person; (b) the making of any deposit with, or advance, loan, or other extension of credit to, any other Person (excluding any such advance, loan, or extension of credit having a term not exceeding ___ days representing the purchase price of inventory or supplies sold by such Person in the ordinary course of business); or (c) the entering into of any Guarantee of, or other contingent obligation with respect to, Debt or other liability of any other Person and (without duplication) any amount committed to be advanced, loaned, or extended to such other Person.

From the standpoint of a lender, the objective of an investments covenant is much like that of the fundamental changes or standalone acquisitions covenant: to control material changes to the business or assets of the borrower upon which the lender's initial credit decision is made. There is considerable overlap between the two covenants (a purchase of 100 percent of the stock of a corporation, for example, constitutes both an investment and an acquisition, and therefore any such purchase needs to satisfy the conditions of both covenants). Investments in securities and debt also represent uses of cash or assets that, if not regulated, potentially lead to cash leakage from the credit group. A $100 million loan from the borrower to a joint venture or unrestricted subsidiary may or may not be a credit-enhancing transaction for the senior lenders but certainly will accrue value to equity holders. By restricting investments in non-guarantor subsidiaries for example, the investments covenant overlaps with the restricted payments covenant in restricting potentially detrimental value extraction from the credit group.

The definition of *investments* is, like other definitions, overexpansive and encompasses not just the acquisition of securities and interests in joint ventures or partnerships, but also extensions of credit, issuance of guarantees, and commitments to make loans or buy equity. Sometimes derivatives or hedging agreements are also swept in (see Section 7.6.10). The term does not normally include extensions of credit by the borrower to customers in the ordinary course of business. Customary credit terms given by a borrower for payment of inventory or services are excluded (though credit terms longer than an agreed period, 90 or 180 days being typical, are treated as investments).

Expansiveness in the definition leads, of course, to a variety of exceptions, as outlined in Sections 7.6.8.1 to 7.6.8.6.

7.6.8.1 Grandfathered Investments

As with grandfathered liens and debt, investments in existence on the closing date are usually listed on a disclosure schedule. The level of detail in the disclosure schedule is normally negotiated between the borrower and the lending syndicate. The borrower may, for practical purposes, not want to identify each $5.00 investment that it has made and will therefore push (with justification) for investments below a threshold to be identified on the schedule by category rather than by specific investment. Grandfathered investments do not normally need to include investments in cash and cash equivalents, which are customarily covered by another exception. Investments in subsidiaries may also not need to be listed depending upon how the subsidiaries exception is drafted.

7.6.8.2 Cash and Cash Equivalents

"*Cash*" incorporates all cash on hand held by the borrower and its subsidiaries, including amounts held in deposit accounts. "Cash equivalents" is a more expansive term and normally sweeps in a wide variety of high-quality liquid investments, such as commercial paper with high ratings from Moody's, Standard & Poor's, or other agreed rating agencies, short-term Treasuries (or short-term repos on Treasuries with strong financial institutions), short-term certificates of deposit, and money-market funds that primarily invest in other securities that fit within the definition of permitted investments. The term is intended to allow investments that will give some (albeit modest) yield to the borrower, but that are of such high quality, short tenor, and market liquidity that they can essentially be treated as equivalent to cash. Accordingly, equity securities are not included because of the potential for market volatility and because, depending upon how thin the market is for a particular security, they may not be readily saleable. Longer-term bonds (even if given the highest rating by Moody's and Standard & Poor's) and longer-term Treasury securities are normally not included because interest-rate volatility can adversely affect their market value.

7.6.8.3 Subsidiaries

This exclusion covers investments in subsidiaries (whether by the borrower or by other subsidiaries). In theory, if the lenders' credit analysis looks at the borrower and its subsidiaries (or restricted subsidiaries more particularly) as one consolidated entity, the lenders should be indifferent to money moving around within the credit group and so investments between and among the borrower and such subsidiaries should be unrestricted. This would be doubly the case if the lending syndicate benefits from guarantees from subsidiaries. Conversely, where there are subsidiaries outside the credit group, as is the case with unrestricted subsidiaries or frequently with foreign subsidiaries and other categories of excluded subsidiaries, lenders will be anything but indifferent to value leaving the credit group to such excluded subsidiaries.

In cases in which the credit analysis of the borrower is based upon its being an entity with operating assets, the lender may want to control the movement of assets from the borrower into subsidiaries and will, therefore, either impose a dollar cap on investments, or limit investments to loans and advances (as distinct from equity investments). This is yet another example of the issue of structural subordination discussed in Section 7.6.4.6. As explained there, the term "structural subordination" reflects that creditors of a subsidiary, in a bankruptcy of the latter, are entitled to be paid in full from the assets of the subsidiary before any money flows up to the borrower. To permit, therefore, the borrower to put additional equity capital into subsidiaries may simply support creditors of the subsidiaries without increasing the claims of the borrower against the subsidiary.

The most obvious way to minimize structural subordination issues is to require that subsidiaries guarantee the credit facility. If subsidiary guarantees are not available, the next best thing is to require that any money invested in a subsidiary be in the form of a loan or advance. This allows the borrower itself to be a creditor of the subsidiary. There are still bankruptcy issues to be overcome—equitable subordination of the borrower's claims against the subsidiaries being one example—but the loan by the borrower to the subsidiary allows the borrower (in theory) to compete with other creditors of the subsidiary on an equal footing.

Another issue sometimes addressed in the exclusion for intergroup investments is loans and advances by subsidiaries to the borrower. Many credit facilities are structured to prohibit such investments outright; it only compounds structural subordination issues by giving creditors of subsidiaries (or a trustee in bankruptcy acting on behalf of those creditors) a claim not only against the subsidiary but also against the borrower! Other credit agreements require that subsidiaries subordinate claims against the borrower to the borrower's obligations under the credit agreement.

7.6.8.4   Guarantees

Guarantees of obligations of others are customarily swept into the definition of *investments*. The underlying theory is that a guarantee is essentially no different than an agreement to make an equity or debt investment in the obligor on the guaranteed debt. If the guarantor pays, it succeeds to or is subrogated (the technical term) to the claims of the beneficiary of the guarantee against the obligor. In effect, the guarantor has lent money to the obligor in an amount equal to the guaranteed claim.

Of course, there is considerable overlap between the debt covenant and the investments covenant, since a guarantee of debt is itself debt. An approach frequently seen is to allow the borrower, for purposes of the investments covenant, to guarantee debt of third parties to the extent that the debt is permitted under the debt covenant.

7.6.8.5   Acquisition Investments

This is an exclusion for investments related to permitted acquisitions. To the extent that a credit agreement allows the company to consummate acquisitions of other companies or businesses, the investments covenant needs to exclude acquisitions permitted under the fundamental changes covenant.

7.6.8.6   Investment Basket

The investment basket allows investments that are not covered by other exceptions, and are usually permitted up to some agreed dollar threshold ("hard cap") or subject to an incurrence-based financial covenant, grower basket, or builder basket. One issue that is addressed in certain investment covenants is valuation of the investment for basket purposes. Since the value of the investment will fluctuate while the basket cap may be static, the question arises of how to treat the borrower's $1,000,000 investment that turned into $10 million, for example. If the original investment was made in reliance on the $5 million basket, is the basket capacity now exhausted due to this successful investment? One (borrower-friendly) approach is to net out returns on the investment up to the cost of the investment, thereby "refreshing" basket capacity for investments that generate a return. Borrowers sometimes object that too many other types of investments need to be squeezed into the basket and so will either push for a relatively high number, or will ask that certain ordinary course of business investments be allowed under a separate basket. Examples of the latter might include security deposits with landlords and utilities, salary and relocation advances to employees, and notes receivable obtained in the course of renegotiating claims against insolvent customers.

7.6.9 Lines of Business

Box 7.43

Neither the Borrower nor any Subsidiary shall engage to any substantial extent in any line or lines of business activity other than [_____] [the types of businesses engaged in on the date hereof by the Borrower and its Subsidiaries plus reasonably related or ancillary businesses or reasonable extensions of such current business lines].

Consistent with the concerns described in Section 7.6.6, lenders make a credit analysis of the borrower based upon the nature of its current business. To take an example, the lenders may not want to see a cable television company enter the fast-food business. Just as could happen with a merger, not only might the borrower's management be unfamiliar with the operation of a fast-food business, but the financial covenants might no longer appropriately measure how the company performs. As a result, many credit agreements contain a line of business covenant that prohibits the borrower from engaging in any substantial or material manner in a line of business different from that in which the borrower is engaged at the closing of the credit agreement. This covenant is not intended to stifle a borrower's expansion into related or similar businesses. After all, the best growth prospects for the borrower's business may lie in such related, ancillary, or extended lines of business. There are no shortage of real-world examples of successful entry of companies into related sectors. Amazon.com began its corporate life as a bookseller but found substantial value from its foray into other areas of ecommerce. Credit agreements generally recognize this corporate reality by permitting such related expansionary activity.

7.6.10 Derivatives

> **Box 7.44**
>
> Neither the Borrower nor any Subsidiary shall enter into any Derivative Transaction except in the ordinary course of business and not for speculative purposes.

Borrowers, regardless of the business they conduct, often need (or want) to enter into derivatives or hedging transactions. Sometimes they are required to do so by the credit agreement itself. As discussed in Section 7.5, lenders may mandate that the borrower hedge against interest rate risks in connection with the credit agreement. In addition, many businesses, particularly those dependent upon commodity prices, may simply as a matter of business prudence need to hedge against future raw-material price swings. A lending syndicate may, however, be concerned that the borrower could "overhedge" (speculate) in currencies, commodities, interest indices, or any of the numerous other products available in the derivatives markets beyond what it strictly needs for its business.

Accordingly, credit agreements (primarily for leveraged borrowers) frequently control the derivatives transactions into which the borrower may enter beyond those required by the lenders in the affirmative covenants. These limitations can be found in a number of places. Sometimes all or some net portion (generally tied to a close out or termination value) of derivatives are deemed to be debt and through this device are limited by the debt covenant and subject to the cross-default provision (see Section 9.1.4). As discussed in Section 7.3.2.1, treating derivatives as debt can have unintended adverse consequences, particularly when it comes to calculating performance with financial covenants. To address the floating contingent nature of hedging obligations, some credit agreements will only include the crystallized close-out value, on a net basis, as debt. A second approach is to treat derivatives as investments subject to the investments covenant on the theory that the value of a derivative behaves much the same as an investment in a debt or equity security. A third approach is simply to deal with derivatives in a standalone covenant along the lines set out in Box 7.44. Credit agreement treatment of derivatives is not limited to the borrower's balance sheet but also frequently covers income statement impact as well. For example, gains on hedging contracts, such as those related to currency risk, may be excluded from net income or EBITDA while losses may be added back.

Regardless of how derivatives are controlled, it is often not terribly practical to limit derivative exposures to a dollar cap, since that requires daily recalculation of the exposure under the derivative as interest, commodity prices, and other relevant indicators change. The more customary approach, therefore, is to avoid dollar caps and allow the borrower to enter into derivative contracts so long as they are entered in the ordinary course of the borrower's financial planning and not for speculative purposes. Of course, a covenant written in this fashion is somewhat vague and nebulous (how, for example, can the parties determine whether a derivative is speculative or not?), but in an extreme case a breach would presumably be clear. The term "speculative" may not be definable but, to paraphrase a famous Supreme Court case,[5] a court will know it when it sees it.

7.6.11   *Guarantees or Contingent Liabilities*

Box 7.45

The Borrower will not, and will not permit any Subsidiary to, directly or indirectly, create or become or remain liable with respect to any obligation, contingent or otherwise, guaranteeing or having the economic effect of guaranteeing any Debt or other obligation of any other Person (the *"primary obligor"*) in any manner, whether directly or indirectly, and including any obligation, direct or indirect, (a) to purchase or pay (or advance or supply funds for the purchase or payment of) such Debt or other obligation or to purchase (or to advance or supply funds for the purchase of) any security for the payment thereof; (b) to purchase or lease property, securities, or services for the purpose of assuring the owner of such Debt or other obligation of the payment thereof; (c) to maintain working capital, equity capital, or any other financial statement condition or liquidity of the primary obligor so as to enable the primary obligor to pay such Debt or other obligation; or (d) as an account party in respect of any letter

---

[5] See *Jacobellis v. Ohio*, 378 U.S. 184, 197 (1964).

of credit or letter of guarantee issued to support such Indebtedness or obligation (any of the foregoing being herein called a *"Guarantee"*) except:

(a) Guarantees by Subsidiaries of the obligations of the Borrower hereunder;

(b) Guarantees consisting of endorsements for collection or deposit in the ordinary course of business; and

(c) Guarantees constituting Debt permitted under Section [*Debt*].

As discussed earlier in this chapter, guarantees are frequently controlled by both the debt covenant (by treating guarantees of debt of a third party as debt of the guarantor) and the investments covenant (by treating guarantees of obligations of a third party as an investment in the third party). Some credit agreements also (or alternatively) control guarantees and other contingent liabilities directly through a stand-alone covenant.

For these purposes, the term "guarantees," as in the sample language in Box 7.45, is defined very broadly to pick up not just a simple guarantee, but also a broad variety of other arrangements, such as the borrower's causing a bank to issue a letter of credit to support the obligations of a third party or the borrower's agreeing to protect a third party against losses that arise out of a commercial transaction. So-called take-or-pay agreements are also captured, in which, for the benefit of a creditor of a third party, the borrower agrees to pay for products (such as oil or processed chemicals) whether or not the third party is able to deliver the products to the borrower. Similarly, support arrangements in which the borrower agrees with the creditor of a subsidiary to maintain the net worth or working capital of the subsidiary regardless of adverse events are treated as a guarantee. If the net worth or working capital must always be positive, the borrower has, in effect, guaranteed the debt of the subsidiary. The breadth of the definition stems from the expectation that borrowers have an infinite capacity to be creative in structuring deals, and so the broader (and more verbose) the "guarantee" concept, the better.

The amount of a guarantee is deemed to be equal to the amount of the claim guaranteed (or, if less, the limit stated in the guarantee instrument). The amount of the guarantee is not reduced by the fact that other parties are jointly and severally obligated with the borrower and that, therefore, the borrower can seek reimbursement from other parties for any payment by it in excess of its pro rata share. So, if the borrower is 1 of 10 guarantors, each of which is obligated on the entire amount of the debt, the full amount of the guarantee is treated as debt under their 10 credit agreements (assuming they each have one).

7.6.12 Dividends and Equity Repurchases

Box 7.46

The Borrower will not, and will not permit any Subsidiary to, declare or make, or agree to pay or make, directly or indirectly, any Dividend Payment, except:

(a) the Borrower may declare and pay dividends with respect to its capital stock payable solely in additional shares of its capital stock (other than Disqualified Stock);

(b) Subsidiaries may declare and pay dividends ratably with respect to their capital stock [ratably to their shareholders];

(c) the Borrower may make Dividend Payments pursuant to and in accordance with stock option plans or other benefit plans for management or employees of the Borrower and its Subsidiaries;

(d) so long as no Default exists or would result therefrom, the Borrower may pay regularly scheduled dividends in respect of its [Series ____] Preferred Stock as in effect on the date hereof; and

(e) so long as no Default exists or would result therefrom, the Borrower may declare and pay _____.

"Dividend Payment" means, collectively, all distributions of the Borrower and its Subsidiaries (in cash, property, or obligations) on, or other payments or distributions on account of, or the setting apart of money for a sinking or other analogous fund for, or the purchase, redemption, retirement, or other acquisition of, any portion of any ownership interest in the Borrower or of any warrants, options, or other rights to acquire any such ownership interest (or any payments to any Person, such as "phantom stock" payments, where the amount thereof is calculated with reference to fair market or equity value of the Borrower or any Subsidiary).

The dividend covenant in a credit agreement limits dividends and distributions by the borrower and its subsidiaries. The covenant is usually not, as is typically the case in bond indentures, controlling both investments and dividends under a shared permitted restricted payment basket. Instead, a credit agreement customarily controls dividends and investments in separate covenants.

As with definitions employed in other negative covenants, the term "dividend payment" (or, simply, *dividend*) is defined expansively.

It not only picks up the layman's understanding of periodic dividends declared by the borrower's board or management body, but also captures any other device by which money could leave the borrower and be paid to equity holders. As a result, it includes distributions, sinking fund payments, purchases of stock, and even "phantom stock" payments whereby a creditor or employee is entitled to an equity-like return as if it held stock without actually owning any equity. It includes those actions if they are undertaken by the borrower; it also includes those actions if they are undertaken by subsidiaries (the theory being that a repurchase of *borrower* stock by a subsidiary is still money out of the consolidated group). Customary exceptions include those outlined in Sections 7.6.12.1 to 7.6.12.5.

7.6.12.1   Stock Dividends

Stock dividends are dividends paid through the issuance of additional shares of capital stock. In the case of corporate borrowers, dividends payable in capital stock (which include not only *common* stock, but also *preferred* stock) are almost always permitted without limit, since they do not represent money that leaves the borrower's consolidated group. In the case of other classes of borrower (partnerships or limited liability companies, for example), equivalent terminology is employed. Dividends paid through the issuance of "Disqualified Stock" (see Box 7.45) will not, however, be entitled to the exclusion.

7.6.12.2   Subsidiary Dividends

This exclusion permits dividend payments made by subsidiaries of the borrower. Unless the borrower is an operating company with sufficient financial resources to service its debt obligations on its own, it will need to receive dividends from subsidiaries to service payments under the credit agreement. For subsidiaries that are wholly owned, 100 percent of their dividends payments are paid to the borrower. For subsidiaries that are less than wholly owned there is some leakage of money from the consolidated group; such dividends are nevertheless normally allowed as long as they are made ratably by the subsidiary to all of its shareholders.

7.6.12.3   Employee Stock Plans

Dividend payments made under stock option or other benefit plans are often entitled to a separate exception. Stock option and other benefit plans are, for many borrowers, a cost of doing business; to attract qualified employees (and keep them happy) most large businesses establish such plans. Once established, the borrower is, of course, required to make payments when employees die or retire or take employment elsewhere. In general, credit agreements allow payments under such plans to be made without limit, though in closely held companies, in which such plans could be a method for insiders to remove large amounts of money from the borrower, an annual dollar cap may be imposed.

7.6.12.4 Preferred Dividends

Dividends on preferred stock are normally permitted only at the level in effect at the closing date. (The language in Box 7.46 refers to "regularly scheduled" dividends, meaning those dividends scheduled under the preferred stock provisions of the borrower's charter as in effect on the date of the credit agreement.) The exclusion does not provide for dividends on future issuances of preferred stock. Normally also, this type of dividend is blocked during an event of default.

7.6.12.5 Dividend Baskets

Dividend payment baskets are based on a simple per annum dollar amount (a "hard cap"); a "grower" basket that is sized on a percentage of total assets, cash flow, or some other metric; or a "builder" basket that is sized on cumulative retained excess cash flow, cumulative net income, equity contributions, and other amounts that may aggregate over time (with the grower and builder concepts being variants of a "soft cap") or a combination of the foregoing. As with preferred dividends, the availability of any dividend basket is normally contingent upon the absence of any default. Sometimes (especially in highly leveraged transactions) the agreement may impose a condition that the borrower deliver an officer's certificate with a supporting calculation that demonstrates compliance with the dividend exception before the dividend is paid.

Lastly, in cases where the corporate organization includes a direct holding company parent and that parent has incurred its own borrowed money indebtedness, the dividends covenant may permit dividends to be upstreamed to pay interest on the holding company debt. Dividends from the borrower to pay principal at maturity or upon mandatory redemption events or defaults are not typically allowed. Payments to service interest obligations are normally (though not always) conditioned upon the absence of any default. The effect of a covenant fashioned in this manner is to bolster the structural seniority of the credit agreement as against debt of the ultimate parent. (See the discussion on subordination generally in Section 6.5.2.)

7.6.13   Tax-Sharing Payments and Permitted Tax Distributions

Box 7.47

Except as contemplated by the Tax-Sharing Agreement, the Borrower and its Subsidiaries will not make payments in respect of income taxes (or in respect of reimbursement for such taxes) to [Parent] in amounts the cumulative sum of which exceeds the cumulative sum of income taxes that the Borrower and its Subsidiaries would have paid in respect of Federal and state income taxes if the Borrower and its Subsidiaries had at all times (including at all times prior to the date hereof) filed a separate consolidated Federal income tax return, with the Borrower as the "common parent" (within the meaning of Section 1504 of the Code), and taking into account all net operating loss carry forwards pursuant to Section 172 of the Code that would have been available to the Borrower and its Subsidiaries had they filed such a separate return.

If the borrower is a domestic corporation that is more than 80 percent owned by another domestic corporation, under the U.S. Internal Revenue Code, it is consolidated with its ultimate parent for tax purposes. This means that the parent is the entity that actually pays taxes to the government (although all entities in the consolidated group are each liable for the full amount of the taxes). The parent, of course, looks to its subsidiaries (including, in this case, the borrower and its subsidiaries) for funds to make the tax payments.

When the borrower is itself the parent this raises no issues (and, as discussed above, it is customary for the subsidiaries to be required to remain free to pay dividends to the borrower). When, however, the borrower is not the parent, credit agreements sometimes limit the aggregate amount of payments that may be made upstream in respect of taxes to an amount deemed to be "fair" from the standpoint of the borrower. The parent might, for example, have other subsidiaries that generate substantially more current income than the borrower; in these circumstances, it would not be appropriate (arguably) for the borrower to pay more to its parent than the amount it would have been required to pay had it been an independent taxpayer. Nor would it be fair (again arguably) for the parent to use up the borrower's valuable loss carry forwards to shelter the income of sister corporations and non-guarantor subsidiaries outside of the credit group.

Typically, these issues are handled in a tax-sharing agreement, and in fact most large corporations have such an agreement to address these issues. In other cases, the credit agreement may include a covenant such as that set out in Box 7.47 to provide overarching principles as to how much may be paid to the parent to cover for taxes. The restriction on tax-sharing payments is often not a separate covenant, but is simply incorporated into either the dividend or the affiliate transactions covenant in the form of baskets permitting such payments. The typical permitted tax distribution basket will be sized to permit the borrower to distribute cash, often whether or not a default exists, to the tax-paying parent in an aggregate amount required to pay U.S. federal, state, local, and/or non-U.S. income or similar taxes imposed on such parent company but only to the extent such income or similar taxes are attributable to the income of the borrower.

7.6.14 Restrictions on Subsidiary Distributions

Box 7.48

The Borrower will not, and will not permit any Subsidiary to, directly or indirectly, enter into, incur, or permit to exist any agreement or other arrangement that prohibits, restricts, or imposes any condition upon the ability of any Subsidiary to pay dividends or other distributions with respect to any shares of its capital stock or to make or repay loans or advances or transfer assets to the Borrower or any other Subsidiary or to Guarantee Debt of the Borrower or any other Subsidiary, except to the extent:

(a) existing on the date hereof identified in Schedule ___ [and extensions, renewals, and replacements thereof that do not expand the scope thereof];

(b) constituting restrictions and conditions imposed by law; and

(c) consisting of customary restrictions and conditions contained in agreements relating to the sale of a Subsidiary or property pending such sale, *provided* such restrictions and conditions apply only to the Subsidiary or property that is to be sold, and such sale is permitted hereunder.

A restriction on subsidiary distributions covenant, also known as a dividend blocker, relates to a dividend covenant in the same way that a negative negative pledge relates to a lien covenant. In other words, a dividend blocker prohibits the borrower from agreeing with third parties that dividends and distributions by subsidiaries to the borrower are constrained. The covenant also typically restricts other kinds of limitations on money or property going "upstream," such as through repayments of intercompany liabilities or debt, or through loans or transfers of assets (including, among other transactions, through sales or mergers). Limitations upon the ability of subsidiaries to guarantee debt of the borrower are also blocked (the lenders want, if anything, to be free to grab guarantees from subsidiaries in the future should the borrower's credit quality decline). The underlying concern of lenders is simple. If the borrower's access to funds is dependent upon money that flows up from subsidiaries, then to restrict that flow could impair the borrower's ability to pay scheduled principal and interest on the loans.

As with the negative negative pledge, a number of customary exceptions are typically incorporated into the dividend blocker covenant, including those outlined in Sections 7.6.14.1 to 7.6.14.5.

7.6.14.1 Grandfathered Restrictions

Agreements that impose restrictions that exist on the date of the agreement will be grandfathered and normally listed on a schedule.

7.6.14.2 Permitted Debt Restrictions

This exclusion includes restrictions arising under the subject credit agreement and documentation governing certain permitted debt. Credit agreements, including the subject credit agreement, and indentures will themselves generally contain dividend blockers. If debt is being permitted to be incurred, then it would defeat the purpose to not likewise permit the customary terms thereof, including dividend blockers. This assumes that such customary provisions under permitted debt instruments do not eviscerate or otherwise conflict with the dividend blockers of the subject credit agreement.

7.6.14.3 Legal Restrictions

This exclusion covers restrictions that are imposed by law. Subsidiaries, for example, may be limited in the amount of dividends they can pay to the aggregate amount of their capital and surplus. Similarly, fraudulent conveyance laws may restrict the amount of debt of a parent that a subsidiary can guarantee. Since these are rules that, in most cases, may not be waived, a specific exclusion to the covenant is normally built in.

7.6.14.4 Sale Restrictions

Restrictions also arise in connection with the sale of a subsidiary or asset. A parallel exclusion is of course customary in the negative negative pledge context. When a company signs an agreement to sell a subsidiary, it is standard to limit the dividends and transfers of assets that can be made by the subsidiary to its parent pending the sale. New guarantees by the subsidiary would also be barred. Even if the subsidiary is simply selling an asset or business unit, it would be customary to forbid the transfer of that asset or unit to another entity within the same corporate group.

7.6.14.5 Limited Customary Restrictions

This exclusion comprises restrictions arising under customary contracts that are limited, and relatively immaterial, in nature. Lease agreements will often restrict assignments, joint venture and shareholder agreements will restrict transfers of ownership interests, and consignment agreements will restrict transfer of the consigned assets. These and other common contractual arrangements may contain limited restrictions on asset transfers that would be captured by the dividend blocker covenant if not for negotiated exceptions.

7.6.15 Modification and Prepayment of Other Debt

Box 7.49

The Borrower will not, and will not permit any Subsidiary to, consent to any modification, supplement, or waiver of any of the provisions of the [specify debt instrument], without in each case the prior written consent of the Administrative Agent (with the approval of the Required Lenders).

The Borrower will not, and will not permit any Subsidiary to, purchase, redeem, retire, or otherwise acquire for value, or set apart any money for a sinking, defeasance or other analogous fund for the purchase, redemption, retirement, or other acquisition of, or make any voluntary payment or prepayment of the principal of or interest on, or any other amount owing in respect of, any such Debt, except for (a) regularly scheduled payments, prepayments, or redemptions of principal and interest in respect thereof required pursuant to the instruments evidencing such Debt and (b) extensions, renewals, and refinancings thereof permitted under Section [*Debt*].

Loans under the credit agreement are often not the borrower's only debt. Subordinated debt and other senior debt may be outstanding, in the form of another credit agreement, a private placement, a bond indenture, or other debt issuance. The credit analysis of the borrower by the lenders takes into account the borrower's closing date capital structure, including the maturity of any other debt and the terms and conditions applicable to the other debt. Changes in the other debt, such as to shorten the tenor, increase amortization, tighten covenants, increase interest rates, or the like, may adversely affect the credit profile of the borrower. Similarly, early payments of the debt may drain precious cash that the lenders assumed would be available to make payments or prepayments on the credit agreement.

To address the risk of junior debt holders leapfrogging the senior lenders, credit agreements control amendments to other debt as well as limit the ability of the borrower to prepay other debt. Borrowers not infrequently object to a blanket prohibition upon changes to the terms of other debt instruments and push either to eliminate the restriction entirely or have it apply only to material modifications. "Material" for these purposes can be defined as any change that would affect adversely the lenders in any *material* respect. This approach may suffer from vagueness; what is perceived as material to the lending syndicate may be viewed as insignificant by the borrower. Therefore, even with a materiality standard, the borrower to be safe will want a consent from the lenders in all cases unless a change is clearly inconsequential. The benefit of a materiality threshold may therefore be slight.

In an attempt nevertheless to give the borrower the benefit of a materiality standard, some agreements have the administrative agent first determine whether a change is material and thus requiring lender consent. The rationale here (from the perspective of the borrower) is that the agent can make a faster and more informed decision than a full lending syndicate, which may not be as familiar with the borrower as the agent. Many agents, however, resist this approach because of the potential for the syndicate to complain (or syndicate members even to sue) if they disagree with the agent's determination. A common response is that the agent is not paid enough to risk exposure to the syndicate when these types of discretionary judgments must be made.

The prepayments limitation applies to voluntary prepayments of other debt; it does not prevent scheduled principal or interest payments nor prohibit mandatory prepayments. The reason to distinguish voluntary from scheduled and mandatory payments is twofold. First, to state the obvious, no borrower wants to agree that it must obtain the lending syndicate's consent before it can honor its payment obligations under another agreement. Second, even if a borrower were cavalier enough to agree to such a restriction, the lending syndicate risks liability under the doctrine of tortious interference with contractual relations discussed in more detail in Section 6.1.5. As stated there, a claim of tortious interference has five elements (for these purposes, assume that the holders of the other debt are the plaintiffs and the lenders are the defendants):

the existence of a valid contract between the plaintiff and a third party (the borrower), defendant's knowledge of that contract, defendant's intentional procurement of the third party's breach of the contract without justification, actual breach of the contract, and damages resulting therefrom. Forcing a borrower to covenant that it will not pay other debt holders likely satisfies the last three elements: procurement of a breach, actual breach (when the borrower fails to pay the other debt), and damages (the missing payment). In the context of a credit facility when the lending syndicate has done normal due diligence, the element of knowledge is probably also satisfied—the lenders will certainly be aware of the other debt. If the other debt agreement is valid (also highly likely), all of the elements for a tortious interference claim by the other debt holders against the lenders will have been met. Credit agreements are consequently careful to carve out any scheduled or mandatory prepayments under other debt agreements from the prepayment limitation covenant. Covenant lite credit agreements will generally permit the borrower to make some amount of prepayment of other debt but only upon meeting certain negotiated conditions such as satisfaction of a leverage-based or other incurrence test.

In cases where debt that exists on the closing date may, under the debt covenant, be extended, renewed, or refinanced, the modification and prepayment covenant often includes a parallel permission. Otherwise, what is permitted in the debt covenant ends up prohibited in the modification and prepayment covenant. However, in more restrictive credit agreements, the covenant may set out a detailed set of criteria, including with respect to amortization and maturity, interest rates, covenants, and redemption or repurchase events, that are applicable to any refinancing indebtedness. This is to prevent the borrower from doing indirectly (say, through a refinancing) what it cannot do directly (by amendment to an outstanding debt document).

7.6.16   Affiliate Transactions

Box 7.50

The Borrower will not, and will not permit any Subsidiary to, sell, lease, or otherwise transfer any property or assets to, or purchase, lease, or otherwise acquire any property or assets from, or otherwise engage in any other transactions with, any of its Affiliates, except (a) in the ordinary course of business at prices and on terms and conditions not less favorable to the Borrower or such Subsidiary than could be obtained on an arm's-length basis from unrelated third parties, (b) transactions between or among the Borrower and its [wholly owned] Subsidiaries not involving any other Affiliate, and (c) transactions otherwise expressly permitted hereunder (including Dividend Payments permitted by Section [*Dividends*]).

* * * * * * * * * * * *

"*Affiliate*" means, with respect to a specified Person, another Person that directly, or indirectly through one or more intermediaries, Controls or is Controlled by or is under common Control with the Person specified. For purposes hereof, "*Control*" means the possession, directly or indirectly, of the power to direct or cause the direction of the management or policies of a Person, whether through the ability to exercise voting power, by contract or otherwise.

The affiliate transactions covenant restricts dealings between the borrower and its affiliates. "Affiliates" are often defined with reference to the SEC standard to be any entity, currently in existence or in the future, that the borrower (or a common parent) "controls" by voting power, contract, or otherwise. Any shareholder with sufficient voting power to control the borrower is accordingly an affiliate; any sister company of the borrower (a company controlled by the borrower's parent) is also an affiliate. Subsidiaries of the borrower, since presumptively controlled by the borrower, fall into the affiliate category as well. The definition may, in some cases, deem a percentage ownership (5 percent or 10 percent) to constitute control regardless of whether that percentage constitutes control under SEC rules. If the borrower is closely held, the term can expressly include family members (and related trusts or other estate planning vehicles) of controlling parties. Officers and directors may not per se qualify as affiliates without the presence of the additional control relationship.

The rationale for the affiliate transactions covenant is the concern that an entity or individual who controls the borrower may be able to unduly influence the terms of transactions with that entity or individual (or with other entities that it or the individual controls) and thereby harm creditors. In a sense, the affiliate transactions covenant is a supplement to the dividend covenant, in that it regulates money going out of the system to equity holders. Thus, while a dividend covenant might prohibit the payment of dividends to the owner of a privately held company, absent a restriction on affiliate transactions, there would be nothing to prevent the company from purchasing pencils at a price of

$1,000 each from the owner or from the owner's wife or son (as opposed to buying them from unaffiliated third parties; regulating against poor business decisions are another matter entirely). In a public company, the securities laws provide a measure of legal protection that may make this kind of abuse less likely. But in the context of a privately held company, the only safeguard other than the borrower's moral conscience (and, perhaps, fraudulent conveyance laws applicable if the borrower is insolvent) is the affiliate transactions covenant.

Given the breadth of the definition (and, particularly, that subsidiaries of a borrower will be "affiliates"), certain obvious carveouts to the covenant are necessary. For example, a credit agreement normally allows transactions between the borrower and affiliates for the purchase or sale of property or engaging in any other transaction in the ordinary course of business if the transaction takes place on terms not less favorable to the borrower than terms that would be applicable to a transaction between two unrelated or disinterested parties. Thus, while buying pencils at $1,000 apiece from an affiliate is prohibited by the covenant, purchasing them at 5¢ each (or whatever the going rate for pencils may be) is allowed. This is the so-called arm's-length exception. Credit agreements may also adopt the approach customarily taken in bond indentures, where the arm's-length exception is applied to any transaction (not just for the purchase and sale of property in the ordinary course of business) and determines compliance with the arm's-length standard based upon either a board resolution (often approved by a majority of disinterested directors) or, if the transaction exceeds a dollar threshold, upon a third-party appraisal.

An affiliate transactions covenant also normally contains exceptions for transactions otherwise expressly permitted under the credit agreement, such as the payment of permitted dividends, and, because directors and senior officers may be deemed to be affiliates, for compensation to directors and officers, loans and advances to officers, and stock and bonus plans. Transactions between and among the borrower and its subsidiaries are allowed at least in facilities where the lenders are looking to the consolidated group to support loans made available to the borrower, although in a credit agreement in which not all of the subsidiaries are guarantors, only transactions between and among the borrower and its guarantor subsidiaries may be permitted. Lastly, the borrower's existing contractual arrangements and past practice may necessitate the inclusion of a specified category of transactions, which may or may not be conducted on a firmly arm's-length basis. Typically such specifically permitted transaction categories will nonetheless be required to be customary or ordinary course.

7.6.17   Amendments to Organic Documents and Other Agreements

Box 7.51

In addition, the Borrower will not, and will not permit any Subsidiary to, consent to any modification, supplement or waiver of any of the provisions of its charter, bylaws, partnership agreement, or limited liability company agreement or [specify material contract], other than (a) minor modifications, supplements, or waivers that do not in any material respect increase the obligations, or limit the rights, of the Borrower or its Subsidiaries thereunder and (ii) nonmaterial modifications that could not reasonably be expected to be materially adverse to the Lenders.

Credit agreements may sometimes limit amendments to the borrower's charter, bylaws, or other organic documents. The fear is that the borrower might amend these instruments in a manner adverse to the lenders, such as by authorizing the issuance of preferred stock that benefits from mandatory dividends or redemption provisions. Similarly, a subsidiary might amend its charter to restrict its ability to declare and pay dividends up to the borrower. In most agreements, these concerns may also be addressed by other covenants (in these examples, the debt, dividend, and dividend blocker covenants).

Credit agreements may in addition limit amendments to material agreements beyond the debt documents discussed in Section 7.6.15. Examples might include a purchase or sale contract pursuant to which a major acquisition financed by the proceeds of the loans is consummated. In this case, the lenders may limit the ability of the borrower to waive rights it may have under the indemnification provisions of the contract. Similarly, if a supply contract is an important source of raw materials for the borrower, or if sales under a requirements contract provide funds critical to servicing the loans, modifications to those contracts could be restricted by the covenant.

One qualification frequently inserted into the covenant, as applied to either organic documents or other material agreements, allows the borrower to effect modifications without the consent of the lenders if the modification is "not adverse" or "not materially adverse" to the lenders, or if the modification does not adversely affect the rights of the borrower under the contract. From the borrower's perspective, these allow it to effect *de minimis* changes (such as modifications to the notice provisions or other routine matters) without the need to obtain the consent of the lenders. There is considerable logic to this type of exclusion (especially since agents and lending syndicates typically do not want to be bothered with nonmaterial modifications), so many credit agreements carve out nonmaterial changes. This is so despite the difficulty of determining what is material in any particular circumstance (though, as discussed in Section 7.6.15 with respect to amendments to debt documents, some agreements permit the administrative agent to decide whether a change is material, and only if it is material is a vote of the required lenders taken).

7.6.18   Fiscal Periods and Accounting Changes

Box 7.52

(a) *GAAP; Changes in Accounting Treatment.* Except as otherwise expressly provided herein, all terms of an accounting or financial nature shall be construed in accordance with GAAP, as in effect from time to time; *provided* that, if the Borrower notifies the Administrative Agent that the Borrower requests an amendment to any provision hereof to eliminate the effect of any change occurring after the date hereof in GAAP or in the application thereof on the operation of such provision (or if the Administrative Agent notifies the Borrower that the Required Lenders request an amendment to any provision hereof for such purpose), regardless of whether any such notice is given before or after such change in GAAP or in the application thereof, then such provision shall be interpreted on the basis of GAAP as in effect and applied immediately before such change shall have become effective until such notice shall have been withdrawn or such provision amended in accordance herewith; *provided, further,* that if such an amendment is requested by the Borrower or the Required Lenders, then the Borrower and the Administrative Agent shall negotiate in good faith to enter into an amendment of the relevant affected provisions (without the payment of any amendment or similar fee to the Lenders) to preserve the original intent thereof in light of such change in GAAP or the application thereof.

(b) *Changes in Fiscal Periods.* To enable the ready and consistent determination of compliance with the covenants set forth in Article [Financial and Negative Covenants], the Borrower will not change the last day of its fiscal year from [December 31] of each year, or the last days of the first three fiscal quarters in each of its fiscal years from [March 31], [June 30] and [September 30] of each year, respectively.

As noted earlier in the discussion of GAAP in Section 7.3.1, the financial covenants set forth in a credit agreement are usually prepared on a base set of "generally accepted accounting principles" that have been "consistently applied." Changes in the application of those principles to the financial statements of the borrower, whether at the borrower's own initiative or as a result of changes in principles themselves, could mean that the financial covenants no longer adequately measure business performance. Two recently announced modifications to accounting principles, namely rules of fair value accounting for debt obligations and lease accounting (and elimination of off-balance-sheet accounting for operating leases), are examples of such changes that could flow through to impact a borrower's financial statements. The lenders, of course, fear that a change might make compliance too easy; the borrower fears that compliance will become too difficult, although the latter is of less worry to it principally because the borrower can normally control the timing and manner of implementation of any change. To address these concerns, credit agreements often allow the borrower or the lenders to force all financial covenants to be calculated in a manner consistent with the generally accepted accounting principles that were in effect before the change. This construct, which is typically found in the interpretation provision, is generally referred to as "frozen GAAP" as opposed to a "rolling GAAP" construct, which would measure financial covenants to be calculated after giving effect to the changed accounting principles. To minimize the expense of the borrower's having to prepare two sets of financial statements (one for its regular financial statements under the newly modified accounting rules and the other for its lenders), the agreement may contemplate that the parties will negotiate appropriate changes to the financial covenants so that the required covenant levels reflect the changed principles or changed application thereof. Absent agreement, the financial covenants are required to be calculated without giving effect to the change.

Financial covenants (and, sometimes, negative covenants) are often prepared with a view to step-ups or step-downs that occur at times of the year and correspond to fiscal quarter or fiscal year end dates. To determine compliance with the covenants is thus straightforward for both the borrower and the lenders. To permit the borrower to change fiscal end dates could either require the lenders to guess whether the borrower is in compliance with these tests or force the borrower to prepare one-off, less reliable financial statements at a date that does not correspond to a fiscal period end. Credit agreements, accordingly, frequently restrict the ability of a borrower to change the end of fiscal periods. This restriction can typically be found as a standalone negative covenant.

7.6.19   Passive Holding Company

> **Box 7.53**
>
> Holdings (i) shall not engage in any material business or material activity other than (1) the ownership of all the outstanding Capital Stock of the Borrower (or, indirectly, other Capital Stock in accordance with clause (ii) below) and activities incidental thereto, (2) activities necessary or advisable to consummate the Transactions, and (3) corporate maintenance activities (including the payment of taxes and similar administrative expenses associated with being a holding company); (ii) shall not own or acquire any material assets (other than Capital Stock of the Borrower or any Immaterial Subsidiary in existence on the Closing Date or, indirectly, other Subsidiaries of the Borrower and cash and Cash Equivalents); (iii) shall not create, incur, assume, or permit to exist any Debt other than in the form of a guarantee of the obligations of the Borrower and its Subsidiaries described in clause (i) above; (iv) shall not create, incur, assume, or permit to exist Lien on the Capital Stock of the Borrower owned by it, other than Liens under the Loan Documents; (v) may make any public offering of its common stock or any other issuance of its Capital Stock not prohibited by Article [*Negative Covenants*] or constituting a Change of Control; (vi) may engage in payment of dividends not otherwise prohibited by Section [*Restricted Payments*], contribute to the capital of the Borrower and its Subsidiaries described in clause (i) above; (vii) may participate in tax, accounting, and other administrative matters as a member of the consolidated group of Holdings and the Borrower; (viii) may provide indemnification to officers and directors; (ix) may engage in activities incidental or reasonably related to the foregoing; and (x) may engage in any transaction that Holdings is otherwise expressly permitted to enter into or consummate under this Article [*Negative Covenants*].

A common corporate structure for loan transactions is for the borrower to have a direct parent holding company. The presence of a holding company parent may assist in achieving tax planning goals as well as financing goals. To the extent the borrower has a direct parent holding company, there are several reasons to subject that holding company to the covenants, or at least the passive holding company covenant of the type shown in Box 7.53.

First, lenders may require a pledge of borrower's equity to provide a single point of enforcement, as opposed to enforcing on pledges from potentially disparate equity holders, in case of any foreclosure. A parallel parent holding company guarantee of borrower's obligations will often accompany this equity pledge. The guaranty and pledge are stronger due to the prohibition on the parent's incurrence of any competing liens, others claims, or claimholders at the parent holding company. More generally, requiring a passive parent without active business operations lessens the risk of competing voluntary or involuntary creditors of the holding company in an enforcement situation. Second, the more liabilities and cash demands that arise at the parent holding company, the greater the likelihood that the holding company will seek capital distributions or other cash payments from the borrower and operating subsidiaries. Therefore, a passive holding company covenant plays a role in protecting the creditworthiness and risk profile of the borrower credit group. To maintain such a "clean" holding company and address the issues described above, lenders will insist on introducing a passive holding company covenant along the lines of that set forth above.

7.7 INCORPORATION BY REFERENCE

Box 7.54

The Borrower agrees, for the benefit of the Lenders and the Administrative Agent, to perform, comply with, and be bound by each of its covenants, agreements, and obligations contained in Sections ___ through ___ of the [Indenture] dated as of [Date] between the Borrower and [Name of Trustee], as trustee (the *"Other Agreement"*), [as modified and supplemented and in effect from time to time, or as last in effect in the event the Other Agreement shall be terminated] [as in effect on the date hereof and without giving effect to any modifications or supplements thereto except to the extent expressly agreed to by the Required Lenders for purposes hereof]. Without limiting the generality of the foregoing, the above-mentioned provisions of the Other Agreement, together with related definitions and ancillary provisions and schedules and exhibits, are hereby incorporated herein by reference and shall continue in effect for the benefit of the Lenders and the Administrative Agent, as if set forth herein in full, *mutatis mutandis; provided* that, as incorporated herein, (a) each reference therein to "this [Agreement]" or "the [Notes] [Bonds]" or the like shall be deemed to be a reference to this Agreement and to promissory notes hereunder (if any), as the case may be; (b) each reference therein to any "[holder of any [Note] [Bond]]" or the like, shall be deemed to be a reference to a Lender hereunder; (c). . . .

From time to time, a credit agreement incorporates covenants from another agreement, such as a bond indenture or private placement. Incorporation can be done in two ways. Most often, incorporation is effected by simply word processing the covenants into the credit agreement directly with such modifications as the parties may agree. An alternative method is to reference the other agreement in the credit agreement itself and "deem" the target covenants to be incorporated. That is the approach of the sample language in Box 7.54. When necessary, these provisions also incorporate related definitions and specify any necessary changes in terminology (the Latin expression used above, *mutatis mutandis*, means "to change those things which need to be changed"). Some adaptations, however, are expressly stipulated. To illustrate, if the covenants to be incorporated are from a bond indenture, the incorporation, for clarity, states that references in the covenants to "notes" and "note holders" are deemed to refer to "loans" and "lenders."

One key question that any incorporation provision must address is whether covenants are to be incorporated "as amended from time to time" or "as in effect" on the date of incorporation. The former removes the ability of the lenders to consent to changes to the incorporated covenants. The latter gives the lenders an independent consent right each time the borrower wants to modify the incorporated provision. Of course, even if incorporated "as amended from time to time," the covenant still needs to address what happens if, say, the bond indenture from which the covenants are incorporated is terminated. In that instance, as demonstrated in the language in Box 7.54, the incorporation provision normally provides that the indenture covenants are incorporated "as last in effect" and that they "continue in effect for the benefit of the Lenders and the Administrative Agent."

7.8 COVENANT LITE

Covenants in credit agreements have historically been different from those usually found in bond indentures. For several reasons, those found in indentures have tended to be somewhat looser. To begin with, the duration of the covenants in an indenture is usually longer, corresponding to the generally longer tenors of bonds as compared with loans. The longer the duration of covenants, the more flexibility the issuer wants to accommodate its planning needs, its growth projections, and unforeseen circumstances that may affect its business. In addition, bonds tend to be more widely held than loans, which makes it more difficult to obtain waivers and amendments for indenture provisions. Knowing this, an issuer of bonds is more reluctant to accept the statement, often heard in credit agreement negotiations, "Don't worry—if the covenant is too tight you can just go for a waiver." Also, the cost of issuing bonds is generally higher than the borrowing cost for loans, and issuers often have the view that a looser covenant package is one of the advantages they are "buying" with the higher priced alternative. Finally, while bank lenders and other noninstitutional investors, for example, have historically been focused on deleveraging and amortization, the typical bond investor has been less focused on paydown during the term of the instrument and content with keeping its money "at work" and accruing interest. Therefore bonds in the past were viewed as more liberal than loans in terms of forcing principal repayment prior to maturity.

Notwithstanding the past differences, at various times in the development of the leveraged finance market (including at the time of this writing) there has been a convergence of terms and conditions for loans and bonds. This convergence has come about at times of high investor demand (including from high-yield bond investors) which result in borrowers enjoying particularly strong negotiating leverage. Not surprisingly in these circumstances, borrowers are able to pick and choose what they like from each market. This was seen for the first time in the late 1990s, when the two markets began to mix and match maturities, interest rates (fixed versus variable), and covenant packages. Starting in about 2005 and ending at the beginning of the last financial crisis in mid-2007 and then again commencing in the postcrisis period circa 2011, the loan market could be described as heavily trending toward so-called "covenant lite" transactions, in which some credit agreements incorporated many of the weaker covenants from typical high-yield securities transactions in place of the more robust covenants typical of leveraged loan transactions. During the first quarter of 2016, more than 65 percent of existing institutional U.S. term loan B loans were covenant lite[6] and approximately 40 percent of existing European institutional term loan B loans were of the covenant lite variety.[7]

The hallmark of covenant lite transactions is the replacement of financial covenants that constitute "maintenance" tests with covenants constituting "incurrence" tests. The distinction between these two types of covenants is discussed in detail in the introductory paragraphs to Section 7.6. For present purposes it suffices simply to restate that a *maintenance* covenant requires the borrower to maintain a given level of financial performance (with a default occurring if that level is not continually satisfied for any reason, voluntary or involuntary), while

---

[6] S&P/LSTA Leveraged Loan Index.
[7] S&P European Leveraged Loan Index.

an *incurrence* covenant simply requires the borrower not to take some action within its control, such as issuing additional debt or paying dividends, unless a given financial ratio meets agreed parameters (with a default occurring only if the borrower nevertheless takes the voluntary action in breach of the parameters).

The increased investor demand that resulted in the growth of covenant lite transactions has largely come from institutional investors providing B term loans. At times, the demand was so strong that A term loans virtually disappeared in the leveraged loan market, and the primary role of traditional commercial banks was reduced to providing revolving credit facilities. This results in a bifurcated approach to financial covenants, in which the B term loans had the benefit of incurrence tests and the revolving credit lenders had the benefit of financial maintenance tests. This structure has sometimes been achieved with two separate credit agreements—one for the term loans and the other for revolving loans—or with a single credit agreement in which the maintenance tests are designed to benefit the term loan A and revolving lenders only. At the height of the latest investor demand cycle, some credit agreements even omitted maintenance tests in revolving credit facilities or (particularly, but not exclusively, in asset-based lending transactions) provide that the maintenance tests, which would usually take the form of a fixed charge coverage test, would apply only if the borrower's liquidity (defined as unrestricted cash-on-hand plus unused availability under the revolving credit facility) fell below a specified level or, conversely, if drawn exposure under the revolving credit facility in the form of loan draws and letters of credit exceeded a specified level.

While covenant lite structures are commonly viewed as more borrower-friendly than traditionally covenanted loans, it is anything but settled whether the growing prevalence of such structures in the loan market is an entirely negative phenomenon. For those sounding the alarm, including banking regulators,[8] the absence of creditor controls, the monitoring mechanism, and credit distress tripwire of sorts that financial covenants provide all combine to make covenant lite structures weaker from the lender's perspective. For those more sanguine about covenant lite structures, they may point to the fact that covenant lite loans still have substantially the same affirmative and negative covenants as traditionally covenanted loans and the absence of financial maintenance covenants is but one of many variables to be concerned about in credit underwriting. The presence of financial

---

[8] *See Interagency Guidance on Leveraged Lending,* March 21, 2013 and revised November 13, 2014; Board of Governors of the Federal Reserve System, FDIC, and OCC and the 2014 SNC Supplement.

maintenance covenants may even provide false comfort where covenant levels are set with generous cushions to the borrower's proposed business model and borrower-friendly elements, such as unlimited cash netting and aggressive add backs (both of which have merited mentions in recent leveraged lending guidance issued by banking regulators), make covenants less meaningful. Finally, in the context of a deep highly liquid secondary loan market where a lender can find many willing and able buyers for its loan if such lender desires to trade out of a position, reduced covenant protections may be less of a concern.

Regardless of one's view of covenants, the advent of the covenant lite structure has been profound and, at the time of this writing, may be the most identifiable hallmark of the current institutional term loan market.

CHAPTER 8

Guarantees and Security

8.1 GUARANTEES AND SECURITY GENERALLY

The obligations of a borrower under a credit agreement may be guaranteed by its parent, by its subsidiaries, and/or by other affiliates. The obligations of the borrower and guarantors may also be secured by collateral. Whether guarantee and security provisions are set forth in the credit agreement or in separate documents is typically a matter of style and convenience. Guarantees are often set out in the credit agreement (primarily for ease of reading); because of their length, security provisions are rarely set forth in the credit agreement, except perhaps in the asset-based lending context.

8.2 GUARANTEES

8.2.1 Guarantees Generally

> **Box 8.1**
>
> The Guarantors hereby jointly and severally guarantee, as primary obligor and not as surety only, to the Administrative Agent and each Lender and their respective successors and assigns the prompt payment in full in cash when due (whether at stated maturity, by acceleration or otherwise) of the principal of and interest on the Loans and all fees, indemnification payments and other amounts whatsoever, whether direct or indirect, absolute or contingent, now or hereafter from time to time owing to the Lenders or the Administrative Agent by the Borrower under the Loan Documents or Specified Hedge Agreement or Cash Management Obligations, in each case strictly in accordance with the terms thereof and including all interest and expenses accrued or incurred subsequent to the

commencement of any bankruptcy or insolvency proceeding with respect to the Borrower, whether or not such interest or expenses are allowed as a claim in such proceeding (collectively, the *"Guaranteed Obligations"*); *provided* that "Guaranteed Obligations" shall exclude any Excluded Swap Obligations (see Section 8.2.11 for discussion of "Excluded Swap Obligations").

Credit agreement guarantees vary in length from a few lines to many pages. There is no right or wrong way to write guarantees and their length relates less to the guarantee language itself than to the scope of the waivers that the drafter believes are necessary to make the guarantee absolute (see Section 8.2.3). In fact, the phrase "payment guaranteed" stamped above an additional signature on a promissory note is effective under case law and the Uniform Commercial Code (UCC) to guarantee a note.

When more than one guarantor guarantees an obligation, the undertaking is generally expressed as "joint and several." Joint and several liability is a common law concept that has been defined as liability that is "apportionable at a [creditor's] discretion either among two or more parties or to only one or a few select members of the group; together and in separation" (*Black's Law Dictionary* 751 (10th ed. 2014)). In the context of a credit agreement, this means that each guarantor is independently obligated for the full amount of the loan. If there are three guarantors, each is obligated for 100 percent of the loan, not just for 33 1/3 percent. No guarantor can refuse to pay on the grounds that the other guarantors are not paying, or even on the grounds that the lenders have not demanded payment from the others. This is a big advantage to the lenders if, for example, one guarantor happens to be insolvent; they need pursue only the remaining, solvent guarantors. Of course, the lenders are entitled to only one recovery (courts may refer to this rule as the "single-satisfaction rule") and if one guarantor pays the full amount of the guaranteed loan it may be entitled to receive contribution from the other guarantors for their ratable shares of the payment.

Credit agreements sometimes diverge from the general rule of joint and several liability, for example when the borrower is a joint venture formed by two or more joint venture partners. In this circumstance, it is not unusual for each joint venture partner to be *severally* obligated in respect of the credit agreement for a percentage equivalent to, say, its percentage ownership interest in the borrower. For example, a 40 percent equity holder might be obligated in respect of only 40 percent of the loans. Failure by one joint venture partner to pay its guarantee would not in this circumstance entitle the lenders to seek payment from the other guarantors for the defaulting partner's obligation.

Many guarantees (the language set out in Box 8.1 is an example) state expressly that the guarantor is obligated to pay interest accruing on the loan after commencement of a bankruptcy or insolvency proceeding, whether or not the interest is allowed as a claim in the proceeding. This language is derived from a concern that a guarantor might not be obligated on a claim for which the borrower itself is not obligated (interest on the underlying debt ceases to accrue after a filing), at least without an express undertaking on the part of the guarantor. This is analogous to the so-called "rule of explicitness" applicable to subordinated indebtedness. Under cases such as *In re Southeast Banking Corp.*, 93 N.Y.2d 178 (1999), if a senior creditor ". . . desires to establish a right to post-petition interest and a concomitant reduction in the dividends due the subordinated creditor, the agreement should clearly show that the general rule that interest stops on the date of filing of the petition is to be suspended, at least vis-à-vis these parties." Bankruptcy attorneys have been concerned that the rule of explicitness could be stretched to apply to guarantees of interest that would otherwise accrue after a bankruptcy case commences and have convinced their drafting colleagues to insert into guarantees explicit language that references post-petition interest.

It is worth noting that the Bankruptcy Code itself (Section 524(e)) provides that discharge of the debt of a bankrupt debtor does not affect the liability of any other entity for such debt. At least two decisions have confirmed that Section 524(e) means that guarantors are not relieved simply because a borrower is discharged from liability for post-petition interest (see *Credit Suisse First Boston Mortg. Capital LLC v. Cohn*, 2004 U.S. Dist. LEXIS 16577 (S.D.N.Y. 2004) and *Keene Corp. v. Acstar Ins. Co.*, 162 B.R. 935 (Bankr. S.D.N.Y. 1994)). This fact notwithstanding, there appears to be little movement to eliminate reference to post-petition interest.

The phrase "as primary obligor and not as surety only" in the sample language in Box 8.1 is antiquated language still seen in many guarantees. Although it purports to say that the guarantee is a *primary* liability, in fact a guarantee is normally payable only if and to the extent of a default by the underlying obligor, and therefore in truth remains *secondary* in nature. When included in guarantee language, the "primary obligor" language is designed to underscore the unconditional nature of the guarantee. Once the guarantee obligation is triggered due to a payment default or other default, that guarantee obligation is noncontingent. No other events need to occur for the primary guarantee to be enforceable and creditors may demand payment from the guarantors of 100 percent of the underlying obligation even if the creditors do not first, or ever, seek to enforce the claim against the borrower. See *In re Lightsquared Inc.*, 2014 Bankr. LEXIS 4577 at 11 (Bankr. S.D.N.Y. 2014). In this way, the guarantee obligation may be viewed as primary or at least on par with the underlying guaranteed obligation. However, prior to the occurrence of a triggering event that crystallizes the guarantee obligation, the guarantee is secondary. Case law indicates, for example, that even when "primary obligor" language is included, other attributes of secondary liability such as the right of subrogation (see Section 8.2.4) remain applicable; see *Chem. Bank v. Meltzer*, 93 N.Y.2d 296 (1999).

8.2.2 Guarantee of Payment versus Guarantee of Collection

Box 8.2

This is a guarantee of payment and not of collection. The Guarantors hereby expressly waive diligence, presentment, demand of payment, protest and all notices whatsoever, and any requirement that the Administrative Agent or any Lender exhaust any right, power or remedy or proceed against the Borrower under the Credit Agreement or any other agreement or instrument referred to herein, or against any other Person under any other guarantee of, or security for, any of the Guaranteed Obligations.

As already noted, a guarantee is a secondary obligation, which means the guarantor becomes obligated to make payment only if the primary obligor (the borrower) fails to do so. However, the nature of this secondary obligation can vary depending upon whether the guarantee is a guarantee of payment or a guarantee of collection. At common law, a guarantee of collection requires the lender to exhaust all remedies against the borrower before it makes a claim under the guarantee (and then only for the ultimate shortfall not paid by the borrower). By contrast, a guarantee of payment obligates the guarantor to pay the lender immediately upon the default of the borrower regardless of whether the lender has taken any action against the borrower, such as to notify the borrower of the default or make a demand upon the borrower.

Guarantees (whether found in credit agreements or otherwise) are almost always stated to be guarantees of payment rather than guarantees of collection. To do otherwise could present significant, even insurmountable, difficulties to a lender. An example can illustrate the problem. If a lender were required to exhaust remedies against the borrower before making a claim on the guarantor, it could, in the worst case, suffer years of costly litigation before it convinces a court to issue a money judgment against the borrower, then additional years of fruitless effort as it attempts to seize assets or foreclose on collateral, and finally a third set of years as it sues the guarantor and proves to a court the amount of its ultimate shortfall. The situation becomes more hopeless if the borrower is in bankruptcy. To take action against the borrower to crystallize the amount of the claim under a guarantee of collection would violate the Bankruptcy Code's automatic stay. No lender would (or could) do this and so the lender could not satisfy the precondition to making a claim against the guarantor until the bankruptcy case is concluded or it persuades the bankruptcy court to lift the automatic stay. For all of these reasons, the customary guarantee includes an explicit waiver by the guarantor of any requirement that the lenders first take action against the borrower before they make a claim on the guarantor. The language set out in Box 8.2 is a typical example of how a guarantee is made a guarantee of payment rather than a guarantee of collection.

8.2.3 Waivers

Box 8.3

The obligations of the Guarantors are absolute and unconditional, joint and several, irrespective of the value, genuineness, legality, validity, regularity or enforceability of the obligations of the Borrower under this Agreement or any other agreement or instrument referred to herein or therein, or any substitution, release or exchange of any other guarantee of or security for any of the Guaranteed Obligations, and, to the fullest extent permitted by applicable law, irrespective of any other circumstance whatsoever that might otherwise constitute a legal or equitable discharge or defense of a guarantor or surety, it being the intent hereof that the obligations of the Guarantors hereunder shall be absolute and unconditional, joint and several, under any and all circumstances. Without limiting the generality of the foregoing, it is agreed that the occurrence of any one or more of the following shall not alter or impair the liability of the

Guarantors hereunder, which shall remain absolute and unconditional as described above:

(i) at any time or from time to time, without notice to the Guarantors, the time for any performance of or compliance with any of the Guaranteed Obligations shall be extended, or such performance or compliance shall be waived;

(ii) any of the acts mentioned in any of the provisions of this Agreement or any other agreement or instrument referred to herein or therein shall be done or omitted;

(iii) any rescission, waiver, amendment or modification of, or any consent to departure from, any of the terms or provisions (including provisions relating to events of default) hereof or any of the other Loan Documents, or any agreement or instrument executed pursuant thereto, or of any other guarantee or security for the Guaranteed Obligations;

(iv) any failure or omission to assert or enforce or agreement or election not to assert or enforce, or the stay or enjoining, by order of court, by operation of law or otherwise, of the exercise or enforcement of, any claim or demand or any right, power or remedy;

(v) the maturity of any of the Guaranteed Obligations shall be accelerated, or any of the Guaranteed Obligations shall be modified, supplemented or amended in any respect, or any right under this Agreement or any other agreement or instrument referred to herein or therein shall be waived or any other guarantee of any of the Guaranteed Obligations or any security therefor shall be released or exchanged in whole or in part or otherwise dealt with;

(vi) any lien or security interest granted to, or in favor of, the Administrative Agent or any other Secured Party as security for any of the Guaranteed Obligations shall be impaired or otherwise fail to be perfected; or

(vii) any other act or thing or omission, or delay to do any other act or thing, which may or might in any manner or to any extent vary the risk of any Guarantor as an obligor in respect of the Guaranteed Obligations.

In most states (California is an exception), no comprehensive statute governs guarantees (as there is, for example, under the civil code in many countries), and guarantees are therefore governed by common law decisions of the courts of the various states. At common law, guarantors are favored over the beneficiaries of guarantees. As a result, court decisions have established a number of qualifications to the obligations of guarantors that, unless waived, can present pitfalls and traps for the lender.

By way of illustration, at common law, the granting of extra time to the borrower, the issuance of a waiver or amendment of the borrower's obligations, the release of security, the release of other guarantors, and a host of other actions by a lender could have the effect of releasing a guarantor from its guarantee liability. Guarantees, therefore, routinely state that they are "absolute and unconditional" and include waivers of these common law defenses. Case law in California counsels that these waivers be as explicit as possible, resulting in long and detailed waiver provisions; in New York, it is common for guarantee waivers to refer specifically to only a few of the circumstances that could release the guarantor at common law, and to rely otherwise on a "sweep-up" phrase that waives "any other circumstance whatsoever that might otherwise constitute a legal or equitable discharge or defense of a guarantor or surety." The language set out in Box 8.3 is an example of a typical New York waiver provision.

8.2.4 Subrogation

Box 8.4

The Guarantors hereby jointly and severally agree that until the payment and satisfaction in full of all Guaranteed Obligations and the expiration or termination of the Commitments of the Lenders they shall not exercise any right or remedy arising by reason of any performance by them of their guarantee, whether by subrogation or otherwise, against the Borrower or any other guarantor of any of the Guaranteed Obligations or any security for any of the Guaranteed Obligations.

Under the common law theory of subrogation, payment by a guarantor under a guarantee does not relieve the borrower of any of its obligations in respect of a loan, but the guarantor rather than the lender is deemed to become the holder of that obligation (at least to the extent of the payment by the guarantor). An example may help to illustrate this. If a borrower has taken a loan of $10,000,000 and then defaults, and the guarantor pays $6,000,000 pursuant to its guarantee, the borrower remains obligated on the full $10,000,000, $6,000,000 of which is now payable to the guarantor and $4,000,000 of which remains payable to the lenders. Payment by the guarantor is not payment by the borrower.

At common law, the transfer of the claim from the lenders to the guarantors is effected pursuant to the doctrine of subrogation. When the guarantor makes payment under its guarantee, it is "subrogated" to the rights of the lender to the extent of its payment. Subject to certain limitations, payment under a guarantee in a credit agreement has the same effect—the guarantor steps into the shoes of the lender up to the amount it has paid. Under subrogation theory, the rights to which the guarantor becomes entitled include any claims against other guarantors and any collateral security for the obligations of the borrower or other guarantors. Subrogation is, in effect, a transfer by the lender to the guarantor of the portion of its claim against the borrower that corresponds to the dollar amount of the payment tendered by the guarantor.

The "transfer" occurs without execution of any written assignment agreement or the like: subrogation arises by operation of law. However, under some agreements (such as in the circumstance where joint venture partners guarantee on a several basis the obligations of the borrower), the guarantee provides that the lenders (or administrative agent on their behalf) execute a subrogation agreement pursuant to which the lenders' claims against the borrower are formally transferred to the relevant guarantor. There can be advantages to this approach for both lenders and guarantors, since a written subrogation agreement may avoid ambiguities that might otherwise arise when subrogation occurs by operation of law. For example, under common law principles a guarantor may not be permitted to exercise subrogation rights until the lender is paid (or if the Box 8.4 formulation was used, "paid and satisfied") in full. Does that prevent the guarantor from voting upon amendments that require 100 percent lender consent? What if the lenders are required to reimburse the administrative agent for costs incurred by the latter? Is it clear that the subrogated guarantor is obligated for its *pro rata* share of those costs? These points can be addressed explicitly in a written subrogation agreement. In cases where a written subrogation agreement is to be executed, a form thereof is typically attached to the credit agreement as an exhibit and not left to negotiation at the time of payment under the guarantee.

Partial subrogation, which can arise if after payment on a guarantee the loan has not been paid in full, can be problematic for a lender. In the example above, if the guarantor is subrogated to the rights of the lender upon payment of the $6,000,000, the lender would find itself competing with the guarantor for payment by the borrower of the remaining $4,000,000. If the borrower can only afford to pay 50¢ on the dollar, the lender ends up short, recovering only $8,000,000 instead of the full $10,000,000 to which it is entitled ($8,000,000 = $6,000,000 (the payment from the guarantor) + $2,000,000 (50 percent of the $4,000,000 remaining to be paid by the borrower)). Yet it should receive a full $10,000,000: $6,000,000 from the guarantor and $4,000,000 from the borrower.

Credit agreement guarantee provisions commonly address this issue by subordinating the subrogation rights of the guarantor to the unpaid loan claims of the lender. In the example above, the exercise of any rights of subrogation are postponed until the lender is paid in full. In other instances the subrogation clause simply bars any right of subrogation (or states that no subrogation right exists) until the lender is paid in full. If there are multiple guarantors, the subrogation clause may also limit any claim (such as a contribution right) that one guarantor may have against another. Regardless of how subrogation provisions are drafted, they generally get to the same point: the lender is entitled to be fully satisfied before any guarantor may seek payment from the borrower or any other guarantor.

8.2.5 Reinstatement

Box 8.5

The obligations of the Guarantors under the guarantee shall be automatically reinstated if and to the extent that for any reason any payment by or on behalf of the Borrower in respect of the Guaranteed Obligations is rescinded or must be otherwise restored by any holder of any of the Guaranteed Obligations, whether as a result of any proceedings in bankruptcy or reorganization or otherwise, and the Guarantors jointly and severally agree that they will indemnify the Administrative Agent, the other Secured Parties and other indemnified parties hereunder or under the other Loan Documents, in each case on demand for all reasonable costs and expenses (including fees of counsel) incurred by them in connection with such rescission or restoration, including any such costs and expenses incurred in defending against any claim alleging that such payment constituted a preference, fraudulent transfer or similar payment under any bankruptcy, insolvency or similar law.

If a borrower makes payment on a loan within 90 days prior to filing for bankruptcy, the payment could potentially be recovered from the lenders as a "preference" under Section 547 of the Bankruptcy Code. A guarantor might, in that instance, claim that payment by the borrower discharged the guarantor even if the borrower (or its successor in bankruptcy) seeks to recover the payment. To avoid the lenders' having to argue with the guarantor as to whether or not the borrower's original payment (now reversed) discharged the guarantee, guarantees generally include an express "reinstatement" clause. The effect of this clause is to revive the guarantee automatically if a payment by the borrower is reversed or recaptured.

The reinstatement clause typically requires the guarantor to indemnify the lenders for any costs that they may incur in resisting the preference claim. The theory is that the lenders' fight in this regard is, in substance, a fight for the account of the guarantor. If the guarantor does not want to have the lender incur costs that are to be reimbursed by the guarantor, it can simply pay the lender an amount equal to the claimed preference, become subrogated to the lender's suit in the bankruptcy proceeding in respect of the preference litigation, and take up the fight itself.

8.2.6   Insolvency of Borrower

Box 8.6

The Guarantors jointly and severally agree that, as between the Guarantors and the Secured Parties, the obligations of the Borrower hereunder may be declared to be forthwith due and payable as provided in Section [*Events of Default*] (and shall be deemed to have become automatically due and payable in the circumstances provided in said Section [*Events of Default*]) for purposes of the guarantee notwithstanding any stay, injunction or other prohibition preventing such declaration (or such obligations from becoming automatically due and payable) as against the Borrower and that, in the event of such declaration (or such obligations being deemed to have become automatically due and payable), such obligations (whether or not due and payable by the Borrower) shall forthwith become due and payable by the Guarantors for purposes of the guarantee.

Lenders may make a demand on a guarantor only for amounts that have not been paid by the borrower when due. What happens if the borrower declares bankruptcy and the automatic stay that arises under the Bankruptcy Code prevents an acceleration of the loans (see the discussion of the automatic stay in Section 9.1.5)? What happens if a court order prevents a loan becoming due (by acceleration or otherwise) outside the context of bankruptcy, such as might happen if a foreign country declares a debt moratorium? To prevent the guarantee being rendered worthless because there is nothing payable by the borrower to be demanded from the guarantor, guarantees include a provision that, if an event of default occurs and for any reason the lenders are prevented from accelerating the loans, the loans are nevertheless deemed to be (or, in effect, may be declared) due and payable for purposes of any claims on the guarantor. So even though the loans are not accelerated as against the borrower, the loans are accelerated as against the guarantor.

8.2.7 Continuing Guarantee

> **Box 8.7**
>
> The guarantee hereunder is a continuing guarantee, and shall apply to all Guaranteed Obligations whenever arising.

A guarantee typically specifies that it is "continuing," which is to say that it covers not only obligations outstanding at the time the guarantee is issued, but also future obligations of the borrower incurred from time to time. Absent this language, a guarantee of revolving loans made at closing might arguably terminate once those particular loans were repaid and subsequent revolving loans would not be guaranteed. The magic language that has been blessed by New York courts is to state that the guarantee is *continuing* and thus that it picks up any future advances.

8.2.8 Summary Procedure

> **Box 8.8**
>
> Each Guarantor hereby acknowledges that its guarantee constitutes an instrument for the payment of money only, and consents and agrees that the Administrative Agent and any Lender, at its sole option, in the event of a dispute by such Guarantor in the payment of any moneys due hereunder, shall have the right to bring motion-action under New York CPLR Section 3213.

A guarantee that is stated to be governed by New York law often includes an acknowledgment by the guarantor that it constitutes "an instrument for the payment of money only" within the meaning of Section 3213 of New York's Civil Practice Law and Rules (CPLR). CPLR Section 3213 provides that such an instrument may be enforced by expedited (or summary) procedure, without the need for a plaintiff to labor through time-consuming and cumbersome matters of proof when the documentary evidence taken alone shows that money is due. "Its purpose was to provide quick relief on documentary claims so presumptively meritorious that a formal complaint is superfluous, and even the delay incident upon waiting for an answer and then moving for summary judgment is needless" (*Weissman v. Sinorm Deli, Inc.*, 88 N.Y.2d 437 (N.Y. 1996)).

Although most court decisions have answered favorably when determining whether guarantees are entitled to the summary procedure contemplated by CPLR Section 3213, courts are not uniform and can be influenced by the language in the guarantee itself. Indeed, in at least one instance a court implied that it was upholding the application of CPLR Section 3213 because the guarantor had expressly acknowledged that summary enforcement was available (see *SCP, Inc., v. Bermudatel Ltd.*, 638 N.Y.S.2d 2 (App. Div. 1st Dep't 1996)). No drafting suggestion made by a court goes ignored and many guarantee forms were quickly revised to include an express statement that CPLR Section 3213 was applicable to enforcement of the guarantee. Saying that a guarantee is an "instrument for the payment of money only" may not make it so (many guarantees include a variety of undertakings beyond the obligation to pay money), so closing opinions frequently take a qualification as to the effectiveness of the guarantor's acknowledgment. Nevertheless, the CPLR acknowledgment has become near-standard language in New York law guarantees.

8.2.9 Guarantee Limitations and Rights of Contribution

Box 8.9

(a) *Guarantee Limitation.* In any action or proceeding involving any state corporate law, or any state or Federal bankruptcy, insolvency, reorganization or other law affecting the rights of creditors generally, if the obligations of any Guarantor hereunder would otherwise, taking into account the provisions of paragraph (b), be held or determined to be void, invalid or unenforceable, or subordinated to the claims of any other creditors, on account of the amount of its liability hereunder, then, notwithstanding any other provision hereof to the contrary, the amount of such liability shall, without any further action by such Guarantor, the Administrative Agent, any Lender or any other Person, be automatically limited and reduced to the highest amount that is valid and enforceable and not subordinated to the claims of other creditors as determined in such action or proceeding.

(b) *Rights of Contribution.* The Obligors[1] hereby agree, as between themselves, that if any Guarantor shall become an Excess Funding Guarantor (as defined below) by reason of the payment by such Guarantor of any Guaranteed Obligations, then each other Guarantor shall, on demand of such Excess Funding Guarantor (but subject to the next sentence), pay to such Excess Funding Guarantor an amount equal to such Guarantor's Pro Rata Share (as defined below and determined, for this purpose, without reference to the properties, debts and liabilities of such Excess Funding Guarantor) of the Excess Payment (as defined below) in respect of such Guaranteed Obligations. The payment obligation of a Guarantor to any Excess Funding Guarantor hereunder shall be subordinate and subject in right of payment to the prior payment in full of the obligations of such Guarantor under the other provisions hereof and such Excess Funding Guarantor shall not exercise any right or remedy with respect to such excess until payment and satisfaction in full of all of such obligations.

For purposes hereof, (i) *"Excess Funding Guarantor"* means, in respect of any Guaranteed Obligations, a Guarantor that has paid an amount in excess of its Pro Rata Share of such Guaranteed Obligations, (ii) *"Excess Payment"* means, in respect of any Guaranteed Obligations, the amount paid by an Excess Funding Guarantor in excess of its Pro Rata Share of such Guaranteed Obligations and (iii) *"Pro Rata Share"* means, for any Guarantor, the ratio (expressed as a percentage) of (x) the amount by which the aggregate fair saleable value of all properties of such Guarantor (excluding any shares of stock or other equity interest of any other Guarantor) exceeds the amount of all the debts and liabilities of such Guarantor (including contingent, subordinated, unmatured and unliquidated liabilities, but excluding the obligations of such Guarantor hereunder and any obligations of any other Guarantor that have been guaranteed by such Guarantor) to (y) the amount by which the aggregate fair saleable value of all properties of the Borrower and all of the Guarantors exceeds the aggregate amount of all the debts and liabilities (including contingent, subordinated, unmatured and unliquidated liabilities, but excluding the obligations of the Obligors hereunder and under the other Loan Documents) of all of the Guarantors, determined (A) with respect to any Guarantor that is a party hereto on the Closing Date, as of the Closing Date, and (B) with respect to any other Guarantor, as of the date such Guarantor becomes a Guarantor hereunder.

---

[1] This is defined to be the borrower and the guarantors, collectively.

Guarantees can be "upstream" (as when a subsidiary guarantees the debt of its parent), "cross-stream" (when a subsidiary guarantees the debt of a "sister" company, with both ultimately owned by the same parent), or "downstream" (when a parent guarantees the debt of a subsidiary). The discussion in Section 6.2.7 illustrates how an upstream or cross-stream guarantee may be vulnerable to attack under federal and state insolvency laws. Except to the extent that the guarantor actually receives the proceeds of the guaranteed loan or other "reasonably equivalent value," one of the two requirements for a "fraudulent conveyance" or "fraudulent transfer" is established. If, after giving effect to the guarantee, the guarantor is "insolvent," then both requirements are established. A downstream guarantee does not suffer the same infirmity because it is presumed that a parent guarantor receives reasonably equivalent value by virtue of its subsidiary receiving the proceeds of the loan.

Guarantees deal with fraudulent transfer risk in two ways. Some incorporate a so-called solvency cap or savings clause (the "Guarantee Limitation" paragraph in Box 8.9), which limits or caps the guarantee at the maximum amount (but not one dollar more) that would allow it to be enforced without resulting in a fraudulent conveyance. To take a simplified example, if the assets of a subsidiary exceed its liabilities by $10,000,000, and it guarantees debt in a face amount of $100,000,000, the aggregate amount of the guarantee is limited automatically to $9,999,999 (to leave an excess of assets over liabilities of $1.00). Through this device, even though the subsidiary may not receive any of the proceeds of the loans, it is (arguably) not rendered insolvent by reason of the guarantee, and so no fraudulent conveyance should arise.

The solvency cap approach is not without weaknesses. One is that it makes the amount of the guarantee unclear inasmuch as the amount of assets and liabilities of the guarantor is subject to later proof; few borrowers are willing (or even able) to prepare detailed subsidiary-by-subsidiary financial statements at the time an agreement is signed that would permit an upfront determination of the guarantee amount. Another weakness is the ambiguity as to when the calculation of assets and liabilities must be made; the law is not clear. In the case of a guarantee of a term loan, the calculation is logically made at the time the term loan is funded. However, a guarantee of loans to be made under a revolving commitment should, perhaps, also be made each time loans are funded. If there are multiple loans and multiple repayments, the calculation quickly becomes quite complex. Perhaps the most serious weakness are court decisions that have found savings clauses to be unenforceable. See *In re TOUSA, Inc.*, 422 B.R. 783 (Bankr. S.D. Fla. 2009) and *In re Exide Techs., Inc.*, 299 B.R. 732 (Bankr. D. Del. 2003).

Other credit agreements address fraudulent transfer risk by inserting a so-called cross-contribution provision (the "Rights of Contribution" paragraph in Box 8.9), whereby the borrower and each of the other guarantors agree that if any guarantor makes payment under its guarantee in an amount greater than the excess of its assets over its liabilities, it is entitled to reimbursement from the borrower and each other guarantor for the amount of the excess. The amount of reimbursement that would be payable by any guarantor to a funding guarantor is normally determined by calculating the ratio of the former's assets over liabilities to the aggregate assets over liabilities of all obligors. This is the approach taken in the language in Box 8.9. The effect of this provision is to give the funding guarantor an additional asset (namely, the contingent reimbursement claim against the borrower and the other guarantors), which should, in theory, prevent the funding guarantor from being rendered insolvent by reason of the guarantee.

The weakness of the contribution rights approach is that for the scheme to work mathematically the consolidated group obligated on the loan (the borrower together with its guaranteeing subsidiaries and affiliates) must be solvent; otherwise, the aggregate of the cross-contribution claims will not exceed the amount of the loans. Credit agreements deal with the question of consolidated group solvency in several ways. First, the solvency representation (discussed in Section 6.2.7) has the borrower confirm that the borrower and its guarantors (together with their subsidiaries) taken as a whole are solvent (thereby affirming that the contingent reimbursement claims are, in fact, money good). The representation may be back-stopped through the delivery by the borrower at closing of a "solvency certificate" that elaborates in more detail how the obligor group is solvent (see Section 5.1.11.2). A prudent lender, as part of its credit approval process, verifies to its own satisfaction that the obligor group meets the solvency tests. All of these efforts notwithstanding, there may be a great temptation on the part of creditors' counsel and courts to conclude that, because a bankruptcy proceeding has been commenced, the borrower must have been insolvent when the loan was first made. Hindsight is always 20/20.

Neither of these solutions may work if an upstream or cross-stream guarantee is given by an entity organized outside the United States. Many countries have so-called financial assistance rules that carry more severe consequences than the fraudulent conveyance and fraudulent transfer doctrines in the United States. If a guarantee renders a guarantor insolvent, violation of such rules can result in personal liability (and even, in some cases, criminal liability) for managers or directors. Savings and cross-contribution clauses such as those described previously may be ineffective. As a result, even in situations in which the tax consequences described in Section 8.6 do not arise, guarantees from foreign subsidiaries may become a patchwork of full guarantees, dollar-capped guarantees, and no guarantees—altogether a confused structure when compared to guarantees from U.S. subsidiaries.

8.2.10   Subordination

> ### Box 8.10
>
> Each Guarantor hereby agrees that any and all debts, liabilities and other obligations owed to such Guarantor by any other Loan Party, including pursuant to Section [*Cross Contribution*], are hereby subordinated to the prior payment in full in cash of the obligations of such other Loan Party hereunder and under the Loan Documents.

Although not uniformly included in credit agreement guarantees, perhaps as a logical extension of the limitation upon subrogation described above, many guarantees include an express subordination by each guarantor of any claim it may have against other parties obligated on the loan (whether the borrower or another guarantor). As with the subrogation clause, the object is to avoid the lenders having to compete with the guarantors for satisfaction from the obligor group's assets. From the lender's perspective, no guarantor should ever be treated as its equal. (For a more detailed discussion of the concept of subordination, see Section 6.5.2.)

8.2.11   Limitations on Guarantee of Hedging Obligations

> ### Box 8.11[2]
>
> (a) *"Excluded Swap Obligation"* means, with respect to any Guarantor, any Swap Obligation if, and to the extent that, all or a portion of the Guarantee of such Guarantor of, or the grant by such Guarantor of a

---

[2] The language in Box 8.11 comes from the LSTA Advisory "Swap Regulations' Implications for Loan Documentation" (February 15, 2013).

security interest to secure, such Swap Obligation (or any Guarantee thereof) is or becomes illegal under the Commodity Exchange Act or any rule, regulation or order of the Commodity Futures Trading Commission (or the application or official interpretation of any thereof) by virtue of such Guarantor's failure for any reason to constitute an "eligible contract participant" as defined in the Commodity Exchange Act and the regulations thereunder at the time the Guarantee of such Guarantor or the grant of such security interest becomes effective with respect to such Swap Obligation. If a Swap Obligation arises under a master agreement governing more than one swap, such exclusion shall apply only to the portion of such Swap Obligation that is attributable to swaps for which such Guarantee or security interest is or becomes illegal.

"Swap Obligation" means, with respect to any Guarantor, any obligation to pay or perform under any agreement, contract or transaction that constitutes a "swap" within the meaning of Section 1a(47) of the Commodity Exchange Act.

(b) *Keepwell.* Each Qualified ECP Guarantor hereby jointly and severally absolutely, unconditionally and irrevocably undertakes to provide such funds or other support as may be needed from time to time by each other [Loan Party] to honor all of its obligations under this Guarantee in respect of Swap Obligations (*provided*, however, that each Qualified ECP Guarantor shall only be liable under this Section [*Guarantee*] for the maximum amount of such liability that can be hereby incurred without rendering its obligations under this Section [*Guarantee*], or otherwise under this Guarantee, voidable under applicable law relating to fraudulent conveyance or fraudulent transfer, and not for any greater amount). The obligations of each Qualified ECP Guarantor under this Section shall remain in full force and effect until a [Discharge of Guaranteed Obligations]. Each Qualified ECP Guarantor intends that this Section ___ constitute, and this Section shall be deemed to constitute, a "keepwell, support, or other agreement" for the benefit of each other Loan Party for all purposes of Section 1a(18)(A)(v)(II) of the Commodity Exchange Act.

"Qualified ECP Guarantor" means, in respect of any Swap Obligation, each [Loan Party] that has total assets exceeding $10,000,000 at the time the relevant Guarantee or grant of the relevant security interest becomes effective with respect to such Swap Obligation or such other person as constitutes an "eligible contract participant" under the Commodity Exchange Act or any regulations promulgated thereunder and can cause another person to qualify as an "eligible contract participant" at such time by entering into a keepwell under Section 1a(18)(A)(v)(II) of the Commodity Exchange Act.

Credit agreements may either require borrowers to enter into swap or other derivative arrangements (referred to here as "swaps") or permit the borrower to enter into certain swaps (see Sections 7.5.6 and 7.6.4, respectively). Under secured credit agreements, often the banks, other financial institutions, or their affiliates who are providing the borrower with the swaps will expressly benefit from the collateral and guarantee package alongside the lenders. This is because the swap providers would have little incentive to enter into a swap arrangement without credit support and certainly there would be even less incentive if secured lenders holding a supposed "blanket" lien were ahead of them in priority. The swap providers generally come from the lender group or are affiliates of lender group members so effectively the existing lenders are providing themselves with additional credit support backing their swap exposure.

However, due to recent changes in law[3] and agency rules,[4] a guarantee of swap obligations may be treated as being equivalent to entering into the underlying swap itself and require guarantors to meet the same enhanced requirements (i.e., minimum asset requirements) that apply to swap participants themselves. Failure to meet these statutory requirements can lead to a determination of illegality and unenforceability of the relevant guarantee and related pledge or even enforcement actions brought by the Commodity Futures Trading Commission. Since not all subsidiary guarantors may meet the applicable minimum asset test on their own (either initially or at any point during the term of the credit agreement), recent credit agreements have addressed these new rules with two parallel solutions. First, any guarantor that fails to meet the minimum asset level requirement is excluded by definition from the guarantor group. This is accomplished by carving out from Guaranteed Obligations (or similar term) any swap obligations that, if guaranteed by such offending entity, would trip the Commodity Exchange Act rules. See the definition of "Excluded Swap Obligation" in Box 8.11. The excluded guarantor would still remain on the hook for all other non-swap obligations. Second, compliance with the minimum asset requirement is achieved by including a keepwell provision. Under the keepwell, those guarantors that satisfy the minimum asset level test contractually undertake to fund or provide other credit support to

---

[3] Section 732(a)(2) of Dodd-Frank Wall Street Reform and Consumer Protection Act, Public Law 111-203, 124 Stat. 1376 (2010).
[4] See No Action Letter, October 12, 2012, Office of General Counsel of U.S. Commodity Futures Trading Commission.

those entities that do not satisfy the minimum asset test. This second method, though, is typically handled in the guarantee agreement itself and clause (b) of Box 8.11 is an example of commonly used keepwell language. A keepwell has been viewed as sufficient under the Commodity Exchange Act to make an otherwise ineligible entity eligible under the minimum asset requirement.

8.3 COLLATERAL PACKAGES

Whole treatises have been written about the legal intricacies of collateral security. This chapter does not treat the topic in depth, but focuses briefly only on how collateral security affects the drafting of a credit agreement.

Normally, whatever collateral security the lending syndicate takes is set out in separate mortgages, security agreements, or other collateral documents. In some cases, the parties may provide in the credit agreement itself for the grant of security, though when this is done, it is only with respect to personal property collateral and never real property collateral. As noted previously, with the exception perhaps of asset-based lending arrangements, incorporating even personal property security provisions into a credit agreement is quite rare. In most instances, therefore, taking collateral security affects only a few very discrete provisions of the credit agreement and does not involve inserting into the agreement the full panoply of boilerplate that a security agreement contains. A more detailed discussion of these provisions is given in other chapters. A brief explanation of each affected provision, and cross-references to the relevant chapters, follows.

8.3.1 Conditions

If a facility is to be secured, the conditions precedent typically include a requirement that whatever actions are necessary for the relevant liens to be perfected and to enjoy the appropriate priority have been taken. These include execution of relevant security documents (security agreements, pledge agreements, mortgages, and the like) as well as the delivery of UCC financing statements, any original stock certificates or promissory notes, or other collateral that must be in the physical possession of the administrative or collateral agent and, in the case of real property mortgages or deeds of trust, the issuance of satisfactory surveys, title insurance policies, and flood hazard determinations and, if required, flood insurance policies. The security package for a large credit facility can easily be much more complicated and so the condition precedent may need to reference the establishment of lock-box arrangements and cash collateral and securities accounts, the execution of intercreditor agreements, and specific actions required to perfect liens under the law of foreign countries (such as the authentication of pledge agreements by notaries, the delivery of notices to account debtors, and the creation of specialized escrow arrangements). However, to the extent that a financing is subject to U.S.-style "certain funds" or "SunGard" conditionality, the required steps with respect to collateral that need to be completed at closing may be narrower and include, for example, only limited filings and delivery of pledged stock certificates. In the SunGard scenario, the other typical collateral-related requirements may be pushed to a later date and become a post-closing requirement. For a full discussion of the typical condition, see Section 5.1.7.

8.3.2   Representations

The credit agreement may include a representation that all action to perfect liens on a first-priority basis has been taken (though, more frequently, this representation is incorporated into the security documents themselves). In a syndicated credit facility, confirmation of perfection and priority is almost always one of the representations required by the term sheet (see Section 6.5.3).

8.3.3   Further Assurances Covenant

For credit facilities to be secured by liens on property of the borrower or other loan parties, the credit agreement typically includes an undertaking on the part of the borrower to execute additional agreements and take other actions in order that the lenders have good liens on the collateral intended to be covered thereby. The further assurances covenant is discussed in detail in Section 7.5.8.

8.3.4   Lien Covenant

The lien covenant not only permits the grant of liens securing the loans incurred under the credit agreement but also permits lien grants in support of other debt and other obligations incurred by the borrower. Thus the lien covenant regulates the extent to which the collateral package is shared on an equal or subordinate (and even senior) basis with competing obligations of the borrower. The lien covenant is discussed in detail in Section 7.6.1.

8.3.5   Defaults

Credit agreements that document a secured credit facility supplement the further assurances covenant by including an event of default triggered in the event the liens created under the security documents fail to be perfected or to have the required priority, or in the event the liens are terminated or the borrower asserts that they are invalid or unenforceable. Materiality and other qualifiers are, from time to time, incorporated (see Section 9.1.10).

8.3.6   Voting

The voting provisions address the level of lender consent required to release collateral or guarantees or subordinate a lien covering collateral. Usually, only releases or subordinations that affect all or substantially all of the collateral or guarantors require unanimous consent; otherwise consent of the required lenders is sufficient. Voting rights generally, as they relate to collateral security as well as sample language, are discussed in more detail in Section 10.3.6.

8.3.7   Expenses

As discussed in Section 12.5, creating and maintaining liens can give rise to their own unique set of costs and expenses: recording and filing fees, stamp taxes, notary fees, and title insurance premiums are but a few examples. Some of these costs can be significant. In secured credit facilities, it is therefore customary to insert additional language that provides for the borrower to pay these costs.

8.3.8   Agent Authorizations

Box 8.12

Collateral and Guarantee Matters (a) The [Secured Parties] irrevocably authorize the Administrative Agent, at its option and in its discretion,

(i) to release any Lien on any property granted to or held by the Administrative Agent under any Loan Document (x) upon termination of all Commitments and payment in full of all Obligations (other than contingent indemnification obligations) and the expiration or termination of all Letters of Credit [(other than Letters of Credit as to which other arrangements satisfactory to the Administrative Agent and the applicable Issuing Bank shall have been made)], (y) that is sold or otherwise disposed of or to be sold or otherwise disposed of as part of or in connection with any sale or other disposition permitted under the Loan Documents, or (z) subject to Section [*Amendments*], if approved, authorized or ratified in writing by the Required Lenders;

(ii) [to subordinate any Lien on any property granted to or held by the Administrative Agent under any Loan Document to the holder of any Lien on such property that is permitted by Section [*Liens Securing Capital Leases, Synthetic Leases and Purchase Money Indebtedness*]]; and

(iii) to release any Guarantor from its obligations under the Guarantee if such Person ceases to be a Subsidiary as a result of a transaction permitted under the Loan Documents.

Upon request by the Administrative Agent at any time, the Required Lenders will confirm in writing the Administrative Agent's authority to release [or subordinate] its interest in particular types or items of property, or to release any Guarantor from its obligations under the Guarantee pursuant to this Section 10.

(b) The Administrative Agent shall not be responsible for or have a duty to ascertain or inquire into any representation or warranty regarding the existence, value or collectability of the Collateral, the existence, priority or perfection of the Administrative Agent's Lien thereon, or any certificate prepared by any Loan Party in connection therewith, nor shall the Administrative Agent be responsible or liable to the Lenders for any failure to monitor or maintain any portion of the Collateral.

Secured lenders often give broad delegations to the administrative agent to release liens and guarantors in connection with permitted transactions such as asset sales. Rather than face the delay and expense of requesting lender consent for lien releases on each asset sale, for example, borrowers may negotiate for the agent to be empowered to process the lien releases on its own. The language quoted in Box 8.12, taken from Section 10 of the Agency section of the LSTA's Model Credit Agreement Provisions, is representative of market-standard for such agent authorization language.

8.4 SPRINGING LIENS

In some cases, the lenders do not take security at closing, but enter into an understanding with the borrower that upon specified future events (generally adverse), the borrower will grant security to the lenders. Often the triggering event is the occurrence of an event of default, but in other instances it is an adverse development in a financial ratio short of an event of default. The future, contingent liens that provisions of this nature contemplate are so-called springing liens. Although the moniker "springing liens" could apply to the liens a borrower is required to grant pursuant to an equal and ratable sharing clause (see Section 7.6.2), the term is not normally applied in that context.

Springing lien covenants are relatively rare; if collateral security is important, the parties normally create and perfect it at closing. Lenders do not want something as significant as security to be dependent upon the future cooperation of the borrower. If the adverse event that is to trigger the springing lien is an event of default, the borrower may see little advantage in granting the liens at the time required unless the default is concurrently being cured (most springing lien clauses do not so provide). Assuming that the borrower cooperates and grants the relevant liens (and takes whatever additional actions are necessary to perfect the liens), the lenders are still not home free: a lien that "springs" necessarily secures an antecedent (preexisting) debt, and thus the lenders cannot know that the lien is enforceable against other creditors of the borrower until the Bankruptcy Code preference period (90 days for noninsiders) has passed. If the borrower commences a bankruptcy case prior to the ninetieth day, the liens will be subject to preference attack and may well be undone by the Bankruptcy Court (see Section 8.2.5).

8.5 COLLATERAL ALLOCATION MECHANISM

In multitranche agreements, it is sometimes not practicable to secure all tranches equally and ratably. For example, if a credit agreement has a revolving credit commitment provided to the borrower in the United States and a term loan commitment provided to a subsidiary in Europe, collateral security granted by the European subsidiary may be able to secure only the term loans because of either the financial assistance rules described in Section 8.2.9 or the potential adverse tax consequences discussed in Section 8.6. Another example can be confronted in New York, where the severe mortgage recording tax for liens on real property discussed in Section 8.3.6 is imposed. In New York, if a term loan is secured by real property, the recording tax need be paid only once. If a revolving credit loan is secured by real property, the tax is payable on each drawing (at least, that is the position of New York State recording offices). To minimize taxes, the parties may want to stipulate that only the term loans are secured by the mortgage.

Notwithstanding these dynamics, a successful syndication may depend upon the credit agreement being structured to allow all lenders to share equally in all collateral. The typical sharing and pro rata provisions discussed in Sections 10.4 and 10.5 do not allow all lenders to share equally in the collateral because those provisions only allocate ratably borrowings and payments in respect of loans in the same tranche made by the same obligors. The mechanism that is often used to accomplish an equalization of credit support across varying tranches is the so-called collateral allocation mechanism, or CAM, provision. A CAM provision, which is used most frequently with cross-border credit facilities, requires each lender to pool the principal, interest, and other obligations owing to it with those owed to the other lenders, some of whom may have different borrowers, varying levels of collateral, and other credit support due to the difference in guarantors and collateral packages between facilities. Once an agreed trigger event occurs, such as a bankruptcy filing of the borrower or other obligor, each lender is deemed to purchase a participation in each other lenders' loans, which effectively creates a common pool of loans that are then reallocated amongst all the lenders on a proportionate basis determined by the ratio of such lender's outstanding obligations owing at such time to the aggregate obligations owing to all lenders. Where there are loan tranches denominated in different currencies, the reallocated loans take the form of loans of a common currency, usually but not necessarily U.S. dollars, based on a spot exchange rate. After the dust settles, each lender—each of whom may have held loans of varying tranches with varying levels of effective credit support—will end up with voting rights in each purchased tranche and claims in bankruptcy whether or not their original borrower filed for bankruptcy.

Under a CAM provision, taking the first scenario described in the opening paragraph above, each tranche, upon realizing on the collateral for its loans, purchases participations in the other tranche. Accordingly, the lenders that made term loans would purchase participations in the revolving loans so that, after giving effect to such purchases, the risks and benefits of the collateral security for both tranches of loans would be shared equally among all lenders. In the second scenario, the term loan lenders would similarly purchase participations in the revolving credit loans so that the proceeds of any foreclosure on mortgaged property in New York would be shared equally among all lenders. To defend against arguments as to the enforceability of a CAM provision, a typical CAM provision will include express acknowledgments to enforceability from all parties as well as undertakings to execute further documents or take further steps to give effect to the CAM provision.

8.6 DEEMED DIVIDENDS

Box 8.13

The guarantee by any Foreign Subsidiary shall be limited to the extent necessary to minimize adverse tax consequences under Section 956 of the Internal Revenue Code, as amended. In no event shall the security interest under the Security Documents in any voting stock of any issuer that is a Foreign Subsidiary exceed 65% of the aggregate issued and outstanding voting stock of such issuer.

A loan to a U.S. borrower that is guaranteed by a non-U.S. subsidiary may raise the so-called deemed dividend problem. Under Section 956 of the U.S. Internal Revenue Code, a guarantee from a non-U.S. subsidiary controlled by a U.S. company is generally deemed to be a dividend by the subsidiary to its U.S. parent (up to the amount of the guarantee) of the earnings and profits of the subsidiary. Although it is not something that affects the enforceability of the guarantee, a deemed dividend can have potentially terrible tax consequences for the U.S. parent, since the parent must include the subsidiary's earnings and profits as taxable income without receiving any cash to pay the associated taxes. As a consequence, most guarantees of debt of a U.S. borrower are restricted to its U.S. subsidiaries or, as the language in Box 8.13 contemplates, are limited to the extent necessary to avoid adverse tax consequences under Section 956.

The deemed dividend problem can also surface if a U.S. borrower pledges the equity of a non-U.S. subsidiary. Under the U.S. Internal Revenue Code, a pledge of more than 66 2/3 percent of the total combined voting power of the non-U.S. subsidiary is deemed to be a dividend to the same degree as a guarantee by the subsidiary. To avoid this result, security agreements customarily limit the percentage of pledged equity of first-tier foreign subsidiaries to 65 percent (though 66 2/3 percent is the number actually set out in the tax rules) and no stock of lower-tier foreign subsidiaries is pledged. Also customarily, the carveout above 65 percent applies to all equity capital of the non-U.S. subsidiary, although the tax rule refers only to voting stock and the pledge of nonvoting stock need not be limited.

Out of an abundance of caution, U.S. borrowers sometimes seek to limit guarantees or pledges from certain domestic subsidiaries substantially all of whose assets consist of controlled foreign subsidiaries' stock. Any such U.S. subsidiary is referred to as a "foreign subsidiary holding company." These borrowers may argue that no such foreign subsidiary holding company can be a guarantor or pledgor on the theory that a pledge of such entities' equity or guarantee may be viewed as, in substance, a pledge or guarantee with respect to the foreign subsidiaries that are owned by the foreign subsidiary holding company. Borrowers may be even more concerned to the extent that any such foreign subsidiary holding company has elected to be treated as a "disregarded entity" for U.S. tax purposes, where technically a pledge of the "disregarded" stock of the foreign subsidiary holding company constitutes a pledge of its assets (i.e., the shares of the foreign subsidiaries).

Section 956 captures only the earnings and profits of a foreign subsidiary that guarantees debt of the parent, or whose stock is pledged by the parent. Many foreign subsidiaries may have valuable assets without having tax earnings and profits (either because of the way tax accounting is performed or because the borrower has adopted a corporate policy of always dividending its earnings and profits to the parent). In some credit agreements, therefore, the Section 956 strictures do not apply and foreign subsidiaries guarantee debt of the U.S. borrower as well as have their stock pledged. Note also that Section 956 applies only to subsidiaries of a U.S. parent; subsidiaries of foreign subsidiaries can (within the other limitations described in this chapter) guarantee debt of their foreign parents without implicating the tax consequences of Section 956.

CHAPTER 9

Defaults and Enforcement

9.1 EVENTS OF DEFAULT

> **Box 9.1**
>
> If any of the following events (*"Events of Default"*) shall occur and be continuing:

Events of default are specified events or circumstances that suggest a decreased likelihood that the borrower will be able to pay its obligations under the credit agreement and that may lead the lenders to want to terminate the credit facility. Credit agreements include the event of default concept to give the lenders the ability to stop extending credit to the borrower if any of the specified events occurs. Events of default also serve as a basis for the lending syndicate to exercise remedies against the borrower, such as to commence suit to recover the loan, exercise a right of setoff, or seize collateral (or all the above!).

Short of terminating the credit facility or exercising remedies, event of default can also trigger a range of interim consequences. For example, default interest (generally in the amount of an additional 2 percent per annum) may begin to accrue, late fees may be incurred in limited cases, and ultimately lenders may charge the borrower fees to waive the default. For those credit agreements containing incurrence-based covenant baskets, these are often available only if there is no event of default. An event of default will therefore prohibit the borrower from undertaking certain discretionary actions under the incurrence-based baskets such as consummating acquisitions or paying dividends. A borrower's right to restrict secondary trading of its loans may all but vanish upon the occurrence of an event of default when its right to consent to an assignment may terminate (other than with respect to disqualified lenders as discussed further in Section 11.2.3). The potentially gravest consequence from an event of default is a cross-default to other debt resulting in a daisy chain of accelerated debt obligations. In addition to the foregoing parade of horribles that may arise under the four corners of the credit agreement, there are indirect consequences that can arise from events of default. If the borrower is a reporting company under the Securities Exchange Act of 1934 and the credit agreement is "material," the borrower is required to disclose any acceleration and may be required to disclose the occurrence of a default or event of default even if it does not result in acceleration. Being forced to tell the world of a default can lead to other problems for a lender. For example, it could scare vendors into tightening credit terms, lead to a decline in stock value, or adversely impact the availability or cost of new borrowings or debt issuances. It could also frighten away business partners for joint ventures and other projects. For these and other reasons, defaults are taken very seriously by borrowers and lenders alike, regardless of whether the lenders contemplate the exercise of remedies.

All events of default are treated the same under a credit agreement. The occurrence of any event of default, no matter the cause, can result in the above-mentioned consequences. However, in reality different events of default may indicate varying levels of borrower distress. Some events of default, such as the commencement of a bankruptcy proceeding, constitute serious and urgent problems. Other events of default relate to lesser nonpayment breaches that may be described as "technical defaults." Some breaches or events constitute immediate events of default while others ripen into events of default only after notice is given or time has elapsed (or, in some cases, after both notice is given and time has elapsed). Prior to the point that a breach or event ripens into an event of default, it is commonly referred to as a "default" or "unmatured default" (a typical formulation defines these terms as "an event that with notice or lapse of time or both will constitute an event of default"). As is discussed in greater detail in Section 9.2, lenders may accelerate the loans only once an actual event of default occurs; they may not do so upon the occurrence of a mere default. The lenders' remedy during the period when a breach or event is merely a default is to decline to extend further credit (and, if the default is a failure of payment, perhaps to sue the borrower for the defaulted amount or to make a demand on the guarantors).

Lenders normally have the ability to act on an event of default only so long as it is continuing (although some credit agreements are not clear on this point). The requirement of continuance has the following effect. If a borrower fails to pay an installment of principal when due, the lenders take no action to accelerate the loans and the borrower later pays the defaulted principal, the event of default is then cured and the lenders may no longer accelerate the loans. A different result occurs if the agreement does not require that the breach or event be continuing. In that case, once a default occurs, even if later cured, the borrower remains vulnerable to acceleration by the lenders. Only a formal waiver by the lenders could restore the parties to their original positions.

Events of default do not have to be events that are within the control of the borrower. For example, a borrower typically has no control over its shareholders' sale of their borrower stock and thus does not have the ability to prevent a change of control. Nevertheless, "change of control" is often included as an event of default. Similarly, a non-U.S. borrower is likely to have no ability to prevent nationalization of its property or a moratorium affecting outstanding debt of its home country, both of which are common events of default for borrowers in non-Organization for Economic Cooperation and Development (OECD) countries.

Some of the events and circumstances that are normally listed as events of default are discussed in the following sections.

9.1.1   Default in Payment

Box 9.2

(a) the Borrower shall fail to pay any principal of any Loan or any reimbursement obligation in respect of any Letter of Credit Disbursement when and as the same shall become due and payable, whether at the due date thereof or at a date fixed for prepayment thereof or otherwise;

(b) the Borrower shall fail to pay any interest on any Loan or any fee or any other amount (other than an amount referred to in clause (a) of this Article) payable under this Agreement, when and as the same shall become due and payable, and such failure shall continue unremedied for a period of ___ Business Days;

The payment event of default for principal and the payment event of default for interest and other amounts are often treated differently. Generally, the failure to pay when due the principal of a loan, or the reimbursement obligation that arises upon the payment of a drawing under a letter of credit, is an immediate event of default. If a loan has a bullet maturity, the principal payment default has little significance since, by definition, the entire principal of the loan becomes due on the maturity date and no acceleration is necessary. The clause has relevance, though, when a loan is payable in installments or if the agreement provides for mandatory partial prepayments. In such circumstances, failure to pay the relevant principal when due results in an event of default that allows the lenders to accelerate the entire principal.

In all cases (including for loans that have a bullet maturity), the clause typically provides that a failure to pay principal on a date fixed for *prepayment* is an event of default. That this should be the case for mandatory prepayments is obvious, since principal becomes due on the date of the prepayment. If an asset sale requires that a portion of the loans be prepaid, the borrower faces an event of default and acceleration of the entire loan if it withholds prepayment. That this should be the case for voluntary prepayments may be less obvious. However, such a default is consistent with the principle that, once a borrower has given notice to the lenders of a voluntary prepayment of a loan (or portion thereof), that loan (or portion) becomes due and payable just as if it had been initially scheduled as an installment. Failure to make a voluntary prepayment on the noticed date therefore constitutes an immediate event of default. An exception to this rule may apply when the voluntary prepayment is being funded by proceeds of a refinancing loan or another transaction, such as an asset sale, that may involve conditions precedent to closing. In such a situation, the borrower faces the dilemma of having to provide prior notice of prepayment while simultaneously facing the risk that the relevant conditions are not satisfied and the predicate transaction not being consummated. Any failure of the predicate transaction to close may lead to a failure to pay the promised principal on the fixed prepayment date. Some credit agreements alleviate this risk for borrowers by expressly allowing a borrower to revoke its prepayment notice and thereby avert a missed prepayment date and trigger an event of default.

A default in the payment of interest, fees, and other amounts often enjoys a grace period (two or three business days is the most common) before it ripens into an event of default. Many credit agreements grant longer grace periods for fees and certain other amounts (such as expense reimbursements), sometimes as long as 15 or 30 days. A short grace period for interest should prevent the occurrence of an event of default based on wire transfer difficulties or administrative error but leaves intact the event of default if the borrower is truly unable to pay by reason of financial difficulties. A longer grace period for fees and the like reflects the lower importance of such payments; typically, these involve claims such as legal fees or other out-of-pocket costs of the agent or lenders.

No borrower wants to treat a grace period as an extension of the date by which it must pay interest, fees, or other amounts since even absent an exercise of remedies by the lenders the borrower can suffer serious and adverse consequences. The most serious may be a cross-default to other debt (see Section 9.1.4). Failure to pay interest could result in acceleration of other debt before the grace period has yet run. Beyond that, failure to pay interest when due even if not yet an "event of default" nevertheless gives rise to a "default." The absence of any default is a condition to additional borrowings under the agreement. Thus, failure to pay interest on the due date, even before it ripens into an event of default, cuts off access to new loans under the credit agreement—even loans that the borrower anticipated would be applied to pay the interest itself.

In contrast to the approach taken in credit agreements, the typical bond indenture has a payment-default grace period (whether for principal or interest) of 30 days. The longer grace period for bonds reflects the practical reality (at least historically) that, if a default occurs, there is greater difficulty in first locating and then obtaining waivers from a disparate and anonymous bondholder group than from lenders under a credit agreement. A similar rationale may explain the longer grace periods for covenant breaches under a bond indenture.

9.1.2 Inaccuracy of Representations

Box 9.3

(c) any representation or warranty made or deemed made by or on behalf of the Borrower or any Subsidiary in or in connection with this Agreement or any of the other Loan Documents, or in any amendment hereof or thereof, or in any report, certificate, financial statement, or other document furnished pursuant to or in connection with this Agreement or any other Loan Document or any amendment hereof or thereof, shall prove to have been incorrect when made or deemed made in any material respect;

An event of default is triggered under the typical credit agreement whenever a representation proves to have been false in any material respect. This applies to representations when made (such as upon the date the credit agreement is signed or a closing certificate affirming the representations is delivered) as well as to representations deemed to be made (such as upon the making of a loan after closing). The default covers not only the representations in the credit agreement, but also those in related agreements, such as security agreements, intercreditor agreements, guarantee agreements, and the like. The default also typically sweeps in representations made in amendments and in certificates and other documents furnished under the credit agreement (including, potentially, preclosing commitment letters) and less frequently may cover representations made "in connection with" the credit agreement. The sample language in Box 9.3 exemplifies this broader "in connection with" formulation.

The justification for including an event of default based upon breach of representations flows from the principle that the representations in a credit agreement encapsulate the critical assumptions upon which the lenders extend credit to the borrower. When representations are untrue, it is not sufficient that lenders be able to sue the borrower for fraud or misrepresentation, or to assert claims against officers for executing false certificates, or even to refuse to make additional loans and thus not increase credit exposure. If, say, financial statements are materially inaccurate or a major litigation has not been disclosed, lenders want the additional leverage of being able to accelerate the debt, an ability that should, in turn, encourage borrowers to make certain the representations are accurate in the first place.

The approach set out in credit agreements contrasts with the market convention in bond indentures. The latter rarely include a default based upon breach of representations. The rationale for the distinction goes beyond the mere absence of representations in the typical bond indenture; a default can always cross-reference the related underwriting agreement or any security or ancillary agreement. The distinction is more likely grounded in market custom (bond purchasers do not expect, and therefore do not insist upon, a representations default) and in the differences between the marketing of bonds and the syndication of loans. For example, bond underwritings are always accompanied by a detailed offering circular, much more comprehensive than the typical bank information memorandum covering most of the areas of concern that are covered by credit agreement representations. A bond is also a security for Securities Exchange Act purposes. If, therefore, the offering circular is inaccurate or incomplete in any material respect, a bondholder may be in a position to make a claim under Rule 10b-5 of the Securities Exchange Act—a much more powerful claim than the common-law fraud claims available to ordinary creditors (those who hold debt instruments that are not treated as securities). A bank information memorandum, by contrast, tends to be much less detailed. Normal commercial loans, moreover, are generally structured so as not to constitute securities for purposes of the Securities Exchange Act (see Section 11.6) and so a lender is not able to assert a 10b-5 claim. Detailed representations are therefore set out in the credit agreement and the default is included to ensure the lenders have an immediate remedy if they are untrue.

As noted, the standard representations default is predicated upon the relevant representation being inaccurate *when made* (or when deemed made, such as upon the making of a loan). Certificates delivered at the time of the initial borrowing to the effect that no default exists can thus be the basis of a default if untrue. Many credit agreements also prescribe a form of "Notice of Borrowing" that includes an affirmation that the representations are true and that no default exists. Even absent a paper statement, the typical credit agreement provides (as noted in Section 5.2) that each time a loan is made the borrower is "deemed" to have affirmed that all representations are true as if made on the date of the loan. The reference in the standard default to "deemed representations" thus picks up those "deemed" affirmations.

In the normal case, as illustrated in the language in Box 9.3, a default arises only if a representation is incorrect when made or deemed made; a representation initially correct that later becomes incorrect does not constitute an event of default, regardless of materiality, unless the representation is "deemed" made again at a later date. Accordingly, if at the closing of a single-draw term loan, the borrower is not a defendant in any material litigation and so affirms in a certificate, but subsequently is sued for a material amount, no default based upon a misrepresentation arises, inasmuch as the representation was true when made. This does not relieve the borrower of any on going requirement to report the existence of the litigation to the lenders, or of any event of default if the litigation is converted into a judgment that goes unpaid (see Section 9.1.6).

In rare instances, the lenders structure the representations default to provide that a breach occurs if, at any time, a representation is untrue if made at such time. This has the effect of turning the representations into a continuing obligation and may result in significant overlap of the covenants and other defaults. The infrequent cases where it is seen arise primarily in the cross-border lending context.

A representations default is also generally predicated upon the inaccuracy being *material*. Thus, an inadvertent failure to list an inactive subsidiary with no assets, no liabilities, and no operations is probably not a default. A failure to list an active subsidiary that has significant assets and liabilities and is also the holding company for a number of other listed subsidiaries is probably material. Sometimes borrowers push for an added "materiality" qualification by requesting that the default arise only if *material* representations are *materially* inaccurate. This approach is problematic. The difficulty is that it implies that some representations are not themselves material. Taken to its logical conclusion, the qualifier could just as easily be inserted into the covenant default (to say, in other words, that an event of default occurs only if a *material* covenant is breached) or even into the payment default (providing that an event of default occurs only if a *material* payment is not made).

Borrowers occasionally request that they be afforded a grace period to cure an inaccurate representation. It is unusual to see this concept incorporated into a credit agreement. If included, it normally affords a grace period only for representations that are curable; most are not. The qualifier should, in any event, largely be unnecessary. A borrower is much more likely than the lenders to know that a representation is inaccurate and, if it is so easily curable, can likely fix the problem itself before it is required to notify the lenders.

9.1.3   Breach of Covenants

Box 9.4

(d) the Borrower shall fail to observe or perform (i) any covenant, condition, or agreement contained in Sections [_____] or (ii) any other covenant, condition, or agreement contained in this Agreement or any of the other Loan Documents (other than those specified in paragraphs (a) or (b) [*Payment Defaults*] or the preceding clause (i)), and such failure shall continue unremedied for a period of [30] days after notice thereof from the Administrative Agent to the Borrower (which notice will be given at the request of any Lender);

Events of default based upon covenant breaches generally fall into two categories: those events of default that occur immediately upon a breach and those events of default that first require a grace period to run or notice to be given after the breach arises. As to who must give the notice, agreements differ. Some allow it to be given by any lender; others provide that only the administrative agent or the required lenders are permitted to do so. Many agreements require that any notice be given *through* the administrative agent (as illustrated in the language in Box 9.4).

Commonly, breaches of negative covenants, financial covenants, and certain affirmative covenants (such as the agreement to maintain corporate existence and provide notice of any default) are immediate;

others require notice, lapse of time, or both. There is no uniform approach for all credit agreements. In many instances the parties negotiate to include or exclude a grace period for particular covenants. Factors that are weighed in determining what is appropriately an immediate event of default include (1) whether a breach, if it occurs, is susceptible of cure, (2) whether the covenant is so important that the lenders should have the right to act without delay, and (3) whether a breach, if it occurs, is the result of intentional action of the borrower. One seemingly benign covenant—the borrower's obligation to notify the lenders promptly after it has obtained knowledge of a default—is generally an immediate event of default, even if the underlying event or circumstance does not constitute an event of default until after notice or a grace period. The reason is simple: if the lenders do not know that a breach or other event has occurred, they are unable to deliver a notice or monitor the lapse of any grace period.

Bond indentures usually have longer grace periods than credit agreements (30 or 60 days is customary) and require that notice be given before the grace period commences; in other words, there are no immediate events of default based on covenant breaches. As noted in Section 9.1.1, this more debtor-favorable approach is probably a function of the greater difficulty (historically) in locating and then obtaining waivers from a group of bondholders.

The event of default picks up not just each "covenant" and "agreement" in the credit agreement, but also each "condition." Thus, if the "leverage ratio" at closing is required to be less than 3.5x and is in fact 3.6x, it is an event of default if the closing is consummated, notwithstanding that the ratio is otherwise in full compliance with the corresponding covenant. A breach of such a condition also constitutes a breach of the representations default if the borrower has delivered a closing certificate averring that the ratio does not exceed 3.5x. In fact, the delivery of closing certificates means that most breaches of conditions also constitute breaches of the representations default. As to other closing conditions, the lenders and their respective counsel should be monitoring satisfaction of the conditions anyway, so the likelihood of the conditions default ever being utilized is limited.

Finally, a word on covenant defaults in a covenant lite credit agreement. As discussed in Section 7.8, a distinguishing characteristic of covenant lite credit agreements is the lack of financial covenants at least with respect to institutional term loan B tranches. While a financial covenant breach triggers an immediate event of default on the pro rata term loan A tranches, the point of covenant lite facilities is that the term loan B tranche, whose financial terms more closely resemble those of a bond, should not benefit from any financial covenants or events of default that are triggered by breaches of such covenants. Therefore the covenant default provision in a covenant lite-style credit agreement will expressly provide that a financial covenant breach will not constitute an event of default for purposes of any loan other than revolving or pro rata term loan A tranches. Once the term loan A lenders accelerate their loans, however, the term loan B lenders should not be disadvantaged when it comes to remedies and are deemed to also have accelerated their loans alongside the pro rata lenders.

9.1.4   Cross-Default; Cross-Acceleration

Box 9.5

(e) the Borrower or any Subsidiary shall fail to make any payment (whether of principal or interest and regardless of amount) in respect of any Material Debt, when and as the same shall become due and payable [(after giving effect to any period of grace)];

(f) any event or condition occurs that results in any Material Debt becoming due prior to its scheduled maturity or that enables or permits [Alternative 1: (with or without the giving of notice, the lapse of time, or both)] [Alternative 2: (with or without the giving of notice, but without any further lapse of time)] the holder or holders of any Material Debt or any trustee or agent on its or their behalf to cause any Material Debt to become due, or to require the prepayment, repurchase, redemption, or defeasance thereof, prior to its scheduled maturity;

The cross-default clause in a credit agreement is one of the most misunderstood provisions; it is also one of the most powerful tools that the lenders have to avoid being disadvantaged as against other creditors. Cross-default clauses come in many flavors and varieties, and a discussion of several key principles may therefore be useful to understand how they work.

9.1.4.1   Why a Cross-Default?

When a borrower defaults on indebtedness owed to other creditors, lenders may have at least three separate concerns. First, the default may indicate that the borrower has credit-related problems that may affect the borrower's ability to repay the loans. Second, the borrower is at risk of the other indebtedness being accelerated, which might not only jeopardize its ability to repay the lenders, but also subject it to other remedial actions, such as foreclosure on collateral (if the other creditors are secured) or a bankruptcy filing. Third, the borrower may enter into negotiations with the other creditors for a waiver or amendment that would eliminate the default or forestall the exercise of remedies. These negotiations could involve the restructuring of the other indebtedness by the borrower in a way that advantages the other creditors (and, thereby, disadvantages the lenders), such as by granting collateral security, changing the average life of the other indebtedness, increasing compensation, or making other concessions. As a result, the default in respect of other indebtedness may create intercreditor issues.

9.1.4.2 What Debt Is Crossed?

In most credit agreements, the cross-default is triggered if debt or hedging and other derivative obligations under another agreement go into default (or, in the case of a derivative, suffer the equivalent of a default, such as a termination event). Sometimes the scope of the obligations to which the credit agreement is crossed is narrower, and covers only indebtedness for borrowed money. Frequently, a term to define all crossed obligations such as "material indebtedness" is used, which sets forth thresholds that the other debt must exceed to trigger the cross-default. The size of the threshold is negotiated based upon the size of the borrower and the amount of other debt outstanding or permitted to be outstanding.

In the case of indebtedness for borrowed money, the cross-default is dependent upon the amount of the threshold, not the dollar amount of the underlying payment default. This is achieved in the language in Box 9.5 by inclusion of the words "regardless of amount" to make clear that it is *not* the amount of the payment default, but rather the principal amount of the debt in respect of which the payment default occurs that determines whether the cross-default is triggered. If the threshold is $10,000,000, any default in respect of such debt can be the basis for a cross-default even if, in the case of a payment default, the amount not paid is a single interest payment of $10,000. The seriousness of the default is best measured by the amount of indebtedness that can be accelerated rather than by the amount needed to effect a cure.

This is in contrast to the cross-default for hedges and other derivatives. The threshold for these is typically measured by reference to the amount payable by the borrower if the arrangement were terminated, rather than by reference to the amount overdue or to the notional amount. Thus, although the notional amount of a hedge may be $100,000,000, if from the perspective of the borrower it is "in the money" and a termination results in a payment made by the hedge counterparty to the borrower, a default on the hedge does not result in a cross-default under the credit agreement.

9.1.4.3 Meanings of "Cross-Default" and "Cross-Acceleration"

The term "cross-default" is often used loosely to describe both cross-default and cross-acceleration clauses. "Cross-default" refers more accurately to a provision that allows the credit agreement to be accelerated whenever a default or event of default occurs in another instrument, *whether or not* the debt under that other instrument has been or may be accelerated. "Cross-acceleration" refers to a provision that allows the credit agreement to be accelerated only when the other debt has actually been accelerated. Some agreements contemplate a third, in-between, category, perhaps best described as "cross-accelerability" or "cross-event of default." This third category would allow the credit agreement to be accelerated only when the other debt may be accelerated immediately without any further notice (other than mere demand) or lapse of time.

Using this terminology, the cross-default clause is the most protective of the lenders. However, from the perspective of the borrower, the cross-default may effectively wipe out grace periods on all of its debt instruments and, as a consequence, cut short the time it needs to cure a default or to work out a problem with other creditors. By way of illustration, if two credit agreements for different syndicates (but the same borrower) each have a cross-default clause, when a default (but not yet an event of default) occurs under one instrument, an event of default immediately occurs under the second. But the occurrence of the event of default in the second, by reason of the cross-default in the first, triggers an event of default in the first as well. Thus the borrower suffers events of default under both agreements for a breach that was, under each, intended to have a grace period.

A cross-acceleration, in contrast, is viewed by lenders as very weak. It arguably defeats the whole purpose of the clause, since it is triggered only when other creditors *actually* accelerate their indebtedness, rather than upon their merely being entitled to do so. The cross-acceleration clause allows those other creditors to threaten and cajole and obtain additional favorable terms without according the lenders any matching bargaining power unless an acceleration actually takes place. Since indebtedness is rarely accelerated, this provides substantially less protection to lenders and is usually seen only in credit agreements for the most highly rated borrowers. It is also the approach taken most often in public debt indentures.

The cross-accelerability clause may strike a middle ground between the two extremes of the cross-default clause and the cross-acceleration clause. By not triggering an event of default until all grace periods have run on the second debt instrument, it avoids the borrower's losing its grace periods, and it avoids the lenders' losing leverage in a workout. The clause should, however, grant clemency only for the original grace periods in the second debt instrument and not for any extensions. In other words, once the original grace periods have run under the second instrument, a default should arise under the first; "grace" should not include lengthy periods of repeated deferrals by the second designed precisely to keep the lenders away from the negotiating table.

In the language in clause (f) in Box 9.5, two bracketed alternatives are included. The first, by using the words "with or without the giving of notice, the lapse of time, or both" is a true cross-default clause. An event of default occurs under the credit agreement whether or not a matured event of default exists under the other debt instrument. The second, which employs the phrase "with or without the giving of notice, *but without any further lapse of time,*" is the more moderate cross-accelerability clause. Here, an event of default occurs under the credit agreement if all grace periods have lapsed under the other debt instrument and the only triggering action from the other creditor that remains is to send a notice.

9.1.4.4 Mandatory Prepayments

Borrowers are sometimes concerned that a breach of a mandatory prepayment provision of another agreement may trigger the cross-default. The language in clause (f) in Box 9.5 is explicit that any event or condition that requires the *prepayment, repurchase, redemption, or defeasance* of "Material Debt" results in a default under the credit agreement. A borrower may argue that its credit agreement should not fall into default merely because an asset sale or other event triggering a mandatory prepayment, redemption, or repurchase occurs under a bond indenture. It reasons that these are "normal" prepayment events and do not necessarily reflect adversely on the financial condition of the borrower. One solution is to limit the triggering event to *defaults* rather than the more encompassing *event or condition* in the language in Box 9.5. This approach, although superficially appealing, may not be logical in all instances. A required change of control prepayment that, for example, results in the entire underlying debt becoming due prematurely should arguably be treated differently than an asset sale, excess cash flow, or casualty event prepayment. Another solution is to limit the triggering event to mandatory prepayments of *unsecured* debt. To the extent that *pari passu* secured debt is permitted under the credit agreement, it should be assumed that such secured debt would include a typical mandatory prepayment triggered by sale of any of its underlying collateral. Again, such "normal" and expected mandatory prepayment, the thinking goes, should not trigger any sort of cross-default. The ultimate resolution of this issue is usually left to negotiation.

9.1.5 Insolvency

Box 9.6

(g) the Borrower or any Subsidiary shall (i) voluntarily commence any proceeding or file any petition seeking liquidation, reorganization, or other relief under any Federal, state, or foreign bankruptcy, insolvency, receivership, or similar law now or hereafter in effect; (ii) consent to the institution of, or fail to contest in a timely and appropriate manner, any proceeding or petition described in clause (h) of this Article; (iii) apply for or consent to the appointment of a receiver, trustee, custodian, sequestrator, conservator, or similar official for the Borrower or any Subsidiary or for a substantial part of its assets; (iv) file an answer admitting the material allegations of a petition filed against it in any such proceeding; (v) make a general assignment for the benefit of creditors; or (vi) take any corporate or other action for the purpose of effecting any of the foregoing;

(h) an involuntary proceeding shall be commenced or an involuntary petition shall be filed seeking (i) liquidation, reorganization, or other relief in respect of the Borrower or any Subsidiary or its debts, or of a substantial part of its assets, under any Federal, state, or foreign bankruptcy, insolvency, receivership, or similar law now or hereafter in effect or (ii) the appointment of a receiver, trustee, custodian, sequestrator, conservator, or similar official for the Borrower or any Subsidiary or for a substantial part of its assets, and, in any such case, such proceeding or petition shall continue undismissed for 60 days or an order or decree approving or ordering any of the foregoing shall be entered;

(i) the Borrower or any Subsidiary shall become unable, admit in writing its inability or fail generally to pay its debts as they become due;

Insolvency of the borrower can usher in the worst of all scenarios for a lender. For proceedings under the Bankruptcy Code, it leads to the nightmare situation in which any action by the lenders (whether or not ordinary course for either the lenders or the borrowers) is subject to court approval, where interest payments and principal amortization may be suspended and where the finely crafted and negotiated covenants inserted into the credit agreement become irrelevant. The lenders' influence over the borrower is radically diminished, the borrower itself cannot undertake nonordinary course actions without approval of the court, and expensive and sometimes litigious creditors' committees are ready to contest every decision made by management, all in a scenario in which the borrower's business suffers the shock and adverse publicity of insolvency.

The dire implications are not limited, however, to insolvency proceedings under the Bankruptcy Code. A variety of other insolvency laws can come into play, including state insolvency statutes, insolvency regimes for specialized businesses (such as insurance companies, banks, savings and loans, and other similar institutions), and foreign bankruptcy laws.

The typical insolvency default is designed to give the lenders a remedy in the event any of these horrible events occurs. It is phrased broadly to pick up not just bankruptcy proceedings against the borrower, but all of the other insolvency-related events (liquidation, reorganization, the appointment of a custodian or receiver, and the like) that have an effect similar to that of a bankruptcy filing. If the borrower or any of its subsidiaries is a bank or an insurance company, the default is also triggered by a receivership or conservatorship or the like (the equivalent terms under the insolvency laws applicable to those entities).

The default is normally divided into three categories illustrated in the three clauses set out in the language in Box 9.6: actions by the borrower (the voluntary default), actions of third parties (the involuntary default), and an admission of insolvency by the borrower (the admissions default).

9.1.5.1 Voluntary

Voluntary default is triggered when the borrower itself commences a voluntary bankruptcy or insolvency proceeding (including applying for a custodian or receiver for its property). It is also triggered if the borrower rolls over and plays dead when any of these actions is instituted by third parties. In most cases, the default includes the borrower's taking corporate or other action (such as a board or shareholder meeting) to effect any of the listed items, as provided in the reference at the end of paragraph (g) in Box 9.6.

The reference to corporate or other action merits some discussion. Lenders might want to invoke this language when financial difficulties first arise by arguing that a default has occurred because the borrower's board or other governing body undertook preliminary consideration of a bankruptcy filing. This argument will likely not succeed. Few cases construe what level of action triggers a bankruptcy default, but those few that exist indicate that merely engaging in contingency planning, or retaining counsel, or discussing the possibility of a filing do not give rise to a default until an actual board of directors' resolution authorizing a filing is passed. See *In re Revere Copper & Brass, Inc.*, 60 B.R. 887 (Bankr. S.D.N.Y. 1985) and *Union Bank of Switz. v. Deutsche Fin. Servs. Corp.*, 2000 U.S. Dist. LEXIS 1481 (S.D.N.Y. 2000).

Because all of the actions described above are voluntary, they constitute immediate events of default, and the borrower does not benefit from any grace period. As is more fully discussed in Section 9.2, they also result in an automatic termination of commitments and automatic acceleration of the loans.

9.1.5.2 Involuntary

The involuntary default normally encompasses all of the actions listed in the voluntary default, if instituted by a third party against the borrower or its property. Under Section 303 of the Bankruptcy Code, an involuntary case can generally be commenced by any three creditors that hold matured claims (or if there are less than 12 creditors in the aggregate, a single creditor that holds a matured claim) against the borrower in excess of a statutorily defined minimal amount. Since such an action may be without merit, the standard insolvency clause allows the borrower a grace period, typically 60 days, to have the case dismissed. If dismissal is not obtained upon expiration of the grace period, the involuntary proceeding ripens into an event of default. And, as noted in Section 9.1.5.1, if the borrower acquiesces in the involuntary proceeding, it becomes an immediate event of default (treated as if it were a voluntary insolvency filing by the borrower). As with the voluntary default, if an involuntary default becomes an event of default, the commitments are automatically terminated and the loans automatically accelerated.

9.1.5.3 Admission

The third category of insolvency default is triggered if the borrower admits in writing its inability, or fails "generally," to pay its debts as they become due. This language is an element of proof required for an involuntary bankruptcy petition to succeed, and so an admission of this type by a borrower may place it in immediate jeopardy of a bankruptcy case being commenced. Also, from a purely practical standpoint, if a borrower makes this type of admission, it is probable that payment and other defaults are imminent. An admissions default constitutes an immediate event of default with no grace period.

9.1.6 Judgment Default

Box 9.7

(j) one or more judgments for the payment of money in an aggregate amount in excess of $[_____] shall be rendered against the Borrower, any Subsidiary, or any combination thereof and the same shall remain undischarged for a period of 30 consecutive days during which execution shall not be effectively stayed, or any action shall be legally taken by a judgment creditor to attach or levy upon any assets of the Borrower or any Subsidiary to enforce any such judgment;

As discussed in Chapter 6, the litigation representation addresses whether any material suit or proceeding is pending against the borrower. In contrast, the judgment default addresses the consequences if the suit or proceeding has been lost. Failure to pay a court judgment gives rise to concerns similar to those that arise when a cross-default occurs. It may indicate that the borrower is unable to meet its financial obligations and that the judgment creditor may be on the verge of exercising remedies, such as to obtain and enforce a judgment lien or institute bankruptcy proceedings.

The default is triggered by an *unpaid* and *unstayed* judgment. If a borrower loses a suit and immediately pays the plaintiff, there is no event of default. If the borrower loses the suit and does not pay, but files an appeal and obtains a stay preventing the plaintiff from taking any enforcement action, there is similarly no event of default. To give the borrower a meaningful opportunity to either pay or appeal the judgment, the customary judgment default includes a grace period (30 to 60 days is typical) from the date of the judgment before an event of default is triggered. The grace period does not apply if the judgment creditor begins to attach or levy upon assets, though most trial or appellate decisions in a litigation do not become final and allow a party to begin enforcement actions until at least 30 days have lapsed.

Obtaining a stay is not an easy task for the losing party in litigation, since it is typically required to post a bond as a condition to the stay. To induce a bonding company to issue an appeal bond, the borrower may be required to pledge cash or post a letter of credit or grant a lien on its assets. If it does not have access to letters of credit, or if the granting of liens on cash or other assets is prohibited by lien covenants in the credit agreement or in other debt instruments, the borrower could find itself unable to obtain a bond. This is the situation that Texaco faced in 1984 when Pennzoil obtained an $11 billion judgment against it for allegedly interfering with Pennzoil's acquisition of Getty Oil. Texaco, which thought it had good grounds to appeal, could not obtain a bond of that size without breaching its debt agreements. It was forced to file for bankruptcy to gain the benefit of the Bankruptcy Code's automatic stay and thereby capture the time it needed to appeal. In the end, after a four-year saga that included its filing for bankruptcy, Texaco settled with Pennzoil for $3 billion.

Like the cross-default, the judgment default generally has a minimum dollar threshold. Since the credit considerations in this context are similar to those for the cross-default, it is quite common for the two thresholds to be the same. In the case of the judgment default, the amount covered by insurance is sometimes excluded on the theory that the borrower does not actually need to go out-of-pocket in the event that the judgment ultimately must be paid. Judgment defaults that exclude portions covered by insurance may sometimes require that the insurer be creditworthy and have first accepted responsibility for the judgment.

The default ordinarily picks up only judgments for *monetary* damages. It does not capture a nonmonetary judgment in the nature of a consent decree or injunction, even one that materially adversely affects the business of the borrower. So if a national trucking company is suddenly enjoined from delivering freight east of the Mississippi, the injunction does not constitute an event of default even though the ultimate monetary impact of the judgment may be severe. An event of this magnitude probably results in a material adverse change (MAC) and, if there is a condition precedent that no MAC has occurred or would result, could thus be used by the lenders as a basis to stop further credit extensions. It may also ultimately lead to a breach of one or more financial covenants as the adverse impact upon earnings is realized. Unless, however, the agreement includes a MAC default of the type described in Section 9.1.12, a consent decree or injunction of this nature is not by itself typically an event of default.

9.1.7   ERISA Events

Box 9.8

(k) an ERISA Event shall have occurred that, in the opinion of the Required Lenders, when taken together with all other ERISA Events that have occurred, could reasonably be expected to [result in a Material Adverse Effect] [result in liability of the Borrower and its Subsidiaries in an aggregate amount exceeding $[_____]];

As discussed in Section 6.2.6, to the extent that a company is obligated to pay retired employees a defined pension benefit, the company is typically required under the Employee Retirement Income Security Act of 1974 (ERISA) to pay into a trust for the benefit of its employees an amount sufficient to cover its future benefit obligations. The trust does not have to be funded at inception (the creation of the pension plan). Rather, the trust is funded through payments usually made over a period of years with the objective that the trust will have sufficient assets to meet pension obligations once employees begin to retire.

If a business fails to meet its funding obligations, the Pension Benefit Guaranty Corporation (PBGC) may be entitled to a statutory lien on the assets of the company. This lien covers not just the assets of the borrower, but those of subsidiaries that are 80 percent or more owned. It could also attach to the assets of any affiliates that are 80 percent or more owned. ERISA also stipulates that, in certain circumstances, a funding deficiency of a pension plan (the difference between the value of the plan assets or amount in the trust and the present value of the benefit obligations of the borrower) can become immediately due and payable. Acceleration of the deficiency could result in a sudden, unanticipated burden on a company's resources. This, coupled with the lien in favor of the PBGC, could in turn severely impair the lenders' legal position.

The risks posed by the PBGC's liens may be partly mitigated in a transaction in which the lenders are fully secured. Subject to certain limited exceptions, the PBGC's lien does not trump prior perfected liens in favor of lenders. Collateral security, however, does not eliminate the risks that ERISA deficiency claims will be accelerated and there is no protection if the credit agreement is unsecured. The typical ERISA event of default is therefore inserted to give the lenders a trigger if any of the described events occurs *and* if the effect is material to the borrower.

Materiality can be measured in several ways. Many agreements include hard dollar thresholds or a percentage of the borrower's net worth (or some other balance-sheet item). Other agreements measure materiality by a more subjective standard, such as whether the event would have a "material adverse effect." In this latter case, many credit agreements allow the required lenders to determine whether the event can be expected to have a "material adverse effect" to remove the burden of proving to the satisfaction of a court that a material adverse event will, in fact, occur. The approach taken in any particular ERISA default is determined by negotiation.

9.1.8   Environmental Events

Box 9.9

(l) a reasonable basis shall exist for the assertion against the Borrower or any of its Subsidiaries of (or there shall have been asserted against the Borrower or any of its Subsidiaries) claims or liabilities, whether accrued, absolute, or contingent, based on or arising from the generation, storage, transport, handling, or disposal of Hazardous Materials by the Borrower or any of its Subsidiaries or any predecessor in interest of the Borrower or any of its Subsidiaries or relating to any site or facility owned, operated, or leased by the Borrower or any of its Subsidiaries, which claims or liabilities (insofar as they are payable by the Borrower or any of its Subsidiaries, but after deducting any portion thereof which is reasonably expected to be paid by other creditworthy Persons jointly and severally liable there for), in the judgment of the Required Lenders, are reasonably likely to be determined adversely to the Borrower or any of its Subsidiaries and the amount thereof is, singly or in the aggregate, reasonably likely to have a Material Adverse Effect;

Although any business can have environmental problems, an event of default tied to possible environmental liabilities is typically inserted only in financing agreements for a company engaged in a manufacturing, refining, chemical processing, extraction, or other similar business, or in facilities that rely upon significant real property security. The language in Box 9.9 is an example. In its most lender-friendly form, the default is triggered by the assertion of claims against the borrower under environmental laws, including fines, penalties, remediation costs, and damage claims by private persons, that could have a material adverse effect upon the borrower or its business or that exceed a specified dollar or balance-sheet threshold. An obvious example is an assertion that the borrower either owns a Superfund site or has contributed hazardous materials to a Superfund site. See the discussion in Section 6.3.8, as to the credit implications of environmental legislation. The default is intended more to address the risks of clean-up liability and less the costs of ongoing compliance with regulatory requirements.

Triggering an event of default upon *assertion* or possible assertion of a claim is in stark contrast to the judgment default, which is triggered only by a *finding of liability* at the end of a losing lawsuit. Many borrowers object to the inclusion of an environmental default for precisely this reason. They argue that only when the borrower is actually required to make payment on an environmental liability, and then fails to pay, should there be a default. This reasoning misses the point. The rationale for an environmental default is more akin to that for the ERISA default than that for the judgment default. What the lenders care about, in other words, is the *possibility* of liability, not merely the actual finding of liability. It is too late for them to take protective action once liability has been assessed by a court or agreed to by the borrower after settlement discussions.

A clean-up problem typically starts with the realization on the part of the borrower (which, in some cases, occurs as a result of a regulatory notice) that it may be required to remediate a groundwater or tainted soil problem on property owned or operated by it, or contribute to the cleanup of a Superfund or other waste site. The full magnitude of the potential costs may not be known until a clean-up plan has been formulated, which can often take years. However, the scope of the worst-case liability (or, in the language in Box 9.9, the scope of liability that is "reasonably likely") is in most cases known much earlier. The objective of the event of default is to give the lenders an opportunity at an early stage to examine the facts, determine the likelihood of liability, and then, if the exposure is deemed sufficiently material, confer on the lenders the leverage of potential acceleration.

Most investment-grade borrowers resist agreeing to an environmental default; it is therefore usually included only in credit agreements for non-investment-grade leveraged borrowers that engage in the types of businesses described above with significant environmentally related exposure. When included, the assertion of an environmental liability is not an event of default unless it can be expected to have a material adverse effect on the borrower, taking into account the likelihood that the claim will be successful. Given the subjective nature of this test, the determination of materiality and likelihood is often left to the judgment of the required lenders, rather than to disputation between the parties and ultimate resolution by a court.

9.1.9 Change of Control or Management

Box 9.10

(m) (i) any Person or group (within the meaning of the Securities Exchange Act of 1934 and the rules of the Securities and Exchange Commission thereunder as in effect on the date hereof) [other than the Grandfathered Shareholders], shall acquire ownership, directly or directly, beneficially or of record of Equity Interests representing more than [__]% of the aggregate ordinary voting power represented by the issued and outstanding Equity Interests of the Borrower; (ii) a majority of the seats (other than vacant seats) on the board of directors of the Borrower shall be occupied by Persons who were neither (x) nominated by the board of directors of the Borrower nor (y) appointed by directors so nominated; or (iii) direct or indirect Control of the Borrower shall be acquired by any Person or group [other than the Grandfathered Shareholders];

As noted in Chapter 4, a change of control may be treated as either a mandatory prepayment event or as an event of default. In contrast to bond indentures, in which changes of control are almost universally mandatory redemption or repurchase events, credit agreements often treat a change of control as a default rather than as a mandatory prepayment. For a more complete discussion of the concept of change of control, see Section 4.7.7.

Change of control provisions sometimes include a change of management concept by providing that it is an event of default if the president, other senior officer, or key person of the borrower (such as the CEO) shall die, become disabled, or otherwise cease to perform his or her management functions (voluntarily or involuntarily) and an acceptable replacement is not appointed. Sometimes the clause goes even further and creates an event of default if the management generally of the borrower shall cease to be satisfactory to the lenders. Although inclusion of a management change is not *per se* inappropriate, if the clause is invoked in an overbearing or deceptive manner, it can expose a lender to potential liability. The classic story of a lender that went too far is found in *State Nat'l Bank v. Farah Mfg. Co.*, 678 S.W.2d 661 (Tex. Ct. App. 1984)—see Section 9.7. As a consequence, because of the risk that the default will be misapplied, management-change clauses are normally limited to death, disability, or other termination events and rarely expanded to the broader requirement that management remain continually satisfactory to the lenders.

9.1.10 Invalidity of Guarantees or Liens

Box 9.11

(n) the Liens created by the Security Documents shall at any time not constitute valid and perfected Liens on any material portion of the collateral intended to be covered thereby (to the extent perfection by filing, registration, recordation, or possession is required herein or therein) in favor of the Administrative Agent, free and clear of all other Liens (other than Liens permitted under Section [*Liens*] or under the respective Security Documents), or, except for expiration in accordance with its terms (or with the consent of the Administrative Agent), any of the Security Documents shall for whatever reason be terminated or cease to be in full force and effect or any action shall be taken by any Loan Party to discontinue or to assert the invalidity or unenforceability of any Security Document;

(o) any Guarantee of the obligations under this Agreement or any other Loan Document shall for any reason cease to be valid and binding on, or enforceable against, any Guarantor, or any Guarantor shall so state in writing;

To supplement the further assurances covenant (see Section 7.5.8), if the loans either have been guaranteed by subsidiaries or other parties or are secured by liens on property of the borrower or guarantors, the credit agreement is likely to include an event of default triggered by the failure of the guarantees or liens to be enforceable. In some instances, the mere assertion by the borrower or a guarantor of any infirmity is an event of default. In the case of liens, the event of default may also be triggered by a lien's not being perfected or entitled to the agreed-upon priority. A failure, therefore, to continue an expiring uniform commercial code financing statement could trigger a default. Failure to deliver a certificate that evidences additional stock issued by a pledged corporate subsidiary could also trigger a default. The clause might also capture a failure to pay any recording or stamp tax payments required to maintain the enforceability of the lien—such as is the case in New York for real property mortgages that secure revolving credit facilities each time a revolving credit loan is made.

With one exception, it is difficult to conceive how this event of default could be triggered in the absence of deliberate acts by the borrower or a guarantor. The exception is a failure to perfect a lien. This could happen with particular items of property if the parties simply do not bother to take the cumbersome additional steps necessary to perfect the lien (such as to note the lien on certificates of title for motor vehicles, or implement control agreements with respect to the borrower's deposit accounts). Recognizing this, borrowers often request a carveout for collateral that does not have material value in relation to their property as a whole, or request that the default be triggered only if a *material* portion of the collateral is not perfected. Materiality in this context is sometimes defined by reference to a dollar amount of collateral. There is considerable logic to this approach given the ease with which insignificant items of property could fall between the (perfection) cracks.

Borrowers sometimes push to have agent action carved out of the event of default. For example, loss of perfection that results if the administrative agent loses stock certificates delivered to it would not trigger a default. Similarly, failure of the administrative agent to file Uniform Commercial Code (UCC) continuation statements necessary to continue the perfection of liens would not result in a default. These provisions are infrequently conceded, probably on the theory that it is the responsibility of both the borrower and the administrative agent to maintain perfection. The issue is also less significant under Article 9 of the UCC and the filing system which permits liens on most possessory collateral to be perfected by filing as well as by possession.

The event of default is also normally triggered by termination of the security documents, or by an assertion by the borrower that a security document is invalid or unenforceable. Of course, a security instrument, once executed, is expected to continue in force until the secured obligations are paid in full and the administrative agent consciously terminates and releases the liens. Nevertheless, this may not be the case with respect to liens where necessary consents are required to be continually maintained (for example from new customers as they become account debtors obligated on pledged receivables). It may also not be the case in jurisdictions where security documents could be required to be time-limited. The event of default gives the lenders an immediate remedy in these circumstances if a particular security agreement or mortgage turns out to be unenforceable.

9.1.11 Foreign Borrowers

Box 9.12

(p) [Country] or any competent authority thereof shall declare a moratorium on the payment of indebtedness by [Country] or any governmental agency or authority thereof or corporations therein, or [Country] shall cease to be a member in good standing of the International Monetary Fund or shall cease to be eligible to utilize the resources of the International Monetary Fund under the Articles of Agreement thereof, or the international monetary reserves of [Country] shall become subject to any Lien;

Loans made to a non-U.S. borrower or guaranteed by a non-U.S. guarantor carry cross-border political risk. The risk is thought to be less if the borrower or guarantor is located in an OECD country. For borrowers located in emerging markets, lenders are concerned with the possibility of (1) expropriation (the taking by a foreign government of property of the borrower or guarantor), (2) moratorium (the prohibition by a foreign government of local companies servicing external debt), (3) loss of any local licenses or approvals (such as foreign exchange approvals) necessary to perform obligations under the credit agreement, and (4) the home country's inability to access the resources of the International Monetary Fund if foreign exchange reserves are depleted. Borrowers frequently argue that such events of default are unnecessary because, if the covered events are truly problematic, their eventual manifestation as payment defaults will protect the lenders. Lenders, on the other hand, consistent with their view on other events of default, wish to be able to take action at the earliest reasonable time to mitigate adverse consequences.

9.1.12 Material Adverse Change

Box 9.13

(q) any event or other condition shall occur and be continuing that is reasonably likely to result in a Material Adverse Effect;

In rare cases, usually cases involving asset-based lending transactions or in cross-border loans, a credit agreement includes an event of default based upon a MAC. (See Section 5.1.6 for a discussion of the meaning of MAC.) Borrowers may strenuously resist a MAC default, arguing that such a provision is inconsistent with the principle that the financial covenants are designed to test the performance of the borrower. It may cause a domestic (U.S.) borrower's accountants to classify the loans as short-term under the accounting principles set forth in Statement No. 6 of the Financial Accounting Standards Board, resulting in the full principal of the loan being treated as current liabilities on the borrower's balance sheet. It may also produce an element of business uncertainty akin to the loans being payable on demand. If the borrower is located in a non-OECD country outside the United States, however, the MAC clause may supplement the specialized events of default for non-U.S. borrowers discussed in Section 9.1.11 and is seen more frequently.

Some lenders also push (even in the domestic context) to include the default in agreements that in their view have no meaningful financial covenants.

9.1.13   Specialized Events of Default

Credit agreements often include additional events of default that are specific to the borrower. For example, if a borrower is in a regulated industry (such as wireless telecommunications or cable television), it may be appropriate to include an event of default based upon the loss of a material portion of the governmental licenses necessary for its business. Similarly, if the borrower's success is dependent on one or more specific contracts remaining in effect, the credit agreement may contain an event of default triggered by the termination of any of those contracts or the default by one of the parties thereunder. Which, if any, of these defaults is included is strictly a matter of the lenders' credit assessment of the borrower and of negotiation between the parties.

9.1.14   Significant Subsidiaries

As discussed in Section 7.1, events of default as applied to subsidiaries are sometimes limited to "significant subsidiaries" or "material subsidiaries." In an agreement in which the covenants only apply to restricted subsidiaries, the events of default are similarly confined to restricted subsidiaries. Whether to limit events of default in this fashion is left to negotiation. Factors that influence the discussion among the parties include the credit quality of the borrower (limiting events of default to significant subsidiaries is more common for investment-grade borrowers), the number and size of subsidiaries (confining defaults to significant subsidiaries may be more logical when a borrower has many small subsidiaries than when it has a few, large subsidiaries), whether the consolidated assets are held primarily through subsidiaries or by the borrower directly (if the latter is the case, limiting the defaults to significant subsidiaries, or excluding subsidiaries entirely, may be appropriate, if coupled with restrictions on transfers of assets to subsidiaries), and whether the subsidiaries are providing credit support (subsidiaries that guarantee the debt of the borrower are almost always included in the events of default).

9.2   REMEDIES

When an event of default occurs, lenders are often faced with difficult choices. In the best of cases, the default may simply arise out of an inadvertent, nonmaterial breach of a negative covenant that the lenders are prepared to waive and let all parties proceed as before. Even if the breach is of a financial covenant, it may be transitory and may not adversely affect the relationship with the borrower assuming new agreed covenant levels can be set. In the worst of cases, however, the occurrence of a default may compel the lenders to want their money back—now! Their first instinct is to ask what remedies they can exercise under the credit agreement and any related security agreements. We focus here on the remedies available under the typical credit agreement; a detailed discussion of the rights of the lenders vis-à-vis collateral security are beyond the scope of this volume.

Whether to exercise remedies upon the occurrence of an event of default is not always an easy determination. To begin with, before any action is taken, the lenders want to be absolutely certain that an event of default has, in fact, occurred, and that it is of sufficient materiality to justify the proposed exercise of remedies. Other considerations come into play as well. Accelerating loans, for example, rarely results in the loans' being immediately repaid by the borrower; if it were that simple, the borrower would presumably have retired the loans before the default ever occurred. Acceleration can also have adverse effects on the borrower, lenders, and other creditors. It often results in an immediate filing by the borrower for protection under the Bankruptcy Code, which in turn is likely to result in significant legal and other costs. Bankruptcy may also shunt the borrower into a long period of uncertainty as the case progresses and will subject nonordinary course decisions to cumbersome court approval. Acceleration (even absent bankruptcy) can scare trade creditors into tightening (or denying) credit terms to the borrower, and thereby exacerbate whatever liquidity problems the borrower already faces and, perhaps, force the lenders to provide *additional* credit to the borrower simply to maintain the status quo. For these reasons, among others, absent borrower obstinacy or evidence of fraud or rank incompetence on the part of management, it is often better for the parties to agree to an out-of-court restructuring of the loans rather than to commence the exercise of remedies.

Subject to these caveats, lenders under the typical credit agreement have at their disposal a wide range of remedies, considered here in ascending order of severity.

9.2.1   Stop Lending

As discussed in Section 5.2.2, it is a condition to the making of any loan (or the issuance of any letter of credit) that no default or event of default exist. Any individual lender, therefore, has the right, absent waiver, to refuse to extend additional credit under the agreement; exercise of this right is not dependent upon a determination by the required lenders to stop lending. Once the default or event of default is cured or waived, assuming that all other conditions are satisfied, the lenders again become obligated to extend credit.

Although stopping additional loans may appear to be a relatively innocuous remedy, depending upon the borrower's circumstances it can have potentially dire consequences. A borrower that relies upon daily funding under the credit agreement may suddenly find that its liquidity has evaporated and that it is no longer able to keep trade creditors current. The latter may, in turn, refuse to deliver raw materials or other inventory necessary in the borrower's business. To decline additional loans may lead to cross-defaults if the proceeds were intended to pay principal or interest on other debt. Of course, this may be precisely what the lenders intend, but it nevertheless highlights the difficult decision that lenders need to make before asserting that a condition is not satisfied.

9.2.2   Terminate Commitments

Box 9.14

. . . then, and in every such event (other than an event with respect to the Borrower described in clauses [*Bankruptcy*]), the Administrative Agent may, and at the request of the Required Lenders shall, by notice to the Borrower, take either or both of the following actions, at the same or different times: (i) terminate the Commitments, and thereupon the Commitments shall terminate immediately, and (ii) . . . ; and in case of any event with respect to the Borrower described in clauses [*Bankruptcy*], the Commitments shall automatically terminate . . .

Upon the occurrence of an event of default, the lenders may at their option terminate any outstanding commitments. This remedy is not typically exercisable by a lender alone, but is a right available only to the required lenders. In some credit agreements, the administrative agent is also given the authority to terminate commitments on its own initiative (though only in the most extreme circumstances would an administrative agent want to do this without authorization from the required lenders). Most credit agreements allow the lenders to terminate the commitments independent of accelerating the loans, which thus affords a remedy short of the "nuclear option" to send a signal to the borrower. Most credit agreements also provide that, if the event of default is based upon an insolvency, the commitments automatically terminate without action by any party (see Section 9.2.3 for the rationale for this). Terminating the commitments terminates additional funding under the credit agreement and can lead to some of the same adverse consequences to the borrower described in Section 9.2.1.

9.2.3 Accelerate

Box 9.15

. . . then, and in every such event (other than an event with respect to the Borrower described in clauses [*Bankruptcy*]), the Administrative Agent may, and at the request of the Required Lenders shall, by notice to the Borrower, take either or both of the following actions, at the same or different times: (i) . . . , and (ii) declare the Loans then outstanding to be due and payable in whole (or in part, in which case any principal not so declared to be due and payable may thereafter be declared to be due and payable), and thereupon the principal of the Loans so declared to be due and payable, together with accrued interest thereon and all fees and other obligations of the Borrower accrued hereunder, shall become due and payable immediately, without presentment, demand, protest, or other notice of any kind, all of which are hereby waived by the Borrower; and in case of any event with respect to the Borrower described in clauses [*Bankruptcy*], . . . the principal of the Loans then outstanding, together with accrued interest thereon and all fees and other obligations of the Borrower accrued hereunder, shall automatically become due and payable, without presentment, demand, protest, or other notice of any kind, all of which are hereby waived by the Borrower.

Upon the occurrence of an event of default, the lenders have the right to declare the loans due and payable. As with the termination of commitments, this right is almost never exercisable by an individual lender, but requires action by the required lenders. By way of contrast, bond indentures and private placements frequently permit acceleration to be effected by a vote of less than a majority of the note holders (25 percent is a figure often seen). In some credit agreements, the administrative agent is permitted to accelerate the loans on its own. As with the termination of commitments, only in extreme circumstances would an administrative agent want to exercise this right on its own; granting this power to an administrative agent can nevertheless be important. Acceleration by the administrative agent is much speedier than acceleration by the required lenders and thus can enable setoff rights to be quickly exercised or other protective actions rapidly taken. An agent acceleration-right also protects the administrative agent (and the lenders) if there is any question as to whether the required lenders in fact authorized the acceleration; since the agent could have declared the loans due and payable on its own, once an acceleration occurs, inquiry into lender votes becomes irrelevant.

In the case of a credit agreement with competitive bid loans, the definition of "required lenders" is adjusted to stipulate that, for purposes of acceleration, the lenders vote not in accordance with their revolving credit commitments, but in accordance with their outstanding loans. This avoids a scenario in which a competitive bid lender with the only outstanding loan under a facility is unable to declare the loan due and payable because the lenders as a group decline to vote their unused commitments in favor of acceleration.

Credit agreements will typically provide that an event of default based upon the borrower's insolvency results in an automatic acceleration of all loans. This is intended to avoid the automatic stay under Section 362 of the Bankruptcy Code, which stipulates that a filing of a voluntary or involuntary petition by or against a debtor results in an automatic prohibition on creditor action against the debtor. Among other things, the stay may bar sending a notice of acceleration or other demand to a borrower. With an acceleration that occurs automatically, the theory goes, no violation of the stay occurs, since no notice or other action need be taken by the lenders. Whether lenders would be in a less advantageous position in a bankruptcy proceeding if their loans were not accelerated is open to question, but when the Bankruptcy Code (which replaced the Bankruptcy Act and incorporated into law a broad concept of automatic stay) was first enacted in 1978, it was deemed important that lenders have an already-liquidated claim at the start of a proceeding. Another (arguably more persuasive) justification is that automatic acceleration allows a full claim to be made against a guarantor (assuming that the guarantor is not itself in bankruptcy). The typical guarantee also includes language to the effect that if acceleration is for any reason prohibited, a full claim may nevertheless be made on the guarantor (see Section 8.2.6).

Sometimes lenders ask that automatic acceleration be expanded beyond insolvency defaults to all events of default. This might seem superficially appealing. It would avoid any vote by the lenders or initiative by the administrative agent, and it might serve as an added incentive for the borrower not to breach the credit agreement in the first place. However, such an approach has the disadvantage that it removes control from the lenders. The lenders would no longer have the option of ignoring a default (which they might choose to do, even though they decline to waive the default, because it is not sufficiently serious). Automatic acceleration might also trigger cross-default or cross-acceleration clauses contained in other debt instruments. As a consequence, except in rare cases, credit agreements provide for automatic acceleration only in the context of insolvency.

9.2.4   Demand Cover for Letters of Credit

If letters of credit are outstanding at the time an event of default occurs, the lenders can demand that the borrower provide "cover" (cash collateral) for any future reimbursement obligations that arise upon payment of drawings under the letters of credit. Demanding cover overcomes the structural difficulty that the liability of a borrower in respect of a letter of credit cannot be accelerated or repaid in the same sense that loans can be accelerated and repaid. Nothing is owed by the borrower to the issuer until a drawing is made by the beneficiary (see Section 4.9). Therefore, to create an obligation that can become due and payable upon the occurrence of an event of default, credit agreements routinely provide that the lenders have the right to demand that cash collateral be posted by the borrower in an amount equal to the future reimbursement obligations that will be payable by reason of drawings under the letter of credit when they occur (plus, as described in Section 2.1.2.10, a cushion of from 2 percent to 5 percent). If the borrower does not immediately post the cash, the lenders then have a claim to which they can apply the proceeds of any collateral or that they can demand be paid by guarantors.

The typical credit agreement provides that, upon insolvency, the obligation to provide cover for outstanding letters of credit becomes automatically due and payable. Unlike the situation when loans are accelerated upon insolvency, a bankruptcy court will not necessarily agree that the full amount of the cash collateral (the full liability of the issuer on the letter of credit) is the appropriate amount of the claim in the bankruptcy proceedings. Section 502(c) of the Bankruptcy Code allows there to be estimated any "contingent or unliquidated claim . . . the fixing or liquidation of which . . . would unduly delay the administration of the case." Some bankruptcy lawyers believe that in a reorganization of a bankrupt debtor a court might assess the likelihood of a drawing under a letter of credit (a contingent and unliquidated claim) and, if it thought that a $10,000,000 letter of credit had only a 10 percent chance of being drawn, would fix the amount of the claim at

$1,000,000. This could particularly be a risk if the letter of credit had a number of years to run before its expiration date. For this reason, even when a credit agreement includes a provision for automatic cover upon bankruptcy, the agreement will in many cases provide that every letter of credit issued under the agreement (subject to any so-called "evergreen" renewals—see Section 2.1.2.3) shall have a term that does not exceed one year. The shorter term reduces the risk (or so the reasoning goes) that a bankruptcy court would employ a probability analysis to determine the amount of a letter of credit claim (and, therefore, the amount of cover) that is due the lenders.

9.2.5   Institute Suit

If a borrower defaults in the payment of any amount under the credit agreement, the lenders can institute suit against the borrower to compel payment for amounts due and unpaid.

Suit is most often instituted by the administrative agent. For a variety of reasons this makes sense for the lenders. It ensures that the legal costs are shared broadly (and ratably) by all the lenders and avoids the risk of individual lenders taking inconsistent positions in separate lawsuits. In addition, a suit by an administrative agent with the backing of all lenders is likely to carry greater weight in the eyes of the court—it looks less like the grumblings of a discontented outlier and more like the reasoned complaint of a truly aggrieved syndicate. Nevertheless, it has long been the view (at least among lending lawyers) that suing for a past-due payment is a remedy available to individual lenders unless expressly barred by the agreement. Few credit agreements explicitly require approval of the required lenders on this issue. Some recent court decisions (discussed in more detail later in Section 9.6), however, have reached a different conclusion so the traditional view should no longer be considered standard.

9.2.6   Demand Payment from Guarantors

To the extent that a loan is guaranteed, a payment default (or acceleration) permits the lenders to make demand upon guarantors. As with suit against the borrower, demand for payment and any attendant litigation against a guarantor is most often undertaken by the administrative agent (for all of the same reasons described in Section 9.2.5). As with suit against the borrower, the traditional view of lending lawyers was that action against a guarantor (as with action against a borrower) is not confined to the administrative agent. The court decisions discussed in Section 9.6 take a contrary view and thus, absent express language in a guarantee, action by an individual lender against a guarantor may not be allowed.

9.2.7 Foreclose on Collateral

To the extent that a loan is secured by collateral, an event of default (or acceleration) normally permits the lenders to commence the exercise of lien remedies. In contrast to litigation against a borrower or guarantor, however, the traditional view is that individual lenders may not exercise remedies in respect of collateral security for a lending syndicate. This follows from the fact that liens are normally granted to the administrative agent (or a collateral agent) for the benefit of the lenders and not directly (severally or otherwise) to each lender. To exercise remedies against collateral therefore requires either the initiative of the administrative agent (or collateral agent) or the instruction of the required lenders.

9.3 RESCISSION

The remedies clause of a credit agreement sometimes gives the required lenders the right to rescind an acceleration after it has occurred. This can be useful flexibility on the part of the lenders. Absent an express provision in this regard, rescission otherwise requires unanimous lender consent, since overriding an acceleration is arguably extending the maturity (albeit accelerated) of the loans, a change that under the typical amendments provision requires the consent of each affected lender (see Section 10.3).

The required lenders are not, however, given complete freedom to annul an acceleration. Any rescission is normally subject to a number of conditions, including requirements that the borrower have cured the original event of default upon which the acceleration was based, that there is no other intervening default or event of default (unless the same are also being cured or have been waived), that any default interest accrued on the accelerated principal during the period of acceleration is paid, and that no judgment or decree has been entered for payment of the loans. In some cases the right is further restricted if the administrative agent or lenders have commenced the exercise of any judicial remedies. The ability to undo an acceleration is not available if the basis for acceleration is a bankruptcy or insolvency default.

Rescission rights are routinely included in bond indentures and private placements; they are less frequently seen in credit agreements.

9.4 WATERFALLS

The expression "waterfall" refers to the provision found in many credit agreements that specifies how monies are to be applied to obligations when the borrower pays an amount that is less than the full amount owing. Traditionally, waterfalls were inserted only into mortgages, security agreements, and the like, but with the increase in credit agreements with multiple tranches, waterfalls have become more common. Waterfalls normally apply just to scheduled payments and mandatory prepayments and do not control the allocation of optional prepayments, which are generally left to the discretion of the borrower (subject to the limitations discussed in Section 4.10).

The typical structure provides for the fees and expenses of the administrative agent (or any collateral agent) to be paid before any other claims, for interest (and breakfunding payments) to be paid before principal, for term loans to be paid before revolving credit loans, and for revolving credit loans to be paid before cover for any outstanding letters of credit (except that during a default, the waterfall requires all principal and cover among all tranches of loans and letters of credit to be paid ratably). In facilities that are secured, the typical waterfall also provides that protective advances made by individual lenders enjoy the same priority as the fees and expenses (and protective advances) of the administrative agent. In a transaction with one or more junior liens, the waterfall requires payment (at least in case of a default) to be made first to the senior lien holders. None of these principles is set in stone (except, perhaps, for the priority given to administrative and collateral agents) and variations are routinely negotiated.

Waterfalls may also be designed to reduce breakfunding costs by requiring that mandatory prepayments be applied first to base rate loans and then to London interbank offered rate (LIBOR) loans in the order in which their outstanding interest periods expire.

9.5 SETOFF

Box 9.16

Without limiting any of the obligations of the Borrower or the rights of the Lenders hereunder or under applicable law (including other rights of setoff), if the Borrower shall fail to pay when due (whether at stated maturity, by acceleration or otherwise) to or for the account of any Lender any amount payable by the Borrower hereunder, such Lender and any

Affiliate thereof may, without prior notice to the Borrower (which notice is expressly waived by it to the fullest extent permitted by applicable law), set off and appropriate and apply against such amount any and all obligations and liabilities (regardless of currency and whether matured or unmatured, and including all deposits, general or special, time or demand, provisional or final) at any time held or owing by such Lender or any branch or agency thereof or such Affiliate to or for the credit or account of the Borrower. Such Lender shall promptly provide notice of such setoff to the Borrower, *provided* that failure by such Lender to provide such notice shall not give the Borrower any cause of action or right to damages or affect the validity of such setoff and application.

The right of setoff (or offset, as it is sometimes called) is one of the oldest nonjudicial remedies available to a lender. It has its genesis in the common law, as created by court decisions derived from principles originally expounded in Roman law. It is now expressly provided by statute in many states (in New York, pursuant to Section 151 of the Debtor and Creditor Law) and in the typical credit agreement by contract. The logic behind the right is simple. If a lender has a monetary obligation to a borrower, such as a deposit liability, and the borrower defaults on a loan payable to the lender, why should the lender pay the deposit liability to the borrower when it has no assurance that the borrower will repay the loan? Why should the lender not be able to apply the deposit against the loan to reduce the latter on a dollar-for-dollar basis?

Under common law, for one creditor to exercise the right of setoff, two key conditions have to be present: the two claims to be offset must be *mutual* and they must be *matured*. Mutuality means that it must be the same two parties, each acting in the same capacity, that are obligated on, and entitled to the benefit of, the obligations to be offset. Thus, the securities affiliate of a bank could not set off amounts payable under a derivatives contract against the loan obligations of a borrower to the bank since the offset would involve three, and not two, parties. Similarly, no mutuality exists if a bank wishes to offset a deposit obligation owed to a borrower against a loan obligation owed to the bank *in a fiduciary capacity*. The requirement of mutuality, depending upon the circumstances, might also interfere with an international bank's setting off a deposit payable by a branch in one country against a loan booked at a different branch in a separate country.

The maturity condition requires that the two obligations each be due and payable. As a consequence, under common law, even though a loan facility may have been accelerated, a bank could not set off against a loan a time deposit that has three months to run. Similarly, even if the deposit was then payable (or was a demand deposit), if neither principal nor interest were payable on the loan, the right of setoff could not be exercised.

In New York, the requirement of maturity (though not of mutuality) has been overridden by statute. Section 151 of the New York Debtor and Creditor Law grants a statutory right of setoff upon the occurrence of a number of specified events (including bankruptcy and execution against property or the issuance of a warrant of attachment against property). The statute provides that every debtor (here, by way of example, the depositary bank) may set off and apply against any indebtedness (the loan) "whether matured or unmatured" of a creditor (the borrower) against any amount (the deposit) owing from the debtor to the creditor "at or at any time after" the happening of the specified setoff events. In this circumstance, neither the loan nor the deposit must be currently payable in order for the right of setoff to be employed by the lender.

Despite the breadth of Section 151 of the New York Debtor and Creditor Law, credit agreements routinely include an explicit contractual right of setoff, typically expressed (as in the sample in Box 9.16) to be in addition to any rights under applicable law. Part of the reason for inclusion of a contractual setoff right is to attempt to override the mutuality requirement which, as noted above, was not addressed by Section 151. Another reason is doubt as to whether Section 151 effectively overrides the maturity requirement (there has not been, as of the date of this volume, any court decision that expressly confirms that Section 151 does this). Finally, and most importantly, since the validity of a setoff is as a general rule governed by the law of the jurisdiction where the deposit is payable, even in a New York law credit agreement Section 151 may be inapplicable if the borrower maintains its deposit accounts with a lender in Kansas.

The language in Box 9.16 attempts to override the mutuality requirement by according to the lender "and any Affiliate thereof" the right to offset obligations payable to the borrower against the loan facility. Not all setoff provisions are as broad as this, but for institutions in which derivatives are routinely contracted for by securities' affiliates, or loans are made by nondepositary sister institutions, having the borrower waive the mutuality condition may be important. Note that the clause leaves unstated how the lender and its affiliate are to make adjustments among themselves, which may raise substantial practical issues. In any event, whether a broad waiver of mutuality such as that illustrated in Box 9.16 will be enforced by a court is unclear and so legal opinions routinely take a qualification as to the validity of the right of setoff.

At common law, and under Section 151 of the New York Debtor and Creditor Law, lenders and borrowers alike may exercise the right of offset. Indeed, although rare, there are cases where it is the borrower that offsets its loan obligation against a deposit when the depositary bank becomes insolvent. See *Fed. Deposit Ins. Corp. v. Mademoiselle of California*, 379 F.2d 660 (9th Cir. 1967). Nevertheless, it is customary for the credit agreement to provide that the borrower waive whatever setoff rights it may have by requiring that all payments be made "without deduction, setoff, or counterclaim." (This is discussed in more detail in Section 4.1.4.)

In New York, no banking institution may exercise a right of setoff against a deposit account unless "prior to or on the same business day" it mails to the depositor notice of the setoff together with the reasons therefor (New York Banking Law § 9-g). Although as a practical matter every lender that exercises the offset right almost certainly provides such notice, the enactment of § 9-g caused considerable consternation for lending syndicates and led to the addition of the references to notice in the standard setoff clause. Without knowing whether the provisions of the Banking Law are waivable, and wanting to guard against the possibility that through some administrative blunder a lender might fail to deliver the notice, setoff clauses were revised to include a waiver by the borrower of any notice rights "to the fullest extent permitted by applicable law." In addition, a statement that failure to provide notice does not affect the validity of any setoff was inserted, although this does little more than parrot the Banking Law provision itself. Nevertheless, on the theory that a lender will look at the setoff language in the credit agreement before exercising a setoff right, the references to notice will presumably assist the lender (or so the reasoning goes) to comply with relevant law.

Exercise by a lender of its right of setoff in a syndicated credit agreement typically triggers an obligation on its part to share the proceeds of the setoff with other lenders (see Section 10.5).

9.6 INDIVIDUAL VERSUS COLLECTIVE ACTION

Box 9.17

[Alternative 1] The amounts payable at any time hereunder to each Lender shall be a separate and independent debt and each Lender shall be entitled to protect and enforce its rights arising out of this Agreement, and it shall not be necessary for any other Lender to be joined as an additional party in any proceeding for such purpose.

[Alternative 2] Each Lender agrees that it shall not take or institute any actions or proceedings, judicial or otherwise, for any right or remedy against any Loan Party or any other obligor under any of the Loan Documents or any Hedging Obligation or Cash Management Obligation (including the exercise of any right of setoff, rights on account of any banker's lien or similar claim or other rights of self-help), or institute any actions or proceedings, or otherwise commence any remedial procedures, with respect to any Collateral or any other property of any such Loan Party, without the prior written consent of the Administrative Agent. The provision of this Section [__] are for the sole benefit of the Lenders and shall not afford any right to, or constitute a defense available to, any Loan Party.

One question frequently asked by lenders when a syndicated loan goes into default is whether an individual lender can enforce a loan on its own or must it only act through the administrative agent and then only if the administrative agent or required lenders decide. As discussed below, case law is supportive of arguments in favor of individual lender action as well as collective action, though the current weight of authority supports the collective action argument in the syndicated loan context. However, as courts in each of these cases have acknowledged, the contractual language is determinative, and credit agreements that address the question directly can provide clarity on the rights of minority lenders in multi-lender scenarios.

A number of standard provisions in the typical credit agreement arguably support the right of individual action. The commitments are stated to be "several," which is to say that no lender is obligated to cover another lender's breach of its obligation to make loans—a provision that implies the credit agreement consists of a bundle of bilateral contracts between each lender and the borrower. Similarly, each lender is entitled to its own note and only in rare cases is a single note payable to the agent for the benefit of all of the lenders. The submission to jurisdiction clause references suit by individual lenders. The jury waiver provision has *each* party waive jury trial—certainly there would be no need for individual lenders to waive their right to a jury trial if they had no individual right to bring suit. The setoff clause requires each lender to share the fruits of any legal action with the other lenders—implying that there could be individual legal action. Individual action clauses such as that excerpted as Alternative 1 in Box 9.17 has been cited approvingly by courts looking to enforce minority lender actions.

These provisions stand in contrast to others that explicitly limit individual action. For example, most credit agreements make it clear that an individual lender may not accelerate the loans (or even its own loans). Acceleration is expressly addressed in the default section and always requires action by either the administrative agent or some minimum percentage of the lenders. Similarly, action against collateral security requires the administrative agent or a percentage of the lenders to decide that to exercise collateral remedies makes sense.

Notwithstanding the view that individual lenders possess some inherent freedom of action, several court decisions have held that individual lender action is precluded unless a credit agreement explicitly grants such authority to each lender. See *Beal Sav. Bank v. Sommer*, 8 N.Y.3d 44 (2007) and *Crédit Français International, S.A. v. Sociedad Financiera de Comercio, C. A.*, 490 N.Y.S. 2d 670 (Sup. Ct., N.Y. County 1985). This is true particularly where it can be found that lender "sacred rights," which require unanimous consent to be modified, are in fact not implicated. These decisions focus on provisions that delegate broad authority to the agent to act on behalf of the lender syndicate. The courts in these cases have cited the clear delegation of remedial rights to agents as well as to things like the absence of the lenders' names on the cover page of the credit agreement as evidence of the "collective design" of syndicated credit agreements. Each court cites the fact that it is the agent that makes interest determinations, the agent that receives and distributes borrower financial statements, and the agent that receives and disburses funds. Each court also emphasizes that the borrower is obligated to make all payments to the agent for the pro rata account of the lenders.

Absent extenuating circumstances, such as conflicts of interest, courts generally give substantial deference to the notion of the administrative agent playing the lead role when it comes to pursuing remedies under or with respect to the credit agreement.

The argument in favor of collective action is aided in those agreements that include a "no-action" provision in a credit agreement along the lines of the sample language described as Alternative 2 in Box 9.17. Credit agreements containing such provisions expressly funnel any claims through the administrative agent and thereby head off any risk of free-agent lenders pursuing their own claims that may or may not be consistent with, or otherwise generally benefit, the broader syndicate. There are two basic features of the typical no-action provision (which has some key differences from the typical bond indenture provision as discussed below). First is the consent requirement whereby any lender is required to first obtain the prior written consent of the administrative agent before taking formal steps to pursue claims. This affirmative consent requirement is in contrast to the typical no-action provision in a bond indenture, which is usually structured as a negative consent. Under a bond indenture, typically the aggrieved bondholder must first make demand on a trustee to pursue the subject claim and then, if and only if the trustee has failed to pursue such claims within a specified period of time (typically 60 days), the bondholder has rights to pursue its claim. Unlike the bond indenture formulation, the credit agreement formulation by its terms does not put such time pressure on the agent to take action. Second, the typical no-action provision may only limit claims against collateral or other property of an obligor. This provides yet another contrast to the typical indenture no-action provision, which usually is more broadly drafted to bar individual claims in respect of the indenture or the related notes. While no-action provisions may still come under attack by a motivated lender looking to pursue its individual claims and possibly extract incremental value, generally courts will enforce them as written to block individual actions. As with most areas discussed in this volume, it pays to be clear in the drafting if parties have particular rights in mind to protect or stifle.

9.7 LENDER LIABILITY RISKS

If a default occurs under the credit facility, the panoply of rights described earlier in this chapter are designed to protect the lender and to enable it to recover the principal of and interest on its loans. A lender is not free, however, to exercise those rights vindictively or in an unreasonable or draconian manner. If it does so, it may expose itself to the risk of so-called "lender liability," a term coined in the late 1980s to cover a wide range of sins that a lender can commit in pressuring its borrower to comply with covenants or repay loans. As used here, the expression describes not the many ways in which a lender's recovery attempts can be thwarted, but rather the ways in which a lender can suffer affirmative liability at the hands of its borrower or third parties. Lender liability claims thus entail a lender's worst nightmare: a borrower or injured third party turning the tables and suing the lender for damages—damages that can easily wipe out what the lender recoups under the credit agreement and, in the worst-case scenario, expose lenders to losses in excess of principal and interest.

The theories upon which lender liability claims are based are grounded in well-known principles of common-law liability, such as breach of contract, including breach of the implied covenant of good faith and fair dealing, misrepresentation, fraud, breach of fiduciary obligation, and tortious interference. They can also be based upon a violation of statutory rules, including under the Racketeer Influenced and Corrupt Organizations Act (RICO), federal and state securities laws, and environmental protection laws. A full discussion of lender liability is beyond the scope of this volume, but it may be useful to describe a few of the ways in which lenders have been bitten by their borrowers and thereby to illustrate the risk a lender can face if it overzealously or maliciously exercises those rights its counsel carefully built into the credit documentation.

9.7.1   Breach of Contract

The most obvious potential liability for a lender is simple breach of contract because, after all, the relationship between a lender and borrower is a contractual relationship. For example, a lender that fails to make loans after conditions have been satisfied and it is therefore required to do so under a loan commitment or the credit agreement could expose itself to a breach claim and liability for resultant damages suffered by the borrower. (See Section 12.6 for a discussion of how the typical credit agreement attempts to limit consequential or punitive damages in connection with a breach of the credit agreement by a lender.) Breaches of contract can also be asserted under other theories, such as breach of the implied covenant of good faith (discussed in detail in Section 13.5).

9.7.2   Creditor Control

Lender liability concerns arise most frequently in connection with troubled credits, when the lenders may take aggressive steps to protect themselves. Often a complaint filed by the borrower alleges that the lenders exercised undue control, or went too far in exercising control, over the borrower's business, resulting in harm to the borrower. Internal bank files that suggest a vindictive or unprofessional motive on the part of the lender—for example, an internal memorandum that signifies the lender's intention to interfere with the borrower's business—can be harmful to the lender's cause. See *Melamed v. Lake County Nat'l Bank*, 727 F.2d 1399 (6th Cir. 1984).

Certain provisions in credit agreements can be lightning rods for legal claims by opening the door to charges of abuse of control. In *K.M.C. Co. v. Irving Trust Co.*, 757 F.2d 752 (6th Cir. 1985), lender control over the borrower's use of cash and other forms of "interference" with the borrower's business led to a lender liability claim. (The case is discussed in more detail in Section 13.5.) Another example is the

State Nat'l Bank v. Farah Mfg. Co. case referred to in Section 9.1.9, in which a provision purported to restrain the borrower from making changes in its management structure without lender consent. The borrower brought suit based in part upon the lender's insistence that management and a board of directors, in each case favorably inclined to the lenders, be installed. The court held that this constituted "duress" over the borrower and "interference" in the business of the borrower. Damages on the order of $15,000,000 for a loan that had originally been only $22,000,000 were assessed against the lender.

9.7.3   Tortious Interference

In addition to claims being brought under contractual causes of action, parties may look to theories of tort such as fraud, negligence, tortious interference, or economic duress (see Section 9.7.7) to pursue deep-pocketed lenders. Tortious interference, discussed in more detail in Sections 6.1.5 and 7.6.15, is the sin that can arise if a lender, through a loan commitment or the credit agreement, requires the borrower to take or refrain from taking action that conflicts with a previous agreement by which the borrower is already bound. To illustrate, if a lender, being aware of the borrower's repayment obligations under a bond indenture, insists that the borrower agree not to make payments on the bonds unless certain financial tests are met, the lender might expose itself to liability directly to the bondholders should the borrower, in order to comply with the credit agreement, not pay the bonds in accordance with their original terms. Another context in which tortious interference claims have been brought against lenders in recent years is with failed acquisitions. In such cases, prospective lenders are alleged to have wrongfully refused (or effectively refused) to fund the loan commitment and the planned acquisition falters as a result. Under the theory that a refusal to honor the loan commitment interferes with the preexisting merger agreement and the consummation of acquisition that it contemplates, spurned sellers have argued that the lenders' cold feet amounts to tortious conduct. See *Clear Channel Commc'ns, Inc. v Citigroup Global Mkts., Inc.*, Cause No. 2008-CI-04864 (225th Jud. Dist., Bexar County, Texas, 2008). Whether lender behavior amounts to tortious interference involves an analysis of, among other things, whether a lender's action was designed as a goal to interfere with the subject preexisting contract or business relationship and whether such action was merely that of a self-interested economic actor or, instead, was focused on achieving a more improper goal. Financing sources for acquisitions are wise to be cognizant of such claims being used as a litigation strategy in busted transactions.

9.7.4   Environmental Liability

Lender liability for costs associated with cleaning up an environmental hazard can be imposed directly under the Comprehensive Environmental Response, Compensation and Liability Act of 1980 (CERCLA). Pursuant to the Eleventh Circuit's decision in *United States v. Fleet Factors Corp.*, 901 F.2d 1550 (11th Cir. 1990), a lender with the mere ability to control management was found liable under CERCLA. However, the Asset Conservation, Lender Liability, and Deposit Insurance Protection Act of 1996 created a safe-harbor provision for lenders by providing that a secured creditor must actually "participate in the management" of the facility before it incurred liability. 42 U.S.C. § 9601(20(E)-(F)). As a result, the mere ability to control could no longer make a lender liable. What activities constitute participation in management is not entirely clear, although, in general, it can relate to decision-making over day-to-day environmental matters or with respect to operational functions. In addition, to maintain liability protection after foreclosure, a lender must divest the property "at the earliest practicable, commercial reasonable time." 42 U.S.C. § 9601(20(E)). CERCLA does not specify a timeline, although it is considered commercially reasonable that the property should be listed within 12 months of foreclosure. Despite changes made by the 1996 Act, some lenders can face additional risks of triggering environmental liability. For example, the post-foreclosure protection would only be available if the lender forecloses on the borrower's property rather than the borrower's equity, and the safe harbor only covers pollution matters on contaminated property. As a result, the CERCLA lender liability protections would not apply. In addition, even if liability is not directed to the lender itself, the lender could indirectly incur a loss if the values of the borrower's property decreased due to the presence of contamination. If other collateral was not available, the cost to remediate the property would effectively be paid by the lender. Further, the CERCLA lender liability protection relates to contamination matters and does not apply to costs associated with general environmental compliance matters, such as air emissions or wastewater discharges. Lenders could also face liability under some state environmental laws.

9.7.5   RICO

RICO (18 U.S.C. § 1962(c)) provides that it shall be unlawful for any person "employed by or associated with any enterprise" in interstate or foreign commerce to conduct the enterprise's affairs through "a pattern of racketeering activity or collection of unlawful debt." In the lending context, as discussed briefly in Section 3.1.1, banks have sometimes been sued by disgruntled borrowers (primarily consumers) who allege interest overcharges because of the disparity between the prime rate (historically defined as the "best" rate) and other interest rates (such as LIBOR) that are in fact better. See *Michaels Bldg. Co. v. Ameritrust Co.*, N.A., 848 F.2d 674 (6th Cir. 1988) and *Haroco, Inc. v. American Nat'l Bank & Trust Co.*, 747 F.2d 384 (7th Cir. 1984), *aff'd*, 473 U.S. 606 (1985). Although the standard definition of "prime rate" has long since been recast by most banks so that this risk is no longer material—see the failed attempt to charge a RICO violation on these grounds in *Lum v. Bank of Am.*, 361 F.3d 217 (3d. Cir. 2004)—the potential for suits under RICO for other alleged "patterns" of misconduct is still present. RICO claims will never completely disappear because of the tempting treble damages recovery of any successful RICO action.

9.7.6 Securities Laws

We discuss in Section 11.6, the considerations that the U.S. Supreme Court has laid down to determine whether a transaction gives rise to a security. We note there that, applying those principles, a number of helpful provisions in the typical credit agreement and elements of the standard syndication process argue for loans not being treated as securities. Depending upon the circumstances of any particular syndication (and the manner in which the related credit agreement is drafted), it is nevertheless possible for a court to conclude that a loan is a security. If that were to occur then potential lender liability claims could arise under Rule 10b-5 promulgated under the Securities Act of 1934, which contains broad antifraud liability provisions that prohibit, among other things, any person in connection with the purchase or sale of any security in interstate commerce from making an untrue statement of a material fact or omitting to state a material fact necessary in order to make statements not misleading. If loans are deemed securities, both arrangers and lenders might be exposed to liabilities that neither contemplated. Arrangers might risk liability because, in syndicating a facility, the information memorandum distributed to prospective lenders may not have complied with the strict disclosure requirements of the securities laws. Lenders could be exposed because, in selling assignments or participations in loans, they may not have made adequate disclosure of material adverse information known to them or may even have made affirmative misstatements of material information (the potential for liability under the securities law for such nondisclosure or misstatements being broader than under common law theories of fraud or misrepresentation).

9.7.7 Wrongful Coercion

As an alternative to immediately exercising remedies, lenders to a distressed borrower may instead wish to negotiate a workout arrangement. A workout is often designed to provide breathing room for the business to address underlying challenges while allowing lenders, for the time being at least, to avoid having to undertake potentially enterprise value-destructive enforcement actions. In exchange for its forbearance, a lender in this situation may bargain for the payment of additional fees, paydown of outstanding principal, exchange debt for equity, provision of additional guarantees or other forms of credit enhancement, granting of liability releases, or a whole host of other possible arrangements. If such arrangements are determined to have come about from wrongful and unlawful threats made to the borrower, they could be challenged as inequitable and ultimately voided by a court.

In the case of *Interpharm, Inc. v. Wells Fargo Bank, N.A.*, 655 F.3d 136 (2d Cir. 2011), Interpharm challenged the enforceability of a broad release that it had agreed to in a forbearance agreement with Wells Fargo. Arguing that it only agreed to the release because it was under severe economic duress and Wells Fargo had wrongfully threatened to drastically reduce Interpharm's access to the revolving credit line, Interpharm alleged that it had been backed into a corner and had no real choice but to agree or file for bankruptcy. Under New York law, courts may not enforce an agreement where it is found that an unlawful threat compelled involuntary acceptance of terms by the threatened party who had no other alternative. The *Interpharm* court ultimately found in favor of Wells Fargo and reaffirmed the notion that financial pressure and unequal bargaining power by itself do not establish wrongful economic duress. A lender who, for example, withheld credit or some other good that it was contractually obligated to provide in order to bend a borrower into submission is different than a lender who bends a borrower into submission by rightfully withholding credit because it has a right to do so under the credit agreement (due to a continuing default, for example) or threatening to enforce its legal rights to enforce remedies. The important point to note is that when it comes to determining equitable conduct of a lender dealing with a distressed borrower, under the law there is a distinction between driving a hard bargain by lawful means, on the one hand, and on the other hand, wrongful threats.

CHAPTER 10

Interlender, Voting, and Agency Issues; Defaulting Lenders

10.1 AGENCY ISSUES

The role of the administrative agent is to interface between the borrower and the lenders, and among the lenders themselves. Executing what might be described as back-office functions, the administrative agent receives financial and other reports from the borrower and ensures that they are made available to the lenders (typically by posting them on a website). It takes delivery of and forwards notices from the parties. The administrative agent also receives and disburses funds between the borrower and the lenders, including the proceeds of loans and payments of principal, interest, and fees. In facilities that are secured, the administrative agent normally also holds the liens on behalf of the lenders and other secured parties. The grant of security is made to the agent "for the benefit of the secured parties," rather than to the lenders and other secured parties directly. This means that action in respect of the collateral may be taken by the agent only, and not by the secured parties (or any individual secured party).

Except for purposes of maintaining the loan register (see Section 11.2.6), the administrative agent is the agent of the lenders and *not* of the borrower. Accordingly, the borrower has no right to instruct the administrative agent to take, or refrain from taking, any particular action. Similarly, actions taken by the administrative agent do not bind the borrower—they bind the lenders only. Execution of an amendment by the administrative agent still requires execution by the borrower to become effective.

The administrative agent, under the typical agency section of a credit agreement, is solely an agent—it is not a trustee or fiduciary for the lenders.

Stated another way, the job of the administrative agent is purely ministerial. It is not required to take discretionary action on its own initiative. Indeed, it is not required to take *any* action unless expressly provided in the credit agreement. Even though not required to exercise its discretion, that does not stop constituencies from attempting to exert pressure to force an action (or a nonaction). With the recent growth of nonbank loan market participants has come a lender class comprised of more activist-inclined hedge funds and similar institutional investors. Compared with a lender group largely comprised of relationship banks, a more activist lender group presents the administrative agent with more varied and potentially disparate or even conflicting bank group politics than had been the case with a more bank-centric syndicate. While the job description on its face is ministerial, that says nothing of the situations when, due to a lack of a clear answer or as a result of agitating lenders pressing the issue, the agent is forced to essentially make a judgment call. Interested constituencies looking to aggressively interpret and enforce the contract may present new challenges to the administrative agency role. The agent's role today reaches well beyond solely back-office administration.

The duties (such as they are) of the administrative agent should not be confused with the *de facto* leadership role often assumed by the arranger or lead bank, even though that is normally the same institution (or an affiliate of the same institution) as the administrative agent. Recommendations made by the lead bank to a syndicate are just that: recommendations of the bank, not of the administrative agent. The exculpatory language in standard agency provisions benefits the arranger by making it clear that each syndicate member makes its own credit decisions and determinations as to what actions to take under the credit agreement, and that syndicate members do not rely upon the administrative agent or any other lender in that regard.

Remembering these basic principles helps in understanding the agency provisions set forth in the typical credit agreement. For reference, market-standard agency language drawn from the LSTA's Model Credit Agreement Provisions is excerpted in sample provisions throughout this chapter.

10.1.1 Appointment

Box 10.1

Each of the Lenders and the Issuing Banks hereby irrevocably appoints [name of initial Administrative Agent] to act on its behalf as the

Administrative Agent hereunder and under the other Loan Documents and authorizes the Administrative Agent to take such actions on its behalf and to exercise such powers as are delegated to the Administrative Agent by the terms hereof or thereof, together with such actions and powers as are reasonably incidental thereto. The provisions of this Article are solely for the benefit of the Administrative Agent, the Lenders and the Issuing Banks, and [the Borrower shall not] [neither the Borrower nor any other Loan Party shall] have rights as a third-party beneficiary of any of such provisions. It is understood and agreed that the use of the term "agent" herein or in any other Loan Documents (or any other similar term) with reference to the Administrative Agent is not intended to connote any fiduciary or other implied (or express) obligations arising under agency doctrine of any applicable law. Instead such term is used as a matter of market custom and is intended to create or reflect only an administrative relationship between contracting parties.

The lenders that are parties to the credit agreement appoint an institution as the administrative agent. As noted earlier, this institution is normally the lead bank. Any lender that becomes a lender under the credit agreement at a later date by post-closing assignment, through operation of the clause, also appoints that institution as administrative agent. The appointment is stated to be irrevocable, although other provisions in the agency clause allow the administrative agent to resign. The appointment is stated to be irrevocable so that, absent the lender's bankruptcy, no lender in the future may attempt to challenge the administrative agent's continuing authority to act for it by purporting to revoke the appointment.

If the credit agreement is secured, the liens will be granted to the administrative agent "for the benefit of" the lenders or secured parties more generally. Therefore other purported secured parties in addition to the lenders, such as secured hedge providers or banks providing overdraft or other cash management services, will also typically appoint the administrative agent as their agent with respect to administration and enforcement of their lien. The notion that an agent can hold a lien on behalf of separate often unrelated parties is not universally accepted across all legal regimes. In credit facilities involving foreign obligors and secured by foreign collateral, certain jurisdictions may not recognize a lien trustee or agent as a matter of law. Civil law jurisdictions such as Spain, France, and Germany, among others, are examples. In such jurisdictions, the idea that an agent can hold a lien securing debt that is not owing to it is generally unrecognized under local law. However, foreign trust arrangements, such as an administrative agency created by New York law, and workarounds, such as a "parallel debt" structure (whereby a debt obligation equal to the loan obligation is created in favor of the agent in order to enable the agent to qualify as a creditor under the applicable civil law rules, though any payment on such "parallel" debt reduces dollar-for-dollar the loan debt), may be upheld in these jurisdictions.

In the case of a financial institution serving in the dual capacity of administrative agent and collateral agent or security agent, all of the same rights and privileges set forth in the agency provisions are written to apply to the bank as collateral agent or security agent as well. Having the administrative agent serve as the collateral agent or security agent is done principally for convenience. The administrative agent is the entity that keeps the records as to what the lenders hold and what they are owed and is therefore in a good position to distribute proceeds of collateral without having to rely upon third parties.

In some cases it may be useful for the collateral agent role to be delegated to a different institution. This can be the case if the collateral security is granted by the borrower equally for the benefit of the lenders and a separate group of creditors. The separate group may prefer that an institution other than the administrative agent under the credit agreement hold (and, therefore, control) the collateral. The administrative agent itself may also prefer not to hold the collateral because of potential conflict of interest issues that may arise. For example, if collateral granted by a borrower in distress secures both a credit agreement that matures in one year (with a lender group therefore anxious for immediate action) and a private placement that matures in 10 years (with a group of insurance companies that prefers to wait for improvement in the borrower's business rather than commence foreclosure now), the role of the administrative agent could be in conflict with that of the collateral agent. If the agent, mindful of its capacity as collateral agent also for the insurance companies, exercises its discretion to give the borrower more time to recover, it may face criticism (or suit) from the lending syndicate; conversely, if the agent chooses to take immediate action, it may face criticism (or suit) from the insurance companies. (See Section 7.6.2.)

Some of the inherent conflict in multiple roles such as these can be resolved through very explicit intercreditor and voting provisions among the secured parties, though all issues cannot be so managed. By definition, the secured parties want to leave the collateral or security agent with some discretion for situations in which quick action is necessary, yet it is precisely the exercise of such discretion that can potentially lead to conflict.

Another instance where there is pressure for a single agent to fill multiple roles comes up in the context of second lien facilities, discussed in Section 2.4. For cost reasons, borrowers often push to have a single institution serve as the collateral agent for both the first lien and second lien lenders. First lien lenders frequently object to this structure (because of the risk that the first and second lien loans will be treated as a single class, with the resulting adverse implications for post-petition interest and plan confirmations elaborated upon in Chapter 2), and many agents do not want to take on such a dual role which, in case of financial difficulties, can place them in a potentially awkward conflict. Borrowers often respond that any potential difficulty can be handled by the particular institution's resigning its second lien agent role when a conflict becomes apparent, but this presents other complications, including determining when to resign (the very act of resignation could alert third parties that the borrower is facing financial difficulties) and how to find a successor agent (see the discussion in Section 10.1.9). For these reasons, many second lien facilities have an agent separate from that for the related first lien facility.

10.1.2   *Rights of Administrative Agent Individually*

Box 10.2

The Person serving as the Administrative Agent hereunder shall have the same rights and powers in its capacity as a Lender as any other Lender and may exercise the same as though it were not the Administrative Agent and the term "Lender" or "Lenders" shall, unless otherwise expressly indicated or unless the context otherwise requires, include the Person serving as the Administrative Agent hereunder in its individual capacity. Such Person and its Affiliates may accept deposits from, lend money to, own securities of, act as the financial advisor or in any other advisory capacity for and generally engage in any kind of business with the Borrower or any Subsidiary or other Affiliate thereof as if such Person were not the Administrative Agent hereunder and without any duty to account therefor to the Lenders.

Consistent with the distinction between its *de facto* role as a lender (or lead bank or arranger) and its *contractual* role as administrative agent, the agency provisions state that the institution that functions as administrative agent in its individual capacity has the same rights as any other lender to engage in other business with the borrower and its related companies. Absent this language, the administrative agent could be constrained in its ability to conduct business dealings with the borrower. Under general agency principles an agent (here, the administrative agent) has a duty of loyalty to its principals (in this case, the lenders). See *Restatement (Third) of Agency, Chapter 8, Title B (2006)*. This includes an obligation not to compete with the principals during the course of the agency relationship. See *Restatement (Third) of Agency, § 8.04 (2006)*.

The principals can, however, waive this obligation and the language cited above constitutes the lenders' consent to the administrative agent's engaging in activities that could otherwise constitute a breach of the duty of loyalty. It allows the administrative agent to undertake any other commercial activity with the borrower or its affiliates "as if [it] were not the Administrative Agent." From the standpoint of the administrative agent this waiver is essential. The institution that serves as administrative agent is typically awarded that role by the borrower precisely because it has the closest business relationship with the borrower. No lender wants to serve as administrative agent under a loan facility if to do so constricts its ability to continue to do other business with the borrower, including to compete for deposits and new financings (whether loan facilities or high-yield or investment-grade bond offerings), engage in derivatives transactions, and generally offer the full range of products that a bank (or other lending institution) makes available to its customers.

10.1.3   No Fiduciary Duty

Box 10.3

The Administrative Agent shall not have any duties or obligations except those expressly set forth herein and in the other Loan Documents and its duties hereunder shall be administrative in nature. Without limiting the generality of the foregoing, the Administrative Agent:

(a) shall not be subject to any fiduciary or other implied duties, regardless of whether a Default has occurred and is continuing;

(b) shall not have any duty to take any discretionary action or exercise any discretionary powers, except discretionary rights and powers expressly contemplated hereby or by the other Loan Documents that the Administrative Agent is required to exercise as directed in writing by the Required Lenders (or such other number or percentage of the Lenders as shall be expressly provided for herein or in the other Loan Documents), *provided* that the Administrative Agent shall not be required to take any action that, in its opinion or the opinion of its counsel, may expose the Administrative Agent to liability or that is contrary to any Loan Document or applicable law including for the avoidance of doubt any action that may be in violation of the automatic stay under any Debtor Relief Law or that may effect a forfeiture, modification or termination of property of a Defaulting Lender in violation of any Debtor Relief Law; and

(c) shall not, except as expressly set forth herein and in the other Loan Documents, have any duty to disclose, and shall not be liable for the failure to disclose, any information relating to the Borrower or any of its Affiliates that is communicated to or obtained by the Person serving as the Administrative Agent or any of its Affiliates in any capacity.

As noted at the beginning of this chapter, the standard agency clause in a credit agreement explicitly states that the administrative agent under a credit facility is not a fiduciary for the lenders. This is intended to modify the general legal principle discussed in Section 10.1.2 that imposes upon an administrative agent a duty of loyalty.

The agency provisions make clear that the administrative agent's responsibilities are ministerial only and expressly negate the kinds of obligations that a fiduciary would otherwise owe to its beneficiaries. As a consequence, the agency clause normally provides that the agent is not required to do anything under the credit agreement except to the extent other provisions of the agreement expressly require it to act. Neither it nor its affiliates are required to disclose information in their possession to the lenders, except as specifically provided in the credit agreement. The agent need not inform the lenders of material adverse information discovered by the bank that serves as administrative agent, or by its securities or derivatives affiliates, in the course of their business dealings (whether before or after the closing). The ministerial nature of an administrative agent's role as crafted in the agency provisions allows the agency functions to be performed by the same personnel that monitor the facility on behalf of the agent bank without the burden of having to pass on that information to the syndicate.

Although the administrative agent may have the authority to take actions on its own initiative to accelerate the loans, to commence enforcement actions, or to realize on collateral, it is not normally obligated under the credit agreement to undertake any of these. It is, however, obligated to take action that the credit agreement stipulates must be taken if instructed by the requisite lenders (this may be an individual lender, in the case of notices, and in other cases either a majority or all of the lenders). However, even in these instances, the administrative agent is relieved from taking action if, in its judgment, the action exposes it to liability or violates applicable law. Thus, the administrative agent could not be compelled to deliver a notice of default to a borrower that is the subject of a bankruptcy proceeding, since to do so without court approval might violate the automatic stay under the Bankruptcy Code. All of these provisions basically elaborate in explicit language one simple principle: the agent's duties are *ministerial* and not *discretionary*.

Broad waivers such as these were upheld in the case of *UniCredito Italiano SpA v. JPMorgan Chase Bank*, 288 F. Supp. 2d 485 (S.D.N.Y. 2003). In that case, which arose out of the bankruptcy of Enron, two lenders that were syndicate members sought recovery from the administrative agents under separate credit facilities on the grounds of fraud or negligent misrepresentation. Both agents allegedly, by virtue of supposed extensive and undisclosed collateral relationships with the borrower, had knowledge of material adverse information regarding the borrower and its affiliates that was not readily available to the syndicate members. The court, nevertheless, supported the principle that no claim based upon these theories can succeed where the relevant agreements are clear that the administrative agent has no duty to disclose information to the syndicate:

> Sophisticated parties such as [the plaintiff lenders] are held to the terms of their contracts . . . Having failed to bargain for the right to rely on the banks as monitors of Enron's compliance with its disclosure, financial condition and other covenants, or for the right to benefit from any knowledge gained by the Defendant banks or their affiliates in connection with their own business dealings with Enron and its affiliates, Plaintiffs cannot, as a matter of law, be held reasonably to have relied on any misrepresentations or omission by the Defendants concerning those matters.[1]

An exception might apply if an agent had "peculiar knowledge" that a syndicate member has no independent means of discovering. The *UniCredito* court noted that the affirmative covenants (see Section 7.5.1) gave each lender substantial access to borrower information (including to request additional financial disclosure) and, therefore, that the allegedly adverse information was not *peculiarly* within the possession of the agent since the borrower had the information as well. The peculiar knowledge exception or the similar "special facts" doctrine (whereby one party is found to have a duty to disclose based on its

---

[1] *UniCredito Italiano SpA v. JPMorgan Chase Bank*, 288 F. Supp. 2d 485 (S.D.N.Y. 2003) at page 499.

superior knowledge of essential facts that render a transaction without disclosure as inherently unfair) is unlikely to apply in the typical syndicated loan facility. Nonetheless, at least one court has found that whether such exceptions apply to nullify the agent waiver may depend on the particular facts and circumstances of a case. See *Harbinger Capital Partners Master Fund I, Ltd. v Wachovia Capital Mkts., LLC*, 910 N.Y.S.2d 762 (N.Y. Sup. Ct. 2010).

Although the *UniCredito* decision certainly supports the objective of administrative agents to have no responsibility to disclose borrower information to lenders, it should not be viewed as according an agent *carte blanche* to conceal from the lending syndicate matters of which it has knowledge. For example, if the administrative agent or its affiliates assisted in helping the borrower conceal material adverse information, the agent might be held liable to the syndicate on the grounds that it aided and abetted the borrower's own fraud.

The administrative agent's role as constituted in the typical credit agreement stands in sharp contrast to the role of a trustee in a bond indenture, which by its very nature has a certain fiduciary quality. This distinction can be especially important in a default scenario.

10.1.4 Exculpation

Box 10.4

The Administrative Agent shall not be liable for any action taken or not taken by it (i) with the consent or at the request of the Required Lenders (or such other number or percentage of the Lenders as shall be necessary, or as the Administrative Agent shall believe in good faith shall be necessary, under the circumstances as provided in Sections [*Amendments*] and [*Exercise of Remedies*]) or (ii) in the absence of its own gross negligence or willful misconduct as determined by a court of competent jurisdiction by final and nonappealable judgment. The Administrative Agent shall be deemed not to have knowledge of any Default unless and until notice describing such Default is given to the Administrative Agent in writing by the Borrower, a Lender or an Issuing Bank.

The Administrative Agent shall not be responsible for or have any duty to ascertain or inquire into (i) any statement, warranty, or representation made in or in connection with this Agreement or any other Loan Document, (ii) the contents of any certificate, report or other document delivered hereunder or thereunder or in connection herewith or therewith, (iii) the performance or observance of any of the covenants, agreements or other terms or conditions set forth herein or therein or the occurrence of any Default, (iv) the validity, enforceability, effectiveness or genuineness of this Agreement, any other Loan Document or any other agreement, instrument or document, (v) the satisfaction of any condition set forth in Article [*Conditions*] or elsewhere herein, other than to confirm receipt of items expressly required to be delivered to the Administrative Agent or (vi) compliance by Affiliated Lenders with the terms hereof relating to Affiliated Lenders.

The Administrative Agent shall not be responsible or have any liability for, or have any duty to ascertain, inquire into, monitor or enforce, compliance with the provisions hereof relating to Disqualified Institutions. Without limiting the generality of the foregoing, the Administrative Agent shall not (x) be obligated to ascertain, monitor or inquire as to whether any Lender or Participant or prospective Lender or Participant is a Disqualified Institution or (y) have any liability with respect to or arising out of any assignment or participation of Loans, or disclosure of confidential information, to any Disqualified Institution.

In addition to making clear that the agent is not a fiduciary for the lenders and that its responsibilities are ministerial only (see Section 10.1.3), the agency provisions include two overarching exculpations: a statement that the agent is not liable for any actions taken by it (other than for its gross negligence or willful misconduct usually as determined by a court of competent jurisdiction by final and nonappealable judgment) and an acknowledgment that the agent is not responsible to monitor the loans on behalf of the lenders.

The reason for the breadth of the agent's exculpation is simple. As a rule, agency fees are minuscule when compared to the total amount of the loan facility. With a typical fee of $100,000 or less per year, an agent is simply not compensated for taking on the risk that an exercise of remedies by it under a multibillion dollar loan facility may turn out to be a mistake. Agents are willing to assume agency responsibilities only if their potential liability is minimal; the exculpation reflects this.

The first of the broad exculpations of an administrative agent is for any action that does not constitute gross negligence or willful misconduct. Whether to impose liability upon an agent (or, in the case of a bond indenture, a trustee) for *mere* negligence as opposed to *gross* negligence was historically the subject of fierce negotiation between agents (and trustees) on the one hand and lenders (or underwriters) on the other. Lenders, for their part, want the agent to behave as a reasonably prudent person under similar circumstances would behave, and to be held responsible if they fail this standard—a short-hand definition of the term "negligence." From their perspective, agents (and trustees) argue that this standard is too vague, that any good plaintiff's lawyer can confuse a judge or jury into believing that if something went wrong there must have been negligence. As a consequence, agents (and trustees) insist, except in rare cases, that they can be liable only for gross negligence, and that is the standard that has now become customary.

Although the distinction between ordinary negligence and gross negligence has been characterized as "shadowy and unsatisfactory," *Dalton v. Hamilton Hotel Operating Co.*, 242 N.Y. 481 (1926), courts now generally adopt a two-pronged definition of the term: ". . . a failure to use even slight care, or conduct that is so careless as to show complete disregard for the rights or safety of others." *Fed. Ins. Co. v. Honeywell, Inc.*, 641 F. Supp. 1560 (S.D.N.Y. 1986) at 1563 (quoting jury instructions summarizing the law of gross negligence). Gross negligence is, in other words, really bad negligence. Many banks have firm policies that preclude them from accepting an agency (or trustee) role unless the standard of liability is one of gross negligence. A similar fear underpins other uses of the "gross negligence and willful misconduct" standard in the credit agreement (see, for example, Section 12.6).

Even when the standard of liability is based upon gross negligence (as in the language in Box 10.4), actions that might otherwise constitute gross negligence may not result in liability for the agent if it either obtains the consent of the requisite lenders for the action or takes the action in the good-faith belief that it is necessary in the circumstances. A foreclosure on stock pursuant to instruction of the lenders that results in the lenders being the proud new owners of a toxic waste dump should not (if the appropriate exculpation is included in the agency provisions) subject the agent to liability to the lenders, even if it knew of the potential risks and a court were to say the foreclosure constituted gross negligence on the part of the lenders and agent. Similarly, an acceleration of the loans by the agent that a court later finds amounted to willful misconduct should not subject the agent to liability to the lenders if it believed in good faith (even if quite stupidly) that to declare the loans due and payable was the best way to maximize the lenders' recovery.

The second of the broad exculpations that benefits the administrative agent addresses its duties (or, rather, lack thereof) vis-à-vis the lenders. The standard agency clause makes clear that the administrative agent is not under any duty to verify the accuracy of information delivered by the borrower, nor to verify whether the borrower is complying with the provisions of the credit agreement or even whether the borrower's obligations under the credit agreement are in fact valid or enforceable as stated in the legal opinions delivered at closing. Also the administrative agent typically disclaims liability for policing assignments and participations to "disqualified institutions" (that is, parties not permitted to be lenders). (See the discussion of disqualified institutions in Section 11.2.3.) A list of disqualified institutions, also referred to as a disqualified lender list or "DQ list," is shared with the agent and lenders before the date of the credit agreement and may be updated with the names of the borrower's competitors after that date. Like any other notice, the agent is typically authorized to post the disqualified lender list or provide it to a lender upon request, but it is not responsible for ensuring that lenders not trade with entities included on that list.

The agent is also not responsible to confirm that conditions to loans are satisfied, other than to confirm receipt of documents required to be delivered to it. Whether the agent should have responsibility to verify satisfaction of conditions can be a point of contention between administrative agents and lenders. Lenders say, with some justification, that the administrative agent is closer to the borrower and more likely to know what is going on at the borrower than any other lender can hope to be. They may balk at the idea that the administrative agent would pass on a borrowing request when the agent is aware that a default exists or is about to arise. The agent, in response, falls back on the principle that its responsibilities are ministerial only and that it is not compensated to undertake more. As a consequence, the approach taken to address this point in the typical agency provisions (usually drafted by agent's counsel and rarely negotiated by the lenders) is to affirm that each lender takes full responsibility for its own credit decisions with respect to the borrower and for obtaining such information as the lender deems appropriate to extend credit to the borrower and to monitor the loan. The language states that the administrative agent is not under any duty to disclose any information that relates to the borrower or any of its affiliates that it obtains in *any* capacity (this has the effect, therefore, of picking up all of its potential roles: agent, lender, arranger, financial advisor, derivatives counterparty, and so forth). In this vein, the language set out in Box 10.4 (taken from the LSTA's Model Credit Agreement Provisions) is explicit in stating that the administrative agent is not deemed to have notice of any default (even payment defaults) unless it has received written notice to such effect by the borrower or a lender. Some agency provisions go further and require that any such notice, to be effective against the administrative agent, must be prominently identified as a "NOTICE OF DEFAULT."

10.1.5 Reliance

Box 10.5

The Administrative Agent shall be entitled to rely upon, and shall not incur any liability for relying upon, any notice, request, certificate, consent, statement, instrument, document, or other writing (including any electronic message, Internet or intranet website posting or other distribution) believed by it to be genuine and to have been signed, sent or otherwise authenticated by the proper Person. The Administrative Agent also may rely upon any statement made to it orally or by telephone and believed by it to have been made by the proper Person, and shall not incur any liability for relying thereon. In determining compliance with any condition hereunder to the making of a Loan that by its terms must be fulfilled to the satisfaction of a Lender, the Administrative Agent may presume that such condition is satisfactory to such Lender unless the Administrative Agent shall have received notice to the contrary from such Lender prior to the making of such Loan. The Administrative Agent may consult with legal counsel (who may be counsel for the Borrower), independent accountants, and other experts selected by it, and shall not be liable for any action taken or not taken by it in accordance with the advice of any such counsel, accountants or experts.

The agency provisions in the typical credit agreement permit the administrative agent to rely upon notices, certificates, and other documents that it believes to be genuine and sent by the proper, authorized person. This language protects the agent in two ways. First, it helps shield the administrative agent against liability for passing on routine notices under the credit agreement. The agent should therefore be protected if it forwards a notice that it believes to be a valid borrowing request even though it later turns out that the person who submitted the request was not a properly authorized officer. In the worst case, it protects the administrative agent against sending the loan proceeds to an imposter's account—at least absent gross negligence or willful misconduct—if it believed the information given it to be genuine.

Second, the language protects the administrative agent in the event that it chooses to act (by, for example, exercising remedies, assuming the contract allows it to do so) based upon adverse financial information received from the borrower. Therefore, while the agency provisions (see Section 10.1.3) stipulate that the administrative agent has no duty to exercise any remedies on its own initiative, the reliance clause gives the administrative agent the option, if it chooses to act, to assume that the information it acts upon is accurate.

The ability to rely upon information received from the borrower often extends to oral (including telephonic) communications as well as written communications. The inclusion of telephonic communications here is useful when the day-to-day operation of a loan agency is taken into account. When administering a loan facility, a significant portion of the communication that passes between the borrower and the administrative agent is not in writing. Borrowing notices, payment notices, interest elections, and even default notices—all are likely conveyed initially over the telephone and probably not recorded on tape. Whether or not later confirmed in writing, the administrative agent will, in most cases, likely have already passed on the relevant notice to the syndicate and might not, as a practical matter, look for a confirmatory fax or e-mail (and to rescind the oral notice previously sent on to the lenders if confirmation is never received). The clause also allows the administrative agent to rely upon Internet or intranet website postings, which, as with unrecorded oral communications, do not necessarily leave a written record of their contents easily retrievable at a later time.

In addition, the clause permits the administrative agent to consult with counsel (which can include the borrower's counsel) and exculpates the administrative agent from any action it takes upon advice of counsel. The reference to reliance upon the borrower's counsel may seem misplaced—should the agent not always talk to its own counsel? The answer in most credit agreements (and bond indentures) is no. Many legal conclusions relevant to the agent likely come from the borrower's side and so to allow reliance upon the latter has become customary in both agency and bond trustee boilerplate. This is not to say that, in determining whether to exercise remedies, the administrative agent should accept the advice of the borrower's counsel; that might very well amount to gross negligence. However, it will protect the agent in other circumstances, such as whether a new board resolution properly authorizes a loan extension or whether a necessary regulatory approval is in effect.

Consistent with the principle that monitoring the loans is the responsibility of each lender and not that of the administrative agent, the reliance clause also allows the administrative agent to assume that conditions to a loan that are to be satisfactory to each lender are met unless the administrative agent has received notice to the contrary prior to making funds available to the borrower (see further discussion of this topic in Section 10.6). An example might be a condition in a credit agreement that certain material contracts are to be reviewed and to be satisfactory to each lender. The agent is entitled to assume that the contracts meet this test unless informed otherwise by a lender.

10.1.6   Delegation

> **Box 10.6**
>
> The Administrative Agent may perform any and all of its duties and exercise its rights and powers hereunder or under any other Loan Document by or through any one or more sub-agents appointed by the Administrative Agent. The Administrative Agent and any such sub-agent may perform any and all of its duties and exercise its rights and powers by or through their respective Related Parties.[2] The exculpatory provisions of this Article shall apply to any such sub-agent and to the Related Parties of the Administrative Agent and any such sub-agent, and shall apply to their respective activities in connection with the syndication of the Facilities as well as activities as Administrative Agent. The Administrative Agent shall not be responsible for the negligence or misconduct of any sub-agents except to the extent that a court of competent jurisdiction determines in a final and nonappealable judgment that the Administrative Agent acted with gross negligence or willful misconduct in the selection of such sub-agents.

The administrative agent may need to act through subagents. This is particularly the case if collateral security is involved and local trustees are necessary to hold the liens. It may also be the case when the agent exercises remedies, since it will act through attorneys retained by it for that purpose. The general rule under New York law is that without specific authority from the principal, an agent may not delegate its responsibilities, except perhaps for matters that are purely ministerial. See *O. A. Skutt, Inc. v. J. & H. Goodwin, Ltd.,* 295 N.Y.S. 772 (App. Div. 4th Dep't 1937). The agency provisions accordingly make it clear that the administrative agent can appoint sub-agents to perform its duties and exercise its powers, and thereby avoid any question that the delegation was authorized.

Some agency language (including the LSTA's Model Credit Agreement Provisions set out in Box 10.6) also makes explicit that the administrative agent is not liable for the negligence or misconduct of

---

[2] "Related Party" is generally defined to include a person's affiliates and the partners, directors, officers, employees, agents, trustees, administrators, managers, advisors, and representatives of that person and of its affiliates.

sub-agents so long as they were selected by the administrative agent with reasonable care and in good faith. This may work to shield the agent against claims by the lenders; it is not a defense to claims asserted by third parties—actions taken by a sub-agent are treated as actions by the agent itself.

10.1.7   Filing Proofs of Claim

Box 10.7

In case of the pendency of any bankruptcy, insolvency or other similar proceeding with respect to the Borrower or any other judicial proceeding relative to any Loan Party, the Administrative Agent (irrespective of whether the principal of any Loan or L/C Obligation shall then be due and payable or whether the Administrative Agent shall have made any demand therefor) shall be entitled and empowered (but not obligated) by intervention in such proceeding or otherwise:

(a) to file and prove a claim in such proceeding for the full amount of the principal and interest owing and unpaid in respect of the Loans, L/C Obligations and all other Obligations that are owing and unpaid and to file such other documents as may be necessary or advisable in order to have the claims of the Lenders, the Issuing Banks and the Administrative Agent (including any claim for the reasonable compensation, expenses, disbursements, and advances of the Lenders, the Issuing Banks and the Administrative Agent and their respective agents and counsel and all other amounts due the Lenders, the Issuing Banks and the Administrative Agent under Sections [*Fees; Expenses, Indemnity*]) allowed in such proceeding; and

(b) to collect and receive any monies or other property payable or deliverable on any such claims and to distribute the same;

and any custodian, receiver, assignee, trustee, liquidator, sequestrator, or other similar official in any such judicial proceeding is hereby authorized by each Lender and Issuing Bank to make such payments to the Administrative Agent and, in the event that the Administrative Agent shall consent to the making of such payments directly to the Lenders and the Issuing Banks, to pay to the Administrative Agent any amount due for the reasonable compensation, expenses, disbursements, and advances of the Administrative Agent and its agents and counsel, and any other amounts due the Administrative Agent under Sections [*Fees; Expenses, Indemnity*].

Nothing contained herein shall be deemed to authorize the Administrative Agent to consent to or accept or adopt on behalf of any

> Lender any plan of reorganization, arrangement, adjustment, or composition affecting the obligations of the Borrower hereunder or the rights of any Lender, or to authorize the Administrative Agent to vote in respect of the claim of any Lender in any such proceeding.

Although the authority granted to administrative agents in standard agency provisions is certainly expansive enough to include filing proofs of claim on behalf of the syndicate, some credit agreements include an express statement to this effect along the lines of the language in Box 10.7. Including explicit language avoids any issue under the Bankruptcy Rules (*Rule § 3001*) that the administrative agent is "authorized" to file a claim on behalf of the lenders. Having the agent file proofs of claim in a bankruptcy proceeding is preferable from the standpoint of all parties (the borrower, the lenders, and the administrative agent); it ensures accuracy, minimizes legal costs, and is normally insisted upon by bankrupt debtors. It also ensures that the lenders are treated fairly as among themselves. The problem of one lender claiming its portion of legal expenses and another claiming only principal and interest will not occur. Even if a credit agreement is silent and does not authorize the administrative agent to file proofs of claim, it is in any event uncertain that an individual lender would be allowed by the bankruptcy court to file its own proof—the court may very well insist that the agent do all filings simply for ease of administration.

Some credit agreements also address the ability of the agent to vote the claims of the lenders to approve (or disapprove) a plan of reorganization. Filing a proof of claim is a ministerial action by the administrative agent—collect the arithmetic data for each lender, complete a proof of claim, and submit it to the court. Voting to approve or reject a plan of reorganization is not a ministerial act. Indeed, it typically requires a lender to make difficult judgments whether a proposed plan is the best way to obtain maximum recovery. Is 80 cents on the dollar and no equity in the reorganized borrower better or worse than 40 cents on the dollar and 10 percent of the equity? These are not issues that any prudent agent wants to decide on behalf of syndicate members, so to include express language in a credit agreement that an agent cannot vote for or against a plan is probably superfluous. That may explain its relative rarity. Nevertheless, some agreements (particularly those that grant an agent an express right to file proofs of claim) explicitly remove any implied authority on the part of the administrative agent to vote in respect of a plan of reorganization.

10.1.8 Credit Bidding

Box 10.8

The holders of the Obligations hereby irrevocably authorize the Administrative Agent, at the direction of the Required Lenders, to credit bid all or any portion of the Obligations (including accepting some or all of the Collateral in satisfaction of some or all of the Obligations pursuant to a deed in lieu of foreclosure or otherwise) and in such manner purchase (either directly or through one or more acquisition vehicles) all or any portion of the Collateral (a) at any sale thereof conducted under the provisions of the Bankruptcy Code, including under Sections 363, 1123, or 1129 of the Bankruptcy Code, or any similar Laws in any other jurisdictions to which a Credit Party is subject or (b) at any other sale or foreclosure or acceptance of collateral in lieu of debt conducted by (or with the consent or at the direction of) the Administrative Agent (whether by judicial action or otherwise) in accordance with any applicable Law.

Instead of ending with a confirmed plan of reorganization, a Chapter 11 case may alternatively end with a sale of the collateral pursuant to Bankruptcy Code Section 363. In a 363 sale, a secured creditor has the right to "credit bid" its secured claim whereby it can use the face amount of its claim as currency against the purchase price of the collateral. A detailed discussion of 363 sales and credit bidding is beyond the scope of this volume but it should be clear that the right to credit bid is a valuable right for secured creditors in the bankruptcy context. If the highest bid for the collateral comes in for an amount that is less than the outstanding claim of the secured lenders, the lenders can just credit bid their claim and win the assets without putting in any additional cash. A question that arises in connection with a 363 sale is whether the agent may credit bid the entire face amount of the lenders claim or whether instead it may only bid the face amount of the claims of those lenders who support the credit bid. Recent court decisions support the agent's right, with approval from the majority lenders, to credit bid the entire debt claim on the collective behalf of the lenders even in the face of objections from holdout minority lenders. While minority lenders may challenge a credit bid as being a *de facto* release of all or substantially all collateral and therefore require unanimous lender consent, courts have not viewed a credit bid as being subject to the amendment provision of a credit agreement. Instead, a credit bid is viewed as an exercise of remedies, an activity that has been held to be firmly within the purview of an agent's delegated rights (as directed by the requisite lenders). In order to forestall minority lender challenges to credit bids, recent credit agreements often try to avoid any ambiguity on the issue by including language along the lines as set forth in Box 10.8. This language serves as an express authorization and lender consent to the agent's credit bid of the entire secured claim.

10.1.9 Successor Agents

> **Box 10.9**
>
> (a) The Administrative Agent may at any time give notice of its resignation to the Lenders, the Issuing Banks, and the Borrower. Upon receipt of any such notice of resignation, the Required Lenders shall have the right, in consultation with the Borrower, to appoint a successor, which shall be a bank with an office in [_____], or an Affiliate of any such bank with an office in [_____]. If no such successor shall have been so appointed by the Required Lenders and shall have accepted such appointment within 30 days after the retiring Administrative Agent gives notice of its resignation (or such earlier day as shall be agreed by the Required Lenders) (the "*Resignation Effective Date*"), then the retiring Administrative Agent may (but shall not be obligated to), on behalf of the Lenders and the Issuing Banks, appoint a successor Administrative Agent meeting the qualifications set forth above; *provided* that in no event shall any such successor Administrative Agent be a Defaulting Lender [or an Affiliated Lender] [or a Disqualified Institution]. Whether or not a successor has been appointed, such resignation shall become effective in accordance with such notice on the Resignation Effective Date.
>
> (b) If the Person serving as Administrative Agent is a Defaulting Lender pursuant to clause (d) of the definition thereof, the Required Lenders may, to the extent permitted by applicable law, by notice in writing to the Borrower and such Person remove such Person as Administrative Agent and, in consultation with the Borrower, appoint a successor. If no such successor shall have been so appointed by the Required Lenders and shall have accepted such appointment within 30 days (or such earlier day as shall be agreed by the Required Lenders) (the "*Removal Effective Date*"), then such removal shall nonetheless become effective in accordance with such notice on the Removal Effective Date.
>
> (c) With effect from the Resignation Effective Date or the Removal Effective Date (as applicable) (i) the retiring or removed Administrative Agent shall be discharged from its duties and obligations hereunder and under the other Loan Documents [(except that in the case of any collateral security held by the Administrative Agent on behalf of the

Lenders or the Issuing Banks under any of the Loan Documents, the retiring or removed Administrative Agent shall continue to hold such collateral security until such time as a successor Administrative Agent is appointed)] and (ii) except for any indemnity payments owed to the retiring or removed Administrative Agent, all payments, communications, and determinations provided to be made by, to, or through the Administrative Agent shall instead be made by or to each Lender and Issuing Bank directly, until such time, if any, as the Required Lenders appoint a successor Administrative Agent as provided for above. Upon the acceptance of a successor's appointment as Administrative Agent hereunder, such successor shall succeed to and become vested with all of the rights, powers, privileges, and duties of the retiring or removed Administrative Agent (other than any rights to indemnity payments owed to the retiring or removed Administrative Agent), and the retiring or removed Administrative Agent shall be discharged from all of its duties and obligations hereunder or under the other Loan Documents. The fees payable by the Borrower to a successor Administrative Agent shall be the same as those payable to its predecessor unless otherwise agreed between the Borrower and such successor. After the retiring or removed Administrative Agent's resignation or removal hereunder and under the other Loan Documents, the provisions of this Article and Section [*Expenses and Indemnity*] shall continue in effect for the benefit of such retiring or removed Administrative Agent, its sub-agents and their respective Related Parties in respect of any actions taken or omitted to be taken by any of them while the retiring or removed Administrative Agent was acting as Administrative Agent.

One of the key concerns of an administrative agent is that it be able to exit its job as agent if it determines that it is necessary or desirable to do so. This may arise when the borrower begins to drift into financial difficulties. The institution that serves as agent may have sold all of its loans and no longer retain an economic interest in the facility, and therefore wants to be relieved of the responsibility of being the administrative agent (even if its obligations are largely ministerial). Indeed, a nightmare scenario for an institution in this circumstance might be to find itself as a "hung agent": wanting to resign, but with no legal right or practical means to do so. Standard agency provisions attempt to address these concerns by including an express right of resignation. Where the resigning agent has also served as issuing bank for letters of credit, the agent and borrower are presented with the issue of dealing with any outstanding letters of credit. The same goes where the resigning agent served as swingline lender and there are outstanding swingline loans. The credit agreement may provide that a resigning agent is deemed to simultaneously and automatically also be resigning from its roles as issuing bank and swingline lender. While such a provision cuts off any obligation to issue new letters of credit or make additional swingline loans, any outstanding letters of credit or swingline loans will remain so following resignation until expiry or repayment, respectively. The resigning agent is no longer a party to the credit agreement but will retain its rights with respect to the outstanding letters of credit and swinglines.

The resignation right is normally contingent upon a successor agent's having been appointed by the required lenders and having accepted the role as administrative agent. If no qualified institution is willing to serve as a successor, the administrative agent is given the authority to appoint a successor. Certain restrictions are normally imposed as to who can be appointed as a successor administrative agent. In the LSTA's Model Credit Agreement Provisions set out in Box 10.9, the successor must be a bank with an office in a named city. Many agreements go beyond this and require that any successor be a *commercial* bank that has capital and surplus exceeding an agreed-upon dollar figure. Limiting the field of eligible successors in this manner is historical—banks have traditionally been the only institutions that possess the operational capacity to perform capably the agency function, and requiring that the successor be of a certain minimum size prevents a small, unsophisticated bank from assuming the agency role. Limiting successors to banks (or commercial banks), however, is increasingly meeting resistance as the universe of syndicate lenders expands beyond banks to encompass funds, insurance companies, and other nonbank financial institutions. Some agreements, therefore, remove the requirement that the successor be a bank or, alternatively, simply require that the successor be one of the lenders that has the effect of expanding the universe to nonbanks (at least those that are lenders).

Limiting successors to those that have an office in an agreed-upon city is also driven by operational considerations. Normally, the city selected is the same as that of the place of payment already specified in the credit agreement. If loan principal and interest is required to be paid at the initial agent's office in New York City (and all times in the agreement are specified with reference to New York City), then the successor should have an office that enables it to receive payments (and disburse funds) in New York City.

The right of an administrative agent to appoint a successor agent if no institution steps forward may be more illusory than real for an agent that desperately wants to resign. Simply having the right to appoint a successor does not mean that any successor can be found that is willing to serve. This can particularly be the case in the very circumstance where the initial agent wants to shed its agency responsibilities—when the borrower goes into workout mode. Many potential successors decline to step forward simply because of the increased profile of the agency role and the complexity of intrasyndicate dynamics that often arise when financial trouble occurs. Credit agreements try to deal with this problem either by allowing the administrative agent to resign anyway and devolve its responsibilities upon the lenders individually or by stipulating that the borrower pay whatever agency fee the market requires in order to find a willing successor. The former is likely to prove impractical; the latter may be somewhat more workable, though borrowers resist this approach because it is tantamount to an open-ended obligation on its part to pay an unknown level of fees to a successor should the administrative agent ever resign. The approach taken in the LSTA's Model Credit Agreement Provisions set out in Box 10.9 is simply to obligate the borrower to pay to a successor whatever fees were payable to the resigning agent. Of course, the agency fee that was appropriate for a borrower that enjoyed a favorable credit rating when the loan facility was first established may not be appropriate for a borrower on the threshold of a workout—the point of reference for any successor agent. There is no simple solution to this issue and the result is that in many cases administrative agents continue their responsibilities beyond their ideal resignation point.

Often borrowers request that they be given approval rights over a successor administrative agent. Superficially there is logic to this. After all, the borrower will have designated the lending institution that it believed merited the agency role when the facility is first established. On an ongoing basis, a substantial portion of the interaction under a credit agreement is between the agent and the borrower. Is the borrower not entitled to be comfortable with the institution with which it has to deal on a day-to-day basis and for the services of which it is paying? These arguments notwithstanding, borrower approval over agent identity is arguably inconsistent with the concept that the administrative agent is an agent of the lenders and not of the borrower. Accordingly, most agency provisions (including the LSTA's Model Credit Agreement Provisions) at most require consultation by the lenders with the borrower in appointing a new agent. If a credit agreement grants a consent right to the borrower, such right normally only applies during periods when no default or event of default exists.

Notwithstanding the lengthy verbiage in the typical credit agreement that permits an agent to resign, most institutions that serve as administrative agents do not cut and run at the first sign of financial problems. Indeed, many agents as a matter of professional reputation consciously continue to function as agent throughout a borrower's bankruptcy to facilitate a maximum recovery for the lenders even though they have long since sold off their loan exposures. To do otherwise might, not incidentally, adversely affect the ability of the agent (or its arranger affiliates) to syndicate future loan facilities for other customers.

Credit agreements may also permit the required lenders to remove an administrative agent but in such cases, the removal right is generally limited to situations when the administrative agent is a Defaulting Lender or is exhibiting signs of financial distress or otherwise having difficulty carrying out its agent duties. The presence of removal rights have historically ebbed and flowed in credit agreements, but following the latest financial crisis, when concerns of failing financial institutions were particularly acute, agency removal rights have consistently appeared in credit agreements. If the administrative agent is bankrupt or near bankrupt, borrower and lender alike should be worried that the agent's focus and resources are placed elsewhere and therefore in such a situation it is only logical to allow interested parties to swap out such an integral intermediary as the administrative agent. In addition to the potential disruption to credit agreement administration, a financially troubled agent raises further concerns that loan advances, principal, interest, or other monies transferred through the agent's accounts could either be deemed to be property of the bankruptcy estate or be trapped or delayed and held up by the bankruptcy proceedings and the automatic stay. These were concerns that were raised during the Lehman bankruptcy due to a Lehman subsidiary serving as administrative agent under dozens of syndicated credit facilities. The Lehman bankruptcy court ultimately found that monies in Lehman's agency accounts were beyond the reach of the bankruptcy estate. Thus monies continued to flow through Lehman in its capacity as agent under these facilities until a successor agent was finally appointed. However, in at least one credit agreement involving a Lehman entity as administrative agent, there was no contractual lender or borrower removal right and the borrower ultimately had to petition for a court order to force the removal. Therefore, to avoid the need to obtain a court order, credit agreements generally make available a right of removal when borrowers and lenders are faced with a financially distressed agent.

Broader removal rights will surely attract resistance from both borrowers and administrative agents (though see the discussion in Section 10.8.7 as it relates to a defaulting lender that happens also to be the administrative agent). The designation as administrative agent is a coveted title for arranging banks. Beyond being one of the indicia of success (rightly or wrongly) reflected in league tables, an agency role can otherwise be valuable. While agency fees alone may not be rich in the grand scheme, any institution serving as agent has substantial visibility into a corporate borrower's day-to-day operations. The informational advantage to respond to a borrower's banking service needs can be quite valuable.

Agents are not inclined to make their removal particularly easy no matter the level of lender dissatisfaction (or rebellion). In addition, if the borrower (absent default) has approval rights over any successor agent, it does not want an agent to be removed without its concurrence. For these reasons, and for the operational difficulties described above that arise whenever a successor agent takes over agency responsibilities, removal rights, other than in the defaulting or distressed lender context, are rare.

10.1.10 Collateral and Guaranty Matters

> #### Box 10.10
>
> (a) The [Secured Parties] irrevocably authorize the Administrative Agent, at its option and in its discretion,
>
> (i) to release any Lien on any property granted to or held by the Administrative Agent under any Loan Document (x) upon termination of all Commitments and payment in full of all Obligations (other than contingent indemnification obligations) and the expiration or termination of all Letters of Credit [(other than Letters of Credit as to which other arrangements satisfactory to the Administrative Agent and the applicable Issuing Bank shall have been made)], (y) that is sold or otherwise disposed of or to be sold or otherwise disposed of as part of or in connection with any sale or other disposition permitted under the Loan Documents, or (z) subject to Section [*Amendments*], if approved, authorized or ratified in writing by the Required Lenders;
>
> (ii) [to subordinate any Lien on any property granted to or held by the Administrative Agent under any Loan Document to the holder of any Lien on such property that is permitted by Section [*Liens Securing Capital Leases, Synthetic Leases, and Purchase Money Indebtedness*]]; and
>
> (iii) to release any Guarantor from its obligations under the Guaranty if such Person ceases to be a Subsidiary as a result of a transaction permitted under the Loan Documents.

> Upon request by the Administrative Agent at any time, the Required Lenders will confirm in writing the Administrative Agent's authority to release [or subordinate] its interest in particular types or items of property, or to release any Guarantor from its obligations under the Guaranty pursuant to this Section.
>
> The Administrative Agent shall not be responsible for or have a duty to ascertain or inquire into any representation or warranty regarding the existence, value, or collectability of the Collateral, the existence, priority, or perfection of the Administrative Agent's Lien thereon, or any certificate prepared by any Loan Party in connection therewith, nor shall the Administrative Agent be responsible or liable to the Lenders for any failure to monitor or maintain any portion of the Collateral.

For avoidance of any doubt that an agent may release or subordinate the bank group's liens in certain situations, credit agreements will often include a provision along the lines of the sample language in Box 10.10. The release language has the effect of relieving the agent from potentially having to go back to the lenders for approval to release a lien in connection with, for example, a permitted asset sale or a refinancing. From the borrower's perspective, this preauthorization language may come in handy where speed is of the essence and, by avoiding a lender consent process, an asset sale or refinancing can occur on an accelerated basis.

The authorization to subordinate liens is often a nonissue and merely an acknowledgment that in certain situations, such as a purchase money debt, the lenders' lien may be junior as a result of statute or otherwise. This is because Article 9 of the Uniform Commercial Code, which has been adopted as law in all 50 states, recognizes that liens in favor of a seller who sells goods on credit (and on which liens secure the deferred purchase price), otherwise known as "purchase money security interests" (or PMSI), have priority over most security interests in the purchased goods notwithstanding that such security interests were perfected prior to the purchase money interest. This priority in the purchased goods is automatic. To empower the administrative agent to formalize such subordination should not be controversial in principle. Whether the agent's authorization to subordinate extends beyond lien subordination to allow for payment subordination or when the authorization extends beyond PMSI and similar statutory or other nonconsensual liens may be more controversial and is a matter for negotiation.

10.1.11 Syndication and Other Agents

Box 10.11

Anything herein to the contrary notwithstanding, neither any Joint Bookrunner nor any person named on the cover page hereof as a Bookrunner, Lead Arranger, or a Documentation Agent shall have any powers, duties, or responsibilities under this Agreement or any of the other Loan Documents, except in its capacity, as applicable, as the Administrative Agent, a Lender, or the Issuing Bank hereunder.

It is typical for a large syndicated credit agreement to have many agency roles in addition to that of administrative agent. Bookrunner, Arranger, Syndication Agent, Documentation Agent, Managing Agent, and Co-Managing Agent are titles commonly set out on the cover page of the credit agreement. All are sought after, not least because certain titles factor into listings on league tables. Occasionally, the credit agreement even provides for these supplementary agents to execute the credit agreement in those capacities. Nevertheless, beyond appearing on the cover page and other syndicate materials (including commemorative tombstones), these supplementary agents rarely, if ever, have any real job. It has therefore become customary for the agency provisions to set out an express statement that none of these other agents has any duties or responsibilities under the credit agreement, whether or not they sign as parties to it. The language is a means to affirm that their role is titular only.

10.2 LENDER INDEMNIFICATION

Box 10.12

[Each Lender shall severally indemnify the Administrative Agent, within 10 days after demand therefor, for (i) any Indemnified Taxes attributable to such Lender (but only to the extent that [the Borrower] [any Loan Party] has not already indemnified the Administrative Agent for such Indemnified Taxes and without limiting the obligation of [the Borrower] [the Loan Parties] to do so), (ii) any Taxes attributable to such Lender's failure to comply with the provisions of Sections [*Successors and Assigns; Participations*] relating to the maintenance of a Participant Register, and (iii) any Excluded Taxes attributable to such Lender, in each case, that are payable or paid by the Administrative Agent in connection with any Loan Document, and any reasonable expenses arising therefrom or with respect thereto, whether or not such Taxes were correctly or legally imposed or asserted by the relevant Governmental Authority. A certificate as to the amount of such payment or liability delivered to any Lender by the Administrative Agent shall be conclusive absent manifest error. Each Lender hereby authorizes the Administrative Agent to set off and apply any and all amounts at any time owing to such Lender under any Loan Document or otherwise payable by the Administrative Agent to the Lender from any other source against any amount due to the Administrative Agent under this paragraph.]

To the extent that the Borrower for any reason fails to indefeasibly pay any amount required under paragraph (a) or (b) of this Section [*Borrower Indemnification*] to be paid by it to the Administrative Agent (or any sub-agent thereof), any Issuing Lender, any Swingline Lender or any Related Party[3] of any of the foregoing, each Lender severally agrees to pay to the Administrative Agent (or any such sub-agent), such Issuing Lender, such Swingline Lender, or such Related Party, as the case may be, such Lender's pro rata share (determined as of the time that the applicable unreimbursed expense or indemnity payment is sought based on each Lender's share of the Total Credit Exposure at such time) of such unpaid amount (including any such unpaid amount in respect of a claim asserted by such Lender); *provided* that with respect to such unpaid amounts owed to any Issuing Bank or Swingline Lender solely in its capacity as such, only the Revolving Lenders shall be required to pay such unpaid amounts, such payment to be made severally among them based on such Revolving Lenders' Applicable Percentage (determined as of the time that the applicable unreimbursed expense or indemnity payment is sought) *provided further* that the unreimbursed expense or indemnified loss, claim, damage, liability, or related expense, as the case may be, was incurred by or asserted against the Administrative Agent (or any such sub-agent), such Issuing Lender, or such Swingline Lender in its capacity as such, or against any Related Party of any of the foregoing acting for the Administrative Agent (or any such sub-agent), such Issuing Lender, or any such Swingline Lender in connection with such capacity. The obligations of the Lenders under this paragraph (__) are subject to the provisions of Section [*Obligations of Lenders Several*].

As discussed in greater detail in Section 12.6, the general rule in credit agreements is that the borrower is obligated to indemnify the administrative agent and each of the lenders against any loss, liability, or other cost suffered or incurred by them in connection with the loan facility. Nothing is for the account of the agent or lenders (with the exception

---

[3] See Footnote 2 to Box 10.6.

of gross negligence or willful misconduct). However, in the case of the administrative agent and, if there is one, the issuer of letters of credit and any swingline lender, it is customary for the lenders to provide a backup indemnification in the event that the borrower, for whatever reason, does not make good on its indemnification obligation. For the agent, this undertaking comes from all of the lenders under the credit agreement. For a letter of credit issuer or swingline lender, the backup indemnification comes only from the lenders that participate in the relevant letters of credit (the revolving credit lenders of the applicable tranche).

The obligations of the lenders (the "Applicable Percentage" in the language quoted in Box 10.12) to the administrative agent or letter of credit issuer is proportionate to their exposures. For the administrative agent this normally means, for any lender, that lender's share of the commitments (for tranches that still have a commitment) combined with that lender's share of the loans (for tranches that have been funded and have no continuing commitments). By way of example, if a lender holds a $5,000,000 revolving commitment out of an aggregate $30,000,000 revolving tranche, and $10,000,000 out of a $70,000,000 term loan, its proportionate share of the backup indemnity is 15 percent: ($5,000,000 + $10,000,000) ÷ ($30,000,000 + $70,000,000). A similar proportionate computation is made to calculate the relative share of a revolving credit lender's responsibility to a letter of credit issuer. In each case the proportionate obligation is several; no lender is responsible for the breach of any other lender but rather solely for its share of the borrower's breach.

Some credit agreements stipulate that the backup indemnification is subject to the same carveouts as are applicable to the borrower, including for gross negligence or willful misconduct by the administrative agent or letter of credit issuer. The LSTA's Model Credit Agreement Provisions do not take this approach, but achieve the same result by providing that the lenders are obligated only to the extent the borrower is obligated to pay and does not. Whatever defenses the borrower has therefore automatically flow through to the lenders.

10.3 VOTING

Box 10.13

Neither this Agreement nor any provision hereof may be waived, amended, or modified except pursuant to an agreement or agreements in writing entered into by the Borrower and the Required Lenders or by the

Borrower and the Administrative Agent with the consent of the Required Lenders; *provided* that no such agreement shall:

(i) increase the Commitment of any Lender without the written consent of such Lender;

(ii) reduce the principal amount of any Loan or Letter of Credit Disbursement or reduce the rate of interest thereon, or reduce any fees payable hereunder, without the written consent of each Lender adversely affected thereby;

(iii) postpone the scheduled date of payment of the principal amount of any Loan or Letter of Credit Disbursement, or any interest thereon, or any fees payable hereunder, or reduce the amount of, waive or excuse any such payment, or postpone the scheduled date of expiration of any Commitment, without the written consent of each Lender adversely affected thereby;

(iv) change Sections _____ [*Pro Rata Provisions*] in a manner that would alter the *pro rata* sharing of payments required thereby, without the written consent of each Lender adversely affected thereby; or

(v) change any of the provisions of this Section or the percentage in the definition of "Required Lenders" or any other provision hereof specifying the number or percentage of Lenders required to waive, amend, or modify any rights hereunder or make any determination or grant any consent hereunder, without the written consent of each Lender;

provided further that no such agreement shall amend, modify, or otherwise affect the rights or duties of the Administrative Agent, the Issuing Bank, or the Swingline Lender hereunder without the prior written consent of the Administrative Agent, the Issuing Lender or the Swingline Lender, as the case may be.

10.3.1 Basic Rule

The voting provisions of a credit agreement are superficially very simple. They mask, however, considerable nuances of market custom (and some law).

The basic rule is that the "majority" or "required" lenders must approve any modification, waiver, or supplement to any provision of the credit agreement. "Majority" or "required" normally means lenders that hold more than 50 percent of the aggregate credit exposure, defined as unused commitments and outstanding loans and letters of credit. In some agreements the percentage is higher (66⅔ percent is common if there is such a so-called "supermajority" voting construct), but this is generally resisted by borrowers. Although acceleration becomes more difficult with a higher percentage, so also does obtaining waivers and consents to changes—between the two, a borrower is likely to worry more about future amendments than about acceleration after default. Sometimes the credit agreement breaks out particular issues and requires a supermajority vote for changes that affect those issues. Borrowing base provisions are an example of this. In so-called club deals (a credit agreement with only a very small number of lenders), the definition of "required lenders" may include a concept that a minimum *number* of lenders, as well as a minimum *percentage* of exposures, vote in favor of a change. A deal with only three lenders, for example, might require that at least two lenders are necessary to make up the required lenders.

10.3.2 Multitranche Agreements

In a multitranche agreement, the amendments provision must address whether the lenders vote as a single pool, or whether each tranche votes separately. The general practice is that all lenders vote together as a pool except where a proposed amendment affects loans of a specific tranche. In a credit agreement with separate term and revolver facilities, the pooling approach can, however, pose a potential risk to revolving credit lenders. For example, if the term loan lenders constitute a majority of the pool, there is nothing to prevent them from agreeing to delete the material adverse change or other condition precedent if that would remove from the revolving credit lenders a basis upon which to refuse to lend. In the typical credit agreement the solution is a clause that requires a separate majority vote of a tranche if a change would adversely affect that tranche without equally affecting all other tranches. Other, more explicit, language seen in many agreements states that no tranche can be required to make loans as a result of an amendment without the consent of a majority of that tranche. In this case, the waiver is still effective to eliminate an event of default but is not effective for purposes of the conditions precedent. Another example of tranche voting comes from the covenant lite context where there will be a separate term loan A, or pro rata, tranche as well as a term loan B, or institutional, tranche. With the fundamental bargain of a covenant lite facility being that the institutional term loan B tranches not benefit from the financial covenants, it follows that they would be excluded from amendments and waivers of the financial covenant. Therefore, only lenders holding a majority of the pro rata facilities will have veto power over modifications of the financial covenant and related waivers.

10.3.3   Consents Requiring More Than a Majority

Although the general rule in all agreements is that no modification, supplement, or waiver can be effective unless it is approved by the majority or required lenders, the typical voting provision goes on to lay out some exceptions for which the consent of additional lenders is required. In these cases, the modification typically requires the approval of the majority or required lenders and the approval of either each lender (unanimous consent) or of each *affected* lender. Occasionally, in the case of affected-lender issues, a credit agreement will permit these modifications with the approval of only the affected lenders (and not the majority or required lenders). The sample language in Box 10.13 shows the typical approach. The modifications or waivers that require approval by this greater percentage of the lenders (or approval of those affected by the relevant modification or waiver) in most *unsecured and unguaranteed* agreements fall into one of four categories: adverse changes to money terms, alterations to the pro rata provisions, changes to the voting provisions, and, sometimes, waivers of initial conditions. Each of these is discussed briefly here.

10.3.3.1   Money Terms

The so-called "money terms" in a credit agreement encompass any provision that relates to principal, interest, or fees. Commitment amounts and commitment expiration dates, principal and interest due dates, principal maturity dates, rates of interest and fees and currency all fall into this category. Any *adverse* change to these terms generally requires consent from more than the majority lenders to become effective. Increases of commitments, extensions of maturity dates, extensions of "scheduled" payment dates, and reductions of interest and fees all require the higher approval threshold. Changes that are *favorable* to the lenders often do not require the higher level of consent. Thus, an increase of interest rates or advancement to an earlier date of a scheduled payment generally requires only majority approval. The rule with respect to changing money terms in a credit agreement is the same that has been followed for decades in other debt instruments, including private placements and bond indentures; all require a higher level of approval whenever adverse changes to money terms are made.

One question that arises frequently in this context is whether a waiver of a mandatory prepayment requirement constitutes a change to a "scheduled" payment date. For years, the consensus among bank lawyers (and bond lawyers in the context of bond indentures) was that required prepayments (or redemptions) are distinct from scheduled payments and that, unless an agreement specified otherwise, the majority or required lenders, without more, could waive a mandatory prepayment or redemption. This historical view was called into question by the decision in *Citadel Equity Fund, Ltd. v. Aquila, Inc.*, 371 F. Supp. 2d 510 (S.D.N.Y. 2005), where the court was asked to determine whether a prepayment made by the borrower (Aquila) was mandatory or optional. The lenders that instituted the suit claimed that, although a prepayment in the amount made by Aquila had originally been mandatory, it had ceased to be so by reason of a unilateral waiver from two-thirds of the lenders. Therefore, they reasoned, when Aquila nevertheless proceeded to make the prepayment, it was doing so *voluntarily*, and consequently a higher prepayment premium was due (the difference in premiums between a mandatory prepayment and an optional prepayment being on the order of $27,000,000).

The court rejected the lenders' arguments and ruled in favor of Aquila. It based its conclusion on several alternative grounds. First, it held that the purported unilateral waiver from the lenders, not requested and not concurred in by the borrower, was ineffective. This conclusion is consistent with prior case law cited in the decision. Alternatively, and more questionably, it held that unanimous consent (and not merely two-thirds approval) was required since the mandatory prepayment date was a "scheduled" prepayment date. It reasoned that since principal became due once the prepayment condition was satisfied, the prepayment became *scheduled*. This is inconsistent with the long-standing view of bank and bond lawyers alike that mandatory prepayment dates are not scheduled due dates. The only distinction between the phrasing in the *Aquila* transaction and the phrasing of a mandatory prepayment or redemption in the typical credit agreement or bond indenture is that the agreement in *Aquila* recited that the loan became "due" rather than that it should be "prepaid in full." Arguably, therefore, a credit agreement that requires the loans to "be prepaid in full" (as opposed to "become due") avoids this portion of the *Aquila* decision. A third, equally questionable ground, is discussed in Section 10.3.4.

In light of *Aquila* and similar case law, some credit agreements now typically make expressly clear that waivers of mandatory prepayments (and possibly of conditions precedent, covenants (or financial definitions used in covenants such as EBITDA) and defaults) are not subject to the unanimous or adversely affected lender consent requirement.

What about waivers after acceleration? The general consensus is that once the loans have been accelerated a new maturity date is established and, therefore, any waiver of the maturity requires more than a majority or required lender vote. The only exception to this is in those agreements that grant the borrower a cure right (see Section 13.7).

10.3.3.2   Pro Rata Provisions

The provisions of the credit agreement that require the lenders (at least all lenders within the same tranche) be treated ratably are fundamental. Each lender is to make loans, and be paid principal and interest, on a strictly ratable basis with all other lenders of the same tranche (see Sections 10.4 and 10.5). Therefore a typical credit agreement will provide for the express requirement that any modification to this approach requires approval from more than just the majority or required lenders. When not provided for, there is a risk that a majority of lenders can engineer around this fundamental notion of ratability to the detriment of a minority of lenders. See *In re LodgeNet Interactive Corp.*, Ch. 11 Case No. 13-10238, Adv. No. 14-02239-SCC (Bankr. S.D.N.Y. 2014).

10.3.3.3   Voting

As contemplated by the language in Box 10.13, certain changes to the voting provisions require a higher level of consent. Changes to the *percentage* in the definition of the majority or required lenders must be approved by all of the lenders. Any other provision of the credit agreement that requires a specified number or percentage of lenders to make a determination or issue a waiver (such as the right set out in the yield protection provision that allows each lender the ability to determine its own increased cost) is also encompassed. Note that, in contrast to changes to money terms, the rule here does not distinguish between *adverse* or *favorable* changes, perhaps because the distinction is hard to make. Would a modification to the Events of Default section that permits acceleration by 25 percent of the lenders (an approach commonly seen in private placements and bond indentures) instead of a majority be favorable or adverse? Arguably, since it makes it easier to accelerate and would be strenuously resisted by the borrower, the change is favorable. By the same token, however, the lenders may object to the potential instability that it introduces in a situation in which the borrower's financial strength is deteriorating.

10.3.3.4   Conditions

In some cases (the practice is not universal), a credit agreement provides that a waiver of initial conditions precedent must be approved by all lenders. Borrowers generally resist this because of the leverage it gives an individual lender. Particularly in complex transactions (for example, in which the credit facility provides funds for an acquisition), waivers of nonmaterial conditions can often occur and to require approval of every lender is impractical. In some cases lenders ask that the unanimous consent right be extended also to ongoing conditions. Few borrowers accede to this request (most lenders concur) because of the risk that, based upon the concerns of an individual lender, the borrower's future credit availability could be cut off and its financial position thereby harmed.

Determining whether a particular amendment requires unanimous consent or instead only requires a lesser consent threshold is sometimes less than certain. As a technical matter, a proposed amendment might not implicate the stated unanimous consent requirements while nonetheless having the *effect* of modifying a money term or similarly sacrosanct provision. For example, an amendment may extend a payment default cure period and thus permit an otherwise defaulting borrower more time to make a payment while not technically extending the scheduled payment date. Does such an amendment require the higher or lower level of lender consent? Similarly, an amendment may alter a key definition (for example, the definition of a leverage ratio) which has the effect of lowering the borrower's leverage from one tier of an interest rate grid to a lower tier of the grid. What level of lender consent is required? As illustrated by the foregoing, voting provisions may contain nuanced and not-so-obvious minefields (or opportunities for creativity, depending on one's perspective). Borrowers and lenders alike are well-advised to pay careful attention to the drafting of voting provisions.

10.3.4 *Unanimous versus Affected Lender Consent*

For those modifications described above that necessitate more than just majority or required lender consent, credit agreements specify two types of higher thresholds. Some changes require the consent of *all* lenders (unanimous consent); others require the consent of only *affected* lenders. Generally speaking, modifications to the voting provisions require the consent of *all* lenders, primarily because it is difficult to see how each lender is not affected by the change. Other modifications (money terms and the pro rata provisions) may require the additional consent of only *affected* lenders. An "affected" lender does not mean each lender in the particular tranche, but only those lenders affected by the change in terms. Thus, an extension of a subset of revolving credit commitments could be effected through consent of the required lenders and those particular revolving credit lenders whose commitments are being extended. Lenders (including revolving credit lenders) whose commitments are not being extended would have no consent right (other than to participate in the required lender vote). Similarly, a subset of the term lenders could extend the maturity date of the particular term loans held by them, without the consent of any term lenders whose maturity remains the same (again, other than the participation by the latter in the required lender vote).

The *Aquila* case (referred to above) weighed in on the meaning of "affected" lender in a manner inconsistent with the principles described in the preceding paragraph. The credit agreement construed in that case stated that any waiver "shall apply equally to each of the Lenders." Based on this language, the court held that any provision requiring the consent of each "affected" lender required the consent of all lenders. This conclusion may have been correct given the particular language in that agreement. One would hope that a well-drafted agreement, however, is more precise on the point (or not include an "apply equally" provision at all) and so the court's construction of the term "affected lender" in the *Aquila* case will presumably not have a general or lasting effect. Certainly, both credit agreements and bond indentures have been drafted for decades with the intention that *affected* lenders mean just that: lenders affected by a change and not all lenders.

10.3.5 *Special Lender Consents*

Although perhaps obvious, changes that affect the rights or obligations of the administrative agent, any swingline lender, or any letter of credit issuer require the consent of that party. This issue comes up most often when a borrower requests changes to funding mechanics that alter notice periods.

10.3.6 *Collateral Security*

Box 10.14

The Administrative Agent may, with the prior consent of the Required Lenders (but not otherwise), consent to any modification, supplement, or waiver under any of the Security Documents, *provided* that without the prior consent of each Lender, the Administrative Agent shall not (i) release all or substantially all of the collateral under the Security Documents, except that no such consent shall be required, and the Administrative Agent is hereby authorized and directed, to release any Lien covering property that is the subject of a disposition of property permitted hereunder or a disposition to which the Required Lenders have consented; (ii) agree to additional obligations being secured by all or substantially all of the collateral under the Security Documents (except that no such consent shall be necessary, so long as the Required Lenders have consented thereto, (x) if such additional obligations shall be junior to the Lien in favor of the other obligations secured by the Security Documents or (y) if such additional obligations consist of one or more additional tranches of loans, or increases in the amount of any tranche, under this Agreement); or (iii) alter the relative priorities of the obligations entitled to the benefits of the Liens created under the Security Documents with respect to all or substantially all of such collateral.

Matters that relate to collateral security and guarantees are usually separately addressed in voting provisions (see Section 8.3.5). The most common approach (borrowed, perhaps, from the bond indenture context) requires the consent of each lender (except in the circumstances described in the next paragraph) for a release of all or substantially all of the collateral security or all or substantially all of the subsidiary guarantees (see the discussion in Section 7.6.6 for the meaning of "all or substantially all"). This allows the majority to consent to nonmaterial releases requested by the borrower. Altering the relative priority of the liens is typically treated as being equivalent to a release of collateral and, if it affects all or substantially all of the collateral, requires unanimous consent. Release of a lien securing $10,000,000 of loans on property worth $20,000,000 is little different than subordinating that lien to other debt worth $100,000,000.

Historically, unanimous consent had been required if the borrower wanted the collateral to secure additional obligations. However, this traditional check on the incurrence of additional competing secured obligations has come under serious challenge in recent years, especially in the leveraged loan arena where the dominant trend has been to mimic the permissive bond indenture baskets for borrowers to incur *pari passu* secured indebtedness via the incremental facility, a "sidecar" basket that permits usage of the incremental facility for incurrence of additional obligations outside of the credit agreement and various other secured debt baskets, which in each case require no additional existing lender consent (see Section 2.2.4.3). Such permitted debt, either incurred under the credit agreement itself or outside of the credit agreement (but subject to an intercreditor agreement) is normally allowed to be secured *pari passu* with other existing loans, so long as the increased obligations are otherwise permitted under the credit agreement or consented to by the lenders.

When additional obligations are secured by junior liens, historically only required lender consent was necessary and not unanimous consent. The general rule of consent by only the required lenders applies even though the creation of the junior lien is likely to necessitate the execution by the administrative agent and the agent for the junior lien holders of an intercreditor agreement that binds *all* of the lenders. Nevertheless, as noted above, in the age of indenture-like flexibility in leveraged loans at least, the incurrence of second-lien or other obligations secured on a junior basis may be pre-baked into a credit agreement and not require any existing lender consent whatsoever.

Voting provisions frequently also address releases of collateral in the context of asset sales that are either permitted under the asset sales or fundamental changes covenant or to which the appropriate lenders have consented. Most credit agreements authorize the administrative agent (or the collateral agent, if there is one) to release collateral in this context without any additional consent from any lender (see Section 10.1.9 and the sample language in the LSTA's Model Credit Agreement Provisions discussed therein). In other words, that a sale is permitted under the covenants or has been consented to by the required lenders (or other percentage) is deemed to carry with it full authorization to the administrative agent to release on its own any liens on the assets to be sold. However, the mere fact that a loan facility is secured does not convert a majority asset sale consent into a unanimous consent even if the required lenders consent to a sale of all or substantially all of the borrower's assets.

Finally, voting provisions sometimes specify that any modification of a security document (not just releases of collateral) requires the consent of each lender. This can be extraordinarily cumbersome in many instances (most amendments to security documents are technical in nature), and the market practice has moved away from this approach by granting the administrative or collateral agent the right to enter into security document amendments with the consent of only the majority lenders.

10.3.7 Vote Splitting

Typically a lender that sells a participation may not contractually allow the participant to control the seller's vote other than on matters that adversely affect money terms or other modifications that require unanimous consent of the lenders. What happens then if, after a lender sells a participation in 50 percent of its loan, the borrower requests an extension of the maturity which the seller is willing to give, but to which the participant objects? The participant might argue that the selling lender should be permitted to split its vote and extend only the portion of the loan not participated while leaving the maturity of the balance unchanged. Although theoretically appealing, credit agreements almost uniformly do not contemplate vote splitting in this manner—the practical solution is for the parties to convert the participation into an assignment (in which case the participant, now assignee, holds a direct interest in its portion of the loan and can vote that portion as it pleases). Of course, this solution works only if the borrower and administrative agent are willing to grant any necessary consents.

10.3.8   Lenders That Default

As discussed in more detail in Section 10.8.2, some agreements stipulate that any lender that breaches its obligation to make loans (or a lender designated as a "defaulting lender" or "potentially defaulting lender") is barred from participating in votes under the credit agreement. Historically uncommon, provisions that disenfranchise defaulting lenders have become more frequent as a result of the recent credit crisis and the attendant insolvency of several prominent lenders.

10.4   PRO RATA TREATMENT

Box 10.15

Except to the extent otherwise provided herein: (i) each Borrowing shall be made from the Lenders, each payment of commitment fees shall be made for account of the Lenders, and each termination or reduction of the amount of the Commitments shall be applied to the respective Commitments of the Lenders, pro rata according to the amounts thereof; (ii) each Borrowing shall be allocated pro rata among the Lenders according to the amounts of their respective Commitments (in the case of the making of Loans), or their respective Loans that are to be included in such Borrowing (in the case of conversions and continuations of Loans); (iii) each payment or prepayment of principal of Loans by the Borrower shall be made for account of the Lenders pro rata in accordance with the respective unpaid principal amounts of the Loans held by them; and (iv) each payment of interest on Loans by the Borrower shall be made for account of the Lenders pro rata according to the amounts of interest on such Loans then due and payable to the respective Lenders.

A general principle in virtually all credit agreements is that the lenders are treated on a "ratable" basis. Lenders in a tranche make loans of that tranche "ratably" in accordance with their commitments of that tranche. Similarly, principal and interest are paid and prepaid "ratably" in accordance with the outstanding amounts of the relevant tranche. Commitments are reduced, and commitment and facility fees are paid, "ratably" in accordance with the commitments of the particular tranche. Much of this is self-operative, since payments are almost always made directly to the administrative agent, and it is the administrative agent that keeps track of the status of outstanding commitments and that remits funds paid by the borrower to the lenders. If a lender should in any circumstance receive more than its pro rata share of any payment, the provisions of the sharing clause discussed below may be triggered.

There are exceptions to the general rule of ratability. First, as discussed in Section 2.1.1.3, competitive bid loans are made on a nonratable basis since each bidding lender makes a loan in the amount it offers to the borrower whether or not other lenders have made similar offers. Second, as discussed in Section 4.10, in some transactions lenders that hold term tranches are permitted, at their election, to decline a voluntary or mandatory prepayment. Also, extensions or increases of commitments under accordion and incremental features (see Section 2.2) are made at the election of lenders and are not required to be ratable. Third, as will be discussed in Sections 11.2.2.3 and 13.10, when credit agreements permit borrowers and their affiliates to buy back loans on the open market or pursuant to Dutch auctions, such buybacks are typically excluded from any ratable requirement.

10.5 SHARING OF SETOFFS AND OTHER CLAIMS

Box 10.16

If any Lender shall, by exercising any right of setoff or counterclaim or otherwise, obtain payment in respect of any principal of or interest on any of its Loans or other obligations hereunder resulting in such Lender receiving payment of a proportion of the aggregate amount of its Loans and accrued interest thereon or other such obligations greater than its pro rata share thereof as provided herein, then the Lender receiving such greater proportion shall (a) notify the Administrative Agent of such fact, and (b) purchase (for cash at face value) participations in the Loans and such other obligations of the other Lenders, or make such other adjustments as shall be equitable, so that the benefit of all such payments shall be shared by the Lenders ratably in accordance with the aggregate amount of principal of and accrued interest on their respective Loans and other amounts owing them; *provided* that:

> (i) if any such participations are purchased and all or any portion of the payment giving rise thereto is recovered, such participations shall be rescinded and the purchase price restored to the extent of such recovery, without interest; and

> (ii) the provisions of this paragraph shall not be construed to apply to (x) any payment made by the Borrower pursuant to and in accordance with the express terms of this Agreement (including the application of funds arising from the existence of a Defaulting Lender or Disqualified Institution), or (y) any payment obtained by a Lender as consideration for the assignment of or sale of a participation in any of its Loans or participations in L/C Disbursements to any assignee or participant, [other than to the Borrower or any Subsidiary thereof (as to which the provisions of this paragraph shall apply)][, other than to the Borrower or any of its Affiliates (other than pursuant to Section [*Successors and Assigns, paragraph (g)*]), as to which the provision of this paragraph shall apply].

[The Borrower] [Each Loan Party] consents to the foregoing and agrees, to the extent it may effectively do so under applicable law, that any Lender acquiring a participation pursuant to the foregoing arrangements may exercise against [the Borrower] [each Loan Party] rights of setoff and counterclaim with respect to such participation as fully as if such Lender were a direct creditor of [the Borrower] [each Loan Party] in the amount of such participation.

As discussed in Section 10.4, subject to limited exceptions, a credit agreement requires that all payments of principal and interest of a particular tranche be made ratably to the lenders that hold obligations in that tranche. Since the credit agreement, as a rule, also requires that all payments to the lenders be made through the administrative agent, pro rata treatment is largely self-operative.

The so-called "sharing clause" covers those instances in which, for whatever reason, a lender nevertheless receives a payment on a nonratable basis in excess of what it is otherwise entitled to under the agreement. It is, in effect, a backstop to the pro rata clause. Although this clause is sometimes called the "sharing of setoff" provision, it is not normally limited to receipt of an excess payment by means of a setoff and includes other payments, such as might arise upon a successful suit on its note. Under the sharing clause, the lender who receives the nonratable payment (in excess of its ratable entitlement) must share the proceeds of its excess nonratable payment with the other lenders, by purchasing either participations or assignments in the loans of the other lenders, or by making other adjustments as are equitable to achieving pro rata treatment. "Other adjustments," although vague, may require the buying and selling lenders to take into account related monetary factors, such as interest accruals for any period between when the nonratable payment is first received by a lender and when that lender implements the sharing by purchasing participations or assignments. It may also require the lenders to take into account the costs incurred by the purchasing lender of obtaining the nonratable payment—litigation costs might be an example.

Sharing clauses can be written in two ways. The most common structure seen in credit agreements requires that the lenders share the benefits of a nonratable payment through the purchase of assignments or participations in the other lenders' loans. An alternative, infrequently used, structure provides that any disproportionate payment received by a lender is deemed to have been a payment by the borrower to all of the lenders, with the recipient lender having collected the excess monies as agent on behalf of the other lenders. This latter structure may, however, raise issues with respect to the effectiveness of the setoff itself. As discussed in Section 9.5, although the standard setoff provisions are written more broadly, absent contractual expansion a setoff is permitted only if the two claims are mutual; a claim by the bank owed to the borrower (the deposit) may only be set off against a claim owed by the borrower to the bank (the loan). A bank might not therefore be permitted to set off a deposit it owes to a borrower against a loan of a third party for which it purports to act as agent.

The assignment–participation structure should avoid these issues relating to the validity of the setoff. It may also have advantages if the borrower, following the setoff, files for bankruptcy. The reason is simple. When a bank exercises a right of setoff with respect to the loans held by it, the result is to reduce that bank's claim while each other lender continues to hold its full exposure. If the lender "shares" the benefit of that setoff without receiving an assignment or participation in return, it may end up in a worse position than the other lenders. An illustration may be helpful. If five banks hold loans of $1,000,000 each and a single bank exercises a right of setoff against a deposit of $200,000, that bank's loan is permanently paid down to $800,000 as a consequence of the setoff. That is the maximum claim the bank is entitled to assert against the borrower in a later bankruptcy or suit. If the bank were simply to distribute the payment to the other lenders (by gift, for example) without receiving anything in return, it would still hold a claim of only $800,000, though it would retain less than the full $200,000 garnered pursuant to the setoff. Each of the other banks, however, would retain its full $1,000,000 claim (plus the generous gift from the offsetting bank).

Ultimately, when the borrower is liquidated, the sharing bank could end up receiving *less* in respect of its loans than the other lenders. To avoid this potentially inequitable result, the sharing clause provides that each lender receiving a portion of the setoff must assign or sell a participation in a portion of its loan so that the aggregate of the claims held by all of the lenders remains the same. The math works as follows. The offsetting bank ends up holding $960,000: $800,000 (the remaining balance of its direct claim) *plus* $160,000 (the sum of the four $40,000 participations it purchases from the other lenders). Each recipient lender likewise ends up holding $960,000: $1,000,000 (its original direct claim against the borrower) *minus* $40,000 (the portion of the direct claim participated to the offsetting bank upon receipt of its share of the proceeds of the setoff).

Historically, the sharing clause applied only to disproportionate payments received *from the borrower*. Although this protected against a borrower colluding with those lenders in the syndicate with whom it had a long-standing relationship (and stiffing all of the other lenders), the narrowness of the approach became a sore point among lenders during the Iran hostage crisis in 1979. After the repudiation by Iran of substantially all of its external debt obligations, lenders under several multibillion dollar loan syndicates set off against Iranian deposits held by them. Consistent with the way the sharing clauses were then drafted, some of the offsetting lenders took the position that an exercise of a right of setoff did not constitute a payment *from the borrower*. Based on this reasoning, they refused to share the proceeds.

As a consequence, sharing clauses were quickly redrafted to sweep in any circumstance whereby a lender "obtained payment" in a disproportionate amount in respect of its loans. The language in Box 10.16 (from the LSTA's Model Credit Agreement Provisions) is typical. It applies the sharing obligation to any payment obtained through the exercise of a "right of setoff, counterclaim, or otherwise." As a consequence, it traps not just payments made directly by the borrower (whether by mistake, or in an attempt to prefer one lender over others), but also any other disproportionate payment of any kind. Any payments obtained through the exercise of a right of setoff are captured. Monies realized by a lender who institutes suit against the borrower and either wins a judgment or enters into a settlement with a borrower are also picked up. (This, not coincidentally, has the effect of discouraging individual action by lenders because of their inability to keep the fruits of any litigation.) The clause as drafted is broad enough even to capture monies received by a lender from the sale of an assignment or participation. This presents an obstacle if the parties intend to allow individual lenders the right to trade loans on the open market and on a non-pro rata basis. Unless the sharing provision is modified, a lender would sell its loan and then be required to turn around and share the proceeds with the lender group and thereby defeat the purpose of non-pro rata trading flexibility. For this reason, for credit agreements permitting non-pro rata sales (including non-pro rata buybacks from the borrower or any of its affiliates), special care must be taken to exclude such permitted assignments and participations from the sharing provision. If such borrower or affiliate loan buybacks are permitted then of course the sharing provision will carve out such proceeds.

The customary sharing clause (consistent with the language in Box 10.16) requires sharing of payments obtained only in respect of the loans or other obligations under the credit agreement. A lender that has a separate mortgage loan to a borrower is free to apply a setoff to that loan without having to pay over anything to the other lenders. Banks with which a borrower keeps its deposits under cash management or lock box arrangements are particularly sensitive to this point. If they extend credit to the borrower both under the credit agreement and under a separate facility, they may want the choice of the obligation (the credit agreement or any separate facility) against which to exercise the right of setoff and permit the proceeds of any setoff against lender-only debt to be retained in full.

In the typical credit agreement, the sharing clause does not set out detailed procedures as to how sharing is to be implemented. This is, perhaps, in part to keep the clause simple by stating broad principles; it is also consistent with the approach customarily taken elsewhere in credit agreements in which interlender rights and obligations are not addressed with the excruciating detail applied to the relationship between the borrower and the lenders. Historically, however, some credit agreements set out explicit procedures spelling out how nonratable payments were to be shared. These clauses provided for a detailed notice to the administrative agent of any setoff (including time, place, and amount), followed by a further detailed notice from the administrative agent to each of the lenders. The proceeds of the setoff were then paid to the agent under equally detailed procedures, followed by calculations as to what each lender was to be paid and payment thereof by the administrative agent. The agent, in other words, was compelled by long-winded language to maintain a book as to what claims were held by each lender (whether through direct loan or through assignment or participation from other lenders), and to issue periodic reports to the lenders that showed their relative positions in the credit. This cumbersome approach has largely disappeared, though it may occasionally crop up in cross-border financings.

The obligation to share is limited to "payments." One question that arises is what happens if a "payment" is not in cash, but is instead effected through the delivery to a lender of an equity interest in the borrower or a subsidiary, or through the transfer of property or other noncash consideration. Absent express language to the contrary, in the typical credit agreement the term "payment" is most sensibly construed to apply only to payments received in cash. Since any sharing must be effected by purchasing "for cash at face value" the fruits of the disproportionate payment, it would be singularly unfair to expect a lender that receives a noncash "payment" to fork over cash to the other lenders as part of the sharing obligation. However, it would also be singularly unfair for a lender who receives noncash consideration to retain the benefit of that consideration when the equity or property is ultimately converted into cash. If that happens, the clause should kick in to require sharing with the lenders that did not collect the noncash consideration. This notion was confirmed in *Prudential Ins. Co. of Am. v. WestLB AG, NY Branch* 2012 N.Y. Misc. LEXIS 4822 (N.Y. Sup. Ct. 2012). In that case, an administrative agent successfully credit bid on behalf of a lender group to take over two ethanol plants that had served as collateral for a bankrupt borrower. Upon taking ownership of the ethanol plants, title to each plant was held by the credit bidding lenders through newly formed limited liability companies. However, preferential equity interests in the owner LLCs were given only to those lenders that participated in funding an exit loan facility that had been provided to the bankrupt debtor. On the theory that the funds from the exit facility had kept the plants operating and in turn generated a higher sales price when both plants were eventually sold, the participating lenders were provided equity distributions and resulting cash proceeds in excess of their pre-petition ratable share. The court held that such nonratable distributions had breached the sharing clause and the sales proceeds from the plants should have been shared ratably.

The typical sharing clause requires the borrower to consent that any lender that acquires a participation or other interest via operation of the sharing provision may, in turn, exercise a right of setoff with respect to the participation interest. This is intended to keep the lenders in the same position after a sharing event as they enjoyed before the sharing event—that is, legally entitled to exercise a right of setoff with respect to their entire loan. Absent an explicit consent from the borrower, it is unclear that a lender who acquires a participation can exercise a right of setoff with respect to a participation interest held by it. As noted above, a setoff right traditionally exists only in respect of *mutual* claims. Since a participation interest does not give the lender direct rights against the borrower (see Section 11.1), it would ordinarily not satisfy the mutuality requirement. This was, in effect, confirmed in the decision of *In re Yale Express System, Inc.*, 245 F. Supp. 790 (S.D.N.Y. 1965), in which the court refused to allow a participant to exercise a right of setoff by applying funds deposited with the participant against the loan participation held by it. The court viewed the setoff as an attempt by the participant to take assets of the borrower to pay claims that the borrower owed to an unrelated third party—namely, the seller of the participation.

The *Yale Express* court implied that its decision might have been different had the borrower in that case consented to the participant's exercise of a right of setoff. As a consequence, since the *Yale Express* decision, sharing clauses have been drafted to incorporate a borrower consent. The law, nevertheless, remains unsettled as to whether such consent rights are enforceable, and some clauses (such as the LSTA's Model Credit Agreement Provisions in Box 10.16) accordingly provide that the participant's ability to exercise a setoff right is limited "to the extent it may effectively do so under applicable law." This language essentially does nothing more than state the obvious, though it may persuade counsel delivering legal opinions at credit agreement closings to omit a qualification with respect to the enforceability of the borrower's consent right.

The effect of the borrower's consent is to allow a participant that holds deposits to suck up the entire deposit amount even though its share of the credit facility may be smaller. This is sometimes referred to as the "black hole" provision. An illustration of the way it works may be useful. Assume that a lender has $1,000,000 in loans in a $5,000,000 syndicate (20 percent of the total loans). Assume also that it holds $1,500,000 of deposits from the borrower. After it has exercised its right of setoff against the deposits and before it purchases participations from the other lenders, it will have $0 in loans and $500,000 of deposits. However, when it purchases participations from the other lenders so that everyone receives the benefit of the setoff ratably, it will have $800,000 of loans (20 percent of $4,000,000). Under the "black hole" clause, it is then entitled to set off the remaining $500,000 of deposits, which leaves it before the second round of participations with $300,000 in loans and $0 in deposits. After the second round of participations, it would hold $700,000 of loans (20 percent of $3,500,000). In practice, if the black hole clause is ever employed, the successive setoffs and participations are effected in one single action, though they would be deemed to have occurred in separate stages as described here.

10.6 THE CLAWBACK CLAUSES

Box 10.17

(a) *Funding by Lenders; Presumption by Administrative Agent.* Unless the Administrative Agent shall have received notice from a Lender [(x) in the case of ABR Loans, [___] hours prior to the proposed time of such Borrowing and (y) otherwise], prior to the proposed date of any Borrowing that such Lender will not make available to the Administrative Agent such Lender's share of such Borrowing, the Administrative Agent may assume that such Lender has made such share available on such date in accordance with Section [*Funding*] and may, in reliance upon such assumption, make available to the Borrower a corresponding amount. In such event, if a Lender has not in fact made its share of the applicable Borrowing available to the Administrative Agent, then the applicable Lender and the Borrower severally agree to pay to the Administrative Agent forthwith on demand such corresponding amount with interest thereon, for each day from and including the date such amount is made available to the Borrower to but excluding the date of payment to the Administrative Agent, at (i) in the case of a payment to be made by such Lender, the greater of the Federal Funds Effective Rate and a rate determined by the Administrative Agent in accordance with banking industry rules on interbank compensation, and (ii) in the case of a payment to be made by the Borrower, the interest rate applicable to ABR Loans. If the Borrower and such Lender shall pay such interest to the Administrative Agent for the same or an overlapping period, the Administrative Agent shall promptly remit to the Borrower the amount of such interest paid by the Borrower for such period. If such Lender pays its share of the applicable Borrowing to the Administrative Agent, then the amount so paid shall constitute such Lender's Loan included in such Borrowing. Any payment by the Borrower shall be without prejudice to any claim the Borrower may have against a Lender that shall have failed to make such payment to the Administrative Agent.

(b) *Payments by Borrower; Presumptions by Administrative Agent.* Unless the Administrative Agent shall have received notice from the Borrower prior to the date on which any payment is due to the Administrative Agent for the account of the Lenders or the Issuing Banks hereunder that the Borrower will not make such payment, the Administrative Agent may assume that the Borrower has made such payment on such date in accordance herewith and may, in reliance upon such assumption, distribute to the Lenders or the Issuing Banks, as the case may be, the amount due. In such event, if the Borrower has not in fact made such payment, then each of the Lenders or the Issuing Banks, as the case may be, severally agrees to repay to the Administrative Agent forthwith on demand the amount so distributed to such Lender or Issuing Bank, with interest thereon, for each day from and including the date such amount is distributed to it to but excluding the date of payment to the Administrative Agent, at the greater of the Federal Funds Effective Rate and a rate determined by the Administrative Agent in accordance with banking industry rules on interbank compensation.

As noted in Section 2.6, virtually all syndicated credit agreements stipulate that funding passes through the administrative agent. Lenders make loans to the borrower by remitting their respective shares to the administrative agent, which then passes the proceeds on to the borrower either by depositing the same into an account with the administrative agent or by wiring the funds to an account designated by the borrower. Similarly, the borrower makes payments to the lenders by sending funds to the administrative agent (the lenders' agent) and the administrative agent then remits the same to the lenders. In an ideal world, routing funds through the administrative agent in this manner works seamlessly; all the administrative agent need do is confirm receipt of monies from the lenders or from the borrower, as applicable, before remitting the same to the intended recipient.

The world is not, however, ideal since the funds transfer system does not work in real time. In many cases it takes hours for a transfer to wend its way through the payments system, and then yet more hours before the administrative agent is able to confirm receipt. If administrative agents always waited until they knew with certainty that funds had arrived, many loans would not be made until either very late in the day of the borrowing (probably too late for the borrower to use them that day) or on the next business day. In addition, many borrowers would suffer repeated (arguably technical) defaults as administrative agents waited to confirm receipt of funds before passing on principal or interest payments to the lenders.

For loans and payments to work smoothly under a credit agreement, administrative agents in effect may need to remit funds to the intended recipients based upon the *expectation* that funds will be remitted by the intended payors (borrower or lender). Agents are not legally required to do this, but any institution that wants to accommodate the other parties might choose to not stand on ceremony and not insist upon receipt of funds before it makes remittance to the borrower or lenders. The clawback clause attempts to cover the legal risk the administrative agent assumes if its expectation should prove wrong, and the failure to receive a payment is discovered after the agent has forwarded to the borrower the full amount of a loan (including the portion that was to have been provided by the defaulting lender) or paid to the lenders the full amount of a principal or interest payment (even though insufficient funds are received from the borrower).

The language set out in Box 10.17, taken from the LSTA's Model Credit Agreement Provisions, is broken into two parts. Under the lender-funding clawback provision, an administrative agent is entitled to presume that a lender is remitting funds to the agent, unless that lender has informed the administrative agent otherwise (customarily at least one business day prior to the date of the borrowing). If the lender fails to so inform the administrative agent and the agent remits that lender's portion of the loan to the borrower, then the agent has a claim against *both* the lender and the borrower (with only one recovery permitted, of course). The lender is obligated to pay such funds immediately to the administrative agent and the borrower is obligated to return the funds sent to it by the administrative agent. The clause expressly reserves to the borrower any rights that it may have against the defaulting lender for having failed to honor its obligation to make the loan.

Under the borrower clawback provision (which addresses payments by the borrower), the administrative agent is permitted to presume, unless the borrower advises it otherwise, that the borrower has remitted the appropriate amount to the administrative agent. As with the lender-funding clawback clause, if the borrower fails to make such payment the administrative agent has a claim against both the borrower and the lenders (with only one recovery permitted). The borrower is obligated to make such payment to the administrative agent and each lender is obligated to return to the administrative agent the payment made to it.

In each of these cases the administrative agent is not required to remit funds to the borrower or to the lenders. At least until the agent can confirm receipt of the relevant funds, disbursing money is legally within its sole discretion (though not, perhaps, from a market standpoint if it wants to preserve its continued standing as a lead bank). Sometimes, however, the borrower (or lenders) may not want to depend upon the agent's being comfortable with the clawback clause but want to ensure that all lenders have funded the full amount of their loans prior to the projected borrowing date. Usually this is effected by the lenders prefunding their loans on the day preceding the closing date. Another option is to enter into a fronting arrangement as describes in Section 5.1.2. The borrower then knows before closing a major acquisition or tender offer that all funds are poised for remittance by the agent. Each lender has comfort that the other lenders have, in fact, funded their "several" obligations to make loans. Normally, such advance funding is effected pursuant to a "prefunding agreement" executed between the agent and the borrower whereby the latter agrees to pay to the lenders an amount equal to the interest they would have earned if the loans had been made on the prefunding date, and agrees to pay breakfunding if the closing does not, in fact, occur on the scheduled borrowing date.

In the case of either clawback, for each day that a lender or the borrower fails to remit relevant funds to the administrative agent, the credit agreement specifies an appropriate interest rate to be payable to the administrative agent on the defaulted amount. The interest rate normally varies depending upon who has defaulted. For lender defaults, perhaps as a last vestige of interbank courtesy, the rate charged by the administrative agent is typically the federal funds effective rate or other rate "customary" for interbank compensation. For borrowers, the rate is the interest rate charged on base rate loans.

10.7 ACCESS TO THE LOAN REGISTER

Box 10.18

The Administrative Agent, acting solely for this purpose as an agent of the Borrower, shall maintain at one of its offices in [New York City] a copy of each Assignment and Assumption delivered to it and a register for the recordation of the names and addresses of the Lenders, and the Commitments of, and principal amounts (and stated interest) of the Loans owing to, each Lender pursuant to the terms hereof from time to time (the "*Register*"). The entries in the Register shall be conclusive absent manifest error, and the Borrower, the Administrative Agent and the Lenders shall treat each Person whose name is recorded in the Register pursuant to the terms hereof as a Lender hereunder for all purposes of this Agreement. The Register shall be available for inspection by the Borrower and any Lender, at any reasonable time and from time to time upon reasonable prior notice.

Pursuant to the assignments clause of a credit agreement, the administrative agent is typically required to maintain a register of loans (discussed in detail in Section 11.2.6). The task of maintaining the register is the only role where the agent is serving as agent for the borrower. Recalling the discussion in 10.1.2 of the general agency principles, an agent would not take on such a role without a clear acknowledgment that it is not simultaneously taking on any extracontractual duties that accompany the typical agency appointment. To drive the point home, some credit agreements specify that such agency role is on a non-fiduciary basis.

The sample register clause set out in Box 10.18 is from the LSTA's Model Credit Agreement Provisions. The register typically identifies the names and addresses of the lenders and the amounts of their respective commitments and loan balances. Although there may be exceptions, most of these clauses provide that the administrative agent make the register available for inspection by the borrower and any lender (usually at "reasonable" times and upon "reasonable" notice). It is worth highlighting that the LSTA has published loan market best practices regarding the sharing of lender lists. Those state that if a request for consent for a material or substantive change to the credit agreement is pending, a lender who wishes to consult with other members of the syndicate in connection therewith may request and receive from the administrative agent a list of the names of the other lenders in the syndicate and their exposures.

In workout situations, the loan register can be an important inter-lender right. Having access to the identity of other lenders allows a lender (or group) that disagrees with suggestions being made by the arranger or lead bank to talk to other lenders directly about alternative solutions. This fact notwithstanding, given that loan participations are not logged into the register, and given the speed and frequency with which loans are traded once financial difficulties emerge, the loan register may not, as a practical matter, be a particularly complete or helpful list of all interested parties.

10.8 DEFAULTING LENDERS

The so-called defaulting lender provisions of a credit agreement address what happens if a lender defaults in performing its obligations under the credit agreement. The term is broad enough to pick up two circumstances in which this can occur: (1) breach by a lender that is perfectly solvent but either maliciously or ineptly declines to lend or pay its other obligations and (2) breach by a lender that is insolvent (or whose parent holding company is insolvent) or unable to obtain funding and no longer able to perform its obligations under the credit agreement. The defaulting lender provisions that appear in credit agreements address both situations, but originate more by reason of the latter circumstance.

Historically, with rare exceptions, credit agreements have ignored what happens if a lender becomes insolvent. One early exception arose in 1991 when the Office of the Comptroller of the Currency declared the Bank of New England insolvent and appointed the FDIC as its receiver. Notwithstanding the fact that the Bank of New England was considered "too big to fail"—and all of its deposits (including those in excess of the then-$100,000 insured limit) were protected—the FDIC as receiver declined to honor lending commitments of the bank under many syndicated loan transactions. This prompted several of the largest arrangers to introduce into their standard forms of syndicated credit agreements what were then called "Bank of New England provisions," contemplating the possibility of defaults by lenders. The principal effect of these provisions was to remove from a defaulting lender its right to vote. Over time these special protections faded away as the memory of the Bank of New England's demise became more distant.

The most recent credit crisis, however, abruptly revived the focus upon defaulting lender provisions. The failure of some lenders (most prominently, Lehman Commercial Paper Inc.) and difficulties that other lenders encountered obtaining funds (whether or not they were insolvent) led to defaults and fears of defaults by lenders in syndicated loan transactions. These defaults have sometimes resulted in lawsuits by borrowers seeking to compel performance and have almost always raised difficult issues of interpretation under syndicated credit agreements that do not contemplate lender defaults.

10.8.1   Defining a Defaulting Lender

Box 10.19

"Defaulting Lender" means, subject to Section [*Defaulting Lender Cure*], any Lender that (a) has failed to (i) fund all or any portion of its Loans within two Business Days of the date such Loans were required to be funded hereunder unless such Lender notifies the Administrative Agent and the Borrower in writing that such failure is the result of such Lender's determination that one or more conditions precedent to funding (each of which conditions precedent, together with any applicable default, shall be specifically identified in such writing) has not been satisfied, or (ii) pay to the Administrative Agent, any Issuing Bank, any Swingline Lender, or any other Lender any other amount required to be paid by it hereunder (including in respect of its participation in Letters of Credit or Swingline Loans) within two Business Days of the date when due, (b) has notified the Borrower, the Administrative Agent or any Issuing Bank or Swingline Lender in writing that it does not intend to comply with its funding obligations hereunder, or has made a public statement to that effect (unless such writing or public statement relates to such Lender's obligation to fund a

Loan hereunder and states that such position is based on such Lender's determination that a condition precedent to funding (which condition precedent, together with any applicable default, shall be specifically identified in such writing or public statement) cannot be satisfied), (c) has failed, within three Business Days after written request by the Administrative Agent or the Borrower, to confirm in writing to the Administrative Agent and the Borrower that it will comply with its prospective funding obligations hereunder (*provided* that such Lender shall cease to be a Defaulting Lender pursuant to this clause (c) upon receipt of such written confirmation by the Administrative Agent and the Borrower), or (d) has, or has a direct or indirect parent company that has, (i) become the subject of a proceeding under any Debtor Relief Law [,or] (ii) had appointed for it a receiver, custodian, conservator, trustee, administrator, assignee for the benefit of creditors or similar Person charged with reorganization or liquidation of its business or assets, including the Federal Deposit Insurance Corporation or any other state or federal regulatory authority acting in such a capacity [or (iii) become the subject of a Bail-in Action];[4] *provided* that a Lender shall not be a Defaulting Lender solely by virtue of the ownership or acquisition of any equity interest in that Lender or any direct or indirect parent company thereof by a Governmental Authority so long as such ownership interest does not result in or provide such Lender with immunity from the jurisdiction of courts within the United States or from the enforcement of judgments or writs of attachment on its assets or permit such Lender (or such Governmental Authority) to reject, repudiate, disavow or disaffirm any contracts or agreements made with such Lender. Any determination by the Administrative Agent that a Lender is a Defaulting Lender under any one or more of clauses (a) through (d) shall be conclusive and binding absent manifest error, and such Lender shall be deemed to be a Defaulting Lender (subject to Section [*Defaulting Lender Cure*]) upon delivery of written notice of such determination to the Borrower, each Issuing Bank, each Swingline Lender and each Lender.

The threshold issue for any defaulting lender provision is to define what the term *"defaulting lender"* means. At a minimum, one would expect this definition to include any lender that (1) has failed (after a grace period) to comply with its obligations to fund a loan or a swingline or letter of credit participation or (2) has become the subject of a bankruptcy

---

[4] "Bail-in Action" means the exercise of any Write-Down and Conversion Powers by the applicable EEA Resolution Authority in respect of any liability of an EEA Financial Institution. Capitalized terms used in this definition are defined in the LSTA's Form of Contractual Recognition Provision published on December 22, 2015. For more on the LSTA's Form of Contractual Recognition Provision, see Appendix III.

or insolvency proceeding or has had a receiver, trustee, or similar entity appointed in respect of its assets. Additional events that may trigger a lender's being treated as "defaulting" include (1) notice or public declaration by a lender that it will not comply with those obligations (either under the applicable credit agreement or under another similar credit agreement to which it is a party), (2) failure by a lender to confirm to the administrative agent or the borrower (in response to a specific request) that it will comply with those obligations, or (3) the occurrence of any of the events referred to here with respect to a parent company of a lender.

No lender will be deemed to be a defaulting lender if it provides notice in reasonable detail that its failure to fund its obligations is due to a bona fide good-faith belief that a condition precedent has not been satisfied. The defaulting lender provisions should only capture truly credit-impaired or deadbeat lenders, not those with legitimate dispute as to whether it is required to fund.

During the most recent financial crisis, bank capital levels became and, at the time of this writing, remain a focal point for global bank regulators. With concerns that equity capital would not be forthcoming, government regulators in the United States, United Kingdom, Europe, and elsewhere took unprecedented steps to prop up imperiled banks by injecting substantial new equity investments into such regulated financial institutions. Does such an equity injection by the government equate to the regulators playing the role of receiver, trustee, or similar entity managing the affairs of a stressed lender? Market convention seems to suggest that the answer is no as the defaulting lender definition has appeared to settle on carving out from defaulting lender triggers any such governmental equity investment. More precisely, an institution finding itself on the receiving end of a regulator's request to accept an equity injection should not be considered a defaulting lender for reason of the forced capital raise alone if such investment does not likewise result in the institution gaining sovereign immunity. However, in a scenario where a lender is the subject of a bail-in action under national legislation implemented pursuant to the European Union's Bank Recovery and Resolution Directive, the LSTA has changed the model "Defaulting Lender" definition to include such affected lender. This modification extends the scope of the LSTA's defaulting lender language to a European lender subject to bail-in because it is not possible to allow for a reduction in any affected lender's commitments (which is the result of a bail-in action) without acknowledging the broader adverse effects of this on the other parties to the agreement. The LSTA believes this offers a pragmatic approach to projecting lenders to fronting exposures and dealing with other provisions affected by a reduction in lender's commitments as a result of a bail-in. This expansion of the defaulting lender construe has the added advantage of using the existing LSTA Model Credit Agreement Provisions and procedures familiar to the market.

The defaulting lender definition attempts to strike a balance between protecting the other parties to the agreement at the earliest possible time without setting a trigger event that is so premature as to be unfair to the borrower (who may be forced to post cash collateral or lose a portion of its benefit under the facilities) or the lender (who may not have actually defaulted yet). In this regard, some agreements contemplate two separate definitions—a "defaulting lender" and a "potential defaulting lender"—with the most draconian consequences reserved for the former. For example, it may be regarded as unfair to disenfranchise a lender or to take away its fees if it has not yet actually defaulted, but at the same time allow fronting banks to seek additional credit protection when a default seems likely. Trigger events for any lender that could become a debtor under the Bankruptcy Code (this would not include banks, but would encompass many other institutional lenders, including funds) are identified so they will be tripped *before* the lender actually becomes subject to a bankruptcy proceeding. A trigger consisting solely of the commencement of a bankruptcy case against the lender (a so-called "*ipso facto* clause") might not be enforceable (and therefore would be too late), and remedies exercised after the commencement of such a case would likely be subject to the automatic stay provisions of the Bankruptcy Code. (See the discussion on the automatic stay in Section 9.2.3.)

Determining whether any of the defaulting lender or potential defaulting lender events has occurred is often made by the administrative agent (in its sole or reasonable discretion, acting in good faith). Relying on an administrative agent determination has the benefit of speed as the defaulting lender provisions can immediately be activated and this avoids the parties having to prove in long-winded court proceedings that the trigger events have in fact happened.

10.8.2   Disenfranchising Defaulting Lenders

Copying the approach used in the Bank of New England clause, many modern defaulting lender provisions stipulate that a lender that breaches its obligation to make loans loses its right to vote except in certain limited circumstances. Typically, this is done by removing the loans held by such lender from both the numerator and the denominator of the "required lender" definition to determine whether the relevant threshold is met. If a defaulting lender holds $10,000,000 of a facility that totals $100,000,000 and lenders who hold $46,000,000 of the commitments have approved an amendment, the amendment becomes effective (assuming it is a majority-consent issue); $46,000,000 is more than 50 percent of $90,000,000 (the total commitments excluding the $10,000,000 of the defaulting lender).

Sometimes these provisions go further and eliminate any requirement for obtaining the consent of a defaulting lender under circumstances where unanimous consent (or consent from "affected" or "directly affected" lenders) would otherwise be required. Exceptions may be made for fundamental matters such as increasing or extending a commitment of the defaulting lender, or reducing the rate of interest or fees payable to the lender or extending a scheduled payment date, or reducing the principal, of any amount owing to the lender. In the case of such "sacred rights" for lenders, defaulting lenders have generally been disenfranchised from voting only to the extent that such amendment or modification does not affect such defaulting lender differently than other affected lenders.

10.8.3 Mitigating Fronting Bank Exposure

As described in Sections 2.1.1.4 and 2.1.2.7, in syndicated credit transactions that include swingline and letter of credit facilities, swingline lenders and letter of credit issuers extend credit to borrowers as fronting lenders for other syndicate members. In both cases, if a borrower defaults in its obligation to pay the swingline lender or letter of credit issuer, the other revolving lenders will be required to purchase participations in the swingline or letter of credit exposure of the fronting lender. Inherent in these facilities, therefore, is an assumption of risk by the fronting institution that other lenders may default when they are required to fund their participations.

Not surprisingly, therefore, swingline lenders and letter of credit issuers are reluctant to make swingline loans or issue letters of credit if a syndicate member becomes either a "defaulting lender" or a "potentially defaulting lender." Several mechanisms have been introduced to protect fronting lenders in these circumstances. One device is to require, either as a condition to the making of a swingline loan or the issuance of a letter of credit or simply at any time during which a lender has been deemed a defaulting lender, that the borrower post cash collateral with the fronting lender in an amount equal to at least the defaulting lender's participation. Another device is to reallocate the participation of the defaulting lender among the non-defaulting lenders (subject to the limitation that the commitment of each nondefaulting lender not be exceeded). Some credit agreements may allow a fronting bank to resign when one or more lenders have become defaulting lenders or potentially defaulting lenders.

If a lender triggers the defaulting or potentially defaulting lender definitions at a time when swingline loans and letters of credit are outstanding, the mechanisms described in the preceding paragraph may be invoked immediately or within a very short time frame. The LSTA's Model Credit Agreement Provisions grant the borrower one business day following the written request of either the administrative agent or any issuing bank to cash collateralize the fronting exposure of the defaulting lender. Thus, the borrower may be required to post cash collateral to cover at least the defaulting lender's exposure or some other higher preagreed amount. Alternatively, the defaulting lender's participation may be automatically reallocated among the other lenders so that the fronting bank exposure to the defaulting institution is eliminated though not all credit agreements will permit such a reallocation of the defaulting lender's exposure to the nondefaulting lenders if an event of default is continuing. No lender ought to be forced to extend additional credit in the face of an event of default, which is, in essence, what would happen if forced to take on reallocated defaulting lender obligations.

In certain cases, the borrower may be required to reduce the fronting lender's outstanding exposure directly by repaying outstanding swingline loans or procuring the reduction or termination of letters of credit in an amount equal to the defaulting lender's participation.

10.8.4   Forfeiture of Fees

Commitment fees, facility fees, and letter of credit fees are intended to compensate a lender for its being ready, willing, and able to fund its obligations under a credit agreement when required. Following up on this logic, many agreements provide that if a lender does not or cannot satisfy these obligations (by triggering the defaulting or potentially defaulting lender definitions), it forfeits its right to be paid these fees. Naturally, to the extent that letter of credit exposure is reallocated among nondefaulting lenders (as described in Section 10.8.3), those nondefaulting lenders are typically entitled to the portion of the letter of credit fee otherwise payable to the defaulting lender (and if that exposure is not reallocated, such portion would be payable to the issuing lender). To the extent a defaulting lender has outstanding loans or it holds a participation in cash collateralized letters of credit, such defaulting lender may argue that despite its default it still maintains the right to its share of any facility fee as the exposure in these situations is not contingent on future performance.

10.8.5   Application of Payments

Many defaulting lender provisions permit the administrative agent to apply amounts received from a borrower for the account of the defaulting lender in accordance with a special defaulting lender waterfall. A common approach allows the agent to apply such funds in the following order: first, to amounts payable by the defaulting lender to the administrative agent (principally indemnities and expense reimbursement); second to any swingline lender or letter of credit issuer for amounts payable by the defaulting lender to such fronting lenders (principally amounts to fund participations and overdue interest thereon); third, to fund any loan or any letter of credit or swingline participation (or cash collateralization of such participation); fourth, to cash collateralize future funding obligations of the defaulting lender if so elected by the borrower; fifth, to cover any amounts owing under any judgments won by the borrower or nondefaulting lenders as a result of the defaulting lender's breach; and sixth, remaining portions may be paid to the defaulting lender. The foregoing waterfall effectively subordinates the claims of the defaulting lender to the claims of the nondefaulting lenders.

10.8.6   Removing Defaulting Lenders from the Syndicate

Even prior to the emergence of the 2008 financial crisis some "yank-a-bank" provisions allowed borrowers to replace or remove lenders that failed to perform their lending obligations. As defaulting lender provisions have become more common as a result of the credit crisis, covering defaulting lenders in yank-a-bank provisions has also become prevalent. One difficulty remains for borrowers. The normal yank-a-bank clause allows a lender to be removed only if a substitute steps into its shoes, and the responsibility to find a replacement remains with the borrower. In circumstances where lending institutions are failing (and, therefore, becoming defaulting lenders), it may be difficult to find substitute lenders willing to assume the defaulting lender's obligations. The benefit of a yank-a-bank right may therefore be ephemeral unless the borrower is given the right to terminate the commitment of the defaulting lender on a nonratable basis while leaving the commitments of the other lenders in place.

10.8.7 Removing a Defaulting Administrative Agent

If the defaulting lender is the administrative agent, the borrowers and the lenders may be concerned that its back-office administrative capabilities will be impaired or that funds received by it in its capacity as administrative agent may be trapped as part of any insolvency proceedings of which it may become the subject. Accordingly, the lenders may wish to have the right (by action of the required lenders) to remove an administrative agent that becomes a defaulting lender. The language in Box 10.9 (from the LSTA's Model Credit Agreement Provisions) provides the required lenders with such a removal right.

CHAPTER 11

Assignments and Participations

11.1 DISTINGUISHING ASSIGNMENTS AND PARTICIPATIONS

Credit agreements typically regulate both assignments and participations. Understanding the legal distinction between the two is important.

Assignments create direct contractual rights between the borrower and the assignee. In a typical assignment, the assignor transfers its rights and obligations (except to the extent explicitly retained) to the assignee. The bundle of transferred rights in a typical assignment include of course the right to payment but also any rights of enforcement. As a result, if the borrower defaults in payment of the loan, the assignee can sue the borrower directly and does not have to join in the suit with the assignor lender from which it originally acquired the loan. Similarly, if the assignment is of a revolving credit commitment and the assignee breaches its obligation to make a loan, the borrower can sue the assignee directly (and if the facility provides for letters of credit, the issuing lender can also directly sue the assignee). The assignee becomes a "lender" under the credit agreement, with full voting and other rights. At the same time, the lender that has transferred a portion of its commitment to an assignee will be relieved of its obligation vis-à-vis the borrower (and any bank that issues letters of credit or makes swingline loans) with respect to the portion sold, and the purchaser concurrently becomes obligated with respect to that portion.

The key documentation used in implementing an assignment of loans are a trade confirmation, which serves the function of confirming key deal points and incorporates the Standard Terms and Conditions of the LSTA's trade confirmation (performing loans of a U.S. borrower typically trade on the LSTA's Par/Near Par Trade Confirmation), and the assignment and assumption agreement which effects the legal transfer of rights and obligations between assignor and assignee lenders.[1] The LSTA form Assignment and Assumption document is attached as an exhibit to the LSTA's Model Credit Agreement Provisions. A form assignment and assumption agreement is likewise often an exhibit to a credit agreement.

In contrast, a participation does not create direct contractual rights between the borrower and the participant. Rather, the participant's rights and obligations vis-à-vis the borrower are derivative of the rights and obligations of the seller of the participation. The participant does not become a "lender" under the credit agreement, does not have direct voting rights and is not obligated directly to the borrower to make loans. The seller of the participation remains fully obligated to the borrower for the full amount of its commitment and is not relieved of the portion of its commitment transferred to the participant. The borrower has no right to sue the participant directly. The participant is entitled to receive only its applicable proportion of monies paid to the seller of the participation by the borrower. If the participant wants to sue the borrower, it must persuade the seller of the participation to institute suit.

The key documentation used in participating a loan and documenting the sale of the participation interest in the loan is the participation agreement. In addition to summarizing the business terms of the participation sale, a participation agreement effects the sale of the participation and sets out rules for issues such as remittance of underlying cash flows, providing the participant's input on credit agreement votes, and "elevation" rights for the participant to become a lender under certain circumstances. The LSTA has published a form of Participation Agreement for Par/Near Par Trades which can be used to settle par trades (i.e., where the parties have traded a performing loan where interest and principal are being timely paid by the borrower) and a form of Participation Agreement for Distressed Trades which can be used for settling distressed trades (i.e., where the borrower is in financial difficulty or has filed for bankruptcy).

Because the rights of an assignee are greater than those of a participant, assignments are often subject to borrower consent (discussed in more detail in later sections), while participations generally may be granted without consent.

---

[1] Distressed trades settle on the form of assignment and assumption agreement attached to the relevant credit agreement and the LSTA's form of Purchase and Sale Agreement.

11.2 ASSIGNMENTS

11.2.1 The General Rule for Successors and Assigns

Box 11.1

Successors and Assigns Generally. The provisions of this Agreement shall be binding upon and inure to the benefit of the parties hereto and their respective successors and assigns permitted hereby, except that [the Borrower may not][neither the Borrower nor any other Loan Party may] assign or otherwise transfer any of its rights or obligations hereunder without the prior written consent of the Administrative Agent and each Lender and no Lender may assign or otherwise transfer any of its rights or obligations hereunder except (i) to an assignee in accordance with the provisions of paragraph [*Required Consents*] of this Section, (ii) by way of participation in accordance with the provisions of paragraph [*Participations*] of this Section, or (iii) by way of pledge or assignment of a security interest subject to the restrictions of paragraph [*Loan Pledges*] of this Section (and any other attempted assignment or transfer by any party hereto shall be null and void).

Most contracts (credit agreements are no different) specify that the agreement is binding upon the "successors and assigns" of the parties. (If one of the parties is an individual, the litany typically expands to "heirs, executors, administrators, successors, and assigns.") A "successor" arises when a corporation or other legal entity merges with another entity; the survivor is the successor. An "assign" arises when a party sells or assigns its interest to a third party. Assignments, technically speaking, transfer only rights and not obligations, though many agreements refer to an "assignment" of obligations. What this language really means is that rights have been *assigned* to a new party and that obligations have been *assumed* by the new party.

The language in Box 11.1, taken from the LSTA's Model Credit Agreement Provisions, is typical in that it does not allow assignment by the borrower nor other obligor loan parties of their rights, or transfer of their obligations, without the consent of the administrative agent and of each lender. This is a fundamental principle. A lender makes a credit judgment when it decides to participate in a loan facility, whether as an initial lender or as a purchaser of loans in the secondary market. If it agrees to lend to a company with an AAA rating, it naturally wants to be able to veto the transfer by the borrow of its rights and obligations to an unrated subsidiary or to an unaffiliated company nearing bankruptcy.

Each lender wants this consent right since each lender has made an individual credit decision to enter into the facility.

What happens if the merger covenant in the credit agreement permits the borrower to merge into or consolidate with a third party without being the survivor (see Section 7.6.6)? May the required lenders consent to such a merger or consolidation and, thereby, bind the whole syndicate even though a new legal entity becomes the borrower? Is this an example of a borrower wanting to "assign or otherwise transfer" its rights and obligations requiring the consent of each lender and the administrative agent? Many credit agreements address this explicitly by having the borrower assignment restriction begin with the lead-in "except as otherwise provided herein." Even absent this language, however, the assignments provision should not be read to prohibit a merger or consolidation (whether separately permitted by the credit agreement or consented to by the required lenders), since neither of these is the type of naked assignment intended to be captured by the clause.

11.2.2   Consent Rights over Lender Assignments

Box 11.2

Required Consents. No consent shall be required for any assignment by a Lender of any of its rights or obligations hereunder except to the extent required by paragraph [*Minimum Amounts*] of this Section and, in addition:

(a) the consent of the Borrower (such consent not to be unreasonably withheld or delayed) shall be required unless (x) [specify appropriate cross-reference to default] has occurred and is continuing at the time of such assignment or (y) such assignment is to a Lender, an Affiliate of a Lender or an Approved Fund; *provided* that the Borrower shall be deemed to have consented to any such assignment unless it shall object thereto by written notice to the Administrative Agent within [5] Business Days after having received notice thereof and *provided, further*, that the Borrower's consent shall not be required during the primary syndication of the Facilities;

(b) the consent of the Administrative Agent (such consent not to be unreasonably withheld or delayed) shall be required for assignments in respect of (i) the Revolving Facility or any unfunded Commitments with respect to the Term Loan Facility if such assignment is to a Person that is not a Lender with a Commitment in respect of such Facility, an Affiliate of such a Lender, or an Approved Fund with respect to such a Lender or (ii) any Term Loans to a Person who is not a Lender, an Affiliate of a Lender or an Approved Fund; and

    (c) the consent of [each Issuing Lender (such consent not to be unreasonably withheld or delayed) and Swingline Lender shall be required for any assignment in respect of the Revolving Facility].

Under New York law, in the absence of clear language expressly prohibiting assignment, contracts are generally assignable. See *Sullivan v. International Fidelity Ins. Co.*, 465 N.Y.S.2d 235 (App. Div. 2d Dep't 1983). At the same time, courts recognize the freedom of parties to contract and, where "clear, definite, and appropriate language" is used, the common law allows the parties to prohibit the assignment of a contract and related claims (including, presumably, subjecting assignments to whatever conditions the parties wish to specify). *Allhusen v. Caristo Const. Corp.*, 303 N.Y. 446 (1952) at page 452. Therefore, with one exception (loan pledges, see Section 11.4), the extent of restrictions upon assignments in credit agreements is an issue that the parties are free to negotiate. The natural inclination of a borrower is to require that assignments be prohibited unless consented to by the borrower. The natural inclination of the lenders is to permit free assignability.

For a lender, the ability to assign or participate interests in loans under a credit agreement is essential to preserve its access to liquidity and manage its loan portfolio. Lenders may have a number of motivations to sell loans. These include raising funds to redeploy into other investment, limiting exposure to particular industries or lending structures or countries, exiting a facility when the borrower's credit quality begins to deteriorate, or simply to make a profit. As a result, syndicate members press for credit agreements to stipulate, subject to limited and negotiated exceptions, that the lenders are free to assign their rights and transfer their obligations under the agreement without the consent of any other party.

That said, even in those instances where a borrower has contractual veto rights over assignments, it wants to exercise those rights only in extreme circumstances. The reason is simple. For a borrower that frequently accesses the bank credit market, it is in its interest that the secondary market for the borrower's loans be as free of impediments as possible. Ultimately, this improves the borrower's access to credit and thereby insures quick and successful syndication of future deals. It may also improve the chances that those future deals enjoy lower pricing. The existence of consent rights therefore does not mean they will necessarily be used to bar assignments.

Although the exceptions to free assignability are customized from deal to deal, some general exclusions and principles apply. The language in Box 11.2, taken from the LSTA's Model Credit Agreement Provisions, is an example of customary consent provisions. To begin with, the privilege of consenting to lender transfers is normally limited to the borrower and to those other parties that are the beneficiaries of the lender's undertakings under the credit agreement, such as the administrative agent (who benefits from the lenders' indemnification obligations) and any swingline lender or letter of credit issuer (who benefits from the lenders' obligations to purchase participations in swingline loans or letters of credit). Subject only to the circumstance described in Section 11.2.2.3, lenders themselves do not have consent rights over assignments by other lenders, even though each lender in a tranche arguably takes some credit risk vis-à-vis other lenders in the tranche when it comes to sharing the proceeds of setoffs (see Section 10.5).

An entity that must take the credit risk of a lender should arguably have the ability to approve an institution that is being substituted for that lender. A borrower, for example, takes the credit risk of a lender when it agrees to accept the commitment of that lender to make a loan. For a term loan commitment, the period during which the borrower is subject to this risk is, of course, limited to the relatively short period during which the commitment is available. For a revolving commitment, the period runs for the entire term of the facility. The same consideration applies for a swingline lender or letter of credit issuer; both take the risk that the other revolving credit lenders will be there to make good on their obligation to purchase participations in the event the borrower should breach its obligation to repay the swingline loans or to reimburse the issuer for letter of credit draws. The same justification applies to the administrative agent, which takes the credit risk of each of the lenders (term and revolver) that they will make good on any indemnification demand if claims are asserted against the administrative agent for actions it takes under the credit agreement.

Apart from concerns over each lender's credit profile, a borrower generally wants the lending syndicate to consist of institutions otherwise satisfactory to it. During the initial syndication process, the borrower likely insisted upon approval rights over, or at least being consulted on, the composition of its lender syndicate. Once the loans have been made and break for trading, the borrower will similarly wish to monitor the composition of the lender group. The borrower may take into account a variety of factors (in addition to creditworthiness) to determine whether a lender is suitable. These could include any negative history between the borrower and a particular institution, whether the institution has had other business dealings with the borrower that deserve to be rewarded with participation in the syndicate, and whether the prospective lender is sufficiently familiar with the borrower and its industry that if the borrower ever requests a waiver, the lender will be willing to listen to, and understand, what the borrower has to say. Can an institution that has never made a loan to a company in the airline business truly understand the specialized accounting and other business considerations that impact the airline industry? Will a fund that has never lent to a mining company understand depletion accounting? Even an institution that passes each of these factors may still be unacceptable to the borrower if, by reason of the legal posture of the assignee, the borrower will become obligated for increased tax indemnification or other yield protection payments. Competitors understandably present additional concerns for borrowers. Lenders have access to regular confidential financial reports and other sensitive or confidential information of the borrower. Lenders have the right to inspect books and make further informational requests. Confidential information, such as trade secrets, and other sensitive information ending up in the wrong hands could be damaging to a company. It is not difficult to see why a borrower would want to restrict any of its competitors from holding its loans; however, this should be balanced against the market's need for liquidity. This issue is discussed in further detail in Section 11.3.

Given these considerations, a borrower often pushes to have a consent right not only over transfers of revolving commitments but also over funded term loans; it wants a syndicate that it can trust to always "do the right thing."

With the above as background, it may be useful to describe some of the qualifications that typically limit consent rights:

11.2.2.1   Defaults

The borrower generally loses its right to consent to assignments upon the occurrence (and for the duration) of certain specified defaults or events of default. In the most lender-friendly approach, the borrower loses its consent right during the continuance of *any* default. In the most borrower-friendly approach, the borrower loses its consent right only upon the occurrence of a payment or bankruptcy event of default (or not at all). The exception to the rule is with assignments to Disqualified Lenders. The prohibition to trade with disqualified lenders typically survives even during a continuing default.

The logic behind removal of the consent right in a default situation is similar to the logic of giving the lenders the ability to accelerate the loan maturity when an event of default occurs. The existence of a default may be an indicator of future financial and other difficulties. Allowing free sale of loans may give a lender a more rational way to cover its losses (even if it requires a sale at 60¢ on the dollar) than holding onto the loan and joining the other members of the syndicate as they attempt to exercise remedies and recover from the borrower. An individual lender forced to remain in the syndicate could easily consume large amounts of officer time in understanding the options available to the lenders, participating in numerous conference calls and meetings as the nuances of the borrower's financial difficulties are explored in depth, and ultimately having little direct influence on the actions taken by the agent because of the relatively small share its loan represents of the whole facility size.

11.2.2.2 Assignments to Lenders and Lender Affiliates

The borrower normally has no consent rights in the case of an assignment by a lender to another institution that is already a lender in the syndicate or to such a lender's affiliate (including funds that are commonly managed or administered). Whether the absence of consent rights in these circumstances is appropriate is, from the perspective of the borrower, a function of both the credit and noncredit factors discussed earlier in this section.

As to the noncredit factors described above (negative history with the lender, wanting to reward a lender, familiarity of the lender with the borrower's business, yield protection payments, and so forth), an assignment by one lender to another should, in normal circumstances, not be troublesome for a borrower. Once a lender has been approved to hold a portion of the facility, the borrower should not object to its increasing its exposure. Additionally, if a lender is deemed sufficiently borrower-friendly to become part of the syndicate, its affiliates and commonly managed funds should presumptively be acceptable (at least if you assume the same ultimate loan personnel are involved).

The borrower might, however, have a legitimate noncredit related interest in controlling assignments to other lenders if one institution is attempting to assemble a large block of loans. Concentrated loan holdings in the hands of one lender could have the effect of shrinking the secondary market for the facility (with the possible adverse effects upon future syndications described earlier) and might also give that lender undue voting influence over the facility. If the "majority lenders" are defined as $66^2/_3$ percent and a single lender holds 33.35 percent of the facility, it has, in effect, a blocking position over all consents and other actions. Nevertheless, instances in which a single lender attempts to collect a significant block normally arise only once financial difficulties (usually manifested by defaults) begin, and in such cases the typical credit agreement stipulates, as discussed above, that borrower consent rights fall away.

From a credit standpoint, the logic behind denying consent rights over assignments to affiliates is less compelling. Certainly, if a borrower has found a lender acceptable to provide a portion of a revolving credit commitment, that lender should be acceptable for all other purposes under the agreement, including as a holder of term loans and as the holder of an increased portion of the revolving credit commitments. (For these purposes, we ignore the subtlety that a lender might have sufficient credit standing and liquidity to provide a $10,000,000 revolving commitment, but not to provide a $100,000,000 revolving commitment.) However, it is less clear that the obverse is true—that a lender holding a term loan will be suitable to provide a revolving commitment to the borrower. And it is quite uncertain that the affiliates and managed funds (each of which has its own assets, liabilities, and liquidity) should be deemed as creditworthy as their related lender.

That said, borrowers (as opposed to agents, issuing lenders, and swingline lenders) are generally less concerned that a lender can make good on its loan commitments than they are that a lender is sophisticated, experienced, and borrower-friendly. This may explain the infrequency of borrowers demanding any consent rights over assignments to affiliates and managed funds, or to revolving commitments being assumed by term lenders.

11.2.2.3 Assignments to Borrower Affiliates

To permit assignments to the borrower or its affiliates arguably allows the assigning lender to in effect receive a non–pro rata payment of a loan, in contravention of the principle that all lenders are treated ratably (see Section 10.4). Allowing such assignments could also change the voting dynamics. Credit agreements, in contrast to bond indentures and private placement agreements, do not usually provide that affiliates of the borrower have no voting rights, yet in a close vote in a situation with a wide disagreement of opinion or approach among the lenders, the ability of affiliates to swing a lender determination could be significant.

Historically lender consent was required for any assignment to the borrower or any of its affiliates. Waiver of this requirement was typically conditioned upon the consent of each lender and not just of the majority or required lenders. This was consistent with the position taken in most credit agreements that nonratable payments, as well as any modification of the voting provisions, are strictly prohibited unless consented to by all of the lenders.

The issue of transfers to the borrower and its affiliates was not always addressed solely through the assignments provision. Many credit agreements had required that the proceeds of any such transfer be shared among the lenders pursuant to the sharing of setoffs provision (see Section 10.5). In this case, the cash proceeds received by a lender from the sale of a loan to a subsidiary of the borrower are treated in the same manner as a payment of the loan through the exercise by a lender of its right of setoff. The lender making the sale to the borrower or its affiliate is required to apply the proceeds of the sale to purchase assignments or participations in the loans of the other lenders so that all of the lenders benefit ratably from the sale. Relying upon the sharing of setoff clause to protect the lenders against nonratable assignments to the borrower does not address the voting issue described above. However, the prospect that a lender will have to share the proceeds of an assignment with other lenders was undoubtedly sufficient to discourage the sale to the borrower or its affiliate in the first place.

Despite the historical resistance, in recent years the ability to assign loans to borrowers and their affiliates has become increasingly commonplace. This is particularly evident with leveraged loan transactions where financial sponsors may find their portfolio company's debt to be an attractive investment and have pushed lenders to include the flexibility. Even with this increased flexibility, credit agreements that permit assignments to borrowers and their affiliates will still typically include a few common safeguards to mitigate risks that arise with a borrower or its affiliates joining the lender syndicate. These are discussed in greater detail in Section 13.9.

11.2.2.4 Agent Consent Rights

As noted in Section 10.2, every lender (term or revolver) indemnifies the administrative agent for any loss, liability, or claim that the agent suffers in its capacity as such. As a consequence, the administrative agent has an interest in knowing that each lender is sufficiently creditworthy to make good on its indemnification obligation. Agents also are likely to share the borrower's concern about the ability of a new lender to fund its revolver commitments, especially if the agent is an issuing bank or swingline lender and is relying on revolving lenders to fund their respective letter of credit and swingline participations. This is discussed further below. Agents, therefore, almost universally reserve to themselves a consent right over assignments by any lender (again, whether term or revolver—though a distinction may be made between a funded and unfunded term loan). The LSTA's Model Credit Agreement Provisions quoted in Box 11.2 are consistent with this approach.

11.2.2.5   Issuing and Swingline Lender Consent Rights

As discussed in Sections 2.1.1.4 and 2.1.2.7, each letter of credit issuer and swingline lender is dependent upon the ability of other revolving credit lenders to purchase and pay for participations in letter of credit drawings and swingline loans in the event that the borrower, for any reason, fails to pay those obligations when due. Letter of credit issuers and swingline lenders thus make the same kind of credit judgment with respect to the other lenders (though limited to those with revolving commitments) as the administrative agent makes with respect to all lenders to support their indemnification obligations. Accordingly, each issuer of letters of credit and each swingline lender normally has a consent right over any assignment of a revolving credit commitment.

11.2.2.6   Unreasonably Withholding or Delaying Consent

The consent rights described above are often qualified by a requirement that the consent not be unreasonably withheld or delayed. Absent inclusion of this language, a party that has a consent right would be permitted to grant or withhold consent in its sole discretion. See *Albion All. Mezzanine Fund, L.P. v. State St. Bank & Trust Co.*, 797 N.Y.S.2d 699 (Sup. Ct. N.Y. County 2003), *aff'd*, 767 N.Y.S.2d 619 (App. Div. 1st Dep't 2003).

From court decisions in the landlord–tenant context certain basic principles can be derived as to the meaning of "not unreasonably withhold or delay." To begin with, the burden of proof to show that withholding a consent was unreasonable lies with the assignor and assignee, not the person holding the consent right. See *Ring v. Mpath Interactive, Inc.*, 302 F. Supp.2d 301 (S.D.N.Y. 2004). Whether the borrower wrongly declines to grant a consent must be analyzed on the basis of objective factors, such as creditworthiness or legality. See *Astoria Bedding v. Northside P'ship*, 657 N.Y.S.2d 796 (App. Div. 3d Dep't 1997). Thus, a borrower could reasonably withhold consent to a transfer of a revolving commitment to an assignee that lacks the credit standing or liquidity to honor its funding obligations under the credit agreement. A borrower could also presumably withhold consent if the assignment would result in materially increased costs to it (under the yield protection or tax gross-up provisions) or would be illegal—such as an assignment to a bank owned by a designated terrorist organization. A borrower could not reasonably withhold consent by conditioning the consent on a decrease in interest rate or the payment to the borrower of a (newly invented) processing fee not already specified in the credit agreement.

Applying these broad principles to the transfer of loans under a credit agreement may raise more questions than answers, particularly if market conventions are taken into account. A few examples can illustrate the problem. It might be reasonable for a borrower to withhold consent to an assignment and assumption of revolving credit commitments if it has reasonable grounds to believe that the proposed assignee is not creditworthy or lacked liquidity. It might not, however, be reasonable for a borrower to insist, as a condition to granting consent, that a prospective assignee have a stronger balance sheet and liquidity profile than other syndicate members already holding loans or commitments. Similarly, it might be reasonable for a borrower to decline to consent to an assignment to a competitor that would thereby obtain sensitive financial information on the borrower. It might not, however, be reasonable if the same credit agreement permits participations without the consent of the borrower and allows confidential information to be freely shared with participants so long as they sign a confidentiality agreement. At least one court has found a reasonable basis for withholding consent where a borrower has both "valid business reasons" (such as a potential lender being actively hostile to management's announced deleveraging turnaround strategy) and, due to the size of its potential loan holdings, where the potential lender can act on such hostility to thwart any amendment or waiver votes. See *Official Committee of Unsecured Creditors v. Credit Suisse (In re Champion Enterprises, Inc.)*, 2012 Bankr. LEXIS 4009 (Bankr. D. Del. 2012). Whether withholding of consent is reasonable will generally require a review of the facts and circumstances of the individual situation.

11.2.2.7 Absolute Consent Rights

In certain cases, the assignment provision states that a consent may be granted or withheld "within the sole discretion" of the consenting party or simply does not include the "unreasonably withheld or delayed" language described in Box 11.2 (the omission of which, as noted in the preceding paragraphs, is equivalent to "sole discretion"). The most frequent examples of an unfettered consent right include that granted to letter of credit issuers and swingline lenders (see Section 11.2.2.5). The rationale here is that, since a letter of credit issuer or swingline lender takes the direct credit risk of other lenders who participate in the issuer's or swingline lender's exposure, the issuer or swingline lender should have a consent right that is absolute. Neither should have to debate in front of a court whether a credit decision made by it with respect to the acceptability of an assignee was "unreasonable" or "delayed." The same logic could be applied to the borrower's consent right (at least as it relates to unfunded commitments), but, as noted above, borrowers place less weight on the creditworthiness of lenders than do banks and other financial institutions, which are in the business of assessing (and charging for the assumption of) credit risks.

Sometimes the absolute consent right is limited solely to creditworthiness issues. In this instance, the consenting party may withhold consent *only* if it has reasonable grounds to believe that the financial wherewithal of the assignee is not equivalent to that of the assignor (or is weaker than that of the assignor). Incorporating this language narrows the scope of the consent right because it removes from consideration other concerns that might arguably give rise to a consent that could be reasonably withheld, such as concerns that a borrower's competitor obtains an interest in the loans (and thus access to confidential information) or another entity, with which the borrower has ongoing disputes on matters not related to the credit agreement, becomes a lender (see Section 11.2.2.6).

11.2.2.8 Consent During Primary Syndication

The lead arrangers for a syndicated credit facility will often request that borrower consent requirement be suspended during the primary syndication period. The rationale for this is purely administrative. Primary syndication is the period when the lenders in the syndicate are taking legal title to the portions of the loan that had been allocated to them. Taking ownership as lender of record is often accomplished through an assignment from the arranging bank (or arranging banks) who frequently is the sole lender who signs the credit agreement at closing. For a borrower focused on a smooth closing process and getting its promised money, it can be a much simpler settlement process for a single lender (or a few lenders) to sign the credit agreement versus collecting signature pages of the dozens of lenders who may comprise a lending syndicate. Since every assignment (subject to the exceptions discussed in this Section 11.2) is subject to borrower consent, the assignment of each lender's loan from the lead arranger would require a consent. Temporarily dispensing with such consent is one option; another common option is to have the borrower either preapprove a list of lenders who subsequently become parties to the credit agreement through postfunding assignments or the borrower will consent to a master assignment and assumption agreement which doles out the loans from the lead bank to the syndicate members.

11.2.2.9 Other Considerations

Although there is constant pressure from the market to remove or weaken borrowers' and administrative agents' consent rights, their removal may raise other legal issues. Borrowers and lenders both have an interest in loans continuing to be treated as a commercial debt relationship and not as securities under federal and state securities laws. A borrower's and an administrative agent's consent rights can, in this context, be a significant factor in determining whether loans are covered by the securities laws. See the discussion in Section 11.6.

11.2.3   Eligible Assignees and Disqualified Lenders

Box 11.3

(h) *Disqualified Institutions.* (i) No assignment or participation shall be made to any Person that was a Disqualified Institution as of the date (the *"Trade Date"*) on which the assigning Lender entered into a binding agreement to sell and assign all or a portion of its rights and obligations under this Agreement to such Person (unless the Borrower has consented to such assignment in writing in its sole and absolute discretion, in which case such Person will not be considered a Disqualified Institution for the purpose of such assignment or participation). For the avoidance of doubt, with respect to any assignee that becomes a Disqualified Institution after the applicable Trade Date (including as a result of the delivery of a notice pursuant to, and/or the expiration of the notice period referred to in, the definition of "Disqualified Institution"), (x) such assignee shall not retroactively be disqualified from becoming a Lender and (y) the execution by the Borrower of an Assignment and Assumption with respect to such assignee will not by itself result in such assignee no longer being considered a Disqualified Institution. Any assignment in violation of this clause (h)(i) shall not be void, but the other provisions of this clause (h) shall apply . . .

(ii) If any assignment or participation is made to any Disqualified Institution without the Borrower's prior written consent in violation of clause (i) above, or if any Person becomes a Disqualified Institution after the applicable Trade Date, the Borrower may, at its sole expense and effort, upon notice to the applicable Disqualified Institution and the Administrative Agent, (A) terminate any Revolving Credit Commitment of such Disqualified Institution and repay all obligations of the Borrower owing to such Disqualified Institution in connection with such Revolving Credit Commitment, (B) in the case of outstanding Term Loans held by Disqualified Institutions, purchase or prepay such Term Loan by paying the [lowest] [lesser] of (x) the principal amount thereof [and][,] (y) the amount that such Disqualified Institution paid to acquire such Term Loans [and (z) the [market price] of such Term Loans], in each case plus accrued interest, accrued fees and all other amounts (other than principal amounts) payable to it hereunder and/or (C) require such Disqualified Institution to assign, without recourse (in accordance with and subject to the restrictions contained in this Section [*Successors and Assigns*]), all of its interest, rights and obligations under this Agreement to one or more Eligible Assignees at the [lowest] [lesser] of (x) the principal amount thereof [and][,] (y) the amount that such Disqualified Institution paid to acquire such interests, rights and obligations [and (z) the [market price] of such Term Loans, in each case plus accrued interest, accrued fees and all other amounts (other than principal amounts) payable to it hereunder.

(iii) Notwithstanding anything to the contrary contained in this Agreement, Disqualified Institutions (A) will not (x) have the right to receive information, reports, or other materials provided to Lenders by the Borrower, the Administrative Agent, or any other Lender, (y) attend or participate in meetings attended by the Lenders and the Administrative Agent, or (z) access any electronic site established for the Lenders or confidential communications from counsel to or financial advisors of the Administrative Agent or the Lenders and (B) (x) for purposes of any consent to any amendment, waiver or modification of, or any action under, and for the purpose of any direction to the Administrative Agent or any Lender to undertake any action (or refrain from taking any action) under this Agreement or any other Loan Document, each Disqualified Institution will be deemed to have consented in the same proportion as the Lenders that are not Disqualified Institutions consented to such matter, and (y) for purposes of voting on any Plan, each Disqualified Institution party hereto hereby agrees (1) not to vote on such Plan, (2) if such Disqualified Institution does vote on such Plan notwithstanding the restriction in the foregoing clause (1), such vote will be deemed not to be in good faith and shall be "designated" pursuant to Section 1126(e) of the Bankruptcy Code (or any similar provision in any other Debtor Relief Laws), and such vote shall not be counted in determining whether the applicable class has accepted or rejected such Plan in accordance with Section 1126(c) of the Bankruptcy Code (or any similar provision in any other Debtor Relief Laws) and (3) not to contest any request by any party for a determination by the Bankruptcy Court (or other applicable court of competent jurisdiction) effectuating the foregoing clause (2).

(iv) The Administrative Agent shall have the right, and the Borrower hereby expressly authorizes the Administrative Agent, to (A) post the list of Disqualified Institutions provided by the Borrower and any updates thereto from time to time (collectively, the "*DQ List*") on the Platform, including that portion of the Platform that is designated for "public side" Lenders and/or (B) provide the DQ List to each Lender requesting the same.

Certain credit agreements will expressly define which persons are eligible to become lenders (while leaving ineligible persons open and undefined); others will expressly define who is ineligible (while leaving eligible persons open and undefined). Still further credit agreements may try a combination of these two approaches. The combined approach is reflected in the LSTA's Model Credit Agreement Provisions in Box 11.3.

Agreements that adopt the first approach and expressly describe *eligible* lenders commonly incorporate the concept of the "eligible assignee." This is sometimes done for the drafting convenience of using a defined term rather than having to set out a definition in the assignments clause itself detailing the entities that can acquire the loans without consent of the borrower. The definition of who is an "eligible assignee" may generically refer to any person (usually other than a natural person) who meets the consent requirements set forth in the assignments clause. Other times, the definition will list categories of usual, customary, and noncontroversial market participants (normally including existing lenders and their affiliates, banks, insurance companies, financial institutions, and investment funds) with whom lenders can trade in the secondary loan market. Whether an entity is a "financial institution" or "investment fund" may be subject to interpretation as at least one court case has found. In *In re Meridian Sunrise Village, LLC*, 2014 U.S. Dist. LEXIS 30833 (W.D. Wash. 2014), the subject credit agreement included as eligible assignees "any lender or affiliate of lender or any commercial bank, insurance company, financial institution, or institutional lender." The *Meridian* court found that a distressed debt hedge fund was in fact not a "financial institution," but it is open to question whether it can categorically be concluded that hedge funds or similar investors are not financial institutions. The LSTA, reflecting the view of the market, takes a broad view of the meaning of "financial institutions," because any restrictions placed on entities active in the distressed debt market could impede the liquidity of the loan market.

Analogous to the "eligible assignee" approach is the so-called "whitelist" approach that, when used, is most often found in European credit facilities. Instead of setting out broad categories of pre-approved transferees as is done with "eligible assignees," the whitelist approach identifies dozens and possibly hundreds of financial institutions or other persons who are essentially preapproved as transferees. The whitelist is usually attached as an exhibit to the credit agreement (this approach is more suited to the European loan market where there are far fewer loan market participants than in the United States). Whether it is the "eligible assignee" construct or a whitelist, the idea with either approach is to affirmatively identity the favored group that borrowers and agents wouldn't mind having in the lender group.

The second approach of defining who is *ineligible* to hold any loan interest has been an increasingly popular alternative (or supplement) to the first approach. Enter the "disqualified institution" or "disqualified lender" concept that is the preferred approach in the U.S. loan market. Among other benefits, the precision of blacklisting particularly controversial entities from holding its loans is helpful to a borrower but must be carefully balanced with the need to maintain liquidity in the loan market. A disqualified lender is an entity that, for one reason or another, is deemed persona non grata as a member of the lender syndicate and is expressly prohibited (even during a default) from holding assignments and participations in the loans. The borrower's competitors are typically deemed disqualified lenders. Since lenders are regularly privy to nonpublic financial reports and other confidential or sensitive information, a competitor-as-lender could present a damaging scenario for a borrower. Also competitors may vote differently than noncompetitor lenders when presented with amendment or waiver requests. In addition to competitors, the other type of would-be lender who can find themselves on the disqualified lender list will be financial institutions that have been deemed sufficiently antagonistic by the borrower for whatever reason (activist funds who have displayed a loan-to-own investment strategy, for example) that they are singled out and specifically prohibited from holding its loans. Also affiliates of competitors and other specified disqualified lenders will often be swept into the disqualified lender category. The underlying rationale is that excluding affiliates blocks a disqualified lender from circumventing the prohibition by buying into a loan through a related party. Some affiliates may not be appropriate to disqualify such as a bona fide separately managed debt fund affiliate who may be more likely to buy loans for pure economic return, rather than what may be viewed by the borrower as antagonistic purposes. (See the discussion of debt fund affiliates in Section 13.10.)

Who may be tagged a disqualified lender may change over time as borrowers are often given the right to adjust the makeup of its disqualified lenders by adding as well as subtracting competitors. How can a lender stay abreast of any such updates? By making available to lenders the most recent list of disqualified lenders (called a "DQ List") so existing lenders can review and avoid entering into trades with disqualified lenders, the goals of the borrower to keep the disfavored out of the lender group are served as is the goal of lenders to have a transparent and efficient secondary market. In July 2014, the LSTA published a memo summarizing its Disqualified Institution Structure, which balances the legitimate interests of the borrower and the need for liquidity in the secondary market, and the LSTA has also published an advisory in February 2015 highlighting the critical importance to the secondary market of making the DQ List easily available to existing lenders.

The disqualified lender concept is a powerful tool for borrowers since even during a default the borrower's specified disfavored institutions are prohibited from owning its loans. The borrower does not have to rely on any of the consent rights discussed in Section 11.2.2, which consent rights can fall away during a default, when it has the disqualified lender concept as its shield.

11.2.4   Minimums

Box 11.4

Minimum Amounts.

(A) in the case of an assignment of the entire remaining amount of the assigning Lender's Commitment and/or the Loans at the time owing to it (in each case with respect to any Facility) or contemporaneous assignments to related Approved Funds (determined after giving effect to such assignments) that equal at least the amount specified in paragraph [(B) below] of this Section in the aggregate or in the case of an assignment to a Lender, an Affiliate of a Lender or an Approved Fund, no minimum amount need be assigned; and

(B) in any case not described in paragraph (A) above, the aggregate amount of the Commitment (which for this purpose includes Loans outstanding thereunder) or, if the applicable Commitment is not then in effect, the principal outstanding balance of the Loans of the assigning Lender subject to each such assignment (determined as of the date the Assignment and Assumption with respect to such assignment is delivered to the Administrative Agent or, if "Trade Date" is specified in the Assignment and Assumption, as of the Trade Date) shall not be less than $5,000,000, in the case of any assignment in respect of the Revolving Facility, or $1,000,000, in the case of any assignment in respect of the Term Loan Facility, unless each of the Administrative Agent and, so long as no [specify appropriate cross-reference to default] has occurred and is continuing, the Borrower otherwise consents (each such consent not to be unreasonably withheld or delayed).

The assignments clause almost always specifies some minimum amount for an assignment, typically $5,000,000 or more for revolving credit loans and A loans and $1,000,000 or more for B loans. The strongest rationale for minimum amounts of this sort is purely administrative. Agents fear that a lending syndicate could become unwieldy if loan amounts are too small. Even with a loan minimum of $1,000,000, a B Tranche of $2,000,000,000 could theoretically have 2,000 lenders. The issue is compounded by the fact that the market standard now allows assignments to lenders and their affiliates or approved funds to be aggregated. The result is that, while a family of funds as a whole may satisfy the minimum-amount requirement, the individual funds within the family (each of which is, from a technical standpoint, a separate "lender") are not subject to any such restrictions. Agents accept this approach, despite the potential administrative burdens, because of market pressure and market custom (and perhaps because of the transfer fees described in Section 11.2.5).

11.2.5 Transfer Fees

> **Box 11.5**
>
> The parties to each assignment shall pay to the Administrative Agent a processing and recordation fee of [$_____]; *provided* that the Administrative Agent may, in its sole discretion, elect to waive such processing and recordation fee in the case of any assignment.

A credit agreement normally provides for a processing and recordation fee (often colloquially called a "transfer fee") to be paid to the administrative agent upon the occasion of each assignment of a loan. A transfer fee of $3,500 is customary but there is nothing other than market custom that could prevent the size of the fee from changing. Although some agreements provide that concurrent assignments to funds within the same family are treated as one assignment for purposes of the fee, many are silent on the point (or leave it within the discretion of the administrative agent to waive the fee). Given the volume of secondary trading in some credit facilities, the aggregate of the transfer fees payable to an agent over the life of a facility may be substantial and can ameliorate the administrative burdens (discussed in Section 11.2.4) of an agent that manages a large syndicate. Who pays the fee, as between the assignor and assignee, is typically left to negotiation and is specified in the assignment agreement.

11.2.6   Loan Register

Box 11.6

The Administrative Agent, acting solely for this purpose as a non-fiduciary agent of the Borrower, shall maintain at one of its offices in [specify office in United States] a copy of each Assignment and Assumption delivered to it and a register for the recordation of the names and addresses of the Lenders, and the Commitments of, and principal amounts (and stated interest) of the Loans owing to, each Lender pursuant to the terms hereof from time to time (the *"Register"*). The entries in the Register shall be conclusive absent manifest error and the Borrower, the Administrative Agent, and the Lenders shall treat each Person whose name is recorded in the Register pursuant to the terms hereof as a Lender hereunder for all purposes of this Agreement. The Register shall be available for inspection by the Borrower and any Lender, at any reasonable time, and from time to time upon reasonable prior notice.

Under the typical assignment provision, such as the excerpt from the LSTA's Model Credit Agreement Provisions in Box 11.6, the administrative agent is required to maintain a register of loans that identifies the name and address of each lender and the amounts of the lenders' commitments and loan balances, including copies of all assignment and assumption agreements. No administrative agent could possibly do its job without already maintaining records that contain this information; the point is that imposing a formal obligation in the credit agreement and designating those records as a "register" creates a single paper location where the borrower and all lenders can obtain information about the loans. Imposing the formal obligation to maintain a register also allows the credit agreement to specify that the register is conclusive absent manifest error.

Besides the administrative necessity of tracking lender identities, there is a tax rationale for maintaining a register. In particular, non-U.S. lenders that are not in treaty jurisdictions or engaged in a U.S. trade or business rely on the "portfolio interest" exemption to receive interest without U.S. withholding tax. The portfolio interest exemption requires that the debt be in registered form for U.S. federal tax purposes. Requiring a register is seen as satisfying the registered form requirement.

A register is rarely consulted (other than by the administrative agent itself). As a practical matter, only in cases where there is disagreement regarding loan balances or a need to track and confirm the counting of lender votes does the borrower or a lender request access to the register. Having the register and the related copies of the assignment agreements readily available also facilitates transfer of the agency role to a successor agent should the administrative agent ever wish to resign.

11.3 PARTICIPATIONS

> ### Box 11.7
>
> (d) *Participations.* Any Lender may at any time, without the consent of, or notice to, the Borrower or the Administrative Agent, sell participations to any Person (other than a natural Person, or a holding company, investment vehicle or trust for, or owned and operated for the primary benefit of, a natural Person, or the Borrower or any of the Borrower's Affiliates or Subsidiaries) (each, a *"Participant"*) in all or a portion of such Lender's rights and/or obligations under this Agreement (including all or a portion of its Commitment and/or the Loans owing to it); *provided* that (i) such Lender's obligations under this Agreement shall remain unchanged, (ii) such Lender shall remain solely responsible to the other parties hereto for the performance of such obligations, and (iii) the Borrower, the Administrative Agent, the Issuing Banks and the Lenders shall continue to deal solely and directly with such Lender in connection with such Lender's rights and obligations under this Agreement. For the avoidance of doubt, each Lender shall be responsible for the indemnity under Section [*Indemnification of the Administrative Agent*] with respect to any payments made by such Lender to its Participant(s).
>
> Any agreement or instrument pursuant to which a Lender sells such a participation shall provide that such Lender shall retain the sole right to enforce this Agreement and to approve any amendment, modification or waiver of any provision of this Agreement; *provided* that such agreement or instrument may provide that such Lender will not, without the consent of the Participant, agree to any amendment, modification or waiver [with respect to the following: _____] [described in Section [*provision relating to amendments requiring unanimous consent of the Lenders*] that affects such Participant]. The Borrower agrees that each Participant shall be entitled to the benefits of Section [*Yield Protection*] (subject to the requirements and limitations therein, including the requirements under Section [*Taxes—Status of Lenders*] (it being understood that the documentation required under Section [*Taxes—Status of Lenders*] shall be delivered to the participating Lender)) to the same extent as if it were a Lender and had acquired its interest by assignment pursuant to paragraph [*Assignments*] of this Section; *provided* that such Participant (A) agrees to be subject to the provisions of Sections [*Mitigation Obligations; Replacement of Lenders*]

as if it were an assignee under paragraph (b) of this Section; and (B) shall not be entitled to receive any greater payment under Sections [*Increased Costs*] or [*Taxes*], with respect to any participation, than its participating Lender would have been entitled to receive, except to the extent such entitlement to receive a greater payment results from a Change in Law that occurs after the Participant acquired the applicable participation. Each Lender that sells a participation agrees, at the Borrower's request and expense, to use reasonable efforts to cooperate with the Borrower to effectuate the provisions of Section [*Replacement of Lenders*] with respect to any Participant.

To the extent permitted by law, each Participant also shall be entitled to the benefits of Section [*Right of Setoff*] as though it were a Lender, *provided* that such Participant agrees to be subject to Section [*Sharing of Payments by Lenders*] as though it were a Lender. Each Lender that sells a participation shall, acting solely for this purpose as a non-fiduciary agent of the Borrower, maintain a register on which it enters the name and address of each Participant and the principal amounts (and stated interest) of each Participant's interest in the Loans or other obligations under the Loan Documents (the "*Participant Register*"); *provided* that no Lender shall have any obligation to disclose all or any portion of the Participant Register (including the identity of any Participant or any information relating to a Participant's interest in any commitments, loans, letters of credit or its other obligations under any Loan Document) to any Person except to the extent that such disclosure is necessary to establish that such commitment, loan, letter of credit or other obligation is in registered form under Section 5f.103-1(c) of the United States Treasury Regulations. The entries in the Participant Register shall be conclusive absent manifest error, and such Lender shall treat each Person whose name is recorded in the Participant Register as the owner of such participation for all purposes of this Agreement notwithstanding any notice to the contrary. For the avoidance of doubt, the Administrative Agent (in its capacity as Administrative Agent) shall have no responsibility for maintaining a Participant Register.

As discussed in Section 11.1, participations (unlike assignments) do not give the participant any direct rights against the borrower, nor do they give the borrower any direct rights against the participant. The seller of the participation remains fully obligated on its commitment (including the portion sold). A lender with a $10,000,000 commitment that has sold a participation in $2,000,000 remains obligated to make a $10,000,000 loan to the borrower if requested (assuming all conditions are satisfied). It cannot (unless otherwise agreed with the borrower) use as an excuse that its participant has failed to fund its $2,000,000 share of the loan. The absence of any direct claim between the borrower and the participant and the continuation of direct claims between the borrower and the seller of the participation means participations can generally be sold without the consent of any party. The exception to this rule, however, is in the case of disqualified lenders. The language in Box 11.3, taken from the LSTA Model Credit Agreement Provisions, provides in typical fashion that disqualified lenders are just as prohibited from purchasing participations as they are with assignments and therefore the selling of a participation to a disqualified lender is subject to first obtaining borrower consent.

As discussed in Section 11.1, assignments of loans are, as a rule, effected pursuant to standard-form assignment and assumption agreements; participations on the other hand are normally effected pursuant to participation agreements (not generally attached as an exhibit to the credit agreement). In the case of participations in an issuer's liability under letters of credit opened under the credit agreement for the account of a borrower (see Section 2.1.2.7), and in the case of the participations that arise upon the exercise of a right of setoff (see Section 10.5) by a lender, the "participation agreement" is the relevant provisions of the credit agreement itself.

Lawyers have tried for decades to pigeonhole participations into recognized types of legal relationships. Does the participant acquire an ownership interest (legal or equitable)? Does a participation create a trust relationship? Is the selling bank an agent of the participant in respect of collections on the loan? Is it a nonrecourse loan by the participant to the selling bank? Is it a joint venture between the seller of the participation and the buyer? Courts have not definitively settled upon any of these theories and it is beyond the scope of this book to delve into the arcana of what theory most closely describes the typical participation.

It is probably best, instead, just to describe how a participation works. Generally speaking, participations have three basic elements. First, subject to the seller's duty of care described below, a participation is normally sold without recourse to the selling lender who is referred to as the participation grantor. If the borrower never makes any payment on the relevant loan then, absent fraud or breach of an agreed representation by the seller, the seller pays nothing to the participant. The typical participation involves an agreement by the seller that *if* and *when* it receives a payment from a borrower, it will pay the participant an amount equal to the agreed participation interest. In other words, the typical participation acts as a true sale of an interest in the underlying loan and participation agreements will generally include language of the intended true sale treatment. A few examples will illustrate the true sale nature of a participation. In the simplest case, if a participant purchases a 20 percent interest in a $100,000,000 loan, then when a principal payment of $5,000,000 is received, the seller passes on 20 percent of that payment, or $1,000,000, to the participant. More complex cases can arise if, for instance, the participation is senior or subordinated. If, for example, the participant acquires a subordinated participation interest, then the seller retains 100 percent of all payments until the final $20,000,000 of payments are made, whereupon 100 percent of subsequent payments are passed on to the participant.

Second, as noted in greater detail in Section 11.1, a participation is a relationship between the seller and the participant only. No direct legal relationship ("*privity*" is the technical term) is created between the borrower and the participant. There is one exception, however; credit agreements sometimes grant narrow direct rights to the participant in respect of yield protection and taxes. In these agreements, the participant is permitted to submit a reimbursement request directly to the borrower (usually capped by the amount of the claim that the seller could have made had the participation not been sold) for increased costs, or tax withholdings, suffered by the participant. The logic here is simple. To provide otherwise arguably gives the borrower a windfall. For example, if a yield protection event occurs that affects all lenders in a credit agreement, a lender that has sold a participation would, to the extent thereof, not suffer a cost and thus be precluded from requesting compensation from the borrower. The participation could thus result in no one submitting a claim for what could very well be a yield event of general applicability. If the underlying theory behind a participation is to give the purchaser a percentage interest in the rights of the selling lender, not to allow the participant to make a direct claim to the borrower for yield protection and tax costs puts the participant in the position (by virtue of the participation itself) of receiving less than its agreed percentage of the selling lender's rights. If the selling lender could have made a claim for an increased cost or tax, the mere fact that the loan has been participated to another institution should not disqualify the participant from being reimbursed for its costs or loss. The borrower is, in any event, protected by the requirement that the participant's recovery is limited to what the selling lender could have claimed.

Third, although participation agreements almost universally provide that the purchaser makes its own credit decision whether to buy the participation, they also impose a standard of care upon the selling lender once the participation is acquired. This is quite different from what happens when a lender takes an assignment of a loan.

In the latter instance, the assignment is without recourse to the assignor (the standard LSTA form of assignment agreement, for example, states that the assignee "will, independently and without reliance on the . . . assignor . . . make its own credit decisions in taking or not taking action under the credit documents"). In addition, the credit agreement agency provisions are explicit that each lender (including, therefore, assignees) takes responsibility for monitoring the loan and determining whether and when to take action against the borrower (see Section 10.1.5). Since a participant has no direct rights against the borrower, it is not workable to impose this burden upon it. Instead, the customary participation agreement requires that the selling lender continues to be responsible (within limits) to monitor the loan. The typical formulation (such as that set out below from the LSTA's sample par/near par participation agreement form) provides that:

> Seller will not be held to the standard of care of a fiduciary but will exercise the same duty of care in the administration and enforcement of the Participation and the Transferred Rights it would exercise if it held the Transferred Rights solely for its own account, and except for losses that result from Seller's bad faith, gross negligence, willful misconduct or breach of any of the express terms and provisions of this Agreement, it shall not be liable for any error in judgment or for any action taken or omitted to be taken by it. Seller may rely on any notice, consent, certificate, request or other written document or communication received by Seller from Buyer or any employee or agent of Buyer and believed by Seller in good faith to be genuine.

A participation, therefore, imposes a continuing burden upon the selling lender to monitor and maintain the loan consistent with what it would do for loans held for its own account. Thus, a selling lender remains obligated to consider carefully whether to consent to an amendment (against the standard of "would I do this myself?"). It remains obligated to watch the borrower and determine whether it remains in compliance with the credit agreement. It remains obligated to decide what to do upon a default. This burden is not without limit. For example, the LSTA form of participation agreement permits a grantor lender the right to refrain from taking any action if in such grantor's good faith determination such action could result in violation of law or contract or reputational damage.

Disputes (and court decisions) as to how participations are characterized have occasionally arisen because the selling bank has become insolvent. The question most frequently raised in these cases is whether the participant is entitled to its full percentage of payments received from the borrower, or whether it receives only the same portion that other creditors of the selling bank receive upon a general distribution of assets of the insolvent bank. Does the participant, in other words, have a special right with respect to funds paid by the borrower or is it merely a general creditor of the selling bank? To the extent that there has been any consistency by the courts on this issue, it is that a participant may have a special claim against payments actually made by a borrower to a selling bank, but not if the payment arises out of the exercise by a borrower or the selling bank of a right of setoff with respect to deposits. See *Fed. Deposit Ins. Corp. v. Mademoiselle of California*, 379 F.2d 660 (9th Cir. 1967). The Lehman bankruptcy further clarified that a true sale participation has a stronger chance of being found to be outside of any bankrupt seller's bankruptcy estate than a participation that is not a true sale. Unlike a participation arrangement where, for example, the seller and participant are described as having a debtor and creditor relationship (as may be found in certain European participations), the Lehman participations were deemed to be true sales and not the property of Lehman debtor's estate. See *In re Lehman Commercial Paper Inc.*, 08-13900 (Bankr. S.D.N.Y. Oct. 6, 2008) (JMP) (Order Pursuant to Sections 105(a), 363(b), 363(c) and 541(d) of the Bankruptcy Code and Bankruptcy Rule 6004 Authorizing Debtor to (A) Continue to Utilize its Agency Bank Account, (B) Terminate Agency Relationships, and (C) Elevate Loan Participations).

As a participant does not become a "lender" under the credit agreement, it is not directly entitled to voting rights; indeed, the borrower typically resists granting the participant even indirect voting rights. A participant could easily circumvent this by contractually restricting the seller of the participation from consenting to amendments or waivers without authorization from the participant. Note that placing more than the usual participant rights in the hands of a participant in an attempt to circumvent credit agreement restrictions may attract scrutiny. See *Empresas Cablevision, S.A.B. De C.V. v. JPMorgan Chase Bank*, 680 F. Supp. 2d 625 (S.D.N.Y. 2010). In any event, participation provisions of credit agreements, in an effort to maintain the participant's intended passive role, commonly limit the ability of a participant to control the seller's voting rights to matters that would adversely affect money terms (such as reductions of interest or principal, maturity, and the like) or terms in which changes require unanimous or affected lender consent under the amendments provision of the agreement. Limitations of this sort upon participant voting rights may, however, be more of a mirage than real. Given the volume of loan trading in today's market, sellers and buyers of assignments and participations are in continual contact on both the buy and sell side of trading activity. They naturally consult upon modifications and, although a participant may not have a legal right to force its seller to vote in a particular way, as a practical matter the seller gives great weight to the views of its participant.

Recently some market participants have raised tax-related concerns that a formal register may be required to be kept for participations as they are for loan assignments. The concern is that participations may represent beneficial ownership in the underlying loan for U.S. federal tax purposes and therefore the participations also need to be registered. Box 11.7 contains the standard language requiring the maintenance of a participant register. It is the individual lender, not the agent, who is the responsible party for maintenance of the participant register and, keeping the theme of not having to provide notice or other disclosure of the participant's identity, no lender is required to disclose the participant register or its contents other than if and when the tax man comes calling.

11.4 LOAN PLEDGES

> **Box 11.8**
>
> Any Lender may at any time pledge or assign a security interest in all or any portion of its rights under this Agreement to secure obligations of such Lender, including any pledge or assignment to secure obligations to a Federal Reserve Bank; *provided* that no such pledge or assignment shall release such Lender from any of its obligations hereunder or substitute any such pledgee or assignee for such Lender as a party hereto.

Many lenders want to have the flexibility to pledge loans to support their own funding needs. Banks may want to pledge loans to the Federal Reserve under its Regulation A (or to any other relevant central bank under analogous regulations in that jurisdiction) to obtain short-term or emergency credit, and B loan lenders may need to pledge the loans held by them to secure the financing contemplated under their organizing indentures (see the related discussion on the issue in Section 5.1.8).

State court decisions are split on the question of whether a restriction on assignment is a restriction upon a pledge. In certain jurisdictions, a limitation on the assignment of loans could be construed as a limitation on a pledge of loans. Although Section 9-406 of the Uniform Commercial Code as enacted in all 50 states and the District of Columbia should override any such restriction, the conventional assignments clause, such as the example set forth in Box 11.8 from the LSTA's Model Credit Agreement Provisions, expressly allows a lender to pledge any loans held by it, with the qualification that no pledge relieves the pledgor of any obligations under the credit agreement.

One of the issues that these provisions leave open is what happens if the pledgee forecloses on the pledge and seeks to take title to the loan. In this instance, any consents otherwise required in the assignments clause arguably still need to be obtained with the effect that, absent the consents required for a true assignment (from the borrower and administrative agent), the pledgee could not become the record holder of the loan, and thus would not be in a position to transfer the loan to a third party.

11.5 THIRD PARTY BENEFICIARIES

Box 11.9

Nothing in this Agreement, expressed or implied, shall be construed to confer upon any Person (other than the parties hereto, their respective successors and assigns permitted hereby, Participants to the extent provided in paragraph [*Participations*] of this Section and, to the extent expressly contemplated hereby, the Related Parties[2] of each of the Administrative Agent and the Lenders) any legal or equitable right, remedy, or claim under or by reason of this Agreement.

Originally, at common law, only the parties to a contract could resort to the courts to enforce the contract. This traditional rule, however, was soon replaced in the United States by a more common-sense rule if it was clear from the contract that a third party (not a signatory) was intended to benefit from the contract. Thus, Smith and Jones might sign a contract in which Smith agrees to sell land to Jones if Jones pays Doe $1,000,000. If Jones fails to close on the agreement, Doe might be able to argue that he is a third-party beneficiary of the contract and entitled to sue Jones for the purchase price.

Over time, courts progressively expanded the third-party beneficiary concept beyond named beneficiaries to any third party that the court determined was intended to benefit from the contract. From the perspective of a lender this can be a slippery slope. For example, if

---

[2] See Footnote 2 to Box 10.6 for a definition of "Related Party."

a credit facility is established to enable a borrower to pay past-due raw material suppliers, are they intended third-party beneficiaries? Could the suppliers sue the lenders in the event that the lenders purport to invoke a material adverse change (MAC) and decline to lend? What about an acquisition facility? If a $1,000,000,000 credit agreement is executed to finance the merger of a target corporation into the borrower, could the target corporation sue if the lenders default on their obligation to make funds available to the borrower? What about the stockholders of the target that suddenly discover they are not converting their target shares into cash?

Because of the risk that a court might expand the universe of intended beneficiaries in the manner described in the paragraph above, credit agreements often include a clause expressly restricting the potential beneficiaries of the agreement. In the sample in Box 11.9, the only third parties apart from the actual signers of the agreement that are entitled to the benefit of the parties' obligations are participants and "related parties" that enjoy the benefit of indemnities. All others are precluded.

11.6 ARE LOANS COVERED BY THE SECURITIES LAWS?

As noted previously, borrowers and lenders both have an interest in loans continuing to be classified as obligations that arise in a commercial debt relationship, and not as securities under federal and state securities laws. For example, treating loans as "securities" could trigger higher capital requirements for investment banks and could also impose formalities that increase execution time (the time to negotiate, draft, and close the agreement) without meaningfully improving the basis upon which a sound credit judgment is made. Ultimately, such treatment could blur the distinction between the loan syndication market and the bond market and thus remove flexibility from the credit system.

The Securities Act of 1933 and the Securities Exchange Act of 1934 define "security" in slightly different ways, although courts have interpreted the definitions similarly. The Securities Act of 1933 defines a security as including, in addition to stock, bonds, debentures, and a long list of other instruments, a "note." Superficially, the definition could be read to include loans under a typical credit agreement since the term "note" has been construed broadly to include any evidence of indebtedness (including, therefore, noteless loans).

The courts have developed a number of tests to determine whether "notes" are securities. The latest word from the Supreme Court—in the case of *Reves v. Ernst & Young*, 494 U.S. 56 (1990)—employs the so-called "family resemblance" test. Under this test, a note is presumed to be a security unless it looks like a nonsecurity. More precisely, a note is presumed to be a security unless, examining it against the four factors described in the next paragraph, there is a "strong resemblance" to one of the types of nonsecurities on a list that has been judicially created over the years. The list of nonsecurities includes (1) a note with a maturity of less than nine months, (2) a note delivered in consumer financing, (3) a note secured by a mortgage on a home, (4) a short-term note secured by a lien on a small business or some of its assets, (5) a note that evidences a "character" loan to a bank customer, (6) a short-term note secured by an assignment of accounts receivable, (7) a note that simply formalizes open-account debt incurred in the ordinary course of business, and (8) a note that evidences a loan made by a commercial bank to finance current operations.

If a note not on the list of nonsecurities comes before a court, the court looks at four factors to determine whether it is a security. First is the motivation for the parties to enter into the transaction. If the purpose of the issuer or borrower is to raise money for the general use of a business enterprise or to finance substantial investments, and if the purchaser or lender is primarily interested in the profit that the note will generate, the instrument is likely to be considered a security. If, however, the note advances a commercial or consumer purpose (such as to facilitate the purchase and sale of a minor asset or to correct for the cash flow swings of the issuer or borrower), the note is probably not a security. Second is the plan of distribution. Is the note an instrument in which there is "common trading for speculation or investment"? Third is the reasonable expectations of the investing public. A court considers instruments to be securities on the basis of public expectations, even when an economic analysis might suggest that the instrument is not a "security" in a particular transaction. Fourth is whether there is some element, such as the existence of another regulatory scheme, that significantly reduces the risk of the instrument, and thereby renders the application of the securities laws unnecessary.

In the context of a credit agreement, the second and third of these factors are most important (the plan of distribution and the expectations of the trading public). Helpfully, various provisions in a typical credit agreement are not compatible with a plan of distribution for "common trading for speculation or investment." These include (1) reliance by the borrower on the credit and liquidity of the lender to make advances, (2) reliance by the administrative agent on indemnities and clawbacks from lenders, (3) the right of lenders to receive periodic information that goes beyond public information, including computations of covenant compliance, (4) visitation rights of lenders to obtain information, (5) the right of lenders (subject to confidentiality undertakings) to furnish nonpublic information to potential purchasers, (6) that assignments are subject to administrative agent and, absent certain defaults, borrower consent, and (7) that assignees are required to be financial institutions (and not, for example, natural persons) or otherwise familiar with the credit judgments needed in the commercial loan market. While not every commercial loan has all these provisions, most commercial loans have some combination of many of them.

As to the expectations of the investing public, credit agreements are quite different from private placements and bond indentures, with respect to which the issuers and the purchasers clearly expect and intend that the notes or bonds be securities. These instruments typically use securities-like terminology. Most credit agreements, however, are carefully constructed to use loan-like terminology and avoid language such as "accredited investors," "qualified institutional buyers," "purchase without a view to distribution," and other securities law buzzwords. Building in provisions designed to create securities law exemptions could create the expectation that the agreement gives rise to securities in the first place. Accordingly, unless done very carefully, exemption wording can have an effect exactly opposite to the desires of the borrower and the lenders.

Commentators have widely acknowledged the increasing convergence between the debt securities market and the syndicated loan market. This is not an altogether recent trend as the size and sophistication of the syndicated loan market has been on a steadily upward trajectory since inception. One could expect that the relatively nascent syndicated loan market would evolve along the lines of other established fixed income markets. What has been relatively pronounced in more recent times, however, has been the convergence between the high-yield or "junk" bond market and the leveraged loan market as the investor base, covenants and other deal terms, pricing dynamics, and liquidity in the two markets have become increasingly integrated and interdependent. However, key distinguishing characteristics of each of the two markets continue to differentiate in important ways that are relevant for Securities Act purposes. As discussed in Section 11.2.2, unlike with bonds, the borrower's consent is usually required for transfers of loans at least when taking the form of an assignment. Loans are predominantly secured by collateral of the borrower while bonds are mostly unsecured, which leads to a higher recovery rate for loans versus bonds and a theoretically safer investment. The interest rates on loans are almost always floating, which mitigates against interest rate risk for holders of loans versus the generally fixed rate bonds. An alternate regulatory regime exists in the loan market in the form of banking regulators that actively monitor the syndicated loan market and regularly review the loan operations of regulated institutions who continue to dominate the arranging of syndicated loans. A recent example of active, if indirect, loan market regulation is the Leveraged Lending Guidance described in Chapter 14. Nonpublic information is regularly shared with the syndicated loan market subject to important safeguards. The price of entry for lenders in the syndicated loan market is much higher than for debt securities as the minimum denomination of term loan notes is frequently $1 million or higher compared to a minimum in the thousands of dollars for bonds. These differences continue to support a difference in regulatory regimes but the debate is not likely to cease anytime soon.

CHAPTER 12

The Boilerplate

12.1 NOTICE PROVISIONS

12.1.1 Notices Generally

Box 12.1

Except in the case of notices and other communications expressly permitted to be given by telephone (and except as provided in paragraph [*Electronic Communications*]), all notices and other communications provided for herein shall be in writing and shall be delivered by hand or overnight courier service, mailed by certified or registered mail, or sent by facsimile as follows

(i) if to the Borrower, to it at _____, Attention of _____ (Facsimile No. ____; Telephone No. ____; Email: ____);

(ii) if to the Administrative Agent, to [Name of Administrative Agent] at _____, Attention of _____ (Facsimile No. _____; Telephone No. _____; Email: ____); and

(iii) if to the [____] in its capacity as Issuing Bank, to it at _____, Attention of _____ (Facsimile No. _____; Telephone No. _____ Email: ____); and if to any other Issuing Bank, to it at the address provided in writing to the Administrative Agent and the Borrower at the time of its appointment as an Issuing Bank hereunder;

(iv) if to a Lender, to it at its address (or facsimile number) set forth in its Administrative Questionnaire.

Notices sent by hand or overnight courier service, or mailed by certified or registered mail, shall be deemed to have been given when received; notices sent by facsimile shall be deemed to have been given when sent (except that, if not given during normal business hours for the recipient, shall be deemed to have been given at the opening of business on the next business day for the recipient). Notices delivered through electronic communications to the extent provided in paragraph [*Electronic Communications*], shall be effective as provided in said paragraph.

Any party hereto may change its address or facsimile number for notices and other communications hereunder by notice to the other parties hereto (or, in the case of any such change by a Lender, by notice to the Borrower and the Administrative Agent). All notices and other communications given to any party hereto in accordance with the provisions of this Agreement shall be deemed to have been given on the date of receipt.

The notice provisions set out the contact information for each party to the credit agreement, although, with respect to lenders, the more prevalent current practice is for the information to be specified in administrative questionnaires collected by the administrative agent during the syndication process or when a lender joins the credit agreement by assignment. Administrative questionnaires avoid the hassle of completing a notice schedule to be appended to the credit agreement in the last minutes prior to the closing as was traditionally done in credit agreements (and as is still the customary practice for private placement documentation). The administrative questionnaire solicits other information as well, such as wire transfer instructions and information relating to whether the lender is subject to tax withholding. Since many lenders want to separate back-office communications from substantive communications, the standard administrative questionnaire also breaks out administrative contacts (operations personnel) from credit contacts (deal personnel). The form LSTA Administrative Questionnaire, for example, solicits the above-mentioned information including the contact information for both administrative contacts as well as credit personnel.

The language in Box 12.1 is excerpted from the LSTA's Model Credit Agreement Provisions. It contemplates that certain provisions of the credit agreement allow notices to be given by telephone. Historically, telephonic communications were considered risky in loan administration because of the issues of proof they can present. Did the borrower say it wanted a $6,000,000 loan for a three-month interest period, or a $3,000,000 loan for a six-month interest period? When was the interest period to start? Who exactly requested the loan, and was he or she an authorized officer of the borrower? The obvious question in these cases is whether the agent and the lenders may rely upon the telephonic notice and proceed to make a loan.

These issues notwithstanding, lenders and agents have long since crossed the telephonic notice bridge. In many cases there is no alternative; for example, because of the short decision periods involved, competitive bid loan mechanics simply would not work if all notices and decisions had to be communicated in writing (see Section 2.1.1.3). Perhaps because agents became comfortable with telephonic notification in the competitive bid context, they have been willing to expand it to other notices, such as for swingline loans and same-day borrowings. The risk of misunderstandings and disputes has also not proved to be significant. The LSTA's Model Credit Agreement Provisions set out in Box 12.1 accordingly allows telephonic notices so long as the particular notice is expressly permitted by other provisions of the credit agreement to be given by telephone. Some agreements go further and require that telephonic notices be confirmed in writing.

The language at the end of the first paragraph of the LSTA's Model Credit Agreement Provisions in Box 12.1 prescribes when notices become effective. This may appear to be silly and unnecessary wording, but it is intended to override what would otherwise be the result under general legal principles, namely that a notice mailed (or, by extension, delivered to a courier service) is effective when dropped into a post-office box (assuming correctly addressed and affixed with sufficient postage) or submitted to the courier company, as applicable. Absent an override, a notice could be binding upon the borrower or lenders even though never ultimately received. Consequently, it is common practice for notice provisions in agreements to stipulate that notices are not effective until actually received. Some agreements in the nonfinance context provide that a mailed notice is "deemed" to be effective three or five business days after posted, but this approach is rare in the credit agreement context.

12.1.2 Electronic Notices

Box 12.2

(b) *Electronic Communications.* Notices and other communications to the Lenders and the Issuing Banks hereunder may be delivered or furnished by electronic communication (including e-mail and Internet or intranet websites) pursuant to procedures set forth herein or otherwise approved by the Administrative Agent, *provided* that the foregoing shall not apply to notices to any Lender or Issuing Bank pursuant to Article [*Funding Mechanics*] if such Lender or Issuing Bank, as applicable, has notified the Administrative Agent that it is incapable of receiving notices under such Article by electronic communication. The Administrative Agent or the Borrower may, in its discretion, agree to accept notices and other communications to it hereunder by electronic communications pursuant to procedures approved by it, *provided* that approval of such procedures may be limited to particular notices or communications.

Unless the Administrative Agent otherwise prescribes, (i) notices and other communications sent to an e-mail address shall be deemed received upon the sender's receipt of an acknowledgment from the intended recipient (such as by the "return receipt requested" function, as available, return e-mail, or other written acknowledgement) and (ii) notices or communications posted to an Internet or intranet website shall be deemed received upon the deemed receipt by the intended recipient at its e-mail address as described in the foregoing clause (i) of notification that such notice or communication is available and identifying the website address therefor, *provided* that for both clauses (i) and (ii), if such notice, e-mail, or other communication is not sent during the normal business hours of the recipient, such notice or communication shall be deemed to have been sent at the opening of business on the next business day for the recipient. . . .

(d) *Platform.* (i) [The Borrower] [Each Loan Party] agrees that the Administrative Agent may, but shall not be obligated to, make the Communications (as defined below) available to the Issuing Banks and the other Lenders by posting the Communications on the Platform. The Borrower acknowledges and agrees that the DQ List shall be deemed suitable for posting and may be posted by the Administrative Agent on the Platform, including the portion of the Platform that is designated for "public side" Lenders.

(ii) The Platform is provided "as is" and "as available." The Agent Parties (as defined below) do not warrant the adequacy of the Platform and expressly disclaim liability for errors or omissions in the Communications. No warranty of any kind, express, implied or statutory, including, without limitation, any warranty of merchantability, fitness for a particular purpose, non-infringement of third-party rights or freedom from viruses or other code defects, is made by any Agent Party in connection with the Communications or the Platform. In no event shall the Administrative Agent or any of its Related Parties (collectively, the "Agent Parties") have any liability to the Borrower [or the other Loan Parties], any Lender or any other Person or entity for damages of any kind, including, without limitation, direct or indirect, special, incidental or consequential damages, losses or expenses (whether in tort, contract or otherwise) arising out of the Borrower's [,any Loan Party's] or the Administrative Agent's transmission of communications through the Platform.

> *"Communications"* means, collectively, any notice, demand, communication, information, document or other material provided by or on behalf of [the Borrower] [any Loan Party] pursuant to any Loan Document or the transactions contemplated therein which is distributed to the Administrative Agent, any Lender or any Issuing Bank by means of electronic communications pursuant to this Section, including through the Platform.

Notification provisions routinely address the treatment of electronic communications such as e-mail, Internet, or extranet-based communication and settlement platforms and the like. In recognition also that Internet and Web-based technology is changing continuously, most agreements do not lock in detailed procedures for electronic notification. The LSTA's Model Credit Agreement Provisions are consistent with this approach and allow the administrative agent to independently issue procedures for the delivery of electronic communications. Market practice has moved to accepting electronic delivery of borrowing notices from the agent to the lenders while historically many lenders had insisted that they receive a fax or other hard copy notice of borrowing. The LSTA's Model Credit Agreement Provisions allow an individual lender to opt out of electronic borrowing notices if the lender advises the administrative agent that it is "incapable" of receiving such notices.

As a practical matter, with the exception of borrowing notices described above, most communications by the borrower and the administrative agent to syndicate members are now conducted by postings to an online platform (such as Intralinks™, Ipreo Debtdomain, or Syndtrak™) coupled with e-mail notification to each lender that new information is available on the site for them to review or react to.

Many agents, perhaps under the influence of their technology lawyers, believe that a court presented with the issue might rule that communication through a website is tantamount to the agent's providing a technology service to the lenders, or warranting the service provided by the maintainer of the third-party website. They fear that an agent could be held liable for any problems that arise from reliance upon Web access for the dissemination of financial and other information and notices. As a consequence, many credit agreements now include warranty-like disclaimers (see LSTA's Model Credit Agreement Provisions in Box 12.2) modeled after language that has become common for websites. The credit agreement disclaimer is designed to eliminate any agent liability for matters that relate to an agent-provided website (often referred to as a "platform"), including whether the website properly functions, whether dissemination of information violates rights of third parties, and whether the website itself will spread software viruses.

Although from the standpoint of an administrative agent it is difficult to object to yet more protective language in a credit agreement, this is probably overkill. For decades agents have passed on information (by hand, mail, or courier) received from borrowers under credit agreements; it is hard to see how the mere fact that such information is now furnished to the lenders in a different method (by e-mail or website) suddenly subjects the agent to responsibility for the content of the information. In any event, this disclaimer is additive and possibly redundant to customary agency provisions (see Section 10.1.4), which should already include a statement that the administrative agent is not responsible for the contents of reports and other information supplied to the lenders under the credit agreement.

12.2 NO DEEMED WAIVERS

Box 12.3

No failure or delay by the Administrative Agent, Issuing Bank or any Lender in exercising any right or power hereunder shall operate as a waiver thereof, nor shall any single or partial exercise of any such right or power, or any abandonment or discontinuance of steps to enforce such a right or power, preclude any other or further exercise thereof or the exercise of any other right or power.

One lender concern is that acquiescence by the lenders in a breach by the borrower could, if continued, establish a course of conduct that might be viewed by the borrower or a court as an implied waiver by the lenders. Lenders also fear that the act of making the loan might itself constitute a waiver if a borrower could charge them with knowledge of a breach at the time a loan is made (by, for example, asserting that the lenders were aware of facts that should lead to a recognition of the breach).

The "no deemed waivers" provision of the credit agreement attempts to address these issues by having the borrower agree at inception that no waivers will be deemed to arise in any circumstance unless they are express and agreed to in writing by the requisite lenders. At least for a credit agreement governed by New York law, Section 15-301 of the General Obligations Law should in theory make such waivers enforceable. That section generally provides that a written agreement that stipulates it may not be waived orally cannot be changed by an "executory agreement" unless the executory agreement is in writing. (An executory agreement is any agreement as to which one party has material unperformed obligations.) The concern in New York is that an oral waiver by a lender might not be "executory" and so not entitled to the benefit of Section 15-301. Consequently, opinions in New York often include a qualification with respect to the effectiveness of the no deemed waivers clause.

Notwithstanding inclusion of the clause in many credit agreements, whenever lenders are aware of a breach that they are neither waiving nor using as a basis to exercise remedies, the borrower often receives a "friendly" reminder from the administrative agent that acquiescence does not constitute waiver.

12.3 CUMULATIVE REMEDIES

Box 12.4

The rights and remedies of the Administrative Agent and the Lenders hereunder are cumulative and are not exclusive of any rights or remedies that they would otherwise have.

The typical credit agreement states expressly that the lenders are entitled to exercise remedies "cumulatively"—that if a medley of actions is available to the lenders, taking one action now does not preclude taking other actions later. Thus, setting off against deposit accounts immediately after acceleration should not preclude later suit or foreclosure; commencing suit against the borrower in New York does not preclude later suit against a guarantor in Canada.

Some states do not recognize a cumulative remedies provision. California's so-called One Form of Action Rule is an example where a cumulative remedies clause is unenforceable. The One Form of Action Rule provides that, if a loan is secured by real property, the lender must foreclose on the property before or at the same time as it brings any other type of legal action to recover a debt. The rule also requires that any judicial action brought by a secured creditor to collect on its debt must include all real property security. If a lender does not include all real property in the action, any lien on nonincluded real property may be lost. The One Form of Action Rule may not be waived in advance of a default.

12.4 COLORADO RIVER CLAUSE

Box 12.5

The Borrower irrevocably waives, to the fullest extent permitted by applicable law, any claim that any action or proceeding commenced by the Administrative Agent or any Lender relating in any way to this Agreement should be dismissed or stayed by reason, or pending the resolution, of any action or proceeding commenced by the Borrower relating in any way to this Agreement whether or not commenced earlier. To the fullest extent permitted by applicable law, the Borrower shall take all measures necessary for any such action or proceeding commenced by the Administrative Agent or any Lender to proceed to judgment prior to the entry of judgment in any such action or proceeding commenced by the Borrower.

Although not a widespread practice in the market, the provision set out above is sometimes inserted into credit agreements in an attempt to give litigation commenced by the lenders precedence over litigation (even earlier litigation) that might have been commenced by the borrower. The clause addresses a variant of the so-called "Colorado River Doctrine" set out by the U.S. Supreme Court in *Colo. River Water Conservation Dist. v. United States*, 424 U.S. 800 (1976). In that case, the court described circumstances in which one court should decline to accept a suit if the parties were already litigating the same issues before another court. In the context of a credit agreement this situation could arise if a borrower, anticipating suit by the lenders in New York (where it has submitted to jurisdiction), institutes an action against the lenders in the borrower's local state court hoping to obtain a more friendly hearing of the issues. Under the Colorado River doctrine, if the lenders were to later start an action in New York there is a possibility that the court in New York would exercise its discretion and decline to take the case.

Since lenders (rightly or wrongly) believe that the time and place of enforcement actions should be within their control, what might be called the "Colorado River clause" is inserted to create a contractual basis to convince the lenders' court to accept the litigation and the borrower's court to decline the litigation. The argument before each court would be that the borrower has agreed that the lenders' action is to take precedence over the borrower's action and that the borrower has consented to dismissal of its litigation once the lenders' own suit is commenced. Failure of the borrower to support the dismissal of the state action would constitute a breach of the credit agreement, or so the lenders might argue.

Whether a Colorado River clause would be honored by a court is the subject of some doubt, since dismissal on this basis is generally within the *discretion* of the court. In *JP Morgan Chase Bank v. Altos Hornos de Mex., S.A. de C.V.*, 412 F.3d 418 (2d Cir. 2005), the court held that, despite the inclusion of the clause in a loan agreement, at least in the context of a foreign bankruptcy proceeding, ". . . regardless of the parties' pre-litigation agreement . . . U.S. courts may defer to the foreign bankruptcy proceeding on international comity grounds." The inclusion of a Colorado River waiver does not automatically preclude a court from exercising its discretion to dismiss the lender action. Accordingly, closing legal opinions take a qualification as to the enforceability of the clause.

12.5 EXPENSES

Box 12.6

The Borrower shall pay (i) all reasonable out-of-pocket expenses incurred by the Administrative Agent and its Affiliates (including the reasonable fees, charges and disbursements of counsel for the Administrative Agent)[, and shall pay all fees and time charges and disbursements for attorneys who may be employees of the Administrative Agent], in connection with the syndication of the Facilities provided for herein, the preparation, negotiation, execution, delivery, and administration of this Agreement and the other Loan Documents or any amendments, modifications, or waivers of the provisions hereof or thereof (whether or not the transactions contemplated hereby or thereby shall be consummated); (ii) all reasonable out-of-pocket expenses incurred by any Issuing Bank in connection with the issuance, amendment, renewal, or extension of any Letter of Credit or any demand for payment thereunder; and (iii) all out-of-pocket expenses incurred by the Administrative Agent, any Lender or any Issuing Bank (including the fees, charges, and disbursements of any counsel for the Administrative Agent, any Lender or any Issuing Bank)[, and shall pay all fees and time charges for attorneys who may be employees of the Administrative Agent, any Lender or any Issuing Bank], in connection with the enforcement or protection of its rights (A) in connection with this Agreement and the other Loan Documents, including its rights under this Section, or (B) in connection with the Loans made or Letters of Credit issued hereunder, including all such out-of-pocket expenses incurred during any workout, restructuring or negotiations in respect of such Loans.

In addition, the Borrower agrees to pay on demand (i) all costs, expenses, taxes, assessments and other charges incurred in connection with any filing, registration, recording or perfection of any security interest contemplated by any Security Document or any other document referred to therein and (ii) all costs, expenses and other charges in respect of title insurance or notary fees procured with respect to the Liens created pursuant to the Mortgages or any of the other Security Documents.

The expenses provision of a credit agreement obligates the borrower to bear several different categories of costs discussed below.

First, the borrower normally agrees to reimburse the administrative agent and its affiliates for costs incurred in connection with negotiating and closing the credit agreement or amendments. These expenses expressly include the "fees, charges, and disbursements of counsel" since, under New York court decisions, attorney costs must be explicitly covered by an indemnification in order for a beneficiary to be entitled to reimbursement. See *A.G. Ship Maint. Corp. v. Lezak*, 69 N.Y.2d 1 (1986).

The reference to affiliates in Box 12.6 is intended to cover costs and expenses incurred by the arranger, who is normally an affiliate of the agent and who often incurs the bulk of the costs in structuring and syndicating any new credit agreement. Under common market practice, except in certain very special circumstances, the expenses of individual lenders incurred prior to closing are not covered. This can sometimes lead syndicate members to request that the arranger's counsel represent all of the lenders, as is common practice in institutional private placements. They argue that to have the arranger's counsel represent everyone avoids the need for individual lenders to have their own counsel conduct due diligence, review the credit documentation, or examine closing deliverables.

These appeals notwithstanding, only in unusual cases (such as when the "syndicate" consists of two or three banks or when the credit agreement documents a restructuring in a workout) is the arranger's counsel styled as counsel for all of the lenders. Among other things, a law firm that purports to represent all of the lenders in a syndicate could be subject to difficult conflicts of interest problems. A law firm's representation of the lead lender is not, however, inconsistent with its communicating with all of the lenders during the negotiation of the deal, nor with its addressing legal opinions to all of the lenders.

The bracketed clause in Box 12.6 that refers to the legal expenses of inside counsel is optional in the LSTA's Model Credit Agreement Provisions. Borrowers sometimes object to paying an administrative agent or arranger for costs of in-house counsel on the basis that the associated costs are not truly "out-of-pocket" since they are determined by banks based upon allocated overhead and salaries of attorneys on staff. Borrowers argue that these are the kinds of expenses intended to be covered by administrative agency fees or upfront underwriting and arrangement fees.

A second category of costs that the expenses clause covers arises in a secured deal. To create and maintain liens can give rise to its own unique blend of costs and expenses: recording and filing fees, stamp taxes (seen most frequently in cross-border transactions), notary fees, and title insurance premiums are but a few examples. Some of these costs can be significant. To record a lien on real property in New York, for example, requires the payment of a mortgage recording tax that, depending upon the county in which the property is located, can vary from just under 1 percent to up to 2.8 percent. A $10,000,000 commercial mortgage on property in Brooklyn (as of the date of this volume) requires the payment of taxes in excess of $280,000. Where practicable, secured facilities deal with costs of these extremes by limiting the amount of the debt secured by the affected property. If the property in Brooklyn is worth only $1,500,000, then the amount of the loans secured by that particular parcel might be appropriately reduced to thereby reduce the recording tax. Whether or not the costs incurred to create and maintain perfected liens can be minimized, the philosophical point from the perspective of the lenders and administrative agent is that all of the associated expenses of liens are for the account of the borrower. It is the borrower's responsibility in a secured facility to deliver the collateral package; the costs of doing that must be paid by it.

A third category of costs covered by the standard expenses provision is costs and expenses associated with enforcement actions. In its most obvious application, the clause covers the lenders for the expenses of suing the borrower to recover on the loans. Some courts have read the term "enforcement" to be exactly that narrow, and to cover litigation costs only. Some courts refuse to read the term to cover other costs, such as the costs the lenders' incur to monitor a bankruptcy proceeding, review credit documentation in preparation of a suit, participate in negotiations for a possible restructuring, and consult with counsel to obtain general advice as to legal rights and remedies. Credit agreements therefore tend to describe enforcement broadly to include not just legal actions, but also out-of-pocket expenses incurred *during* any workout, restructuring, or negotiations in respect of the loans. Some clauses go further, as in the example in Box 12.6, and are explicit that enforcement costs also include expenses associated with litigation involving the expenses clause itself.

Credit agreements take two approaches as to who is entitled to reimbursement for enforcement costs. Some credit agreements, in response to pressure from borrowers, permit only enforcement expenses of the administrative agent to be reimbursed or permit only reimbursement of the expenses of one, common counsel for all of the lenders. Other agreements cover the expenses of any lender (the LSTA's Model Credit Agreement Provisions in Box 12.6 take this approach) consistent with the underlying theory that each lender is entitled to enforce its own claims (though see Section 9.6). Regardless of the language in any particular credit agreement, there may actually be little practical difference between these two approaches in the context of many workouts. Certainly, if the borrower, after default, seeks lender agreement to a restructuring for which a 100 percent vote is necessary, any lender can condition its consent upon agreement that its legal expenses be paid regardless of the scope of the expenses clause set forth in the original credit agreement. Even in a bankruptcy, an expenses provision that allows every lender to be individually reimbursed would, as a practical matter, still require each lender to convince a judge that its request for expenses was reasonable.

12.6 BORROWER INDEMNIFICATION; CONSEQUENTIAL DAMAGES

Box 12.7

The Borrower shall indemnify the Administrative Agent (and any sub-agent thereof), each Lender and each Issuing Bank, and each Related Party[1] of any of the foregoing Persons (each such Person being called an *"Indemnitee"*) against, and hold each Indemnitee harmless from, any and

---

[1] See Footnote 2 to Box 10.6 for a definition of "Related Party."

all losses, claims, damages, liabilities and related expenses (including the fees, charges and disbursements of any counsel for any Indemnitee)[, and shall indemnify and hold harmless each Indemnitee from all fees and time charges and disbursements for attorneys who may be employees of any Indemnitee], incurred by any Indemnitee or asserted against any Indemnitee by any Person (including the Borrower [or any other Loan Party]) [other than such Indemnitee and its Related Parties] arising out of, in connection with, or as a result of (i) the execution or delivery of this Agreement, any other Loan Document or any agreement or instrument contemplated hereby or thereby, the performance by the parties hereto of their respective obligations hereunder or thereunder or the consummation of the transactions contemplated hereby or thereby, (ii) any Loan or Letter of Credit or the use or proposed use of the proceeds therefrom (including any refusal by any Issuing Bank to honor a demand for payment under a Letter of Credit if the documents presented in connection with such demand do not strictly comply with the terms of such Letter of Credit), (iii) any actual or alleged presence or Release of Hazardous Materials on or from any property owned or operated by the Borrower or any of its Subsidiaries, or any Environmental Liability related in any way to the Borrower or any of its Subsidiaries, or (iv) any actual or prospective claim, litigation, investigation or proceeding relating to any of the foregoing, whether based on contract, tort or any other theory, whether brought by a third party or by the Borrower or any other Loan Party, and regardless of whether any Indemnitee is a party thereto, *provided* that such indemnity shall not, as to any Indemnitee, be available to the extent that such losses, claims, damages, liabilities or related expenses (x) are determined by a court of competent jurisdiction by final and nonappealable judgment to have resulted from the gross negligence or willful misconduct of such Indemnitee or (y) result from a claim brought by the Borrower or any other Loan Party against an Indemnitee for breach in bad faith of such Indemnitee's obligations hereunder or under any other Loan Document, if the Borrower or such Loan Party has obtained a final and nonappealable judgment in its favor on such claim as determined by a court of competent jurisdiction. This Section [*Indemnification*] shall not apply with respect to Taxes other than any Taxes that represent losses, claims, damages, etc. arising from any non-Tax claim.

It is customary for lenders to obtain from the borrower a general indemnification against loss or liability suffered by the lenders in connection with the credit agreement. This indemnification is separate from the borrower's agreement (discussed in Section 12.5) to reimburse costs and expenses incurred in connection with the credit agreement.

Traditionally, credit agreements did not include a general indemnification from the borrower. However, when bank financing of hostile acquisitions became widespread in the late 1970s, and targets began to sue lenders that provided funds to the hostile bidder, indemnification clauses began to appear. In turn, once the concept of suing lenders became a possibility, lenders soon found themselves potentially exposed to other sorts of claims (borrowers who complained that loan funding had been wrongfully withheld, third-party creditors that asserted the lenders had driven the borrower into financial distress, and syndicate members that contended the arranger had misrepresented the borrower's financial condition during syndication). No good idea goes unpunished, and the clauses soon became routine, to the point where their inclusion is now the market standard.

Courts construe indemnities narrowly. Accordingly, the indemnification provision contains a long list of items for which the borrower is to indemnify the lenders: "losses, claims, damages, liabilities, and related expenses" is the litany in the excerpt from the LSTA's Model Credit Agreement Provisions quoted in Box 12.7. The indemnity picks up not just litigation expenses that a lender is forced to pay to defend against a lawsuit that arises out of the credit agreement, but (subject to the exceptions discussed below) any claim or other liability a lender is forced to pay in the event it loses the lawsuit.

Indemnification clauses (in any contract, not only credit agreements) customarily require that the indemnifying party not just *indemnify* the beneficiary of the clause, but also *hold harmless* the beneficiary, in each case against the covered items (losses, claims, damages, liabilities, and related expenses). Historically, these terms had distinct meanings. The term "indemnity" referred to the borrower's obligation to reimburse the lenders against losses and other indemnified risks that they might suffer vis-à-vis third parties. The term "hold harmless" referred to the borrower's not asserting a claim against the lenders. It meant "to absolve another party from any responsibility for damage or other liability arising from the transaction." *Black's Law Dictionary* (10th ed. 2014). The distinction is best illustrated by an example. If a lender is sued by a competitor of the borrower for having provided financing to the borrower, the borrower's *indemnification* protects the lender as against the third party. If the lender is sued by the borrower, the *hold harmless* language protects the lender against having to pay the borrower. Whether the distinction still has any force is questionable. Much like "representation and warranty," the two expressions are nearly always used in conjunction and treated as interchangeable phrases.

Even with a clause that both *indemnifies* and *holds harmless* one party against the full set of loss items (losses, claims, damages, liabilities, and related expenses), the New York Court of Appeals has held that unless a contract is "unmistakably clear," a court should not infer that an indemnification covers attorney's fees incurred by the beneficiary in prosecuting (or defending) an action against (or by) the very party giving the indemnity. See *Hooper Assocs. Ltd. v. AGS Computers, Inc.*, 74 N.Y.2d 487 (1989). The clause must contain language "clearly permitting plaintiff [the beneficiary] to recover from defendant [the indemnifying party] the attorney's fees incurred in a suit [by the indemnifying party] against defendant" (*id.* at 492). The model LSTA language quoted in Box 12.7 attempts to satisfy the requirements of the *Hooper* decision by expressly stating that the indemnity covers not only attorney's fees and the like arising out of claims asserted by third parties, but also those arising out of claims asserted *by the borrower*.

The borrower indemnity is deliberately broad and covers not only the lenders, but affiliates of the lenders (such as securities affiliates that may have acted as arrangers of the credit facility) and their officers, directors, professional advisors, and others. The indemnity also covers a broad range of events that might give rise to losses, including costs of investigations and litigation. Often, the clause explicitly covers any environmental claims that might be asserted against the lenders in the event that they take over property from the borrower. However, it typically excludes liability based upon "gross negligence" or "willful misconduct," as finally determined by a court of competent jurisdiction. (For a discussion of "gross negligence," see Section 10.1.4.)

Some borrowers may seek to exclude liability for breach of contract by the lenders. This can be a sensitive point, since it is most likely to arise in a crisis situation, such as when the lenders refuse to honor a borrowing request because they believe that a material adverse change (MAC) has occurred. The LSTA's Model Credit Agreement Provisions provide that the indemnification is lost in this context only if there is a breach "in bad faith" by the indemnified party of its obligations under the credit agreement. Thus, if a lender determines that a MAC has occurred and a court later holds that it was wrong, the indemnity is not lost so long as the determination was not made in bad faith.

Because of concerns arising out of court cases that involve "lender liability," it is common for an indemnity to state that the lenders shall have no liability for any "indirect, consequential, or punitive damages." The words *indirect* and *consequential* are alternative ways to refer to damages that were not reasonably in the contemplation of the parties when the contract was made. For example, if the failure of a lender to make a loan results in the borrower's not being able to consummate an acquisition, consequential damages might include the loss of future profits for the borrower because it did not own the business it sought to acquire. Punitive damages are damages of unpredictable amount, beyond any actual damages, that are awarded by juries to punish what they see as a party's wrongful behavior. Under New York law, punitive damages have been held to be appropriate only where necessary to deter parties from engaging in conduct that may be characterized as "gross" and "morally reprehensible" and of such "wanton dishonesty" as to imply a criminal indifference to civil obligations. Additionally, in the context of a breach of contract (such as a failure to lend under a credit agreement), the conduct that gives rise to the damages must, among other things, be egregious and "part of a pattern directed at the public generally." See *N.Y. Univ. v. Cont'l Ins. Co.*, 87 N.Y.2d 308 (1995). It is difficult to see how such behavior could arise in the context of a credit agreement, but it is customary nevertheless to address the issue in credit agreements. The LSTA's Model Credit Agreement Provisions take this approach.

12.7 GOVERNING LAW

Box 12.8

This Agreement and the other Loan Documents and any claims, controversy, dispute, or cause of action (whether in contract or tort or otherwise) based upon, arising out of or relating to this Agreement or any other Loan Document (except, as to any other Loan Document, as expressly set forth therein) and the transactions contemplated hereby and thereby shall be governed by, and construed in accordance with, the law of the State of [New York].

A credit agreement—indeed, virtually every contract—includes a "choice of law" provision, by which the parties agree which jurisdiction's law shall be applied to determine the validity of the contract and its interpretation. The contractually chosen law does not govern such matters as the borrower's existence and its power to enter into the financing (which are matters governed by the law of its jurisdiction of organization), nor does it govern issues such as perfection and priority of security interests (here the relevant governing law is determined by statute). It is, however, relevant to many (equally important) questions, such as general contractual validity, which jurisdiction's usury laws apply, and how to interpret the words in the contract.

A choice of law provision is different from a "submission to jurisdiction" clause (see the discussion in Section 12.8.1). The latter relates to the possible locale for litigation, while the former relates to which state's substantive law is applied in whatever locale is used. Courts are accustomed to applying the law of other jurisdictions where required, although the content of such law must be demonstrated to the court (often by the use of expert witnesses).

As a general principle, the law chosen by the parties to govern a contract must, if the choice is to be upheld, bear a reasonable relation to the transaction. What constitutes a "reasonable relation" is not well defined. However, if the loans are to be disbursed (and payments by the borrower are required to be made) in New York and the administrative agent or lead lenders are in New York, the reasonable relation standard is probably satisfied. In addition, for any transaction of $250,000 or more, a New York statute (Section 5-1401 of New York's General Obligations Law) allows the parties to choose New York law regardless of whether there is otherwise a reasonable relation to New York. California has a virtually identical provision (California Civil Code, Section 1646.5).

New York commercial law is relatively extensive, stable, and "creditor-friendly," and this fact, coupled with Section 5-1401 of the General Obligations Law, makes it a favored choice as the governing law for credit agreements. Nevertheless, the parties may choose other jurisdictions. For example, financings led and managed outside the United States are often governed by English law, for many of the same reasons that New York law is considered attractive. It is *not*, however, considered advisable in cross-border lending to provide that the credit agreement shall be governed by the law of the borrower's jurisdiction; selecting the borrower's jurisdiction forces the lenders into the difficult position of having to understand how a different legal regime would construe the standard provisions of a credit agreement, and may subject the lenders to increased risk of adverse changes in the applicable substantive law. It may also be against many lenders' internal credit policies.

A typical choice of law clause, as the language in Box 12.8 taken from the LSTA's Model Credit Agreement Provisions illustrates, provides not only that the agreement be governed by and construed in accordance with the law of the chosen jurisdiction (New York, in this example) but also that any related claims, controversies, disputes, causes of action (whether in contract or tort or otherwise), and transactions be interpreted under the chosen body of law. This litany of related actions is a meaningful inclusion. Choice of law provisions in contracts are generally viewed as having just wide enough scope to sweep in only contract claims such as breach of contract and similar claims arising within the four corners of the credit agreement. However, tort claims, such as fraud, are ordinarily seen as outside of the choice of law provision's reach unless the provision is drafted broadly enough to show that the parties intended to include torts, in which case New York courts will apply the chosen law to tort claims as well. The foregoing litany has been viewed by at least one court as sufficiently broad to cover any tort claims relating to the contract. See *Finance One Public Co., Ltd. v. Lehman Brothers Special Financing Inc.*, 417 F.3d 325 (2d Cir. 2005).

Sometimes the clause goes on to exclude "conflicts of law" rules, out of concern that the chosen jurisdiction's choice of law rules may direct the court to apply the law of a jurisdiction with more extensive contacts with the transaction than the chosen law—for example, the law of the borrower's jurisdiction. This is both unnecessary and undesirable. The reference to "the law" of the chosen jurisdiction is generally understood to mean that jurisdiction's *internal* law. Excluding conflicts of law principles could exclude the principle that the intentions of the parties should be given effect and, in the New York context, might be telling a court not to look to Section 5-1401 of New York's General Obligations Law to uphold the choice of New York law. If the parties wish to cover the point, an alternative and better (though wordier) approach is to exclude those conflicts of law rules "that would otherwise direct application of the law of another jurisdiction."

Occasionally credit documentation incorporates a "split" choice of law, meaning that the governing law provision selects more than one jurisdiction's law as the applicable law. There are several possible varieties of split choice of law. In one variety, the credit agreement is stated to be governed by, say, English law, except that the covenant sections are stated to be governed by New York law (this approach is sometimes taken, for example, when the financing is being placed in the London market, but the covenants and related provisions are drawn from existing credit agreements or indentures governed by New York law, and the borrower wishes to assure consistency of interpretation in its various financings). A New York court should uphold such a "split." Section 5-1401 of the General Obligation Law itself indicates that a contract may be governed "in whole or in part" by New York law. However, when implementing any such split, ambiguity can result if covenants are governed by one jurisdiction's law, but defined terms used in them are to be construed in accordance with a different law.

In another "split law" formulation, the credit documentation may provide that it is governed by New York law, except that it shall be governed by the law of the borrower's jurisdiction if enforcement takes place there. The effect of this kind of "split" is somewhat more difficult to analyze; it could theoretically raise questions whether there was a meeting of the minds at the time of contracting (an element of contract formation), since a contractual provision might be given a different meaning or effect under different bodies of law. However, such a provision does appear in cross-border lending (it is, for example, a routine aspect of promissory notes issued by Mexican borrowers under international credit agreements).

Other forms of split choice of law are, of course, possible—the variations are limited only by the imagination of bankers and borrowers. There are, however, limits as to their enforceability. A split choice of law may not be honored if it creates too much uncertainty in the mind of the court. For example, a provision to the effect that a contract shall be governed by the law of the jurisdiction of any assignee of rights under the contract has been held to fail the "meeting of the minds" test since at the time of contracting there was no way to know where future assignees would be located. See *Sterling Nat'l Bank v. Kings Manor Estates LLC*, 808 N.Y.S.2d 920 (Civ. Ct. N.Y. County 2005).

12.8 ENFORCEMENT PROVISIONS

12.8.1 Jurisdiction; Process Agents

Box 12.9

The Borrower [and each other Loan Party] irrevocably and unconditionally agrees that it will not commence any action, litigation, or proceeding of any kind or description, whether in law or equity, whether in contract or in tort or otherwise, against the Administrative Agent, any Lender, any Issuing Bank, or any Related Party of the foregoing in any way relating to this Agreement or any other Loan Document, or the transactions relating hereto or thereto, in any forum other than the courts of the State of [New York] sitting in [New York] County, and of the United States District Court of the [Southern District of New York], and any appellate court from any thereof, and each of the parties hereto irrevocably and unconditionally submits to the jurisdiction of such courts and agrees that all claims in respect of any such action, litigation, or proceeding may be heard and determined in such [New York] State court or, to the fullest extent permitted by applicable law, in such federal court.

Each of the parties hereto agrees that a final judgment in any such action, litigation, or proceeding shall be conclusive and may be enforced in other jurisdictions by suit on the judgment or in any other manner provided by law. Nothing in this Agreement or in any other Loan Document shall affect any right that the Administrative Agent, any Lender, or any Issuing Bank may otherwise have to bring any action or proceeding relating to this Agreement or any other Loan Document against the Borrower [or any other Loan Party] or its properties in the courts of any other jurisdiction.

Each party hereto irrevocably consents to service of process in the manner provided for notices in Section [*Notices*]. Nothing in this Agreement will affect the right of any party hereto to serve process in any other manner permitted by applicable law.

Lenders always prefer to enforce a credit agreement, should it come to that, in New York or some other "home" jurisdiction. Commencing litigation in the borrower's jurisdiction can entail incremental travel and other expenses, be less certain of a proper outcome, and, of course, eat up more loan officer time. This is particularly true when the borrower is organized outside the United States, where additional factors come into play, such as the potential difficulty of communication with local counsel and the possibility that a local court would favor a local company and perhaps misconstrue New York law.

Court jurisdiction comes in two shapes and sizes: "subject matter" and "personal." Subject-matter jurisdiction refers to the power of a particular court to hear a particular kind of case. Personal jurisdiction refers to the power of a court over a particular entity.

For the most part, subject-matter jurisdiction cannot be created by agreement among the parties. Parties cannot by agreement, for example, force a tax or customs court to hear a landlord–tenant dispute. Parties to a credit agreement could not require the New York Family Court to pass judgment on an interest-rate provision in a commercial loan agreement. The subject-matter jurisdiction of a federal court in the context of a commercial loan generally depends on the circumstance of "diversity of citizenship," a concept in the U.S. Constitution that requires that, in any litigation, the plaintiffs and defendants be from different jurisdictions (and that there not be "aliens" on both sides of the controversy). Other sources of federal subject-matter jurisdiction include where the borrower is a "foreign state" (see Section 12.8.3) and where litigation involves a U.S. national bank or other entity organized under U.S. federal law (12 U.S.C. § 632).

State courts (except for specialized courts, such as family courts, traffic courts, and landlord–tenant courts) have far fewer limitations on their subject-matter jurisdiction. As a result, even though there may be no federal court jurisdiction to hear a particular controversy, it may generally be heard in a state court. A dispute under a credit agreement with a non-U.S. borrower and a group of non-U.S. lenders could be heard in New York State courts even though there are "aliens" on both sides of the dispute. However, even state courts of general jurisdiction may have jurisdictional limitations. For example, a so-called door-closing statute in New York precludes an action in a New York State court by one non-New York entity against another unless, among other exceptions, the contract is performable in New York—loans payable in New York probably satisfy this requirement (Section 1314 of New York's Business Corporation Law).

Personal jurisdiction, which (as noted previously) refers to the power of a court over a particular defendant, consists of two components, each of which can be established by contract. First, there must be a "basis" for jurisdiction, and, second, notice must have been given to the defendant. A basis for personal jurisdiction over a borrower may be created simply by having the borrower consent (or "submit") to the court's jurisdiction. Most credit agreements, therefore, include a formal submission by the borrower to the jurisdiction of the federal courts in New York (or other home jurisdiction), and of the state courts of New York (or other home jurisdiction). Personal jurisdiction, which (as noted previously) refers to the power of a court over a particular defendant, consists of two components, each of which can be established by contract. First, there must be a "basis" for jurisdiction, and, second, notice must have been given to the defendant. A basis for personal jurisdiction over a borrower may be created simply by having the borrower consent (or "submit") to the court's jurisdiction. Most credit agreements, therefore, include a formal submission by the borrower to the jurisdiction of the federal courts in New York (or other home jurisdiction), and of the state courts of New York (or other home jurisdiction). The submission is customarily either fully exclusive, whereby all parties to the credit agreement agree that the specified courts are the only possible places for bringing suit, or exclusive as to the borrower only. In this latter formulation, the borrower is limited to bringing suit in the specified courts while the agent and lenders may expressly preserve their right to bring suit in other jurisdictions in pursuit of loan parties and collateral located in such other jurisdictions. This permits the agents and lenders to preserve their right to sue before any other court that has the proper subject-matter and personal jurisdiction while the borrower agrees to only bring suit in the chosen and exclusive forum.

Notice can generally be effected in any manner agreed to by the borrower. For a U.S. borrower, the typical approach is to have the borrower consent to receiving process (the papers that commence a lawsuit) by mail delivered to its "address for notices" specified in the credit agreement. For non-U.S. borrowers, credit agreements usually have the borrower appoint an agent in New York to which process can be delivered. This agent is defined as a "process agent." The more formal approach for non-U.S. borrowers is designed to avoid a non-U.S. court's refusing to enforce a New York judgment on the grounds that notice was inadequate.

Sovereign borrowers sometimes ask to appoint their own embassies as process agents; this is generally inadvisable from a lender's point of view because the embassy's own diplomatic immunity may prevent service of process. A consulate has more limited (consular) immunity and appointment of a consulate is sometimes proposed. In general, it is preferable from a lender's standpoint to use a commercial process agent, as is normally done with private borrowers.

12.8.2 Venue and Forum Non Conveniens

Box 12.10

The Borrower [and each other Loan Party] irrevocably and unconditionally waives, to the fullest extent permitted by applicable law, any objection that it may now or hereafter have to the laying of venue of any action or proceeding arising out of or relating to this Agreement or any other Loan Document in any court referred to in this Section [*Submission to Jurisdiction*]. Each of the parties hereto hereby irrevocably waives, to the fullest extent permitted by applicable law, the defense of an inconvenient forum to the maintenance of such action or proceeding in any such court.

In addition to the limitations of subject-matter and personal jurisdiction, actions in federal and state courts are typically also subject to "venue" rules. Thus, although a federal court might have subject-matter jurisdiction to hear a suit, the federal venue statute might stipulate that only a court in a state where one of the parties has a place of business may take on the suit. Venue requirements are generally waivable, and so it is customary in credit agreements for there to be a waiver of venue by the borrower.

Even if a court has subject-matter jurisdiction and venue is proper (or has been waived), the court may still have the discretion to decline a case if it believes there is a more convenient forum for the suit. This is the so-called *forum non conveniens* doctrine. A court might thus force transfer of the case if that would be more convenient for the parties, taking into account such factors as the location of documents and witnesses, the place where relevant events occurred, and the like. It is customary to require the borrower to waive objection on *forum non conveniens* grounds. A federal court is free to dismiss the case on this ground despite a waiver. A New York court, however, is precluded from doing so by Section 327 of New York's civil procedure statute (the New York Civil Practice Law and Rules) if the credit agreement provides for loans of $1,000,000 or more and contains both a choice of New York law and a submission to New York court jurisdiction.

12.8.3 Waiver of Sovereign Immunity

Box 12.11

To the extent that the Borrower may be or become entitled, in any jurisdiction in which judicial proceedings may at any time be commenced with respect to this Agreement, to claim for itself or its properties or revenues any immunity from suit, court jurisdiction, attachment prior to judgment, attachment in aid of execution of a judgment, execution of a judgment, or from any other legal process or remedy relating to its obligations under this Agreement or any other Loan Document to which it is a party, and to the extent that in any such jurisdiction there may be attributed such an immunity (whether or not claimed), the Borrower hereby irrevocably agrees not to claim and hereby irrevocably waives such immunity to the fullest extent permitted by the laws of such jurisdiction.

Sovereign immunity refers to the special status that a borrower has if it is a "foreign state" as defined in the U.S. Foreign Sovereign Immunities Act of 1976 (FSIA), namely, immunity from court jurisdiction and immunity of its property from attachment or execution. As a general principle, a foreign state cannot be forced to appear in a court in the United States (federal or state) and cannot have its property in the United States seized to pay a judgment. However, the Act permits sovereign immunity to be waived.

The term *foreign state* is defined broadly under the FSIA. It includes not only a foreign government, but any political subdivision of a foreign state and any agency or instrumentality (such as a ministry or central bank) of a foreign state. It also sweeps in any entity that is majority owned by a foreign state or political sub-division thereof (if it is organized under the laws of the same country). Therefore even a private company becomes entitled to sovereign immunity if a majority of its shares are acquired by its home country after the closing, so sovereign immunity waivers are standard in all cross-border credit agreements, even with private borrowers, and cover future immunity as well as any immunity to which the borrower may already be entitled.

Although the FSIA broadly upholds waivers of sovereign immunity, there are some limits on their validity. In particular, even with a waiver, the FSIA does not authorize attachment of noncommercial property. Thus, a lending syndicate could not attach the Kurbian consulate in New York, or its embassy in Washington, DC, when it sues to enforce payment of a sovereign loan to the Republic of Kurbia. Similarly, the property of a foreign central bank or monetary authority "held for its own account" is immune from attachment and execution, unless there is an *explicit* (as opposed to implied) waiver as to such property. There can be no attachment of or execution upon property that is or is intended to be used in connection with a military activity if such property is of a military character (such as military weapons) or is under the control of a military authority or defense agency.

Property of a foreign state that is used for a commercial activity in the United States may be subject to attachment as a provisional remedy (that is, not to satisfy a court judgment, but to secure an eventual judgment) only if the foreign state has explicitly waived its immunity from attachment prior to judgment. For this reason, as shown in the language in Box 12.11, a sovereign immunity waiver generally includes specific reference to "attachment prior to judgment."

Certain organizations enjoy immunity under authority separate from the FSIA. Under the International Organizations Immunities Act, an "international organization," defined in 22 U.S.C. § 288 as a public international organization in which the United States participates by treaty or Act of Congress and which is designated by Executive Order, enjoys the same immunity from suit and judicial process as a foreign government, except to the extent explicitly waived. Examples include the International Monetary Fund (IMF), the International Bank for Reconstruction and Development (IBRD), the Organization for Economic

Cooperation and Development (OECD), and many others. In addition, some institutions in which the United States does not participate are granted equivalent status (for example, the African Union).

12.8.4 Waiver of Jury Trial

Box 12.12

EACH PARTY HERETO HEREBY IRREVOCABLY WAIVES, TO THE FULLEST EXTENT PERMITTED BY APPLICABLE LAW, ANY RIGHT IT MAY HAVE TO A TRIAL BY JURY IN ANY LEGAL PROCEEDING DIRECTLY OR INDIRECTLY ARISING OUT OF OR RELATING TO THIS AGREEMENT OR ANY OTHER LOAN DOCUMENT OR THE TRANSACTIONS CONTEMPLATED HEREBY OR THEREBY (WHETHER BASED ON CONTRACT, TORT OR ANY OTHER THEORY). EACH PARTY HERETO (A) CERTIFIES THAT NO REPRESENTATIVE, AGENT OR ATTORNEY OF ANY OTHER PERSON HAS REPRESENTED, EXPRESSLY OR OTHERWISE, THAT SUCH OTHER PERSON WOULD NOT, IN THE EVENT OF LITIGATION, SEEK TO ENFORCE THE FOREGOING WAIVER AND (B) ACKNOWLEDGES THAT IT AND THE OTHER PARTIES HERETO HAVE BEEN INDUCED TO ENTER INTO THIS AGREEMENT AND THE OTHER LOAN DOCUMENTS BY, AMONG OTHER THINGS, THE MUTUAL WAIVERS AND CERTIFICATIONS IN THIS SECTION.

Unpredictable jury awards in "lender liability" cases have led lenders for many years to require borrowers to waive the right to trial by jury, so that any litigation is tried before a presumably more sophisticated judge. The right to a jury trial is set out in the U.S. Constitution as well as in state constitutions and statutes. Insofar as federal law is concerned, a waiver that is voluntary and knowing is generally enforceable. See *K.M.C. Co. v. Irving Trust Co.*, 757 F.2d 752 (6th Cir. 1985). In the context of commercial credit agreements in which the borrowers are sophisticated and represented by counsel, there is generally no question as to the voluntary and knowing nature of such a waiver. New York similarly upholds jury waivers. See *Brian Wallach Agency, Inc. v. Bank of New York*, 428 N.Y.S.2d 280 (App. Div. 2d Dep't 1980). In a few states a waiver of the state constitutional jury right may not be enforceable even if it is voluntary and knowing (California is an example, because of a provision in its constitution).

Whether a jury-waiver provision is enforceable is a function of the court before which a case is being tried. So if a New York law credit agreement is being enforced in a New York court, the judge looks to New York principles to determine whether a waiver is valid. If the case is being tried in a federal court, it is federal principles that are relevant. And if suit is commenced in the borrower's home state of Nebraska, the court looks to Nebraska cases to decide if the waiver is to be upheld. Because of different approaches to the issue in different states, and because there is authority in some states (particularly in the area of consumer finance) that such waivers must be conspicuous, it has become customary in the lending market to make the jury-waiver provision likewise conspicuous by placing it in all capital letters with bold text. The reluctance of courts to enforce jury waivers may also explain the tendency in most agreements to make the waiver mutual, to have *both* the borrower and the lenders waive their right to a jury trial.

Under New York law, the requirement that the waiver be conspicuous is probably unnecessary in a financing between sophisticated parties represented by counsel. See *Am. Equities Group Inc. v. Ahava Dairy Prods. Corp.*, 2007 U.S. Dist. LEXIS 93511 (S.D.N.Y. 2007) and *Barclays Bank of New York, N.A. v. Heady Electric Co.*, 571 N.Y.S.2d 650 (App. Div. 3d Dep't 1991). However, since enforcement of an agreement can easily occur in a federal court, federal rules are also relevant in this context and they may put more weight upon a waiver being conspicuous, consistent with the requirement that the waiver be knowing and voluntary. See *Nat'l Equip. Rental, Ltd. v. Hendrix*, 565 F.2d 255 (2d Cir. 1977). The LSTA's Model Credit Agreement Provisions in Box 12.12 both place the jury waiver in conspicuous text (e.g., all capital letters with bold text) and adopt the mutuality approach.

12.8.5 Judgment Currency

Box 12.13

This is an international loan transaction in which the specification of Dollars and payment in New York City is of the essence, and the obligations of the Borrower under this Agreement to make payment to or for account of a Lender in Dollars shall not be discharged or satisfied by any tender or recovery pursuant to any judgment expressed in or converted into any other currency or in another place except to the extent that such tender or recovery results in the effective receipt by such Lender in New York City of the full amount of Dollars payable to such Lender under this Agreement.

If for the purpose of obtaining judgment in any court it is necessary to convert a sum due hereunder in Dollars into another currency (in this Section called the *"judgment currency"*), the rate of exchange that shall be applied shall be that at which in accordance with normal banking procedures the Administrative Agent could purchase such Dollars at the principal office of the Administrative Agent in New York City with the judgment currency on the Business Day next preceding the day on which such judgment is rendered. The obligation of the Borrower in respect of any such sum due from it to the Administrative Agent or any Lender hereunder (in this Section called an *"Entitled Person"*) shall, notwithstanding the rate of exchange actually applied in rendering such judgment, be discharged only to the extent that on the Business Day following receipt by such Entitled Person of any sum adjudged to be due hereunder in the judgment currency such Entitled Person may in accordance with normal banking procedures purchase and transfer Dollars to New York City with the amount of the judgment currency so adjudged to be due; and the Borrower hereby, as a separate obligation and notwithstanding any such judgment, agrees to indemnify such Entitled Person against, and to pay such Entitled Person on demand, in Dollars, the amount (if any) by which the sum originally due to such Entitled Person in Dollars hereunder exceeds the amount of the Dollars so purchased and transferred.

A judgment currency clause is inserted either when the credit agreement provides for nondollar loans or when the borrower is located outside the United States. It addresses the problem that arises when a debt is denominated in one currency but judgment on the debt is rendered in another. This situation comes up most often when the winning party in a lawsuit seeks to transport a judgment rendered by a court in one country (say, the administrative agent's) to a second country that has a different currency (say, the borrower's). An example might arise if a borrower that is organized and has all of its assets in Germany is obligated on a loan denominated in U.S. dollars made available in New York by a group of U.S. lenders. If a judgment for U.S. $1,000,000 is rendered against the borrower in New York, the lenders may eventually need to present the New York judgment to a German court and request that it order the borrower to pay. A German court, however, will likely render its own judgment in Euros in an amount equal to the equivalent of U.S. $1,000,000. Between the time that the German court issues a judgment and the borrower actually pays the stipulated Euros, the value of the Euro may fall, and thus, when the lenders convert those Euros into U.S. dollars, they may end up short. The judgment currency clause allows the lenders to go back to the New York court and request a new judgment in the amount of the shortfall, which could then be similarly enforced in Germany against the borrower.

As of this writing, no court in New York has ruled on the validity of the core principle of the judgment currency clause, namely that a lender can go back to court to obtain a supplemental judgment if currency fluctuations render the initial judgment amount insufficient. Accordingly, legal opinions delivered at closing normally include an exception as to the enforceability of the clause.

12.9 SEVERABILITY; COUNTERPARTS; INTEGRATION; CAPTIONS

12.9.1 Severability

> **Box 12.14**
>
> Any provision of this Agreement held to be invalid, illegal, or unenforceable in any jurisdiction shall, as to such jurisdiction, be ineffective to the extent of such invalidity, illegality or unenforceability without affecting the validity, legality, and enforceability of the remaining provisions hereof; and the invalidity of a particular provision in a particular jurisdiction shall not invalidate such provision in any other jurisdiction.

Courts have long struggled with what happens when a single contract contains multiple obligations (such as the typical credit agreement) and a promise of one party (a particular clause of the agreement) turns out to be illegal or unenforceable. This concern can be especially acute in cases in which the borrower is located in a jurisdiction other than the jurisdiction whose law governs the agreement. Would, for example, an entire New York law credit agreement for an Arizona borrower fail because, say, the indemnification clause might be illegal in Arizona, or against the public policy of Arizona? Would the answer be different if the clause were simply unenforceable and not illegal? The general rule under New York law is that if the illegal provision is so interwoven with the other provisions of the agreement that they form "one and the same contract," the whole contract may be illegal. "The court will not allow itself to become the means of enforcing such an agreement, but will leave the contracting parties where it finds them." See *Sturm v. Truby*, 282 N.Y.S. 433 (App. Div. 4th Dep't 1935).

Severability clauses are an attempt to avoid these concerns. They are inserted as an expression of intent that the parties do not want the whole contract to fall simply because one provision may offend legal rules. However, whether the severability clause itself will be given effect is questionable. Courts, while willing to take such a clause into consideration in deciding if an offending provision can be severed, have also taken into account other factors such as whether the offending clause may be severed without destroying the intent of the contract. A credit agreement might thus be enforced even though the currency indemnity is unenforceable or illegal. A credit agreement might not be enforced, however, if the purpose of the loan is to establish an illegal gambling operation and the lender is given, as additional interest, a share of the profits.

12.9.2 Counterparts; Effectiveness

Box 12.15

This Agreement may be executed in counterparts (and by different parties hereto in different counterparts), each of which shall constitute an original, but all of which when taken together shall constitute a single contract. Except as provided in Section [*Conditions Precedent*], this Agreement shall become effective when it shall have been executed by the Administrative Agent and when the Administrative Agent shall have received counterparts hereof that, when taken together, bear the signatures of each of the other parties hereto.

The counterparts clause is one of those provisions that is frequently overlooked, but has great practical significance. It permits a credit agreement to be executed by having each party sign a different copy, or an individual signature page, with all of the respective copies or signature pages then assembled into one, single agreement. This is now routine practice in the United States for most credit documentation and quite different from the method used in many non-U.S. jurisdictions where a contract, to be enforceable, must be executed by all parties on a single document at a single time.

Under New York contract law, mere execution of the signature pages by the parties, even without furnishing originals or copies of these signature pages to the borrower and the administrative agent, could be sufficient for an agreement to become effective. For a variety of reasons, the parties to a credit agreement do not want this to happen. Accordingly, the counterparts clause is usually also accompanied by an effectiveness provision. The latter makes it explicit that the agreement does not become effective until all parties have delivered counterpart signature pages to the administrative agent so that a fully executed agreement can be compiled.

12.9.3   Integration

Box 12.16

This Agreement and the other Loan Documents, and any separate letter agreements with respect to fees payable to the Administrative Agent, constitute the entire contract among the parties relating to the subject matter hereof and supersede any and all previous agreements and understandings, oral or written, relating to the subject matter hereof.

The integration clause in a credit agreement stipulates that the agreement reflects the entire understanding between the parties and that all prior agreements between the parties are superseded. The purpose of an integration clause (sometimes referred to as a "merger clause") is to preclude a court from applying the so-called "parol evidence rule" to introduce extrinsic evidence to alter, vary, or contradict the terms of the agreement. The integration clause establishes the parties' intent that the written agreement is to be considered a fully integrated agreement. See *DDCLAB Ltd. v. E.I. Du Pont De Nemours & Co.*, 2005 U.S. Dist. LEXIS 2721 (S.D.N.Y. 2005). It acts as a shield against the borrower's (or the lenders') introducing earlier extraneous writings and oral conversations as a way to undercut the clear language of the agreement. Such materials can still be used to *clarify* ambiguous provisions in a credit agreement, but may not be used either to contradict, or to make ambiguous, the already clear language of an agreement.

Note that an integration clause is not intended to exclude written and oral communications that arise *after* an agreement is executed, but only communications that occur prior to (and, in certain circumstances, contemporaneously with) the execution of the agreement. Communications after an agreement is executed are covered either by the amendments provision (which requires them to be in writing and to be authorized and executed by the relevant parties) or by the no deemed waivers provision (see Section 12.2).

In the context of a credit agreement, the integration clause supersedes all the many term sheets, business models, PowerPoint presentations, notes, e-mails, and other communications that go back and forth between the parties during the marketing, syndication, and negotiation process for the credit agreement. Some of this material, since prepared at early stages of the process, may be completely inconsistent with the credit documentation as ultimately negotiated. Absent an integration clause, the final business deal, as reflected in the credit agreement, could be unwound before a court by the borrower (or lenders) introducing into evidence the earlier, contradictory, material.

In addition to superseding prior writings, the integration clause supersedes earlier oral communications. This prevents the borrower, when a deal goes sour, for example, from alleging the existence of prior understandings as to whether and when remedies might be invoked. It also prevents a borrower or lenders from introducing conversations as to how covenants should be interpreted or calculated if the financial and related definitions are not ambiguous.

Courts generally uphold integration clauses, and thus exclude parol evidence, absent evidence of fraud, or evidence that the extraneous material actually reflects a *separate* agreement (with *separate consideration*) and does not contradict express or implied provisions of the main agreement. In the context of a credit agreement, most side letters or similar agreements are not considered sufficiently separate for a court to allow them to be enforced. Fee letters that set out the fee understandings with the arranger and the agent fall into this category. The customary integration clause consequently excludes fee letters from the operation of the clause. The provision in Box 12.16 is from the LSTA's Model Credit Agreement Provisions and takes this approach.

Side letters, and commitment and engagement letters, are less frequently carved out of the integration clause and thus are at risk of being merged into the credit agreement. This can be a trap for parties if they execute a "side letter" at closing—such as a side letter in which the agent waives selected conditions to the making of the initial loans so long as the conditions are satisfied within 30 days. The borrower may not actually have 30 days grace if the side agreement is effectively nullified by reason of the integration clause, though a lending syndicate would be hard-pressed to accelerate a loan in the face of a writing executed by the agent (even without the knowledge or consent of the syndicate).

12.9.4 Captions

> **Box 12.17**
>
> Article and Section headings and the Table of Contents used herein are for convenience of reference only, are not part of this Agreement, and shall not affect the construction of, or be taken into consideration in interpreting, this Agreement.

The table of contents and the section and paragraph headings of a credit agreement can be useful to help find relevant provisions in the document. Courts, however, have been known to look to captions to interpret the meaning of an ambiguous clause. For example, a poorly captioned debt covenant intended to limit both debt of the borrower and debt of its subsidiaries, but which is labeled "Subsidiary Debt," could be construed against the lenders to restrict only subsidiary debt in the event of an ambiguity in the covenant itself. To prevent a party from using captions in this way to induce a court to misconstrue words, the captions clause provides that captions and the table of contents are not to have interpretive effect and are inserted for "convenience of reference" only. Of course, the ultimate protection for the parties is to ensure that the underlying agreements are clear and accurately reflect the business deal they have agreed to.

12.10 ELECTRONIC EXECUTION

> **Box 12.18**
>
> Delivery of an executed counterpart of a signature page of this Agreement and any other Loan Document or Assignment and Assumption by facsimile or electronic (i.e., "pdf" or "tif") format shall be effective as delivery of a manually executed counterpart of this Agreement, other Loan Document or Assignment or Assumption.

The words "execution," "signed, "signature," and words of like import in any Assignment and Assumption shall be deemed to include electronic signatures or the keeping of records in electronic form, each of which shall be of the same legal effect, validity, or enforceability as a manually executed signature or the use of a paper-based recordkeeping system, as the case may be, to the extent and as provided for in any applicable law, including the Federal Electronic Signatures in Global and National Commerce Act, the New York State Electronic Signatures and Records Act, or any other similar state laws based on the Uniform Electronic Transactions Act.

Lawyers may worry whether receipt of a fax, photocopy, pdf by e-mail, or other electronically delivered signature page of an agreement is sufficient for enforcement purposes against the party that submits the signature page. Two historical legal doctrines have led to this concern. The first, the so-called "best evidence rule," which was originally developed through court decisions and incorporated into statutes beginning more than a century ago, required that if a party wished to enforce a contract, it must produce an original of the contract or the "best evidence" of the execution of the contract. A mere copy of the contract, or oral testimony of the contract, would not suffice unless it could be shown that the original was not available. The second is the statute of frauds, in force throughout the United States (in New York it is codified in General Obligations Law Section 5-701), which requires that certain types of contracts be in writing to be enforceable. Credit agreements (except short-term facilities) almost always fall within one of the covered categories, since statutes of frauds generally apply to any contract that is not to be performed within one year. In the face of these two legal doctrines, would an electronic signature or record really be the "best" evidence? Would it constitute a "writing"? Given that bankers and lawyers have long since dispensed with the exchange of original signature pages, these are not insignificant questions.

Modern statutes, enacted at both the federal and state levels, support standard market practice for the exchange of signature pages by fax and e-mail. At the federal level, in 2000 the United States enacted the Electronic Signatures in Global and National Commerce Act (or "E-Sign" for short). The Act applies to any transaction "in or affecting interstate or foreign commerce," which almost certainly encompasses most credit agreements, and provides that a signature may not be objected to "solely because it is in electronic form."

The federal act, however, may have little practical effect since it expressly stipulates that it is preempted by any state enactment of the "Uniform Electronic Transactions Act" (virtually all states have done this, although New York is one of the few that has not) and by any state statute that specifies "alternative procedures and requirements" consistent with the federal act and that is "technologically neutral" (does not prefer one type of technology over another). In 1999 New York adopted the Electronic Signatures and Records Act, which arguably qualifies under the second of the exceptions in the federal act. Revisions passed in 2002 were intended to harmonize the New York Act with the federal act and probably allow the New York law to avoid preemption by the federal law. The issue of preemption of the New York law has, however, not yet been construed by any court decision.

As a consequence, essentially all states (including New York) allow electronically delivered signature pages. Both the federal act and the New York Act provide that a signature, contract, or other record may not be denied legal effect, validity, or enforceability solely because it is in electronic form or because an "electronic signature" or "electronic record" (terms of art defined in the Acts) were used in its formation. Thus, whether the federal law or New York law applies to agreements governed by New York law the result should be the same. The Acts do not mandate the use of electronic signatures; rather, recognizing the ever-expanding use of e-mail and database record-keeping, they approve the use of electronic methods to form and maintain records of contracts regardless of the technology used. New York courts have confirmed that a typed signature at the bottom of an e-mail satisfies the "writing" requirement of the New York statute of frauds. See *Naldi v. Grunberg*, 80 A.D.3d 1 (N.Y. App. Div. 1st Dep't 2010).

In addition to New York's Electronic Signatures and Records Act, other revisions to the New York and federal "best evidence rule," and to the statute of frauds, now treat an "electronic record" as equivalent to the original. As a result, the hurdles historically presented by both the "best evidence rule" and the statute of frauds have largely disappeared.

This fact notwithstanding, electronic signature acts are not a panacea to overcome all challenges to the execution of agreements. They do not prevent a party in an appropriate instance from challenging the authenticity of an agreement on the grounds of fraud, forgery, alteration, or other forms of deception. A forged signature page to a contract does not gain authenticity simply because it is e-mailed as a pdf to a counterparty. To avoid fraud, basic documentary closing conditions and due diligence must remain an essential element of any transaction.

Electronic signature acts may not be helpful if a signature originates in a non-U.S. jurisdiction. In the United States, if the parties to an agreement validly select a particular law to govern the agreement, the formalities necessary to make an enforceable contract are determined by the law selected, although the contract is also enforced if the formalities satisfy the requirements of the place of execution (*Restatement of Conflict of Law 2d, § 199*). This is a win–win scenario. If a contract is executed by a borrower in Kentucky (which has enacted the Uniform Electronic Transactions Act) and the borrower delivers its signature as a pdf by e-mail, the contract is enforced without regard to whether New York allows pdfs by e-mail. Similarly, if the agreement specifies New York law as the governing one and New York would uphold a pdf by e-mail signature, then the contract is enforced without reference to Kentucky law. This is not necessarily the case if the agreement is executed in, say, Brazil. A Brazilian court could insist that an agreement, to be enforceable, must be executed in accordance with Brazilian formalities. If those formalities do not permit electronic execution, or pdf by e-mail or fax, or require notarization, those are the procedures that should be followed and not the procedures allowed in U.S. jurisdictions. For this reason, in any cross-border transaction (where the lenders are in the United States but the borrower is organized and doing its principal business outside of the United States and executes a contract outside of the United States) the "due execution" opinion confirms to the lenders that local formalities were followed (see Section 5.1.4).

12.11 SURVIVAL

Box 12.19

All covenants, representations, and warranties made by the Borrower herein or in connection herewith shall survive the execution and delivery of this Agreement and the making of any Loans, regardless of any investigation made by any party and notwithstanding that the Administrative Agent or any Lender had notice or knowledge of any Default or incorrect representation or warranty at the time any Loan is made, and shall continue in full force and effect so long as any Loan or other amount payable under this Agreement is outstanding and the Commitments have not expired or terminated. The provisions of Sections [*Yield Protection; Indemnification of Agent; Indemnification By Borrower; Expenses*] shall survive and remain in full force and effect regardless of the repayment of the Loans or the termination of the Commitments or this Agreement.

The typical survival provision comes in two parts. The first of these, which supplements the no deemed waivers provision (described in Section 12.2), specifies that a lender has not waived a breach of a representation, or the existence of a default, simply because it may be aware of the breach or default at the time a loan is made. The survival clause carries this further by making clear that all representations survive regardless of the lender's having notice or knowledge of the breach or default at the time of the loan. The provision is intended to preempt any implication that arises under law that a representation or warranty no longer has any force once a loan is made and that, as a consequence, the lender is estopped from later accelerating the loan based upon the breach or default.

The second part of the survival clause overrides traditional legal doctrine that, unless an agreement stipulates otherwise, once the transactions contemplated by the agreement have been completed, the agreement terminates. In the context of a loan facility, this would mean that when the loan has been repaid, the credit agreement ceases to be in force and all obligations expire. The parties may, however, want certain obligations to continue. For example, the lenders want the yield protection provisions to survive inasmuch as they may not know at the time of payoff whether future claims related to the agreement will be made against them. Likewise agents want their indemnity protection, as well as rights to claim unpaid or contingent amounts owing to them from indemnitors, to survive post-closing. Even litigation ongoing against the lenders at the time of repayment may not reach a conclusion until years after the loan is repaid in full. If the suit is covered by the borrower's agreement to reimburse the lender for defense costs and ultimate judgment, the lender does not want the indemnification to lapse upon repayment of the loan. Similarly, a regulatory agency could impose costs retroactively for periods during which the loan was outstanding that, had the loan not been repaid, would be covered by the yield protection provisions.

The borrower also wants certain provisions to survive, such as the undertaking of the lenders to keep borrower information confidential. Sensitive financial information in the hands of the lenders does not cease to be sensitive simply because the loan is repaid (see Section 13.9).

While Box 12.19 provides an example of a single survival provision, survival language is, just as commonly, sprinkled within the relevant provisions to specify the intention of the parties that such provision survive.

12.12 USA PATRIOT ACT

> **Box 12.20**
>
> Each Lender subject to the Act hereby notifies the Borrower that pursuant to the requirements of the USA PATRIOT Act (Title III of Pub. L. 107-56 (signed into law October 26, 2001)) (the "Act"), it may be required to obtain, verify, and record information that identifies the Borrower, which information includes the name and address of the Borrower and other information that will allow such Lender to identify the Borrower in accordance with the Act.

Shortly after the attacks of September 11, 2001, the United States enacted the so-called USA PATRIOT Act. The term abbreviates the rather meandering, artificially crafted title "Uniting and Strengthening America by Providing Appropriate Tools Required to Intercept and Obstruct Terrorism Act of 2001." Under the Act, "United States Persons" are prohibited from engaging in a wide variety of transactions with known or suspected terrorists or terrorist organizations or other blocked persons identified on a list issued and regularly updated by the U.S. Treasury Department of "Persons Who Commit, Threaten to Commit, or Support Terrorism." The Act also requires the Treasury Department to prescribe regulations that set out procedures for financial institutions to verify the identity of customers, maintain records relating to customers, and consult the Department's list to determine whether customers appear on the list.

It is these latter regulations that have led to the provision set out in Box 12.20 that is now commonly included in the credit agreement boilerplate. The regulations issued under the Act require subject financial institutions to develop and implement customer identification programs whenever they open an *account* with a *customer*. Financial institutions must provide borrowers with prior notice of their intent to compile the required information.

"Account" is defined broadly to include an extension of credit, so that it picks up the execution and delivery between a lender and a borrower of an agreement that establishes a credit facility. The term does not encompass other relationships in the typical credit agreement, such as that between the arranger and the borrower, or between the lenders and the agent. The regulations also state that an "account" is not established when an assignee or participant acquires an interest in a loan pursuant to a secondary trade.

"Customer" also has its generally understood meaning, except that it excludes any public company and any existing customer if the financial institution has a reasonable belief that it knows the true identity of the borrower. As a technical matter, therefore, the exclusion is broad enough to exempt most customers from the notice requirement. Nevertheless, for simplicity's sake, it has become common for credit agreements to include a PATRIOT Act notice for all borrowers, even public companies and existing customers. Some agreements also include a condition precedent that requires the borrower to have delivered whatever information is necessary for each lender to determine that the PATRIOT Act is complied with, as well as a representation as to PATRIOT Act compliance (see Section 5.1.11.5).

The LSTA has issued "Know Your Customer Considerations for Syndicated Lending and Loan Trading: Guidelines for the Application of Customer Identification Programs, Foreign Correspondent Account Due Diligence, and Other Consideration" (the "KYC Guidelines"), available on its website (www.lsta.org). The KYC Guidelines include a suggested notice provision (see the language in Box 12.20). To ensure compliance with the Treasury Department's regulations, the FDIC instructs bank examiners to confirm that banks are satisfying the customer identification program requirements, including the notice requirement.

CHAPTER 13

Borrower Rights

13.1 THE RIGHT THAT LENDERS MAKE LOANS

> **Box 13.1**
>
> Subject to the terms and conditions set forth herein, each Lender agrees to make Loans to the Borrower from time to time during the Availability Period in an aggregate principal amount that will not result in (a) such Lender's Loans exceeding such Lender's Commitment or (b) the aggregate principal amount of outstanding Loans exceeding the total Commitments.

Perhaps the most fundamental right that a borrower has under a credit agreement is to require that the lenders make the loans such lenders have committed to make. As discussed in Section 2.2.1, when a group of lenders undertakes to make loans to a borrower, each lender is individually obligated, assuming all relevant conditions are satisfied, to extend credit up to the full amount of its commitment. These obligations are "several," in the sense that no lender is responsible for the failure of any other lender to make its loan, and the failure of one lender to make its loan does not relieve any other lender of its separate obligation to make loans.

Any lender that fails to make a loan requested by the borrower when all conditions precedent are satisfied is in breach of its commitment under the credit agreement. The same applies to lenders who have committed to finance a loan transaction pursuant to a standalone commitment letter. We discussed in more detail in Section 10.8, the so-called "defaulting lender" provisions that emerged following the most recent credit crisis, which give a borrower (and the agent and to a certain extent even other lenders) certain contractual remedies against a defaulting lender, such as to remove its right to vote, to require it to post cash collateral for participation obligations in respect of swingline loans or letters of credit, and, in some cases, to subordinate its claims to those of the other lenders. However, even assuming that the defaulting lender provisions are triggered, the borrower likely still prefers that the lender not default in the first instance. What can the borrower do?

As with any breach of contract, the borrower theoretically has two remedies available to it: seek a mandatory injunction to force the lender to make its loans or sue for damages. As a practical matter, injunctive relief is not likely to be helpful. To begin with, courts rarely order a lender to specifically perform on a contract to lend money. One lender's money is just as good as another lender's money, and a jilted borrower can borrow money from another lender and sue for any damages resulting from higher pricing or any other damages suffered from having to borrow from a replacement lender. Where damages provide for an adequate remedy at law, courts will not order specific performance. See *BT Triple Crown Merger Co., Inc. v Citigroup Global Mkts. Inc.*, 866 N.Y.S.2d 90 (describing the general rule that New York courts will not order specific performance of a contract to lend money and the limited exceptions thereto) (unpublished opinion). Even if a borrower were to pursue the remedies of injunctive relief or specific performance, it would probably take months of long-winded court proceedings before an order is issued—a time frame that doubtless means the injunction will be too late to satisfy time-critical funding needs.

For all practical purposes, therefore, the remedy available to a borrower (beyond rights it may have under any "defaulting lender" provisions) is to recover damages from the defaulting lender. However, under common law principles and the credit agreement itself, the amount of damages that the borrower can obtain will not be the amount of the loan, but rather the extra costs (higher interest, up-front fees, and other expenses) that the borrower must expend to procure alternative financing. Damages, such as the harm to its business or business opportunities that result from the failure of the lender to fund, are normally constrained by the standard indemnification provisions in a credit agreement, which eliminate the borrower's ability to claim consequential or punitive damages from the lenders for any breach (see Section 12.6).

The latest financial crisis predictably resulted in litigation involving skittish lenders (and often equally skittish acquirers or potential acquirers) being sued for failing to close and fund on their financing commitments. Some of these lawsuits involved parties that were not party to any definitive credit agreement but rather were party to a commitment letter pursuant to which the committed lenders had allegedly undertaken to fund subject to satisfaction of specified conditions precedent. Unlike a credit agreement, a commitment letter is inherently a preliminary agreement. Preliminary agreements can range from mere "agreements to agree," where courts will only hold the parties to the obligation to negotiate in good faith toward a binding agreement but not require an obligation to consummate the transaction, to a binding commitment that may require a legal obligation to consummate the ultimate transaction. The likelihood that a lender can be found to have breached for failing to fund a commitment is much weaker if the commitment letter is found to fit into the "agreements to agree" category and stronger if found to actually involve an enforceable binding commitment. While a detailed discussion of commitment letters is beyond the scope of this volume, the broader point is that whether dealing with a commitment letter or a credit agreement, borrowers have rights to enforce legally binding commitments of their lenders if the applicable funding conditions have been satisfied.

13.2 THE RIGHT THAT LENDERS MITIGATE COSTS

Box 13.2

If any Lender requests compensation under Section [*Increased Costs*], or requires the Borrower to pay any Indemnified Taxes or additional amounts to any Lender or any Governmental Authority for the account of any Lender pursuant to Section [*Taxes*], then such Lender shall (at the request of the Borrower) use reasonable efforts to designate a different lending office for funding or booking its Loans hereunder or to assign its rights and obligations hereunder to another of its offices, branches or affiliates, if, in the judgment of such Lender, such designation or assignment (i) would eliminate or reduce amounts payable pursuant to Section [*Increased Costs*] or [*Taxes*], as the case may be, in the future, and (ii) would not subject such Lender to any unreimbursed cost or expense and would not otherwise be disadvantageous to such Lender. The Borrower hereby agrees to pay all reasonable costs and expenses incurred by any Lender in connection with any such designation or assignment.

> *"Indemnified Taxes"* means (a) Taxes, other than Excluded Taxes, imposed on or with respect to any payment made by or on account of any obligation of [the Borrower] [any Loan Party] under any Loan Document and (b) to the extent not otherwise described in (a), Other Taxes.

Credit agreements normally require that any lender that requests compensation under the increased costs or taxes clauses use "reasonable" efforts either to book loans at a different branch or office or to transfer loans to an affiliate if these actions would reduce or eliminate costs. The purpose of this language is to minimize yield protection losses and expenses that are passed on to the borrower. What is "reasonable" for these purposes varies from lender to lender. For example, it would probably not be reasonable to force a lender to move a loan to an affiliate that is not in the business of lending or that makes loans only in Latin America and thus would not know how to evaluate or monitor a loan to a software company in California. Likewise it would not be reasonable to force a lender to violate applicable legal and regulatory restrictions (e.g., banking licensure or other rules) by transferring loans to an unlicensed entity. It might, however, be reasonable to require the lender to transfer a loan to an affiliate that already has a multibillion dollar portfolio of similar loans.

The obligation to use reasonable efforts to mitigate costs typically also provides that any action taken not be "otherwise disadvantageous" to the lender. This is intended, among other things, to override any requirement that the lender book a loan in a particular jurisdiction if doing so would violate an internal lending policy of the institution. Some lenders, for example, may have a policy that all London interbank offered rate (LIBOR) loans be booked in offshore offices (to distinguish LIBOR from other short-term interest rates that may be offered by the lender) and consequently would not want to move those loans to a domestic office. In other cases, transfers to affiliates may use valuable interaffiliate transactional baskets (such as those under Section 23A of the Federal Reserve Act) and thus assignment of the loan could be "disadvantageous" to the lender.

Although the provision illustrated in Box 13.2 (taken from the LSTA's Model Credit Agreement Provisions) confines the obligation of the lenders to mitigate costs solely to changing the booking location of loans, borrowers sometimes request that this obligation be broadened. A borrower might, for example, ask that the lenders take "any and all" actions to eliminate or reduce compensable costs. Even if this request is limited to "reasonable" actions or actions that would not otherwise be "disadvantageous," lenders generally reject this approach because of its breadth and ambiguity.

13.3 THE "YANK-A-BANK" PROVISION

Box 13.3

If any Lender requests compensation under Section [*Increased Costs*], or if the Borrower is required to pay any Indemnified Taxes or additional amounts to any Lender or any Governmental Authority for the account of any Lender pursuant to Section [*Taxes*] and, in each case, such Lender has declined or is unable to designate a different lending office in accordance with Section [*Designation of a Different Lending Office*], or if any Lender is a Defaulting Lender or a Non-Consenting Lender, then the Borrower may, at its sole expense and effort, upon notice to such Lender and the Administrative Agent, require such Lender to assign and delegate, without recourse (in accordance with and subject to the restrictions contained in, and consents required by, Section [*Successors and Assigns*]), all its interests, rights (other than its existing rights to payments pursuant to Section [*Increased Cost*] or Section [*Taxes*]) and obligations under this Agreement and the related Loan Documents to an Eligible Assignee that shall assume such obligations (which assignee may be another Lender, if a Lender accepts such assignment); *provided* that (i) the Borrower shall have paid to the Administrative Agent the assignment fee (if any) specified in Section [*Successors and Assigns*]; (ii) such Lender shall have received payment of an amount equal to the outstanding principal of its Loans and participations in L/C Disbursements, accrued interest thereon, accrued fees and all other amounts payable to it hereunder and under the other Loan Documents (including any amounts under Section [*Breakfunding*]) from the assignee (to the extent of such outstanding principal and accrued interest and fees) or the Borrower (in the case of all other amounts); (iii) in the case of any such assignment resulting from a claim for compensation under Section [*Increased Costs*] or payments required to be made pursuant to Section [*Taxes*], such assignment will result in a reduction in such compensation or payments thereafter; (iv) such assignment does not conflict with applicable law; and (v) in the case of any assignment resulting from a Lender becoming a Non- Consenting Lender, the applicable assignee shall have consented to the applicable amendment, waiver or consent. A Lender shall not be required to make any such assignment or delegation if, prior thereto, as a result of a waiver by such Lender or otherwise, the circumstances entitling the Borrower to require such assignment and delegation cease to apply.

> *"Non-Consenting Lender"* means any Lender that does not approve any consent, waiver or amendment that (i) requires the approval of all or all affected Lenders in accordance with the terms of Section [*Required Consents*] and (ii) has been approved by the Required Lenders [and, in the case of amendments that require the approval of all or all affected Lenders of a particular Class, Required Class Lenders of such Class].

If it is not feasible for a lender to mitigate costs as described in Section 13.2, the so-called "yank-a-bank" provision (usually captioned "Replacement of Lenders") permits a borrower to replace a lender that requests reimbursement for increased costs or taxes. The clause will often also allow the borrower to replace a lender that has been deemed a "defaulting lender" and, as discussed below, to replace a lender who declines to consent to certain waivers or amendments requested by the borrower.

As normally written, the borrower is responsible for finding a replacement lender and also for paying any associated transfer fees or other expenses relating to the substitution. The new lender takes an assignment (and not merely a participation) of loans and commitments from the lender being replaced. The replaced lender is entitled to the full amount of its principal, interest, and any related breakfunding costs or fees (or, if applicable, premium). The fact that the replaced lender has the right to receive 100 cents on the dollar for its loan can make the yank-a-bank an unappealing remedy for the borrower and replacement lender alike if the debt is trading below par in the secondary market. Typically, the replacement must result in a reduction of costs that the borrower would otherwise be required to pay or, in the case of a nonconsenting lender, the replacement with an amenable consenting lender. The borrower cannot, in other words, use the increased cost event as an excuse to rid itself of a lender it does not like solely on the basis of its antipathy. To induce a replacement lender to accept a transfer of the loan, the borrower may, of course, be required to pay a fee to cover, among other things, the transferee's administrative costs and any funding losses it may incur if the current LIBOR is higher than the LIBOR accruing on the transferred loans. Although arguably inconsistent with the principle that the replacement is to result in a reduction of costs, the yank-a-bank provision does not normally limit the right of the borrower to pay inducement fees of this sort.

Language traditionally found in yank-a-bank clauses required a borrower to replace *all* lenders that request coverage for increased costs (if there is more than one), and restricted its right to pick and choose who it wanted to replace (or, perhaps, to replace a lender demanding lesser increased costs than another). Historically, the yank-a-bank provision would not allow replacement of fewer than all such lenders. This practice has now largely disappeared and the language quoted in Box 13.3 (taken from the LSTA's Model Credit Agreement Provisions) is typical—the borrower, at its option, can choose to replace one or some or all of the lenders that request increased costs.

Although considered inadvisable by some lenders, as noted above, a yank-a-bank provision often allows a borrower to replace a lender that has declined to consent to a proposed amendment. This can be a powerful tool not only for the borrower, but also for arrangers (and even lenders) in those cases where all but one or two lenders wish to consent to a modification that they and the borrower agree is beneficial to both the borrower and the lenders—such as one that avoids a cross-default to other debt. If the yank-a-bank clause allows nonconsenting lenders to be yanked, an amendment that needs unanimous or affected lender approval cannot be held up by a small group of lenders trying to extract a higher amendment fee or other concession. The borrower can always replace those lenders with more compliant institutions. It used to be that, in some cases, the aggregate percentage of the lenders that could be so replaced was limited (5 percent was frequently seen), but the market has moved to greater flexibility and there is typically no express cap on the percentage of lenders that can be replaced. Furthermore, while historically replacement was allowed only for issues that required unanimous consent, it is now common to see the yank-a-bank provision apply to consents that require affected lenders as well as those consents that require unanimous lender consent. Whether unanimous lender consents or affected lender consents are at issue, in both cases the required lenders (or required class lenders if applicable) must have provided their consents before the yank-a-bank right is triggered.

As with other assignments under the relevant credit agreement, the formalities for assignment must be complied with to effect the substitution. A replaced lender is obligated to sign an assignment agreement to transfer its loan to the chosen assignee. Should the replaced lender fail to execute and deliver the necessary assignment documentation, some yank-a-bank provisions explicitly authorize the administrative agent to act as attorney in fact for the replaced lender and execute and deliver the assignment documentation on behalf of such lender.

13.4 DOCUMENTATION FROM LENDERS

Box 13.4

A certificate of a Lender or Issuing Bank setting forth the amount or amounts necessary to compensate such Lender or Issuing Bank or its holding company, as the case may be, as specified paragraph (a) [*Increased Costs Generally*] or (b) [*Capital Requirements*] this Section [*Increased Costs*] and delivered to the Borrower, shall be conclusive absent manifest error. The Borrower shall pay such Lender or Issuing Bank, as the case may be, the amount shown as due on any such certificate within 10 days after receipt thereof.

Borrowers request documentation from lenders in four principal situations: requests for yield protection; payments of interest, fees, or expenses; tax forms showing that payments of interest are exempt from withholding; and when effecting a loan assignment. The first of these is illustrated in the language in Box 13.4, taken from the Yield Protection provisions of the LSTA's Model Credit Agreement Provisions and discussed in some detail in Section 3.7.1. It generally applies to the increased costs clause (which covers changes to reserve requirements and taxation), to the capital adequacy clause (which protects the lender against increases to the capital and liquidity costs of the lender or its holding company), and to the breakfunding provision (which compensates the lenders for funding losses in connection with early payments of principal or failures to borrow after a request has been made). A borrower prefers a *certificate* as opposed to a *statement* from a lender. Although there may be little practical difference between the two, a certificate may be perceived as having greater formality and perhaps making it easier for a borrower to assert fraud or misrepresentation on the part of the lender in the event the determination by the lender is incorrect.

The second type of documentation that borrowers frequently request from lenders is a statement of the amount of interest, fees, or reimbursable expenses due—an invoice, in effect. Although lenders may provide such statements in the normal course, they resist any contractual requirement to do so. To begin with, no lender or administrative agent wants to give an excuse to a borrower not to pay. "I received no invoice, so nothing was due and payable" is not an argument any lender or agent wants to hear. Rather, a credit agreement (like a bond indenture or private placement) provides simply that interest and principal (and fees and expenses) are due and payable on fixed dates; the responsibility to make timely payment is left to the borrower. Default occurs if the borrower fails to make that payment regardless of whether it has received a piece of paper with a calculation of what is owed.

Third, the taxes clause of a credit agreement normally includes a right on the part of the borrower to request documentation that either minimizes taxes for which the borrower must pay a gross-up or evidences that a lender is entitled to an exemption from withholding. Also for tax-related reasons, recent credit agreements have increasingly required lenders to maintain a participant register, akin to the register held by the administrative agent, denoting any participations that it has sold in its loans. For more discussion of the participant register, see Section 11.3. Although the participant register is not required to be disclosed to the borrower, each lender who maintains a participant register does so as a nonfiduciary agent of the borrower, which mirrors the administrative agent's maintenance of the loan register as agent for the borrower. In both situations, the borrower taxpayer is required to have a withholding agent under U.S. tax rules.

Fourth, lenders are generally required to make available documentation in connection with loan assignments. When loan assignments are subject to borrower consent, the borrower will be provided with the name of the assignee and other information set forth in the related Assignment and Assumption. Increasingly, loan trading is conducted via electronic platforms so no actual "documents" are provided but nonetheless information, whether in documentary paper form or otherwise, is provided by the agent to the borrower.

13.5 IMPLIED COVENANT OF GOOD FAITH AND FAIR DEALING; NO IMPLIED FIDUCIARY DUTIES

There is a general principle of New York law that every contract contains an implied covenant of "good faith and fair dealing." See *Dalton v. Educ. Testing Serv.*, 87 N.Y.2d 384 (1995). No party to an agreement may do anything that has the effect of destroying or injuring the right of the other parties "to receive the fruits of the contract." In the context of a credit agreement, this has been held in certain cases to limit the ability of a lender to exercise remedies, at least without reasonable prior notice (even though the underlying agreement says no notice is necessary). In the case of *K.M.C. Co. v. Irving Trust Co.*, 757 F.2d 752 (6th Cir. 1985), all funds generated by the borrower in the ordinary course of its business were required to be deposited directly into a blocked account under the control of the lender. The court held that, since the exercise of remedies by the lender effectively left the entire existence of the borrower "at the whim or mercy" of the lender, the lender had such a degree of control over the borrower and its funds that the lender could not decline to make the balance of the unused commitments available to the borrower without prior notice even though the financing agreement itself gave the lender that right. The lender's termination of credit available to the borrower was held to constitute a breach by the lender of its covenant of "good faith and fair dealing." At least one court has found a lender to have breached the implied covenant of good faith and fair dealing when it entered into a nonstandard participation agreement that the court believed amounted to a disguised assignment. In the case of *Empresas Cablevision, S.A.B. De C.V. v. JPMorgan Chase Bank, N.A.*, 680 F. Supp. 2d 625 (S.D.N.Y 2010), the court found JPMorgan to have evaded a borrower's right to veto a loan assignment by effecting the trade via this bespoke participation agreement.

A breach of the implied covenant of good faith can hurt a lender in two ways. First, it could be used as a defense by the borrower to an action by a lender that seeks to collect on the debt. Second, it could subject the lender to damage claims, including potentially extreme damage claims, at least in the absence of a waiver of any right on the part of the borrower to assert consequential damages against the lenders (inclusion of such a waiver is normally the case; see Section 12.6). In the *K.M.C. Co.* decision, the lender was ordered to pay damages measured by the potential value of the business purportedly destroyed by its actions ($7,500,000), more than double the amount of the loan facility itself ($3,500,000).

The duty of good faith and fair dealing is not without limits, and no obligation can be implied that would be inconsistent with other terms of the contractual relationship. Nevertheless, some worry that courts might expand the implied covenant of good faith and fair dealing beyond the *K.M.C. Co.* facts and apply it in a broader range of cases, such as when a lender exercises remedies based upon allegedly technical or nonmaterial breaches of the agreement. Indeed, breach of the implied covenant of good faith is routinely raised in litigation between borrowers and lenders, though the instances in which a court actually finds such a breach on the part of lenders are relatively rare.

The implied covenant of good faith should not be confused with the question of whether a lender owes a fiduciary duty to the borrower. New York law generally provides that the usual relationship between a borrower and a lender is purely contractual (that of debtor and creditor) and does not give rise to a fiduciary relationship between the lender and the borrower (or any guarantors). See *SNS Bank, N.V. v. Citibank, N.A.*, 777 N.Y.S.2d 62 (App. Div. 1st Dep't 2004) and *Aaron Ferer & Sons, Ltd. v. Chase Manhattan Bank, Nat'l Ass'n*, 731 F.2d 112 (2d Cir. 1984). Courts have held this to be the rule even if an entity has borrowed money from the same lender for several years. If the rule were otherwise and a lender were deemed a fiduciary in a lending relationship, it would radically alter the borrower–lender relationship. A fiduciary owes a duty of paramount loyalty to its beneficiary, even to the extent of subordinating its own interests and profits to that of its beneficiary. Were a lender a fiduciary, its ability to demand payment of a loan after default and to exercise remedies might be limited by what is best for the borrower rather than what is appropriate for the lender, and thus severely constrain the lender's exercise of its carefully negotiated rights. Because the consequences of being deemed a fiduciary are so dramatic, lenders will typically require an express (and increasingly lengthy) provision under which the borrower will have disclaimed and waived any fiduciary or extracontractual claims against the lenders and their affiliates.

13.6 THE RIGHT TO DESIGNATE ADDITIONAL BORROWERS

Credit agreements sometimes permit the borrower to designate subsidiaries or, less frequently, affiliates as additional borrowers. This right is often granted with respect to foreign subsidiaries, when for tax or other reasons, such as currency availability or the need for immediate funding in the subsidiary's time zone, the subsidiary needs direct access to funds. Typically, in the case of subsidiary borrowers, the subsidiary is required to be a wholly-owned subsidiary in order to avoid loan proceeds going to benefit parties outside of the credit group and beyond the reach of the secured parties. The obligations of the subsidiary borrowers are guaranteed by the borrower as well as each other subsidiary borrower. Absent such a borrower guarantee, any such borrower designation would normally require an independent credit approval (and hence consent) by each affected lender.

Designation of an additional borrower (even when its obligations under the agreement are to be fully guaranteed by the initial borrower) can raise issues for the lenders, including, among others, whether under applicable laws the lender can legally extend credit to such new borrower (particularly if the new borrower is a foreign borrower) and relatedly whether the lender is operationally set up to extend credit, issue letters of credit, and make other accommodations for any such new borrower.

Also the multiple borrower issues, discussed in Section 4.12, will require attention and, to the extent such new borrower is a foreign subsidiary, deemed dividend issues discussed in Section 8.6, may arise. Credit agreements often set out in an exhibit a form of "Designation Letter" pursuant to which the subsidiary or affiliate is designated as a new borrower and the new borrower makes certain basic representations to the lenders. Although the guarantee by the initial borrower is stated to be absolute and unconditional regardless of any defense that the new borrower may have (such as illegality of the credit agreement), the lenders do not want to invite litigation or contravene local law even if it is not directly applicable to them. The lenders therefore want the new borrower to make the usual legal representations to confirm that it is duly organized; that its obligations under the credit agreement are duly authorized; that the agreement is legal, valid, binding, and enforceable; and that all requisite government approvals in connection with the credit agreement have been obtained while also requiring delivery of officer certificates and legal opinions supporting such representations. The lender also needs to collect information with respect to the new designated borrower under the PATRIOT Act's "know your customer" rules and comply with OFAC regulations (see Section 5.1.11.5).

13.7 EQUITY CURE RIGHTS

As discussed in Section 9.1, a breach of the credit agreement con-stitutes an event of default only so long as the breach continues. If a borrower fails to pay an installment of principal and then 10 days later (before the lenders have accelerated the maturity of the loans) pays the full amount that is past due, the event of default that originally arose upon failure to pay no longer continues. It has been cured (so long as the credit agreement contains the requirement that the default be continu-ing to constitute an event of default) and the lenders may no longer be able to accelerate the loans.

By their nature, certain types of breaches cannot be cured. If a borrower defaults on an interest coverage covenant at the end of a fiscal quarter, no cure is possible (at least without time travel). Interest coverage measures aggregate earnings before interest, taxes, depreciation, and amortization (EBITDA) for a period (often the most recent four fiscal quarters) against interest payable in respect of that period (see Section 7.4). Once the period has elapsed and the borrower compiles its financial results and realizes that a default has occurred it is too late to fix the breach. It cannot retroactively either increase EBITDA or reduce interest paid or accrued.

However, a different result occurs if the credit agreement contains an equity cure rights provision. An equity cure right grants the borrower a period within which it can wipe out a financial covenant default after the fact, even though it is otherwise incurable. Under the cover of equity cure rights, borrowers are provided an alternative to approaching lenders for default waivers and forbearance requests and the accompanying fees that may be associated with such requests. Therefore an equity cure right provides valuable flexibility to a borrower. During the cure period, the lenders are barred from accelerating the loans or exercising other remedies even though an event of default exists. Taking the example of an interest coverage default, the borrower might be allowed to cure a default if (1) its parent puts in additional cash equity capital or subordinated debt, (2) the borrower applies the proceeds thereof to repay outstanding loans or other senior interest-bearing debt, and (3) the interest coverage ratio, when recalculated on a *pro forma* basis (as if the amount of debt outstanding during the period covered by the covenant were reduced by the amount of the repayment), at least equals the level required at the end of the relevant period. Another approach might allow the borrower to treat the infusion of capital as additional EBITDA for the relevant period to the extent necessary to bring the covenant into compliance after the fact. The former requires a larger infusion of funds compared to the latter and is therefore favored by lenders (if a cure right is to be granted at all). While lenders are barred from exercising remedies during the cure period, typically borrowers are also subject to consequences during a cure period since a continuing event of default does in fact exist. Namely, a typical equity cure provision will expressly stipulate that revolving credit facilities under the credit agreement are unavailable during a cure period and prior to a cure being effected.

Lenders may be reluctant to include equity cure rights in a credit agreement, not only because they defer a potential acceleration, but also because they disrupt the performance benchmarks the covenants are designed to measure. Curing a financial covenant breach by allowing an infusion of equity or subordinated debt to reduce senior debt or to bump up EBITDA may do nothing to solve the underlying problem of low earnings. There is no assurance that the borrower's parent will make a similar injection of funds in the succeeding quarter should EBITDA continue to slide. For these reasons, equity cure rights, if granted at all, are subject to limits. To begin with, they are usually exercisable only during a relatively short period, the duration of which is subject to negotiation, but typically runs up to 10 to 15 days *after* the date upon which financial statements for the relevant accounting period are (or are required to be) delivered. The reasoning here is that the borrower should have time after a default is verified (and the amount of any cure payment calculated) before the cure right expires. In addition, the frequency and number of times they may be exercised is often limited, for example, by disallowing use in consecutive fiscal quarters or restricting total exercises in any period of four fiscal quarters or over the term of the credit agreement. The borrower is thus precluded from indefinitely extending the day of reckoning as its business declines. Also the amount of the permitted cure amount may be capped at an amount solely equal to comply with the relevant covenant and not a dollar more. The cap on the cure amount prohibits an "overcure" thereby limiting the masking effect on the underlying performance of the business. Cure rights, as in the illustration above, are also not commonly granted unless a parent holding company or other equity holder invests additional monies into the borrower either as equity capital or subordinated debt. In other words, the borrower is not usually permitted to cure the breach after the fact by taking funds on hand and reducing debt or "increasing" EBITDA.

Where a credit agreement contains a leverage-based pricing grid for the determination of the interest spread or contains incurrence-based covenants that permit a borrower to take an action so long as its debt to EBITDA or EBITDA to fixed charges or interest ratios are sufficiently healthy, the artificial inflation of EBITDA from an equity cure presents unwanted and, from a lender's perspective, unmerited benefit and flexibility for the borrower. Therefore it is commonly made clear in the equity cure provision that EBITDA is deemed to be increased only for the narrow purpose of calculating the financial covenant ratios for cure purposes and not, for example, for purposes of calculating ratios for interest rate pricing grid purposes. Also equity cure contributions are not included for purposes of negative covenant exceptions in the form of builder baskets (see Section 7.6). Once the equity contribution has been made, the borrower then will need to find a restricted payment covenant exception to reverse gears and distribute such contributed equity in the form of a dividend.

Because of reluctance on the part of lenders to accept equity cure rights, the provision tends to wax and wane with market conditions. In a market in which competitive pressures among lenders are particularly strong, and especially where a borrower's parent companies are financial sponsors, one is more likely to encounter robust equity cure rights. In other circumstances, equity cure rights are nonexistent or significantly diluted.

A cure right should not be confused with a grace period (see Section 9.1). A grace period determines when a breach ripens from a mere default into an event of default that can be the basis for immediate acceleration by the lenders. If a failure to pay interest enjoys a five-day grace period, the borrower can cure the breach by paying the defaulted interest at any time during the five-day period. It can also cure the breach by paying the defaulted interest after the expiration of the grace period if there has been no acceleration of the loan. A cure right, by contrast, does at least two things more. First, as described above, in the case of an otherwise incurable breach (such as an interest coverage ratio), a cure right allows the borrower to wipe out a default entirely; a grace period does nothing more than give the borrower talking time with the lenders before the event of default kicks in. This is true even if both the borrower and the lenders know with certainty that the financial statements for the relevant fiscal period will, when delivered, show a default. Second, also as noted earlier, a cure right for financial covenants is typically tacked on to the period within which financial statements for the relevant period must be delivered. By way of example, if the borrower has 60 days after the end of a fiscal quarter in which to furnish financial statements and the cure period is an additional 15 days beyond, the lenders are effectively barred from accelerating for a 75-day period after the end of the fiscal period (the date the breach actually occurs). Cure rights provisions are thus both more powerful and of longer duration than simple grace periods.

13.8 CONFIDENTIALITY

> ### Box 13.5
>
> Each of the Administrative Agent, the Lenders, and the Issuing Banks agree to maintain the confidentiality of the Information (as defined below), except that Information may be disclosed (a) to its Affiliates and to its Related Parties (it being understood that the Persons to whom such disclosure is made will be informed of the confidential nature of such Information and instructed to keep such Information confidential); (b) to the extent required or requested by any regulatory authority purporting to have jurisdiction over such person or its Related Parties (including any self-regulatory authority, such as the National Association of Insurance Commissioners); (c) to the extent required by applicable laws or regulations or by any subpoena or similar legal process; (d) to any other party hereto; (e) in connection with the exercise of any remedies hereunder or under any other Loan Document or any action or proceeding relating to this Agreement or any other Loan Document or the enforcement of rights hereunder or thereunder; (f) subject to an agreement containing provisions substantially the same as those of this Section, to (i) any assignee

of or Participant in, or any prospective assignee of or Participant in, any of its rights and obligations under this Agreement or (ii) any actual or prospective party (or its Related Parties) to any swap, derivative or other transaction under which payments are to be made by reference to the Borrower and its obligations, this Agreement or payments hereunder (it being understood that the DQ List may be disclosed to any assignee or Participant, or prospective assignee or Participant, in reliance on this clause (f)); (g) on a confidential basis to (i) any rating agency in connection with rating the Borrower or its Subsidiaries or the Facilities or (ii) the CUSIP Service Bureau or any similar agency in connection with the issuance and monitoring of CUSIP numbers with respect to the Facilities; (h) with the consent of the Borrower; or (i) to the extent such Information (x) becomes publicly available other than as a result of a breach of this Section or (y) becomes available to the Administrative Agent, any Lender , any Issuing Bank or any of their respective Affiliates on a nonconfidential basis from a source other than the Borrower. In addition, the Administrative Agent and the Lenders may disclose the existence of this Agreement and information about this Agreement to market data collectors, similar service providers to the lending industry and service providers to the Agents and the Lenders in connection with the administration of this Agreement, the other Loan Documents, and the Commitments.

For purposes of this Section, *"Information"* means all information received from the Borrower or any of its Subsidiaries relating to the Borrower or any of its Subsidiaries or any of their respective businesses, other than any such information that is available to the Administrative Agent, any Lender or any Issuing Bank on a nonconfidential basis prior to disclosure by the Borrower or any of its Subsidiaries; *provided* that, in the case of information received from the Borrower or any of its Subsidiaries after the date hereof, such information is clearly identified at the time of delivery as confidential. Any Person required to maintain the confidentiality of Information as provided in this Section shall be considered to have complied with its obligation to do so if such Person has exercised the same degree of care to maintain the confidentiality of such Information as such Person would accord to its own confidential information.

13.8.1   The Confidentiality Clause

Credit agreements require borrowers to deliver (both in writing and sometimes orally in calls or in meetings) a substantial volume of financial and other information to lenders. This substantial information flow can be broadly divided into four basic categories. The first category is public information. Public information may include information included in a press release, posted on the borrower's corporate website, or otherwise generally disseminated. The second category is confidential information that a borrower provides (typically through an administrative agent or arranger) to its lenders or prospective lenders. Regular financial reports, borrowing requests, amendments, and other similar information made available to the entire lender syndicate are included in this category. Such information is referred to as "syndicate information." The third category is comprised of confidential information not meant to be shared with the entire lending group (and therefore is not syndicate information) due to its highly sensitive nature and is disclosed on a limited and less than syndicate-wide basis. This category is referred to as "borrower restricted information." Proprietary information provided to a lender's steering committee during the course of a restructuring negotiation would be characterized as borrower restricted information. Finally, there is confidential information that does not contain any material nonpublic information, or MNPI. Such information is deemed "bank loan nonrestricting information." Borrower information not containing MNPI is deemed as nonrestricting because recipients are not restricted under federal securities law from trading securities of the borrower on the basis of mere receipt of this type of information. The antifraud and related provisions of the U.S. federal securities laws generally prohibit the trading of securities while in possession of MNPI relating to the issuer. Therefore a recipient of MNPI is restricted from trading in the borrower's securities. Both syndicate information and borrower restricted information may contain MNPI and therefore the handling of such information raises concerns for the recipient and borrower alike. For the recipient, there is a clear risk that it becomes tainted with MNPI and can't trade in the borrower's securities. On the borrower's side, public reporting borrowers will have to consider the Securities and Exchange Commission's (SEC's) Regulation FD, which prohibits selective disclosure of MNPI. Although revealing information to lenders without disclosing it publicly could be deemed "selective" disclosure, Regulation FD contains an exemption for information delivered pursuant to a confidentiality agreement. The confidentiality clause discussed below serves that purpose. The important point to note here is that while not all confidential information is MNPI, there is always the risk that confidential information may at times contain MNPI. For more on the treatment of confidential information and MNPI in the loan market see "Statement of Principles for the Communication and Use of Confidential Information by Loan Market Participants" (December 2006).

However the information is characterized, with the exception of public information, borrowers want this sensitive information kept confidential. Disclosure could adversely affect their position with customers, competitors, and employees. A confidentiality provision in the credit agreement is meant to protect against such adverse disclosure. The fairly typical example in Box 13.5 is the confidentiality clause from the LSTA's Model Credit Agreement Provisions.

Many wonder why a confidentiality clause in a credit agreement is even necessary. After all, are banks not already required by law to keep information they receive from their customers confidential? This is a common misconception. Absent an agreement, there is no general legal duty imposed upon lenders, as such, to keep information confidential. The confusion may originate from a 1961 Idaho Supreme Court decision that held that a deposit by a customer in a bank created an implied contract that no information be disclosed by a bank concerning its customer or the customer's account. See *Peterson v. Idaho First Nat'l Bank*, 367 P.2d 284 (Idaho 1961). The court used fearsome and expansive language to describe the bank's duty to its customer. "Inviolate secrecy is one of the inherent and fundamental precepts of the relationship of the bank and its customers or depositors" (367 P.2d at 290). This pronouncement notwithstanding, the *Peterson* holding has not been expanded beyond the narrow relationship of deposit-taking. Subsequent decisions in New York and other states have held that a "mere debtor–creditor relationship," such as that which arises when a loan is made, does not give rise to a duty of confidentiality, at least when a bank does not broadcast the information to the public. See *Graney Development Corp. v. Taksen*, 400 N.Y.S.2d 717 (Sup. Ct. Monroe County 1978) and *ADT Operations, Inc. v. Chase Manhattan Bank, N.A.*, 662 N.Y.S.2d 190 (Sup. Ct. N.Y. County 1997). This rule may not help a lender that also acts as an arranger and has undertaken to advise a borrower on its strategic plans or a restructuring. But it does mean that, in the typical loan relationship, if a borrower wants to obligate the lender to keep information confidential, the credit agreement must include a confidentiality clause.

Confidentiality provisions have developed over the years into a format generally consistent with the LSTA language shown in Box 13.5. A number of relatively standard qualifiers have also developed.

To begin with, the confidentiality undertaking customarily applies only to "information." Often, this term is defined. Typically, it encompasses any information that (1) is received from (or on behalf of) the borrower, (2) relates to the borrower, and (3) is clearly identified as confidential at the time of delivery. The last requirement (identification) merits some discussion. It is not uniformly included in confidentiality clauses. Borrowers, from their perspective, argue that *all* information sent by them to lenders should be treated confidentially, notwithstanding that a borrower–lender relationship does not give rise to a general duty of secrecy. Lenders counter that if a borrower really wants information to remain confidential the borrower should take the (relatively) simple step of clearly identifying it as "confidential." (Identification for these purposes need not be limited to a red-letter caption on the information itself, but could be as simple as a cover memorandum or e-mail that indicates confidentiality). Lenders also counter, in the case of companies that are public filers, that they will not know whether information is confidential or is public without it being appropriately identified. Even in the case of nonpublic companies, a lender may plead that there should be no duty of nondisclosure as to information received from third-party sources and not identified as being confidential.

This is not to say that information, unless otherwise identified (or known to be) as confidential, will be blithely published by lenders to third parties. As a practical matter lenders are not in the habit of broadcasting financial information, whether public or not. Nevertheless, knowing whether information is confidential is relevant to a lender's day-to-day operations in several ways. For example, arrangers often include comparative financial information when preparing pitch pieces for new business. Knowing the boundaries of what is public and what is not helps assure that nonpublic information is kept confidential. In addition, although under the typical confidentiality provision, lenders are free to share confidential information with affiliates, they may not want to give such information to affiliates (such as the trading desk) that limit themselves exclusively to public information and will not want to risk any such confidential information being further deemed to be material non-public information. Having a clear understanding of what is confidential and what is not helps the lender with its own compliance requirements under the securities laws.

In addition to defining the scope of the information that is subject to the confidentiality undertaking, the typical clause also sets out a number of common exceptions. These are discussed briefly in Sections 13.8.1.1 through 13.8.1.8.

13.8.1.1 Disclosure to Regulators

Banks are subject to examination by regulators: the Comptroller of the Currency, in the case of national banks, and the Federal Deposit Insurance Corporation, in the case of most state banks, as well as the Board of Governors of the Federal Reserve for any bank that is a member of the Federal Reserve system. In addition, certain institutional lenders (insurance companies are an example) have created self-regulatory bodies that undertake a similar examination function. An examiner has broad so-called "visitation rights," which allow it to see basically any customer file (including loan files) held by a bank. By law, the bank must allow unfettered access to examiners. Any confidentiality clause, to be workable, needs to permit such access; carveouts for regulatory authorities (governmental and self-regulatory) have therefore become routine.

13.8.1.2   Disclosure Required by Law or Subpoena

Although sharing information with regulators, as discussed above, is probably the best example, other disclosures might also be "required by law." For example, a bank might be required under securities laws to disclose information about specific loans in default, or under bankruptcy laws if a court mandates disclosure of financial information as part of a valuation hearing. Similarly, a subpoena delivered to a lender that orders delivery of loan files has the force of law. The last thing that a lender wants to face is a choice between breaching a confidentiality agreement to keep documents secret and ignoring a court order to produce those same documents. For these reasons, it has become customary for confidentiality provisions to allow disclosure required by law or subpoena.

13.8.1.3   Disclosure to Other Agreement Parties

Another common exception to the confidentiality undertaking permits disclosure to any other party to the credit agreement. This may seem like an obvious point, but can have unexpected consequences. For example, it means that if a lender exercises its right under the information or visitation covenant to obtain additional financial detail from the borrower, the lender is free to share whatever it obtains with the administrative agent and any other lender. Distribution of information to one lender should therefore be seen as distribution to all. This is logical. Except in certain special deal structures, all of the lenders in a credit agreement hold claims of the same rank against the borrower; it follows that the lenders must be able to discuss their legal position vis-à-vis the borrower without the constraint of the confidentiality clause. Any other approach could complicate the lenders' exercise of remedies or the dialogue that lenders engage in when they debate a difficult amendment or waiver.

13.8.1.4   Exercise of Remedies

Another common exception to the confidentiality clause permits disclosure of information in connection with the exercise of remedies or the enforcement of rights under the credit agreement. This is an exception born of necessity. For example, to prove the existence of a material default (and thus justify acceleration), lenders may need to disclose financial information in court. Similarly, in a bankruptcy proceeding, lenders may be forced to introduce financial statements (projected cash flows, for example) as part of a fight to resist the use of cash collateral or to obtain adequate protection if use of cash collateral is to be allowed. Without an exception for enforcement action the ability of the lenders to recover their loan could be significantly impaired.

Some confidentiality clauses confuse the exercise of remedies exception with the subpoena exception and assume that the latter is sufficient to cover the former. This is incorrect. When a lender uses information in its possession to pursue an action, no subpoena is involved. A lender does not subpoena information it already has. Subpoenas are employed when a party wishes to obtain information held by another, or when a third party wants to obtain information in the possession of the lender.

13.8.1.5 Under Confidentiality Agreement

As discussed in Chapter 11, a lender's ability to "manage its portfolio" through selling assignments or participations in the loans held by it is critical to its managing risk. However, no one wants to take an assignment or purchase a participation without first reviewing financial information relating to the borrower. If the borrower is a public filer, the requisite information is likely available in an instant off the Internet. For nonpublic borrowers, however, the lender may need to supply confidential information it possesses to the prospective purchaser before the purchaser even considers acquiring an interest in the loan. The borrower, of course, wants the purchaser to be bound by the confidentiality clause to the same extent as the selling lender. Hence, there has developed a customary exception that permits disclosure in connection with assignments and participations if the intended assignee or participant agrees to keep the information confidential, consistent with the clause in the credit agreement. In recent years as the size and sophistication of the secondary loan trading market, not to mention the ecosystem of intermediaries supporting this market, have expanded, the universe of parties potentially dealing in borrower information has likewise expanded. The enlarged role of rating agencies in the loan market is a primary example of this trend. For example, in 2009 Standard & Poor's reported rating approximately 230 leveraged loans globally; in 2013 the number of rated loans had more than quadrupled to approximately 930 loans globally. In connection with each rating, the rating agencies will undertake a similar credit analysis to that performed by lenders and will likewise require access to similar types of borrower information which may include the confidential variety. As reflected in Box 13.5, the customary exception permitting confidential information disclosure will often include disclosures to rating agencies. Disclosure to the CUSIP Service Bureau is also increasingly permitted as industry-wide efforts to assign CUSIP identifier numbers to syndicated loans have gained momentum.

Another category of confidentiality exceptions relates to the disqualified lender list. A borrower may not want the world to know that it or its financial sponsor has effectively blacklisted specified financial institutions from holding its loan obligations. Therefore, disqualified lender lists are commonly treated as confidential information. Balanced against the borrower's desire for confidentiality, however, is the loan market participants' desire to maintain a secondary market that is as liquid and frictionless as possible. With this aim in mind, the LSTA's proposed best practices (embodied in the LSTA's Market Advisory, "Disqualified Institutions/DQ Structure" dated February 20, 2015) advocate for regular and free lender access to the disqualified lender list. Regular and free lender access can be accomplished by having the administrative agent post the list to the online platform, if there is one, for all lenders to see and/or to make the list available upon inquiry to any lender who asks, which is the approach taken in the LSTA's model provisions. Permitting disclosure in this fashion facilitates overall secondary market liquidity as lenders are effectively put on notice of the identity of prohibited parties and are in a better position to avoid entering into trades with such prohibited parties. At the same time, a borrower's sensitive information is managed in a way that is consistent with other confidential borrower information.

Also, with the recent growth of credit default swaps and other derivative transactions in the loan market, the scope of parties requiring disclosure of borrower information has likewise expanded to include counterparties under such arrangements. These parties are effectively making credit decisions like any lender and likewise need financial and other borrower information in order to underwrite. Therefore specific exceptions to permit disclosure to swap or similar counterparties is customarily included. An example of such exception can be seen in Box 13.5.

Some credit agreements attach as an exhibit a form of confidentiality agreement to be executed by prospective assignees and participants before they are supplied information on the borrower. This has the advantage of providing a form ready-at-hand for execution. Borrowers may also prefer this approach because it eliminates any ambiguity as to exactly what a prospective holder must agree to. It has the disadvantage of locking in the parties to particular language on a deal-specific basis rather than letting the lender and potential assignee or participant rely upon a master confidentiality agreement applicable to all transactions between the two. The LSTA has published a form of Master Confidentiality Agreement for such purposes.

13.8.1.6   With Consent of Borrower

This is perhaps an obvious exception to the confidentiality clause. A confidentiality undertaking is for the benefit of the borrower; if the borrower consents to disclosure, the disclosing lender should not be in breach of the clause. Note that the standard notice provision requires that all consents (including this one) be in writing (see Section 12.1). As a practical matter many lenders are content with oral authorization from the borrower. Nevertheless, from the perspective of the lender it is far better to follow the old adage—"get it in writing."

13.8.1.7   Information Already Public

Confidentiality clauses typically do not apply to information that is either already public (other than as a result of a breach of the clause) or that becomes available to the lenders on a nonconfidential basis. Of course, the carveout for information already public would probably be read into the clause even if not expressly stated; once information is publicly available, a borrower would be hard-pressed to prove that disclosure by a lender results in any damage. The carveout for information that a lender obtains independently might also be effectively read in for the same reasons, though it protects the lender in a different scenario. A lender can implement controls relatively easily over information it receives directly from the borrower (assuming the information is clearly identified at the time of delivery as being confidential). Not so for information that comes from third parties. Such information is more likely to fall outside of any controls and thus disclosure by the lender could trap it into a breach of the clause absent a carveout.

13.8.1.8   Confidential Tax Treatment

Some credit agreements contain a general carveout for matters that relate to the "tax treatment" of the credit facility. A typical formulation provides that the borrower may ". . . disclose to any and all persons, without limitation of any kind, the U.S. tax treatment and U.S. tax structure of the facility and all materials of any kind (including opinions and other tax analyses) that are provided to it relating to such U.S. tax treatment and U.S. tax structure."

This language arose out of an early, misguided, version of regulations issued by the Internal Revenue Services (IRS) in 2003 designed to crack down on confidential tax structures or schemes. The regulations required parties participating in any transaction (these would have included lenders under credit agreements) to submit a report to the IRS disclosing the existence of the transaction. Basically, the rule was that if the "tax treatment" (broadly defined) of a transaction was confidential, it must be reported to the IRS. The regulations, however, presumed that a transaction was not "confidential" if express written authorization allowed the parties to disclose to any person, without limitations, the transaction's tax treatment and tax structure and all materials provided to them, including opinions and other tax analyses. The standard confidentiality provision such as the sample set out in Box 13.5 makes *all* information confidential, including information that relates to the tax treatment of the credit facility. This would have meant that lenders arguably were required to file a report with the IRS describing any credit agreement that contained a confidentiality clause. No one (neither borrowers nor lenders) wanted the responsibility of doing this or to highlight a transaction to the IRS that was otherwise plain vanilla. Consequently, credit agreements quickly began to insert language like that quoted in Box 13.5 to defeat any argument that the tax treatment of the transaction was confidential and thus needed to be reported.

Thankfully, the IRS in December 2003 narrowed the regulations to require reporting only if an advisor (but not the parties to the transaction) is entitled to fees in excess of certain thresholds and restricts disclosure of the transaction's tax structure and tax treatment with the object of protecting the confidentiality of the advisor's tax strategies. As a result, two parties to an agreement that imposes confidentiality on each other in ordinary course commercial transactions generally should not trigger the "reportable transaction" rules. However, if the loans provided under a credit facility are part of a larger transaction that utilizes a sophisticated tax strategy, particularly when the institution that makes the loan or its affiliates have advisory involvement (such as financing a cross-border merger in which a complex loan structure is designed to minimize taxes), the lenders might be required to report (or at least confirm that the borrower has reported) the transaction to the IRS.

Despite the narrower regulation (and its likely inapplicability), some lenders out of an excess of caution continue to insert the tax treatment exception into confidentiality provisions. In addition, lenders may see the exception in older credit agreements. This fact notwithstanding, the appearance of the tax treatment qualifier is becoming increasingly rare.

13.8.2 Remedies

What are the remedies available to a borrower if the confidentiality covenant in a credit agreement is breached by a lender? Agreements are generally silent on this point. The standard language in most credit agreements provides that the borrower's obligations are absolute and that it cannot assert a counterclaim against a lender as an excuse not to make payment (see Section 4.1.4). That leaves the borrower with a damage claim against any breaching lender, though the indemnification provision normally restricts the borrower from asserting consequential or punitive damages (see Section 12.6). However, proving direct damages, as opposed to speculative damage, to its business may be difficult. Some agreements may also incorporate an express acknowledgment on the part of the lenders that damages from a breach of the clause are difficult to measure and that, accordingly, the borrower should be entitled to obtain an injunction to prevent breach of the clause by a lender. Though not particularly objectionable to a lender, such language in most instances does not help the borrower; rarely will the borrower discover in advance that information is to be released.

13.8.3 Use Restrictions

Sometimes, as part of a confidentiality clause, borrowers request that lenders agree to a so-called use restriction to the effect that information disclosed to lenders be used only "in connection with" the loans or the credit agreement. This can be problematic. Most banks have a single internal credit review function for all business dealings with a borrower, including loans, derivatives transactions, cash management services, letters of credit, deposit services, and the like. Revealing information to a credit officer in connection with a credit agreement necessarily means the information is being used for other purposes as well. In addition, in their overall portfolio management lenders want freedom to use all information available to them from any source that relates to their borrower customers, arguably a use that is not "in connection with" a specific agreement. Thus, from the standpoint of the lenders, use restrictions are not terribly practical, and are infrequently seen in credit agreements. To the extent found at all, a use restriction may simply have the lenders affirm that they are aware of their responsibilities under applicable securities laws and will not use any information "in contravention of" the securities laws. Even the latter is not required under Regulation FD if a confidentiality agreement is in force, as the SEC has made clear in its *Manual of Publicly Available Telephone Interpretations.*

Simply because a credit agreement permits disclosure to affiliates and does not incorporate a use restriction does not exempt a lender and its affiliates from complying with restrictions under the securities laws against using material nonpublic information in buying or selling securities.

13.8.4   Destruction of Records

Confidentiality provisions sometimes require a lender to "destroy" information once the loan has been paid off or, in the case of an institution that is considering an assignment or participation, once the institution has determined that it does not want to take the assignment or participation. Although superficially reasonable, such a requirement raises a number of issues. To begin with, bank lenders may be subject to regulatory constraints on the destruction of records even after a loan has been repaid. Bank examiners may expect to be able to review past loan files to determine whether a practice they see is common or an aberration. In addition, most lenders (bank and nonbank) have internal policies mandating the retention of loan documentation files at least until relevant statutes of limitations have passed. No lender wants to be faced with a lender liability claim lodged by a borrower and not have access to its historical loan files.

Destruction of such information may also run up against a technological hurdle. Given that financial information and other records are now almost uniformly transmitted by e-mail and stored on computer files, how exactly is it feasible to destroy anything? Mere deletion of the relevant computer files is not sufficient given the availability of sophisticated recovery software. Locating the files to be deleted may be impracticable given the ease with which information can disseminate to computers within an organization. Information is not necessarily stored in institution-wide databases only, but may also be stored on employee hard drives. Even assuming, therefore, that a lender was willing to destroy borrower-supplied information, given the near-impossibility of destroying all computer records, a certification of destruction may simply be untrue. As a consequence, any request that files be wiped clean of information supplied by a borrower may be impossible for a careful lender to agree to. Probably the best that a lender could say is that *physical* copies had been destroyed.

For these reasons, most confidentiality clauses do not include an undertaking on the part of lenders to destroy borrower information.

13.9 LOAN BUYBACKS

13.9.1 Documentary Impediments

For a variety of reasons, borrowers have always wanted to be able to pay lenders on a nonratable basis, either through selective voluntary prepayments or by selective repurchases of loans. Many provisions, however, in the typical credit agreement historically prohibited exactly this type of action. To begin with, as discussed in Section 10.4, most agreements required that any voluntary prepayment of the loans of any tranche be applied ratably to the loans in that tranche. It is not permissible for a borrower to, say, favor lender A by prepaying it in full while leaving lenders B through Z to continue holding the principal amount of their loans. Apart from constituting a breach of the agreement, any such prepayment would have triggered the obligations of the receiving lender under the sharing clause (see Section 10.5) thus forcing the lender to share the proceeds with other lenders in the same tranche through purchasing participations (or taking assignments) of an appropriate percentage of their loans. Many credit agreements also historically precluded a borrower from repurchasing its loans (whether selectively or ratably), and many agreements went further to preclude affiliates or subsidiaries from doing the same. Even if a credit agreement were to permit such a repurchase, the sharing provisions would again have prevented any lender from retaining the proceeds of the repurchase since it would be required to share those proceeds with the other lenders in the tranche.

Other impediments to prepaying or repurchasing loans were also found in the typical credit agreement. A purchase of a loan by the borrower or a subsidiary may constitute an investment prohibited by the investments covenant (see Section 7.6.8). In addition, the cash flow mandatory prepayment (see Section 4.7.6) may allow reduction of the required prepayment only to the extent of ordinary voluntary prepayments and not a buyback prepayment. This could require the borrower to apply the same dollars twice—the buyback prepayment and its mandatory cash sweep.

13.9.2 Overcoming Documentary Issues

Box 13.6

(a) *Assignments to Affiliated Lenders.* Notwithstanding anything in this Agreement to the contrary, any Term Lender may, at any time, assign all or a portion of its Term Loans on a non-pro rata basis to an

Affiliated Lender through open-market purchases, subject to the following limitations:

(i) In connection with an assignment to a Non-Debt Fund Affiliate, (A) the Non-Debt Fund Affiliate shall have identified itself in writing as an Affiliated Lender to the assigning Term Lender and the Administrative Agent prior to the execution of such assignment and (B) the Non-Debt Fund Affiliate shall be deemed to have represented and warranted to the assigning Term Lender and the Administrative Agent that the requirements set forth in this clause (a) (i) and clause (iv) below, shall have been satisfied upon consummation of the applicable assignment;

(ii) Non-Debt Fund Affiliates will not (A) have the right to receive information, reports or other materials provided solely to Lenders by the Administrative Agent or any other Lender, except to the extent made available to the Borrower, (B) attend or participate in meetings attended solely by the Lenders and the Administrative Agent, or (C) access any electronic site established for the Lenders or confidential communications from counsel to or financial advisors of the Administrative Agent or the Lenders;

(iii) (A) for purposes of any consent to any amendment, waiver or modification of, or any action under, and for the purpose of any direction to the Administrative Agent or any Lender to undertake any action (or refrain from taking any action) under, this Agreement or any other Loan Document, each Non-Debt Fund Affiliate will be deemed to have consented in the same proportion as the Term Lenders that are not Non-Debt Fund Affiliates consented to such matter, unless such matter requires the consent of all or all affected Lenders and adversely affects such Non-Debt Fund Affiliate more than other Term Lenders in any material respect, (B) for purposes of voting on any plan of reorganization or plan of liquidation pursuant to any Debtor Relief Laws (a *"Plan"*), each Non-Debt Fund Affiliate hereby agrees (x) not to vote on such Plan, (y) if such Non-Debt Fund Affiliate does vote on such Plan notwithstanding the restriction in the foregoing clause (x), such vote will be deemed not to be in good faith and shall be "designated" pursuant to Section 1126(e) of the Bankruptcy Code (or any similar provision in any other Debtor Relief Laws), and such vote shall not be counted in determining whether the applicable class has accepted or rejected such Plan in accordance with Section 1126(c) of the Bankruptcy Code (or any similar provision in any other Debtor Relief Laws) and (z) not to contest any request by any party for a determination by the Bankruptcy Court (or other applicable court of competent jurisdiction) effectuating the foregoing clause (y), in each case under this clause (iii) (B) unless such Plan adversely affects such

Non-Debt Fund Affiliate more than other Term Lenders in any material respect, and (C) each Non-Debt Fund Affiliate hereby irrevocably appoints the Administrative Agent (such appointment being coupled with an interest) as such Non-Debt Fund Affiliate's attorney-in-fact, with full authority in the place and stead of such Non-Debt Fund Affiliate and in the name of such Non-Debt Fund Affiliate (solely in respect of Term Loans therein and not in respect of any other claim or status such Non-Debt Fund Affiliate may otherwise have), from time to time in the Administrative Agent's discretion to take any action and to execute any instrument that the Administrative Agent may deem reasonably necessary or appropriate to carry out the provisions of this clause (iii), including to ensure that any vote of such Non-Debt Fund Affiliate on any Plan is withdrawn or otherwise not counted;

(iv) the aggregate principal amount of [any Class or tranche of] Term Loans held at any one time by Non-Debt Fund Affiliates may not exceed [__]% of the aggregate outstanding principal amount of [any Class or tranche of] Term Loans;

(v) the Affiliated Lender will not be entitled to bring actions against the Administrative Agent, in its role as such, or receive advice of counsel or other advisors to the Administrative Agent or any other Lenders or challenge the attorney client privilege of their respective counsel; and

(vi) the portion of any Loans held by Debt Fund Affiliates in the aggregate in excess of 49.9% of the amount of Loans and Commitments required to be held by Lenders in order for such Lenders to constitute "Required Lenders" shall be disregarded in determining Required Lenders at any time.

Each Affiliated Lender that is a Term Lender hereunder agrees to comply with the terms of this paragraph (a) (notwithstanding that it may be granted access to the Platform or any other electronic site established for the Lenders by the Administrative Agent), and agrees that in any subsequent assignment of all or any portion of its Term Loans it shall identify itself in writing to the assignee as an Affiliated Lender prior to the execution of such assignment.

(b) *Borrower Buybacks*. Notwithstanding anything in this Agreement to the contrary, any Term Lender may, at any time, assign all or a portion of its Term Loans on a non-pro rata basis to the Borrower in accordance with the procedures set forth on Exhibit [__], pursuant to an offer made available to all Term Lenders on a pro rata basis (a *"Dutch Auction"*), subject to the following limitations:

(i) The Borrower shall represent and warrant, as of the date of the launch of the Dutch Auction and on the date of any such assignment, that neither it, its Affiliates nor any of its respective directors or officers has any Excluded Information that has not been disclosed to the Term Lenders generally (other than to the extent any such Term Lender does not wish to receive material non-public information with respect to the Borrower or its Subsidiaries or any of their respective securities) prior to such date;

(ii) immediately and automatically, without any further action on the part of the Borrower, any Lender, the Administrative Agent or any other Person, upon the effectiveness of such assignment of Term Loans from a Term Lender to the Borrower, such Term Loans and all rights and obligations as a Term Lender related thereto shall, for all purposes under this Agreement, the other Loan Documents and otherwise, be deemed to be irrevocably prepaid, terminated, extinguished, cancelled and of no further force and effect and the Borrower shall neither obtain nor have any rights as a Term Lender hereunder or under the other Loan Documents by virtue of such assignment;

(iii) the Borrower shall not use the proceeds of any Revolving Loans for any such assignment; and

(iv) no Default or Event of Default shall have occurred and be continuing before or immediately after giving effect to such assignment.

These provisions notwithstanding, during the turmoil in the credit markets during the depths of the last financial crisis, there was severe downward pressure on the secondary market prices of bank loans. Perhaps driven as much by the need for B lenders to obtain liquidity as by a deterioration in borrower credit quality, the depressed secondary market affected not only loans of distressed borrowers but also loans for borrowers that were relatively strong. Not unexpectedly, the dramatic fall in prices created tempting opportunities for borrowers and their affiliates to retire loans at a discount. By doing so, borrowers could deleverage at bargain prices, affiliates could profit from acquiring undervalued assets, and, in some cases, financial sponsors could remedy defaults at their portfolio companies less expensively than by exercising equity cure rights.

As a consequence, some borrowers began to push for amendments to their outstanding credit facilities to allow nonratable prepayments or repurchases of term loans at a discount. Other borrowers pressed for pre-baked permission to do the same in credit agreements being newly executed. This was so notwithstanding that the circumstances in which the buyback right is useful to borrowers (and not unacceptable to lenders) arguably depends upon a rare confluence of two events:

a borrower with sufficient available cash to repurchase its loans and a general, market-driven, decline in loan-trading values. Depending upon the terms of the particular agreement, changing prepayment, repurchase, and other provisions to permit buybacks might require either a majority or unanimous consent from the lenders.

Lenders, at least initially, did not view buyback provisions favorably. An initial objection was based on principle. It seemed unfair (bordering, in the minds of some, on immoral) to allow borrowers and their affiliates in effect to profit from lower secondary market loan prices at the expense of the very lenders that extended the loans in the first place. However (except when buybacks were proposed to be made with the proceeds of their own newly advanced loans), hard reality soon set in and it became difficult for lenders rationally to distinguish buybacks by borrowers and their affiliates from open market purchases by unaffiliated third parties, especially at a time of relative illiquidity for secondary market sales.

Lenders instead began to focus on other issues; out of this process certain fundamental principles have emerged. These principles are embodied in the LSTA's Model Credit Agreement Provisions quoted in Box 13.6. Postfinancial crisis, it is more the exception than the rule to find a credit agreement that does not contain buyback provisions substantially similar to the LSTA model provisions.

One of the key principles evident in recent versions of buyback provisions is the distinction between borrower buybacks, on the one hand, and buybacks by affiliates of the borrower, on the other hand. With the former relying on cash that would otherwise be reinvested in the business while the latter is funded from a sponsor or other equity holders' own funds (which may or may not be derived from the borrower's business), it is reasonable for lenders to view these as not identical. In addition, within the category of buybacks by borrower affiliates, recent practice has drawn a finer distinction between affiliates in the form of the equity holder or financial sponsor and affiliates in the form of credit investment funds. While the credit investment fund may be housed under the same roof as the financial sponsor, the credit fund, the thinking goes, is separately managed by different personnel as compared with those who led the borrower equity investment and who manage a different pot of money with different limited partner investors to whom independent and distinct duties run (as compared with those duties that run to limited partner investors in the equity investment fund). The credit investment funds are referred to as "debt fund affiliates" while the pure private equity investment side of the affiliated sponsor is referred to as a "nondebt fund affiliate."

When lenders are concerned about a borrower or its subsidiaries using its or their own resources for the buyback and thereby depleting liquidity, they may insist that the buyback be made directly by, or with the proceeds of equity contributions from, other affiliates of the borrower and not from the proceeds of new loans under the facility (or even other new debt of the borrower). If it is anticipated that loans bought by affiliates remain outstanding (in some cases the documents will require that they be immediately retired, though this is increasingly rare), it is likely that lenders will require that the affiliates forfeit voting rights under the credit agreement and agree not to participate as a creditor in discussions with other lenders, in each case in order to avoid any taint resulting from a conflict.

13.9.3   Buyback Methodologies

Buyback methodologies can be grouped into two broad categories: pro rata offered buybacks available to all lenders and non-pro rata open market purchases that are made available on a narrower basis to individual lenders. In the former category, there are two principal methodologies that have developed to determine the price and total amount of the loans to be prepaid or acquired: a fixed-price tender offer and a reverse (or modified) Dutch auction. While there is no particular magic to using these methodologies, the market has come to regard them as fair and transparent—two considerations of utmost importance to lenders. Each lender (or at least each lender of a certain tranche for tranche-specific buybacks) is offered the opportunity to sell its loan and, even if it passes on the offer, at least the borrower cannot be accused of favoritism. In the category of open market purchases, a borrower is allowed to negotiate one-on-one with individual lenders to repurchase loans up to a pre-agreed dollar amount. This approach is the most borrower-friendly, but may not pass the "fair and transparent" tests.

In a fixed-price tender offer, the borrower or its affiliate (referred to here as the "initiating party"), specifies a price, and all loans tendered by lenders of the relevant tranche at that price are accepted. The offer is structured so that all lenders in the tranche receive notice of the offer and sufficient time to react. If the borrower has specified a maximum amount of loans that it wishes to prepay or repurchase (or, alternatively, if the agreement sets out a cap on the total amount that may be repaid or repurchased), and tenders by the lenders exceed these amounts, the tendered loans will be retired ratably.

In a reverse (or modified) Dutch auction, instead of the borrower conjuring a specified price the initiating party specifies a *range* of acceptable prices and either the total amount of loans it is seeking to purchase (or prepay) or the total purchase price (or prepayment amount) it is willing to pay. In this way, the Dutch auction aims to solicit offers from lenders within a predetermined range. Each lender that wishes to bid tenders an amount of loans that it is willing to include in the buyback and the price at which it is willing to offer those loans. The highest price is then determined that clears the market for the total amount of loans or total purchase price specified by the initiating party. All lenders that tender at or below that price will have their loans included in the buyback. If the total amount of the loans tendered or the total purchase price (or prepayment amount) to be paid at that price would otherwise exceed the limits set by the initiating party (these limits may sometimes be increased at the discretion of the initiating party), the buyback procedures set forth an allocation mechanism to keep the buyback within those limits. Generally, the allocation would result either in all loans tendered at or below the market clearing price receiving ratable treatment or in loans tendered at the lowest prices being the first ones to be included in the buyback with the ratable cutback to be applied only to the loans tendered at the market clearing price.

Regardless of the methodology, certain other requirements may be imposed on the buyback. There may be, for example, a requirement that the buyback not be allowed if a default or event of default exists. As noted above, the market has permitted borrower buybacks on the assumption that the borrower's liquidity is not adversely impacted and, as a way to police liquidity, minimum liquidity levels may be required to be maintained and often the borrower is prohibited from using its revolving credit facility for funding buybacks. Typically, an aggregate dollar or percentage cap will limit the total amount of loans that may be bought back by a borrower and its subsidiaries or any nondebt fund affiliates—rarely will such parties be permitted to effect buybacks in excess of one-third (more typically 20 percent to 30 percent) of the entire principal of the tranche. This percentage is not arbitrary as in bankruptcy, creditor class acceptance of a plan requires two-thirds in dollar amount and one-half in number of the class and a borrower or nondebt fund affiliate of the borrower holding a third of the amount could find itself in a critical blocking position for adoption of a plan of reorganization. Such leverage can change the dynamics of any workout negotiations to the detriment of the lenders.

13.9.4   Effect upon Amortization

Typically, for any term loan payable in installments, the prepay-ment clause will specify the manner in which a prepayment is applied to the installments—inverse order, direct order, ratably, or other cus-tomized allocation (see Section 4.6). As a consequence, the buyback provision can, once made, have an odd effect upon future amortization. An illustration may be helpful. Assume that voluntary prepayments under an agreement reduce installments in the inverse order. If prin-cipal amortization is applied to the outstanding loans ratably (this will normally be the case under the pro rata provisions of the agreement), once a buyback is concluded the effect will be to *increase* the installment amount of those lenders that did not receive the buyback repayment since the amount of the principal held by them has increased relative to the principal held by the buyback lenders. So while the buyback may nominally have been applied to installments in the inverse order of maturity, the buyback would end up shortening the maturity of all of the loans, not just the buyback loans.

The buyback lenders might of course object to this: they may argue that, from their perspective, all of the retired buyback principal should have precedence in the reduction of buyback loan installments. After all, they were the ones willing to accept the discount in the first place. Why, so they might reason, should the benefit of the reduction in installments be shared with the other lenders? To solve this, the buyback lenders may press for the adjustment to be applied only to the installments of the buyback loans. This would keep the payment amounts for the install-ments of the non-buyback loans at their original levels. However, if as a result the buyback loans are repaid in full before the non-buyback loans (as might occur if the buyback prepayment is applied to installments in the inverse order of maturity), then the aggregate installment payments to be made by the borrower would, at that point, be reduced (after all, only the non-buyback loans would be outstanding). This approach could thus undercut the original purpose of having prepayments applied to the loans in the inverse order so that the borrower's payment obligation is not reduced. There is no obvious solution to this problem.

13.10   AMEND-AND-EXTEND AND REFINANCING FACILITIES

To paraphrase the old adage, a borrower may get consents from all lenders some of the time, and some of the lenders all of the time, but a borrower certainly should not expect to get consents from all of the lenders all of the time. It is this steep climb of obtaining unanimous lender consent that is behind the recent increased adoption (particularly in larger syndicated facilities involving financial sponsors) of so-called amend-and-extend provisions as well as refinancing facility provisions. Both of these provisions permit a borrower to modify maturity, pricing, and other key terms on a portion of its debt without having to seek the unanimous lender consent that typically comes with such "sacred rights" amendments. Particularly in a broadly syndicated loan with many disparate lenders, meeting the required consent threshold is difficult at best. Additionally, both amend-and-extend and refinancing facility provisions help avoid the pro rata sharing obligations found in every syndicated credit agreement. As discussed further below, the added flexibility offered by these provisions gives a challenged borrower an alternate path for navigating the consent gauntlet.

Under an amend-and-extend provision, a borrower may amend the final maturity date on an individual lender-by-lender basis for those lenders who consent to an extension and avoid having to secure 100 percent lender consent. Amend-and-extend provisions often will include an express exclusion from the amendment provision (and its 100 percent lender consent requirement for maturity extensions) or will include an express approval of all lenders so as to capture the 100 percent consent up-front. In exchange for their agreement to extend the maturity of their loan, extending lenders are frequently given consent fees, improved pricing, or other incentives. During the recent credit crisis, amend-and-extend capabilities allowed borrowers to create breathing room from impending maturities in an environment when refinancing options were severely constrained.

Just as the amend-and-extend provision permits a borrower to make targeted bite-sized (or larger) modifications to its debt while avoiding the often insurmountable hurdle of all-lender negotiations, a refinancing facility provision allows a borrower to refinance a portion (and not all) of its debt with either new tranches under the credit agreement or new loan facilities or bonds under an entirely separate facility. Therefore partial refinancings can be accomplished without having to obtain lender consent for nonratable refinancings that may run afoul of pro rata sharing requirements. Also since the refinancing is partial, the hurdle of finding enough debt to replace the existing facility in full is avoided. Under refinancing facility provisions, this new refinancing debt can also share on a *pari passu* basis or junior basis with the existing debt.

The individualized approach embodied in both the amend-and-extend provision and refinancing provisions may seem inconsistent with the collective approach that is in many ways a fundamental operating principle of syndicated credit facilities. There is a balance to be struck in these provisions between the enhanced borrower freedom to proactively manage its capital structure, on the one hand, and the right of the lender syndicate to be protected from selective and possibly coercive maneuvers. The balance is embodied in common safeguards included in both amend-and-extend and refinancing facility provisions. The LSTA's Model Credit Agreement Provisions for amend-and-extend transactions (see Box 2.22 and the related discussion in Section 2.7) exemplify typical lender protections that may apply in both the amend-and-extend context as well as in the refinancing facility context. These safeguards include, among other things, requirements that terms and conditions of the amended-and-extended or refinanced debt have substantially similar terms as the existing debt or at least not have materially better terms when taken as a whole (excluding economic terms that are the incentives borrowers have to entice extensions or refinancings) when compared to the terms of the nonextended or non-refinanced debt, requirements that such newly created debt not participate on a greater-than-ratable basis in payments or prepayments as compared to the nonaffected debt and other protections aimed to prevent the nonaffected debt from becoming effectively subordinated or otherwise disadvantaged from a credit perspective relative to the newly created debt. Also the amend-and-extend and refinancing provisions are usually not available to a borrower if there is continuing default or event of default under the existing loans, therefore forcing the borrower to deal with its current lenders. Lastly, no lender is obligated to extend its maturity or refinance its debt if a borrower exercises its prerogative under either of these two provisions. (For a further discussion of amend-and-extend transactions and refinancing facilities, see Sections 2.7 and 2.8.)

CHAPTER 14

Regulatory Developments

The commercial loan market is subject to a wide range of regulations, a number of which are discussed in this volume. The offshore Eurocurrency funding market, letters of credit, customer identification, margin lending, anti-bribery and anti-corruption rules, sanctions and flood insurance are just a few of the regulated areas reviewed herein. In addition to these discrete regulated areas, bank lending activities are subject to the broad regulatory expectation that they be conducted in a safe and sound manner. The federal bank regulatory agencies, namely the Federal Reserve Board, the Office of the Comptroller of the Currency, and the Federal Deposit Insurance Corporation (collectively, "the Agencies"), have broad authority and examination powers to ensure the safety and soundness of regulated lenders. A bank's loan portfolio, lending policies, credit review process, and other related internal processes are all subject to monitoring and regular examination. In fact, since 1977 the Agencies have conducted reviews of all syndicated loans or loan commitments of at least $20 million that are shared by three or more unaffiliated federally supervised institutions. In 2016 there were 10,837 credit facilities to 6,676 borrowers totaling $4.1 trillion that met this threshold. This review, formally referred to as the Shared National Credit (SNC) Review Program, is typically conducted by regulators traveling onsite to the regulated institutions to review books and records and ask questions. While SNC reviews have historically been conducted on an annual basis, at the time of this writing the Agencies have initiated a semi-annual examination schedule on a selective basis. The Agencies also publish examination manuals that provide in-depth descriptions on the continually evolving supervisory expectations and priorities with respect to commercial lending.[1] In addition to laying out broad criteria applicable across a bank's loan

---

[1] See *Commercial Bank Examination Manual*, Board of Governors of the Federal Reserve System.

portfolio, the examination manuals also describe certain categories of loans, such as real estate lending, subprime lending, energy lending, leveraged lending, and asset-based lending (just to name a few), that may merit a more tailored examination to address historical and unique issues typically applicable to those areas.

A discussion of credit agreements and current market practices relating to credit agreements would not be complete without mention of how deeply the U.S. regulatory environment has evolved in response to the 2008 financial crisis. The numerous new statutes, regulations, interpretations, and formal and informal guidance that have been promulgated since the crisis have impacted, among other things, credit agreement terms, loan origination and syndication practices and participants, and underwriting standards. As discussed below, leveraged lending is an area that has been particularly impacted by this new regulatory regime.

14.1 2013 LEVERAGED LENDING GUIDANCE

In March 2013, the Agencies issued an *Interagency Guidance on Leveraged Lending* (Guidance), updating and replacing a previous guidance issued in 2001. The Agencies issued the Guidance in response to a marked growth in the volume of leveraged credit that had taken place since 2001, as well as the growing participation of unregulated investors in such credits. In the Guidance, the Agencies warned of a general deterioration in underwriting standards, describing their goal to help institutions strengthen their risk management frameworks so that leveraged lending activities—and in particular, the origination and distribution of poorly underwritten loans—would not heighten risk in the banking system or the financial system at large.

The standards in the Guidance apply to all financial institutions for which one of the three Agencies is the primary federal supervisor. For U.S. banking organizations, the Guidance applies on an enterprisewide basis, regardless of where a loan is booked. For foreign institutions, the Guidance applies to all leveraged loans that are both originated and distributed in the United States. Additionally, the Guidance applies to all leveraged lending activity, whether the originating institution intends to participate in a loan or to distribute all of it.

Although the Guidance contains few bright-line standards, it discusses the Agencies' expectations with respect to virtually every aspect of the leveraged lending process. Key topics addressed by the Guidance include:

- *Definition of Leveraged Lending*: Financial institutions should define "leveraged lending" using institution-specific criteria and in a manner sufficiently detailed to ensure consistent application across all business lines.

- *Participations Purchased*: Financial institutions purchasing participations and assignments in leveraged lending transactions should apply the same standards of prudence, credit assessment and approval criteria, and in-house limits that would be used if they had originated the loan.

- *Underwriting Standards*: Financial institutions should have clear, written, and measurable underwriting standards reflecting that specific institution's risk appetite for leveraged transactions.

- *Valuation Standards*: Financial institutions should rely on valuation methods that give supportable and credible results. The Guidance states that the income method is generally considered the most reliable, while enterprise value estimates are often imprecise and may not be realized.

- *Pipeline Management*: Financial institutions should have robust controls in place over transactions in the pipeline, including the ability to differentiate transactions by tenor, investor class, structure, and key borrower characteristics.

- *Reporting and Analytics*: Financial institutions must diligently monitor their leveraged loan portfolio and must have processes in place to provide management and the board with quarterly updates.

- *Risk Rating Leveraged Loans*: Financial institutions should review whether a borrower has the ability to fully amortize their senior secured debt or the ability to repay at least 50 percent of their total debt within five to seven years. The Guidance also warns that leverage levels in excess of six times total debt divided by EBITDA raises concerns for most industries.

- *Financial Sponsors*: Financial institutions relying (explicitly or impliedly) on a financial sponsor as a secondary source of repayment should implement procedures to evaluate the financial sponsor and regularly monitor the sponsor's financial health.

- *Credit Review and Stress-Testing*: Financial institutions must conduct traditional reviews of their leveraged finance portfolios at least annually and must conduct stress-test reviews of their leveraged finance portfolios periodically.

- *Conflicts of Interest and Compliance*: Financial institutions should implement policies and procedures to identify and prevent conflicts of interest, and must periodically have their independent compliance team review their entire leveraged lending portfolio.

14.2 AGENCY FAQS

In part due to its lack of bright-line standards, the Guidance left a wide range of interpretive ambiguities unaddressed. In November 2014, in connection with the Agencies' annual Shared National Credit review, the Agencies issued a set of frequently asked questions (FAQs) on the Guidance (*see* the Agencies' *Frequently Asked Questions for Implementing March 2013 Interagency Guidance on Leveraged Lending* (Nov. 7, 2014)). In the FAQs, the Agencies reiterated that the definition of "leveraged lending" should be institution-specific and take into account the institution's individual risk management framework and risk appetite. The Agencies also rejected definitions of "leveraged lending" that would require a loan to meet a "purpose test" (for example, that a loan be used for a buyout or acquisition) in order to be considered a leveraged loan, stating that excluding loans on the basis of a purpose test would be inconsistent with a comprehensive risk framework for leveraged lending. At the same time, the FAQs noted that loans that meet one common characteristic—such as exceeding three times senior debt/EBITDA or four times total debt/EBITDA—would not *automatically* be considered leveraged loans. Rather, leverage should be treated as an important indicator that would be considered in relation to other loan characteristics.

Other topics addressed by the FAQs include the refinancing of criticized loans (lenders may refinance an existing loan, but should demonstrate that an action is being taken to correct or mitigate the structural or credit-related concerns that resulted in an adverse rating); whether leverage levels exceeding six times EBITDA would necessarily be adversely rated (six times EBITDA is not a bright line, but excessive levels of leverage raise supervisory concerns and may draw additional regulatory scrutiny with respect to the sustainability of the capital structure and repayment capacity of the borrower); and "covenant-lite" loans (loans with relatively few or weak covenants should have other mitigating factors to ensure appropriate credit quality).

14.3   IMPACT OF THE GUIDANCE

While nominally a "guidance" rather than a rule, institutions view compliance with the Guidance as essentially mandatory. In the several years since the Guidance became effective, the Agencies have sought (at times, aggressively) to dispel the notion that institutions have leeway to participate in a certain number of noncompliant deals a year. The Federal Reserve's *Commercial Bank Examination Manual* contains detailed procedures requiring examiners to assess compliance with virtually every aspect of the Guidance, and any shortcomings could expose institutions to a range of formal or informal enforcement actions, including those brought on the basis of unsafe and unsound banking practices.

From the time the Guidance became effective to the time of this writing, the overall impact of the Guidance has been to both decrease the total volume of leveraged lending activity as well as to push leveraged lending activity from regulated financial institutions toward nonbank entities not subject to the Guidance. In recent years, regulators have warned that this migration of leveraged loan origination to the so-called "shadow banking system" poses a potential emerging threat to financial stability.[2] At the same time, regulators have noted a slight decrease in debt to EBITDA ratios in leveraged loans and a sharp decrease in the number of leveraged buyouts financed with debt multiples of seven or higher.[3]

---

[2] See *2015 Annual Report, Financial Stability Oversight Council.*
[3] See *2016 Annual Report, Financial Stability Oversight Council.*

Table of Authorities

CASES

Model
Credit Agreement
Provisions

August 8, 2014

Model Credit Agreement Provisions

Table of Contents

Table of Contents

Exhibits and Appendices

MODEL CREDIT AGREEMENT PROVISIONS

Definitions

"*Administrative Questionnaire*" means an Administrative Questionnaire in a form supplied by the Administrative Agent.

"*Affiliate*" means, with respect to a specified Person, another Person that directly or indirectly through one or more intermediaries, Controls or is Controlled by or is under common Control with the Person specified.

"*Affiliated Lender*" means, collectively, any Affiliate of the Borrower [or the Sponsor] (other than [Holdings], the Borrower and [their respective][its] Subsidiaries).

"*Applicable Percentage*" means with respect to any Revolving Lender, the percentage of the total Revolving Credit Commitments represented by such Revolving Lender's Revolving Credit Commitment. If the Revolving Credit Commitments have terminated or expired, the Applicable Percentages shall be determined based upon the Revolving Credit Commitments most recently in effect, giving effect to any assignments.

"*Approved Fund*" means any Fund that is administered or managed by (a) a Lender, (b) an Affiliate of a Lender or (c) an entity or an Affiliate of an entity that administers or manages a Lender.

"*Assignment and Assumption*" means an assignment and assumption entered into by a Lender and an Eligible Assignee (with the consent of any party whose consent is required by Section *Successors and Assigns*]), and accepted by the Administrative Agent, in substantially the form of Exhibit ___ or any other form approved by the Administrative Agent.

"*Cash Collateralize*" means, to [deposit in a Controlled Account or to] pledge and deposit with or deliver to the Administrative Agent, for the benefit of one or more of the Issuing Banks or Lenders, as collateral for L/C Obligations or obligations of Lenders to fund participations in respect of L/C Obligations, cash or deposit account balances or, if the Administrative Agent and each applicable Issuing Bank shall agree in their sole discretion, other credit support, in each case pursuant to documentation in form and substance satisfactory to the Administrative Agent and each applicable Issuing Bank. "*Cash Collateral*" shall have a meaning correlative to the foregoing and shall include the proceeds of such cash collateral and other credit support.

"*Change in Law*" means the occurrence, after the date of this Agreement, of any of the following: (a) the adoption or taking effect of any law, rule, regulation or treaty, (b) any change in any law, rule, regulation or treaty or in the administration, interpretation, implementation or application thereof by any Governmental Authority or (c) the making or issuance of any request, rule, guideline or directive (whether or not having the force of law) by any Governmental Authority; *provided* that notwithstanding anything herein to the contrary, (x) the Dodd-Frank Wall Street Reform and Consumer Protection Act and all requests, rules, guidelines or directives thereunder or issued in connection therewith and (y) all requests, rules, guidelines or directives promulgated by the Bank for International Settlements, the Basel Committee on Banking Supervision (or any successor or similar authority) or the United States or foreign regulatory authorities, in each case pursuant to Basel III, shall in each case be deemed to be a "Change in Law", regardless of the date enacted, adopted or issued.

"*Code*" means the Internal Revenue Code of 1986.

"*Connection Income Taxes*" means Other Connection Taxes that are imposed on or measured by net income (however denominated) or that are franchise Taxes or branch profits Taxes.

"*Control*" means the possession, directly or indirectly, of the power to direct or cause the direction of the management or policies of a Person, whether through the ability to exercise voting power, by contract or otherwise. "*Controlling*" and "*Controlled*" have meanings correlative thereto.

["*Controlled Account*" means each [deposit account and securities account] that is subjec to an account control agreement in form and substance satisfactory to the Administrative Agent and each applicable Issuing Bank.]

"*Debt Fund Affiliate*" means an Affiliated Lender that is a bona fide debt fund or ar investment vehicle that is primarily engaged in making, purchasing, holding or otherwise investing ir commercial loans, bonds and similar extensions of credit in the ordinary course of business and with respect to which none of the Borrower [or the Sponsor] or any Affiliate of the Borrower [or the Sponsor makes investment decisions or has the power, directly or indirectly, to direct or cause the direction of such Affiliated Lender's investment decisions.

"*Debtor Relief Laws*" means the Bankruptcy Code of the United States of America, and all other liquidation, conservatorship, bankruptcy, assignment for the benefit of creditors, moratorium rearrangement, receivership, insolvency, reorganization, or similar debtor relief Laws of the United State or other applicable jurisdictions from time to time in effect.

"*Defaulting Lender*" means, subject to Section [*Defaulting Lender Cure*], any Lender that (a has failed to (i) fund all or any portion of its Loans within two Business Days of the date such Loans were required to be funded hereunder unless such Lender notifies the Administrative Agent and the Borrowe in writing that such failure is the result of such Lender's determination that one or more condition precedent to funding (each of which conditions precedent, together with any applicable default, shal be specifically identified in such writing) has not been satisfied, or (ii) pay to the Administrative Agent any Issuing Bank, any Swingline Lender or any other Lender any other amount required to be paid by it hereunder (including in respect of its participation in Letters of Credit or Swingline Loans) within two Business Days of the date when due, (b) has notified the Borrower, the Administrative Agent or any Issuing Bank or Swingline Lender in writing that it does not intend to comply with its funding obligation hereunder, or has made a public statement to that effect (unless such writing or public statement relate to such Lender's obligation to fund a Loan hereunder and states that such position is based on such Lender's determination that a condition precedent to funding (which condition precedent, together with any applicable default, shall be specifically identified in such writing or public statement) cannot be satisfied), (c) has failed, within three Business Days after written request by the Administrative Agent c the Borrower, to confirm in writing to the Administrative Agent and the Borrower that it will comply with its prospective funding obligations hereunder (*provided* that such Lender shall cease to be a Defaulting Lender pursuant to this clause (c) upon receipt of such written confirmation by the Administrative Agen and the Borrower), or (d) has, or has a direct or indirect parent company that has, (i) become the subject c a proceeding under any Debtor Relief Law, or (ii) had appointed for it a receiver, custodian, conservato trustee, administrator, assignee for the benefit of creditors or similar Person charged with reorganizatio or liquidation of its business or assets, including the Federal Deposit Insurance Corporation or an other state or federal regulatory authority acting in such a capacity; *provided* that a Lender shall not be Defaulting Lender solely by virtue of the ownership or acquisition of any equity interest in that Lende or any direct or indirect parent company thereof by a Governmental Authority so long as such ownershi interest does not result in or provide such Lender with immunity from the jurisdiction of courts withi the United States or from the enforcement of judgments or writs of attachment on its assets or perm such Lender (or such Governmental Authority) to reject, repudiate, disavow or disaffirm any contract or agreements made with such Lender. Any determination by the Administrative Agent that a Lende is a Defaulting Lender under any one or more of clauses (a) through (d) above shall be conclusive an binding absent manifest error, and such Lender shall be deemed to be a Defaulting Lender (subject t Section [*Defaulting Lender Cure*]) upon delivery of written notice of such determination to the Borrowe each Issuing Bank, each Swingline Lender and each Lender.

"*Disqualified Institution*" means, on any date, (a) any Person designated by the Borrowe as a "Disqualified Institution" by written notice delivered to the Administrative Agent on or prior the date hereof and (b) any other Person that is a Competitor[1] of the Borrower or any of its Subsidiarie which Person has been designated by the Borrower as a "Disqualified Institution" by written notice [the Administrative Agent and the Lenders (including by posting such notice to the Platform) not les

---

[1] To be defined with specificity in reference to the particular Borrower and its business.

than [_] Business Day[s] prior to such date][2]; *provided* that "Disqualified Institutions" shall exclude any Person that the Borrower has designated as no longer being a "Disqualified Institution" by written notice delivered to the Administrative Agent from time to time.

"*DQ List*" has the meaning set forth in Section [*Successors and Assigns*](h)(iv).

"*Dutch Auction*" has the meaning set forth in Section [*Successors and Assigns*](g).

"*Eligible Assignee*" means any Person that meets the requirements to be an assignee under Section [*Successors and Assigns*](b)(iii), (v) and (vi) (subject to such consents, if any, as may be required under Section [*Successors and Assigns*] (b)(iii)) For the avoidance of doubt, any Disqualified Institution is subject to Section [*Successors and Assigns*](h).

"*Excluded Information*" means any non-public information with respect to the Borrower or its Subsidiaries or any of their respective securities to the extent such information could have a material effect upon, or otherwise be material to, an assigning Term Lender's decision to assign Term Loans or a purchasing Term Lender's decision to purchase Term Loans.

"*Excluded Taxes*" means any of the following Taxes imposed on or with respect to a Recipient or required to be withheld or deducted from a payment to a Recipient, (a) Taxes imposed on or measured by net income (however denominated), franchise Taxes, and branch profits Taxes, in each case, (i) imposed as a result of such Recipient being organized under the laws of, or having its principal office or, in the case of any Lender, its applicable lending office located in, the jurisdiction imposing such Tax (or any political subdivision thereof) or (ii) that are Other Connection Taxes, (b) in the case of a Lender, U.S. federal[3] withholding Taxes imposed on amounts payable to or for the account of such Lender with respect to an applicable interest in a Loan or Commitment pursuant to a law in effect on the date on which (i) such Lender acquires such interest in the Loan or Commitment (other than pursuant to an assignment request by the Borrower under Section [*Replacement of Lenders*]) or (ii) such Lender changes its lending office, except in each case to the extent that, pursuant to Section [*Taxes*], amounts with respect to such Taxes were payable either to such Lender's assignor immediately before such Lender became a party hereto or to such Lender immediately before it changed its lending office, (c) Taxes attributable to such Recipient's failure to comply with Section [*Taxes – Status of Lenders*] and (d) any U.S. federal withholding Taxes imposed under FATCA.

"*Extended Revolving Credit Commitment*" means any Class of Revolving Credit Commitments the maturity of which shall have been extended pursuant to Section [*Amend and Extend Transactions*].

"*Extended Revolving Loans*" means any Revolving Loans made pursuant to the Extended Revolving Credit Commitments.

"*Extended Term Loans*" means any Class of Term Loans the maturity of which shall have been extended pursuant to Section [*Amend and Extend Transactions*].

"*Extension*" has the meaning set forth in Section [*Amend and Extend Transactions*](a).

"*Extension Amendment*" means an amendment to this Agreement (which may, at the option of the Administrative Agent and the Borrower, be in the form of an amendment and restatement of this Agreement) among the Loan Parties, the applicable extending Lenders, the Administrative Agent and, to the extent required by Section [*Amend and Extend Transactions*], the Issuing Bank and/ or the Swingline Lender implementing an Extension in accordance with Section [*Amend and Extend Transactions*].

"*Extension Offer*" has the meaning set forth in Section [*Amend and Extend Transactions*](a).

Parties to consider appropriate method for noticing updates to the DQ List, and depending on the method of notification, the appropriate time period for effectiveness of such notice.

The appropriate scope of the carve-out for day 1 withholding taxes will vary, depending on the nature of any exceptions to any applicable withholding taxes. Generally there should not be a carve-out for day 1 withholding taxes with respect to any Loan unless the Loan can be syndicated and traded in the secondary market exclusively among Lenders that are exempt from such day 1 withholding taxes. In addition, a carve-out for day 1 withholding taxes is less common for non-U.S. borrowers.

"*FATCA*" means Sections 1471 through 1474 of the Code, as of the date of this Agreement (or any amended or successor version that is substantively comparable and not materially more onerous to comply with), any current or future regulations or official interpretations thereof and any agreement entered into pursuant to Section 1471(b)(1) of the Code.

"*Foreign Lender*" means (a) if the Borrower is a U.S. Person, a Lender that is not a U.S. Person, and (b) if the Borrower is not a U.S. Person, a Lender that is resident or organized under the laws of a jurisdiction other than that in which the Borrower is resident for tax purposes.

"*Fronting Exposure*" means, at any time there is a Defaulting Lender, (a) with respect to any Issuing Bank, such Defaulting Lender's Applicable Percentage of the outstanding L/C Obligations with respect to Letters of Credit issued by such Issuing Bank other than L/C Obligations as to which such Defaulting Lender's participation obligation has been reallocated to other Lenders or Cash Collateralized in accordance with the terms hereof, and (b) with respect to any Swingline Lender, such Defaulting Lender's Applicable Percentage of outstanding Swingline Loans made by such Swingline Lender other than Swingline Loans as to which such Defaulting Lender's participation obligation has been reallocated to other Lenders.

"*Fund*" means any Person (other than a natural Person) that is (or will be) engaged in making, purchasing, holding or otherwise investing in commercial loans, bonds and similar extension of credit in the ordinary course of its activities.

"*Governmental Authority*" means the government of the United States of America or any other nation, or of any political subdivision thereof, whether state or local, and any agency, authority, instrumentality, regulatory body, court, central bank or other entity exercising executive, legislative, judicial, taxing, regulatory or administrative powers or functions of or pertaining to government (including any supra-national bodies such as the European Union or the European Central Bank).

"*Indemnified Taxes*" means (a) Taxes, other than Excluded Taxes, imposed on or with respect to any payment made by or on account of any obligation of [the Borrower] [any Loan Party] under any Loan Document and (b) to the extent not otherwise described in (a), Other Taxes.

"*IRS*" means the United States Internal Revenue Service.

"*Issuing Bank*" means [_____], in its capacity as issuer of Letters of Credit hereunder, or such other Lender as the Borrower may from time to time select as an Issuing Bank hereunder pursuant to Section [*Letters of Credit*]; *provided* that such Lender has agreed to be an Issuing Bank.

"*Lenders*" means the Persons listed on Schedule [__] and any other Person that shall have become party hereto pursuant to an Assignment and Assumption, other than any such Person that cease to be a party hereto pursuant to an Assignment and Assumption. Unless the context requires otherwise the term "Lenders" includes the Swingline Lenders.

["*Loan Document*" means this Agreement and any notes, security agreements or other documents entered into in connection herewith.][4]

["*Loan Party*" means each of the Borrower and each Guarantor].

"*Minimum Collateral Amount*" means, at any time, (i) with respect to Cash Collateral consisting of cash or deposit account balances, an amount equal to [__]% of the Fronting Exposure of all Issuing Banks with respect to Letters of Credit issued and outstanding at such time and (ii) otherwise, a amount determined by the Administrative Agent and the Issuing Banks in their sole discretion.

"*Non-Consenting Lender*" means any Lender that does not approve any consent, waiver or amendment that (i) requires the approval of all or all affected Lenders in accordance with the terms of Section [__] and (ii) has been approved by the Required Lenders [and, in the case of amendments that require the approval of all or all affected Lenders of a particular Class, Required Class Lenders of such Class].

"*Non-Debt Fund Affiliate*" means an Affiliated Lender that is not a Debt Fund Affiliate.

"*Non-Defaulting Lender*" means, at any time, each Lender that is not a Defaulting Lender at such time.

---

[4] Definition to be tailored for each transaction.

"*Other Connection Taxes*" means, with respect to any Recipient, Taxes imposed as a result of a present or former connection between such Recipient and the jurisdiction imposing such Tax (other than connections arising from such Recipient having executed, delivered, become a party to, performed its obligations under, received payments under, received or perfected a security interest under, engaged in any other transaction pursuant to or enforced any Loan Document, or sold or assigned an interest in any Loan or Loan Document).

"*Other Taxes*" means all present or future stamp, court or documentary, intangible, recording, filing or similar Taxes that arise from any payment made under, from the execution, delivery, performance, enforcement or registration of, from the receipt or perfection of a security interest under, or otherwise with respect to, any Loan Document, except any such Taxes that are Other Connection Taxes imposed with respect to an assignment (other than an assignment made pursuant to Section [*Mitigation Obligations; Replacement of Lenders – Replacement of Lenders*]).

"*Participant*" has the meaning specified in Section [*Successors and Assigns*](d).

"*Participant Register*" has the meaning specified in Section [*Successors and* Assigns](d).

"*Person*" means any natural Person, corporation, limited liability company, trust, joint venture, association, company, partnership, Governmental Authority or other entity.

"*Plan*" has the meaning specified in Section [*Successors and Assigns*](f)(iii).

"*Platform*" means Debt Domain, Intralinks, Syndtrak or a substantially similar electronic transmission system.

"*Recipient*" means (a) the Administrative Agent, (b) any Lender or (c) any Issuing Bank, as applicable.

"*Related Parties*" means, with respect to any Person, such Person's Affiliates and the partners, directors, officers, employees, agents, trustees, administrators, managers, advisors and representatives of such Person and of such Person's Affiliates.

["*Required Class Lenders*" means, at any time with respect to any Class of Loans or Commitments, Lenders having Total Credit Exposures with respect to such Class representing more than [50]% of the Total Credit Exposures of all Lenders of such Class. The Total Credit Exposure of any Defaulting Lender with respect to such Class shall be disregarded in determining Required Class Lenders at any time.]

"*Required Lenders*" means, at any time, Lenders having Total Credit Exposures representing more than [50]% of the Total Credit Exposures of all Lenders. The Total Credit Exposure of any Defaulting Lender shall be disregarded in determining Required Lenders at any time.

"*Revolving Credit Exposure*" means, as to any Revolving Lender at any time, the aggregate principal amount at such time of its outstanding Revolving Loans and such Revolving Lender's participation in L/C Obligations and Swingline Loans at such time.

"*Swingline Lender*" means [_____], in its capacity as lender of Swingline Loans hereunder, or such other Lender as the Borrower may from time to time select as the Swingline Lender hereunder pursuant to Section [*Swingline Loans*]; *provided* that such Lender has agreed to be a Swingline Lender.

"*Taxes*" means all present or future taxes, levies, imposts, duties, deductions, withholdings (including backup withholding), assessments, fees or other charges imposed by any Governmental Authority, including any interest, additions to tax or penalties applicable thereto.

"*Total Credit Exposure*" means, as to any Lender at any time, the unused Commitments, Revolving Credit Exposure and outstanding Term Loans of such Lender at such time.

"*Trade Date*" has the meaning specified in Section [*Successors and Assigns*](h)(i).

"*U.S. Borrower*" means any Borrower that is a U.S. Person.

"*U.S. Person*" means any Person that is a "United States Person" as defined in Section 7701(a)(30) of the Code.

"*U.S. Tax Compliance Certificate*" has the meaning specified in Section [*Taxes – Status of Lenders*](f).

"*Withholding Agent*" means [the Borrower] [any Loan Party] and the Administrative Agent.

Terms Generally

The definitions of terms herein shall apply equally to the singular and plural forms of the terms defined. Whenever the context may require, any pronoun shall include the corresponding masculine, feminine and neuter forms. The words "include," "includes" and "including" shall be deemed to be followed by the phrase "without limitation." The word "will" shall be construed to have the same meaning and effect as the word "shall." Unless the context requires otherwise (a) any definition of or reference to any agreement, instrument or other document herein shall be construed as referring to such agreement, instrument or other document as from time to time amended, supplemented or otherwise modified (subject to any restrictions on such amendments, supplements or modifications set forth herein), (b) any reference herein to any Person shall be construed to include such Person's successors and assigns, (c) the words "herein," "hereof" and "hereunder," and words of similar import, shall be construed to refer to this Agreement in its entirety and not to any particular provision hereof, (d) all references herein to Articles, Sections, Exhibits and Schedules shall be construed to refer to Articles and Sections of, and Exhibits and Schedules to, this Agreement, (e) any reference to any law or regulation herein shall, unless otherwise specified, refer to such law or regulation as amended, modified or supplemented from time to time, and (f) the words "asset" and "property" shall be construed to have the same meaning and effect and to refer to any and all tangible and intangible assets and properties, including cash, securities, accounts and contract rights.

Yield Protection

SECTION 1. *Increased Costs.*

(a)   *Increased Costs Generally.* If any Change in Law shall:

(i)   impose, modify or deem applicable any reserve, special deposit, compulsory loan, insurance charge or similar requirement against assets of, deposits with or for the account of, or credit extended or participated in by, any Lender (except any reserve requirement reflected in the Adjusted LIBO Rate) or any Issuing Bank;

(ii)   subject any Recipient to any Taxes (other than (A) Indemnified Taxes, (B) Taxes described in clauses (b) through (d) of the definition of Excluded Taxes and (C) Connection Income Taxes) on its loans, loan principal, letters of credit, commitments, or other obligations, or its deposits, reserves, other liabilities or capital attributable thereto; or

(iii)   impose on any Lender or any Issuing Bank or the London interbank market any other condition, cost or expense (other than Taxes) affecting this Agreement or Loans made by such Lender or any Letter of Credit or participation therein;

and the result of any of the foregoing shall be to increase the cost to such Lender or such other Recipient of making, converting to, continuing or maintaining any Loan or of maintaining its obligation to make any such Loan, or to increase the cost to such Lender, such Issuing Bank or such other Recipient of participating in, issuing or maintaining any Letter of Credit (or of maintaining its obligation to participate in or to issue any Letter of Credit), or to reduce the amount of any sum received or receivable by such Lender, Issuing Bank or other Recipient hereunder (whether of principal, interest or any other amount) then, upon request of such Lender, Issuing Bank or other Recipient, the Borrower will pay to such Lender, Issuing Bank or other Recipient, as the case may be, such additional amount or amounts as will compensate such Lender, Issuing Bank or other Recipient, as the case may be, for such additional costs incurred or reduction suffered.

(b)   *Capital Requirements.* If any Lender or Issuing Bank determines that any Change in Law affecting such Lender or Issuing Bank or any lending office of such Lender or such Lender's or Issuing

Bank's holding company, if any, regarding capital or liquidity requirements, has or would have the effect of reducing the rate of return on such Lender's or Issuing Bank's capital or on the capital of such Lender's or Issuing Bank's holding company, if any, as a consequence of this Agreement, the Commitments of such Lender or the Loans made by, or participations in Letters of Credit or Swingline Loans held by, such Lender, or the Letters of Credit issued by any Issuing Bank, to a level below that which such Lender or Issuing Bank or such Lender's or Issuing Bank's holding company could have achieved but for such Change in Law (taking into consideration such Lender's or Issuing Bank's policies and the policies of such Lender's or Issuing Bank's holding company with respect to capital adequacy), then from time to time the Borrower will pay to such Lender or Issuing Bank, as the case may be, such additional amount or amounts as will compensate such Lender or Issuing Bank or such Lender's or Issuing Bank's holding company for any such reduction suffered.

(c)   *Certificates for Reimbursement.* A certificate of a Lender or Issuing Bank setting forth the amount or amounts necessary to compensate such Lender or Issuing Bank or its holding company, as the case may be, as specified in paragraph (a) or (b) of this Section and delivered to the Borrower, shall be conclusive absent manifest error. The Borrower shall pay such Lender or Issuing Bank, as the case may be, the amount shown as due on any such certificate within 10 days after receipt thereof.

(d)   *Delay in Requests.* Failure or delay on the part of any Lender or Issuing Bank to demand compensation pursuant to this Section shall not constitute a waiver of such Lender's or Issuing Bank's right to demand such compensation; *provided* that the Borrower shall not be required to compensate a Lender or Issuing Bank pursuant to this Section for any increased costs incurred or reductions suffered more than nine months prior to the date that such Lender or Issuing Bank, as the case may be, notifies the Borrower of the Change in Law giving rise to such increased costs or reductions, and of such Lender's or Issuing Bank's intention to claim compensation therefor (except that, if the Change in Law giving rise to such increased costs or reductions is retroactive, then the nine-month period referred to above shall be extended to include the period of retroactive effect thereof).

SECTION 2. *Taxes.*

(a)   *Defined Terms.* For purposes of this Section [*Taxes*], the term "Lender" includes any Issuing Bank and the term "applicable law" includes FATCA.

(b)   *Payments Free of Taxes.* Any and all payments by or on account of any obligation of [the Borrower] [any Loan Party] under any Loan Document shall be made without deduction or withholding for any Taxes, except as required by applicable law. If any applicable law (as determined in the good faith discretion of an applicable Withholding Agent) requires the deduction or withholding of any Tax from any such payment by a Withholding Agent, then the applicable Withholding Agent shall be entitled to make such deduction or withholding and shall timely pay the full amount deducted or withheld to the relevant Governmental Authority in accordance with applicable law and, if such Tax is an Indemnified Tax, then the sum payable by [the Borrower] [the applicable Loan Party] shall be increased as necessary so that after such deduction or withholding has been made (including such deductions and withholdings applicable to additional sums payable under this Section) the applicable Recipient receives an amount equal to the sum it would have received had no such deduction or withholding been made.

(c)   *Payment of Other Taxes by the Borrower.* [The Borrower] [The Loan Parties] shall timely pay to the relevant Governmental Authority in accordance with applicable law, or at the option of the Administrative Agent timely reimburse it for the payment of, any Other Taxes.

(d)   *Indemnification by the Borrower.* [The Borrower] [The Loan Parties] shall [jointly and severally][5] indemnify each Recipient, within 10 days after demand therefor, for the full amount of any Indemnified Taxes (including Indemnified Taxes imposed or asserted on or attributable to amounts payable under this Section) payable or paid by such Recipient or required to be withheld or deducted from a payment to such Recipient and any reasonable expenses arising therefrom or with respect thereto, whether or not such Indemnified Taxes were correctly or legally imposed or asserted by the relevant Governmental Authority. A certificate as to the amount of such payment or liability delivered to the Borrower by a Lender (with a copy to the Administrative Agent), or by the Administrative Agent on its own behalf or on behalf of a Lender, shall be conclusive absent manifest error.

---

[5] Only include "jointly and severally" when there is more than one indemnitor.

(e)   *Indemnification by the Lenders.* Each Lender shall severally indemnify the Administrative Agent, within 10 days after demand therefor, for (i) any Indemnified Taxes attributable to such Lender (but only to the extent that [the Borrower] [any Loan Party] has not already indemnified the Administrative Agent for such Indemnified Taxes and without limiting the obligation of [the Borrower] [the Loan Parties] to do so), (ii) any Taxes attributable to such Lender's failure to comply with the provisions of Section [*Successors and Assigns – Participations*] relating to the maintenance of a Participant Register and (iii) any Excluded Taxes attributable to such Lender, in each case, that are payable or paid by the Administrative Agent in connection with any Loan Document, and any reasonable expenses arising therefrom or with respect thereto, whether or not such Taxes were correctly or legally imposed or asserted by the relevant Governmental Authority. A certificate as to the amount of such payment or liability delivered to any Lender by the Administrative Agent shall be conclusive absent manifest error. Each Lender hereby authorizes the Administrative Agent to set off and apply any and all amounts at any time owing to such Lender under any Loan Document or otherwise payable by the Administrative Agent to the Lender from any other source against any amount due to the Administrative Agent under this paragraph (e).

(f)   *Evidence of Payments.* As soon as practicable after any payment of Taxes by [the Borrower] [any Loan Party] to a Governmental Authority pursuant to this Section [Taxes], [the Borrower] [such Loan Party] shall deliver to the Administrative Agent the original or a certified copy of a receipt issued by such Governmental Authority evidencing such payment, a copy of the return reporting such payment or other evidence of such payment reasonably satisfactory to the Administrative Agent.

(g)   *Status of Lenders.* (i) Any Lender that is entitled to an exemption from or reduction of withholding Tax with respect to payments made under any Loan Document shall deliver to the Borrower and the Administrative Agent, at the time or times reasonably requested by the Borrower or the Administrative Agent, such properly completed and executed documentation reasonably requested by the Borrower or the Administrative Agent as will permit such payments to be made without withholding or at a reduced rate of withholding. In addition, any Lender, if reasonably requested by the Borrower or the Administrative Agent, shall deliver such other documentation prescribed by applicable law or reasonably requested by the Borrower or the Administrative Agent as will enable the Borrower or the Administrative Agent to determine whether or not such Lender is subject to backup withholding or information reporting requirements. Notwithstanding anything to the contrary in the preceding two sentences, the completion, execution and submission of such documentation (other than such documentation set forth in Section [*Taxes—Status of Lenders*] (ii)(A), (ii)(B) and (ii)(D) below) shall not be required if in the Lender's reasonable judgment such completion, execution or submission would subject such Lender to any material unreimbursed cost or expense or would materially prejudice the legal or commercial position of such Lender.

(ii)   Without limiting the generality of the foregoing, in the event that the Borrower is a U.S. Borrower,

(A) any Lender that is a U.S. Person shall deliver to the Borrower and the Administrative Agent on or prior to the date on which such Lender becomes a Lender under this Agreement (and from time to time thereafter upon the reasonable request of the Borrower or the Administrative Agent), executed copies of IRS Form W-9 certifying that such Lender is exempt from U.S. federal backup withholding tax;

(B) any Foreign Lender shall, to the extent it is legally entitled to do so, deliver to the Borrower and the Administrative Agent (in such number of copies as shall be requested by the recipient) on or prior to the date on which such Foreign Lender becomes a Lender under this Agreement (and from time to time thereafter upon the reasonable request of the Borrower or the Administrative Agent), whichever of the following is applicable:

(1) in the case of a Foreign Lender claiming the benefits of an income tax treaty to which the United States is a party (x) with respect to payments of interest under any Loan Document, executed copies of IRS Form W-8BEN establishing an exemption from, or reduction of, U.S. federal withholding Tax pursuant to the "interest" article of such tax treaty and (y) with respect to any other applicable payments under any Loan Document, IRS Form W-8BEN establishing an exemption from, or reduction of, U.S. federal withholding Tax pursuant to the "business profits" or "other income" article of such tax treaty;

(2) executed copies of IRS Form W-8ECI;

(3) in the case of a Foreign Lender claiming the benefits of the exemption for portfolio interest under Section 881(c) of the Code, (x) a certificate substantially in the form of Exhibit [J]-1 to the effect that such Foreign Lender is not a "bank" within the meaning of Section 881(c)(3)(A) of the Code, a "10 percent shareholder" of the Borrower within the meaning of Section 881(c)(3)(B) of the Code, or a "controlled foreign corporation" described in Section 881(c)(3)(C) of the Code (a "*U.S. Tax Compliance Certificate*") and (y) executed copies of IRS Form W-8BEN; or

(4) to the extent a Foreign Lender is not the beneficial owner, executed copies of IRS Form W-8IMY, accompanied by IRS Form W-8ECI, IRS Form W-8BEN, a U.S. Tax Compliance Certificate substantially in the form of Exhibit [J]-2 or Exhibit [J]-3, IRS Form W-9, and/or other certification documents from each beneficial owner, as applicable; *provided* that if the Foreign Lender is a partnership and one or more direct or indirect partners of such Foreign Lender are claiming the portfolio interest exemption, such Foreign Lender may provide a U.S. Tax Compliance Certificate substantially in the form of Exhibit [J]-4 on behalf of each such direct and indirect partner;

(C) any Foreign Lender shall, to the extent it is legally entitled to do so, deliver to the Borrower and the Administrative Agent (in such number of copies as shall be requested by the recipient) on or prior to the date on which such Foreign Lender becomes a Lender under this Agreement (and from time to time thereafter upon the reasonable request of the Borrower or the Administrative Agent), executed copies of any other form prescribed by applicable law as a basis for claiming exemption from or a reduction in U.S. federal withholding Tax, duly completed, together with such supplementary documentation as may be prescribed by applicable law to permit the Borrower or the Administrative Agent to determine the withholding or deduction required to be made; and

(D) if a payment made to a Lender under any Loan Document would be subject to U.S. federal withholding Tax imposed by FATCA if such Lender were to fail to comply with the applicable reporting requirements of FATCA (including those contained in Section 1471(b) or 1472(b) of the Code, as applicable), such Lender shall deliver to the Borrower and the Administrative Agent at the time or times prescribed by law and at such time or times reasonably requested by the Borrower or the Administrative Agent such documentation prescribed by applicable law (including as prescribed by Section 1471(b)(3)(C)(i) of the Code) and such additional documentation reasonably requested by the Borrower or the Administrative Agent as may be necessary for the Borrower and the Administrative Agent to comply with their obligations under FATCA and to determine that such Lender has complied with such Lender's obligations under FATCA or to determine the amount to deduct and withhold from such payment. Solely for purposes of this clause (D), "FATCA" shall include any amendments made to FATCA after the date of this Agreement.

Each Lender agrees that if any form or certification it previously delivered expires or becomes obsolete or inaccurate in any respect, it shall update such form or certification or promptly notify the Borrower and the Administrative Agent in writing of its legal inability to do so.

(h) *Treatment of Certain Refunds.* If any party determines, in its sole discretion exercised in good faith, that it has received a refund of any Taxes as to which it has been indemnified pursuant to this Section [*Taxes*] (including by the payment of additional amounts pursuant to this Section [*Taxes*]), it shall pay to the indemnifying party an amount equal to such refund (but only to the extent of indemnity payments made under this Section with respect to the Taxes giving rise to such refund), net of all out-of-pocket expenses (including Taxes) of such indemnified party and without interest (other than any interest paid by the relevant Governmental Authority with respect to such refund). Such indemnifying party, upon the request of such indemnified party, shall repay to such indemnified party the amount paid over pursuant to this paragraph (h) (plus any penalties, interest or other charges imposed by the relevant Governmental Authority) in the event that such indemnified party is required to repay such refund to such Governmental Authority. Notwithstanding anything to the contrary in this paragraph (h), in no event will the indemnified party be required to pay any amount to an indemnifying party pursuant to this paragraph (h) the payment of which would place the indemnified party in a less favorable net after-Tax position than the indemnified party would have been in if the Tax subject to indemnification and giving rise to such refund had not been deducted, withheld or otherwise imposed and the indemnification payments or additional amounts with respect to such Tax had never been paid. This paragraph shall not be construed to require any indemnified party to make available its Tax returns (or any other information relating to its Taxes that it deems confidential) to the indemnifying party or any other Person.

(i) *Survival*. Each party's obligations under this Section [*Taxes*] shall survive the resignation or replacement of the Administrative Agent or any assignment of rights by, or the replacement of, a Lender, the termination of the Commitments and the repayment, satisfaction or discharge of all obligations under any Loan Document.

SECTION 3. *Mitigation Obligations; Replacement of Lenders.*

(a)   *Designation of a Different Lending Office.* If any Lender requests compensation under Section [*Increased Costs*], or requires the Borrower to pay any Indemnified Taxes or additional amounts to any Lender or any Governmental Authority for the account of any Lender pursuant to Section [*Taxes*], then such Lender shall (at the request of the Borrower) use reasonable efforts to designate a different lending office for funding or booking its Loans hereunder or to assign its rights and obligations hereunder to another of its offices, branches or affiliates, if, in the judgment of such Lender, such designation or assignment (i) would eliminate or reduce amounts payable pursuant to Section [*Increased Costs*] or [*Taxes*], as the case may be, in the future, and (ii) would not subject such Lender to any unreimbursed cost or expense and would not otherwise be disadvantageous to such Lender. The Borrower hereby agrees to pay all reasonable costs and expenses incurred by any Lender in connection with any such designation or assignment.

(b)   *Replacement of Lenders.*[6] If any Lender requests compensation under Section [*Increased Costs*], or if the Borrower is required to pay any Indemnified Taxes or additional amounts to any Lender or any Governmental Authority for the account of any Lender pursuant to Section [*Taxes*] and, in each case, such Lender has declined or is unable to designate a different lending office in accordance with Section 3(a), or if any Lender is a Defaulting Lender or a Non-Consenting Lender, then the Borrower may, at its sole expense and effort, upon notice to such Lender and the Administrative Agent, require such Lender to assign and delegate, without recourse (in accordance with and subject to the restrictions contained in, and consents required by, Section [*Successors and Assigns*]), all of its interests, rights (other than its existing rights to payments pursuant to Section [*Increased Cost*] or Section [*Taxes*]) and obligations under this Agreement and the related Loan Documents to an Eligible Assignee that shall assume such obligations (which assignee may be another Lender, if a Lender accepts such assignment); *provided* that:

(i)   the Borrower shall have paid to the Administrative Agent the assignment fee (if any) specified in Section [*Successors and Assigns*];

(ii)   such Lender shall have received payment of an amount equal to the outstanding principal of its Loans and participations in L/C Disbursements, accrued interest thereon, accrued fees and all other amounts payable to it hereunder and under the other Loan Documents (including any amounts under Section [*Breakfunding*]) from the assignee (to the extent of such outstanding principal and accrued interest and fees) or the Borrower (in the case of all other amounts);

(iii)   in the case of any such assignment resulting from a claim for compensation under Section [*Increased Costs*] or payments required to be made pursuant to Section [*Taxes*], such assignment will result in a reduction in such compensation or payments thereafter;

(iv)   such assignment does not conflict with applicable law; and

(v)   in the case of any assignment resulting from a Lender becoming a Non-Consenting Lender, the applicable assignee shall have consented to the applicable amendment, waiver or consent.

A Lender shall not be required to make any such assignment or delegation if, prior thereto, as a result of a waiver by such Lender or otherwise, the circumstances entitling the Borrower to require such assignment and delegation cease to apply.

---

[6] Please note that the Breakfunding section in the Credit Agreement should expressly include any amounts payable as a result of an assignment required by this Section.

Right of Setoff

If an Event of Default shall have occurred and be continuing, each Lender, each Issuing Bank, and each of their respective Affiliates is hereby authorized at any time and from time to time, to the fullest extent permitted by applicable law, to set off and apply any and all deposits (general or special, time or demand, provisional or final, in whatever currency) at any time held, and other obligations (in whatever currency) at any time owing, by such Lender, such Issuing Bank or any such Affiliate, to or for the credit or the account of the Borrower [or any other Loan Party] against any and all of the obligations of the Borrower [or such Loan Party] now or hereafter existing under this Agreement or any other Loan Document to such Lender or such Issuing Bank or their respective Affiliates, irrespective of whether or not such Lender, Issuing Bank or Affiliate shall have made any demand under this Agreement or any other Loan Document and although such obligations of the Borrower [or such Loan Party] may be contingent or unmatured or are owed to a branch, office or Affiliate of such Lender or such Issuing Bank different from the branch, office or Affiliate holding such deposit or obligated on such indebtedness; provided that in the event that any Defaulting Lender shall exercise any such right of setoff, (x) all amounts so set off shall be paid over immediately to the Administrative Agent for further application in accordance with the provisions of Section [Defaulting Lenders] and, pending such payment, shall be segregated by such Defaulting Lender from its other funds and deemed held in trust for the benefit of the Administrative Agent, the Issuing Banks, and the Lenders, and (y) the Defaulting Lender shall provide promptly to the Administrative Agent a statement describing in reasonable detail the Obligations owing to such Defaulting Lender as to which it exercised such right of setoff. The rights of each Lender, each Issuing Bank and their respective Affiliates under this Section are in addition to other rights and remedies (including other rights of setoff) that such Lender, such Issuing Bank or their respective Affiliates may have. Each Lender and Issuing Bank agrees to notify the Borrower and the Administrative Agent promptly after any such setoff and application; provided that the failure to give such notice shall not affect the validity of such setoff and application.

Amend and Extend Transactions[7,8]

(a)   The Borrower may, by written notice to the Administrative Agent from time to time, request an extension (each, an *"Extension"*) of the maturity date of any Class of Loans and Commitments to the extended maturity date specified in such notice. Such notice shall (i) set forth the amount of the applicable Class of Revolving Credit Commitments and/or Term Loans that will be subject to the Extension (which shall be in minimum increments of $[AMOUNT] and a minimum amount of $[AMOUNT]), (ii) set forth the date on which such Extension is requested to become effective (which shall be not less than [ten (10)] Business Days nor more than [sixty (60)] days after the date of such Extension notice (or such longer or shorter periods as the Administrative Agent shall agree in its sole discretion)) and (iii) identify the relevant Class of Revolving Credit Commitments and/or Term Loans to which such Extension relates. Each Lender of the applicable Class shall be offered (an *"Extension Offer"*) an opportunity to participate in such Extension on a pro rata basis and on the same terms and conditions as each other Lender of such Class pursuant to procedures established by, or reasonably acceptable to, the Administrative Agent and the Borrower. If the aggregate principal amount of Revolving Credit Commitments or Term Loans in respect of which Lenders shall have accepted the relevant Extension Offer shall exceed the maximum aggregate principal amount of Revolving Credit Commitments or Term Loans, as applicable, subject to the Extension Offer as set forth in the Extension notice, then the Revolving Credit Commitments or Term Loans, as applicable, of Lenders of the applicable Class shall be extended ratably up to such maximum amount based on the respective principal amounts with respect to which such Lenders have accepted such Extension Offer.

(b)   The following shall be conditions precedent to the effectiveness of any Extension: (i) no Default or Event of Default shall have occurred and be continuing immediately prior to and immediately after giving effect to such Extension, (ii) the representations and warranties set forth in Article [*Representations and Warranties*] and in each other Loan Document shall be deemed to be made and

---

See Appendix I for alternate formulation.

If the facility is secured by improved real property in the United States, the flood insurance requirements must be satisfied prior to the extension.

shall be true and correct in all material respects on and as of the effective date of such Extension, (iii) the Issuing Bank and the Swingline Lender shall have consented to any Extension of the Revolving Credit Commitments, to the extent that such Extension provides for the issuance or extension of Letters of Credit or making of Swingline Loans at any time during the extended period and (iv) the terms of such Extended Revolving Credit Commitments and Extended Term Loans shall comply with paragraph (c) of this Section.

(c)   The terms of each Extension shall be determined by the Borrower and the applicable extending Lenders and set forth in an Extension Amendment; *provided* that (i) the final maturity date of any Extended Revolving Credit Commitment or Extended Term Loan shall be no earlier than the Revolving Credit Maturity Date or the Term Loan Maturity Date, respectively, (ii)(A) there shall be no scheduled amortization of the loans or reductions of commitments under any Extended Revolving Credit Commitments and (B) the average life to maturity of the Extended Term Loans shall be no shorter than the remaining average life to maturity of the existing Term Loans, (iii) the Extended Revolving Loans and the Extended Term Loans will rank pari passu in right of payment and with respect to security with the existing Revolving Loans and the existing Term Loans and the borrower and guarantors of the Extended Revolving Credit Commitments or Extended Term Loans, as applicable, shall be the same as the Borrower and Guarantors with respect to the existing Revolving Loans or Term Loans, as applicable, (iv) the interest rate margin, rate floors, fees, original issue discount and premium applicable to [any Extended Revolving Credit Commitment (and the Extended Revolving Loans thereunder) and] Extended Term Loans shall be determined by the Borrower and the applicable extending Lenders, (v)(A) the Extended Term Loans may participate on a pro rata or less than pro rata (but not greater than pro rata) basis in voluntary or mandatory prepayments with the other Term Loans and (B) borrowing and prepayment of Extended Revolving Loans, or reductions of Extended Revolving Credit Commitments, and participation in Letters of Credit and Swingline Loans, shall be on a pro rata basis with the other [Revolving Loans] or [Revolving Credit Commitments] (other than upon the maturity of the non-extended [Revolving Loans] and [Revolving Credit Commitments]) and (vi) the terms of the Extended Revolving Credit Commitments or Extended Term Loans, as applicable, shall be substantially identical to the terms set forth herein (except as set forth in clauses (i) through (v) above).

(d)   In connection with any Extension, the Borrower, the Administrative Agent and each applicable extending Lender shall execute and deliver to the Administrative Agent an Extension Amendment and such other documentation as the Administrative Agent shall reasonably specify to evidence the Extension. The Administrative Agent shall promptly notify each Lender as to the effectiveness of each Extension. Any Extension Amendment may, without the consent of any other Lender, effect such amendments to this Agreement and the other Loan Documents as may be necessary or appropriate, in the reasonable opinion of the Administrative Agent and the Borrower, to implement the terms of any such Extension, including any amendments necessary to establish Extended Revolving Credit Commitments or Extended Term Loans as a new Class or tranche of Revolving Credit Commitments or Term Loans, as applicable, and such other technical amendments as may be necessary or appropriate in the reasonable opinion of the Administrative Agent and the Borrower in connection with the establishment of such new Class or tranche (including to preserve the pro rata treatment of the extended and non-extended Classes or tranches and to provide for the reallocation of Revolving Credit Exposure upon the expiration or termination of the commitments under any Class or tranche), in each case on terms consistent with this section.

Cash Collateral[9]

At any time that there shall exist a Defaulting Lender, within one Business Day following the written request of the Administrative Agent or any Issuing Bank (with a copy to the Administrative Agent) the Borrower shall Cash Collateralize the Issuing Banks' Fronting Exposure with respect to such Defaulting

---

[9] If the Facilities are secured (e.g., by a "blanket lien"), consider ensuring (i) that Cash Collateral provided to secure the Issuing Banks' Fronting Exposure remains subject to the security interest granted to the Lenders and other secured parties pursuant to the Loan Documents (as contemplated by bracketed language in clause (a)), (ii) that the Loan Documents provide that the payment of amounts owing to the Issuing Bank ranks ahead of amounts payable to other Lenders to the extent of the Cash Collateral so provided (as contemplated by clause (b) of this Section) and (iii) that there is no "release" of the security interest granted to the Lenders and the other Secured Parties upon termination of the requirements under this Section (as contemplated by the bracketed second proviso to clause (c) of this Section).

Lender (determined after giving effect to Section [*Defaulting Lender – Reallocation of Participations to Reduce Fronting Exposure*] and any Cash Collateral provided by such Defaulting Lender) in an amount not less than the Minimum Collateral Amount.

(a)   *Grant of Security Interest.* The Borrower, and to the extent provided by any Defaulting Lender, such Defaulting Lender, hereby grants to the Administrative Agent, for the benefit of the Issuing Banks, and agrees to maintain, a first priority security interest in all such *Cash Collateral* as security for the Defaulting Lenders' obligation to fund participations in respect of L/C Obligations, to be applied pursuant to clause (b) below. If at any time the Administrative Agent determines that Cash Collateral is subject to any right or claim of any Person other than the Administrative Agent and the Issuing Banks as herein provided [(other than [specify applicable Permitted Liens])], or that the total amount of such Cash Collateral is less than the Minimum Collateral Amount, the Borrower will, promptly upon demand by the Administrative Agent, pay or provide to the Administrative Agent additional Cash Collateral in an amount sufficient to eliminate such deficiency (after giving effect to any Cash Collateral provided by the Defaulting Lender).

(b)   *Application.* Notwithstanding anything to the contrary contained in this Agreement, Cash Collateral provided under this Section [*Cash Collateral*] or Section [*Defaulting Lender*] in respect of Letters of Credit shall be applied to the satisfaction of the Defaulting Lender's obligation to fund participations in respect of L/C Obligations (including, as to Cash Collateral provided by a Defaulting Lender, any interest accrued on such obligation) for which the Cash Collateral was so provided, prior to any other application of such property as may otherwise be provided for herein.

(c)   *Termination of Requirement.* Cash Collateral (or the appropriate portion thereof) provided to reduce any Issuing Bank's Fronting Exposure shall no longer be required to be held as Cash Collateral pursuant to this Section [Cash Collateral] following (i) the elimination of the applicable Fronting Exposure (including by the termination of Defaulting Lender status of the applicable Lender), or (ii) the determination by the Administrative Agent and each Issuing Bank that there exists excess Cash Collateral; *provided* that, subject to Section [*Default Lenders*]] the Person providing Cash Collateral and each Issuing Bank may agree that Cash Collateral shall be held to support future anticipated Fronting Exposure or other obligations [and *provided further* that to the extent that such Cash Collateral was provided by the Borrower, such Cash Collateral shall remain subject to the security interest granted pursuant to the Loan Documents].

Defaulting Lenders

(a)   *Defaulting Lender Adjustments.* Notwithstanding anything to the contrary contained in this Agreement, if any Lender becomes a Defaulting Lender, then, until such time as such Lender is no longer a Defaulting Lender, to the extent permitted by applicable law:

(i)   *Waivers and Amendments.* Such Defaulting Lender's right to approve or disapprove any amendment, waiver or consent with respect to this Agreement shall be restricted as set forth in the definition of Required Lenders.

(ii)   *Defaulting Lender Waterfall.* Any payment of principal, interest, fees or other amounts received by the Administrative Agent for the account of such Defaulting Lender (whether voluntary or mandatory, at maturity, pursuant to Article [*Events of Default*] or otherwise) or received by the Administrative Agent from a Defaulting Lender pursuant to Section [*Right of Setoff*] shall be applied at such time or times as may be determined by the Administrative Agent as follows: *first*, to the payment of any amounts owing by such Defaulting Lender to the Administrative Agent hereunder; *second*, to the payment on a pro rata basis of any amounts owing by such Defaulting Lender to any Issuing Bank or Swingline Lender hereunder; *third*, to Cash Collateralize the Issuing Banks' Fronting Exposure with respect to such Defaulting Lender in accordance with Section [*Cash Collateral*]; *fourth*, as the Borrower may request (so long as no Default or Event of Default exists), to the funding of any Loan in respect of which such Defaulting Lender has failed to fund its portion thereof as required by this Agreement, as determined by the Administrative Agent; *fifth*, if so determined by the Administrative Agent and the Borrower, to be held in a deposit account and released pro rata in order to (x) satisfy such

Defaulting Lender's potential future funding obligations with respect to Loans under this Agreement and (y) Cash Collateralize the Issuing Banks' future Fronting Exposure with respect to such Defaulting Lender with respect to future Letters of Credit issued under this Agreement, in accordance with Section [*Cash Collateral*]; *sixth*, to the payment of any amounts owing to the Lenders, the Issuing Banks or Swingline Lenders as a result of any judgment of a court of competent jurisdiction obtained by any Lender, the Issuing Banks or Swingline Lenders against such Defaulting Lender as a result of such Defaulting Lender's breach of its obligations under this Agreement; *seventh*, so long as no Default or Event of Default exists, to the payment of any amounts owing to the Borrower as a result of any judgment of a court of competent jurisdiction obtained by the Borrower against such Defaulting Lender as a result of such Defaulting Lender's breach of its obligations under this Agreement; and *eighth*, to such Defaulting Lender or as otherwise directed by a court of competent jurisdiction; *provided* that if (x) such payment is a payment of the principal amount of any Loans or L/C Disbursements in respect of which such Defaulting Lender has not fully funded its appropriate share, and (y) such Loans were made or the related Letters of Credit were issued at a time when the conditions set forth in Section [*Conditions to All Credit Extensions*] were satisfied or waived, such payment shall be applied solely to pay the Loans of, and L/C Disbursements owed to, all Non-Defaulting Lenders on a pro rata basis prior to being applied to the payment of any Loans of, or L/C Disbursements owed to, such Defaulting Lender until such time as all Loans and funded and unfunded participations in L/C Obligations and Swingline Loans are held by the Lenders pro rata in accordance with the Commitments under the applicable Facility without giving effect to Section [*Defaulting Lender – Reallocation of Participation to Reduce Fronting Exposure*]. Any payments, prepayments or other amounts paid or payable to a Defaulting Lender that are applied (or held) to pay amounts owed by a Defaulting Lender or to post Cash Collateral pursuant to this Section [*Defaulting Lender Waterfall*] shall be deemed paid to and redirected by such Defaulting Lender, and each Lender irrevocably consents hereto.

(iii)   *Certain Fees*. (A) [ALT 1 – for Commitment Fees: No Defaulting Lender shall be entitled to receive any Commitment Fee for any period during which that Lender is a Defaulting Lender (and the Borrower shall not be required to pay any such fee that otherwise would have been required to have been paid to that Defaulting Lender)] [ALT 2 – for Facility/Utilization Fee: Each Defaulting Lender shall be entitled to receive a Facility Fee [or Utilization Fee] for any period during which that Lender is a Defaulting Lender only to extent allocable to the sum of (1) the outstanding principal amount of the Revolving Loans funded by it, and (2) its Applicable Percentage of the stated amount of Letters of Credit for which it has provided Cash Collateral pursuant to Section [Cash Collateral]].

(B)   Each Defaulting Lender shall be entitled to receive [L/C Fees] for any period during which that Lender is a Defaulting Lender only to the extent allocable to its Applicable Percentage of the stated amount of Letters of Credit for which it has provided Cash Collateral pursuant to Section [*Cash Collateral*].

(C)   With respect to any [Facility Fee, Utilization Fee or L/C Fee] not required to be paid to any Defaulting Lender pursuant to clause (A) or (B) above, the Borrower shall (x) pay to each Non-Defaulting Lender that portion of any such fee otherwise payable to such Defaulting Lender with respect to such Defaulting Lender's participation in L/C Obligations or Swingline Loans that has been reallocated to such Non-Defaulting Lender pursuant to clause (iv) below, (y) pay to each Issuing Bank and Swingline Lender, as applicable, the amount of any such fee otherwise payable to such Defaulting Lender to the extent allocable to such Issuing Bank's or Swingline Lender's Fronting Exposure to such Defaulting Lender, and (z) not be required to pay the remaining amount of any such fee.

(iv)   *Reallocation of Participations to Reduce Fronting Exposure*. All or any part of such Defaulting Lender's participation in L/C Obligations and Swingline Loans shall be reallocated among the Non-Defaulting Lenders in accordance with their respective Applicable Percentages (calculated without regard to such Defaulting Lender's Commitment) but only to the extent that such reallocation does not cause the aggregate

Revolving Credit Exposure of any Non-Defaulting Lender to exceed such Non-Defaulting Lender's Revolving Credit Commitment. No reallocation hereunder shall constitute a waiver or release of any claim of any party hereunder against a Defaulting Lender arising from that Lender having become a Defaulting Lender, including any claim of a Non-Defaulting Lender as a result of such Non-Defaulting Lender's increased exposure following such reallocation.

(v)   *Cash Collateral, Repayment of Swingline Loans.* If the reallocation described in clause (iv) above cannot, or can only partially, be effected, the Borrower shall, without prejudice to any right or remedy available to it hereunder or under law, (x) first, prepay Swingline Loans in an amount equal to the Swingline Lenders' Fronting Exposure and (y) second, Cash Collateralize the Issuing Banks' Fronting Exposure in accordance with the procedures set forth in Section [*Cash Collateral*].

(b)   *Defaulting Lender Cure.* If the Borrower, the Administrative Agent and each Swingline Lender and Issuing Bank agree in writing that a Lender is no longer a Defaulting Lender, the Administrative Agent will so notify the parties hereto, whereupon as of the effective date specified in such notice and subject to any conditions set forth therein (which may include arrangements with respect to any Cash Collateral), that Lender will, to the extent applicable, purchase at par that portion of outstanding Loans of the other Lenders or take such other actions as the Administrative Agent may determine to be necessary to cause the Loans and funded and unfunded participations in Letters of Credit and Swingline Loans to be held pro rata by the Lenders in accordance with the Commitments under the applicable Facility (without giving effect to Section [*Defaulting Lender – Reallocation of Participations to Reduce Fronting Exposure*), whereupon such Lender will cease to be a Defaulting Lender; *provided* that no adjustments will be made retroactively with respect to fees accrued or payments made by or on behalf of the Borrower while that Lender was a Defaulting Lender; and *provided, further,* that except to the extent otherwise expressly agreed by the affected parties, no change hereunder from Defaulting Lender to Lender will constitute a waiver or release of any claim of any party hereunder arising from that Lender's having been a Defaulting Lender.

(c)   *New Swingline Loans/Letters of Credit.* So long as any Lender is a Defaulting Lender, (i) the Swingline Lender shall not be required to fund any Swingline Loans unless it is satisfied that it will have no Fronting Exposure after giving effect to such Swingline Loan and (ii) no Issuing Bank shall be required to issue, extend, renew or increase any Letter of Credit unless it is satisfied that it will have no Fronting Exposure after giving effect thereto.

Sharing of Payments by Lenders

If any Lender shall, by exercising any right of setoff or counterclaim or otherwise, obtain payment in respect of any principal of or interest on any of its Loans or other obligations hereunder resulting in such Lender receiving payment of a proportion of the aggregate amount of its Loans and accrued interest thereon or other such obligations greater than its pro rata share thereof as provided herein, then the Lender receiving such greater proportion shall (a) notify the Administrative Agent of such fact, and (b) purchase (for cash at face value) participations in the Loans and such other obligations of the other Lenders, or make such other adjustments as shall be equitable, so that the benefit of all such payments shall be shared by the Lenders ratably in accordance with the aggregate amount of principal of and accrued interest on their respective Loans and other amounts owing them; *provided* that:

(i)   if any such participations are purchased and all or any portion of the payment giving rise thereto is recovered, such participations shall be rescinded and the purchase price restored to the extent of such recovery, without interest; and

(ii)   the provisions of this paragraph shall not be construed to apply to (x) any payment made by the Borrower pursuant to and in accordance with the express terms of this Agreement (including the application of funds arising from the existence of a Defaulting Lender or Disqualified Institution), or (y) any payment obtained by a Lender as consideration for the assignment of or sale of a participation in any of its Loans or participations in L/C Disbursements to any assignee or participant, [other than to the Borrower or any

Subsidiary thereof (as to which the provisions of this paragraph shall apply)][, other than to the Borrower or any of its Affiliates (other than pursuant to Section [*Successors and Assigns, paragraph (g)*]), as to which the provision of this paragraph shall apply][10].

[The Borrower] [Each Loan Party] consents to the foregoing and agrees, to the extent it may effectively do so under applicable law, that any Lender acquiring a participation pursuant to the foregoing arrangements may exercise against [the Borrower] [each Loan Party] rights of setoff and counterclaim with respect to such participation as fully as if such Lender were a direct creditor of [the Borrower] [each Loan Party] in the amount of such participation.

Administrative Agent's Clawback

(a)   *Funding by Lenders; Presumption by Administrative Agent.* Unless the Administrative Agent shall have received notice from a Lender [(x) in the case of ABR Loans, [____] hours prior to the proposed time of such Borrowing and (y) otherwise], prior to the proposed date of any Borrowing that such Lender will not make available to the Administrative Agent such Lender's share of such Borrowing, the Administrative Agent may assume that such Lender has made such share available on such date in accordance with Section [*Funding*] and may, in reliance upon such assumption, make available to the Borrower a corresponding amount. In such event, if a Lender has not in fact made its share of the applicable Borrowing available to the Administrative Agent, then the applicable Lender and the Borrower severally agree to pay to the Administrative Agent forthwith on demand such corresponding amount with interest thereon, for each day from and including the date such amount is made available to the Borrower to but excluding the date of payment to the Administrative Agent, at (i) in the case of a payment to be made by such Lender, the greater of the Federal Funds Effective Rate and a rate determined by the Administrative Agent in accordance with banking industry rules on interbank compensation, and (ii) in the case of a payment to be made by the Borrower, the interest rate applicable to ABR Loans. If the Borrower and such Lender shall pay such interest to the Administrative Agent for the same or an overlapping period, the Administrative Agent shall promptly remit to the Borrower the amount of such interest paid by the Borrower for such period. If such Lender pays its share of the applicable Borrowing to the Administrative Agent, then the amount so paid shall constitute such Lender's Loan included in such Borrowing. Any payment by the Borrower shall be without prejudice to any claim the Borrower may have against a Lender that shall have failed to make such payment to the Administrative Agent.

(b)   *Payments by Borrower; Presumptions by Administrative Agent.* Unless the Administrative Agent shall have received notice from the Borrower prior to the date on which any payment is due to the Administrative Agent for the account of the Lenders or the Issuing Banks hereunder that the Borrower will not make such payment, the Administrative Agent may assume that the Borrower has made such payment on such date in accordance herewith and may, in reliance upon such assumption, distribute to the Lenders or the Issuing Banks, as the case may be, the amount due. In such event, if the Borrower has not in fact made such payment, then each of the Lenders or the Issuing Banks, as the case may be, severally agrees to repay to the Administrative Agent forthwith on demand the amount so distributed to such Lender or Issuing Bank, with interest thereon, for each day from and including the date such amount is distributed to it to but excluding the date of payment to the Administrative Agent, at the greater of the Federal Funds Effective Rate and a rate determined by the Administrative Agent in accordance with banking industry rules on interbank compensation.

Agency

ARTICLE [___]

AGENCY

SECTION 1   *Appointment and Authority.* Each of the Lenders and the Issuing Banks hereby irrevocably appoints [name of initial Administrative Agent] to act on its behalf as the Administrative

---

[10] To replace immediately preceding bracketed language if the Borrower or its Subsidiaries are permitted to purchase Term Loans from Term Lenders.

Agent hereunder and under the other Loan Documents and authorizes the Administrative Agent to take such actions on its behalf and to exercise such powers as are delegated to the Administrative Agent by the terms hereof or thereof, together with such actions and powers as are reasonably incidental thereto. The provisions of this Article are solely for the benefit of the Administrative Agent, the Lenders and the Issuing Banks, and [the Borrower shall not] [neither the Borrower nor any other Loan Party shall] have rights as a third-party beneficiary of any of such provisions. It is understood and agreed that the use of the term "agent" herein or in any other Loan Documents (or any other similar term) with reference to the Administrative Agent is not intended to connote any fiduciary or other implied (or express) obligations arising under agency doctrine of any applicable law. Instead such term is used as a matter of market custom, and is intended to create or reflect only an administrative relationship between contracting parties.

SECTION 2. *Rights as a Lender.* The Person serving as the Administrative Agent hereunder shall have the same rights and powers in its capacity as a Lender as any other Lender and may exercise the same as though it were not the Administrative Agent, and the term "Lender" or "Lenders" shall, unless otherwise expressly indicated or unless the context otherwise requires, include the Person serving as the Administrative Agent hereunder in its individual capacity. Such Person and its Affiliates may accept deposits from, lend money to, own securities of, act as the financial advisor or in any other advisory capacity for, and generally engage in any kind of business with, the Borrower or any Subsidiary or other Affiliate thereof as if such Person were not the Administrative Agent hereunder and without any duty to account therefor to the Lenders.

SECTION 3. *Exculpatory Provisions.* (a) The Administrative Agent shall not have any duties or obligations except those expressly set forth herein and in the other Loan Documents, and its duties hereunder shall be administrative in nature. Without limiting the generality of the foregoing, the Administrative Agent:

(i)   shall not be subject to any fiduciary or other implied duties, regardless of whether a Default has occurred and is continuing;

(ii)   shall not have any duty to take any discretionary action or exercise any discretionary powers, except discretionary rights and powers expressly contemplated hereby or by the other Loan Documents that the Administrative Agent is required to exercise as directed in writing by the Required Lenders (or such other number or percentage of the Lenders as shall be expressly provided for herein or in the other Loan Documents); *provided* that the Administrative Agent shall not be required to take any action that, in its opinion or the opinion of its counsel, may expose the Administrative Agent to liability or that is contrary to any Loan Document or applicable law, including for the avoidance of doubt any action that may be in violation of the automatic stay under any Debtor Relief Law or that may effect a forfeiture, modification or termination of property of a Defaulting Lender in violation of any Debtor Relief Law; and

(iii)   shall not, except as expressly set forth herein and in the other Loan Documents, have any duty to disclose, and shall not be liable for the failure to disclose, any information relating to the Borrower or any of its Affiliates that is communicated to or obtained by the Person serving as the Administrative Agent or any of its Affiliates in any capacity.

(b)   The Administrative Agent shall not be liable for any action taken or not taken by it (i) with the consent or at the request of the Required Lenders (or such other number or percentage of the Lenders as shall be necessary, or as the Administrative Agent shall believe in good faith shall be necessary, under the circumstances as provided in Sections [*Amendments*] and [*Exercise of Remedies*]), or (ii) in the absence of its own gross negligence or willful misconduct as determined by a court of competent jurisdiction by final and nonappealable judgment. The Administrative Agent shall be deemed not to have knowledge of any Default unless and until notice describing such Default is given to the Administrative Agent in writing by the Borrower, a Lender or an Issuing Bank.

(c)   The Administrative Agent shall not be responsible for or have any duty to ascertain or inquire into (i) any statement, warranty or representation made in or in connection with this Agreement or any other Loan Document, (ii) the contents of any certificate, report or other document delivered hereunder or thereunder or in connection herewith or therewith, (iii) the performance or observance of any of the covenants, agreements or other terms or conditions set forth herein or therein or the occurrence of any Default, (iv) the validity, enforceability, effectiveness or genuineness of this Agreement, any other Loan Document or any other agreement, instrument or document, [or] (v) the satisfaction of any condition set forth in Article [*Conditions*] or elsewhere herein, other than to confirm receipt of items expressly required to be delivered to the Administrative Agent [or (vi) compliance by Affiliated Lenders with the terms hereof relating to Affiliated Lenders].[11]

(d)   The Administrative Agent shall not be responsible or have any liability for, or have any duty to ascertain, inquire into, monitor or enforce, compliance with the provisions hereof relating to Disqualified Institutions. Without limiting the generality of the foregoing, the Administrative Agent shall not (x) be obligated to ascertain, monitor or inquire as to whether any Lender or Participant or prospective Lender or Participant is a Disqualified Institution or (y) have any liability with respect to or arising out of any assignment or participation of Loans, or disclosure of confidential information, to any Disqualified Institution.

SECTION 4.   *Reliance by Administrative Agent.* The Administrative Agent shall be entitled to rely upon, and shall not incur any liability for relying upon, any notice, request, certificate, consent, statement, instrument, document or other writing (including any electronic message, Internet or intranet website posting or other distribution) believed by it to be genuine and to have been signed, sent or otherwise authenticated by the proper Person. The Administrative Agent also may rely upon any statement made to it orally or by telephone and believed by it to have been made by the proper Person, and shall not incur any liability for relying thereon. In determining compliance with any condition hereunder to the making of a Loan, or the issuance, extension, renewal or increase of a Letter of Credit, that by its terms must be fulfilled to the satisfaction of a Lender or an Issuing Bank, the Administrative Agent may presume that such condition is satisfactory to such Lender or Issuing Bank unless the Administrative Agent shall have received notice to the contrary from such Lender or Issuing Bank prior to the making of such Loan or the issuance of such Letter of Credit. The Administrative Agent may consult with legal counsel (who may be counsel for the Borrower), independent accountants and other experts selected by it, and shall not be liable for any action taken or not taken by it in accordance with the advice of any such counsel, accountants or experts.

SECTION 5.   *Delegation of Duties.* The Administrative Agent may perform any and all of its duties and exercise its rights and powers hereunder or under any other Loan Document by or through any one or more sub-agents appointed by the Administrative Agent. The Administrative Agent and any such sub-agent may perform any and all of its duties and exercise its rights and powers by or through their respective Related Parties. The exculpatory provisions of this Article shall apply to any such sub-agent and to the Related Parties of the Administrative Agent and any such sub-agent, and shall apply to their respective activities in connection with the syndication of the Facilities as well as activities as Administrative Agent. The Administrative Agent shall not be responsible for the negligence or misconduct of any sub-agents except to the extent that a court of competent jurisdiction determines in a final and nonappealable judgment that the Administrative Agent acted with gross negligence or willful misconduct in the selection of such sub-agents.

SECTION 6.   *Resignation of Administrative Agent.* (a) The Administrative Agent may at any time give notice of its resignation to the Lenders, the Issuing Banks and the Borrower. Upon receipt of any such notice of resignation, the Required Lenders shall have the right, in consultation with the Borrower, to appoint a successor, which shall be a bank with an office in [_____], or an Affiliate of any such bank with an office in [_____]. If no such successor shall have been so appointed by the Required Lenders and shall have accepted such appointment within 30 days after the retiring Administrative Agent gives notice of its resignation (or such earlier day as shall be agreed by the Required Lenders) (the "*Resignation Effective Date*"), then the retiring Administrative Agent may (but shall not be obligated to), on behalf of the Lenders and the Issuing Banks, appoint a successor Administrative Agent meeting the qualifications set forth above; *provided* that in no event shall any such successor Administrative Agent be a Defaulting Lender [or an Affiliated Lender] [or a Disqualified Institution]. Whether or not a successor has been appointed, such resignation shall become effective in accordance with such notice on the Resignation Effective Date.

---

[11] To be added if Affiliated Lenders are permitted to purchase Term Loans from Term Lenders.

(b)   If the Person serving as Administrative Agent is a Defaulting Lender pursuant to clause (d) of the definition thereof, the Required Lenders may, to the extent permitted by applicable law, by notice in writing to the Borrower and such Person remove such Person as Administrative Agent and, in consultation with the Borrower, appoint a successor. If no such successor shall have been so appointed by the Required Lenders and shall have accepted such appointment within 30 days (or such earlier day as shall be agreed by the Required Lenders) (the *"Removal Effective Date"*), then such removal shall nonetheless become effective in accordance with such notice on the Removal Effective Date.

(c)   With effect from the Resignation Effective Date or the Removal Effective Date (as applicable) (i) the retiring or removed Administrative Agent shall be discharged from its duties and obligations hereunder and under the other Loan Documents [(except that in the case of any collateral security held by the Administrative Agent on behalf of the Lenders or the Issuing Banks under any of the Loan Documents, the retiring or removed Administrative Agent shall continue to hold such collateral security until such time as a successor Administrative Agent is appointed)] and (ii) except for any indemnity payments owed to the retiring or removed Administrative Agent, all payments, communications and determinations provided to be made by, to or through the Administrative Agent shall instead be made by or to each Lender and Issuing Bank directly, until such time, if any, as the Required Lenders appoint a successor Administrative Agent as provided for above. Upon the acceptance of a successor's appointment as Administrative Agent hereunder, such successor shall succeed to and become vested with all of the rights, powers, privileges and duties of the retiring or removed Administrative Agent (other than any rights to indemnity payments owed to the retiring or removed Administrative Agent), and the retiring or removed Administrative Agent shall be discharged from all of its duties and obligations hereunder or under the other Loan Documents. The fees payable by the Borrower to a successor Administrative Agent shall be the same as those payable to its predecessor unless otherwise agreed between the Borrower and such successor. After the retiring or removed Administrative Agent's resignation or removal hereunder and under the other Loan Documents, the provisions of this Article and Section [*Expenses and Indemnity*] shall continue in effect for the benefit of such retiring or removed Administrative Agent, its sub-agents and their respective Related Parties in respect of any actions taken or omitted to be taken by any of them while the retiring or removed Administrative Agent was acting as Administrative Agent.

SECTION 7.   *Non-Reliance on Administrative Agent and Other Lenders.* Each Lender and Issuing Bank acknowledges that it has, independently and without reliance upon the Administrative Agent or any other Lender or any of their Related Parties and based on such documents and information as it has deemed appropriate, made its own credit analysis and decision to enter into this Agreement. Each Lender and Issuing Bank also acknowledges that it will, independently and without reliance upon the Administrative Agent or any other Lender or any of their Related Parties and based on such documents and information as it shall from time to time deem appropriate, continue to make its own decisions in taking or not taking action under or based upon this Agreement, any other Loan Document or any related agreement or any document furnished hereunder or thereunder.

SECTION 8.   *No Other Duties, Etc.* Anything herein to the contrary notwithstanding, none of the Bookrunners, Arrangers or [other titles as necessary] listed on the cover page hereof shall have any powers, duties or responsibilities under this Agreement or any of the other Loan Documents, except in its capacity, as applicable, as the Administrative Agent, a Lender or an Issuing Bank hereunder.

SECTION 9.   [*Administrative Agent May File Proofs of Claim.* In case of the pendency of any proceeding under any Debtor Relief Law [or any other judicial proceeding relative to any Loan Party,] the Administrative Agent (irrespective of whether the principal of any Loan or L/C Obligation shall then be due and payable as herein expressed or by declaration or otherwise and irrespective of whether the Administrative Agent shall have made any demand on the Borrower) shall be entitled and empowered (but not obligated) by intervention in such proceeding or otherwise:

(a)   to file and prove a claim for the whole amount of the principal and interest owing and unpaid in respect of the Loans, L/C Obligations and all other Obligations that are owing and unpaid and to file such other documents as may be necessary or advisable in order to have the claims of the Lenders, the Issuing Banks and the Administrative Agent (including any claim for the reasonable compensation, expenses, disbursements and advances of the Lenders, the Issuing Banks and the Administrative Agent and their respective agents and counsel and all other amounts due the Lenders, the Issuing Banks and the Administrative Agent under Sections [*Letter of Credit Fees; Fees; Expenses, Indemnity*]) allowed in such judicial proceeding; and

(b)   to collect and receive any monies or other property payable or deliverable on any such claims and to distribute the same;

and any custodian, receiver, assignee, trustee, liquidator, sequestrator or other similar official in any such judicial proceeding is hereby authorized by each Lender and Issuing Bank to make such payments to the Administrative Agent and, in the event that the Administrative Agent shall consent to the making of such payments directly to the Lenders and the Issuing Banks, to pay to the Administrative Agent any amount due for the reasonable compensation, expenses, disbursements and advances of the Administrative Agent and its agents and counsel, and any other amounts due the Administrative Agent under Sections [*Fees; Expenses, Indemnity*]].

[SECTION 10.   *Collateral and Guaranty Matters.* (a) The [Secured Parties] irrevocably authorize the Administrative Agent, at its option and in its discretion,

(i)   to release any Lien on any property granted to or held by the Administrative Agent under any Loan Document (x) upon termination of all Commitments and payment in full of all Obligations (other than contingent indemnification obligations) and the expiration or termination of all Letters of Credit [(other than Letters of Credit as to which other arrangements satisfactory to the Administrative Agent and the applicable Issuing Bank shall have been made)], (y) that is sold or otherwise disposed of or to be sold or otherwise disposed of as part of or in connection with any sale or other disposition permitted under the Loan Documents, or (z) subject to Section [*Amendments*], if approved, authorized or ratified in writing by the Required Lenders;

(ii)   [to subordinate any Lien on any property granted to or held by the Administrative Agent under any Loan Document to the holder of any Lien on such property that is permitted by Section [Liens Securing Capital Leases, Synthetic Leases and Purchase Money Indebtedness]]; and

(iii)   to release any Guarantor from its obligations under the Guaranty if such Person ceases to be a Subsidiary as a result of a transaction permitted under the Loan Documents.

Upon request by the Administrative Agent at any time, the Required Lenders will confirm in writing the Administrative Agent's authority to release [or subordinate] its interest in particular types or items of property, or to release any Guarantor from its obligations under the Guaranty pursuant to this Section 10.

(b)   The Administrative Agent shall not be responsible for or have a duty to ascertain or inquire into any representation or warranty regarding the existence, value or collectability of the Collateral, the existence, priority or perfection of the Administrative Agent's Lien thereon, or any certificate prepared by any Loan Party in connection therewith, nor shall the Administrative Agent be responsible or liable to the Lenders for any failure to monitor or maintain any portion of the Collateral.]

Notices; Effectiveness; Electronic Communication

(a)   *Notices Generally.* Except in the case of notices and other communications expressly permitted to be given by telephone (and except as provided in paragraph (b) below), all notices and other communications provided for herein shall be in writing and shall be delivered by hand or overnight courier service, mailed by certified or registered mail or sent by facsimile as follows:

(i)   if to the Borrower [or any other Loan Party], to it at _____, Attention of _____ (Facsimile No. _____; Telephone No. _____);

(ii)   if to the Administrative Agent, to [Name of Administrative Agent] at _____, Attention of _____ (Facsimile No. _____; Telephone No. _____;

(iii)   if to [_____] in its capacity as Issuing Bank, to it at _____, Attention of _____ (Facsimile No. _____; Telephone No. _____), and if to any other Issuing Bank, to it at the address provided in writing to the Administrative Agent and the Borrower at the time of its appointment as an Issuing Bank hereunder;

(iv)   if to a Lender, to it at its address (or facsimile number) set forth in its Administrative Questionnaire.

Notices sent by hand or overnight courier service, or mailed by certified or registered mail, shall be deemed to have been given when received; notices sent by facsimile shall be deemed to have been given when sent (except that, if not given during normal business hours for the recipient, shall be deemed to have been given at the opening of business on the next business day for the recipient). Notices delivered through electronic communications, to the extent provided in paragraph (b) below, shall be effective as provided in said paragraph (b).

(b)   *Electronic Communications.* Notices and other communications to the Lenders and the Issuing Banks hereunder may be delivered or furnished by electronic communication (including e-mail and Internet or intranet websites) pursuant to procedures approved by the Administrative Agent,[12] *provided* that the foregoing shall not apply to notices to any Lender or Issuing Bank pursuant to Article [*Funding Mechanics*] if such Lender or Issuing Bank, as applicable, has notified the Administrative Agent that it is incapable of receiving notices under such Article by electronic communication. The Administrative Agent or the Borrower may, in its discretion, agree to accept notices and other communications to it hereunder by electronic communications pursuant to procedures approved by it; *provided* that approval of such procedures may be limited to particular notices or communications.

Unless the Administrative Agent otherwise prescribes, (i) notices and other communications sent to an e-mail address shall be deemed received upon the sender's receipt of an acknowledgement from the intended recipient (such as by the "return receipt requested" function, as available, return e-mail or other written acknowledgement), and (ii) notices or communications posted to an Internet or intranet website shall be deemed received upon the deemed receipt by the intended recipient, at its e-mail address as described in the foregoing clause (i), of notification that such notice or communication is available and identifying the website address therefor; *provided* that, for both clauses (i) and (ii) above, if such notice, email or other communication is not sent during the normal business hours of the recipient, such notice or communication shall be deemed to have been sent at the opening of business on the next business day for the recipient.

(c)   *Change of Address, etc.* Any party hereto may change its address or facsimile number for notices and other communications hereunder by notice to the other parties hereto.

(d)   *Platform.*

(i)   [The Borrower] [Each Loan Party] agrees that the Administrative Agent may, but shall not be obligated to, make the Communications (as defined below) available to the Issuing Banks and the other Lenders by posting the Communications on the Platform. The Borrower acknowledges and agrees that the DQ List shall be deemed suitable for posting and may be posted by the Administrative Agent on the Platform, including the portion of the Platform that is designated for "public side" Lenders.

(ii)   The Platform is provided "as is" and "as available." The Agent Parties (as defined below) do not warrant the adequacy of the Platform and expressly disclaim liability for errors or omissions in the Communications. No warranty of any kind, express, implied or statutory, including, without limitation, any warranty of merchantability, fitness for a particular purpose, non-infringement of third-party rights or freedom from viruses or other code defects, is made by any Agent Party in connection with the Communications or the Platform. In no event shall the Administrative Agent or any of its Related Parties (collectively, the "*Agent Parties*") have any liability to the Borrower [or the other Loan Parties], any Lender or any other Person or entity for damages of any kind, including,

---

[12] Administrative Agents may wish to prescribe procedures for electronic communications and to disseminate those procedures to Lenders.

without limitation, direct or indirect, special, incidental or consequential damages, losses or expenses (whether in tort, contract or otherwise) arising out of the Borrower's [, any Loan Party's] or the Administrative Agent's transmission of communications through the Platform. "*Communications*" means, collectively, any notice, demand, communication, information, document or other material provided by or on behalf of [the Borrower] [any Loan Party] pursuant to any Loan Document or the transactions contemplated therein which is distributed to the Administrative Agent, any Lender or any Issuing Bank by means of electronic communications pursuant to this Section, including through the Platform.

Expenses; Indemnity; Damage Waiver[13]

(a)   *Costs and Expenses.* The Borrower shall pay (i) all reasonable out-of-pocket expenses incurred by the Administrative Agent and its Affiliates (including the reasonable fees, charges and disbursements of counsel for the Administrative Agent)[, and shall pay all fees and time charges and disbursements for attorneys who may be employees of the Administrative Agent][14], in connection with the syndication of the Facilities, the preparation, negotiation, execution, delivery and administration of this Agreement and the other Loan Documents, or any amendments, modifications or waivers of the provisions hereof or thereof (whether or not the transactions contemplated hereby or thereby shall be consummated), (ii) all reasonable out-of-pocket expenses incurred by any Issuing Bank in connection with the issuance, amendment, renewal or extension of any Letter of Credit or any demand for payment thereunder, and (iii) all out-of-pocket expenses incurred by the Administrative Agent, any Lender or any Issuing Bank (including the fees, charges and disbursements of any counsel for the Administrative Agent, any Lender or any Issuing Bank)[, and shall pay all fees and time charges for attorneys who may be employees of the Administrative Agent, any Lender or any Issuing Bank], in connection with the enforcement or protection of its rights (A) in connection with this Agreement and the other Loan Documents, including its rights under this Section, or (B) in connection with the Loans made or Letters of Credit issued hereunder, including all such out-of-pocket expenses incurred during any workout, restructuring or negotiations in respect of such Loans or Letters of Credit.

(b)   *Indemnification by the Borrower.* The Borrower shall indemnify the Administrative Agent (and any sub-agent thereof), each Lender and each Issuing Bank, and each Related Party of any of the foregoing Persons (each such Person being called an "*Indemnitee*") against, and hold each Indemnitee harmless from, any and all losses, claims, damages, liabilities and related expenses (including the fees, charges and disbursements of any counsel for any Indemnitee)[, and shall indemnify and hold harmless each Indemnitee from all fees and time charges and disbursements for attorneys who may be employees of any Indemnitee], incurred by any Indemnitee or asserted against any Indemnitee by any Person (including the Borrower [or any other Loan Party]) other than such Indemnitee and its Related Parties arising out of, in connection with, or as a result of (i) the execution or delivery of this Agreement, any other Loan Document or any agreement or instrument contemplated hereby or thereby, the performance by the parties hereto of their respective obligations hereunder or thereunder or the consummation of the transactions contemplated hereby or thereby, (ii) any Loan or Letter of Credit or the use or proposed use of the proceeds therefrom (including any refusal by any Issuing Bank to honor a demand for payment under a Letter of Credit if the documents presented in connection with such demand do not strictly comply with the terms of such Letter of Credit), (iii) any actual or alleged presence or Release of Hazardous Materials on or from any property owned or operated by the Borrower or any of its Subsidiaries, or any Environmental Liability related in any way to the Borrower or any of its Subsidiaries, or (iv) any actual or prospective claim, litigation, investigation or proceeding relating to any of the foregoing, whether based on contract, tort or any other theory, whether brought by a third party or by the Borrower [or any other Loan Party], and regardless of whether any Indemnitee is a party thereto; *provided* that such indemnity shall not, as to any Indemnitee, be available to the extent that such losses, claims, damages, liabilities or related expenses (x) are determined by a court of competent jurisdiction by final and nonappealable judgment to have resulted from the gross negligence or willful misconduct of such Indemnitee or (y) result from a claim brought by the Borrower or any other Loan Party against an Indemnitee for

---

[13] A reference to this Section should be included in the Survival Section, if any, of the Credit Agreement.

[14] For insertion in instances where appropriate.

breach in bad faith of such Indemnitee's obligations hereunder or under any other Loan Document, if the Borrower or such Loan Party has obtained a final and nonappealable judgment in its favor on such claim as determined by a court of competent jurisdiction. This Section [___](b) shall not apply with respect to Taxes other than any Taxes that represent losses, claims, damages, etc. arising from any non-Tax claim.

(c)   *Reimbursement by Lenders.* To the extent that the Borrower for any reason fails to indefeasibly pay any amount required under paragraph (a) or (b) of this Section to be paid by it to the Administrative Agent (or any sub-agent thereof), any Issuing Bank, any Swingline Lender or any Related Party of any of the foregoing, each Lender severally agrees to pay to the Administrative Agent (or any such sub-agent), such Issuing Bank, such Swingline Lender or such Related Party, as the case may be, such Lender's pro rata share (determined as of the time that the applicable unreimbursed expense or indemnity payment is sought based on each Lender's share of the Total Credit Exposure at such time) of such unpaid amount (including any such unpaid amount in respect of a claim asserted by such Lender); *provided* that with respect to such unpaid amounts owed to any Issuing Bank or Swingline Lender solely in its capacity as such, only the Revolving Lenders shall be required to pay such unpaid amounts, such payment to be made severally among them based on such Revolving Lenders' Applicable Percentage (determined as of the time that the applicable unreimbursed expense or indemnity payment is sought) *provided, further*, that the unreimbursed expense or indemnified loss, claim, damage, liability or related expense, as the case may be, was incurred by or asserted against the Administrative Agent (or any such sub-agent), such Issuing Bank or such Swingline Lender in its capacity as such, or against any Related Party of any of the foregoing acting for the Administrative Agent (or any such sub-agent), such Issuing Bank or any such Swingline Lender in connection with such capacity. The obligations of the Lenders under this paragraph (c) are subject to the provisions of Section [*Obligations of Lenders Several*].

(d)   *Waiver of Consequential Damages, Etc.* To the fullest extent permitted by applicable law, the Borrower shall not assert, and hereby waives, any claim against any Indemnitee, on any theory of liability, for special, indirect, consequential or punitive damages (as opposed to direct or actual damages) arising out of, in connection with, or as a result of, this Agreement, any other Loan Document or any agreement or instrument contemplated hereby, the transactions contemplated hereby or thereby, any Loan or Letter of Credit, or the use of the proceeds thereof. No Indemnitee referred to in paragraph (b) above shall be liable for any damages arising from the use by unintended recipients of any information or other materials distributed by it through telecommunications, electronic or other information transmission systems in connection with this Agreement or the other Loan Documents or the transactions contemplated hereby or thereby.

(e)   *Payments.* All amounts due under this Section shall be payable [promptly/not later than [ ] days] after demand therefor.

(f)   *Survival.* Each party's obligations under this Section shall survive the termination of the Loan Documents and payment of the obligations hereunder.

Successors and Assigns

(a)   *Successors and Assigns Generally.* The provisions of this Agreement shall be binding upon and inure to the benefit of the parties hereto and their respective successors and assigns permitted hereby, except that [the Borrower may not][neither the Borrower nor any other Loan Party may] assign or otherwise transfer any of its rights or obligations hereunder without the prior written consent of the Administrative Agent and each Lender, and no Lender may assign or otherwise transfer any of its rights or obligations hereunder except (i) to an assignee in accordance with the provisions of paragraph (b) of this Section, (ii) by way of participation in accordance with the provisions of paragraph (d) of this Section, or (iii) by way of pledge or assignment of a security interest subject to the restrictions of paragraph (e) of this Section (and any other attempted assignment or transfer by any party hereto shall be null and void). Nothing in this Agreement, expressed or implied, shall be construed to confer upon any Person (other than the parties hereto, their respective successors and assigns permitted hereby, Participants to the extent provided in paragraph (d) of this Section and, to the extent expressly contemplated hereby, the Related Parties of each of the Administrative Agent and the Lenders) any legal or equitable right, remedy or claim under or by reason of this Agreement.

(b)   *Assignments by Lenders.* Any Lender may at any time assign to one or more assignees all or a portion of its rights and obligations under this Agreement (including all or a portion of its Commitment and the Loans at the time owing to it); *provided* that (in each case with respect to any Facility) any such assignment shall be subject to the following conditions:

(i)   *Minimum Amounts.*

(A)   in the case of an assignment of the entire remaining amount of the assigning Lender's Commitment and/or the Loans at the time owing to it (in each case with respect to any Facility) or contemporaneous assignments to related Approved Funds (determined after giving effect to such assignments) that equal at least the amount specified in paragraph (b)(i)(B) of this Section in the aggregate or in the case of an assignment to a Lender, an Affiliate of a Lender or an Approved Fund, no minimum amount need be assigned; and

(B)   in any case not described in paragraph (b)(i)(A) of this Section, the aggregate amount of the Commitment (which for this purpose includes Loans outstanding thereunder) or, if the applicable Commitment is not then in effect, the principal outstanding balance of the Loans of the assigning Lender subject to each such assignment (determined as of the date the Assignment and Assumption with respect to such assignment is delivered to the Administrative Agent or, if "*Trade Date*" is specified in the Assignment and Assumption, as of the Trade Date) shall not be less than $5,000,000,[15] in the case of any assignment in respect of the Revolving Facility, or $1,000,000, in the case of any assignment in respect of the Term Loan Facility, unless each of the Administrative Agent and, so long as no [*Institution to select appropriate cross-reference to default*] has occurred and is continuing, the Borrower otherwise consents (each such consent not to be unreasonably withheld or delayed).

(ii)   *Proportionate Amounts.* Each partial assignment shall be made as an assignment of a proportionate part of all the assigning Lender's rights and obligations under this Agreement with respect to the Loan or the Commitment assigned, except that this clause (ii) shall not prohibit any Lender from assigning all or a portion of its rights and obligations among separate Facilities on a non-pro rata basis.

(iii)   *Required Consents.* No consent shall be required for any assignment except to the extent required by paragraph (b)(i)(B) of this Section and, in addition:

(A)   the consent of the Borrower (such consent not to be unreasonably withheld or delayed) shall be required unless (x) [*institution to select appropriate cross-reference to default*] has occurred and is continuing at the time of such assignment, or (y) such assignment is to a Lender, an Affiliate of a Lender or an Approved Fund; *provided* that the Borrower shall be deemed to have consented to any such assignment unless it shall object thereto by written notice to the Administrative Agent within [5] Business Days after having received notice thereof and *provided, further*, that the Borrower's consent shall not be required during the primary syndication of the Facilities;

(B)   the consent of the Administrative Agent (such consent not to be unreasonably withheld or delayed) shall be required for assignments in respect of (i) the Revolving Facility or any unfunded Commitments with respect to the Term Loan Facility if such assignment is to a Person that is not a Lender with a Commitment in respect of such Facility, an Affiliate of such Lender or an Approved Fund with respect to such Lender, or (ii) any Term Loans to a Person who is not a Lender, an Affiliate of a Lender or an Approved Fund; and

(C)   the consent of each Issuing Bank and Swingline Lender shall be required for any assignment in respect of the Revolving Facility.

---

[15] Consider whether a lower minimum assignment amount for the revolving facility (but in no event less than $1,000,000) is appropriate.

(iv)   *Assignment and Assumption.* The parties to each assignment shall execute and deliver to the Administrative Agent an Assignment and Assumption, together with a processing and recordation fee of [$_____]; *provided* that the Administrative Agent may, in its sole discretion, elect to waive such processing and recordation fee in the case of any assignment. The assignee, if it is not a Lender, shall deliver to the Administrative Agent an Administrative Questionnaire.

(v)   *No Assignment to Certain Persons.* No such assignment shall be made to (A) the Borrower or any of the Borrower's Affiliates or Subsidiaries [except, solely with respect to Term Loans, as permitted by paragraphs (f) and (g) of this Section] or (B) to any Defaulting Lender or any of its Subsidiaries, or any Person who, upon becoming a Lender hereunder, would constitute a Defaulting Lender or a Subsidiary thereof.

(vi)   *No Assignment to Natural Persons.* No such assignment shall be made to a natural Person (or a holding company, investment vehicle or trust for, or owned and operated for the primary benefit of, a natural Person).

(vii)   *Certain Additional Payments.* In connection with any assignment of rights and obligations of any Defaulting Lender hereunder, no such assignment shall be effective unless and until, in addition to the other conditions thereto set forth herein, the parties to the assignment shall make such additional payments to the Administrative Agent in an aggregate amount sufficient, upon distribution thereof as appropriate (which may be outright payment, purchases by the assignee of participations or subparticipations, or other compensating actions, including funding, with the consent of the Borrower and the Administrative Agent, the applicable pro rata share of Loans previously requested but not funded by the Defaulting Lender, to each of which the applicable assignee and assignor hereby irrevocably consent), to (x) pay and satisfy in full all payment liabilities then owed by such Defaulting Lender to the Administrative Agent, each Issuing Bank, each Swingline Lender and each other Lender hereunder (and interest accrued thereon), and (y) acquire (and fund as appropriate) its full pro rata share of all Loans and participations in Letters of Credit and Swingline Loans in accordance with its Applicable Percentage. Notwithstanding the foregoing, in the event that any assignment of rights and obligations of any Defaulting Lender hereunder shall become effective under applicable law without compliance with the provisions of this paragraph, then the assignee of such interest shall be deemed to be a Defaulting Lender for all purposes of this Agreement until such compliance occurs.

Subject to acceptance and recording thereof by the Administrative Agent pursuant to paragraph (c) of this Section, from and after the effective date specified in each Assignment and Assumption, the assignee thereunder shall be a party to this Agreement and, to the extent of the interest assigned by such Assignment and Assumption, have the rights and obligations of a Lender under this Agreement, and the assigning Lender thereunder shall, to the extent of the interest assigned by such Assignment and Assumption, be released from its obligations under this Agreement (and, in the case of an Assignment and Assumption covering all of the assigning Lender's rights and obligations under this Agreement, such Lender shall cease to be a party hereto) but shall continue to be entitled to the benefits of Sections *[Yield Protection]* and *[Expenses, Indemnity; Damage Waiver]* with respect to facts and circumstances occurring prior to the effective date of such assignment; *provided*, that except to the extent otherwise expressly agreed by the affected parties, no assignment by a Defaulting Lender will constitute a waiver or release of any claim of any party hereunder arising from that Lender's having been a Defaulting Lender. Any assignment or transfer by a Lender of rights or obligations under this Agreement that does not comply with this paragraph shall be treated for purposes of this Agreement as a sale by such Lender of a participation in such rights and obligations in accordance with paragraph (d) of this Section.

(c)   *Register.* The Administrative Agent, acting solely for this purpose as an agent of the Borrower, shall maintain at one of its offices in [_____][16] a copy of each Assignment and Assumption delivered to it and a register for the recordation of the names and addresses of the Lenders, and the Commitments of, and principal amounts (and stated interest) of the Loans owing to, each Lender pursuant to the terms hereof from time to time (the *"Register"*). The entries in the Register shall be

---

[5] Office must be in the United States of America.

conclusive absent manifest error, and the Borrower, the Administrative Agent and the Lenders shall treat each Person whose name is recorded in the Register pursuant to the terms hereof as a Lender hereunder for all purposes of this Agreement. The Register shall be available for inspection by the Borrower and any Lender, at any reasonable time and from time to time upon reasonable prior notice. .

(d)   *Participations.* Any Lender may at any time, without the consent of, or notice to, the Borrower or the Administrative Agent, sell participations to any Person (other than a natural Person, or a holding company, investment vehicle or trust for, or owned and operated for the primary benefit of, a natural Person, or the Borrower or any of the Borrower's Affiliates or Subsidiaries) (each, a *"Participant"*) in all or a portion of such Lender's rights and/or obligations under this Agreement (including all or a portion of its Commitment and/or the Loans owing to it); *provided* that (i) such Lender's obligations under this Agreement shall remain unchanged, (ii) such Lender shall remain solely responsible to the other parties hereto for the performance of such obligations, and (iii) the Borrower, the Administrative Agent, the Issuing Banks and Lenders shall continue to deal solely and directly with such Lender in connection with such Lender's rights and obligations under this Agreement. For the avoidance of doubt, each Lender shall be responsible for the indemnity under Section [*Indemnification of the Administrative Agent*] (d) with respect to any payments made by such Lender to its Participant(s).

Any agreement or instrument pursuant to which a Lender sells such a participation shall provide that such Lender shall retain the sole right to enforce this Agreement and to approve any amendment, modification or waiver of any provision of this Agreement; *provided* that such agreement or instrument may provide that such Lender will not, without the consent of the Participant, agree to any amendment, modification or waiver [with respect to the following: _____] [described in Section *[provision relating to amendments requiring unanimous consent of the Lenders]*] that affects such Participant. The Borrower agrees that each Participant shall be entitled to the benefits of Sections [*Increased Costs*], [*Breakage Indemnity*] and [*Taxes*] (subject to the requirements and limitations therein, including the requirements under Section [*Taxes – Status of Lenders*] (it being understood that the documentation required under Section [*Taxes – Status of Lenders*] shall be delivered to the participating Lender)) to the same extent as if it were a Lender and had acquired its interest by assignment pursuant to paragraph (b) of this Section; provided that such Participant (A) agrees to be subject to the provisions of Sections [*Mitigation Obligations; Replacement of Lenders*] as if it were an assignee under paragraph (b) of this Section; and (B) shall not be entitled to receive any greater payment under Sections [*Increased Costs*] or [*Taxes*], with respect to any participation, than its participating Lender would have been entitled to receive, except to the extent such entitlement to receive a greater payment results from a Change in Law that occurs after the Participant acquired the applicable participation. Each Lender that sells a participation agrees, at the Borrower's request and expense, to use reasonable efforts to cooperate with the Borrower to effectuate the provisions of Section [*Replacement of Lenders*] with respect to any Participant. To the extent permitted by law, each Participant also shall be entitled to the benefits of Section [*Right of Setoff*] as though it were a Lender; *provided* that such Participant agrees to be subject to Section [*Sharing of Payments by Lenders*] as though it were a Lender. Each Lender that sells a participation shall, acting solely for this purpose as a non-fiduciary agent of the Borrower, maintain a register on which it enters the name and address of each Participant and the principal amounts (and stated interest) of each Participant's interest in the Loans or other obligations under the Loan Documents (the *"Participant Register"*); *provided* that no Lender shall have any obligation to disclose all or any portion of the Participant Register (including the identity of any Participant or any information relating to a Participant's interest in any commitments, loans, letters of credit or its other obligations under any Loan Document) to any Person except to the extent that such disclosure is necessary to establish that such commitment, loan, letter of credit or other obligation is in registered form under Section 5f.103-1(c) of the United States Treasury Regulations. The entries in the Participant Register shall be conclusive absent manifest error, and such Lender shall treat each Person whose name is recorded in the Participant Register as the owner of such participation for all purposes of this Agreement notwithstanding any notice to the contrary. For the avoidance of doubt, the Administrative Agent (in its capacity as Administrative Agent) shall have no responsibility for maintaining a Participant Register.

(e)   *Certain Pledges.* Any Lender may at any time pledge or assign a security interest in all or any portion of its rights under this Agreement to secure obligations of such Lender, including any pledge or assignment to secure obligations to a Federal Reserve Bank; *provided* that no such pledge or assignment shall release such Lender from any of its obligations hereunder or substitute any such pledgee or assignee for such Lender as a party hereto.

[(f)   *Assignments to Affiliated Lenders.* Notwithstanding anything in this Agreement to the contrary, any Term Lender may, at any time, assign all or a portion of its Term Loans on a non-pro rata basis to an Affiliated Lender through open-market purchases, subject to the following limitations:

(i)   In connection with an assignment to a Non-Debt Fund Affiliate, (A) the Non-Debt Fund Affiliate shall have identified itself in writing as an Affiliated Lender to the assigning Term Lender and the Administrative Agent prior to the execution of such assignment and (B) the Non-Debt Fund Affiliate shall be deemed to have represented and warranted to the assigning Term Lender and the Administrative Agent that the requirements set forth in this clause (f)(i) and clause (iv) below, shall have been satisfied upon consummation of the applicable assignment;

(ii)   Non-Debt Fund Affiliates will not (A) have the right to receive information, reports or other materials provided solely to Lenders by the Administrative Agent or any other Lender, except to the extent made available to the Borrower, (B) attend or participate in meetings attended solely by the Lenders and the Administrative Agent, or (C) access any electronic site established for the Lenders or confidential communications from counsel to or financial advisors of the Administrative Agent or the Lenders;

(iii)   (A) for purposes of any consent to any amendment, waiver or modification of, or any action under, and for the purpose of any direction to the Administrative Agent or any Lender to undertake any action (or refrain from taking any action) under, this Agreement or any other Loan Document, each Non-Debt Fund Affiliate will be deemed to have consented in the same proportion as the Term Lenders that are not Non-Debt Fund Affiliates consented to such matter, unless such matter requires the consent of all or all affected Lenders and adversely affects such Non-Debt Fund Affiliate more than other Term Lenders in any material respect, (B) for purposes of voting on any plan of reorganization or plan of liquidation pursuant to any Debtor Relief Laws (a *"Plan"*), each Non-Debt Fund Affiliate hereby agrees (x) not to vote on such Plan, (y) if such Non-Debt Fund Affiliate does vote on such Plan notwithstanding the restriction in the foregoing clause (x), such vote will be deemed not to be in good faith and shall be "designated" pursuant to Section 1126(e) of the Bankruptcy Code (or any similar provision in any other Debtor Relief Laws), and such vote shall not be counted in determining whether the applicable class has accepted or rejected such Plan in accordance with Section 1126(c) of the Bankruptcy Code (or any similar provision in any other Debtor Relief Laws) and (z) not to contest any request by any party for a determination by the Bankruptcy Court (or other applicable court of competent jurisdiction) effectuating the foregoing clause (y), in each case under this clause (iii)(B) unless such Plan adversely affects such Non-Debt Fund Affiliate more than other Term Lenders in any material respect, and (C) each Non-Debt Fund Affiliate hereby irrevocably appoints the Administrative Agent (such appointment being coupled with an interest) as such Non-Debt Fund Affiliate's attorney-in-fact, with full authority in the place and stead of such Non-Debt Fund Affiliate and in the name of such Non-Debt Fund Affiliate (solely in respect of Term Loans therein and not in respect of any other claim or status such Non-Debt Fund Affiliate may otherwise have), from time to time in the Administrative Agent's discretion to take any action and to execute any instrument that the Administrative Agent may deem reasonably necessary or appropriate to carry out the provisions of this clause (iii), including to ensure that any vote of such Non-Debt Fund Affiliate on any Plan is withdrawn or otherwise not counted;

(iv)   the aggregate principal amount of [any Class or tranche of] Term Loans held at any one time by Non-Debt Fund Affiliates may not exceed [__]% of the aggregate outstanding principal amount of [any Class or tranche of] Term Loans[17];

(v)   the Affiliated Lender will not be entitled to bring actions against the Administrative Agent, in its role as such, or receive advice of counsel or other advisors to the Administrative Agent or any other Lenders or challenge the attorney client privilege of their respective counsel; and

(vi)   the portion of any Loans held by Debt Fund Affiliates in the aggregate in excess of 49.9% of the amount of Loans and Commitments required to be held by Lenders in order for such Lenders to constitute "Required Lenders" shall be disregarded in determining Required Lenders at any time.

Each Affiliated Lender that is a Term Lender hereunder agrees to comply with the terms of this paragraph (f) (notwithstanding that it may be granted access to the Platform or any other electronic

---

[7] Parties to consider specifying remedies for assignments in excess of the threshold.

site established for the Lenders by the Administrative Agent), and agrees that in any subsequent assignment of all or any portion of its Term Loans it shall identify itself in writing to the assignee as an Affiliated Lender prior to the execution of such assignment.][18]

[(g)   *Borrower Buybacks.* Notwithstanding anything in this Agreement to the contrary, any Term Lender may, at any time, assign all or a portion of its Term Loans on a non-pro rata basis to the Borrower in accordance with the procedures set forth on Exhibit L, pursuant to an offer made available to all Term Lenders on a pro rata basis (a *"Dutch Auction"*), subject to the following limitations:

(i)   The Borrower shall represent and warrant, as of the date of the launch of the Dutch Auction and on the date of any such assignment, that neither it, its Affiliates nor any of its respective directors or officers has any Excluded Information that has not been disclosed to the Term Lenders generally (other than to the extent any such Term Lender does not wish to receive material non-public information with respect to the Borrower or its Subsidiaries or any of their respective securities) prior to such date;

(ii)   immediately and automatically, without any further action on the part of the Borrower, any Lender, the Administrative Agent or any other Person, upon the effectiveness of such assignment of Term Loans from a Term Lender to the Borrower, such Term Loans and all rights and obligations as a Term Lender related thereto shall, for all purposes under this Agreement, the other Loan Documents and otherwise, be deemed to be irrevocably prepaid, terminated, extinguished, cancelled and of no further force and effect and the Borrower shall neither obtain nor have any rights as a Term Lender hereunder or under the other Loan Documents by virtue of such assignment;

(iii)   the Borrower shall not use the proceeds of any Revolving Loans for any such assignment; and

(iv)   no Default or Event of Default shall have occurred and be continuing before or immediately after giving effect to such assignment.][19]

(h)   *Disqualified Institutions.* (i) No assignment or participation shall be made to any Person that was a Disqualified Institution as of the date (the *"Trade Date"*) on which the assigning Lender entered into a binding agreement to sell and assign all or a portion of its rights and obligations under this Agreement to such Person (unless the Borrower has consented to such assignment in writing in its sole and absolute discretion, in which case such Person will not be considered a Disqualified Institution for the purpose of such assignment or participation). For the avoidance of doubt, with respect to any assignee that becomes a Disqualified Institution after the applicable Trade Date (including as a result of the delivery of a notice pursuant to, and/or the expiration of the notice period referred to in, the definition of "Disqualified Institution"), (x) such assignee shall not retroactively be disqualified from becoming a Lender and (y) the execution by the Borrower of an Assignment and Assumption with respect to such assignee will not by itself result in such assignee no longer being considered a Disqualified Institution. Any assignment in violation of this clause (h)(i) shall not be void, but the other provisions of this clause (h) shall apply.

(ii)   If any assignment or participation is made to any Disqualified Institution without the Borrower's prior written consent in violation of clause (i) above, or if any Person becomes a Disqualified Institution after the applicable Trade Date, the Borrower may, at its sole expense and effort, upon notice to the applicable Disqualified Institution and the Administrative Agent, (A) terminate any Revolving Credit Commitment of such Disqualified Institution and repay all obligations of the Borrower owing to such Disqualified Institution in connection with such Revolving Credit Commitment, (B) in the case of outstanding Term Loans held by Disqualified Institutions, purchase or prepay such Term Loan by paying the [lowest] [lesser] of (x) the principal amount thereof [and][,] (y) the amount that such Disqualified Institution paid to acquire such Term Loans [and (z) the [market price][20] of such Term Loans], in each case plus accrued interest, accrued fees and all other amounts (other than principal amounts) payable to it hereunder and/or (C) require such Disqualified Institution to assign, without recourse (in accordance with and subject to the restrictions contained in this Section [*Successors and Assigns*]), all of its interest, rights and obligations under this Agreement to one or more Eligible Assignees

---

[18] Clause (f) to be added if Affiliated Lenders are permitted to purchase Term Loans from Term Lenders.

[19] Clause (g) to be added if the Borrower or its Subsidiaries is permitted to purchase Term Loans from Term Lenders.

[20] Parties to consider appropriate mechanism for determining market price.

at the [lowest] [lesser] of (x) the principal amount thereof [and][,] (y) the amount that such Disqualified Institution paid to acquire such interests, rights and obligations [and (z) the [market price] of such Term Loans[21], in each case plus accrued interest, accrued fees and all other amounts (other than principal amounts) payable to it hereunder.

(iii)   Notwithstanding anything to the contrary contained in this Agreement, Disqualified Institutions (A) will not (x) have the right to receive information, reports or other materials provided to Lenders by the Borrower, the Administrative Agent or any other Lender, (y) attend or participate in meetings attended by the Lenders and the Administrative Agent, or (z) access any electronic site established for the Lenders or confidential communications from counsel to or financial advisors of the Administrative Agent or the Lenders and (B) (x) for purposes of any consent to any amendment, waiver or modification of, or any action under, and for the purpose of any direction to the Administrative Agent or any Lender to undertake any action (or refrain from taking any action) under this Agreement or any other Loan Document, each Disqualified Institution will be deemed to have consented in the same proportion as the Lenders that are not Disqualified Institutions consented to such matter, and (y) for purposes of voting on any Plan, each Disqualified Institution party hereto hereby agrees (1) not to vote on such Plan, (2) if such Disqualified Institution does vote on such Plan notwithstanding the restriction in the foregoing clause (1), such vote will be deemed not to be in good faith and shall be "designated" pursuant to Section 1126(e) of the Bankruptcy Code (or any similar provision in any other Debtor Relief Laws), and such vote shall not be counted in determining whether the applicable class has accepted or rejected such Plan in accordance with Section 1126(c) of the Bankruptcy Code (or any similar provision in any other Debtor Relief Laws) and (3) not to contest any request by any party for a determination by the Bankruptcy Court (or other applicable court of competent jurisdiction) effectuating the foregoing clause (2).

(iv)   The Administrative Agent shall have the right, and the Borrower hereby expressly authorizes the Administrative Agent, to (A) post the list of Disqualified Institutions provided by the Borrower and any updates thereto from time to time (collectively, the "*DQ List*") on the Platform, including that portion of the Platform that is designated for "public side" Lenders and/or (B) provide the DQ List to each Lender requesting the same.

Cashless Settlement

Notwithstanding anything to the contrary contained in this Agreement, any Lender may exchange, continue or rollover all or a portion of its Loans in connection with any refinancing, extension, loan modification or similar transaction permitted by the terms of this Agreement, pursuant to a cashless settlement mechanism approved by the Borrower, the Administrative Agent and such Lender.

Governing Law; Jurisdiction; Etc.[22]

(a)   *Governing Law.* This Agreement and the other Loan Documents and any claims, controversy, dispute or cause of action (whether in contract or tort or otherwise) based upon, arising out of or relating to this Agreement or any other Loan Document (except, as to any other Loan Document, as expressly set forth therein) and the transactions contemplated hereby and thereby shall be governed by, and construed in accordance with, the law of the State of [New York].

(b)   *Jurisdiction.* The Borrower [and each other Loan Party] irrevocably and unconditionally agrees that it will not commence any action, litigation or proceeding of any kind or description, whether in law or equity, whether in contract or in tort or otherwise, against the Administrative Agent, any Lender, any Issuing Bank, or any Related Party of the foregoing in any way relating to this Agreement or any other Loan Document or the transactions relating hereto or thereto, in any forum other than the courts of the State of [New York] sitting in [New York] County, and of the United States District Court of the [Southern District of New York], and any appellate court from any

---

[1] Parties to consider appropriate mechanism for determining market price.
[2] Revise as appropriate where Credit Agreement is not governed by New York law. In cases where the Credit Agreement is not governed by New York law, counsel may wish to consider completing this Section in all capital letters. Counsel should also consider the appropriateness of the Jurisdiction clause for transactions that include non-U.S. Loan Parties.

thereof, and each of the parties hereto irrevocably and unconditionally submits to the jurisdiction of such courts and agrees that all claims in respect of any such action, litigation or proceeding may be heard and determined in such [New York] State court or, to the fullest extent permitted by applicable law, in such federal court. Each of the parties hereto agrees that a final judgment in any such action, litigation or proceeding shall be conclusive and may be enforced in other jurisdictions by suit on the judgment or in any other manner provided by law. Nothing in this Agreement or in any other Loan Document shall affect any right that the Administrative Agent, any Lender or any Issuing Bank may otherwise have to bring any action or proceeding relating to this Agreement or any other Loan Document against the Borrower [or any other Loan Party] or its properties in the courts of any jurisdiction.

(c)   *Waiver of Venue.* The Borrower [and each other Loan Party] irrevocably and unconditionally waives, to the fullest extent permitted by applicable law, any objection that it may now or hereafter have to the laying of venue of any action or proceeding arising out of or relating to this Agreement or any other Loan Document in any court referred to in paragraph (b) of this Section. Each of the parties hereto hereby irrevocably waives, to the fullest extent permitted by applicable law, the defense of an inconvenient forum to the maintenance of such action or proceeding in any such court.

(d)   *Service of Process.* Each party hereto irrevocably consents to service of process in the manner provided for notices in Section [*Notices*]. Nothing in this Agreement will affect the right of any party hereto to serve process in any other manner permitted by applicable law.

Waiver of Jury Trial

EACH PARTY HERETO HEREBY IRREVOCABLY WAIVES, TO THE FULLEST EXTENT PERMITTED BY APPLICABLE LAW, ANY RIGHT IT MAY HAVE TO A TRIAL BY JURY IN ANY LEGAL PROCEEDING DIRECTLY OR INDIRECTLY ARISING OUT OF OR RELATING TO THIS AGREEMENT OR ANY OTHER LOAN DOCUMENT OR THE TRANSACTIONS CONTEMPLATED HEREBY OR THEREBY (WHETHER BASED ON CONTRACT, TORT OR ANY OTHER THEORY). EACH PARTY HERETO (A) CERTIFIES THAT NO REPRESENTATIVE, AGENT OR ATTORNEY OF ANY OTHER PERSON HAS REPRESENTED, EXPRESSLY OR OTHERWISE, THAT SUCH OTHER PERSON WOULD NOT, IN THE EVENT OF LITIGATION, SEEK TO ENFORCE THE FOREGOING WAIVER AND (B) ACKNOWLEDGES THAT IT AND THE OTHER PARTIES HERETO HAVE BEEN INDUCED TO ENTER INTO THIS AGREEMENT AND THE OTHER LOAN DOCUMENTS BY, AMONG OTHER THINGS, THE MUTUAL WAIVERS AND CERTIFICATIONS IN THIS SECTION.

Counterparts; Integration; Effectiveness; Electronic Execution

(a)   *Counterparts; Integration; Effectiveness.* This Agreement may be executed in counterparts (and by different parties hereto in different counterparts), each of which shall constitute an original, but all of which when taken together shall constitute a single contract. This Agreement and the other Loan Documents, and any separate letter agreements with respect to fees payable to the Administrative Agent, constitute the entire contract among the parties relating to the subject matter hereof and supersede any and all previous agreements and understandings, oral or written, relating to the subject matter hereof. Except as provided in Section [*Conditions Precedent*], this Agreement shall become effective when it shall have been executed by the Administrative Agent and when the Administrative Agent shall have received counterparts hereof that, when taken together, bear the signatures of each of the other parties hereto. Delivery of an executed counterpart of a signature page of this Agreement by facsimile or in electronic (i.e., "pdf" or "tif") format shall be effective as delivery of a manually executed counterpart of this Agreement.

(b)   *Electronic Execution of Assignments.* The words "execution," "signed," "signature," and words of like import in any Assignment and Assumption shall be deemed to include electronic signatures or the keeping of records in electronic form, each of which shall be of the same legal effect, validity or enforceability as a manually executed signature or the use of a paper-based recordkeeping system, as the case may be, to the extent and as provided for in any applicable law, including the Federal Electronic Signatures in Global and National Commerce Act, the New York State Electronic Signatures and Records Act, or any other similar state laws based on the Uniform Electronic Transactions Act.

Treatment of Certain Information; Confidentiality

Each of the Administrative Agent, the Lenders and the Issuing Banks agree to maintain the confidentiality of the Information (as defined below), except that Information may be disclosed (a) to its Affiliates and to its Related Parties (it being understood that the Persons to whom such disclosure is made will be informed of the confidential nature of such Information and instructed to keep such Information confidential); (b) to the extent required or requested by any regulatory authority purporting to have jurisdiction over such Person or its Related Parties (including any self-regulatory authority, such as the National Association of Insurance Commissioners); (c) to the extent required by applicable laws or regulations or by any subpoena or similar legal process; (d) to any other party hereto; (e) in connection with the exercise of any remedies hereunder or under any other Loan Document or any action or proceeding relating to this Agreement or any other Loan Document or the enforcement of rights hereunder or thereunder; (f) subject to an agreement containing provisions substantially the same as those of this Section, to (i) any assignee of or Participant in, or any prospective assignee of or Participant in, any of its rights and obligations under this Agreement[23], or (ii) any actual or prospective party (or its Related Parties) to any swap, derivative or other transaction under which payments are to be made by reference to the Borrower and its obligations, this Agreement or payments hereunder (it being understood that the DQ List may be disclosed to any assignee or Participant, or prospective assignee or Participant, in reliance on this clause (f)); (g) on a confidential basis to (i) any rating agency in connection with rating the Borrower or its Subsidiaries or the Facilities or (ii) the CUSIP Service Bureau or any similar agency in connection with the issuance and monitoring of CUSIP numbers with respect to the Facilities; (h) with the consent of the Borrower; or (i) to the extent such Information (x) becomes publicly available other than as a result of a breach of this Section, or (y) becomes available to the Administrative Agent, any Lender, any Issuing Bank or any of their respective Affiliates on a nonconfidential basis from a source other than the Borrower. In addition, the Administrative Agent and the Lenders may disclose the existence of this Agreement and information about this Agreement to market data collectors, similar service providers to the lending industry and service providers to the Agents and the Lenders in connection with the administration of this Agreement, the other Loan Documents, and the Commitments.

For purposes of this Section, *"Information"* means all information received from the Borrower or any of its Subsidiaries relating to the Borrower or any of its Subsidiaries or any of their respective businesses, other than any such information that is available to the Administrative Agent, any Lender or any Issuing Bank on a nonconfidential basis prior to disclosure by the Borrower or any of its Subsidiaries; *provided* that, in the case of information received from the Borrower or any of its Subsidiaries after the date hereof, such information is clearly identified at the time of delivery as confidential. Any Person required to maintain the confidentiality of Information as provided in this Section shall be considered to have complied with its obligation to do so if such Person has exercised the same degree of care to maintain the confidentiality of such Information as such Person would accord to its own confidential information.

---

[*] Parties to consider an express prohibition on disclosure to Disqualified Institutions, subject to appropriate qualifications for inadvertent disclosure to entities that are not known to be Disqualified Institutions at the time of disclosure.

ASSIGNMENT AND ASSUMPTION[24]

This Assignment and Assumption (the "*Assignment and Assumption*") is dated as of the Effective Date set forth below and is entered into by and between [the][each][25] Assignor identified in item 1 below ([the][each, an] "*Assignor*") and [the][each][26] Assignee identified in item 2 below ([the][each, an] "*Assignee*"). [It is understood and agreed that the rights and obligations of [the Assignors][the Assignees][27] hereunder are several and not joint.][28] Capitalized terms used but not defined herein shall have the meanings given to them in the Credit Agreement identified below (as amended, the "*Credit Agreement*"), receipt of a copy of which is hereby acknowledged by [the][each] Assignee. The Standard Terms and Conditions set forth in Annex 1 attached hereto are hereby agreed to and incorporated herein by reference and made a part of this Assignment and Assumption as if set forth herein in full.

For an agreed consideration, [the][each] Assignor hereby irrevocably sells and assigns to [the Assignee][the respective Assignees], and [the][each] Assignee hereby irrevocably purchases and assumes from [the Assignor][the respective Assignors], subject to and in accordance with the Standard Terms and Conditions and the Credit Agreement, as of the Effective Date inserted by the Administrative Agent as contemplated below (i) all of [the Assignor's][the respective Assignors'] rights and obligations in [its capacity as a Lender][their respective capacities as Lenders] under the Credit Agreement and any other documents or instruments delivered pursuant thereto to the extent related to the amount and percentage interest identified below of all of such outstanding rights and obligations of [the Assignor] [the respective Assignors] under the respective facilities identified below (including without limitation any letters of credit, guarantees, and swingline loans included in such facilities), and (ii) to the extent permitted to be assigned under applicable law, all claims, suits, causes of action and any other right of [the Assignor (in its capacity as a Lender)][the respective Assignors (in their respective capacities as Lenders)] against any Person, whether known or unknown, arising under or in connection with the Credit Agreement, any other documents or instruments delivered pursuant thereto or the loan transactions governed thereby or in any way based on or related to any of the foregoing, including, but not limited to, contract claims, tort claims, malpractice claims, statutory claims and all other claims at law or in equity related to the rights and obligations sold and assigned pursuant to clause (i) above (the rights and obligations sold and assigned by [the][any] Assignor to [the][any] Assignee pursuant to clauses (i) and (ii) above being referred to herein collectively as [the][an] "*Assigned Interest*"). Each such sale and assignment is without recourse to [the][any] Assignor and, except as expressly provided in this Assignment and Assumption, without representation or warranty by [the][any] Assignor.

1. Assignor[s]:   _____

                                                 _____

2. Assignee[s]:   _____

                                                 _____

    [Assignee is an [Affiliate][Approved Fund] of [*identify Lender*]

3. Borrower(s):   _____

---

[24] The LSTA's Form of Assignment Agreement has been drafted so that parties need not tailor the agreement depending on the identity of each assignee. In this way, electronic settlement platforms do not need to create "pop-ups", ie, questions which appear or "pop-up" on the screen of the person completing the assignment agreement and which must be answered before the assignment agreement can be populated and finalised. By avoiding "pop-ups", the loan market can operate more efficiently, for trades will be able to settle more promptly.

[25] For bracketed language here and elsewhere in this form relating to the Assignor(s), if the assignment is from a single Assignor, choose the first bracketed language. If the assignment is from multiple Assignors, choose the second bracketed language.

[26] For bracketed language here and elsewhere in this form relating to the Assignee(s), if the assignment is to a single Assignee choose the first bracketed language. If the assignment is to multiple Assignees, choose the second bracketed language.

[27] Select as appropriate.

[28] Include bracketed language if there are either multiple Assignors or multiple Assignees.

4. Administrative Agent: _____, as the administrative agent under
   the Credit   Agreement

5. Credit Agreement: [The [*amount*] Credit Agreement dated as of _____ among [*name of Borrower(s)*], the Lenders parties thereto, [*name of Administrative Agent*],
   as
   Administrative Agent, and the other agents parties thereto]

6. Assigned Interest[s]:

Assignor[s][29]	Assignee[s][30]	Facility Assigned[31]	Aggregate Amount of Commitment/Loans for all Lenders[32]	Amount of Commitment/Loans Assigned[8]	Percentage Assigned of Commitment/ Loans[33]	CUSIP Number
			$	$	%	
			$	$	%	
			$	$	%	

[7. Trade Date: _____][34]

[Page break]

List each Assignor, as appropriate.

List each Assignee, as appropriate.

Fill in the appropriate terminology for the types of facilities under the Credit Agreement that are being assigned under this Assignment (e.g., "Revolving Credit Commitment," "Term Loan Commitment," etc.)

Amount to be adjusted by the counterparties to take into account any payments or prepayments made between the Trade Date and the Effective Date.

Set forth, to at least 9 decimals, as a percentage of the Commitment/Loans of all Lenders thereunder.

To be completed if the Assignor(s) and the Assignee(s) intend that the minimum assignment amount is to be determined as of the Trade Date.

Effective Date: _____ ___, 20___ [TO BE INSERTED BY ADMINISTRATIVE AGENT AND WHICH SHALL BE THE EFFECTIVE DATE OF RECORDATION OF TRANSFER IN THE REGISTER THEREFOR.]

The terms set forth in this Assignment and Assumption are hereby agreed to:

ASSIGNOR[S][35]
[NAME OF ASSIGNOR]

By:_____
  Title:

[NAME OF ASSIGNOR]

By:_____
  Title:

ASSIGNEE[S][36]
[NAME OF ASSIGNEE]

By:_____
  Title:

[NAME OF ASSIGNEE]

By:_____
  Title:

[Consented to and][37] Accepted:

[NAME OF ADMINISTRATIVE AGENT], as
 Administrative Agent

By: _____
  Title:

[Consented to:][38]

[NAME OF RELEVANT PARTY]

By: _____
  Title:

---

[35] Add additional signature blocks as needed. Include both Fund/Pension Plan and manager making the trade (if applicable).

[36] Add additional signature blocks as needed. Include both Fund/Pension Plan and manager making the trade (if applicable).

[37] To be added only if the consent of the Administrative Agent is required by the terms of the Credit Agreement.

[38] To be added only if the consent of the Borrower and/or other parties (e.g., Swingline Lender, Issuing Bank) is required by the terms of the Credit Agreement.

[_____]³⁹

STANDARD TERMS AND CONDITIONS FOR
ASSIGNMENT AND ASSUMPTION

1. *Representations and Warranties.*

1.1 *Assignor[s].* [The][Each] Assignor (a) represents and warrants that (i) it is the legal and beneficial owner of [the][the relevant] Assigned Interest, (ii) [the][such] Assigned Interest is free and clear of any lien, encumbrance or other adverse claim, (iii) it has full power and authority, and has taken all action necessary, to execute and deliver this Assignment and Assumption and to consummate the transactions contemplated hereby and (iv) it is not a Defaulting Lender; and (b) assumes no responsibility with respect to (i) any statements, warranties or representations made in or in connection with the Credit Agreement or any other Loan Document⁴⁰, (ii) the execution, legality, validity, enforceability, genuineness, sufficiency or value of the Loan Documents or any collateral thereunder, (iii) the financial condition of the Borrower, any of its Subsidiaries or Affiliates or any other Person obligated in respect of any Loan Document, or (iv) the performance or observance by the Borrower, any of its Subsidiaries or Affiliates or any other Person of any of their respective obligations under any Loan Document.

1.2. *Assignee[s].* [The][Each] Assignee (a) represents and warrants that (i) it has full power and authority, and has taken all action necessary, to execute and deliver this Assignment and Assumption and to consummate the transactions contemplated hereby and to become a Lender under the Credit Agreement, (ii) it meets all the requirements to be an assignee under Section [*Successors and Assigns*] of the Credit Agreement (subject to such consents, if any, as may be required thereunder)⁴¹, (iii) from and after the Effective Date, it shall be bound by the provisions of the Credit Agreement as a Lender thereunder and, to the extent of [the][the relevant] Assigned Interest, shall have the obligations of a Lender thereunder, (iv) it is sophisticated with respect to decisions to acquire assets of the type represented by the Assigned Interest and either it, or the Person exercising discretion in making its decision to acquire the Assigned Interest, is experienced in acquiring assets of such type, (v) it has received a copy of the Credit Agreement, and has received or has been accorded the opportunity to receive copies of the most recent financial statements delivered pursuant to Section ___ thereof, as applicable, and such other documents and information as it deems appropriate to make its own credit analysis and decision to enter into this Assignment and Assumption and to purchase [the][such] Assigned Interest, (vi) it has, independently and without reliance upon the Administrative Agent or any other Lender and based on such documents and information as it has deemed appropriate, made its own credit analysis and decision to enter into this Assignment and Assumption and to purchase [the] [such] Assigned Interest, and (vii) if it is a Foreign Lender⁴² attached to the Assignment and Assumption is any documentation required to be delivered by it pursuant to the terms of the Credit Agreement, duly completed and executed by [the][such] Assignee; and (b) agrees that (i) it will, independently and without reliance on the Administrative Agent, [the][any] Assignor or any other Lender, and based on such documents and information as it shall deem appropriate at the time, continue to make its own credit decisions in taking or not taking action under the Loan Documents, and (ii) it will perform in accordance with their terms all of the obligations which by the terms of the Loan Documents are required to be performed by it as a Lender.

Describe Credit Agreement at option of Administrative Agent.

The term "Loan Document" should be conformed to that used in the Credit Agreement.

By confirming that it meets all the requirements to be an assignee under the Successors and Assigns provision of the Credit Agreement, the assignee is also confirming that it is not a Disqualified Institution (see section (h) of the Successors and Assigns provision).

The concept of "Foreign Lender" should be conformed to the section in the Credit Agreement governing withholding taxes and gross-up. If the Borrower is a U.S. Borrower, the bracketed language should be deleted.

2. *Payments.* From and after the Effective Date, the Administrative Agent shall make all payments in respect of [the][each] Assigned Interest (including payments of principal, interest, fees and other amounts) to [the][the relevant] Assignor for amounts which have accrued to but excluding the Effective Date and to [the][the relevant] Assignee for amounts which have accrued from and after the Effective Date.[43] Notwithstanding the foregoing, the Administrative Agent shall make all payments of interest, fees or other amounts paid or payable in kind from and after the Effective Date to [the][the relevant] Assignee.

3. *General Provisions.* This Assignment and Assumption shall be binding upon, and inure to the benefit of, the parties hereto and their respective successors and assigns. This Assignment and Assumption may be executed in any number of counterparts, which together shall constitute one instrument. Delivery of an executed counterpart of a signature page of this Assignment and Assumption by telecopy shall be effective as delivery of a manually executed counterpart of this Assignment and Assumption. This Assignment and Assumption shall be governed by, and construed in accordance with the law of the State of New York [*confirm that choice of law provision parallels the Credit Agreement*].

---

[43] The Administrative Agent should consider whether this method conforms to its systems. In some circumstances, the following alternative language may be appropriate:

"From and after the Effective Date, the Administrative Agent shall make all payments in respect of [the][each] Assigned Interest (including payments of principal, interest, fees and other amounts) to [the][the relevant] Assignee whether such amounts have accrued prior to, on or after the Effective Date. The Assignor[s] and the Assignee[s] shall make all appropriate adjustments in payments by the Administrative Agent for periods prior to the Effective Date or with respect to the making of this assignment directly between themselves."

EXHIBIT [J]-1

[FORM OF]

U.S. TAX COMPLIANCE CERTIFICATE

(For Foreign Lenders That Are Not Partnerships For U.S. Federal Income Tax Purposes)

Reference is hereby made to the Credit Agreement dated as of [   ] (as amended, supplemented or otherwise modified from time to time, the *"Credit Agreement"*), among [   ], and each lender from time to time party thereto.

Pursuant to the provisions of Section [*Taxes*] of the Credit Agreement, the undersigned hereby certifies that (i) it is the sole record and beneficial owner of the Loan(s) (as well as any Note(s) evidencing such Loan(s)) in respect of which it is providing this certificate, (ii) it is not a bank within the meaning of Section 881(c)(3)(A) of the Code, (iii) it is not a ten percent shareholder of the Borrower within the meaning of Section 871(h)(3)(B) of the Code and (iv) it is not a controlled foreign corporation related to the Borrower as described in Section 881(c)(3)(C) of the Code.

The undersigned has furnished the Administrative Agent and the Borrower with a certificate of its non-U.S. Person status on IRS Form W-8BEN. By executing this certificate, the undersigned agrees that (1) if the information provided on this certificate changes, the undersigned shall promptly so inform the Borrower and the Administrative Agent, and (2) the undersigned shall have at all times furnished the Borrower and the Administrative Agent with a properly completed and currently effective certificate in either the calendar year in which each payment is to be made to the undersigned, or in either of the two calendar years preceding such payments.

Unless otherwise defined herein, terms defined in the Credit Agreement and used herein shall have the meanings given to them in the Credit Agreement.

[NAME OF LENDER]

By:_____
    Name:
    Title:

Date: _____ __, 20[ ]

EXHIBIT [J]-2

[FORM OF]

U.S. TAX COMPLIANCE CERTIFICATE
(For Foreign Participants That Are Not Partnerships For U.S. Federal Income Tax Purposes)

Reference is hereby made to the Credit Agreement dated as of [　] (as amended, supplemented or otherwise modified from time to time, the "*Credit Agreement*"), among [　], and each lender from time to time party thereto.

Pursuant to the provisions of Section [*Taxes*] of the Credit Agreement, the undersigned hereby certifies that (i) it is the sole record and beneficial owner of the participation in respect of which it is providing this certificate, (ii) it is not a bank within the meaning of Section 881(c)(3)(A) of the Code, (iii) it is not a ten percent shareholder of the Borrower within the meaning of Section 871(h)(3)(B) of the Code, and (iv) it is not a controlled foreign corporation related to the Borrower as described in Section 881(c)(3)(C) of the Code].

The undersigned has furnished its participating Lender with a certificate of its non-U.S. Person status on IRS Form W-8BEN. By executing this certificate, the undersigned agrees that (1) if the information provided on this certificate changes, the undersigned shall promptly so inform such Lender in writing, and (2) the undersigned shall have at all times furnished such Lender with a properly completed and currently effective certificate in either the calendar year in which each payment is to be made to the undersigned, or in either of the two calendar years preceding such payments.

Unless otherwise defined herein, terms defined in the Credit Agreement and used herein shall have the meanings given to them in the Credit Agreement.

[NAME OF PARTICIPANT]

By:_____
　　Name:
　　Title:

Date: _____ __, 20[ ]

EXHIBIT [J]-3

[FORM OF]

U.S. TAX COMPLIANCE CERTIFICATE

(For Foreign Participants That Are Partnerships For U.S. Federal Income Tax Purposes)

Reference is hereby made to the Credit Agreement dated as of [   ] (as amended, supplemented or otherwise modified from time to time, the *"Credit Agreement"*), among [   ], and each lender from time to time party thereto.

Pursuant to the provisions of Section [*Taxes*] of the Credit Agreement, the undersigned hereby certifies that (i) it is the sole record owner of the participation in respect of which it is providing this certificate, (ii) its direct or indirect partners/members are the sole beneficial owners of such participation, (iii) with respect such participation, neither the undersigned nor any of its direct or indirect partners/members is a bank extending credit pursuant to a loan agreement entered into in the ordinary course of its trade or business within the meaning of Section 881(c)(3)(A) of the Code, (iv) none of its direct or indirect partners/members is a ten percent shareholder of the Borrower within the meaning of Section 871(h)(3)(B) of the Code and (v) none of its direct or indirect partners/members is a controlled foreign corporation related to the Borrower as described in Section 881(c)(3)(C) of the Code.

The undersigned has furnished its participating Lender with IRS Form W-8IMY accompanied by one of the following forms from each of its partners/members that is claiming the portfolio interest exemption: (i) an IRS Form W-8BEN or (ii) an IRS Form W-8IMY accompanied by an IRS Form W-8BEN from each of such partner's/member's beneficial owners that is claiming the portfolio interest exemption. By executing this certificate, the undersigned agrees that (1) if the information provided on this certificate changes, the undersigned shall promptly so inform such Lender and (2) the undersigned shall have at all times furnished such Lender with a properly completed and currently effective certificate in either the calendar year in which each payment is to be made to the undersigned, or in either of the two calendar years preceding such payments.

Unless otherwise defined herein, terms defined in the Credit Agreement and used herein shall have the meanings given to them in the Credit Agreement.

[NAME OF PARTICIPANT]

By:_____
    Name:
    Title:

Date: _____ __, 20[ ]

EXHIBIT [J]-4

[FORM OF]

U.S. TAX COMPLIANCE CERTIFICATE
(For Foreign Lenders That Are Partnerships For U.S. Federal Income Tax Purposes)

Reference is hereby made to the Credit Agreement dated as of [   ] (as amended, supplemented or otherwise modified from time to time, the *"Credit Agreement"*), among [   ], and each lender from time to time party thereto.

Pursuant to the provisions of Section [*Taxes*] of the Credit Agreement, the undersigned hereby certifies that (i) it is the sole record owner of the Loan(s) (as well as any Note(s) evidencing such Loan(s)) in respect of which it is providing this certificate, (ii) its direct or indirect partners/members are the sole beneficial owners of such Loan(s) (as well as any Note(s) evidencing such Loan(s)), (iii) with respect to the extension of credit pursuant to this Credit Agreement or any other Loan Document, neither the undersigned nor any of its direct or indirect partners/members is a bank extending credit pursuant to a loan agreement entered into in the ordinary course of its trade or business within the meaning of Section 881(c)(3)(A) of the Code, (iv) none of its direct or indirect partners/members is a ten percent shareholder of the Borrower within the meaning of Section 871(h)(3)(B) of the Code and (v) none of its direct or indirect partners/members is a controlled foreign corporation related to the Borrower as described in Section 881(c)(3)(C) of the Code.

The undersigned has furnished the Administrative Agent and the Borrower with IRS Form W-8IMY accompanied by one of the following forms from each of its partners/members that is claiming the portfolio interest exemption: (i) an IRS Form W-8BEN or (ii) an IRS Form W-8IMY accompanied by an IRS Form W-8BEN from each of such partner's/member's beneficial owners that is claiming the portfolio interest exemption. By executing this certificate, the undersigned agrees that (1) if the information provided on this certificate changes, the undersigned shall promptly so inform the Borrower and the Administrative Agent, and (2) the undersigned shall have at all times furnished the Borrower and the Administrative Agent with a properly completed and currently effective certificate in either the calendar year in which each payment is to be made to the undersigned, or in either of the two calendar years preceding such payments.

Unless otherwise defined herein, terms defined in the Credit Agreement and used herein shall have the meanings given to them in the Credit Agreement.

[NAME OF LENDER]

By:_____
    Name:
    Title:

Date: _____ __, 20[ ]

EXHIBIT [L]

[FORM OF]

AUCTION PROCEDURES

This outline is intended to summarize certain basic terms of procedures with respect to certain Borrower buy-backs pursuant to and in accordance with the terms and conditions of Section [Successors and Assigns, paragraph (g)] of the Credit Agreement to which this Exhibit [L] is attached. It is not intended to be a definitive list of all of the terms and conditions of a Dutch Auction and all such terms and conditions shall be set forth in the applicable auction procedures documentation set for each Dutch Auction (the "*Offer Documents*"). None of the Administrative Agent, [NAME OF AUCTION MANAGER] (or, if [NAME OF AUCTION MANAGER] declines to act in such capacity, an investment bank of recognized standing selected by the Borrower) (the "*Auction Manager*") or any of their respective Affiliates makes any recommendation pursuant to the Offer Documents as to whether or not any Term Lender should sell by assignment any of its Term Loans pursuant to the Offer Documents (including, for the avoidance of doubt, by participating in the Dutch Auction as a Term Lender) or whether or not the Borrower should purchase by assignment any Term Loans from any Term Lender pursuant to any Dutch Auction. Each Term Lender should make its own decision as to whether to sell by assignment any of its Term Loans and, if so, the principal amount of and price to be sought for such Term Loans. In addition, each Term Lender should consult its own attorney, business advisor or tax advisor as to legal, business, tax and related matters concerning any Dutch Auction and the Offer Documents. Capitalized terms not otherwise defined in this Exhibit [L] have the meanings assigned to them in the Credit Agreement.

Summary. The Borrower may purchase (by assignment) Term Loans on a non-pro rata basis by conducting one or more Dutch Auctions pursuant to the procedures described herein; *provided* that no more than one Dutch Auction may be ongoing at any one time and no more than [four] Dutch Auctions may be made in any period of four consecutive fiscal quarters of the Borrower.

1.   *Notice Procedures.* In connection with each Dutch Auction, the Borrower will notify the Auction Manager (for distribution to the Term Lenders) of the Term Loans that will be the subject of the Dutch Auction by delivering to the Auction Manager a written notice in form and substance reasonably satisfactory to the Auction Manager (an "*Auction Notice*"). Each Auction Notice shall contain (i) the maximum principal amount of Term Loans the Borrower is willing to purchase (by assignment) in the Dutch Auction (the "*Auction Amount*"), which shall be no less than $[AMOUNT] or an integral multiple of $[AMOUNT] in excess of thereof, (ii) the range of discounts to par (the "*Discount Range*"), expressed as a range of prices per $1,000 of Term Loans, at which the Borrower would be willing to purchase Term Loans in the Dutch Auction and (iii) the date on which the Dutch Auction will conclude, on which date Return Bids (as defined below) will be due at the time provided in the Auction Notice (such time, the "*Expiration Time*"), as such date and time may be extended upon notice by the Borrower to the Auction Manager not less than 24 hours before the original Expiration Time. The Auction Manager will deliver a copy of the Offer Documents to each Term Lender promptly following completion thereof.

2.   *Reply Procedures.* In connection with any Dutch Auction, each Term Lender holding Term Loans wishing to participate in such Dutch Auction shall, prior to the Expiration Time, provide the Auction Manager with a notice of participation in form and substance reasonably satisfactory to the Auction Manager (the "*Return Bid*") to be included in the Offer Documents, which shall specify (i) a discount to par that must be expressed as a price per $1,000 of Term Loans (the "*Reply Price*") within the Discount Range and (ii) the principal amount of Term Loans, in an amount not less than $[AMOUNT], that such Term Lender is willing to offer for sale at its Reply Price (the "*Reply Amount*"); *provided* that each Term Lender may submit a Reply Amount that is less than the minimum amount and incremental amount requirements described above only if the Reply Amount equals the entire amount of the Term Loans held by such Term Lender at such time. A Term Lender may only submit one Return Bid per Dutch Auction, but each Return Bid may contain up to [three] component bids, each of which may result in a separate Qualifying Bid (as defined below) and each of which will not be contingent on any other component bid submitted by such Term Lender resulting in a Qualifying Bid. In addition to the

Return Bid, a participating Term Lender must execute and deliver, to be held by the Auction Manager, an assignment and acceptance in the form included in the Offer Documents which shall be in form and substance reasonably satisfactory to the Auction Manager and the Administrative Agent (the *"Auction Assignment and Acceptance"*). The Borrower will not purchase any Term Loans at a price that is outside of the applicable Discount Range, nor will any Return Bids (including any component bids specified therein) submitted at a price that is outside such applicable Discount Range be considered in any calculation of the Applicable Threshold Price (as defined below).

3. *Acceptance Procedures.* Based on the Reply Prices and Reply Amounts received by the Auction Manager, the Auction Manager, in consultation with the Borrower, will calculate the lowest purchase price (the *"Applicable Threshold Price"*) for the Dutch Auction within the Discount Range for the Dutch Auction that will allow the Borrower to complete the Dutch Auction by purchasing the full Auction Amount (or such lesser amount of Term Loans for which the Borrower has received Qualifying Bids). The Borrower shall purchase (by assignment) Term Loans from each Term Lender whose Return Bid is within the Discount Range and contains a Reply Price that is equal to or less than the Applicable Threshold Price (each, a *"Qualifying Bid"*). All Term Loans included in Qualifying Bids received at a Reply Price lower than the Applicable Threshold Price will be purchased at a purchase price equal to the applicable Reply Price and shall not be subject to proration. If a Term Lender has submitted a Return Bid containing multiple component bids at different Reply Prices, then all Term Loans of such Term Lender offered in any such component bid that constitutes a Qualifying Bid with a Reply Price lower than the Applicable Threshold Price shall also be purchased at a purchase price equal to the applicable Reply Price and shall not be subject to proration.

4. *Proration Procedures.* All Term Loans offered in Return Bids (or, if applicable, any component bid thereof) constituting Qualifying Bids equal to the Applicable Threshold Price will be purchased at a purchase price equal to the Applicable Threshold Price; *provided* that if the aggregate principal amount of all Term Loans for which Qualifying Bids have been submitted in any given Dutch Auction equal to the Applicable Threshold Price would exceed the remaining portion of the Auction Amount (after deducting all Term Loans purchased below the Applicable Threshold Price), the Borrower shall purchase the Term Loans for which the Qualifying Bids submitted were at the Applicable Threshold Price ratably based on the respective principal amounts offered and in an aggregate amount up to the amount necessary to complete the purchase of the Auction Amount. For the avoidance of doubt, no Return Bids (or any component thereof) will be accepted above the Applicable Threshold Price.

5. *Notification Procedures.* The Auction Manager will calculate the Applicable Threshold Price no later than the [___] Business Day after the date that the Return Bids were due. The Auction Manager will insert the amount of Term Loans to be assigned and the applicable settlement date determined by the Auction Manager in consultation with the Borrower onto each applicable Auction Assignment and Acceptance received in connection with a Qualifying Bid. Upon written request of the submitting Term Lender, the Auction Manager will promptly return any Auction Assignment and Acceptance received in connection with a Return Bid that is not a Qualifying Bid.

6. *Additional Procedures.* Once initiated by an Auction Notice, the Borrower may withdraw a Dutch Auction by written notice to the Auction Manager no later than 24 hours before the original Expiration Time so long as no Qualifying Bids have been received by the Auction Manager at or prior to the time the Auction Manager receives such written notice from the Borrower. Any Return Bid (including any component bid thereof) delivered to the Auction Manager may not be modified, revoked, terminated or cancelled; *provided* that a Term Lender may modify a Return Bid at any time prior to the Expiration Time solely to reduce the Reply Price included in such Return Bid. However, a Dutch Auction shall become void if the Borrower fails to satisfy one or more of the conditions to the purchase of Term Loans set forth in, or to otherwise comply with the provisions of Section [*Successors and Assigns, paragraph (g)*] of the Credit Agreement to which this Exhibit L is attached. The purchase price for all Term Loans purchased in a Dutch Auction shall be paid in cash by the Borrower directly to the respective assigning Term Lender on a settlement date as determined by the Auction Manager in consultation with the Borrower (which shall be no later than ten (10) Business Days after the date Return Bids are due), along with accrued and unpaid interest (if any) on the applicable Term Loans up to the settlement date. The Borrower shall execute each applicable Auction Assignment and Acceptance received in connection with a Qualifying Bid.

All questions as to the form of documents and validity and eligibility of Term Loans that are the subject of a Dutch Auction will be determined by the Auction Manager, in consultation with the Borrower, and the Auction Manager's determination will be conclusive, absent manifest error. The Auction Manager's interpretation of the terms and conditions of the Offer Document, in consultation with the Borrower, will be final and binding.

None of the Administrative Agent, the Auction Manager, any other Agent or any of their respective Affiliates assumes any responsibility for the accuracy or completeness of the information concerning the Borrower, the Subsidiaries or any of their Affiliates contained in the Offer Documents or otherwise or for any failure to disclose events that may have occurred and may affect the significance or accuracy of such information.

The Auction Manager acting in its capacity as such under a Dutch Auction shall be entitled to the benefits of the provisions of Article [*Agency*] and Section [*Expenses; Indemnity*] of the Credit Agreement to the same extent as if each reference therein to the "Administrative Agent" were a reference to the Auction Manager, each reference therein to the "Loan Documents" were a reference to the Offer Documents, the Auction Notice and Auction Assignment and Acceptance and each reference therein to the "Transactions" were a reference to the transactions contemplated hereby and the Administrative Agent shall cooperate with the Auction Manager as reasonably requested by the Auction Manager in order to enable it to perform its responsibilities and duties in connection with each Dutch Auction.

This Exhibit [L] shall not require the Borrower or any Subsidiary to initiate any Dutch Auction, nor shall any Term Lender be obligated to participate in any Dutch Auction.

APPENDIX I TO MODEL CREDIT AGREEMENT PROVISIONS

Extension of Commitment Termination Date[44]

(a)   *Requests for Extension.* The Borrower may, by notice to the Administrative Agent (who shall promptly notify the Lenders) not earlier than 45 days and not later than 35 days prior to the Commitment Termination Date then in effect hereunder (the *"Existing Commitment Termination Date"*), request that each Lender extend such Lender's Commitment Termination Date for an additional 364 days from the Existing Commitment Termination Date.

(b)   *Lender Elections to Extend.* Each Lender, acting in its sole and individual discretion, shall, by notice to the Administrative Agent given not earlier than 30 days prior to the Existing Commitment Termination Date and not later than the date (the *"Notice Date"*) that is 20 days prior to the Existing Commitment Termination Date, advise the Administrative Agent whether or not such Lender agrees to such extension (and each Lender that determines not to so extend its Commitment Termination Date (a *"Non-Extending Lender"*) shall notify the Administrative Agent of such fact promptly after such determination (but in any event no later than the Notice Date) and any Lender that does not so advise the Administrative Agent on or before the Notice Date shall be deemed to be a Non-Extending Lender. The election of any Lender to agree to such extension shall not obligate any other Lender to so agree.

(c)   *Notification by Administrative Agent.* The Administrative Agent shall notify the Borrower of each Lender's determination under this Section no later than the date 15 days prior to the Existing Commitment Termination Date (or, if such date is not a Business Day, on the next preceding Business Day).

(d)   *Additional Commitment Lenders.* The Borrower shall have the right on or before the Existing Commitment Termination Date to replace each Non-Extending Lender with, and add as "Lenders" under this Agreement in place thereof, one or more Eligible Assignees (each, an *"Additional Commitment Lender"*) with the approval of the Administrative Agent and the Issuing Banks (which approvals shall not be unreasonably withheld), each of which Additional Commitment Lenders shall have entered into an agreement in form and substance satisfactory to the Borrower and the Administrative Agent pursuant to which such Additional Commitment Lender shall, effective as of the Existing Commitment Termination Date, undertake a Commitment (and, if any such Additional Commitment Lender is already a Lender, its Commitment shall be in addition to such Lender's Commitment hereunder on such date).

(e)   *Minimum Extension Requirement.* If (and only if) the total of the Commitments of the Lenders that have agreed so to extend their Commitment Termination Date and the additional Commitments of the Additional Commitment Lenders shall be more than [___%] of the aggregate amount of the Commitments in effect immediately prior to the Existing Commitment Termination Date, then, effective as of the Existing Commitment Termination Date, the Commitment Termination Date of each Extending Lender and of each Additional Commitment Lender shall be extended to the date falling 364 days after the Existing Commitment Termination Date (except that, if such date is not a Business Day, such Commitment Date as so extended shall be the next preceding Business Day) and each Additional Commitment Lender shall thereupon become a "Lender" for all purposes of this Agreement.

(f)   *Conditions to Effectiveness of Extensions.* Notwithstanding the foregoing, the extension of the Commitment Termination Date pursuant to this Section shall not be effective with respect to any Lender unless:

(x)   no Default or Event of Default shall have occurred and be continuing on the date of such extension and after giving effect thereto;

---

[44] This language is suggested for Additional Provisions Agreements in which the Commitments are scheduled to expire within one year and in which the parties desire to specify an extension mechanism consistent with the Risk-Based Capital Adequacy Guidelines issued by the Board of Governors of the Federal Reserve (12 CFR 108, appendix A) for commitments that are to have a zero percent conversion factor (i.e., commitments with an original maturity of one year or less).

(y)   the representations and warranties contained in this Agreement are true and correct on and as of the date of such extension and after giving effect thereto, as though made on and as of such date (or, if any such representation or warranty is expressly stated to have been made as of a specific date, as of such specific date); and

(z)   on or before the Commitment Termination Date of each Non-Extending Lender, (1) the Borrower shall have paid in full the principal of and interest on all of the Advances made by such Non-Extending Lender to the Borrower hereunder and (2) the Borrower shall have paid in full all other amounts owing to such Lender hereunder.

Termination of Defaulting Lender

The Borrower may terminate the unused amount of the Commitment of any Revolving Lender that is a Defaulting Lender upon not less than [____] Business Days' prior notice to the Administrative Agent (which shall promptly notify the Lenders thereof), and in such event the provisions of Section [*Defaulting Lender Waterfall*] will apply to all amounts thereafter paid by the Borrower for the account of such Defaulting Lender under this Agreement (whether on account of principal, interest, fees, indemnity or other amounts); *provided* that (i) no Event of Default shall have occurred and be continuing, and (ii) such termination shall not be deemed to be a waiver or release of any claim the Borrower, the Administrative Agent, any Issuing Bank, the Swingline Bank or any Lender may have against such Defaulting Lender.

Resignation of Issuing Bank

Any Issuing Bank may resign at any time by giving 30 days' prior notice to the Administrative Agent, the Lenders and the Borrower. After the resignation of an Issuing Bank hereunder, the retiring Issuing Bank shall remain a party hereto and shall continue to have all the rights and obligations of an Issuing Bank under this Agreement and the other Loan Documents with respect to Letters of Credit issued by it prior to such resignation, but shall not be required to issue additional Letters of Credit or to extend, renew or increase any existing Letter of Credit.

Resignation of Swingline Lender

Any Swingline Lender may resign at any time by giving 30 days' prior notice to the Administrative Agent, the Lenders and the Borrower. After the resignation of a Swingline Lender hereunder, the retiring Swingline Lender shall remain a party hereto and shall continue to have all the rights and obligations of a Swingline Lender under this Agreement and the other Loan Documents with respect to Swingline Loans made by it prior to such resignation, but shall not be required to make any additional Swingline Loans.

LSTA Form of Contractual Recognition Provision

LSTA

EU Bail-In Rule
Form of Contractual Recognition Provision
LSTA Variant[1]

Acknowledgement and Consent to Bail-In of EEA Financial Institutions[2].
Notwithstanding anything to the contrary in any Loan Document or in any other agreement, arrangement or understanding among any such parties, each party hereto acknowledges that any liability of any EEA Financial Institution arising under any Loan Document, to the extent such liability is unsecured, may be subject to the write-down

---

[1] This model provision has been prepared for inclusion in a New York law governed credit agreement and will be included in the LSTA's Model Credit Agreement Provisions (MCAPs). Further background on the scope and requirements of the European bail-in rules can be found here in the LSTA's September 2015 Market Advisory. Affected European institutions and their counterparties incorporating these model provisions into any agreements are responsible for making an independent determination of their suitability for the transactions in question, their individual circumstances, and compliance with any applicable law.

[2] Affected European institutions are required to include certain specified elements in contractual recognition provisions. Those requirements are set out in the technical standards published on July 3, 2015 by the European Banking Authority for adoption by the European Commission for application in all EU Member States (which can be found at https://www.eba.europa.eu/documents/10180/1132911/EBA-RTS-2015-06+RTS+on+Contractual+Recognition+of+Bail-in .pdf. This provision incorporates the elements appropriate for the typical liabilities of lenders party to a credit agreement but would need to be adapted for use in other situations, e.g., for an affected European institution as borrower, or in a contract or instrument pursuant to which it has issued equity.

The draft technical standards also require a description of the write-down and conversion powers of each applicable EEA Resolution Authority in accordance with the national law implementing the European Bail-In Rules. The applicable definitions, therefore, contain a reference to the EU Bail-In Legislation Schedule published on the website of the Loan Market Association (LMA) which set forth the relevant national implementing legislation and write-down and conversion powers.

and conversion powers of an EEA Resolution Authority and agrees and consents to, and acknowledges and agrees to be bound by:

(a) the application of any Write-Down and Conversion Powers by an EEA Resolution Authority to any such liabilities arising hereunder which may be payable to it by any party hereto that is an EEA Financial Institution; and

(b) the effects of any Bail-in Action on any such liability, including, if applicable:

  (i) a reduction in full or in part or cancellation of any such liability;

  (ii) a conversion of all, or a portion of, such liability into shares or other instruments of ownership in such EEA Financial Institution, its parent undertaking, or a bridge institution that may be issued to it or otherwise conferred on it, and that such shares or other instruments of ownership will be accepted by it in lieu of any rights with respect to any such liability under this Agreement or any other Loan Document; or

  (iii) the variation of the terms of such liability[3] in connection with the exercise of the write-down and conversion powers of any EEA Resolution Authority.

"Bail-In Action" means the exercise of any Write-Down and Conversion Powers by the applicable EEA Resolution Authority in respect of any liability of an EEA Financial Institution.

"Bail-In Legislation" means, with respect to any EEA Member Country implementing Article 55 of Directive 2014/59/EU of the European Parliament and of the Council of the European Union, the implementing law for such EEA Member Country from time to time which is described in the EU Bail-In Legislation Schedule.[4]

"EEA Financial Institution" means (a) any credit institution or investment firm established in any EEA Member Country which is subject to the supervision of an EEA Resolution Authority, (b) any entity

---

[3] As the typical U.S. credit agreement contains many provisions regulating the liabilities and relationship between other parties that are not EEA Financial Institutions, this provision makes clear by its inclusion of the words "of such liability" that the required acknowledgment of the powers of the applicable EEA Resolution Authority is limited to the liabilities of the affected EEA Financial Institution to other parties under the agreement, and not to the provisions of the agreement as they may otherwise apply to the other parties thereto.

[4] The LMA variant of the contractual recognition clause offers an option to anticipate future bail-in legislation in countries outside the EEA. This is not required for compliance with the EU Bail-In legislation.

established in an EEA Member Country which is a parent of an institution described in clause (a) of this definition, or (c) any financial institution established in an EEA Member Country which is a subsidiary of an institution described in clauses (a) or (b) of this definition and is subject to consolidated supervision with its parent;

"EEA Member Country" means any of the member states of the European Union, Iceland, Liechtenstein, and Norway.

"EEA Resolution Authority" means any public administrative authority or any person entrusted with public administrative authority of any EEA Member Country (including any delegee) having responsibility for the resolution of any EEA Financial Institution.

"EU Bail-In Legislation Schedule" means the EU Bail-In Legislation Schedule published by the Loan Market Association (or any successor person), as in effect from time to time. [5]

"Write-Down and Conversion Powers" means, with respect to any EEA Resolution Authority, the write-down and conversion powers of such EEA Resolution Authority from time to time under the Bail-In Legislation for the applicable EEA Member Country, which write-down and conversion powers are described in the EU Bail-In Legislation Schedule.

*****

"Defaulting Lender"[6] means, subject to Section [*Defaulting Lender Cure*], any Lender that (a) has failed to (i) fund all or any portion of its Loans within two Business Days of the date such Loans were required to be funded hereunder unless such Lender notifies the Administrative Agent and the Borrower in writing that such failure is the result of such Lender's determination that one or more conditions precedent to funding (each of which conditions precedent, together with any applicable default, shall be specifically identified in such writing) has not been satisfied, or (ii) pay to the Administrative Agent, any Issuing Bank, any Swingline Lender or any other Lender any other amount required to be paid by it hereunder (including in respect of its participation in Letters of Credit or Swingline Loans) within two Business Days of the date

---

[5] The EU Bail-In Legislation Schedule may be found at http://www.lma.eu.com/pages .aspx?p=499.

[6] These provisions contemplate a modification of the LSTA MCAPs Defaulting Lender Language to extend their scope to a European Lender subject to bail-in, as it is not possible to allow for a reduction in commitments without considering the broader effects of this on the other parties to the agreement. This offers a pragmatic approach to arrangements relating to fronting exposures and other provisions affected by a reduction in commitments and the reinstatement of bailed-in commitments using existing LSTA MCAPs and procedures familiar to the market.

when due, (b) has notified the Borrower, the Administrative Agent or any Issuing Bank or Swingline Lender in writing that it does not intend to comply with its funding obligations hereunder, or has made a public statement to that effect (unless such writing or public statement relates to such Lender's obligation to fund a Loan hereunder and states that such position is based on such Lender's determination that a condition precedent to funding (which condition precedent, together with any applicable default, shall be specifically identified in such writing or public statement) cannot be satisfied), (c) has failed, within three Business Days after written request by the Administrative Agent or the Borrower, to confirm in writing to the Administrative Agent and the Borrower that it will comply with its prospective funding obligations hereunder (provided that such Lender shall cease to be a Defaulting Lender pursuant to this clause (c) upon receipt of such written confirmation by the Administrative Agent and the Borrower), or (d) has, or has a direct or indirect parent company that has, (i) become the subject of a proceeding under any Debtor Relief Law, (ii) had appointed for it a receiver, custodian, conservator, trustee, administrator, assignee for the benefit of creditors or similar Person charged with reorganization or liquidation of its business or assets, including the Federal Deposit Insurance Corporation or any other state or federal regulatory authority acting in such a capacity, *or (iii) become the subject of a Bail-in Action*; provided that a Lender shall not be a Defaulting Lender solely by virtue of the ownership or acquisition of any equity interest in that Lender or any direct or indirect parent company thereof by a Governmental Authority so long as such ownership interest does not result in or provide such Lender with immunity from the jurisdiction of courts within the United States or from the enforcement of judgments or writs of attachment on its assets or permit such Lender (or such Governmental Authority) to reject, repudiate, disavow or disaffirm any contracts or agreements made with such Lender. Any determination by the Administrative Agent that a Lender is a Defaulting Lender under any one or more of clauses (a) through (d) above shall be conclusive and binding absent manifest error, and such Lender shall be deemed to be a Defaulting Lender (subject to Section [*Defaulting Lender Cure*]) upon delivery of written notice of such determination to the Borrower, each Issuing Bank, each Swingline Lender and each Lender.

****

(i) *Reallocation of Participations to Reduce Fronting Exposure.* All or any part of such Defaulting Lender's participation in L/C Obligations and Swingline Loans shall be reallocated among the Non-Defaulting Lenders in accordance with their respective Applicable Percentages (calculated without regard to such Defaulting Lender's Commitment) but only to the extent that such reallocation does not cause the aggregate Revolving Credit Exposure of any Non-Defaulting Lender to exceed such Non-Defaulting Lender's Revolving Credit Commitment. Subject to Section [*Acknowledgment and Consent to EEA Financial Institution Bail-In*], no reallocation hereunder shall constitute a waiver or release of any claim of any party hereunder against a Defaulting Lender arising from that Lender having become a Defaulting Lender, including any claim of a Non-Defaulting Lender as a result of such Non-Defaulting Lender's increased exposure following such reallocation.

INDEX